Capital Management and Budgeting in the Public Sector

Arwiphawee Srithongrung
University of Illinois at Springfield, USA

Natalia B. Ermasova
Governors State University, USA

Juita-Elena (Wie) Yusuf
Old Dominion University, USA

A volume in the Advances in Public Policy and Administration (APPA) Book Series

IGI Global
DISSEMINATOR OF KNOWLEDGE

Published in the United States of America by
IGI Global
Business Science Reference (an imprint of IGI Global)
701 E. Chocolate Avenue
Hershey PA, USA 17033
Tel: 717-533-8845
Fax: 717-533-8661
E-mail: cust@igi-global.com
Web site: http://www.igi-global.com

Library of Congress Cataloging-in-Publication Data

Names: Srithongrung, Arwiphawee, editor. | Ermasova, Natalia, editor. | Yusuf, Juita-Elena Wie, 1976- editor.
Title: Capital management and budgeting in the public sector / Arwiphawee Srithongrung, Natalia B. Ermasova, and Juita-Elena (Wie) Yusuf, editors.
Description: Hershey, PA : Business Science Reference, [2019]
Identifiers: LCCN 2018023856| ISBN 9781522573296 (hardcover) | ISBN 9781522573302 (ebook)
Subjects: LCSH: Budget. | Capital budget. | Public investments. | Finance, Public.
Classification: LCC HJ2005 .C358 2019 | DDC 352.4/8--dc23 LC record available at https://lccn.loc.gov/2018023856

This book is published in the IGI Global book series Advances in Public Policy and Administration (APPA) (ISSN: 2475-6644; eISSN: 2475-6652)

British Cataloguing in Publication Data
A Cataloguing in Publication record for this book is available from the British Library.

Advances in Public Policy and Administration (APPA) Book Series

ISSN:2475-6644
EISSN:2475-6652

Mission

Proper management of the public sphere is necessary in order to maintain order in modern society. Research developments in the field of public policy and administration can assist in uncovering the latest tools, practices, and methodologies for governing societies around the world.

The **Advances in Public Policy and Administration (APPA) Book Series** aims to publish scholarly publications focused on topics pertaining to the governance of the public domain. APPA's focus on timely topics relating to government, public funding, politics, public safety, policy, and law enforcement is particularly relevant to academicians, government officials, and upper-level students seeking the most up-to-date research in their field.

Coverage

- Government
- Law Enforcement
- Political Economy
- Politics
- Public Administration
- Public Funding
- Public Policy
- Resource Allocation
- Urban Planning

IGI Global is currently accepting manuscripts for publication within this series. To submit a proposal for a volume in this series, please contact our Acquisition Editors at Acquisitions@igi-global.com or visit: http://www.igi-global.com/publish/.

The Advances in Public Policy and Administration (APPA) Book Series (ISSN 2475-6644) is published by IGI Global, 701 E. Chocolate Avenue, Hershey, PA 17033-1240, USA, www.igi-global.com. This series is composed of titles available for purchase individually; each title is edited to be contextually exclusive from any other title within the series. For pricing and ordering information please visit http://www.igi-global.com/book-series/advances-public-policy-administration/97862. Postmaster: Send all address changes to above address.

Titles in this Series

For a list of additional titles in this series, please visit: www.igi-global.com/book-series

Handbook of Research on Advocacy, Promotion, and Public Programming for Memory Institutions
Patrick Ngulube (University of South Africa, South Africa)
Information Science Reference • copyright 2019 • 453pp • H/C (ISBN: 9781522574293) • US $265.00 (our price)

Marketing Peace for Social Transformation and Global Prosperity
Alexandru-Mircea Nedelea (Stefan cel Mare University of Suceava, Romania) and Marilena-Oana Nedelea (Stefan cel Mare University of Suceava, Romania)
Information Science Reference • copyright 2019 • 304pp • H/C (ISBN: 9781522574644) • US $195.00 (our price)

Mathematical Approaches to Understanding Democracy Emerging Research and Opportunities
Alberto Arteta (Troy University, USA)
Information Science Reference • copyright 2019 • 148pp • H/C (ISBN: 9781522575580) • US $165.00 (our price)

Advanced Methodologies and Technologies in Government and Society
Mehdi Khosrow-Pour, D.B.A. (Information Resources Management Association, USA)
Information Science Reference • copyright 2019 • 726pp • H/C (ISBN: 9781522576617) • US $275.00 (our price)

Handbook of Research on Promoting Peace Through Practice, Academia, and the Arts
Mohamed Walid Lutfy (London School of Economics, UK) and Cris Toffolo (Northeastern Illinois University, USA)
Information Science Reference • copyright 2019 • 553pp • H/C (ISBN: 9781522530015) • US $275.00 (our price)

Handbook of Research on Military Expenditure on Economic and Political Resources
Ramesh Chandra Das (Katwa College, India)
Information Science Reference • copyright 2018 • 564pp • H/C (ISBN: 9781522547785) • US $325.00 (our price)

Technology and the New Generation of Active Citizens Emerging Research and Opportunities
Paolo Beneventi (Independent Researcher, Italy)
Information Science Reference • copyright 2018 • 173pp • H/C (ISBN: 9781522537700) • US $135.00 (our price)

Examining the Private Sector's Role in Wealth Creation and Poverty Reduction
Scott A. Hipsher (Webster University, Thailand)
Information Science Reference • copyright 2018 • 325pp • H/C (ISBN: 9781522531173) • US $185.00 (our price)

Handbook of Research on Examining Global Peacemaking in the Digital Age
Bruce L. Cook (Chicago ORT Technical Institute, USA)
Information Science Reference • copyright 2018 • 435pp • H/C (ISBN: 9781522530329) • US $295.00 (our price)

IGI Global
DISSEMINATOR OF KNOWLEDGE

701 East Chocolate Avenue, Hershey, PA 17033, USA
Tel: 717-533-8845 x100 • Fax: 717-533-8661
E-Mail: cust@igi-global.com • www.igi-global.com

Editorial Advisory Board

List of Reviewers

Table of Contents

Detailed Table of Contents

This chapter presents an analysis of four main components of the German capital budgeting system including (1) long-term public capital planning, (2) annual public budgeting and financing, (3) project execution, and (4) public infrastructure evaluation. Germany provides good conditions for capital investments. This chapter explains main reasons for it: institutional framework, healthy public finance, structural reform, and special investment and redemption fund that gave a boost to investments in infrastructure. This case describes the capital budgeting process in Germany and explains the recent trends of public capital investments.

This chapter offers a macro-level review of the capital budgeting process and practices, capital investment projects, and capital funding in the post-Soviet Republic of Uzbekistan. The chapter discusses some of the major challenges related to capital investment and capital budgeting that Uzbekistan faced after the collapse of the Soviet Union, how the country has overcome some of these challenges in 27 years of independence, and what issues remain unresolved. The chapter additionally describes the most sizeable and impactful recent capital investment projects and the role government played in their financing. Finally, the chapter provides a comparison between capital budgeting practices in Uzbekistan, some post-Soviet republics, and the United States.

This chapter discusses the budget process for public capital investments in Ukraine, presents controversies in the current process, and offers several avenues for improvement. In doing so, the author provides a description of the country's normative capital public budgeting framework, presents the institutional setup, and tracks Ukraine's public capital expenditure trends for nearly three decades (1991-2016). The study then discusses implementation, audit, and performance issues in Ukraine's public capital expenditure management and provides recommendations. Because of the country's limited fiscal capacity as compared to its massive infrastructure needs, the author posits that Ukraine can no longer afford to delay or ignore its most pressing public capital investment needs. Because the current list of capital investment proposals is underfunded and too long, the author suggests that the government focuses on finishing strategic, high-priority public projects, while other capital spending proposals target private sector financing once it becomes more readily available.

In this chapter, the authors provide an overview of Taiwan's public infrastructure system using the recommended normative framework presented in Chapter 1. In general, most of Taiwan's practices fit the requirements suggested in Chapter 1. However, there are still rooms for improvements in prioritization, debt affordability analysis, and infrastructure maintenance. In addition, the build-operate-transfer (BOT) model and the so-called "Mosquito Buildings" also feature Taiwan's capital management and budgeting process and are discussed in this chapter. Nowadays, Taiwanese governments place much emphasis on disaster prevention, environmental protection, and renewable energy. These new trends may also affect Taiwan's capital management and budgeting process.

Divided into four parts, this chapter examines infrastructure investment in Vietnam through the lens of a normative framework for capital management and budgeting. Part 1 provides an overview of the country's socio-economic, political, and financial background that would affect the capital management processes. Part 2 introduces the status of Vietnam's infrastructure and its challenges. Part 3 is a comprehensive review of current procedures and processes of capital planning, budgeting, implementation, and maintenance being practiced in Vietnam. The authors then compare and contrast Vietnam's practices with the recommended provisions of the normative framework. Part 4 reviews the probable consequences associated with infrastructure inefficiency, which are implied by Vietnam's inconsistent practices with the framework. This chapter culminates with conclusions and recommendations for capital management and budgeting that are more specific to a developing country like Vietnam.

This chapter evaluates the 12 countries' capital management practices according to the systematic public capital management and budgeting process described in Chapter 1. The chapter characterizes and classifies the management practices of the twelve countries based on the authors' evaluation using the case study descriptions. The authors offer some initial observations based on comparisons across the case study countries and analysis of relationships between capital management and budgeting practices and political, economic, and public sector variables. The chapter proposes a tentative theory of public investment behavior and offers five propositions regarding the factors driving different practices across the case study countries and the consequences of a systematic capital management and budgeting process.

Preface

Public infrastructure systems are vitally important components of a country's economic system. The size of a country's infrastructure stock; the cumulative investment in public infrastructure systems such as roads, sewers, bridges, and electrical distribution systems; the net of accumulated depreciation on the investments; and the quality and availability of the infrastructure to a nation's population play an important role in facilitating economic growth. These public infrastructure systems are key inputs into private sector production processes.

The International Monetary Fund (IMF, 2017) describes public investment as a key input for a network of physical assets including economic infrastructure (e.g., roads, bridges, railroads, airports, and utilities) and social infrastructure (e.g., schools, parks, and hospitals.) Srithongrung and Kriz (2012) find that it is not only the monetary value of public investment that contributes to this physical public infrastructure across countries, but that public capital management practices further enhance the quality and quantity of public infrastructure systems. Combined, the public investments itself and the practices used to decide on public investments enhance the availability and quality of public infrastructure. This finding is substantiated by the IMF's public capital stock data (2017) suggesting that, over time, countries may be investing in equal amounts of public capital but the investments will not yield the same quantity or quality of public capital stock.

Public infrastructure systems are also important in another way. Public capital investments can comprise the largest, single spending item for governments. Building an extension to a transit line or a highway interchange, for example, can easily cost tens of millions or hundreds of millions of dollars. Because of the upfront cost of capital investment, these projects are most often financed using debt, requiring much more deliberate analysis in support of decision making.

Public infrastructure systems vary across countries in terms of size, availability to the population, and quality. The IMF (2017) estimates that in 2015, among 170 countries, the value of China's public infrastructure stock is the world's largest at about $26.8[1] trillion. The world's second and third largest public infrastructure systems are those of the U.S.A. and Japan, equal to $10.9 trillion and $5.5 trillion, respectively. In the same year, the world's three smallest public infrastructure systems are St. Kitts and Nevis, Antigua and Barbuda, and Comoros at about $0.95 billion, $0.99 billion, and $1.2 billion, respectively.

In terms of availability to the public, the IMF (2017) reports that per capita public infrastructure stock remains unequal across countries. OECD countries such as the U.S.A., Canada, Italy, France, German, Spain, Norway, Sweden, and Finland exhibit high public infrastructure availability. In contrast, lower-income countries such as Ethiopia, Tanzania, Malawi, and Zimbabwe have more limited public infrastructure investment (IMF, 2017). In terms of quality, the World Bank (2018) reports that public infrastructure in Germany, Japan, and Sweden rank highest for quality in trade- and transport-related infrastructure (e.g., roads, bridges, ports, railroads and information technology).

This book describes the public capital management and budgeting practices of 12 case study countries – U.S.A., Germany, Taiwan, Korea, Thailand, Vietnam, Burkina Faso, Albania, Moldova, Russia, Ukraine, and Uzbekistan – and the resulting capital investment outcomes. Figure 1 below presents the growth rate of public capital investment and infrastructure stock in the 12 countries during the period from 1990 to 2015. As shown in the figure, the countries have demonstrated different rates of capital investment over time and have had varying success in growing their public capital stock. The highest rates of public capital investment are in Taiwan, Thailand, Burkina Faso, Korea, Vietnam, and the U.S.A. The fastest growth rate of public capital accumulation is in Vietnam, followed by Burkina Faso, Korea, Thailand, and Taiwan. Germany, Moldova, Russia, Ukraine, and Uzbekistan lag behind the other case study countries on both metrics.

Figure 1 also demonstrates the relative efficiency of public investment. The relative height of the bars in this bar chart demonstrates the ability of a country to grow its capital stock beyond that which is offered by direct investment. From this perspective, Albania, Burkina Faso, Korea, Moldova, and Vietnam seem to be doing a good job at growing their capital stock relative to the amount of investment the country is making in infrastructure. Germany, Ukraine, Russia, Taiwan, Thailand, and U.S.A. seem to have experienced challenges in growing capital stock relative to their levels of public investment.

Owing to the importance of public capital management and budgeting practices, the main purpose of this book is to describe capital management and budgeting practices in each of the twelve case study countries shown in Figure 1. An understanding of the differences in public capital budgeting and management practices across the twelve countries should provide a foundation toward building a theory of

Figure 1. Public capital investment and infrastructure stock in the 12 case study countries, 1990-2015
Source: Editors' calculation using IMF (2017) Public Infrastructure Investment and Stock data

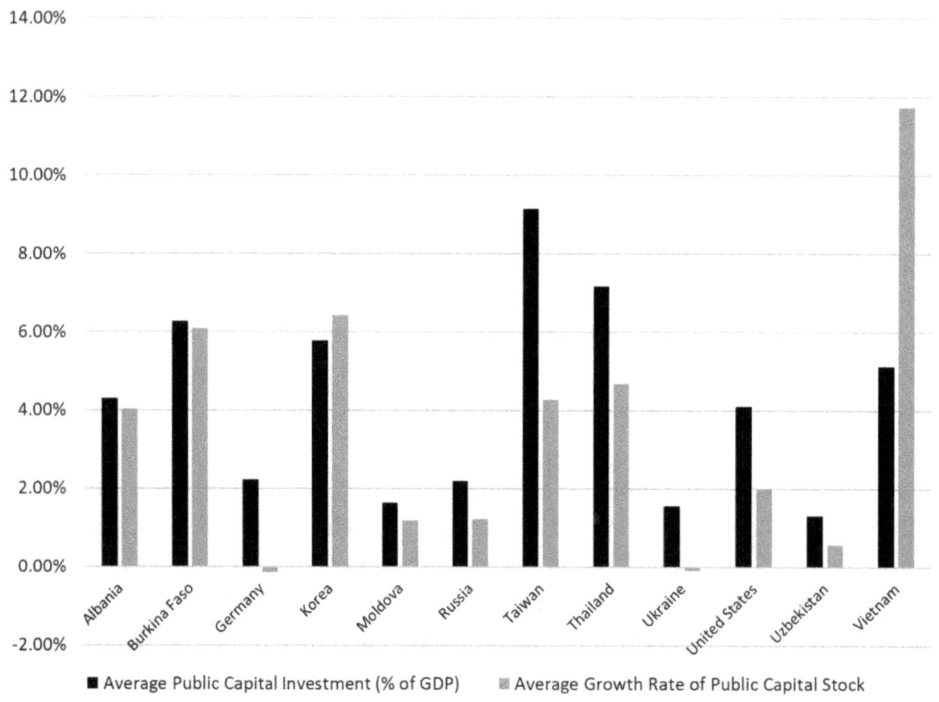

public capital management that explains variations in practices and the outcomes observed from public capital investment. Based on the rich case study descriptions provided in this book and the comparisons of capital management and budgeting practices across the case study countries, public management and international development scholars may develop better understanding of how countries approach capital management and budgeting and explanation of the causes and consequences of public investment and the capital management and budgeting practices that underpin public investment decisions.

This book is comprised of 14 chapters, including an introduction chapter, twelve individual country case studies of public capital management and budgeting practices, and an analysis and conclusion chapter. In the first chapter – the introduction chapter – concepts relevant to the normative theory of public capital budgeting and management are discussed. This normative framework, which takes the form of a systematic public capital management and budgeting process, is drawn from the public budgeting and financial management literature. The normative process is comprised of four main components: (1) long-term capital planning, (2) capital budgeting and financial management, (3) capital project execution and project management, and (4) maintenance processes. Combined, these four components and the practices they encompass constitute the systematic capital management and budgeting process. This process is used as an underlying framework for all country case studies in this book.

The case studies described in Chapters 2 through 13 provide in-depth discussion of the capital management and budgeting process within each country. To the extent possible, the chapters' authors compare the country's capital management and budgeting process with the systematic capital budgeting and management process presented in Chapter 1. For example, the Germany case study (Chapter 3) shows how the country's practices adhere to the four main components of the systematic capital management and budgeting process with the exception that the national government does not have a separate capital budget document. Despite some political issues in government finance, the majority of subnational governments in the U.S.A. (presented in Chapter 2) adhere to all components of the systematic process except for maintenance planning and funding since maintenance funding sources are limited. As described in Chapter 12, the process in Taiwan is similar to those of the subnational governments in the U.S.A. The Taiwanese government is highly committed to a long-term capital planning process, and the country has a robust accounting system. However, like the U.S.A. and many other country case studies included in this book, the Taiwanese government falls short on the last component of the framework in that it has less robust maintenance practices. As the authors of the Vietnam case study (Chapter 13) note, the Vietnamese government tends to perform well in all four components. However, the country experiences institutional problems such as management and bureaucratic expertise, transparency, and forecasting ability. Korea's (Chapter 11) and Thailand's (Chapter 10) performance are similar given that the two countries adopt some activities related to long-term capital planning, while performing less well in the remaining the three components. Burkina Faso (Chapter 9) has its own unique characteristics in that public capital financing has mainly relied on external grants and aid, and as a result, capital management and budgeting practices are underdeveloped.

The transitioning country group includes Uzbekistan (Chapter 4), Ukraine (Chapter 5), Russia (Chapter 6), Moldova (Chapter 7), and Albania (Chapter 8). Albania seems to be the leading country in this group for capital project acquisition and maintenance since the Albanian government is a pioneer in adopting public-private partnerships to finance public roads that are in high demand. Moldova is a leader for capital budgeting and financial management for the transitioning country group. The country has no separate capital budget document, but in practice, the Moldovan government treats capital budget decisions separately from operational budget decisions. Russia performs poorly in all four components of the systematic capital management and budgeting process. Given that capital planning in Russia is fragmented, public spending is not implemented objectively. Ukraine seems to perform better than Russia in terms of project prioritization process. For Ukraine, the case study author notes that the national government adheres to all four components, but does not provide detailed information on specific practices that are consistent with the systematic process. Uzbekistan appears to do well in financial management and project execution compared to the rest of the countries in the transitioning economies group. However, the country does not use long-term debt, and finances capital projects with 100 percent current revenue. This could reduce investment efficiency given that there is a relatively large opportunity cost in committing capital resources to the public projects that can last for several years in the future.

The book concludes with a final chapter that summarizes public capital management and budgeting practices across the country case studies and compares these practices across the different countries. In this chapter the editors discuss possible reasons why some practices included in the systematic capital management and budgeting process are not adopted in some of the case study countries. The chapter also describes the obstacles in adopting these practices, such as the lack of legal requirements, the lack of technical expertise, corruption, or political infeasibility. This chapter provides analysis that shows how capital management and budgeting practices are related to various political, economic, and public sector factors. We develop a tentative theory along with several propositions that connect the systematic capital management and budgeting process to possible antecedents and outcomes. We hope that this tentative theory of public investment behavior offers some suggestions for future in-depth research on why and how countries approach public capital management and budgeting differently, and what are the implications of the systematic approach to capital management and budgeting in terms of public investment outcomes and related institutional and governance factors.

REFERENCES

International Monetary Fund. (2017). *Estimating the stock of public capital in 170 countries (Jan 2017 update).* Retrieved December 10, 2018, from https://www.imf.org/external/np/fad/publicinvestment/pdf/csupdate_jan17.pdf

OECD. (2018). *Purchasing power parities (PPP) (indicator).* Retrieved December 10, 2018, from https://data.oecd.org/conversion/purchasing-power-parities-ppp.htm

Srithongrung, A., & Kriz, K. A. (2012). From public infrastructure to national economic growth: Do systematic investment practices matter? *International Public Management Review*, *13*(2), 19–50.

World Bank. (2018). *International LPI, Global Rankings 2018.* Retrieved December 19, 2018, from https://lpi.worldbank.org/international/global

ENDNOTE

1 The units are in constant international dollars with a base year of 2011. According to the World Bank (2018), an international dollar would buy in the cited country a comparable amount of goods and services a U.S. dollar would buy in the United States. The international dollar is used in conjunction with Purchasing Power Parity (PPP) dollar. The public infrastructure stock data were derived from the International Monetary Fund (2017) in 2011 international dollar value and then converted to U.S. Dollars using the PPP indicators from the OECD (2018).

Acknowledgment

The editors would like to acknowledge the help of everyone involved in this project and, more specifically, the authors, editorial board members, and reviewers. Without their support, this book would not have become a reality.

First, the editors would like to thank the authors for their contributions, insight and interest in advancing the theories and practice of capital management and budgeting in the public sector. Our sincere appreciation goes to the authors for their time and expertise.

Second, the editors wish to acknowledge the valuable contributions of the editorial board members and reviewers for improving the quality, coherence, and content of the country case studies and the book as a whole.

Arwiphawee Srithongrung
University of Illinois at Springfield, USA

Natalia B. Ermasova
Governors State University, USA

Juita-Elena (Wie) Yusuf
Old Dominion University, USA

Section 1

Capital Management and Budgeting in Developed Economies

Chapter 1
A Systematic Public Capital Management and Budgeting Process

Arwiphawee Srithongrung
University of Illinois at Springfield, USA

Juita-Elena (Wie) Yusuf
https://orcid.org/0000-0003-3599-1417
Old Dominion University, USA

Kenneth A. Kriz
https://orcid.org/0000-0001-8050-8506
University of Illinois at Springfield, USA

ABSTRACT

This chapter introduces the readers to a public capital management and budgeting process and its role in generating public infrastructure networks. The main purpose of the chapter is to describe the normative public capital management and budgeting practices that are recommended by the public finance literature. These normative practices are segregated into four main components: (1) long-term capital planning, (2) capital budgeting and financial management, (3) capital project execution and project management, and (4) infrastructure maintenance. Given that the literature recommends specific practices to maximize efficiency in public capital spending, the four main components, combined, are referred to as the systematic capital management and budgeting process. The systematic process discussed in detail in this chapter is used as a common framework for each of the 12 country case studies in describing their respective public capital management and budgeting practices.

DOI: 10.4018/978-1-5225-7329-6.ch001

INTRODUCTION

Public infrastructure systems, such as roads, highways, government buildings, sewerage and water systems, school facilities, police and fire stations, and recreational parks, generate economic and social benefits. At the national level, public infrastructure such as highway networks, the electrical grid, telephone lines and towers, water and sewage systems, and fiber optic lines increase national productivity through two pathways. In the first pathway, national public infrastructure subsidizes private production costs through better services with lower transportation, utility, and communication costs. Through the second pathway, national public infrastructure systems can attract more foreign investment. At the subnational level (i.e., state, county, city, districts), public infrastructure adds valuable amenities into a community, thus increasing housing values and expanding local property tax bases (Yinger, Bloom, Börsch-Supan, Ladd, 1988). At this level, public infrastructure also plays an important role in cushioning local economies, for example, by attracting new businesses and employment into a community (Srithongrung & Kriz, 2012). Public infrastructure plays a critical role in promoting economic growth and development (Munnell, 1992) and in fulfilling basic public health and safety needs (Pagano & Perry, 2008). In the USA, increased interstate highway spending significantly increased economic growth through increased earnings in the manufacturing, retail trade, services, and utilities sectors (Chandra and Thompson (2000)). At the subnational level, many empirical studies have found that public capital spending enhances local economic growth given that public infrastructure, such as roads, bridges, and government buildings, is another input in the local production process (Holtz-Eakin & Schwartz, 1995; Lobo & Rantisi, 1999; Storm & Feiock, 1999; Moomaw, Mullen & Williams, 2002). Further, U.S. states adopting systematic capital budgeting and management practices saw increased public capital stocks and faster economic growth rates in the short run (Srithongrung, 2008).

Given the high value, long lifespan, and tangible nature of capital assets, comprehensive and systematic planning, management, and maintenance efforts are very important (Pagano & Perry, 2008; Steiss, 2005). Coupled with the importance of public infrastructure for national and subnational economies, public capital management and budgeting processes should be carefully and systematically practiced so that a government can meet the public infrastructure needs of society while maintaining strong financial condition. Theoretically, the normative literature suggests that careful and systematic public capital management and budgeting should include four main components: (1) long-term capital planning, (2) capital budgeting and financial management, (3) project execution, and (4) infrastructure maintenance. This systematic approach to capital planning and management introduces efficiency and effectiveness to public investment (Srithongrung, 2008; Wigfall & Lynch, 2003). "Infrastructure management that is based on comprehensive capital planning, effective project oversight, and adequate asset preservation can benefit the economy and society" (Jimenez & Pagano, 2012, p. 125).

THE NORMATIVE FRAMEWORK FOR A SYSTEMATIC CAPITAL MANAGEMENT AND BUDGETING PROCESS

Providing facilities and services for the public good is one of the principle functions of government (Steiss, 2005). Public capital budgeting is defined as a "process or system of administrative procedures which relate long-term capital improvement program with the methods which will be used to pay for those improvements and provides for the implementation of these long-term financial and physical plans"

(Howard, 1973). The capital budgeting literature recommends a systematic capital management and budgeting process (Gatti, 2012; Mikesell, 1999). Ebdon (2004), for example, identifies three essential components of a capital management system: capital planning and budgeting, project management, and asset maintenance. Ammar, Duncombe, and Wright (2001) suggest that the capital management and budgeting process should be comprised of four main components: long-term capital planning, capital budgeting and financial management, execution and project management, and infrastructure maintenance. These components combine fundamental decision-making and detailed action plans that a government will follow to manage its public infrastructure. Building on the literature, we suggest a normative, systematic capital management and budgeting process that can be organized into four components: (1) long-term capital planning, (2) capital budgeting and financial management, (3) centralized execution and project management, and (4) infrastructure maintenance. Figure 1 presents these four main components. The first two components – long-term capital planning and capital budgeting and financial management – comprise the pre-commitment stages of public investment, while centralized execution and project management occur during the post-commitment stage, and infrastructure maintenance reflects the post-completion stage (Jacobs, 2008; Spackman, 2001). Importantly, while each component can be considered separately, the strength of the overall capital management and budgeting system depends on all activities in each of the components (Ebdon, 2004; Ammar et al, 2001).

Long-Term Capital Planning

The first component of the systematic capital management and budgeting process is long-term capital planning which involves four key elements: strategic and comprehensive planning, needs assessment, long-term fiscal planning, and a capital improvement plan. The comprehensive plan (or master plan)

Figure 1. A normative model of the capital management and budgeting process
Source: Srithongrung (2006), adapted from Ammar et al. (2001)

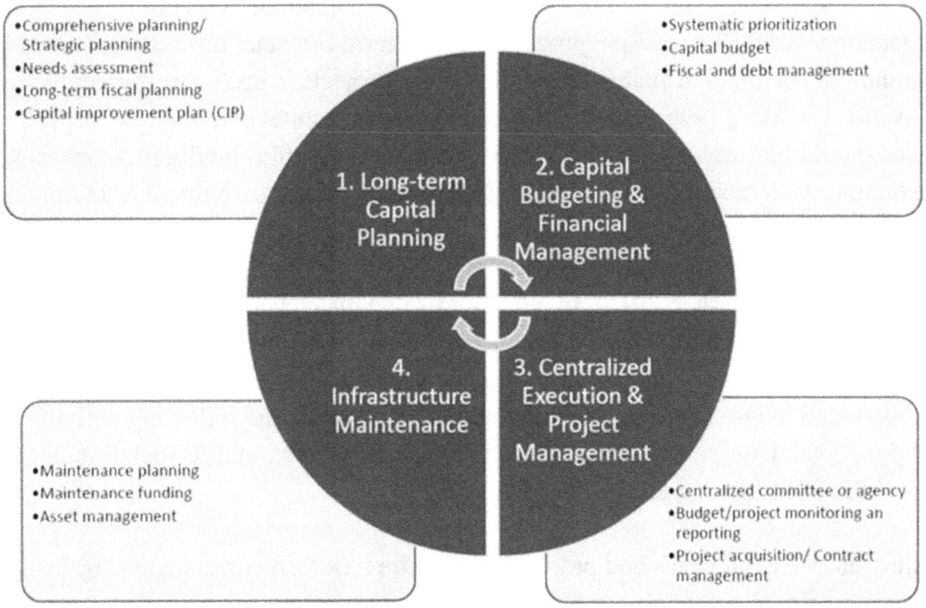

provides a broad policy spelling out future land use and the objectives of community expansion and containment over a relatively lengthy period (Srithongrung, 2006). Strategic planning refers to setting specific strategies that will make the best use of available resources in moving from the present stage to the future stage inspired by the comprehensive plans (Srithongrung, 2006). The goals, objectives, and strategies identified in the strategic plan will have implications for capital needs and provide the basis for identifying capital requirements (Beckett-Camarata, 2008; Robinson, 1993). The literature emphasizes the importance of coordinating capital planning with the strategic and comprehensive plans (Ammar et al., 2001; Beckett-Camarata, 2003; Dowall, 2001; Halachmi & Sekwat, 1997; Mikesell, 1999; Price, 2002; Robinson, 1993), and a good comprehensive plan should contain a capital component (Ammar et al., 2001; Mikesell, 1999). As such, a strategic and comprehensive capital plan will be based on a variety of long-term factors, such as estimates of population growth, demographics and changes in demographics, changes in the underlying economic base, transportation growth, technological changes, and the needs and demands of the citizens (Dowall, 2001; Jimenez & Pagano, 2012; Mikesell, 1999; Stich & Eagle, 2005).

A needs assessment can be used to link comprehensive planning and strategic planning to capital investment needs. The needs assessment should include an assessment of capital assets and the organization's mission, strategic planning, and programmatic-based activities. Information about existing assets is important for determining capital resources that are currently available and the resources that are needed (U.S. General Accounting Office, 1998). According to the U.S. National Advisory Council on State and Local Budgeting (NACSLB), assessment of capital assets as a best practice includes inventorying capital assets and assessing the conditions of these assets and the factors that could affect the need for or ability to maintain the assets in the future (Westerman & Casey, 2007).

Long-term capital planning must include long-term fiscal planning, which is comprised of revenues, expenditures, and debt burden forecasts; otherwise, capital project acquisition would be impossible (Ammar et al., 2001; Aronson & Schwartz, 2004). A government should project its future revenues from different sources including tax and non-tax revenues (such as road user fees and charges, earmarked taxes, and other public service fees), potential external grants, and long-term debt to identify the aggregated level of public resources (Steiss, 2005). This aggregated level of public resources needs to be separated from annual operational spending so that public investment is not competing with public consumption in the resource allocation and decision-making processes. Long-term financial projections should identify the aggregate amount of resources available for public capital projects in each year, based on the individual sources of revenue (Singhvi, 1996). Furthermore, in long-term capital planning, the benefits of a public capital project should be carefully matched with its sources of public funding (Aronson & Schwartz, 2004). For example, a toll road should be used to finance public roads, earmarked restaurant taxes should be used to finance a local entertainment complex or a baseball stadium, and local property taxes should be used to finance local fire stations. This is done to ensure that the public dollars spent correspond with the benefits received (Fisher, 2016). In other words, the match between public project benefits and sources of funding assures that social costs are distributed in an efficient manner.

Effective long-term capital planning that incorporates strategic and comprehensive planning with needs assessment and long-term fiscal planning should encompass the following activities (Ammar et al., 2001; Ebdon, 2004; Government Performance Project, 2005; National Association of State Budgeting Officers, 1999; 2014; Srithongrung, 2006):

- Identification of capital needs and projections that are based on current and projected statistics of capital inventories, demographic, and economic conditions;

- Development of capital inventories;
- Identification of capital needs and projections for a five-year period with longer-term projections presented for programs with reasonably predictable longer-term needs;
- Identification of capital needs and projections that are presented independently of financing requirements or opportunities;
- Comprehensive assessment of capital project cost and financing;
- Determination of the full financial burden and funding opportunities of programs and of individual projects, considering external resources such as grants and aids; and
- Analysis of alternative methods of financing capital programs and projects are described and assessed, including debt financing and use of current revenues.

If the above activities are carefully practiced, a government should be able to establish a Capital Improvement Program (CIP), which is "a list of the major capital projects and acquisitions needed over a five- to six-year period, appropriation of expenditures to be incurred by the identified projects, financial sources for the project funding, and the impacts of the projected outcomes on the future operating budget" (Vogt, 2004, p. 19). An effective CIP should not only identify the location, scale, and timing of capital projects and include a fiscal plan to fund the projects but also include the impacts of a capital projects (Beckett-Camarata, 2008). An essential feature of the CIP is that it apportions capital expenditures across the years covered by the CIP. Since the CIP ranks projects in priority order, it is considered an important blue print for a government to understand its capital needs and to direct government execution (Beckett-Camarata, 2008). The CIP facilitates systematic government investment by answering two managerial questions: (1) when to invest in what projects, and (2) how to finance the projects over a multiple-year period (usually around 5-6 years). Furthermore, in a transparent capital budgeting process, the CIP contains descriptions of the capital projects, their justification, and a glossary or user's guide (Ammar et al., 2001). The process for developing the CIP should also provide opportunities for stakeholder involvement (Westerman & Casey, 2007).

The public capital budgeting and financial management literature recommends the activities in this first component because long-term planning promotes investment efficiency by targeting types and locations for capital resources allocation (Gatti, 2012; Srithongrung, 2006; Steiss & Nwagwu, 2001). Comprehensive planning is expected to provide public infrastructure that supports economic development in the community (Gianakis & McCue, 1999). The CIP lays a foundation for capital investment in a multi-year time frame so that management can schedule investment timing in a way that corresponds to resource availability and construction phases (Moak & Killian, 1963). Finally, capital planning is useful in justifying the proposed capital projects, and hence preventing arbitrary cuts that often occur when political projects with low-ranked priorities are requested for investment in the first year (Adams, 1998). A case study from the U.S. state of Minnesota found that capital planning and the CIP document alleviate "one-shot" and "on-the-spot" decisions that are haphazard and politically driven (King 1995).

Capital Budgeting and Financial Management

The CIP must be annually revised to update capital project needs, remove funded projects and add new projects. In general, the capital projects proposed in the annual capital budget document are first-year projects listed in the CIP (Robinson, 1993). The capital budget is "a plan of proposed outlays and the means of financing them for the current fiscal period" (Moak & Hillhouse, 1975, p.2). The capital budget "provides a mechanism to smooth out peaks and valleys, regularize construction activity in an effort to avoid local bottlenecks that can delay projects and inflate their cost, avoid excessive drains on the tax base when projects must be paid for, and balance spending with the resources available within political, economic, and legal tax and debt limits" (Mikesell, 1999, p. 226). The Government Finance Officers Association (GFOA) recommends state and local governments in the U.S. prepare a separate capital budget and include the following information for each project: description of the project's purpose, estimated total project costs and costs for the budget period, identified funding sources, timetable for completion, links to other plans (such as strategic plan or comprehensive plan), and the operating impact of the project (Government Finance Officers Association, 2016). Essentially, a community that has a capital budget that is *separate* from its operational budget is better able to focus on the capital resource allocation process. This is because capital projects have long-term benefits and should be financed through long-term debt (Mikesell, 2017). If the community does not separate the capital budget from the operational budget, short-term consumption will be competing with long-term investment, resulting in inefficient and ineffective use of public resources (Murdick & Deming, 1968).

In addition to annual budgeting, the systematic capital management and budgeting process includes two other elements: project prioritization and fiscal and debt management. The normative literature suggests that governments should prioritize capital projects and maintain prudential fiscal and debt management. The first activity is intended to match resources with needs, while the second is intended to promote fiscal stability, maintain and improve the government's bond rating, and maintain an optimal balance between investment and consumption expenditures. Capital needs generally exceed public capital resources; thus, project prioritization is necessary. Systematic project prioritization supports evidence-based decision-making by including an extensive set of capital projects and applying a wide set of criteria reflecting project benefits, the needs for spending effectiveness, public values, and legitimacy for relatively large public spending (Marcelo, Mandri-Perrott, House, and Schwartz, 2016). Given the needs for evidence, comprehensiveness, effectiveness, value, and legitimacy, governments should establish a systematic project prioritization process. This process should include clear and objective criteria for project selection that reflect community priorities and investment targets. The process should facilitate consistent comparison of proposed capital projects based on criteria determined to be important by the community or jurisdiction (Ammar et al., 2001; Ebdon, 2004; Robinson, 1993) and improve objectivity in decision making (Calia, 2001). For state and local governments in the USA, the Government Finance Officers Association (GFOA, 2016) recommends including information on how capital projects are evaluated and prioritized in the capital budget.

Cost-benefit analysis is the main method for systematic project selection, allowing a government to compare the benefits of the projects with investment costs, while adding policy effectiveness and social values into decision-making through the measurement of social benefits (Burger & Hawkesworth, 2013). There are various cost-benefit analysis measures available for governments, including net present value (NPV), benefit-cost ratio (BCR), payback period, and internal rate of return (IRR). The NPV and BCR are superior to the payback period, given that they account for time-value money, which is an opportunity cost in committing capital resources to a public project (Mikesell, 2017). The BCR is not appropriate for comparing projects with relatively small cost, as the benefit-cost ratio of the projects will be inflated. NPV is the most useful approach to the public projects since it does not use cost size to standardize the public projects and incorporates time value money of the projects. In the USA, the federal government requires departments and agencies proposing capital projects submitting cost-benefit analysis to use discount factors for time-value money announced by the Office of Management and Budget – OMB's

Circular No. A-94, "Guidelines and Discount Rates for Benefit-Cost Analysis of Federal Programs." In South African state-owned companies, NPV and IRR were the most common cost-benefit analysis methods (Hall and Mutshutshu, 2013). Among Canadian municipal governments, payback period was the dominant measure (Chan, 2004). However, at the subnational level, there is some evidence suggesting that cost benefit analysis is not used in project prioritization processes due to technical capacity limitation in measuring the benefits of the public projects (Stanley & Block, 1984).

Beyond cost-benefit analysis, multiple-criteria decision techniques are often used to prioritize public projects at the subnational level in the USA. The techniques range from simple project ranking criteria to weighting systems in which each criterion is assigned a weight based on public values. Tables 1 and 2 present a simple project prioritization approach using multiple criteria and a weighting system, respectively. In the simple project prioritization approach (Table 1), budget analysts and agency heads proposing capital projects answer questions such as whether the project is legally required, reduces hazards, enhances the executive's policy priorities, and supports the economic environment, and the consequences of not funding the projects. Cost-benefit analysis results are included (the sixth criterion in Table 1). Then all scores would be combined as shown in the table.

In the weighting system, each criterion is assigned different points and weights are based on community values. Table 2 presents the weighting system used by Chatham County, North Carolina (USA) to prioritize the capital projects (Vogt, 2004). As an example of the system, the operating budget impact criterion is assigned 15 points, and its weight equals to 11.34 percent. The operating budget impact is defined as whether the project will decrease future operating expenses. The financing criterion is defined as the extent to which a project can be financed with non-general fund revenue sources. It has an equal score and weight to those of the operating budget impact. This suggests that the County is concerned about its financial condition after committing to large capital projects and hence, reflects such values into its prioritization criterion's scores and weight. The simplest ranking criteria is a set of subjective categories containing such criterion as "Essential, Desirable, Acceptable, and Deferrable". This type of system is often found in local governments in the USA (Tigue, 1996). The multiple-criteria project prioritization system has several benefits, including allowing a government to prioritize its projects based on its community's goals, making best use of available information across the set of proposed projects, and encouraging explicit *ex ante* identification of decision criteria (Marcelo et al., 2016). Based on

Table 1. Simple project ranking system using multiple criteria

Rating Question	Clearly No Clearly Yes						
Is the request legally mandated?	0	1	2	3	4	5	6
Does the request eliminate or reduce a hazard or a threat to public health or safety?	0	1	2	3	4	5	6
Does the request fit with or advance the goals and objectives of the governing board?	0	1	2	3	4	5	6
Does the project support economic development in the community?	0	1	2	3	4	5	6
Would the consequences be severe if the request were not funded?	0	1	2	3	4	5	6
Do the benefits balance or exceed the cost?	0	1/1	2/1	3/1	4/1	5/1	6/1
Total score or rating	**0**						**36**

Source: Vogt, 2004.

Table 2. Weighted project prioritization system

Rating Criteria	Definition	Maximum Points	Percentage Weighting
Functional area priority	Priority of project among requests in functional area: 5 for top-ranked project to 0 for any project ranked sixth or below priority.	5	3.79
Safety	Extent to which project eliminates, prevents, or reduces an immediate hazard to safety.	14	10.61
Mandates	Extent to which project helps county meet existing or new mandates.	13	9.83
Timing/Linkages	Extent to which project is timely, a continuation of a project currently under way related to other high-priority projects, etc.	12	9.09
Economic Impact	Extent to which project enhances economic development in county, while it protects the environment, or directly or indirectly adds to the tax base.	11	8.33
Efficiencies	Extent to which project contributes to savings in county operating or capital spending.	10	7.58
Maintaining current level of service	Extent to which project is necessary for county to continue to provide one or more services at current standards.	9	6.82
Improving access	Extent to which project improves the quality of existing services.	8	6.1
Service Improvement	Extent to which project improves the quality of existing services.	7	5.3
Service addition	Extent to which project increases the quantity of existing services.	3	2.3
Operating budget impact	Project that decrease future operating expenses receive a positive score, ranging from 0 to 15. Projects that have no effect on operating expenses receive a score of 0. Projects that increase operating expenses score anywhere from 0 to -15.	0-15, 0, or 0-(-15)	11.34
Community support and county long-term plans	Extent to which project has broad and/or string support from the community and is consistent with the county strategic plan or other long-term pans.	10	7.58
Financing	Extent to which project can be financed with non-general fund revenue sources.	15	11.34
Maximum points, all categories		**132**	**100**

Source: Vogt, 2004.

these benefits, the World Bank also recommends the multi-criteria project ranking approach (Marcelo et al., 2016).

For fiscal and debt management, the normative literature advocates budgetary forecasts, debt affordability analysis, and clear debt and financial management policies in capital financing. First, governments should conduct multi-year revenue and expenditure forecasting to identify net cash flow (total projected revenue minus total projected operating expenditures). The net cash flow is then compared with capital investment expenditures required in future years as identified in the CIP. This activity marries capital planning to fiscal planning. It also helps governments locate gaps between capital needs and resources and to prepare financially for increasing capital project demands. Multi-year fiscal forecasting indicates the government's capacity for capital funding and thus, whether the activity will be beneficial in promoting fiscal stability (Aronson & Schwartz, 2004). Spackman (2002), following the guidelines of the OECD (Richard & Daniel, 2001; The World Bank, 1998), recommends the medium-term budget framework which forms the basis for multi-year spending ceilings for capital budgeting, especially for developing and transitional economies whose government budgets are prepared once a year.

Second, debt affordability analysis should be conducted before issuing bonds to ensure that the amount of debt does not exceed the ability of the tax and revenue base (Johansen & Cooper, 2007; GFOA, 2001; Vogt 2004, Steiss, 2005). Debt affordability analysis involves calculating debt or debt service obligation on a per capita basis or as a ratio to total revenues or expenditures and a ratio to local property taxes. The per capita debt burden is not comprehensive given that it does not tie any income or financial capacity of a jurisdiction in paying debt services. However, such an approach is used often since it is convenient to benchmark debt levels in a jurisdiction with another. The ratio of debt service to total revenue or expenditure is used often in the U.S. state governments since it presents debt capacity relative to a state government's budget sizes (Vogt, 2004). The ratio of total net outstanding debt to property value is used often at the municipal levels in the USA since it is directly tied with the sources to pay debt services and is also convenient in comparing with statutory debt limits in which local governments in the USA are often subject to (Braun, 2006). In the USA, the two common approaches that are used to judge whether a government's debt obligation is too high are: (1) comparing per capita debt with other similar governments or to a group average (e.g., national average) and (2) using benchmarks, such as debt service as a percent of operating expenditures that is considered low if 5 percent or less, moderate if less than 10 percent, and high if more than 15 percent (Simonsen, Robbins & Brown, 2003). In addition to calculating debt burden, debt affordability should also be tied to characteristics of the community, such as population size, wealth, growth rate, and attitudes toward taxation and debt (Johansen & Cooper, 2007; Vogt 2004).

Third, governments should maintain an operating reserve (i.e., a "rainy-day" fund) to cover unanticipated revenue shortfalls or unexpected expenditures. Fitch (2002) suggests that the appropriate size of the rainy-day fund depends on a government's revenues, expenditures, and the economic environment. Governments should have clear debt management policies such as debt limits and debt disclosure. Subnational governments in the U.S. that issue municipal debt must comply with Securities and Exchange Commission (SEC) Rule 15c2-12, which requires that bond issuing governments must submit annual financial information and provide notice of certain events material to their bonds or notes. Fitch (2002) also suggests that "superior debt disclosure" should be conducted. In addition to complying with the Rule 15c2-12, debt disclosure should include not only the management's discussion and analysis section of the financial report but also supplementary information, including economic outlook, demographic trends, net outstanding debts, and tax assessments.

Finally, governments should establish a clear guideline for capital financing, e.g., what kinds of public projects should be financed through current revenue (e.g., taxes, external grants and user charges as well as earmarked taxes) and what kinds of public projects should be financed through long-term debt. Table 3 presents capital financing methods, types of public projects suitable for each method, and advantages and disadvantages of each method. Mikesell (2017) suggests that public capital projects which have long useful lives and generate long-term benefits to the public (e.g., roads and bridges as well as public facilities) should be financed through long-term debts with debt service coming from general revenues or taxes. In the U.S., the interest on most bonds issued by state and local governments for a public purpose are not subject to federal income taxes and state income taxes to the extent that the bondholder is a resident of the state where the government is located. Public projects that are secured by a dedicated revenue stream, such as public utility plants and sewerage systems using user charges, should be financed by revenue bonds. Public projects that have relatively short useful lives, such as police cars, equipment, or computer software, should be financed through current revenue. Vogt (2004) observes that relatively fast-growing communities tend to use borrowing to finance about 80 percent of total capital projects given that the community will experience economic growth. Meanwhile, communities with

Table 3. Summary of public capital financing methods

Funding Mechanism and Assets/Projects	*Advantages*	*Disadvantages*
Pay As You Go (PAYGO) • Assets that are not expensive, have short useful lives, benefit is achieved early, requiring matching local funds • Projects that can be reasonably phased given annual expenditures	• Saves interest and other issuance costs • Preserves financial flexibility • Protects borrowing capacity • Enhances credit quality	• Generally insufficient for capital needs • Discourages intergenerational equity • Creates uneven flow of issuing debt
Tax-Exempt Bonds • Assets with long useful lives • Projects that are expensive to acquire or that exceed the capacity of the PAYGO program	• Permits acquisition of assets as needed • Promotes intergenerational equity • Smooths capital expenditures	• Adds financial and administrative costs of procuring capital assets
Certificates of Participation • Projects that are expensive to acquire or that exceed the capacity of the PAYGO program • Purchases of equipment, buildings, real property	• Permits acquisition of assets as needed • Voter approval not needed	• Higher interest costs relative to issuing debt
Grants • Assets qualifying for grant assistance (e.g., transportation projects)	• Expands size of capital program with little or no cost to local taxpayers	• Limited amounts • Availability may not coincide with priorities • Administrative or compliance costs
Impact Fees/ Exactions • Projects benefitting new developments (e.g., water, sewer, and transportation facilities)	• Initial capital outlay can be funded at no cost to taxpayers	• Does not address ongoing maintenance or replacement costs • May be politically unpopular
Revolving Loan Programs • Assets qualifying for loan assistance (e.g., wastewater treatment projects)	• May lower financing costs	• Availability may not coincide with priorities • Administrative or reporting costs
State Bond Banks • Projects of small governments appropriate for debt financing	• May lower financing costs	• May not be available when needed • May impose burdensome requirements
Public/Private Partnerships • Projects appropriate for franchising agreements, service contracts, or joint development	• Lowers capital and/or operating costs	• Additional staff resources to negotiate, coordinate, monitor
Private Contributions • Facilities adjacent to private properties	• Lowers capital and/or operating costs	• Additional staff resources to identify contributors and coordinate activities

Source: Adapted from Tigue (1996)

slower growth rates will tend to use current revenues for about half of their capital project needs, while at the same time looking to employ innovative financing strategies.

Innovative financing methods such as Certificates of Participation (COPs) are often used by communities that have little borrowing capacity available, at least under legal debt limits (most states limit the amount of debt that municipalities can issue) or who have other difficulties accessing the long-term debt market. In a COP arrangement, a government leases property or equipment from a private party (known as the lessor), which acquires the property through issuing debt; the government then leases the property and makes payments to the lessor, who then makes the debt payments (with a mark-up).

Another innovative capital financing method used by state governments in the U.S. is creating a state revolving fund. In this method, a state government issues long-term bonds and then lends the bond proceeds, along with other financing sources, such as a portion of general revenue, federal grants and special taxes, to local governments with relatively low interest rates. Repayments by the local government help to "recapitalize" the revolving fund. This financial tool is often used to help small governments in the U.S. obtain financing for sanitation public projects, such as water plants and sewerage systems (Levine & Augustino, 1994).

Other innovative financing methods used by U.S. subnational governments include impact fees and bond banks. Impact fees are widely used in California as communities are expanding rapidly while referenda passed by citizens restricted the growth of property tax revenues. Impact fees are development fees collected from commercial and residential developers with the revenues being used to pay for debt service on debt issued to make public improvements demanded by individuals living or working in the development. State bond banks are state entities that borrow to capitalize themselves, and then give loans to local (generally smaller) governments who would normally borrow at higher interest rates. This mechanism is similar to revolving loan funds in that local governments can borrow at lower rates and with lower costs of issuance due to economies of scale. Public-private partnerships (PPP) are a method used to finance public projects through franchising agreement, service contracts, or joint development. The PPP helps a government adopt public projects in a timely manner, share risks and technologies with its private partners, and save project acquisition cost, but it may add staff time in managing contracts (Tigue, 1996).

King (1995) observes that systematic capital budgeting and financial management practices support an investment policy goal (i.e., investment effectiveness). The practices provide a mechanism to finance multi-year capital programs without having to alter them for unstable fiscal situations. Furthermore, the practices help enhance bond ratings, which in turn reduces project acquisition cost. For example, in the U.S., well-constructed, project prioritization criteria helped the State of Minnesota stay focused on its investment proposals, using critical versus strategic criteria to prevent the government from committing to unbalanced capital spending between new and maintenance projects. The critical criteria directed the government to focus on repairing and replacing obsolete facilities to save future maintenance cost, reducing infrastructure backlogs, and reducing the need to develop public projects on an emergency basis. The strategic criteria helped the government focus on new construction to strategically expand public infrastructure systems.

Forte (1989) observes that a good forecast helps a government invest in capital projects at a stable rate across time. A government investing at a stable rate does not need to increase tax rates (Forte, 1989), yielding taxpayers' and voters' satisfaction, while at the same time being responsive to public needs. For example, the City of McKinney, Texas identified $21 million in capital resources without increasing taxes by conducting a debt affordability analysis, budgetary forecast, and debt service capacity study (Forte, 1989). Darr (1998) asserts that because of debt management policies, including statutory debt limits, rainy day funds, and innovative capital financing, the Commonwealth of Virginia has been able to preserve its superior bond rating profile over a 30-year period. The Virginia state government created a diversified fund reserve to support the operating budget during recessions and for use in financing capital projects when interest rates were high. For some state governments in the U.S., operational costs of new facilities are incorporated into the evaluation of capital project proposals. In others, the annual budget document is likely to have a special section that presents major capital projects and acquisitions that are up for approval and funding that year (Ermasova, 2013). Through their commitment to long-range fiscal planning, governments can ensure fiscal discipline and stable infrastructure funding by maintaining an optimal balance between consumption and investment.

Centralized Execution and Project Management

The centralized execution and project management component of the systematic capital management and budgeting process is an essential step that ensures capital projects are delivered on time and within budget (Ammar et al., 2001). The normative literature recommends that governments identify a central committee or agency to supervise project construction, monitor project performance, track the use of funds, and report funded project progress to the public and central government (Dupont-Morales & Harris, 1994; Government Performance Project, 2005; Westerman, 2004; Sermier & Macone, 1993). This recommendation is based on the idea that centralized project management increases government accountability, capital program effectiveness, and funding efficiency (Sermier & Macone, 1993). Furthermore, Burger and Hawkesworth (2013) suggest that strong oversight and review by a central authority may mitigate perverse incentives and budget maximization tendencies.

Project management by itself is also a key element of a systematic approach to capital management and budgeting. Project management concerns the implementation of decisions made during capital planning. With this component, government seeks to minimize delays, cost overruns, threats to worker and citizen safety, and other problems by detecting such issues in a timely way and correcting them quickly (Ebdon, 2004; Jimenez & Pagano, 2012). The key to strong project management is careful monitoring of progress against the schedule and budget and frequent reporting of project status (through management reports) at both the agency and central levels. The project monitoring reports should include information such as percent of project completed, percent of project budget expended, progress on key project milestone, contract status information (including time remaining and percentage used), revenue and expenditure activities, cash flow and investment maturities, funding commitment, available appropriation, and comparison of results in relation to established performance measures (GFOA, 2007). In addition, delay estimates, budget overruns, revised cost estimates, and overrun explanations should also be included in projects status report (Dupont-Morales & Harris, 1994).

The Government Finance Officers Association (2017) recommends that governments in the U.S. regularly monitor capital projects' financial and project activity. The best practices for project monitoring include the following activities (Government Finance Officers Association, 2017):

- Confirmation that a project plan exists that identifies all required resources and milestone work products and assurance that it is being followed.
- Confirmation that the project's scope has been clearly identified and the project stays within scope or that changes to scope have been made consistent with an established process.
- A review of project-related financial transactions to support budget review, auditing, and asset management.
- A review of expenditures.
- A review of project retainages, warranties, or other conditional performance schedules.
- Review of encumbrances and estimates of planned expenditure activity.
- Confirmation of continued availability and appropriateness of revenue sources.
- Confirmation of the adequacy of cash flow.
- Review of the timing of investment maturities disbursements.
- Review of sources and project uses of bond proceeds and grants.
- Results compared to established measures of performance.

Governments tend to contract out large project acquisition for several reasons. Theoretically, for competitive and transparent biding processes, multiple producers are competing for contracts; the best contractor who can deliver public projects at lowest cost with highest quality in a shortest time frame would be awarded the contract (Savas, 2000; Dastidar & Mukherjee, 2014). Contracting out promotes efficiency through economies of scales, since public projects may require several administrative units. It is argued that once the contractors are responsible for project management, a government can have a reasonably sized administrative team to monitor contractors' performance rather than managing the projects itself (Savas, 2000). In capital project management, risks are defined as "the potentials for realization of unwanted, negative consequences of an event" (Baldry, 1998, p. 36). Public capital projects have different risks than private projects. For example,

- Commencement, execution and completion of a project rely on the higher authority of a public organization, which may not be the direct sponsor of the project. For example, a large expressway project may be contracted by the Department of Transportation; however, project initiation may depend on elected and appointed officers in a legislative body;
- Profits are not a major goal of public projects. The benefits sought are usually public benefits except when the public project can serve the public while at the same time generating some tangible revenue in terms of by-products (e.g., utilities);
- A broad range of procurement methods are involved, including commercial contracts, lease purchases and PPPs;
- Success in project management and acquisition is defined according to citizen and stakeholder perspectives, including functional satisfaction, aesthetic merits, environmental impacts and hazard removal. Monetary benefits of the project are rarely a focus;
- Project implementation is conducted within the public domain and is subject to formal review by statutory bodies and informal scrutiny by the media and the public. (Baldry, 1998, p. 36).

Given such characteristics, Baldry (1998) observes that public organizations possessing good project management skills tend to be aware of and recognize the broad impacts of risks while coordinating contracts. A government skilled in project management is aware that it may have to underwrite significant financial resources that arise due to exigencies such as postponement, cancellation, or non-performance of the contracted projects. Such events may have damaging effects on public service delivery (Baldry, 1998). These risks are retained within a government and should be added to the project cost as contingencies. Public organizations may try to reduce risk by carefully writing contract terms to establish the culture, relationship, and expectation with the private sector to avoid future risk exposure (Baldry, 1998). Research suggests that in contract management, project risks are fewer and more manageable when a government contracts with businesses that have similar management cultures and values (Liu, Meng & Fellows, 2015).

Effective project implementation can be achieved if governments detect and address problems in capital project execution as early as possible. Project monitoring prevents cost overruns for large and time-consuming projects, thus increasing funding efficiency. Performance measurement can be implemented in several ways, including measuring cost per unit output and identifying project outcomes, such as a community economic growth and tax base expansion. It is important to note that output is different than outcomes. Output is directly related to public capital project implementation processes.

For example, the number of daily passengers for a transit project is an output measure. Outcomes, on the other hand, are impacts of the public project and are indirectly related to the public capital investment. For example, clean air, reduced traffic congestion, and reduced commute time from residential areas to business areas are outcomes of transit projects. Outcome measures capture both the effect of the public capital project and the values of the community, while output measures reflect efficiency and effectiveness in capital project planning and implementation. Performance measurement should include both types of measures in capturing program effectiveness and efficiency (Kamensky, 1993). In addition to quantitative measurement, the Government Finance Officers Association (GFOA, 2007) recommends that an organization responsible for project acquisition should solicit stakeholder feedback to aid in designing and implementing projects. The GFOA (2007) recommends that in addition to output and outcome measurement, a government should conduct performance review for project acquisition to assess the following:

- Project acquisition is closed out appropriately with all systems used to manage, monitor, and report on the project;
- All remaining contract encumbrances are properly handled;
- Established procedures for user acceptance of the project are functioning and final project completion procedures have been followed;
- All reporting requirements by grantors and bond covenants have been completed;
- Project data is properly recorded on fixed asset schedules and government capital assets are added to the account for future tracking; and
- Project acquisition is disclosed, properly documented, and reported.

Performance measurement and evaluation is important in the project execution phase because it provides information to help project managers adjust their capital-related activities (Kamensky, 1993). This information helps officials understand how projects are accomplished and helps managers choose the least costly projects from all projects that serve similar goals. Interviews with former budget analysts, department heads, and the Planning Director of the Illinois (USA) Department of Transportation (IDOT) revealed the perception that centralized project management can yield investment effectiveness through two mechanisms: (1) by detecting construction problems and assuring that construction meets standards, and (2) by providing information that facilitates a new round of capital planning (Srithongrung, 2006). The Government Performance Project or GPP (2005) also reported that IDOT practices in centralized monitoring for project execution helped in detecting cost overruns and project inefficiency, and enhancing the quality of construction work. The GPP (2005) further noted that IDOT can correct delays and safety compliance within approximately two to three weeks for poor quality and cost overruns, and one to two months for project inefficiency and cost delays.

Infrastructure Maintenance

Once completed, capital assets are consumed and used for their designated purposes. Existing capital will decay, requiring on-going and preventive maintenance, and eventually will need to be replaced. Once a government decides to invest in a specific infrastructure, it is responsible for maintaining the facility in proper condition (Jimenez & Pagano, 2012). Asset maintenance is important for maximizing the use of capital assets, especially since operating and maintaining costs can far exceed the initial cost

(Ebdon, 2004). The infrastructure maintenance component of the systematic capital management and budgeting process is comprised of two main activities: maintenance planning and maintenance funding (Ammar et al., 2001).

Maintenance planning involves conducting public asset management by evaluating the conditions and useful life of public infrastructure, projecting the capacity of public facilities in the current and future years, and finally, comparing its service capacity to current and future usage. Regular condition assessment is important for establishing capital planning and establishing a CIP based on actual needs. Maintenance planning, on the other hand, is tied directly to the assessment of the condition of the capital stock, using an asset management system (Pagano, 1984). By dedicating more funding to maintenance, governments can defer capital investment needs and avoid larger, more expensive capital project needs in the future. A maintenance plan should include actions and expenditures that extend the useful life of capital assets, including upgrades and replacements of building systems such as structures, enclosures, mechanical, plumbing, and electrical systems (Pagano, 1984). To perform good asset maintenance, governments need regularly updated information to know what they own and the condition of their assets. In the U.S., the majority of the states have developed asset management systems "designed to assess the condition of and to estimate the intensity and timing of maintenance and repair investments for facilities in transportation, corrections, office buildings, the state capitol, libraries and parks, and recreation" (Jimenez & Pagano, 2012, pp. 132-133).

Table 4 presents four commonly used methods of capital asset inventory determination: engineering assessment, performance measurement, service impact indicators, and perpetual inventory methods (Tigue, 1998). Engineering assessment, such as road and bridge condition evaluation, is used when service quality of the public infrastructure is the focus. Methods of engineering assessment can be arbitrary, and the comprehensibility of results may be confined to professional groups. Performance measurement generally focuses on quantity of output. The strength of this method is that it can be readily tied to the demand for capital projects. The disadvantage of this method is that it does not focus on quality of public projects. The service impact indicator is a type of outcome mentioned previously. This method incorpo-

Table 4. Capital asset inventory approaches

METHOD AND UNDERLYING CONCEPT	EXAMPLES	ADVANTAGES	DISADVANTAGES
Engineering Assessment (focus on service quality)	Bridge condition rating ranging from 0-10, Road pavement thickness, Deferred maintenance ($), Infrastructure backlog ($)	Focuses on quality of service rather than quantity	Can be costly, can be subjective if not done by technical specialists
Performance Measurement (focus on service quantity or output)	Per capita lane miles, numbers of population per 1,000 square footage, number of service calls for water line repairs/month	Focuses on capacity to serve citizens, can be easily tied with master plan and community profile data	Excludes quality of public infrastructure system
Service Impact Indicator (focus on service impact or outcome)	Commuting times to work, Annual % increase in housing units/ business permits	Involves both quality and quantity dimensions	Not necessarily related to service levels
Perpetual Inventory Method (focus on accounting)	Record of capital outlays in the past period, applied appreciate rate and useful life of each assets	Practical	Needs good records/book keeping

Source: Excerpted and adapted from Tigue (1996)

rates both quantity and quality of public infrastructure. However, given that the outcome is the impact of the projects, the linkage between the project and a social outcome is not always explicit. Finally, the perpetual inventory method is an accounting method in which capital project expenditure is recorded throughout time, and a depreciation rate is applied in order to yield the monetary value of public stock. This method requires good bookkeeping which some governments cannot afford.

Maintenance funding involves setting aside public resources for repair and replacement. This practice helps a government reduce project costs by avoiding long-term debt with relatively high interest rates, especially when an emergency occurs and a public project must be implemented immediately. For example, a local bridge may become damaged in a natural disaster and require immediate repair. In this situation, a maintenance fund could be accessed to make a large down payment and thereby reduce the amount of debt that needs to be issued. Maintenance funding can also help a government avoid accumulating public infrastructure backlogs since annual repairs can extend the useful life of a project. Pagano (1984) and Jacob (2008) suggest that linking capital and operating budgets provides assurance that maintenance funding is undertaken. For example, by using dedicated revenues to finance public facility depreciation, a government will be able to ensure annual appropriation for a regular maintenance schedule (Afonso, 2014).

In the state of Illinois, USA, maintenance planning is an indispensable element of the agency proposal development process. Condition assessment information is used to justify project proposals and communicate needs to upper-level managers and elected officials (Srithongrung, 2006). The state central budget office supports maintenance funding, both in terms of prioritization and earmarking funds for this purpose. Additionally, in terms of higher education infrastructure, the earmarked funds help relieve the need for higher education projects, which compete with corrections projects at the state level, as both types of facilities are funded by the same sources. According to Srithongrung (2006), the Illinois experience illustrates two points: (1) maintenance funding must be continuously supported by top-level management to effectively relieve emergency needs, and (2) when the capital renewal fund and a regular fund (for programmatic purposes) are separated, the projects that serve different purposes (maintenance versus programmatic) do not compete against each other, which allows a focus on strategic and programmatic planning.

More recently, several U.S. states have moved maintenance from the capital budget into the departmental operating budgets. Other states have developed a system to rate maintenance projects as part of the effort to preserve facilities, for example, by placing additional emphasis on the planning and execution of preventive maintenance (Ermasova, 2013). The Oregon (USA) Department of Administrative Services uses an atypical financing system for maintenance – it recovers funds for preservation through "uniform rent" charges to agencies. Statutory mechanisms exist for agencies that own facilities to include in their budgets what would effectively be an internal rent charge. Agencies could then set aside these rents in a separate fund for use in addressing capital needs, such as replacing systems at the end of their useful life or by providing ongoing maintenance. State governments have funded maintenance using various budget approaches, such as: (1) including maintenance in the operating budget; (2) including maintenance in the capital budget; (3) including most routine maintenance (except maintenance for building renewal) funding in the operating budget; and (4) having a separate appropriation bill or a special maintenance and repair budget (Ermasova, 2013).

CONCLUSION

This chapter introduces the systematic capital management and budgeting process which is used as a framework in describing public capital management and budgeting practices in each of the twelve country case studies included in this book. The systematic capital management and budgeting process is comprised of four main components: long-term capital planning, capital budgeting and financial management, centralized execution and project management, and infrastructure maintenance. This systematic process, as recommended by the literature, parallels the strategic management process in which a government's strategic goal is utilized to frame courses of action (Koteen, 1989). A systematic approach to capital management and budgeting should enhance public spending efficiency given that practices encompassed in a systematic process sets the directions for government in deciding when to spend on a particular public project, where to locate the public project relative to public demands, how to finance projects and what should be done in project acquisition. As empirically shown by Srithongrung (2006; 2008), the resulting efficient public investment ensures quality infrastructure that can affectively enhance local economic growth.

REFERENCES

Adams, C. T. (1988). *The Politics of Capital Investment: The Case of Philadelphia*. Albany, NY: State University of New York Press.

Afonso, W. B. (2014). Local Government Capital Spending During and After Recessions: A Cause for Concern? *International Journal of Public Administration, 37*(8), 494–505. doi:10.1080/01900692.2013.865646

Ammar, S., Duncombe, W., & Wright, R. (2001). Evaluating capital management: A new approach. *Public Budgeting & Finance, 21*(4), 47–69. doi:10.1111/0275-1100.00058

Aronson, J. R., & Schwartz, E. (2004). *Management Policies in Local Government Finance* (5th ed.). Washington, DC: International National City/County Management Association.

Baldry, D. (1998). The Evaluation of risk management in public sector capital projects. *International Journal of Project Management, 16*(1), 35–41. doi:10.1016/S0263-7863(97)00015-X

Beckett-Camarata, J. (2003). An examination of the relationship between the municipal strategic plan and the capital budget and its effect on financial performance. *Journal of Public Budgeting, Accounting &. Financial Management, 15*(1), 23–40.

Beckett-Camarata, J. (2008). Capital Budgeting. In J. Rabin (Ed.), *Encyclopedia of Public Administration and Public Policy*. Taylor & Francis.

Braun, P. J. (2006). Infrastructure Demands Versus Debts. In Managing Local Government Finance. International City and County Management Association (ICMA) Publishers.

Burger, P., & Hawkesworth, I. (2013). Capital Budgeting and Procurement Practices. *OECD Journal on Budgeting, 13*(1), 57–104. doi:10.1787/budget-13-5k3w580lh1q7

Calia, R. (2001). Are all public spending programs equal? Priority setting approaches for government budgeting. *Government Finance Review, 17*(4), 18–18.

Chan, Y.-C. L. (2004). Use of Capital Budgeting Techniques and an Analytic Approach to Capital Investment Decisions in Canadian Municipal Governments. *Public Budgeting & Finance, 24*(2), 40–58. doi:10.1111/j.0275-1100.2004.02402003.x

Chandra, A., & Thompson, E. (2000). Does public infrastructure affect economic activity? Evidence from rural interstate highway system. *Journal of Regional Science, 27*(3), 419–437.

Darr, D. (1998). The Benefits of Long-Range Capital Planning—The Virginia Experience. *Public Budgeting & Finance, 18*(3), 42–53. doi:10.1046/j.0275-1100.1998.01141.x

Dastidar, K. G., & Mukherjee, D. (2014). Corruption in delegated public procurement auctions. *European Journal of Political Economy, 35*, 122–127. doi:10.1016/j.ejpoleco.2014.05.003

Dowall, D. E. (2001). Rethinking statewide infrastructure policies: Lessons from California and beyond. *Public Works Management & Policy, 6*(1), 5–17. doi:10.1177/1087724X0161002

Dupont-Morales, M. A., & Harris, J. E. (1994). Strengthening Accountability: Incorporating Strategic Planning and Performance Measurement into Budgeting. *Public Productivity & Management Review, 17*(3), 231–239. doi:10.2307/3380655

Ebdon, C. (2004). Capital Management Practices in U.S. Counties. *Public Works Management & Policy, 8*(3), 192–202. doi:10.1177/1087724X03259604

Ermasova, N. (2013). The capital budgeting at the state level during the Great Recession: The results of survey. *State & Local Government Review, 45*(2), 119–130. doi:10.1177/0160323X13487079

Fisher, R. C. (2016). *State and local public finance*. New York: Routledge.

Forte, D. (1989). From reactive to proactive fiscal planning: The results of strategic planning in McKinney, Texas. *Government Finance Review, 54*(4), 7–11.

Gatti, S. (2012). *Project Finance in Theory and Practice: Designing, Structuring, and Financing Private and Public Projects*. Waltham, MA: Elsevier.

Gianakis, G. A., & McCue, C. P. (1999). *Local government budgeting: A managerial approach*. Westport, CT: Quorum Books.

Government Finance Officer Association—GFOA. (2007). *Best Practice in Capital Project Monitoring and Reporting*. Retrieved October 15, 2018, from http://www.gfoa.org/capital-project-monitoring-and-reporting

Government Finance Officers Association. (2001). *GFOA Recommended Practices: Debt Management. Recommended Practices for State and Local Governments: 89-127 (Development of a Debt Policy, revised 2003)*. Retrieved from http://www.gfoa.org/services/rp/debt/debtmanagement-policy.pdf

Government Finance Officers Association. (2016). *GFOA Best Practice: Incorporating the Capital Budget into the Budget Document* Retrieved from http://www.gfoa.org/incorporating-capital-budget-budget-document

Government Finance Officers Association. (2017). *GFOA Best Practice: Capital Project Monitoring and Reporting*. Retrieved from http://www.gfoa.org/capital-project-monitoring-and-reporting

Government Performance Project—GPP. (2005). *Grading the States 2005: A look inside*. Retrieved September 13, 2005, from http://results.gpponline.org/States.aspx

Halachmi, A., & Sekwat, A. (1997). Strategic capital budgeting and planning: Prospects at the county level. *Journal of Public Budgeting, Accounting & Financial Management*, *8*(4), 578.

Hall, J. H., & Mutshutshu, T. (2013). Capital budgeting techniques employed by selected South African state-owned companies. *Corporate Ownership & Control*, *10*(2), 177–187.

Holtz-Eakin, D., & Schwartz, A. (1995a). Infrastructure in a structural model of economic growth. *Regional Science and Urban Economics*, *25*(2), 131–151. doi:10.1016/0166-0462(94)02080-Z

Howard, K. (1973). *Changing state budgeting*. Lexington, KY: Council of State Government.

Jacobs, D. F. (2008). *A review of capital budgeting practices*. IMF Working Paper, WP/08/160. International Monetary Fund.

Jimenez, B. S., & Pagano, M. A. (2012). What Factors Affect Management Quality? State Infrastructure Management and the Government Performance Project. *Public Works Management & Policy*, *17*(2), 124–151. doi:10.1177/1087724X11419308

Johansen, E., & Cooper, J. H. (2007). Common Funding Options for Capital Projects. In J. P. Casey & M. J. Mucha (Eds.), *Capital Project Planning and Evaluation: Expanding the Role of the Finance Officer* (Vol. 8, pp. 59–80). Chicago, IL: Government Finance Officers Association.

Kamensky, J. (1993). Program performance measures: Designing a system to manage for results. *Public Productivity & Management Review*, *16*(4), 395–402. doi:10.2307/3381017

King, L. M. (1995). Operating and capital budget reform in Minnesota: Managing public finances like the future matters. *Government Finance Review*, *11*(1), 7–10.

Koteen, J. (1989). *Strategic Management in Public and Non-profit Organizations*. Praeger.

Levine, S., & Augustino, J. (1994). State revolving funds: A model for financing drinking water programs. *Government Finance Review*, *12*, 26–44.

Liu, J., Meng, F., & Fellows, R. (2015). An exploratory study of understanding project risk management from the perspective of national culture. *International Journal of Project Management*, *33*(3), 564–575. doi:10.1016/j.ijproman.2014.08.004

Lobo, J., & Rantisi, N. (1999). Investment in infrastructure as determinant of metropolitan productivity. *Growth and Change*, *30*(1), 106–127. doi:10.1111/0017-4815.00106

Marcelo, D., Mandri-Perrott, C., House, S., & Schwartz, J. (2016). *An Alternative Approach to Project Selection: The Infrastructure Prioritization Framework*. World Bank Working Paper.

Mikesell, J. L. (1999). *Fiscal administration: Analysis and applications for the public sector* (5th ed.). New York: Harcourt Brace College Publishers.

Mikesell, J. L. (2017). *Fiscal administration* (10th ed.). Boston, MA: Cengage Learning.

Moak, L., & Hillhouse, A. (1975). *Concepts and practices in local government finance*. Chicago, IL: Municipal Finance Officer Association.

Moak, L. L., & Killian, K. W. (1963). *Capital programming and capital budgeting*. Chicago, IL: Municipal Finance Officer Association.

Moomaw, R., Mullen, K., & Williams, M. (2002). Human and knowledge capital: A contribution to empirics of state economic growth. *American Economic Journal, 30*(1), 48–59.

Munnell, A. H. (1992). Policy Watch: Infrastructure Investment and Economic Growth. *The Journal of Economic Perspectives*, *6*(4), 189–198. doi:10.1257/jep.6.4.189

Murdick, R. G., & Deming, D. D. (1968). *The Management of Capital Expenditures*. New York City, NY: McGraw Hill.

National Association of State Budget Officers (NASBO). (1999). *Capital budgeting in the States-paths to success: A comparative analysis of capital budgeting practices in the States.* Retrieved July 14, 2018, from https://www.nasbo.org/mainsite/reports-data/capital-budgeting-in-the-states/capital-budgeting-archive

National Association of State Budget Officers (NASBO). (2014). *Capital budgeting in the States.* Retrieved July 14, 2018, from https://higherlogicdownload.s3.amazonaws.com/NASBO/9d2d2db1-c943-4f1b-b750-0fca152d64c2/UploadedImages/Reports/Capital%20Budgeting%20in%20the%20States.pdf

Pagano, M. A. (1984). Notes on capital budgeting. *Public Budgeting & Finance*, *4*(3), 31–40. doi:10.1111/1540-5850.00648

Pagano, M. A., & Perry, D. (2008). Financing Infrastructure in the 21st Century City. *Public Works Management & Policy*, *13*(1), 22–38. doi:10.1177/1087724X08321015

Price, W. (2002). Innovation in Public Finance: Implications for the Nations Infrastructure. *Public Works Management & Policy*, *7*(1), 63–78.

Ratings, F. (2002). *The twelve habits of highly successful finance officers*. Retrieved April 15, 2006, from www.fitchratings.com

Richard, A., & Daniel, T. (2001). *Managing Public Expenditure: A Reference Book for Transition Countries*. Paris: OECD Publishing.

Robinson, S. G. (1993). Capital Planning and Budgeting. In J. E. Petersen & D. R. Strachota (Eds.), *Local Government Finance: Concepts and Practices* (pp. 65–84). Washington, DC: Government Finance Officers Association.

Savas, E. S. (2000). *Privatization and Public-Private Partnerships*. New York: Seven Bridges Press.

Sermier, E., & Marcone, P. (1993). The Challenge of Governing: Getting Things Done. *Public Productivity & Management Review*, *16*(4), 409–414. doi:10.2307/3381019

Simonsen, B., Robbins, M. D., & Brown, R. (2003). Debt affordability. In J. Rabin (Ed.), *Encyclopedia of Public Administration and Public Policy* (pp. 308–312). New York: Marcel Dekker.

Singhvi, S. (1996). Using an affordability analysis to budget capital expenditure. *Healthcare Financial Management, 50*(6), 70–76. PMID:10158243

Spackman, M. (2001). Public investment and discounting in European Union member states. *OECD Journal on Budgeting, 1*(2), 213–260. doi:10.1787/budget-v1-art13-en

Spackman, M. (2002, April). *Multi-year Perspective in Budgeting and Public Investment Planning*. Draft background paper for discussion at session III.1 of the OECD Global Forum on Sustainable Development: Conference on Financing Environmental Dimension of Sustainable Development. Retrieved from http://www.oecd.org/unitedkingdom/2081306.pdf

Srithongrung, A. (2006). *The impact of state capital budget and management programs on state capital budget decisions and economic performance* (Unpublished D.P.A. Dissertation). Available from Dissertations & Theses @ University of Illinois at Springfield.

Srithongrung, A. (2008). The impacts of state capital management programs on state economic performance: An empirical analysis. *Public Budgeting & Finance, 28*(3), 83–107. doi:10.1111/j.1540-5850.2008.00912.x

Srithongrung, A., & Kriz, K. A. (2012). From Public Infrastructure to National Economic Growth: Do Systematic Investment Practices Matter? *International Public Management Review, 13*(2), 19–50.

Stanley, M. T., & Block, S. B. (1984). A survey of multinational capital budgeting. *Financial Review, 19*(1), 36–54. doi:10.1111/j.1540-6288.1984.tb01083.x

Steiss, A. W. (2005). *Strategic Facilities Planning: Capital Budgeting and Debt Administration*. Lanham, MD: Lexington Books.

Steiss, A. W., & Nwagwu, E. O. C. (2001). *Financial planning and management in public organizations*. New York: Marcel-Dekker.

Stich, B., & Eagle, K. (2005). Planning to Include the Public: Transportation Policy Implementation With Effective Citizen Involvement. *Public Works Management & Policy, 9*(4), 319–340. doi:10.1177/1087724X05275672

Storm, R., & Feiock, R. (1999). Economic development consequences of state support for higher education. *State & Local Government Review, 31*(2), 97–105. doi:10.1177/0160323X9903100204

The World Bank. (1998). *Public Expenditure Management Handbook*. Washington, DC: The International Bank for Reconstruction and Development.

The World Bank. (2018). *International LPI - Global Rankings 2018*. Retrieved from https://lpi.worldbank.org/international/global?order=Infrastructure&sort=asc

Tigue, P. (1996). *Capital Improvement Programming: A Guide for Smaller Governments*. Chicago, IL: Government Finance Officers Association.

U.S. General Accounting Office. (1998). *Executive Guide: Leading Practices in Capital Decision-Making*. Washington, DC: U.S. General Accounting Office. Retrieved from https://www.gao.gov/special.pubs/ai99032.pdf

Vogt, A. J. (2004). *Capital budgeting and finance: A guide for local governments*. Washington, DC: International City/County Management Association.

Westerman, N. (2004). Managing the Capital Planning Cycle: Best Practice Examples of Effective Capital Program Management. *Government Finance Review*, *20*(3), 26–32.

Westerman, N., & Casey, J. P. (2007). Cost Estimation and Budgeting. In J. P. Casey & M. J. Mucha (Eds.), *Capital Project Planning and Evaluation: Expanding the Role of the Finance Officer* (Vol. 8, pp. 27–44). Chicago: Government Finance Officers Association.

Wigfall, P., & Lynch, T. D. (2003). Capital Budgeting Practices in Local Governments. *Case Studies in Public Budgeting and Financial Management*, 241-252.

Yinger, J., Bloom, H., Börsch-Supan, A., & Ladd, H. (1988). *Property Taxes and House Values: The Theory and Estimation of Intrajurisdictional Property Tax Capitalization, Studies in Urban Economics*. Boston: Academic Press.

Chapter 2
The Case of Public Capital Budgeting and Management Processes in the United States

Natalia B. Ermasova
Governors State University, USA

Carol Ebdon
University of Nebraska at Omaha, USA

ABSTRACT

This chapter provides a case study from the United States regarding public capital budgeting and management on the federal, state, and local levels. The U.S. case of the public investment process (or positive theory for United States public investment) is described and compared with the normative theory outlined in Chapter 1 to understand the deviation between the positive and normative theories. This chapter presents an analysis of four main components of the USA capital budgeting system including (1) long-term public capital planning, (2) annual public budgeting and financing, (3) project execution, and (4) public infrastructure evaluation. In addition, this chapter shows public infrastructure needs and financing issues in the United States.

INTRODUCTION

The availability and quality of services provided by public infrastructure are critical factors in improving economic growth. Current levels of funding are far below what is needed to properly maintain, improve and expand system capacity to accommodate future demand and avoid the economic costs and inefficiencies associated with system underperformance (Business Roundtable, 2016). According to a 2013 survey, 65 percent of U.S. manufacturers believe that American infrastructure will be unable to meet the demands of a growing economy over the next 10 to 15 years (National Association of Manufacturers and Building America's Future Educational Fund, 2013). The American Society of Civil Engineers "grades" the country's infrastructure every four years. The overall grade for 2017 was a D+, and ranged from a B for the rail system to a D- for transit (American Society of Civil Engineers, 2017).

DOI: 10.4018/978-1-5225-7329-6.ch002

According to the Department of the Treasury and the Council of Economic Advisers (2010), "well designed infrastructure investments can raise economic growth, productivity, and land values, while also providing significant positive spillovers to areas such as economic development, energy efficiency, public health and manufacturing." Investing in infrastructure is an engine for long-term economic growth, increasing GDP, employment, household income, and exports. Batina (1998, p.263) found that "innovations in public capital have long lasting effects on output, labor, and private capital, and innovations to output, labor, and private capital also have long lasting effects on public capital." According to Lynde and Richmond (1992), the reduction in spending on public capital was found to account for approximately 40% of the slowdown in the growth of labor productivity from 1958 to 1989.

We find several major themes in capital management in the United States. First, there has been an increased effort to institutionalize recommended practices in capital budgeting at all levels of government, particularly related to long-term planning and project management. Some governments are lagging, though, and others have theoretically good processes but decisions are ultimately still based largely on political calculation rather than driven by objective prioritization criteria. At the federal level, the ability to gain perspective on capital assets is also hampered by the lack of a separate capital budget. Second, the country is said to be in an infrastructure "crisis" due to the large level of unfunded maintenance needs. This situation is being addressed to some extent in two ways. Organizations are increasing the use of asset management systems to improve their understanding of maintenance needs in the short-term and over the life of an asset. In addition, innovative practices and funding mechanisms are being utilized, especially at the state and local levels. Third, decentralization and fragmentation of infrastructure systems in the United States pose significant challenges to finding solutions to the issues related to planning and maintenance. Coordination and consensus across political boundaries are difficult to achieve.

This chapter begins with a 'Background' section that includes discussion of the different levels of government. The next section provides an overview of capital budgeting at the federal level. State and local capital management processes and issues are then described. This section provides an overview of existing knowledge about capital planning, project management, and asset maintenance in state and local governments. The following section discusses the current status of infrastructure systems across the country, along with suggested solutions to the so-called "crisis" of underfunded maintenance and expansion. Finally, the conclusion addresses variations between positive and normative theory.

BACKGROUND

The United States is a federal country with a population of 321.6 million. The GDP per capita in the United States, USD 56 000, is 36% above the OECD average, ranking the United States the 5th richest in the OECD. It is ranked 7th in the OECD on public spending decentralization, as 47.9% of its government expenditures are undertaken at the subnational level (OECD, 2016).

The U.S. structure differs from many other countries in the relationships between the federal government and other levels. According to U.S. Census Bureau (2012), there are 90,106 state and local governments in the United States. This includes 50 states, 38,910 general purpose governments (cities and counties), 12,880 school districts, and 38,266 special districts (e.g., fire protection or water supply districts). These entities have a great deal of autonomy and responsibility for capital related to the services that they provide. Capital spending was $334.2 billion in 2014-15 for state and local governments combined, which was 13% of total direct expenditures in that year for these organizations (U.S. Census Bureau, 2015).

States are responsible for capital assets such as state highways, prisons, state university facilities, state parks, office buildings, and technology hardware and software. Local governments are responsible for their own assets, such as local streets and bridges, school buildings, police and fire facilities and equipment, airports, public hospitals, local parks, libraries, parking garages, water and sewer systems, buses and subways, jails and courts, and sometimes gas and electric utilities. These governments operate to a large extent in a decentralized manner, where they are primarily responsible for their own capital assets and financing, and spend more on physical capital investment than does the federal government. For example, in fiscal year 2015, total direct capital spending was $483.4 billion, of which 31% was federal spending and 69% state and local (authors' calculations based on U.S. Census Bureau, 2015 and Office of Management and Budget, 2017b).

While governments have primary responsibility for their own assets, there are some regulatory and financing relationships between different levels of government. The federal government controls military capital assets, national parks, national highways, and many federal office buildings. However, state and local governments manage their own assets, as noted above. There is some relationship between levels; for example, federal and state governments regulate water systems, and state governments fund a significant share of local school district spending which can include capital. Commercial airports are typically owned and operated by local governments, but are heavily regulated by the Federal Aviation Administration and receive some financing for airport capital improvements from the federal government's Aviation Trust Fund which is funded primarily from airline ticket excise taxes (Federal Aviation Administration, 2017). Streets and highways are more complex, as they include national and state highways, as well as local roads; some funding is from own-source revenues, while other revenues are shared between levels of government (e.g., the federal Highway Trust Fund). Because of the large role of state and local governments, it is important to understand capital management at these other levels as well as in the federal government.

CAPITAL BUDGETING AND MANAGEMENT AT THE FEDERAL LEVEL

Capital Planning at the Federal Government Level

The federal budget generally measures spending and revenues on a unified basis, including all the government's activities in one place. The budget makes no distinction between capital investments and operating expenses. Capital spending, social insurance outlays, and operating expenses are treated the same. Payroll taxes, income taxes, user fees, and proceeds from bond sales are treated as current revenue. The U.S. federal budget presents the government's expenditures and revenues for each fiscal year. It serves many purposes: (1) enables policymakers to allocate resources to serve national objectives, (2) provides the basis for agencies' management of federal programs, (3) gives the Treasury needed information for its management of cash and the public debt, and (4) provides businesses and individuals with information to make an informed assessment about the government's spending and resources (Potter & Diamond,1999).

The *Financial Report of the United States Government* provides financial statement information related to capital assets owned by the federal government (Congressional Budget Office, 2006). Capital leases are also included, but most federal lands—including military bases, national parks, and forests—are excluded from this report (Office of Management and Budget, 2018). For example, in fiscal year 2017, the direct federal spending for major public physical capital investment was $172.4 billion; $134.0 billion was for defense and $38.4 billion for nondefense. An additional $38.4 billion was spent for grants to state and local governments for physical capital purposes (Office of Management and Budget, 2018).

The Office of Management and Budget (OMB, 2017a) defines federal capital assets as "land, structures, equipment, intellectual property (e.g., software), and information technology (including IT service contracts) used by the Federal Government and having an estimated useful life of two years or more." The Government Accountability Office (GAO) provides a broader definition of federal investment as "...federal spending, either direct or through grants, specifically intended to enhance the private sector's long-term productivity. This definition includes spending on (1) some intangible activities, such as research and development (R&D), (2) human capital designed to increase worker productivity, particularly education and training, and (3) physical assets to improve infrastructure, such as highways, bridges, and air traffic control systems" (GAO, 1997). The President's Commission to Study Capital Budgeting distinguished between *federal* capital and *national* capital: federal capital refers to only those assets that belong to the federal government (like buildings or military aircraft); national capital includes all government spending aimed at delivering long-term benefits to the nation (President's Commission to Study Capital Budgeting, 1999).

OMB reports federal investment spending by category: major public physical capital investment (outlays for construction and rehabilitation, major equipment, and the purchase or sale of land and structures); conduct of research and development (outlays for activities that increase basic scientific knowledge or promote research and development); and conduct of education and training (activities to promote a more skilled and productive labor force, a category that consists mostly of financial assistance and loan subsidies for higher education). Inflows and outflows are recorded mostly on a cash basis because those transactions are readily verifiable and they provide policymakers and the public with a close approximation of the government's annual cash deficit or surplus (GAO, 2004).

The OMB issued the 1997 *Capital Programming Guide* A-11 to provide agencies a foundation for establishing an effective process for planning, budgeting, and making investment decisions (Office of Management and Budget, 2015). The *Guide* includes information on four phases of capital programming: Planning, Budgeting, Procurement, and Management-In-Use. It includes information about linking capital decisions to strategic goals and objectives, analyzing and ranking potential investments, and making informed decisions based on the full cost and risk of a project. According to the GAO (2004), "the *Capital Programming Guide* integrates executive office and statutory asset management initiatives into a single, integrated process to ensure that capital investments contribute to the achievement of agency goals and objectives."

OMB's *Capital Programming Guide* and GAO's *Executive Guide* emphasize the importance of developing a long-term capital investment plan that covers from 5 to 6 years to guide the implementation of organizational goals and objectives and help decision makers establish priorities over time (U.S. General Accounting Office, 1998). The long-term plan should clearly describe an entity's performance gap, the resources needed to bridge it, and a clear justification for new acquisitions proposed for funding with links of proposed investments to an organization's long-term strategic goals. Presidential policy estimates for the nine years following the budget year enable an analysis of the long-term consequences of proposed programs or tax policy initiatives (Office of Management and Budget, 2016).

GAO's *Executive Guide* (U.S. General Accounting Office, 1998) provides general principles for capital investment decisions: (1) integrate organizational goals into the capital decision-making process, (2) evaluate and select capital assets using an investment approach, (3) balance budgetary control and managerial flexibility when funding capital projects, (4) use project management techniques to optimize project success, and (5) evaluate results and incorporate lessons learned into the decision-making process.

To support effective planning over the long run, the budgetary treatments of capital indicate the costs that will be borne by future generations as a result of decisions made today. Since capital projects are on-budget and must be approved by the OMB, they are subject to benefit-cost assessment requirements, which also support long-term considerations. Total life-cycle costs and benefits, including the total budget authority required for the asset, are applied to all major capital projects (OMB, 1992). The benefits of a capital project accrue over the long-term. A capital project should yield positive net benefits to society in order for it to be approved. An analysis of the risk of the investment includes how risks will be isolated, minimized, monitored, and controlled. The Chief Financial Officer provides an evaluation and estimation of the probability of achieving the proposed cost goals for major programs. Agencies and departments use a performance-based management system (e.g., earned value management) for estimation of cost, schedule, and performance goals for the investment throughout the acquisition process. The discounted present value of a capital lease or lease-purchase over the life of the contract is also scored upfront, which helps guard against perverse incentives that result in inefficient decision-making (Office of Management and Budget, 2016a).

According to the *Capital Programming Guide* (2016), investments in major capital assets should: (1) support core/priority mission functions that need to be performed by the Federal Government; (2) reduce costs, improve effectiveness, and make maximum use of commercial, off-the-shelf technology; (3) demonstrate a projected return on the investment that is clearly equal to or better than alternative uses of available public resources; (4) reduce risk by avoiding or isolating custom-designed components and using fully tested pilots, simulations, or prototype implementations (Office of Management and Budget, 2016b).

Careful financial planning and efficient management of budget delivery are essential. Both planning and management work well only if the budget information systems are comprehensive, timely, accurate, and reliable and if all the departments involved cooperate closely. For example, GAO (2004) found that "the Park Service prepares a service wide 5-year construction plan that results from its rigorous review and selection process; however, the plan itself is merely a list of planned projects with estimated costs and schedule data rather than a narrative justification supporting an identified performance gap and linkage to organizational goals." The Park Service construction plan does not include all of the agency's construction needs or its major equipment and land acquisitions.

GAO (2004) evaluated agency experiences with the capital planning policies and found that "the agencies' capital planning processes generally link to their strategic goals and objectives, and they all consider a range of alternatives to bridge an identified performance gap." The majority of agencies have established processes to review and select from competing project proposals, strongly emphasizing linkage to strategic goals. However, the agencies have had limited success with using agency wide asset inventory systems and data on asset condition to identify performance gaps. According to GAO (2004), "none of the agencies prepares an agency wide long-term capital investment plan. Some have long-term capital planning documents that could serve as a base for development of a comprehensive agency wide plan."

Capital Budgeting and Financial Management at the Federal Government Level

The Budgeting Phase begins with the agency's budget submission to OMB and ends with congressional approval and OMB apportionment of funding. OMB is the integrator of specific capital project proposals into the larger budget process. OMB considers agency obligation rates, the overall budget request, and agency strategic plans during reviews of agency budget requests for capital acquisitions. Requests for obligation are initiated through many systems (the procurement system, human resources system, travel system, etc.). Requests for obligation initiate a verification of funds availability in the core accounting system.

Agencies work with OMB to determine the effect of proposals on budget authority, collections, and outlays based on economic and technical assumptions related to interest rates, housing prices inflation rates, outlay rates, caseloads, and estimates for offsetting collections or receipts (Office of Management and Budget, 2016).

OMB's *Guide* suggests that options other than acquiring new assets be considered, such as through regulation or user fees or by using human capital instead of physical capital assets. According to GAO (2004), once detailed requirements are defined, management should answer these questions before planning to acquire capital assets:

1. *Does the investment in a major capital asset support core/priority mission functions that need to be performed by the federal government?*
2. *Does the investment need to be undertaken by the requesting agency because no alternative private sector or governmental source can better support the function?*
3. *Does the investment support work processes that have been simplified or otherwise redesigned to reduce costs, improve effectiveness, and make maximum use of commercial-off-the-shelf technology?*

If a federal agency is requesting funds in support of capital facilities projects, including new construction, full and partial building renovation/modernization, or facility investments, the agency must provide supporting information. This includes documentation of compliance with federal capital policies, life cycle cost analysis, a housing plan (indicating at a minimum the FTE to be housed and the types of facility space and square footage), and environmental/energy efficiency analysis (Office of Management and Budget, 2016). OMB's *Guide* encourages applying risk management that includes how risks will be isolated, minimized, monitored, and controlled for each major capital project. According to OMB (2016) Circular A-11, "failure to analyze and manage the inherent risk in all capital asset acquisitions may contribute to cost overruns, schedule shortfalls, and acquisitions that fail to perform as expected."

The government provides budgetary data in two forms: budget authority and budget outlays. Budget authority includes all the funding that has been authorized in a given year, whether or not it is expected to be spent in that year. For example, the entire estimated expense for a new building might be appropriated in the budget authority in next year's budget, although the spending is expected to take place over several years. Budget outlays, the amount actually spent, or expected to be spent in a given year, are also reported in the budget. This "cash basis" reporting of outlays increases transparency and provides a better idea of the government's annual cash deficit or surplus (Congressional Budget Office, 2008).

The legislative budget process is driven by Congressional subcommittees that appropriate by agency or department. The federal agency executives provide the various Congressional committees with information relative to their capital needs and the decision making processes they used to assess those needs. The differences between full funding with regular appropriations in the budget year and full funding for a capital project (investment) over several years with regular appropriations for the first year and advance appropriations for subsequent years are as follows: (1) full funding with regular appropriations in the budget year leads to tradeoffs within the budget year with spending for other capital assets and with spending for purposes other than capital assets: (2) full funding for a capital project (investment) over several years may bias tradeoffs in the budget year in favor of the proposed asset because with advance appropriations the full cost of the asset is not included in the budget year (Office of Management and Budget, 2016). OMB (2016) highlights the problems of large, temporary, year-to-year increases in budget authority (lumps or spikes) that may create a bias against the acquisition of justified capital assets. Agencies can avoid this bias through the aggregation of capital acquisitions in separate accounts. It would reduce spikes within an agency or bureau by providing roughly the same level of spending for acquisitions each year and help to identify and explain the source of spikes.

Centralized Execution and Project Management at the Federal Government Level

The Management-In-Use Phase begins with operational analysis and includes the execution of an operation and maintenance plan, a post implementation review—to evaluate the overall effectiveness of the agency's capital planning and acquisition process, and the execution of an asset disposal plan. According to OMB's *Guide* (2016, p.3), "budget authority sufficient to complete a useful segment of a capital project (or investment) (or the entire capital project, if it is not divisible into useful segments) must be appropriated before any obligations for the useful segment (or project or investment) may be incurred."

Agencies and departments use performance-based management systems (earned value or similar system) to provide contractor and government management visibility on the achievement of investment goals until the asset is accepted and operational. The performance-based management systems allow for early identification of problems, potential corrective actions, and changes to the original goals needed to complete the investment and necessary for agency portfolio analysis decisions (OMB, 2016, p.5). This allows agencies to recommend modifications for increased funding to the Congress or termination of the investment, based on its revised expected return on investment in comparison to alternative uses of the funds.

Congress enacted the Federal Acquisition Streamlining Act of 1994 to improve the federal acquisition process and the Clinger-Cohen Act in 1996 to improve the implementation and management of information technology investments. Federal agencies also use a variety of acquisition strategies for reducing the risk of cost escalation and the risk of failure to achieve schedule and performance goals. Budgetary resources may be appropriated in separate capital asset acquisition accounts, to enhance transparency and clarity of funding, and budget authority may be apportioned for specific segments of a project. Thresholds are also established for acquisition cost, schedule, and performance goals, including return on investment. Contracts and pricing mechanisms are determined based on efficiency and their ability to incentivize contractors to allocate risk appropriately between the contractor and the Government. In addition, the performance-based management systems are used to monitor project cost, schedule, and performance goals.

According to the OMB Guide, senior management should conduct a portfolio analysis if the progress of capital investments is not within 90 percent of goals, or if new information is available that would indicate a greater return on investment from alternative uses of funds. This analysis should determine the continued viability of the investment with modifications or the termination of the investment, and the start of exploration for alternative solutions if it is necessary to fill a gap in agency strategic goals and objectives (Office of Management and Budget, 2016a, p.5).

According to the National Academies Federal Facilities Council, facilities investments are not often immediately measurable but are evident over a period of years, and it is important that agencies track the outcomes of those investments to improve decision making about those investments and to improve asset management (National Research Council, 2005). The federal agencies need to establish facilities asset management performance goals that have a time frame for attainment, among other things (GAO, 2016).

Infrastructure Maintenance at the Federal Government Level

Asset management decisions and infrastructure maintenance are based on the *Capital Programming Guide (*OMB, 2004*)*, the Federal Real Property Council's Guidance for Real Property Inventory Reporting (General Services Administration, 2012 and Federal Real Property Council, 2016), and the National Academies Federal Facilities Council's *Key Performance Indicators of Federal Facilities Portfolios* (National Research Council, 2005). The growing focus on guideline changes over times that emphasize mounting attention to long-range planning and life-cycle costs to meet the crisis of under-funding for maintenance.

Deferred maintenance and repairs are measured using one of three methods. *Condition assessment surveys* are periodic inspections of government-owned property to determine the current condition and estimated cost to bring the property to an acceptable condition. *Life-cycle cost forecasts* consider the full costs of operation, maintenance, and other costs over an investment's life-cycle, in addition to the asset acquisition costs. *Management analysis* is founded on inflation-adjusted reductions in maintenance funding since the base year (Department of the Treasury, 2014).

OMB states that the use of tools such as the asset priority index (API) helps managers identify the most important assets and provides logical guidance for directing limited funding. API is important for planning for recurring maintenance and preventive maintenance. The facility condition index (FCI) is used in facilities management to provide a benchmark to compare the relative condition of a group of facilities. FCI is a method of measuring the current condition of an asset to assess how much work, if any, is recommended to maintain or change its condition to acceptable levels to support organizational missions. It is calculated by dividing the deferred maintenance associated with an asset by its current replacement value, and the lower the asset FCI value, the better the condition of the asset. For example, a new asset would likely have little or no deferred maintenance associated with it and therefore have a low FCI.

Graphical representations of a distribution of assets according to their importance to mission and their condition can be a useful tool in segmenting and presenting asset portfolios. By plotting an asset according to API and FCI, an agency can determine when an asset no longer supports the mission of the site or bureau or is a candidate for disposal because it has a low API and high FCI (GAO, 2016). For example, GAO (2016) finds that the Department of the Interior's National Park Service (Park Service) allocated $1.16 billion annually to maintain assets that accounted for about one-third (or $1.08 billion) of the agency's total funding of $3.3 billion in 2015. The Park Service uses the ratio of API to FCI to assign assets to a level of maintenance priority, called an optimizer band. The Park Service applies the Capital Investment Strategy to score projects that will be funded by various funding sources in the Project Management Information System. Projects are scored from 1 to 1,000 based partially on elements of financial sustainability, resource protection, visitor use, and health and safety (GAO, 2016).

The current budgeting process does not require the federal government to budget for depreciation of assets. In ad valorem appraisal, deferred maintenance is not normally included in a valuation consideration.

This would have the effect of punishing agencies who kept a property in good condition and rewarding those who let properties run down. Deferred maintenance is the practice of postponing maintenance activities in order to save costs or meet budget funding levels. The policy of continued deferred maintenance could lead to asset deterioration, ultimately asset impairment, and result in higher costs, asset failure, and in some cases, health and safety implications (American Society of Civil Engineers, 2017). According to the U.S. Department of Treasury (2014), "the consequences of not performing regular maintenance and repairs could include increased safety hazards, poor service to the public, higher costs in the future, and inefficient operations." Using condition assessment surveys, the amount of estimated deferred maintenance and repairs for the federal government as of September 30, 2017 was $170.2 billion, which was actually a decrease of $15 billion from the prior year (U.S. Department of the Treasury, 2018).

Deferred maintenance information is included as required supplementary information in federal financial reports that makes it difficult to hold agencies accountable for proper use and management of assets (Federal Accounting Standards Advisory Board, 2011). For example, the National Park Service hosts about 307 million visitors per year at more than 75,000 constructed assets, while the U.S. Army Corps of Engineers is responsible for 12 million acres at 403 lake and river projects which attract 370 million visitors annually (American Society of Civil Engineers, 2017). The GAO (2016, pp. 6-7) found that the Park Service alone estimated that its deferred maintenance had grown from $11.5 billion in 2012 to $11.9 billion in 2015. According to the Park Service, maintenance needs are almost double the annual funding, which leads to an annual increase in deferred maintenance.

Analysis of Federal Capital Practices

As of September 30, 2017, the net cost of property, plant, and equipment for the U.S. Government (after accumulated depreciation) was $1.034 trillion, of which $761.7 billion was for defense assets and $272.8 billion for nondefense assets (U.S. Government, 2017). This represents a significant ownership of capital assets. The Congress, OMB, and GAO all have identified the need for more effective planning and management of capital asset investments due to increasing budget pressures and demands to improve performance in all areas. According to GAO (2004), "Effective capital programming requires long-range planning and a disciplined decision-making process as the basis for managing a portfolio of assets to achieve performance goals and objectives with minimal risk, lowest life-cycle costs, and greatest benefits to the agency's business" (p.22).

The U.S. federal government does not have a separate capital budget. The idea of changing the process to have a distinct capital plan and budget has been discussed, but is controversial. Proponents argue that there would be a number of advantages to segregating capital from operating budgets. They note that a long-term federal government capital plan and capital budget would help with financial management by estimating revenues and expenses associated with capital projects, determining the best financing method, and addressing issues of intergenerational equity (Axelrod, 1988; Istrate & Puentes, 2009). It may make more sense to borrow for capital projects with long useful lives that will benefit future generations who can then pay for them, rather than with current operating funds; a separate capital budget can enhance efficiency and equity by considering these long-term flows in budget and financing decisions. Mikesell (2007) suggests that capital budgets can also help to smooth out tax rates over time in governments where "projects are large enough to significantly influence tax rates" through the use of debt-financing and making careful decisions about project timing. In addition, capital projects typically have a long life; the use of separate capital budgets is said to increase the review of these projects which can reduce expensive errors and can also help in the need to "balance spending with the resources available within political, economic, and legal tax and debt limits" (p.245).

Other proponents of a separate capital budget suggest that it would change the incentive structure so that Congress would no longer favor consumption over investment, and would allow for more informed choices through better information. In addition, Congress could use a capital budget as a budget enforcement tool to limit federal borrowing to the amounts needed to finance capital investment, while balancing the operating budget (Gershberg & Benning, 1999). GAO (1996) suggested that there was not enough attention to the mix between long-term and short-term needs in the federal budget format. A capital budget could also be a useful counter-cyclical economy policy tool to speed up capital spending in times of economic downturns (Gershberg & Benning, 1999).

However, there is opposition to the concept of a separate capital budget. The President's Commission to Study Capital Budgeting (PCSCB) and the President's Commission on Budget Concepts (Kennedy et al., 1967).) note that there are technical challenges to making this change, and they fear that it would lead to reduced transparency, increased borrowing, and inefficient allocation of spending. The increased borrowing might occur because there are a wide range of federal activities that could be broadly construed as "investments," including human capital, which could lead to incentives to increase the capital budget and therefore debt financing (Mikesell, 2007, p.291). In addition, there is an argument that a separate capital budget is not necessary at the federal level because of its size; in smaller governments, the lumpiness of large capital projects may influence tax rates, but that is not the case with the federal government where "smoothing" is not required for this purpose (Mikesell, 2007).

In many ways, the federal government has improved its capital management practices in recent years. Agencies are doing more long-term planning, at least in a decentralized fashion, and guidelines are available to assist in these efforts. Increasing use of asset management systems are helpful in making data-driven decisions better understanding needs. However, practices vary across and within agencies, and there are significant levels of unfunded deferred maintenance. In addition, the lack of a separate capital budget and short-term orientation of the annual budget process incentivize elected officials to prioritize other programs and services over investment in infrastructure.

CAPITAL BUDGETING AND MANAGEMENT IN STATE AND LOCAL GOVERNMENTS

Capital Planning in State and Local Governments

Each state and local government has significant autonomy, so there are differing approaches to capital management in these 90,000 entities. According to Srithongrung (2018), "from 1988 to 2012, the per capita U.S. state capital outlay fluctuated at rates as high as 521 percent" (p.47). The Government Performance Project analyzed capital management capacity (along with management in other areas) in states and in a sample of 40 large counties and 35 cities in the late 1990s/early 2000s (Ingraham, 2007). Some similarities were found, but there were also significant variations across governments. Overall, only 10-14% of these governments (depending on the type of government) were graded in the "A" range, with another 43-63% receiving a grade in the "B" range; a substantial number received lower grades (Ebdon, 2007). Two later rounds of analysis were conducted for the states, based on slightly different criteria; in both years, 8% of states were graded in the "A" range, and 4% in the "D" range, with 42-50%

in the "B" range and 38-46% in the "C" range (Jimenez & Pagano, 2012). Few studies have been done on smaller cities and counties or schools or special districts, so little is known about capital management in these jurisdictions.

Development of a long-term capital improvement plan is common in states, and in large cities and counties. For example, the vast majority of the governments analyzed in the Government Performance Project had capital plans that covered five or more years, although a few had no plan at all (Ebdon, 2007). A more recent study found that only two states did not have long-term capital budgets as of 2012 (Ermasova, 2012; Ermasova, 2013). Governments have significantly different definitions of capital expenditures and useful lives, though (Vermeer, Patton & Styles, 2011). The format and information contained in capital plans also varies greatly (Ebdon, 2007; Ermasova, 2013). State and local governments that have a CIP tend to have a separate capital budget because these appropriations for capital projects require special analysis and approval from voters (Forrester 1993; Mikesell 2007; Sekwat 1999; Srithongrung, 2018)

Elements of the capital plan at the state level usually include (Ermasova, 2012):

1. Assessment and projection of need.
    a. Capital needs and projections are based on current and projected statistics of capital inventories and on state demographic and economic conditions.
    b. Capital inventories encompass all state-financed capital programs.
    c. The capital needs and projections are for a five-year period, with longer-term projections presented for programs with reasonably predictable longer-term needs.
    d. Capital needs and projections are presented independently of financing requirements or opportunities.
2. Comprehensive cost and financing assessment.
    a. Amounts appropriated and expended for the current fiscal year and for the preceding fiscal year are indicated for capital programs and for individual projects.
    b. Amounts proposed to be appropriated for the following fiscal year and for each of the four years thereafter are indicated for capital programs and for individual projects.
    c. The capital costs of programs and of individual projects are presented in full for the entire period of their development.
    d. The operating costs, both actual and prospective, of capital programs and of individual projects are presented in full for the entire period of their development and expected useful life.
    e. The financial burden and funding opportunities of programs and of individual projects are presented in full, including federal, state, and local government shares, and any private participation.
    f. Alternative methods of financing capital programs and projects are described and assessed, including debt financing and use of current revenues.

Recommended best practices for capital project selection include ranking systems based on selected criteria, use of committees to obtain varying perspectives, and coordination with strategic plans and operating budgets. For example, Fairfax County, Virginia has a prioritization process for facilities that includes compliance with mandates, asset age, healthy/safety issues, condition assessment, and needs identified by users. An 11-member citizens advisory board in Hennepin County, Minnesota reviews capital requests and makes recommendations to the county board (Ebdon, 2004). The State of New York ranks projects based on permanent job creation, revenue production, and risk assessment (Ermasova,

2013). However, these prioritization practices have not been widely found to be adopted in state and local governments (Ebdon, 2007). For example, a case study of Illinois found significant use of political negotiation in project decision-making (Srithongrung, 2010).

According to Srithongrung (2010), "highly systematic capital management programs positively alter the relationship between the state's capital spending levels and the state's economic growth rate" (p.83). States have increased their capital planning assessments over time, primarily due to enhanced requirements from the federal government related to highway planning. "All states receive federal-aid money for transportation. As a condition of aid, a state must create a Statewide Transportation Improvement Program (STIP) that lists all federal projects ordered by priority and by funding sources....In effect, the federal grant requires a minimum level of transportation planning for every state or what might be thought of as the 'floor' for infrastructure planning in any state" (Jimenez & Pagano, 2012, p.130).

Capital Budgeting and Financial Management in State and Local Governments

There have been five waves of establishing capital budgets at the state level: (1) 1929-1935; (2) 1940-1950; (3) 1955-1968; (4) 1972-1982; (5) 1995-2003 (Ermasova, 2012). Many states began capital budgeting after the Great Depression and World War II. For example, Wisconsin launched their capital budgeting process in 1949 with the establishment of the Building Commission. Specifically, the Laws of 1949, Chapter 563, provided that the State of Wisconsin Building Commission be created to oversee state facilities from the stages of planning, all the way to improvement and maintenance (Wisconsin Division of State Facilities, 2010).

Mikesell (2007) suggests that half of the state governments have a separate executive capital budget that is passed in legislative processes. Many states produce two capital budget documents (Arizona, Maryland, New York, Washington, and Texas). For example, Maryland produces a Five-Year Capital Improvement Program (CIP), also known as the Capital Budget Volume of the State Budget documents, and the Consolidated Transportation Program or CTP. Arizona produces a one-year plan, the Executive Recommendation and Capital Outlay Bill, and a three-year plan, the Capital Improvement Plan. Texas has a two-year capital budget for items in the General Appropriation Act (GAA) *Capital Budget Riders*; five years for projects in the Community Education Partner (CEP). Long-term financial management refers to resource analysis in terms of debt-affordability, future revenue and expenditure analysis, debt payment policy, and strategic capital infrastructure financing (Johnson, 1995; Levine & Augustino, 1994; Suren 1996; Srithongrung, 2018; Vogt 2004). The most common durations of the Capital Improvement Program are two-year, five-year, and six-year capital plans. Only the State of New Jersey uses a nine-year CIP. The evaluation of capital management practices in the states revealed some large differences in the capital planning process, project revenue estimation, and capital spending.

Ermasova (2013) classified the states' capital budgeting practices into three levels:

Level 1: The first level of capital budgeting is found in several states throughout the United States, where recurring capital needs are modest, and major capital projects arise infrequently. Capital budgeting at Level 1 takes place mainly or entirely within the annual budget process and has the following characteristics: (1) Capital financing comes mainly or entirely from annual revenues and operating fund balances. The occasional large project is financed from these sources and paid by cash. One example is North Dakota. (2) Procedures and formats used for budgeting assets are the same as those used for capital outlays within the operating or annual budget process. If there is a large project, planning for it is project-specific and done by a consulting engineer or architect. Examples of these are South Dakota and Hawaii. A few state governments operating at this first level issue GO bonds or other basic debt to finance major projects. Appropriations for capital spending are usually made in the annual or operating budget ordinance (e.g., South Dakota).

Level 2: Capital budgeting at Level 2 takes place mainly or entirely within the multiyear capital planning. Capital financing comes from operating revenues and balances, earmarked revenues or reserves, and basic debt instruments. Capital budgeting practices at Level 2 are significantly more developed than those at Level l. The states use special formats and procedures for requesting and reviewing major capital projects, and acquisitions are used within the context of the operating or annual budget process. Capital budgeting is coordinated with the operating budget in several ways. First, each capital project or capital program that is funded with cash from any source is budgeted in the operating budget and subject to the constraints of the revenues that support such projects and programs. Second, each capital project request is accompanied with an operating budget impact statement to estimate the additional cost of opening new facilities or of renovating and expanding existing facilities. These estimates are either included in the annual operating budget or are used to forecast the cost of these facilities and their impact on the need for future state operating expenses. The evaluation of the operational costs of new facilities is incorporated into the evaluation of capital project proposals (California, Florida, Minnesota, Mississippi, Missouri, Montana, and Nebraska). The operating or annual budget document is likely to have a special section that presents major capital projects and acquisitions that are up for approval and funding that year (Arizona). Capital expenditure decisions are based on a medium-term budget perspective. These states produce capital improvement plans of at least four years' duration; these states also have a special prioritization section in the capital budget and have some type of formal project management system (Arkansas, Georgia, Maine, Montana, Nebraska, Nevada, and Vermont). The states use the following methods of estimating project costs: national estimating guides; professional cost estimators; estimates provided by departments' architects and engineers. Major capital projects or acquisitions are financed from operating fund balances, if available; grants; basic debt instruments, such as GO bonds for general government projects and revenue bonds for enterprise projects; general and special capital reserve funds; and lease- or installment-purchase agreements for equipment.

Level 3: Capital budgeting practices reflect or approach the postmodern forms of organization and strategic capital management. Multiyear and jurisdiction-wide capital planning, network, and financial forecasting occur on this level of capital budgeting. Capital financing comes from a wide variety of pay-as-go sources and debt sources. Special budgeting procedures and formats are used for capital projects in a separate capital authorization and budget process. A majority of states at Level 3 require that operating costs accompany capital project requests; these states have an enforcement mechanism that requires agencies to develop operating cost estimates over several years. The planning capacity at Level 3 is stronger than in a Level 2 state. There is a jurisdiction-wide, multiyear CIP and usually an accompanying multiyear financial forecast. The capital construction budgets are expected to include pre-construction planning budgets as appropriate. Information on maintenance needs and deferred maintenance is also a required element of the budget. Level 3 capital budgeting has a special form as the basis for cross-sectoral analysis and methodology development, and for continuous improvements in the planning and investment process (Indiana, Maryland, Oregon, Texas, Utah, Virginia, Washington, Wisconsin, and West Virginia). A majority of states at Level 3 of capital budgeting practices have a State Board or Advisory Committee that submits its capital development recommendations and priorities to the Legislature for approval and prioritization. The Board or Advisory Committee makes recommendations on behalf of all state agencies, commissions, departments, and institutions (Indiana, Oregon, Texas, Utah, Washington, and Wisconsin). A budget director or budget officer is responsible for capacity generation, promotion of the flow of information within the Central Budget Agency and between agencies, synchronization of the key organizations, examination of mutual capabilities, and calibration of organizing structures to external needs. The states at Level 3 of capital budgeting practices have a complex system of strategic capital management.

The states' capital budgets usually include estimates for a specific number of years and adhere to particular standards. States use a variety of cost estimation methods, for example, preparing cost options, considering life-cycle costs, and considering the cost standards building type. Techniques include value engineering, life-cycle cost analysis, construction and material indices, and square footage estimates. Almost all states use cost standards according to a particular type of building and space utilization standards to estimate costs, while about one half to two-thirds of the states prepare cost options and use life-cycle costs for cost estimating. Particular state officials (for example, engineers, architects, or one or more outside consultants) help requesting agencies with the more technical parts of their requests, such as construction or major equipment cost estimates. In general, requesting agencies may use a combination of following methodologies to develop estimates: (1) relying on their own staff; (2) employing the assistance of architects and engineer; (3) using historical data on past projects and national estimating guides; (4) relying on professional cost estimators. States use certain procedures to evaluate the accuracy of capital budget estimates presented in the capital plan. There are formal reporting systems to track capital projects in many states.

Execution and Project Management in State and Local Governments

Various state agencies involved in the development process including the Governor's Office, Legislative Budget Board, Higher Education Coordinating Boards, Facilities Commission, and other agencies. Through the input of information of these organizations, the Central Budget Office develops program guidelines, instructions and a formal application process for submitting capital project requests based on the legislative mandate. From a budgetary and capital planning standpoint, there are a number of state agencies that work together in varying degrees to coordinate the budgetary and capital reporting and approval process of state agencies. The central budget office coordinates the submission of capital projects, develops the report and determines the effect of the additional capital requests on the state's budget and debt capacity. The completed plan is then forwarded for use in their development of recommended appropriations to the Legislature. The Legislature makes the final decision on which projects will be funded. The central budget office (CBO) develops the Capital Projects Database (CPD), which is a statewide, web-based, secure application that will be used to capture agency capital project information.

States define the types of expenditures allowed in capital budgets to include such items as construction, improvements, land acquisition, site improvements, major renovations, and equipment. Definitions of what constitutes a capital outlay range from the fairly standard (e.g., the useful design life of a building as 20 years in Hawaii, 40 years in Oregon, 50 years in Delaware; outlays greater than $50,000 in West Virginia or $1,000,000 in South Carolina for a project that provides benefits beyond the immediate year) to some that are normally considered operating outlays (Ermasova, 2013; NASBO, 2015).

States use different systems to handle unexpected portions of appropriations for projects that are not complete at fiscal year end. In Connecticut, the funds automatically carry forward. In Indiana, unexpended funds are encumbered and carried over to subsequent years until the project is complete. In some states, the appropriations for investment projects are valid for several years (California, Iowa, Nebraska, and Washington). A third approach involves state agencies requesting to reappropriate; in Arizona, this occurs through the use of its Reappropriation Request Manual (Ermasova, 2012).

Strong project management processes help to reduce delays and cost overruns and to maintain high quality work. The states and the large cities and counties included in the Government Performance Project were found to be stronger in this area than in planning or maintenance. The vast majority of these governments had formal tracking procedures with some degree of central control, and had project management systems that met their needs. They also produce formal project reports on a monthly or quarterly basis that generally include information such as revised cost estimates, budget overruns and explanations, change orders, scheduled completion date, and delay estimates (Ebdon, 2007; NASBO, 2015; Srithongrung, 2010). According to Srithongrung (2018), “adopting a separate capital budget as a special tool to review capital projects can reduce capital spending volatility. Likewise, using dedicated revenue for capital projects to finance total outlay can reduce volatility” (p.65).

State and local governments have increasingly utilized innovations to minimize costs and complete projects in a more timely manner. For example, governments have traditionally used a “design-bid-build” approach where design and construction are separately bid; a “design-build” approach is increasingly being used in which the two phases overlap and are considered together. The State of Massachusetts has reduced project times by up to six years with this approach, while the State of Utah expected a savings of five years for a $1.6 billion highway project (Ebdon, 2007).

A number of other methods are also being increasingly used for project management. Fairfax County, for example, used performance contracting with energy; they used utility cost savings estimated at $485,000 to finance improvements. Baltimore County saves an estimated $1.5 million in a few years with a gainsharing approach; project teams are incentivized by sharing in any cost savings (Ebdon, 2007).

Maintenance in State and Local Governments

Many scholars say that the U.S. has an infrastructure crisis. Three horrific stories highlight the issues of poor infrastructure systems. First, over 1,800 people died when Hurricane Katrina hit the Gulf Coast in 2005. While this weather event was a force of nature, the failure of the levee system contributed to the disaster. The US Army Corps of Engineers admitted that levees were inadequately designed and built, largely due to a lack of funding (Lopez, 2015). Second, a busy bridge over the Mississippi River in downtown Minneapolis collapsed in 2007 during rush hour traffic. Thirteen people were killed and 145 injured. The bridge was rated as being “structurally deficient” before the collapse (Karnowski, 2017). Third, the city of Flint, Michigan experienced a crisis after they attempted to reduce water system costs by switching their source to the Flint River. Anti-corrosion measures were not used and lead leached into the water supply from aged pipes, leading to high lead levels in homes. Lead exposure has dangerous health effects, especially in children (CNN, 2018).

According to the American Society of Civil Engineers (2017), the overall grade for 2017 was a D+. Other systems in the “D” range include aviation, dams, drinking water, energy, hazardous waste, inland waterways, levees, parks and recreation, roads, schools, and wastewater. Systems graded in the “C” range include bridges, ports, and solid waste (American Society of Civil Engineers, 2017). Table 1 provides the estimated cumulative investment needs for select categories based on current trends extended to the year 2020. For these five categories alone, the estimated gap is $1.44 trillion. Details of the dire situation for several types of infrastructure will be discussed below.

America's surface transportation system is extensive, including over four million miles of roads and about 614,000 bridges. Approximately 20% of road pavement is in poor condition, although the total miles rated as poor has decreased in recent years. Forty percent of bridges are at least 50 years old, and about nine percent of bridge are structurally deficient. Congestion is also increasing. By 2025, around one million jobs are expected to be lost due to the economic impacts of deteriorating transportation infrastructure (American Society of Civil Engineers, 2017). Table 1 demonstrates investment funding gap.

Another problem is aging water and wastewater systems. Nearly 156,000 public drinking water systems and 15,000 wastewater treatment plants are located across the United States. There are an estimated 240,000 water main breaks each year, and discharge of about 900 billion gallons of untreated sewage. At current rates, it would take 200 years to replace the water pipes, which is double their useful life. However, U.S. drinking water quality is still considered to be the safest in the world. The economic impact of funding shortfalls are expected to result in the loss of almost 500,000 jobs by 2025 (American Society of Civil Engineers, 2017). The statistics for other infrastructure systems are equally pessimistic. For example, 53% of schools would need improvements in order to be considered in good condition. The electric transmission grids are at full capacity. Seventeen percent of dams have been identified as having high-hazard potential, and 53% of people are living within three miles of a hazardous waste site (American Society of Civil Engineers, 2017).

How did we get to this level of deterioration? Lack of adequate funding across the complex, largely decentralized infrastructure systems is considered to be the primary reason. Elected officials are wary of increasing taxes and sometimes user fees. Also, as noted earlier, maintenance needs often compete with other operating budget priorities (Pagano & Perry, 2008). Surface transportation funding is a good example. National motor fuel taxes have historically been the source of funding for the Highway Trust Fund, which is then used to partially fund transportation projects at all three government levels. These taxes are a fixed amount of cents per gallon, and the federal rates have not been increased since 1993. In addition, fuel economy standards have reduced the amount of gas purchased. This has resulted in significant revenue issues, but Congress has been unwilling to increase the tax rates to make up for these losses (Kirk & Mallett, 2018). In addition, construction costs have increased over time at a greater pace

Table 1. Investment Funding Gap in Selected Infrastructure Systems Through 2025 (Dollars in $2015 billions)

Infrastructure System	Total Needs	Funded	Funding Gap
Surface Transportation	$2,042	$941	$1,101
Water/Wastewater Infrastructure	$150	$45	$105
Electricity	$934	$757	$177
Airports	$157	$115	$42
Inland Waterways & Marine Ports	$37	$22	$15
TOTALS	$3,320	$1,880	$1,440

Source: (The American Society of Civil Engineers, 2017).

than revenue growth, and federal mandates related to infrastructure have also increased requirements for states and especially local governments (Chen & Bartle, 2017).

Federal spending was 38% of total public investment in transportation infrastructure in 1977, which declined to less than 25 percent by 2016 (Business Roundtable, 2016). This was partly due to the divergence between major capital expenditures and spending on operations and maintenance. Public spending on the latter has been rising steadily since the 1960s, while spending on capacity expansions, major upgrades or new construction projects has grown at a much slower rate and has been in decline since the 2000s (Sabol & Puentes, 2014). Federal spending accounts for 12 percent of total public spending on infrastructure operation and maintenance and nearly 40 percent of capital expenditures. The gap between spending on basic upkeep versus major system improvements is consistent with the growing gap between federal versus state and local infrastructure spending in these areas (Congressional Budget Office, 2015).

Asset maintenance has been found to be the weakest area in capital management at the state and local levels. Ebdon (2007) suggests: "Capital assets need to be maintained in good working order to prevent excessive long-term costs and safety hazards. This requires good information systems and regular, comprehensive condition assessments to determine the status of assets, the cost of maintaining them in good condition, and the financing available to pay for the maintenance needs" (p.66).

Many governments do not have basic information on condition assessments and maintenance needs. For example, only 23% of the cities in the Government Performance Project analysis conducted regular building inspections. Information technology systems also did not meet the needs for many of the states and local governments in the analysis; however, new governmental accounting standards (GASB Statement 34) implemented in the early 2000s required reporting on infrastructure assets for the first time, which led many governments to develop inventory and asset condition management systems (Ebdon, 2007).

While many governments do not know the amount of funding relative to maintenance needs, most reported that they had funded less than 50% of needs in the years prior to the Government Performance Project analysis (Ebdon, 2007). In the most recent state analysis, over one-half of those responding noted underfunded maintenance by more than 25% (Jimenez & Pagano, 2012). Maintenance funding is often funded at the department level through the operating budget, so these needs compete with basic operating needs such as correction workers, school teachers, and police officers. For example, 40% of states responding to a survey fund maintenance in the operating budget, while 15% use the capital budget; 27.5% include routine maintenance in the operating budget with building renewal maintenance in the capital budget (Ermasova, 2013). In difficult economic times, it is common to defer funding for maintenance because it is less visible than other priorities on a day-to-day basis (Marlowe, 2013).

Some governments, though, have implemented funding mechanisms to focus on reducing maintenance needs. For example, the State of North Carolina has a repair and renovation reserve for deferred maintenance that is 3% of the value of state buildings, while Maricopa County developed a reserve fund through a dedicated sales tax to finance maintenance of jail facilities (Ebdon, 2007). The State of Oregon charges "rent" to agencies and uses these funds for maintenance (Ermasova, 2013).

Analysis of State and Local Capital Practices

Overall, state governments and large cities and counties generally use many "best practices" in capital planning and project management, and improvements have been seen in these areas over time. Long-term, detailed capital plans are common, and many governments use specific decision criteria for prioritizing projects. Project tracking systems are also widely used in order to keep projects as close as possible to being completed on time and on budget. There are significant variations across governments, though, and we know very little about practices and circumstances in smaller jurisdictions and in single-purpose special districts such as schools.

However, as with the federal government, asset maintenance is a significant issue. Many state and local governments have high levels of deferred maintenance. These problems are due to a combination of poor data and constrained resources. Only in recent years have many governments begun to have the technology and capacity to track and analyze the condition of their capital assets, and life-cycle costs, in order to make better procurement decisions and enhance the ability to develop appropriate maintenance schedules and target the most critical needs. Limited funding has also been a serious challenge to capital maintenance; when budgets are tight, it is easier to defer maintenance than to reduce important public services such as police officers or teachers.

The fragmentation of the U.S. government and infrastructure structure can exacerbate the capital issues. The highway system, as we noted, is a good example of this. There are federal, state, and local roads, and each level shares in responsibilities and funding for this complex system. The decline in federal gas tax dollars in recent years has put a serious strain on the ability to develop and maintain roads and highways. Other major infrastructure systems are experiencing similar challenges.

ANALYSIS

Infrastructure planning and maintenance is critical for America's economic growth and competitiveness. Every $1 of federal money spent on infrastructure as part of the efforts to stimulate the economy after the Great Recession increased economic activity by between $1 and $2.50 via job creation, system improvements and stimulated aggregate demand (American Society of Civil Engineers, 2013). Researchers from the University of Maryland concluded that an $83 billion infrastructure investment package — the equivalent of approximately 0.6 percent of GDP — would create 1.7 million jobs in the first three years, accounting for both direct and indirect employment effects (Werling & Horst, 2014). Increasing U.S. infrastructure investment by the equivalent of 1 percent of GDP per year could boost annual output across a range of industries by up to $320 billion (McKinsey Global Institute, 2013). According to the Federal Reserve Bank of San Francisco, every $1 spent on federal highway grants increases the recipient state's GDP by $2 over 10 years, although the multiplier can be as high as $8, depending upon the specific characteristics of the project (Leduc & Wilson, 2013).

Despite its importance, most experts believe that the country is underinvesting in infrastructure. Many argue that the lack of a separate capital budget on the federal level systematically penalizes capital investment because the political incentives embedded in the budgeting process are such that Congress is most likely to fund popular consumption-based programs whose impact is felt right away (Frankel and Wachs, 2017). According to the Congressional Budget Office (2008), "proponents of capital budgeting assert that the current budgetary treatment of capital investment creates a bias against capital spending and that additional spending would benefit the economy by boosting productivity. They note that capital budgeting could better match budgetary costs with benefit flows and eliminate some of the spikes in programs' budgets from new investments" (p.3). There is a "macro bias" against capital spending because decision-makers are likely to be particularly averse to the budget spikes created by capital projects when their budget authority is constrained by some type of cap (Brown, 1999).

The short-term orientation of the yearly (operating) budget cycle influences Congress to systematically under-invest in public infrastructure in favor of the more politically popular consumption-based programs. The opponents of a distinct federal capital budget argue that it is a Trojan horse designed to destroy the budget discipline of a balanced budget policy that would encourage more undesirable federal borrowing; and it would not achieve the objectives proponents claim (Gershberg & Benning, 1999, p.21).

As we have seen, state and local governments also have difficulty with capital funding. The cumulative impact of this underinvestment in the nation's transportation infrastructure, the natural aging process and accelerating demand pressures is a massive gap between projected investment needs and projected investment levels over the next several years, on the order of $1 trillion by 2020 (American Society of Civil Engineers, 2013a).

There is general acceptance that infrastructure needs require attention in the U.S. A number of potential solutions have been proposed and tried. They can be classified into several categories (Chen & Bartle, 2017). First, additional funding sources would be helpful. For example, increasing the federal gas tax rates by one cent would increase revenues for transportation by an estimated $1.5 billion per year. However, this is politically challenging for the federal government. Kirk and Mallett (2018) suggest that "increasing the rate of the fuel taxes has never been popular. The last three increases were accomplished with difficulty and were influenced by the broader budgetary environment and the politics of the time" (p.7). Some states have increased their fuel tax rates, while others use variable rates. Movement to a vehicle miles traveled charge has also received attention, particularly for trucks, along with other methods to better align road damage with taxes (Yusuf & O'Connell, 2013).

A second category of solutions involves new financing mechanisms. This involves new types of intergovernmental loans, such as state revolving funds for local government water systems. State infrastructure banks have also been used to provide low-interest loans and credit enhancements; as of 2015, $5.8 billion of loans from SIBs had been provided to state and local governments for transportation projects. New types of debt instruments are also being used, such as "green bonds" and social impact bonds (Chen & Bartle, 2017). Increasing highway expenses at the state level, for example, have been substantially funded by debt (Yusuf & O'Connell, 2013).

Third, public-private partnerships are increasingly being used for capital projects, in a variety of different forms. At one end of the spectrum are activities where philanthropists make donations to build facilities or make park or library improvements (Ebdon & Landow, 2012). At the other end are full-scale P3 arrangements where governments partner with private entities to design, finance, build, and operate and/or maintain infrastructure. The U.S. has been slower than other countries in the use of P3. A recent example is the PortMiami Tunnel project, where the state and local governments will make availability payments to the concessionaire under a 35-year agreement. Legislation authorizing P3 has been adopted in 34 states as of June 2016, although the laws vary across states (Chen & Bartle, 2017).

Finally, existing structural and governance models for infrastructure have been questioned. Frankel and Wachs (2017) highlight that "infrastructure comprises a huge portion of our shared wealth, and it crosses political boundaries. Effectively managing and enhancing our collective assets are among the most pressing challenges to contemporary government and require actions beyond merely spending more money" (p.6). Some argue, for example, that the federal government should have very little role in financing infrastructure, while some consider it necessary to take account of national and multi-jurisdictional externalities. In addition, about 65% of Americans live in 100 metropolitan regions, each of which include numerous governmental jurisdictions. Metropolitan planning organizations have been created to help in coordination of major infrastructure systems, but there are issues with this approach. Frankel and Wachs

(2017) find: "Few of these agencies are geographically aligned with the functional regions within which infrastructure requires coordination and management. Fewer still can cope effectively with power grids and intercity rail networks that define corridors in which movement and commerce are concentrated. Water districts, transit agencies, and power authorities often have separate and single-purpose governance structures and fail to collaborate even though the systems which they manage interact constantly" (p.9).

There are a variety of challenges to capital asset issues in the U.S. Numerous methods have been proposed to address these challenges, and many of these are being used across the country, primarily at state and local levels. Given the complex, decentralized nature of infrastructure systems in this country, it is unlikely that a national policy in this area will be developed.

CONCLUSION

Capital budgeting and management are important for a variety of reasons. For example, government infrastructure can affect efficiency of service provision, economic development, and tax and spending levels. Tragedies such as the Flint water crisis and the devastation from Hurricane Katrina are strong evidence of the potential negative consequences of ignoring infrastructure issues.

Normative theory calls for comprehensive, long-term capital planning and decision making, effective monitoring of capital projects, and data systems and funding to enable adequate maintenance of capital assets. Srithongrung (2018) suggests that "long-term capital planning and management may help to counterbalance the undesirable effects of uncertainties such as fiscal stresses, political decisions, and unexpected revenue shortfall" (p.66). We have good knowledge of actual practices at the federal government level and at the state level. There are a large number of local governments, and they are very diverse, so we have much more limited information at that level, and what we do know tends to relate to larger cities and counties. Generally speaking, governments at all levels utilize at least some of the best practices related to capital planning and project management. Asset maintenance, however, is typically an area that could use significant improvement.

We highlighted three main themes in U.S. capital management. First, there has been an increase in the efforts to institutionalize recommended best practices in capital budgeting at all levels of government. This is not universally true. Some governments are lagging in implementation of these processes, while others "look good on paper" but still base decisions largely on political calculation rather than objective criteria. At the federal level, there is evidence of increased use of guidelines and planning within agencies, but the lack of a separate capital budget hinders the ability to gain perspective on capital asset decisions. At least in theory, though, the overall increase in planning and data-driven decisions should help to reduce long-term life-cycle costs and result in more efficient and effective use of resources.

Second, the U.S. is suffering from an infrastructure "crisis" due to the large level of unfunded maintenance needs at the federal, state, and local levels. This situation is being addressed to some extent in two ways. Organizations are increasing the use of asset management systems to improve their understanding of maintenance needs in the short-term and over the life of an asset. These practices can aid in targeting funding to the highest needs and ultimately reducing the life-cycle costs of an asset. In addition, innovative practices and funding mechanisms are being utilized, especially at the state and local levels. These include, for example, public-private partnerships, state infrastructure banks, and regional collaboration.

Third, decentralization and fragmentation of infrastructure systems in the United States pose significant challenges to finding solutions to the issues related to planning and maintenance. Each government is responsible for their own assets, and state and local governments accounted for 69% of total direct capital outlay in fiscal year 2015 (authors' calculations from U.S. Census Bureau, 2015 and Office of Management and Budget, 2017b). The national highway system has the largest level of federal involvement, but even that system is owned, operated, and financed through a complex approach that is largely the responsibility of state and local governments. This makes it difficult to achieve consensus on any type of a national policy, and complicates efforts at coordination of systems across jurisdiction boundaries.

The magnitude of the investment funding gap is so large that it is not likely to be solved solely through relatively small-scale innovations by individual or groups of governments. According to The American Society of Civil Engineers (2013), "While infrastructure investment must be increased at all levels, it must also be prioritized and executed according to well-conceived plans that both complement the national vision and focus on system wide outputs...The plans must reflect a better defined set of federal, state, local, and private sector roles and responsibilities and instill better discipline for setting priorities and focusing funding to solve the most pressing problems." It is encouraging that governments have implemented new policies and processes for long-term planning and asset management, and that state and local governments are searching for innovative practices to address infrastructure needs. Srithongrung (2018) suggests that "good financial management practices manifested through high quality bond rating appear to help reduce capital spending volatility" (p.65).

However, as suggested by the American Society of Civil Engineers (2013a), leadership by the federal government is likely needed to facilitate action across governments and to provide stable funding mechanisms to supplement those available from states and localities.

REFERENCES

American Society of Civil Engineers. (2013). *Failure to act: The impact of current infrastructure investment on America's economic future.* Retrieved May 2, 2018, from https://www.asce.org/uploadedFiles/Issues_and_Advocacy/Our_Initiatives/Infrastructure/Content_Pieces/failure-to-act-economic-impact-summary-report.pdf

American Society of Civil Engineers. (2013). *The 2013 report card.* Retrieved May 2, 2018, from http://www.infrastructurereportcard.org/a/documents/2013-Report-Card.pdf

American Society of Civil Engineers. (2017). *The infrastructure report card.* Retrieved May 2, 2018, from https://www.infrastructurerportcard.org/wp-content-uploads/2016/10/Grades-Chart.png

Axelrod, D. (1988). *Budgeting for modern government.* St. Martin's Press.

Batina, R. G. (1998). On the long run Effects of public capital and disaggregated public capital on aggregate output. *International Tax and Public Finance*, *5*(1), 259–263.

Brown, K. (1999). *Report of the president's commission to study capital budgeting.* Washington, DC: U.S. Government Printing Office.

Business Roundtable. (2016). *Road to growth: The case for investing in America's transportation infrastructure.* Retrieved January 28, 2018, from http://businessroundtable.org/sites/default/files/2015.09.16%20Infrastructure%20Report%20-%20Final.pdf

Chen, C., & Bartle, J. (2017). *Infrastructure financing: A guide for local government managers. A policy issue white paper for ICMA and GFOA*. Retrieved May 28, 2018, from https://digitalcommons.unomaha.edu/cgi/viewcontent.cgi?article=1076&context=pubadfacpub

CNN. (2018, April 8). *Flint water crisis fast cacts. CNN.* Retrieved April 28, 2018, from https://www.cnn.com/2016/03/04/us/flint-water-crisis-fast-facts/index.html

Commission to Study Capital Budgeting. (1999). *Report of the president's commission to study capital budgeting*. Retrieved May 2, 2016, from https://clintonwhitehouse2.archives.gov/pcscb/report.pdf

Congressional Budget Office. (2006). *Comparing budget and accounting measures of the federal government's fiscal condition*. Retrieved May 2, 2017, from https://www.cbo.gov/publication/18262

Congressional Budget Office. (2008). *Capital budgeting*. Retrieved May 2, 2017, from https://www.cbo.gov/publication/41689

Congressional Budget Office. (2014). *Estimated impact of the American recovery and reinvestment act on employment and economic output in 2013.* Retrieved May 2, 2017, from https://www.cbo.gov/publication/45122

Congressional Budget Office. (2015). *Public spending on transportation and water infrastructure: 1956 to 2014.* Retrieved May 2, 2017, from https://www.cbo.gov/publication/49910

Department of the Treasury. (2014). *Deferred maintenance. Financial management service, United States government supplemental information (Unaudited) for the years ended September 30, 2013, and 2012.* Retrieved May 8, 2017, from https://www.fiscal.treasury.gov/fsreports/rpt/finrep/finrep13/supp_info/fr_supplement_info_defer_maint.htm

Department of the Treasury & Council of Economic Advisers. (2010). *An economic analysis of infrastructure investment, a report.* Retrieved May 22, 2018, from http://www.treasury.gov/resource-center/economic-policy/Documents/infrastructure_investment_report.pdf

Ebdon, C. (2004). Capital management practices in U.S. counties. *Public Works Management & Policy, 8*(3), 192–202. doi:10.1177/1087724X03259604

Ebdon, C. (2007). Underpinning government: Capital and infrastructure management in state and local government. In P. Ingraham (Ed.), *In pursuit of performance: Management systems in state and local government* (pp. 57–81). Johns Hopkins University Press.

Ebdon, C., & Landow, P. (2012). The balancing act: Using private money for public projects. *Public Budgeting & Finance, 32*(1), 58–79. doi:10.1111/j.1540-5850.2011.01002.x

Ermasova, N. (2012). *Capital budgeting at the state level: An empirical analysis from the economic downturn through the present* (PhD Dissertation). SPEA, IU.

Ermasova, N. (2013). Capital budgeting in the states after the great recession. *State & Local Government Review, 45*(2), 119–130. doi:10.1177/0160323X13487079

Federal Accounting Standards Advisory Board. (2011). *Deferred maintenance and repairs amending statements of federal financial accounting standards 6, 14, 29 and 32: Statement of federal financial accounting standards exposure draft*. Retrieved May 22, 2018, from http://fasab.gov/pdffiles/exposure_dmr_2011jun27.pdf

Federal Aviation Administration. (2017). *Airport and airway trust fund*. Retrieved May 24, 2018, from http://www.faa.gov/about/budget/aatf

Federal Real Property Council. (2016). 2016 *guidance for real property inventory reporting*. Retrieved May 24, 2018, from https://www.gsa.gov/cdnstatic/FY_2016_FRPP_Data_Dictionary_May_16__2016.pdf

Forrester, J. P. (1993). Municipal capital budgeting: An examination. *Public Budgeting & Finance*, *3*(1), 85–103. doi:10.1111/1540-5850.00977

Frankel, E., & Wachs, M. (2017). More than money: Infrastructure and governance. *Public Works Management & Policy*, *22*(1), 6–11. doi:10.1177/1087724X16667728

GAO. (1997). *GAO/AIMD-97-88, federal investment outlays*. Fiscal Years 1981-2002 (Letter report, 05/21/1997).

GAO. (2004). *Agency implementation of capital planning principles is mixed*. GAO-04-138.

GAO. (2016). *Process exists for prioritizing asset maintenance decisions, but evaluation could improve efforts*. GAO-17-136.

General Services Administration. (2012). *Federal real property council 2012 guidance for real property inventory reporting*. Washington, DC: Author.

Gershberg, A., & Benning, J. (1999). *Federal capital investment and the balanced budget amendment: The pros and cons of a federal capital budget* (Research paper). The Nelson A. Rockefeller Institute of Government.

Ingraham, P. (2007). *In pursuit of performance: Management systems in state and local government*. Johns Hopkins Press.

Istrate, E., & Puentes, R. (2009). *Investing for success examining a federal capital budget and a national infrastructure bank*. Retrieved March 2, 2017, from http://www.brookings.edu/~/media/Files/rc/reports/2009/1210_infrastructure_puentes.pdf

Jimenez, B., & Pagano, M. (2012). What factors affect management quality? State infrastructure management and the government performance project. *Public Works Management & Policy*, *17*(2), 124–151. doi:10.1177/1087724X11419308

Johnson, C. (1995). Managing financial resources to meet environmental infrastructure needs: The case of state revolving funds. *Public Productivity and Management Review*, *18*(3), 263–275. doi:10.2307/3380847

Karnowski, S. (2017, July 30). Minnesota bridge collapse still reverberates 10 years later. *The Chicago Tribune*. Retrieved May 8, 2018, from http://www.chicagotribune.com/news/nationworld/midwest/ct-minnesota-bridge-collapse -anniversary-20170730-story.html

Kennedy, D. (1967). *Report of the president's commission on budget concepts.* Washington, DC: U.S. Government Printing Office.

Kirk, R., & Mallett, W. (2018). *Funding and financing highways and public transportation, congressional research service, January 11, 2018.* Retrieved May 28, 2018, from http://fas.org/sgp/crs/misc/R44674.pdf

Leduc, S., & Wilson, D. (2013). Roads to prosperity or bridges to nowhere? Theory and evidence on the impact of public infrastructure investment. *NBER Macroeconomics Annual, 27*(1), 89–142. doi:10.1086/669173

Levine, S., & Augustino, J. (1994). State revolving funds: A model for financing drinking water programs. *Government Finance Review, 12*, 26–44.

Lopez, G. (2015, August 28). Hurricane Katrina in 7 essential facts. *VOX.* Retrieved May 28, 2018, from https://www.vox.com/2015/8/23/9191907/hurricane-katrina

Lynde, C., & Richmond, J. (1992). The role of public capital in production. *The Review of Economics and Statistics, 74*(1), 37–44. doi:10.2307/2109540

Marlowe, J. (2013). Strategy, priority-setting, and municipal capital budget reform: Three cases from the great recession. *Journal of Public Budgeting, Accounting & Financial Management, 25*(4), 693–718.

McKinsey Global Institute. (2013). *Game changers: Five opportunities for U.S. growth and renewal.* Retrieved April 2, 2018, from https://www.mckinsey.com/featured-insights/americas/us-game-changers

Mikesell, J. (2007). *Fiscal administration: Analysis and applications for the public sector* (8th ed.). Belmont, CA: Thomson Wadsworth.

National Association of Manufacturers and Building America's Future Educational Fund. (2013). *Infrastructure: Essential to manufacturing competitiveness.* Retrieved April 2, 2018, from http://www.nam.org/Data-and-Reports/NAM-BAF-Infrastructure-Survey/NAM-BAF-Infrastructure-Survey.pdf

National Association of State Budget Officers (NASBO). (2015). *Budget processes in the states.* Retrieved April 2, 2018, from http://www.nasbo.org/publications-data/budget-processes-in-the-states

National Research Council. (2005). *Key performance indicators for federal facilities portfolios: Federal facilities council technical report number 147.* Washington, DC: The National Academies Press; doi:10.17226/11226

OECD. (2016). *Regional outlook survey.* Retrieved May 21, 2018, from https://www.oecd-ilibrary.org/urban-rural-and-regional-development/oecd-regional-outlook-2016/united-states_9789264260245-48-en

Office of Management and Budget. (1992). *Circular A–94: Guidelines and discount rates for benefit-cost analysis of federal programs.* Author.

Office of Management and Budget. (2015). *Capital programming guide, V 3.0, supplement to office of management budget circular A-11: Planning, budgeting, and acquisition of capital assets.* Retrieved April 2, 2017, from https://obamawhitehouse.archives.gov/sites/default/files/omb/assets/a11_current_year/a11_2016.pdf

Office of Management and Budget. (2016). *Appendix A - Scorekeeping guidelines* (OMB Circular A-11). Author.

Office of Management and Budget. (2016). *Appendix J - Principles in budgeting for capital asset acquisitions (OMB Circular A-11).* Retrieved April 2, 2018, from https://obamawhitehouse.archives.gov/sites/default/files/omb/assets/a11_current_year/app_j.pdf

Office of Management and Budget. (2017). *Circular A-11.* Retrieved April 2, 2018, from https://www.whitehouse.gov/sites/whitehouse.gov/files/omb/assets/a11_current_year/a11_2017.pdf

Office of Management and Budget. (2017). *Budget of the U.S. government, analytical perspectives, fiscal year 2017.* Retrieved September 26, 2018, from https://www.gpo.gov/fdsys/pkg/BUDGET-2017-PER/pdf/BUDGET-2017-PER-6-4.pdf

Office of Management and Budget. (2018). *Budget of the U.S. government, analytical perspectives, fiscal year 2019.* Retrieved May 24, 2018, from https://fraser.stlouisfed.org/files/docs/publications/usbanalytical/BUDGET-2019-PER.pdf

Pagano, M., & Perry, D. (2008). Financing infrastructure in the 21st century city. *Public Works Management & Policy*, *13*(1), 22–38. doi:10.1177/1087724X08321015

Potter, B., & Diamond, J. (1999). *Guidelines for public expenditure management.* Retrieved May 24, 2018, from https://www.imf.org/external/pubs/ft/expend/guide5.htm

Sabol, P., & Puentes, R. (2014). Why isn't cheap debt supporting more infrastructure investment? In The Avenue: Rethinking Metropolitan America, Metropolitan Infrastructure Initiative. The Brookings Institution.

Sekwat, A. (1999). Capital budgeting practices among Tennessee municipal governments. *Government Finance Review*, *15*(3), 15–19.

Srithongrung, A. (2008). The impacts of state capital management programs on state economic performance. *Public Budgeting & Finance*, *28*(3), 83–107. doi:10.1111/j.1540-5850.2008.00912.x

Srithongrung, A. (2010). State capital improvement programs and institutional arrangements for capital budgeting: The case Of Illinois. *Journal of Public Budgeting, Accounting & Financial Management*, *22*(3), 407–430.

Srithongrung, A. (2018). Capital budgeting and management practices: Smoothing out rough spots in government outlays. *Public Budgeting & Finance*, *38*(1), 47–71. doi:10.1111/pbaf.12167

Suren, S. (1996). Using an affordability analysis to budget capital expenditure. *Healthcare Financial Management*, *50*(6), 70–76. PMID:10158243

U.S. Census Bureau. (2012). *Government organization summary report 2012.* Retrieved May 22, 2018, from https://www.census.gov/content/dam/Census/library/publications/2013/econ/g12-cg-org.pdf

U.S. Census Bureau. (2015). *Government finances.* Retrieved May 22, 2018 from https://www.census.gov/govs/local/

U.S. Department of the Treasury. (2018). *FY2017 financial report of the United States government.* Retrieved September 26, 2018, from https://www.fiscal.treasury.gov/fsreports/rpt/finrep/fr/17frusg/02142018_FR(Final).pdf

U.S. General Accounting Office. (1998). Executive guide: Leading practices in capital decision-making. GAO/AIMD-99-32. Washington, DC: Author.

U.S. Government. (2017). *Financial report, FY 2017.* Retrieved May 22, 2018, from https://www.gao.gov/assets/700/690123.pdf

Vermeer, T., Patton, T., & Styles, K. (2011). Reporting of general infrastructure assets under GASB statement no. 34. *Accounting Horizons*, *25*(2), 381–407. doi:10.2308/acch-10029

Vogt, J. A. (2004). *Capital budget and finance: A guide for local governments.* International City/ County Management Association.

Werling, J., & Horst, R. (2014). *Catching up: Greater focus needed to achieve a more competitive infrastructure.* National Association of Manufacturers. Retrieved May 28, 2018, from http://www.nam.org/Issues/Infrastructure/Surface-Infrastructure/Infrastructure-Full-Report-2014.pdf

Yusuf, J.-E., & O'Connell, L. (2013). The crisis in state highway finances: Its roots, current effects, and some possible remedies. *Journal of Public Budgeting, Accounting & Financial Management*, *25*(3), 502–521.

Chapter 3
The Case of Public Capital Budgeting and Management Process in Germany

Natalia B. Ermasova
Governors State University, USA

ABSTRACT

This chapter presents an analysis of four main components of the German capital budgeting system including (1) long-term public capital planning, (2) annual public budgeting and financing, (3) project execution, and (4) public infrastructure evaluation. Germany provides good conditions for capital investments. This chapter explains main reasons for it: institutional framework, healthy public finance, structural reform, and special investment and redemption fund that gave a boost to investments in infrastructure. This case describes the capital budgeting process in Germany and explains the recent trends of public capital investments.

INTRODUCTION

According to the World Economic Forum (WEF) Global Competitiveness Report (2017), Germany's infrastructure ranked tenth in the world. Germany provides good conditions for capital investments. The main reasons for it are healthy public finances, robust institutional framework, structural reforms, and public investments to boost competitiveness. The public investment in Germany has increased significantly in the last thirty years. The government gross fixed capital formation increased by 37 percent in 2018 in comparison to 1990 (German Finance Ministry, 2018). The government gross fixed capital formation in relation to nominal GDP (the investment-to-GDP ratio) was 2.6 percent in 2018, compared with 1.7 percent in 2001. The proportion of spending on public investments increased from 8.5 percent of the federal budget in 2014 to 9.5 percent in 2015 (Federal Ministry for Economic Affairs and Energy, 2016, p.11) Germany's gross fixed capital formations increased from €137 billion in 2015 to €149 billion in 2018 (Trading Economics, 2018).

DOI: 10.4018/978-1-5225-7329-6.ch003

The capital budgeting is integrated into the ordinary budget process in Germany. Capital investments are identifiable in the budget but are treated as any other expenditure in the process. Capital budgeting does not have a separate framework. Federal Ministry of Defense, Federal Ministry of Transport and Digital Infrastructure, Federal Ministry of Food and Agriculture, Federal Ministry of the Interior, Building and Community, Federal Ministry for Economic Affairs and Energy, Federal Ministry of Labor and Social Affairs, Federal Ministry of Health, Federal Ministry for the Environment, Nature Conservation, and Nuclear Safety requests for funding are resolved in negotiation between the respective ministry and the Federal Ministry of Finance prior to the budget being submitted to Parliament. It is a key role for the Federal Ministry of Finance to ensure that the capital project portfolio fits into the long-term capital budget (CIP). The Federal Ministry of Finance must give its approval for the project to move forward at the end of the preparation stage and the procurement stage. Investment spending at the federal level mainly happens in the sectors of transport and defense, and it was around 2 percent of the federal budget expenditures in 2017. The majority of capital investment activity takes place at the regional (the Länder) and municipal level.

The political level plays a key role in deciding which projects will be part of the portfolio appropriation. The political support for a project can be more important than cost-benefit estimates. During budget execution, the appropriation framework allows some possibility for the government to change and reallocate the funding within the investment portfolio.

This chapter examines the effects of budget reforms on changes in capital budgeting practices with main focus on federal level. The specific practices discussed in the chapter are the following: (1) long-term public capital planning, (2) annual public budgeting and financing, (3) project execution, and (4) public infrastructure evaluation. This analysis provides links to best practices by exploring innovative solutions in capital budgeting and financing in Germany. This study provides a valuable starting point for future research on comparative studies of capital budgeting in different countries.

BACKGROUND

Germany has Europe's largest economy and second most populous nation (80,594,017 people). Germany is a key member of the continent's economic, political, and defense organizations (CIA, 2018). Germany was in two devastating World Wars in the first half of the 20th century. After World War II, two German states were formed in 1949, the western Federal Republic of Germany (FRG) and the eastern German Democratic Republic (GDR). The democratic FRG embedded itself in key western economic and security organizations, the European Community (EC), which became the European Union (EU), and NATO, while the communist GDR was on the front line of the Soviet-led Warsaw Pact (CIA, 2018). Germany had the reunification in 1990. Based on the Consolidation Assistance Act (Gesetz zur Gewährung von Konsolidierungshilfen), the federal government provides a fixed amount of financial assistance to five regions (Länder) that were parts of the eastern German Democratic Republic with the goal to eliminate the structural deficit in those five Länder by 2020. Since 1990, Germany has expended considerable funds to bring eastern productivity and wages up to western standards.

The German economy is the fifth largest economy in the world (CIA, 2018). GDP per capita was $45,551 in 2017 compared to $45,253 in 2016 (Table 1). Table 1 presents main GDP indicators including GDP, Gross Fixed Capital Formation, GDP from different sectors of German economy, and Gross National Product from 2016 to 2017.

Table 1. The main GDP indicators from 2016 to 2017

Indicators	2017	2016
GDP ($ bln)	3466.76	3363.60
Gross National Product (bln. €)	840.62	836.67
Gross Fixed Capital Formation (bln. €)	149.03	148.98
GDP per capita ($)	45551.51	45253.60
GDP from agriculture (bln. €)	4.79	5.59
GDP from construction (bln. €)	40.61	38.88
GDP from manufacturing (bln. €)	168.23	171.76
GDP from public administration (bln. €)	140.80	133.76
GDP from services (bln. €)	120.76	121.42

Source: Trading Economics (2018)

Reforms launched by the government of Chancellor Gerhard Schroeder (1998-2005) contributed to strong economic growth. The German Government introduced a minimum wage in 2015 that increased to $9.79 (€8.84) in January 2017 (CIA, 2018). Financial stimulus and stabilization efforts were initiated in 2008 and 2009. During a financial crisis, the government introduced tax cuts that increased Germany's total budget deficit, including federal, state, and municipal to 4.1 percent in 2010. The slower spending (during financial crisis) and higher tax revenues (after crisis) reduced the deficit to 0.8 percent in 2011 and in 2017 (CIA, 2018). A constitutional amendment (2009) approved the limits to structural deficits of the federal government no more than 0.35 percent of GDP per year. This target (deficits of no more than 0.35 percent of GDP per year) was reached in 2012.

The German general government comprises federal, regional (the *Länder)*, local governments, and social security funds. The German general government comprises federal, state and local government and social security funds. The German general government had surplus of €23.7 billion at the end of 2016 that equivalent to 0.8 percent of GDP, compared with surplus of €19.2 billion (0.6 percent of GDP) in 2015. It was the biggest surplus that was recorded since German reunification. The main reasons for this surplus are the increase of government's revenues to €1,411.4 billion due to a large increase in income tax and property tax payments (6.5 percent) and in social contributions (4.6 percent). Government expenditures increased to €1,387.7 billion in 2016, driven by higher expenditure on intermediate consumption (8.7 percent) and a marked increase in expenditure on social benefits in kind (6.2 percent). According to Trading Economics (2018), the largest surplus in 2016 was achieved by social insurance funds (€8.2 billion), followed by central government (€7.7 billion), state government (€4.7 billion) and local government (€3.1 billion). The government budget in Germany averaged -2.09 percent of GDP from 1995 until 2016, reaching an all-time high of 0.90 percent of GDP in 2000, very low -4.2 percent of GDP in 2010, and a record low of -9.40 percent of GDP in 1995 (Table 2). Germany reached budget surplus of 0.7 percent in 2017 and 1.2 percent in 2018 (Trading Economics, 2018). Table 2 demonstrates main indicators for the government budget of Germany in 2017.

Germany is a federal parliamentary republic with laws and key institutions of state grounded upon a Basic Law (Grundgesetz). The president of Federal Republic of Germany is indirectly elected by a Federal Convention consisting of all members of the Federal Parliament (Bundestag) and an equivalent number

Table 2. The main indicators for government budget of Germany in 2017

Germany Government	2017
Government Debt to GDP (%)	68.30
Government Spending (bln. €)	139.50
Government Spending to GDP (%)	44.30
Government Revenues (bln. €)	346.12
Government Debt (bln. €)	2,092.64
Fiscal Expenditure (bln. €)	332.75
Military Expenditure (bln. €)	40.98

Source: Trading Economics (2018)

of delegates indirectly elected by the state parliaments. The President serves a 5-year term (eligible for a second term). The last election was held on 12 February 2017.

Based on the Basic Law (2017) and constitutional provisions, the federation must adopt a Budget Act each year setting out its expenditures for the year ahead and how they will be "covered" (financed) through revenues and any necessary borrowing (OECD, 2014, p.15). The draft Budget Act is presented to, debated, amended, and approved by the Bundestag. The consent of the Bundesrat (the upper house of parliament in which the Länder are represented) is not required. The federal budget consists of the annual Budget Act and its appended budget documentation, aggregate budget and departmental budgets. The Federal Ministry of Finance is responsible for organizing the annual budget preparations, including capital budget. Federal Ministry of Finance "proposes allocations for each line ministry (on the basis of continuity with the indicative allocations from the previous cycle), receives "bids" from each ministry, and has the right to amend and adjust these bids (after consultation with the ministries concerned) to ensure consistency with the overall budgetary constraint" (OECD, 2014, p.16).

The Basic Law (2017) provides fundamental requirements of the budget process and prescribes the fiscal relationship between the federation (the federal level of government) and the state regions (Länder). The subnational governments are responsible for 47 percent of public expenditures, ranking Germany 8th in the OECD in terms of decentralization (OECD, 2016b). Germany consists of 16 states (Länder). The states (Länder) have a high level of autonomy. The Länder also participate in the legislative process of the federation through their representation in the Bundesrat (upper house of the bicameral legislature). The tasks assigned to Germany's Länder include: (1) compensation of civil servants (including teachers), (2) regional roads, (3) regional hospitals, (4) regional museums, (5) provision of administrative, regional and district courts, (6) police, (7) culture, sports, education, (8) spatial planning, and (9) water management (Gamper, 2012, p.4). The federation and the Länder are autonomous on managing their budgets.

Municipalities in Germany have three types of tasks: (1) the local registry, the administration of living and social subsidies, construction planning, and the administration of municipal elections, (2) waste management, spatial planning, provision of day care, (3) libraries, museums, retirement homes, traffic and others. The districts are responsible for cross-municipal tasks like transport systems, museums, nature reserves, district roads or waste management. In addition, this could include also hospitals or primary schools.

The Basic Law requires that the federation and the Länder have to balance their public finances. They can borrow at the federal level during economic cycle and in response to exceptional events. They must work jointly to fulfil EU-related obligations as regards fiscal discipline. Each level of government (federal and Länder) should finance its own expenditure, although, there are specified grounds upon which financial aid may pass from the federal to Land level (OECD, 2014). The "debt brake" (Schuldenbremse) rule's main purpose is to strengthen and operationalize the balanced budget principle that is included (since 2009) in the Basic Law. The "debt brake" (Schuldenbremse) policy instrument requires structural balanced budgets at the federal and Länder level in accordance with the European Stability and Growth Pact. When the debt brake came into force at the federal level in 2016 to 2020, structural deficits would be forbidden for the Länder. This policy goes partially against the recommendations of the international organizations, such as the IMF and the OECD. They have called on Germany to step up public investment, as this would not only stimulate demand in the near term but would also improve the growth potential of the economy (Van der Putten, 2017).

Germany has the resource allocation process from the outset, resulting in a distinctive form of "top-down budgeting" since 2010. This approach to budget formation is distinct from the 'bottom up' approach whereby the resource demands from line ministries and agencies are a key determinant in the final macro-fiscal outcome. In Germany, all ministries and the Federal Chancellery signal their new funding priorities and strategic orientations for the budget year. The Federal Ministry of Finance handles resolving the policy and funding issues that arise in the first instance. The contentious issues are discussed and settled at the political level. The culmination of this "top-down budgeting" process is the 'key figures decision' whereby the government agrees to overall allocations for each line ministry. According to OECD (2014), the annual budget cycle is organized around three distinct phases: (1) the preparation of the key figures decision in March, which also leads to the annual Stability Program in April, (2) the preparation of the draft federal budget and five-year Financial Plan, which are submitted to the federal parliament in August, and (3) the consideration and adoption of the budget by the parliament with a particularly strong role for the Budget Committee of the Bundestag.

LONG-TERM INFRASTRUCTURE EVALUATION AND PUBLIC INVESTMENTS IN GERMANY

Germany has a reputation for excellent infrastructure. The infrastructure is a key driver of economic growth, competitiveness, and social well being of citizens (Ammar, Duncombe & Wright, 2001; Ermasova, 2013). The public investment in Germany has increased significantly from 1990 to 2018. The government gross fixed capital formation increased by 37 percent in 2018 in comparison to 1990 (German Finance Ministry, 2018).

Public investments are around 10 percent of total investments in Germany. The federal government, the *Länder,* and the local authorities each accounted for roughly a third of total government investment (German Finance Ministry, 2015). Table 4 presents the public investments on federal, the *Länder,* local levels, and by social insurance funds in 2016. Table 3 shows that Net Investments (Gross investments - Depreciation) were negative on local level due high depreciation.

The high growth rates of government gross fixed capital formation were in 1990 to 1994 years (Table 5). The investment-to-GDP ratio did decline significantly from 2002 to 2004. The reason for this situation was the ongoing wind-down of the construction boom that followed German reunification (Ministry of Finance of Germany, 2014). The situation improved from 2005 to 2009, but during financial crisis, the gross fixed capital formations decreased by 10.1 percent in 2010.

Table 3. The gross and net public investments across levels of government in 2016 (bln. €)

Indicators	Total Investments	Total Public Investments	Federal Level	The *Länder* Level	Local Level	Social Insurance Funds
Gross investments	603,591	66.3	20.1	22.0	23.3	0.9
Depreciation	552,291	68.6	18.4	19.8	29.3	1.2
Net investments	51,300	-2.3	1.7	2.8	-5.9	-0.3

Source: Statistisches Bundesamt (Destatis), 2018

Germany started to use a new European System of Accounts (ESA) in 2010 that provided a general revision of its national accounts (OECD, 2015a). The research and development spending is now classified as investment, not as consumption. The additional government research centers are considered as a part of the public sector. These modifications have raised levels of government investment. As a result, the average annual investment-to-GDP ratio increased from 1.9 percent to 2.4 percent for the period from 1991 to 2013 and from 1.6 percent to 2.2 percent for the year 2013 (German Finance Ministry, 2015). The classification of R&D expenditures as investment was the main factor contributing to this increase. In addition, military weapon systems, which are now classified as equipment, also served to boost the investment ratio.

General government investments are focused on defense, healthcare, social protection, and environment protection. Most of subnational investments in Germany are dedicated to economic affairs (transport, general economic, commercial affairs, industry, agriculture, etc.). Subnational governments are responsible for building and maintaining public roads and public transport (OECD, 2015b, 2017). Other major categories of investment spending include education and general public services. Table 4 demonstrates the public investments by general and subnational governments in 2014.

Table 5 demonstrates the growth of gross fixed capital formation (adjusted for price) from 1990 to 2017. The dynamics of Ratio Gross Fixed Capital Formation to GDP show that the highest ratio was in 2001 (26.1 percent). The ratio decreased from 23.8 percent to 13.3 percent from 2002 to 2011 due to financial crisis.

According to the Global Economic Forum (2008), Germany was ranked third on a list of countries with the best infrastructure. Due to decreasing of capital investments during global financial crisis, Germany had seventh place in 2013 and tenth place in 2017 (WEF Global Competitiveness Report, 2017). Table 6 demonstrates the ranking of countries based on conditions of their infrastructure in 2017.

Table 4. Multi-level governance of public investment in 2014

	General Government	Subnational Governments
USD billion	79.8	55.6
USD per capita	995	687
% of GDP	2.1	1.5
% of public expenditure	4.8	7.1
% of total public direct investment	100	69.7

Source: OECD (2016a), Subnational governments in OECD countries: Key data, 2016 edition (brochure).

Table 5. The growth of gross fixed capital formation (adjusted for price) from 1990 to 2017

Years	GDP ($ bln €)	Gross Fixed Capital Formation Adjusted for Price (bln. €)	Growth of Gross Fixed Capital Formation (%)	Ratio Gross Fixed Capital Formation to GDP (%)
1990	1,592	422.4	+8.0	26.5
1991	1,868	442.3	+4.7	23.6
1992	2,127	460.5	+4.1	21.6
1993	2,069	441.2	-4.2	21.3
1994	2,210	457.2	+3.6	20.6
1995	2,593	457.1	+0.0	17.6
1996	2,504	454.8	-0.5	18.1
1997	2,221	458.4	+0.8	20.6
1998	2,246	458.4	+0.8	20.3
1999	2,202	476.2	+3.9	21.6
2000	1,995	498.3	+4.6	24.9
2001	1,951	510.0	+2.3	26.1
2002	2,085	497.1	-2.5	23.8
2003	2,510	468.4	-5.8	18.6
2004	2,822	462.2	-1.3	16.3
2005	2,866	462.4	+0.0	16.1
2006	3,004	465.8	+0.7	15.4
2007	3,444	500.8	+7.5	14.5
2008	3,770	521.2	+4.1	13.8
2009	3,426	529.2	+1.5	15.4
2010	3,423	475.8	-10.1	13.8
2011	3,761	501.4	+5.4	13.3
2012	3,545	537.4	+7.2	15.1
2013	3,753	533.9	-0.7	14.2
2014	3,896	527.8	-1.1	13.5
2015	3,377	545.9	+3.4	16.1
2016	3,479	555.2	+1.7	15.9
2017	3,686	569.3	+2.5	15.4

Source: Ministry of Finance of Germany, 2018

For decades, the world envied Germany for its network or roads and railways, and this capital starts to crumble (Jung, Müller, Sauga, Schmergal, Traufetter & Witsch, 2014). The quality of road infrastructure dropped from the 5th position in the 2009 to 2010 report to the 16th position in the 2015 to 2016 report (Van der Putten, 2017). The German Institute for Economic Research (DIW) president Fratzscher (2014) offers a detailed picture of the problems of German investment and illustrates the sectors with the most serious problems in his book *Germany illusions (Die Deutschland-Illusion)*. For example, a famous highway on the Sauerland route between Dortmund and Giessen in western Germany, the "Queen

Table 6. The ranking of countries based on conditions of their infrastructure in 2017

Ranking	Countries	Score
1	Hong Kong	6.7
2	Singapore	6.5
3	Netherlands	6.4
4	Japan	6.3
5	United Arab Emirates	6.3
6	Switzerland	6.3
7	France	6.1
8	Korea, Rep	6.1
9	United States	6.0
10	Germany	6.0
11	United Kingdom	6.0
12	Spain	5.9

of the Autobahns", became one of Germany's most expensive autobahns. The stretch of this highway passing through the state of Hesse includes 22 large bridges that were built in the 1960s, and 20 of them will have to be refurbished in the next few years. According to Tarek Al-Wazir, transportation minister in Hesse, the need for these renovations has arisen "well ahead of the lifespan calculated at the time of construction" (Jung et al., 2014). According to DIW calculations, this negative trend could be stopped, but to do so, Germany would have to invest at least an additional €10 billion a year. That includes €3.8 billion for maintenance of capital infrastructure and €2.65 billion for renovations that were neglected in the past period (Jung et al., 2014).

CAPITAL PLANNING

Act on the Principles of Federation and Länder Budgetary Law (Haushaltsgrundsätzegesetz (Gesetz über die Grundsätze des Haushaltsrechts des Bundes und der Länder) is a fundamental piece of legislation that establishes the principles of budgeting with which the federal and Länder budget rules must comply. The main principles of budgeting in Germany are financial sufficiency and necessity, annuality, efficiency and economy, and universality. The Act allows use of either cash or double-entry accounting systems, and it permits carryover of expenditures in certain circumstances. It prescribes that the budget should be allocated by departments and divided into chapters and titles. Some titles may be combined into title groups where they relate to a common purpose (e.g. IT expenditure). The financial detail is supplemented with budget notes, and some of which have binding effect on specifying or restricting the uses of the funds. The departmental budgets are supplemented with numerous budget summaries. Since 2013, some departmental budgets and chapters are accompanied by a one-page foreword to provide the strategic context for departmental activities and objectives. The Act on the Principles of Federation and Länder Budgetary Law also prescribes that authorization, which involves a commitment to spend money in future years (beyond the budget year), requires the prior consent by Ministry of Finance.

On the federal level, the annual budget must be accompanied with a 'finance report', a report on the current state of the public finances and their fiscal outlook. The Federal Budget Code provides rules for the 'blocking' of certain budget items, so that they may not be drawn down for expenditure without express authorization from the Federal Ministry of Finance (OECD, 2014).

The Act to Promote Economic Stability and Growth (Gesetz zur Förderung der Stabilität und des Wachstums der Wirtschaft) was established in 1967. This Act provides a principle that federal and Land budgets shall 'observe the requirements of overall economic equilibrium'. Based on this Act, the Federal Government presents an annual economic report to the Bundestag in January of each year, which should include a response to the most recent Annual Report from the Council of Independent Economic Experts. The networks of independent and technical experts contribute their expertise at various stages of the budgetary and economic forecasts. The Council of Economic Experts presents its wide-ranging economic report, provides independent views of a range of economic subjects, and creates budgetary forecasts for capital investments. The Council is an independent statutory body and its report is not a part of the government's budget preparation process (OECD, 2014). Based on these official macroeconomic forecasts, the Federal Ministry of Finance prepares an internal tax revenue forecast. The federal government's forecasts compared the current forecast by national and international institutions. The Working Party on Tax Revenue Forecasts is an independent advisory council that includes outside economic experts as well as Ministry officials. It prepares a tax revenue forecast. In parallel, and informed by these analyses, the Federal Ministry of Finance draws together its estimate of the national budget parameters. These budget estimates reflect the constraints imposed by Germany's fiscal rules framework. The Federal Ministry of Finance seeks to accommodate policy pressures and new priorities, as signaled from the political system, within the available resources. The combination of a strong rules-based fiscal constraint, which makes explicit the ceiling on resources, and the ex-ante phase of deliberating on political priorities makes for a distinctive 'top-down' style of budgeting in Germany (OECD, 2014). This process leads to cabinet agreement on the "key figures" or "benchmark figures" decision, including indicative expenditure allocations at the federal level.

An important feature of the Act to Promote Economic Stability and Growth is the stipulation that the federal budget should be managed based on a rolling five-year planning period. This five-year Financial Plan must be set each year by the Federal Ministry of Finance. This plan is not binding and can be corrected based on the economic and financial situation in Germany. This Act also states that a reserve fund must be established for counter-balancing cyclical fluctuations. The Federal Ministry of Finance is responsible for organizing the annual budget preparations. The budget documentation is very extensive and detailed, and it includes numerous summary, aggregate tables, and allocations for each line ministry based on continuity with the indicative allocations from the previous cycle. The Federal Ministry of Finance receives 'bids' from each ministry and has the right to amend and adjust these bids, after consultation with the ministries concerned, to ensure consistency with the overall budgetary constraint.

Capital Budgeting and Financial Management

Capital budgeting for infrastructure projects is integrated into the ordinary budget process like in the most OECD countries. Capital investments do not have a separate framework and process that are identifiable in the budget, but it is treated as any other expenditure in the process. The majority of federal investment spending is in the sectors of transport and defense and was around 2 percent of the federal budget in 2017. The capital investment activities at the state level are predominantly in road building, schools, and higher education. The investments spending on municipal level are in the sectors of water supply and waste disposal.

The infrastructure and network plans are coordinated at the federal level by the Federal Ministry of Finance. The detailed coordination, budgeting, and planning efforts take place at the sectoral level. When the requirement plans have been passed, they are operationalized into the five-year framework investment plan. This five-year framework investment plan aligns with the medium-term financial planning framework and forms the basis for the budgeting for specific investment projects.

The following are infrastructure and network plans in Germany:

- Federal Transport Infrastructure Plan
- Federal Regional Policy Plan
- Trans-European Transport Networks
- Energy Network
- EU-Habitats Directive
- 16 Länder-level plans, regional development plans & programs, regional project plans
- Sector-specific plans such as energy plan or mining in North Rhine-Westphalia.

The Federal Ministry of Finance plays a key role in capital budgeting to ensure that the capital project portfolio fits into the long-term capital budget envelope. The appropriation allocated in the budget is not for a single capital project but in a portfolio of capital projects within a relevant category (e.g. road or rail investment). The political support for a project can be more important than what technical cost/benefit estimates. According to OECD (2014, p.56), "during budget execution the appropriation framework allows some possibility for the government to change and reallocate the funding within the portfolio. This has, however, been subject to intense debate as some members of parliament disapprove of the executive using such flexibility with regards to the allocation of appropriated funds."

The Federal Ministry of Finance monitors the investment projects as they moves from the project identification stage to the preparation stage, procurement stage, and implementation stage. At the end of both the preparation stage and the procurement stage, the Federal Ministry of Finance must give its approval for the capital project to move forward and notify the Parliament's Budget Committee. Section 24 of the federal budget code specifies the documentation that has to accompany the project appropriation: plans, cost calculations, qualitative explanations of the project, proposed method of financing, and the timetable for the project. The project documentation must include an estimate of the required annual operational expenditure.

The Federal Ministry of Transport uses a multiannual, planning framework in the form of the federal transport infrastructure plan. The previous plan, endorsed by the government, covered the period 2003 to 2015. The federal transport infrastructure plan takes the form of a "long list" of projects that are evaluated according to cost-benefit analysis. The "long list" of projects is constructed on the basis of the ministry's assessment of pressing economic infrastructure and regional development needs, which in turn, are informed by inputs from the political level, sub-national governments, and other stakeholders. Due the noticeable links to the Länder' transport responsibilities, detailed agreements across levels of government have to be reached before the investment plan is adopted. This process of coordination ensures that the investment plan is realistic and supported on different levels of government. The federal government, in the planning act, then adopts the federal transport infrastructure plan and prepares the amendment of the requirement plans. The requirement plans are set in federal law, regarding federal roads and rail. When the requirement plans have been approved by parliament, they are operationalized into the five-year framework investment plan (OECD, 2014, p.55).

The Federal Ministry of Finance negotiates the budget for the planned projects for a given year with the Federal Ministry of Transport. For example, for the federal trunk roads, the projects are listed in the Road Construction Plan (2013) and are attached to the federal budget as a supplement. Major projects in the sectors of rail and waterways are listed in the budget itself. The Federal Ministry of Finance checks any important draft contracts in the railway sector, which provide the legal basis for financial relations with the state owned rail company Deutsche Bahn AG. The Federal Ministry of Finance checks contracts with regard to their soundness, realism, and budgetary viability. According to Section 24 of the federal budget code, the Federal Ministry of Finance has to approve the necessary documents for construction of buildings before expenditure is allocated in the budget. If these documents are not available during the preparation of the budget, the expenditure is blocked until they are presented to the Ministry of Finance, where a unit of architects and engineers is employed to check and approve them.

Execution and Project Management at the Federal Level

Monitoring and evaluating public investment project systems have been established program-wide on federal and Länder' levels. Federal Ministry for Economic Affairs and Energy (2016, p.10) highlights in his National Reform Program 2016: "investment is key to securing long-term growth and employment potential and to continued survival in the face of global competition for the best ideas, products and talents." The Federal Government focuses economic policy on investment and sustainable growth. It has increased public investment made by the Federation and plans to provide more than €45 billion in financial relief to the Länder and municipalities until 2019 to boost their scope for investment. The Federal Government is also making special efforts to promote private investment.

The Joint Task for the Improvement of Regional Economic Structure (GRW) was created in 1969. The Joint Task for the Improvement of Regional Economic Structure (GRW) and its multiannual Coordination Framework, as well as EU Structural Funds, are the basis of national level regional development policy. It is a consensus-based, coordination framework, and activities are jointly financed by federal and Länder authorities (OECD, 2016b, p.IV). Around two-thirds of GRW budget are spent on investment incentives for firms and one-third for business-related infrastructure. The Joint Tasks (Gemeinschaftsaufgabe) is a long-established collaboration between the Länder and the central government and is responsible for regional economy, extension and construction of higher education facilities, improvement of the agricultural structures and coastal areas, labor market tasks, IT infrastructure, and the environment (Gamper, 2012, p.3). The basic aim of the GRW is to reduce the regional disadvantages faced by structurally weak regions (Länder). The main goal of GRW is to facilitate the participation of Länder in broader economic development processes and to reduce overall developmental disparities. The following are key attributes of the GRW: "a transparent indicator-based system for assessing regional problems; a consensus-based coordination framework which allows equal problems to be treated equally; a systematic rules-based approach to awarding or granting aid; facility for coordinating EU and national regional policy interests; and the ability to provide a coordinating framework for other policy fields with spatial effects" (OECD, 2017, p.4).

The National Development Policy is jointly established by the German Congress of Municipal Authorities, the Association of Towns and Municipalities, and the Conference of the Building Ministers of the Länder (OECD, 2016c, 2017). The National Development Policy carries out and coordinates investment projects on the Länder and municipalities levels. The National Development Policy relies strongly on citizens' participation. For example, the decision to build a new runway at Frankfurt Airport was accompanied by a mediation process initiated by the Länder government of Hesse. It had the goal of reconciling concerns about noise and other environmental effects with the economic case for the new runway. According to OECD (2017), "the process was initiated prior to the decision to build the runway and included extensive consultations with proponents and opponents of the new runway. After the end of the mediation process, a regional forum continued to the dialogue between stakeholders until the planning process for the new runway was completed and construction started"(p.3).

The project management of a public investment project on federal level is based on a cost-benefit analysis that includes the following components: reduced transportation costs, travel time, safety benefits, security, regional economic and social impact, job creation, and derived economic effects (OECD, 2014, p.55). When the result of a cost-benefit analysis is positive (a benefit to cost ratio above one), the investment project is included in the plan. However, the ambiguity and uncertainty involved in quantifying and assigning a monetary value to intangible items like perception of safety, human life, and time in a traffic jam, could lead to an inaccurate cost benefit analysis. Investment projects are ranked according to their score, the expected need for the project, and the assessed urgency in constructing the asset. The process is transparent, and methodology of analysis of a public investment project is made publicly available.

The financing part in particular is equally divided between the federal government, the states, and local authorities. It includes projects in urban restructuring, the preservation of urban monuments (OECD, 2015b, 2017). The basis for the budgeting for specific investments projects aligns with the medium-term financial planning framework. However, the fact that an infrastructure project is accepted does not mean that its financing is assured. Financing for an investment project is allocated as part of the ordinary budget process.

Execution and Project Management on Länder' Levels

Public fixed capital formations in the regions are sustained through co-funding from the federal government and EU support based on the operational programs. For example, Brandenburg received a federal subsidy of EUR 457.1 million due to co-financing requirements for regional and local governments in 2012. Seventy percent of the financing was mandated for municipal infrastructure development. Brandenburg increased this share to 84 percent. The law required a minimum of 65 percent of the support to go to educational infrastructure, the rest to other types of infrastructure. In addition, the Brandenburg Land government used the program to top off the funding for less economically developed areas. (Gamper, 2012, p.7)

Local government carries out more than 60 percent of all public investment. The municipalities have reduced their investments because of increased social spending and financial problems. Local governments spending on capital investments dropped from 17 percent of their total expenditure in 1995 to only 9.7 percent in 2015 (Van der Putten, 2017). The local governments' fixed assets decreased by € 60 billion between 2003 and 2015. These changes in capital investments are largely a result of the expansion of municipalities' responsibilities in the area of social security. The municipal social spending increased two times from 2002 to 2010. KFW (2015) shows that municipal projects are often not undertaken or taken with a certain delay because of uncertainty concerning the division of costs between the state and the municipality and lack of administrative capacity for the planning and implementation. According to the KfW Survey, the total observed backlog amounted to € 136 billion in 2015, € 4 billion more than in the preceding year. Maintaining the capital infrastructure at the same level requires a permanent increase in spending by at least € 4 billion (Van der Putten, 2017, p.2).

The Centre of Excellence for Sustainable Procurement, which is within the Procurement Office of the Federal Ministry of the Interior, supports public contracting authorities at the federal, Länder, and municipality level in taking sustainability criteria into consideration in procurement projects. The KNB website (central portal for sustainable procurement) was launched by the Chancellor on 13 May 2013.

The regional development bank in Brandenburg (Investitionsbank des Landes Brandenburg – ILB) provides support to the regional and local governments. For innovation and R&D investments, for example, although the Land's innovation agency determines the allocation of innovation grants, the ILB manages the application process, especially the financial and technical assessments of the client's application (OECD, 2017). ILB offers support to municipalities in the areas of PPPs and waste/sewage treatment facilities. ILB combines consultancy and financing functions when giving grants to help reduce the debts of municipalities.

On Länder' levels, rigorous evaluations are generally not carried out for all infrastructure investments, partly due to the often challenging time horizons of the investment (Gamper, 2012). For the tourism sector, evaluation is viewed as being difficult, and the region points out that the ILB only controls how the money is spent on particular projects rather than evaluating its impacts. There is, however, a clear interest on the part of the Land to conduct evaluations, even if it is the central level that carries them out. In fact, the region has several evaluation questions in mind that it seeks to investigate, such as the effect of the number of contracted or leased staff on a company's performance, but the funding for conducting such studies remains limited.

The introduction of the Emissions Law was accompanied by a set of indicators, such as the number of people affected by certain levels of fine dust or the number of people exposed to significant levels of noise. Every specific project implemented to reduce negative environmental impacts from emissions needs to monitor the indicators whose information is aggregated to measure the achievement of their target values. The same process is carried out for the Joint Task program, where an M&E framework has been developed to accompany the achievement of its objectives. One of the indicators in the Joint Task framework is, for example, the creation of jobs of economic development programs.

The monitoring conducted by the ILB focuses on the eligibility of the use of its funds but also has outcome-oriented features. For example, during the five-year period after which a company has received funding from the ILB, the beneficiary must provide certain information, such as employment levels or equipment financed. However, the monitoring is confined to the actual use of the grants rather than the economic success of the company. The more risky the investment for the ILB, the more "rigorous" the monitoring seems to be.

A possible solution for improving the country's infrastructure would be the setting up of public-private partnerships. Investments taking place using the Public-Private Partnership procurement model (PPP- ÖPP in German) are budgeted into the annual budget on the basis of the annual charge that has to be paid to the operator. The federal budget documentation contains an annex that gives an overview of all PPP projects and life cycle commitments of the federal government derived from the PPP contract (OECD, 2014, p.56). In the ÖPP partnerships, an investor funds projects with private capital or borrowed money and in return, receives a fee from users or from the government. A standard life span of these ÖPP partnerships is 30 years in Germany. One example of these ÖPP partnerships is the A1 autobahn extension between Bremen and Hamburg with a length of 73 kilometers (45 miles). A consortium that includes engineering and services group, Bilfinger, financed the construction. This consortium receives a monthly payment from the government from 2008 to 2038. Those payments come from truck tolls and depend on the volume of truck traffic along the stretch of highway A1 autobahn extension between Bremen and Hamburg. According to Jung et al. (2014), many ÖPP partnerships projects, including the extension of the A1 autobahn, were finished ahead of schedule.

However, a study by the Federal Audit Office has found that costs of financing infrastructure via public-private partnerships were higher for ÖPP project than they were for conventionally funded enterprises. The Federal Audit Office examined seven large, privately financed road-construction projects and found that five of them would have been cheaper if government without ÖPP partnerships would have paid them. The total savings were estimated at €1.9 billion. The Transportation Ministry found that the public-private partnership planned that ÖPP partnerships would be 40 percent cheaper than tax financing in the A1 expansion project, but the final cost was about thirty percent higher than it was planned.

The Federal Audit Office concludes that ÖPP projects "did not achieve significant goals," and projects conducted to date have been "uneconomical," the auditors concluded. According to Jung et al. (2014, p.6), "the private consortiums are more expensive because they must pay an average of 6 percent interest on their loans, which is about four percentage points higher than the federal government pays in interest on long-term borrowing." Berlin infrastructure economist Thorsten Beckers found that the capital costs of such ÖPP partnerships projects amount to almost 28 percent of construction costs. Beckers argues that the supposed financial advantages of ÖPP autobahn expansion projects are "extremely implausible." Moreover, a temporary fiscal stimulus in Germany can support investment growth in the rest of the Eurozone. The German *Schuldenbremse*, "debt brake," a 2009 provision that limits the ability of German governments to run a deficit, prohibits unlimited borrowing. ÖPP projects provide the possibility to avoid this "debt brake". The Federal Audit Office warns that this could provide additional incentive to turn over the construction of roads and building to private investors even though the conventional approach would be more affordable. In addition, in the case of highways, public-private partnerships have been met with great resistance by citizens who opposed to the introduction of tolls for passenger cars.

According to Federal Ministry for Economic Affairs and Energy (2016, p.10), Federal Government will restructure and strategically realign the public-private partnership advisory company, ÖPP Deutschland AG. The ÖPP Deutschland AG offers the public sector, particularly the municipalities, nationwide advisory services regardless of the selected procurement method. The aim is to support the municipalities in planning and carrying out investment projects to improve their efficiency.

Infrastructure Maintenance

Under the Basic Law (2017), the Federal Government is responsible for funding the construction and structural maintenance of the federal transport infrastructure (the federal motorways, federal highways, and the federal waterways). German sea and inland ports, airports, and freight villages are not part of the federal transport infrastructure. The planning, construction, and maintenance of these facilities are the responsibility of the federal states, local authorities, or private sector operators. However, the Federal Government is responsible for connecting these facilities to the federal transport infrastructure network and provides funds for this purpose.

On the other hand, the Länder have the responsibility of administering the federal highways within their territory, a task that they carry out under the supervision of the federation (Basic Law, article 90). This administrative responsibility includes setting up and maintaining the agencies that administer federal highway construction and maintenance (Basic Law, Article 85).

Germany does not have a dedicated fund for building and maintaining highways. According to the Highway Construction Financing Act (Strassenbaufinanzierungsgesetz), the annual federal budget has a highway construction plan that describes ongoing and planned construction projects and lists the federal revenues that are earmarked to highway construction and maintenance. The important earmarked revenues are the tolls imposed on truck traffic on federal highways, gasoline taxes (Energiesteuergesetz), and motor vehicle tax (Kraftfahrzeugsteuergesetz) (Energy Tax Act, 2006; Federal Highway Toll Act, 2011; Motor Vehicle Tax Act, 2002). In addition, there is some miscellaneous income, such as fees and concessions. The remainder of the needed funds for federal highway construction and maintenance comes from general revenue. In the federal budget, €12.3 billion was earmarked for investment in transport for 2016. The investments in transport infrastructure increases to €13.4 billion in 2018. The focus of investments remains on maintaining the existing transport infrastructure (Federal Ministry for Economic Affairs and Energy, 2016, p.11).

The Federal Transport Infrastructure Plan (FTIP) is the Federal Government's most important transport infrastructure planning tool for maintenance and reconstructions. The Federal Transport Infrastructure Plan (FTIP) 2030 was developed by the Federal Ministry of Transport and Digital Infrastructure with the support of consultants and had been adopted by the Federal Cabinet from 2013 to 2014. The FTIP comprises necessary capital maintenance investment and investment in replacement and upgrading infrastructure as well as new construction projects. The forecast requirements for structural maintenance and replacement have been included in the plan as a total amount for each type of transport. The FTIP focuses on projects that have significant impacts on large areas and develop a significant capacity-enhancing and/or quality-improving impact.

According to FTIP 2030, the Federal Government is focusing its investment primarily on the spheres of structural maintenance/replacement and the removal of traffic jams. The total level of funding provided by the FTIP 2030 is around €269.6 billion (roughly $300 billion) on construction and modernization of the country's infrastructure over the next 15 years (Goubau, 2018). The major priorities are the structural maintenance and replacement of the existing road, rail, and waterway networks. The structural maintenance of the existing road, rail, and waterway networks alone will require around €141.6 billion between 2016 and 2030. This plan prioritizes repairing existing systems with 70 percent of funds allocated toward maintenance (Schulze, 2016). The Federal Ministry of Transport and Digital Infrastructure significantly increases the level of funding for maintenance compared with the FTIP 2003, which earmarked investment of around €83 billion for this purpose.

The Federal Transport Infrastructure Plan (FTIP) 2030 earmarks an investment of €98.3 billion for upgrading and new construction of road infrastructure. It is thus necessary to stabilize the investment for transport infrastructure at a high level. For the structural maintenance and upgrading of the transport networks, the target in the FTIP period from 2016 to 2030 has an average level of funding of around €15 billion per year. Of the total level of funding of the FTIP 2030 (including structural maintenance), the roads accounts for 49.3 percent, the rails accounts for 41.6 percent and the waterway accounts for 9.1 percent of total funds. For upgrading and new construction projects from 2016 to 2030, the roads' share is higher at 53.6 percent (€2.3 billion per annum on average). According to the Federal Transport Infrastructure Plan (FTIP) 2030, the railways will receive a share of 42.1 percent (€1.8 billion per annum on average) and the waterways will receive a share of 4.3 percent (€0.2 billion per annum on average). The FTIP 2030 focuses on the major transport arteries and junctions of the transport networks. These projects' share of the total level of funding for upgrading and new construction is significantly lower in the new Federal Transport Infrastructure Plan (in the period from 2016 to 2030) than in the FTIP 2003 (in the period from 2001 to 2015) – 40 percent as against 72 percent.

The Federal Ministry of Transport and Digital Infrastructure (2016, p.10) suggests: "the large number and varying nature of municipal construction projects necessitates administrative skills and capacities which are not adequately available in-house to all municipalities." Germany lacks coordination between federal and local governments when it comes to funding investment projects. A study by development bank, KfW, found that German municipalities needed nearly $40 billion in road and transport infrastructure last year. Only one in twenty municipalities was able to ensure comprehensive maintenance of local transport infrastructure, according to the report (Schulz, 2016). For example, Berlin's Brandenburg Airport remains closed after more than 10 years under construction. Federal government plans bring together the requisite capacities and skills and to make them available to municipal administrations as needed (Federal Ministry of Transport and Digital Infrastructure, 2016, p.10).

ANALYSIS

In 1990, Germany had a growth rate of gross fixed capital formation of 8.0 percent. This growth rate decreased during global financial crisis in 2010 to -10.1 percent and in 2013-2014 to -1.1 percent. Due to decreasing of capital investments, Germany decreased from third on a list of countries with the best infrastructure in 2008 to seventh place in 2013 and tenth place in 2017. The reason for Germany's relative decline of infrastructure conditions is the lack of public investment spending on infrastructure. Following the reunification-related investment boom in the early 1990s, public capital spending has settled at around 2.2 percent of GDP. This is one of the lowest rations in the EU. For comparison, in France, public investment was 3.5 percent in 2015.

From 2013 to 2014, both public and private investment had declined dramatically, and officials were increasingly concerned about how to solve this problem. Government investment increased continually up to 2013; the slight decline in the investment-to-GDP ratio is because GDP grew at a faster rate. In 2015, the investment-to-GDP ratio began to increase again at 1.7-2.5 percent as overall economic conditions improved. The investment-to-GDP ratios were -0.7 percent in 2013 and -1.1 percent in 2014. The investment ratio in the German private economy decreased from 20 percent in 2000 to 17 percent in 2013. According to the German Institute for Economic Research (DIW), the investment shortfall between 1999 and 2012 amounted to about 3 percent of gross domestic product, in period from 2010 to 2012; the gap was 3.7 percent (Jung et al., 2014).

Germany also has financing problems with the infrastructure investment project, *Energiewende* (energy transition). For example, the new bituminous coal unit of the Rheinhafen power plant was built to fulfill an important task for the *Energiewende,* operating whenever there is too little wind or not enough sun to offer a reliable supply of renewable energies. The plant cost €1.3 billion to build, but it was generating losses for its operator, EnBW. German electricity customers paid more than €23 billion in 2014 via an allocation charge for renewable energy. Fratzscher (2018) sees Germany's shift to renewables as "one of the biggest challenges of our generation," and he also sees it as a hurdle for investment. In his opinion, if the *Energiewende* succeeds, it will create a new, nuclear-free infrastructure worth hundreds of billions of euros, but if the project ends in chaos, it could lead to losses on a similar scale.

To solve this problem, more than €30 billion, or 1 percent of GDP, will have to be invested annually in network infrastructure, renewable-energy generation, combined heat and power systems, and storage technologies in the coming decades (Fratzscher, 2015). Matthias Machnig, State Secretary at the German Federal Ministry for Economic Affairs and Energy, highlighted that "Investment activity in Germany and Europe has been subdued for years. As part of its investment strategy, the German Federal Government has already initiated numerous measures to stimulate private and public investments in Germany" (KFM, 2015). The German project from the European Fund for Strategic Investments (EFSI), the "Juncker fund," has been launched at the German Federal Ministry for Economic Affairs and Energy in 2015. The German Federal Government contributed €8 billion to the "Juncker" fund. The main purposes of the "Juncker" fund are promoting start-ups in Germany and stimulating private and public investments. The funds primarily flow into strategic investments in key areas, such as infrastructure and innovation, in addition to promoting small and medium-sized enterprises by providing venture capital and guarantees.

The majority of the federal government's spending is earmarked for the long term, and it was difficult to make additional investments. The municipalities have reduced their investments because of increased social spending and financial problems. The Länder are also cutting back on capital spending in preparation of tighter budget rules that will come into force in 2020. While some of these investment funds will come from public budgets, the vast majority should be provided by the private sector. According to Federal Ministry for Economic Affairs and Energy (2016), 90 percent of all investments in Germany are private investments. The willingness of private companies to invest depends on hard-to-influence factors, like the overall economic situation, expected profits, and interest rates. Fratzscher (2015) suggests that R&D spending should be raised from less than 3 percent to at least 3.5 percent of GDP. The government's stimulus programs were established in response to the decline of investment activity in Germany. In 2013, the Christian Democratic Union and the Social Democrats set a goal of raising public and private investment by 3 percent of GDP, or €90 billion ($100.8 billion) annually, to reach the OECD average (Fratzscher, 2015). A special investment and redemption fund was created in 2009. This fund pooled the investments contained in the government's second stimulus package. This Fund gave a particular boost to government investment, and the investment-to-GDP ratio peaked at 2.3 percent in 2013. For example, The Federal Ministry of Transport and Digital Infrastructure (Federal Ministry of Transport) had an investment budget of EUR 10.7 billion in 2013. The state and federal governments are spending €207 million to renovate bridges in 2014. Based on National Reform Program 2016, the Federal Government has already undertaken a large number of measures designed to create an attractive investment environment and will press ahead with other measures.

German government created expert committees, government's stimulus programs, and a "national investment pact" to help local governments' investment programs. In 2014, the German government appointed a 21-member committee of experts from business, labor unions, finance, and academia to determine how to achieve the goal of raising public and private investment by 3 percent of GDP. This expert committee recommended to keep investment levels at least as high as the rate of depreciation of state assets and to use unexpected budget surpluses for public investment. The expert committee recommends an investment focus on developing the sectors that will dominate future economy: research and development (R&D), digital economy, network infrastructure, renewable-energy generation, combined heat and power systems, and storage technologies. The German government created the Stability Council that consists of the Minister of Finance, the Minister of Economy, and the finance ministers of all the Länder. The Stability Council is responsible for regularly monitoring the budgets of the federal government and the governments of the Länder and function as an early warning system (OECD, 2017).

According to Federal Ministry for Economic Affairs and Energy (2016, p.13), the Federal government increased financial support to Municipalities (Table 7). Table 7 presents Federal programs of financial support and investments to municipalities from 2013 to 2016.

The German government's plan to invest €15 billion during 2016 to 2018 was intended to spur needed private investment (CIA, 2018). These programs reinforced the positive trend of capital investments in Germany. The growth rates of government gross fixed capital formation were 1.57 percent in 2016 and 2.5 percent in 2017 year. The Chair of the German Council of Economic Experts, Christoph M. Schmidt, highlights, "The solid economic situation provides an ideal opportunity to re-adjust economic policy in order to prepare Germany for the challenges of the future" (German Council of Economic Experts, 2018). The federal government expects the investment trend with an average annual increase of 4.75 to 5 percent to continue over the period to 2020. In other words, growth in government investment will continue to outpace the growth in government spending as a whole (German Finance Ministry, 2018).

In order to support local investment, the committee proposes creating a "national investment pact" to enable municipalities to increase investment by at least €15 billion over the next three years. In addition, this committee recommended establishing a public advisory institution to help municipalities realize their investment projects of which there is currently a €118 billion backlog (Fratzscher, 2015). The expert committee proposed the creation of two publicly owned investment funds, one raising money from institutional investors and the other from individuals. The committee suggests that public projects financed by the funds would provide sufficient efficiency gains to attract private financing.

The Länder and municipalities have special operational programs for infrastructure investment (Table 8). Table 8 presentsthe main regional, urban, and rural investments operational programs.

To improve the efficiency of investments in infrastructure, the Federal Government is planning to set up a transport infrastructure company as part of the reform of the administration of federal highways. This company will be responsible for planning, construction, maintenance, operation, and financing of federal highways. Work on the design concept of the transport infrastructure company is still an ongoing process because the reform of contract management in the field of federal highways requires an agreement between the Federation and the Länder. Federal Minister of Transport and Digital Infrastructure (2014, p.2) highlights that "structural maintenance and replacement plus the evolution of infrastructure that is efficient on a sustained basis are priority policy areas."

Table 7. Federal programs of financial support and investments to municipalities

Years of Starting Support	Measures	Financing
2013-2015	Act to Promote Investment by Municipalities with Inadequate Financial Resources	Financial assistance via Municipal Investment Promotion Fund: €3.5bn total in 2015–2018
2015	Expansion of daycare for children under three	Investment costs: €580.5 million from 2013 and €550 million total in 2016–2018
2014	The Act Unbundling Joint Tasks and Financial Aid	€2.6 bln. in 2014–2019
2016	Increase in regionalization funding	Increase by €600m in 2016 to €8bn; from 2017–2031 rising by 1.8%

Table 8. Main regional, urban and rural investments operational programs

Policy Instrument	Examples
Transport Infrastructure investments	Cross-border Operational Programs with focus on transportation
Other Infrastructure investments	Most Länder Operational Programs intend to invest in education and research infrastructure Rural: the Rural Development Program intends to invest in infrastructure relevant to agriculture as well as recreational infrastructure
Clusters/technology platforms/ centers of expertise	Most Länder Operational Programs have cluster programs to invest in technology, innovation and knowledge transfer
Business development/ innovation support	Länder Operational Programs focus on SME competitiveness and innovation support. Rural: the Rural Development Program intends to diversify rural economies and contributes to innovation as a cross-cutting objective

Source: OECD (2016b)

Based on National Reform Program, the Federal Government will work with the Länder to consider how the funding of infrastructure can be improved in the context of the Joint Task for the "Improvement of the Regional Economic Structure". The Council of the European Union recommends that Germany take action to increase public investment in infrastructure, education, and research: "to foster private investment, take measures to improve the efficiency of the tax system, in particular by reviewing the local trade tax and corporate taxation and by modernizing the tax administration; use the ongoing review to improve the design of fiscal relations between the Federation, Länder and municipalities, particularly with a view to ensuring adequate public investment at all levels of government" (Federal Ministry for Economic Affairs and Energy, 2016, p.9).

CONCLUSION

Capital investments do not have a separate framework; they are identifiable in the budget and are treated as any other expenditure in the process. The investment infrastructure plans are coordinated at the federal level by the Federal Ministry of Finance. The fifteen-year and five-year framework investments plan align with the long-term and medium-term financial planning framework and forms the basis for the budgeting for specific investment projects. The capital budgeting process is transparent.

The analysis of a public investment project is based on a cost-benefit analysis. Main ranking principles are safety, reduced transportation costs, travel time, security, regional economic impact, job creation, social impact, and derived economic effects. Investment projects are ranked according to their score, the expected need for the project, and the assessed urgency in constructing the asset. The methodology of analysis of a public investment project is made publicly available.

The Federal Ministry of Finance plays a key role in capital budgeting to ensure that the capital project portfolio fits into the long-term capital budget envelope. The appropriation allocated in the budget is not for a single capital project but in a portfolio of capital projects within a relevant category (e.g. road or rail investment). The Federal Ministry of Finance monitors the investments projects from the project identification stage to the preparation stage on procurement and implementation stages.

Germany also uses the Public-Private Partnership procurement model (PPP- ÖPP in German) for capital investments. These investments are budgeted into the annual budget on the basis of the annual charge that has to be paid to the operator. The federal budget documentation contains an annex that gives an overview of all PPP projects (ÖPP partnerships). A standard life span of the ÖPP partnerships is 30 years in Germany.

The "debt brake" (Schuldenbremse) rule (2009 provision) limits the ability of German governments to run a deficit and prohibits unlimited borrowing. This rule is affecting the federal and the Länder' investment spending. Van der Putten (2017, p.2) suggests that "public investment is likely to come under increased pressure in the coming years because of the application of the "debt brake" (Schuldenbremse). As the Länder may not borrow anymore for structural purposes, they may have to reduce their investment spending by about EUR 20 billion." Some Länder renounced tapping federal or European investment funds because they are unable to contribute their share in the co-financing arrangements. Appendix 1 provides summary of capital budgeting and management in Germany.

Germany's combination of strong economic growth, low unemployment, favorable financing conditions, healthy public finance, and structural reform give a great opportunity for capital investments. With increased investment in infrastructure, high level of education system, and more investment-friendly business conditions, it can place German economy on a stronger footing for the future.

ACKNOWLEDGMENT

This research was supported by the German Academic Exchange Service (DAAD) [grant number 57378441] and the Ludwigsburg University of Public Administration and Finance (Hochschule für öffentliche Verwaltung und Finanzen). I am very thankful to Professor Oliver Sievering (Hochschule für öffentliche Verwaltung und Finanzen) for his advices and suggested edits.

REFERENCES

Ammar, A., Duncombe, R., & Wright, A. (2001). Evaluating capital management: A new approach. *Public Budgeting & Finance*, *2*(1), 47–69. doi:10.1111/0275-1100.00058

Basic Law. (2017). *Basic law* [Grundgesetz]. Berlin: German Bundestag Public Relations Division. Retrieved May 21, 2018, from https://www.btg-bestellservice.de/pdf/80201000.pdf

CIA. (2018). *Germany*. Retrieved April 14, 2018, from https://www.cia.gov/library/publications/the-world-factbook/geos/gm.html

Energy Tax Act. (2006). *Energiesteuergesetz*. Retrieved May 21, 2018, from https://hylaw.eu/database/national-legislation/germany/energy-tax-act-energiesteuergesetz-energiestg

Ermasova, N. (2013). The capital budgeting at the state level during the Great Recession: The results of survey. *State & Local Government Review*, *45*(2), 119–130. doi:10.1177/0160323X13487079

Federal Highway Toll Act. (2011). *Gesetz über die Erhebung von streckenbezogenen Gebühren für die Benutzung von Bundesautobahnen und Bundesstrassen*, July 12, 2011, BGBl. I at 1378, § 11.

Federal Minister of Transport and Digital Infrastructure. (2014). *Federal transport infrastructure plan till 2030*. Retrieved May 24, 2018, from https://www.bmvi.de/SharedDocs/EN/Documents/G/ftip-2030.pdf?__blob=publicationFile

Federal Ministry for Economic Affairs and Energy. (2016). *National reform programme 2016*. Retrieved May 22, 2018, from https://www.bmwi.de/Redaktion/EN/Publikationen/national-reform-programme-2016.pdf?__blob=publicationFile&v=7

Fratzscher, M. (2014). *Die Deutschland-Illusion: Warum wir unsere Wirtschaft überschätzen und Europa brauchen*. Berlin: Carl Hanser Verlag.

Fratzscher, M. (2015*). Why Germany needs to invest. World Economic Forum*. Retrieved April 15, 2018, from https://www.weforum.org/agenda/2015/05/why-germany-needs-to-invest/

Fratzscher, M. (2018). *The Germany illusion: Between economic euphoria and despair*. London: Oxford Press. doi:10.1093/oso/9780190676575.001.0001

Gamper, C. (2012). Public investment across levels of government: The case of Brandenburg, Germany. Report for the 28th OECD Territorial Development Policy Committee, 4-5 Dec 2012.

German Council of Economic Experts. (2018). *Annual report 2017/2018*. Retrieved April 18, 2018, from http://www.wiwi.ruhr-uni-bochum.de/news/dekanat/news01324.html.en

German Finance Ministry. (2014). *Weak investment in Germany? German finance ministry's March 2014 monthly report*. Retrieved April 12, 2018, from https://www.bundesfinanzministerium.de/Content/DE/Monatsberichte/2014/03/Inhalte/Kapitel-3-Analysen/3-3-investitionsschwaeche.html

German Finance Ministry. (2015). *Public investment trends in Germany*. Retrieved April 12, 2018, from http://www.bundesfinanzministerium.de/Content/EN/Standardartikel/Topics/Fiscal_policy/Articles/2015-01-12-public-investment-trends-germany.html

German Finance Ministry. (2018). *Gesamtwirtschaftliches produktionspotenzial und konjunkturkomponenten des bundes: Kapitalstock und investitionen*. Retrieved April 12, 2018, from https://www.bundesfinanzministerium.de/Monatsberichte/2017/01/Inhalte/Kapitel-6-Statistiken/6-3-06-kapitalstock-und-investitionen.html

Global Economic Forum. (2008). *Global Report*. Retrieved April 15, 2018, from https://www.weforum.org/reports/world-economic-forum-annual-meeting-2008

Goubau, T. (2018). *Germany infrastructure projects over US $129 billion of investment*. Retrieved May 21, 2018, from https://www.aproplan.com/blog/quality-management-plan-construction/germany-infrastructure-projects-us129-billion-investment

Highway Construction Financing Act (Strassenbaufinanzierungsgesetz). (2006). Mar. 28, 1960, BGBL. I at 201, *as last amended* by Verordnung, Oct. 31, 2006, BGBL. I at 2407, art. 3.

Jung, A., Müller, A. K., Sauga, M., Schmergal, C., Traufetter, G., & Witsch, K. (2014). Germany ailing infrastructure. *Spiegel*. September 18, 2014. Retrieved April 15, 2018, from http://www.spiegel.de/international/germany/low-german-infrastructure-investment-worries-experts-a-990903.html

KFW. (2015). *European fund for strategic investments (EFSI) launched in Germany. News of KFW Group*. Retrieved April 17, 2018, from https://www.kfw.de/KfW-Group/Newsroom/Aktuelles/News/News-Details_300288.html

Motor Vehicle Tax Act. (2002). *Kraftfahrzeugsteuergesetz, repromulgated* Sept. 26, 2002, BGBL. I at 3818, *as amended*, Retrieved May 21, 2018, from http://www.gesetze-im-internet.de/kraftstg/BJNR005090927.html

OECD. (2014). Budget review: Germany. *OECD Journal on Budgeting*, *2*(1), 1–83.

OECD. (2015a). *OECD National Accounts Statistics* (database). Retrieved May 21, 2018, from doi:10.1787/na-dataen

OECD. (2015b). *Implementation toolkit, effective public investment across levels of government*. Retrieved May 21, 2018, from http://www.oecd.org/effective-public-investment-toolkit/

OECD. (2016a). *Subnational governments in OECD countries*. Key data, 2016 edition (brochure).

OECD. (2016b). *Regional Outlook Survey*. Retrieved May 21, 2018, from http://www.oecd.org/regional/oecd-regional-outlook-2016-9789264260245-en.htm

OECD. (2016c). *Overview and preliminary proposal on indicators of co-ordination of public investment for regional development*. Room document discussed in the April 2016 RDPC meeting, unpublished material.

OECD. (2017). *Effective public investments across levels of government: Germany*. Retrieved May 17, 2018, from https://www.oecd.org/effective-public-investment-toolkit/Germany.pdf

OECD. (2018). *National accounts statistics*. Retrieved May 17, 2018, from http://www.oecd.org/sdd/na/

Road Construction Plan. (2013). *Bundeshaushaltsplan*. Retrieved May 21, 2018, from http://www.bundeshaushalt-info.de/fileadmin/de.bundeshaushalt/content_de/dokumente/2013/soll/Haushaltsplan-2013.pdf

Schulz, E. (2016). Germany — yes, Germany — has an infrastructure problem. *CBNC*. Retrieved May 17, 2018, from https://www.cnbc.com/2016/09/14/germany-has-a-crumbling-infrastructure-problem.html

Statistisches Bundesamt. (2018). *Volkswirtschaftliche Gesamtrechnungen: Arbeitsunterlage Investitionen*. Retrieved July 7, 2018, from https://www.destatis.de/DE/Publikationen/Thematisch/VolkswirtschaftlicheGesamtrechnungen/Inlandsprodukt/InvestitionenPDF_5811108.pdf?__blob=publicationFile

Trading Economics. (2018). *Germany government budget*. Retrieved April 15, 2018, from https://tradingeconomics.com/germany/government-budget

Van der Putten, R. (2017). Germany: Infrastructure under threat. *Economic Research by PNP Paribas*. Retrieved April 17, 2018, from economic-research.pnpparibas.com

WEF Global Competitiveness Report. (2017). *Germany*. Retrieved March 17, 2018, from http://reports.weforum.org/global-competitiveness-index-2017-2018/countryeconomy-profiles/#economy=DEU

World Bank. (2018). *Gross fix capital formation in Germany*. Retrieved May 17, 2018, from https://data.worldbank.org/indicator/NE.GDI.FTOT.CD?locations=DE

APPENDIX

Table 9. Summary of capital budgeting and management in Germany

Normative Recommendations	Practices
Long-Term Capital Planning	
Comprehensive/Master Planning	Five-year Financial Plan There are following infrastructure and network plans in Germany: • Federal Transport Infrastructure Plan • Federal Regional Policy Plan • Trans-European Transport Networks • Energy Network • EU-Habitats Directive • 16 Länder-level plans, regional development plans & programs, regional project plans • Sector-specific plans such as energy plan or mining in North Rhine-Westphalia.
Strategic Planning	National Development Policy; The Joint Task for the Improvement of Regional Economic Structure; Twenty-Year, Ten-Year, Five-year framework investment plans, for example, Integrated Transport Plan till 2030
Long-term Fiscal Planning	Five-year fiscal planning
Asset Inventory Analysis/Need Analysis	Monitoring of Asset Inventory The expert committee recommends an investment focus on developing the sectors that will dominate future economy: research and development (R&D), digital economy, network infrastructure, renewable-energy generation, combined heat and power systems, and storage technologies
Capital Improvement Program	15 year CIP for transport infrastructure investments; 5 year CIP
Capital Budgeting and Financial Management	
Systematic Priority Ranking	All ministries signal their new funding priorities and strategic orientations for the budget year. Investment projects are ranked according to cost-benefit analysis, the expected need for the project, and the assessed urgency in constructing the asset
Multi-year Fiscal Forecasting	Multi-year Tax Revenue Forecasts and estimation of the national budget parameters. An important feature of the Act to Promote Economic Stability and Growth is the stipulation that the federal budget should be managed based on a rolling five-year planning period. The Council of Economic Experts presents its wide-ranging economic report, provides independent views of a range of economic subjects, and creates budgetary forecasts for capital investments.
Capital Budgeting Process	Yes. Germany has the resource-allocation process from the outset, resulting in a distinctive form of "top-down budgeting" since 2010. Yes. The budgeting for capital projects are integrated into the ordinary budget process in Germany. It is a key role for the Federal Ministry of Finance to ensure that the capital project portfolio fits into the long-term capital budget (CIP). Balanced budget rule with no exception for capital spending, programmatic resource allocation decisions, no separate capital budget document
Debt Affordability Analysis	Yes The "debt brake" (Schuldenbremse) policy instrument requires structural balanced budgets at federal and Länder level, in accordance with the European Stability and Growth Pact. When the debt brake would came into force at the federal level in 2016 and from 2020, structural deficits would be forbidden for the Länder.
Operating Reserve	Yes. The Act establishes that a reserve fund must be established for counter-balancing cyclical fluctuations

continued on following page

Table 9. Continued

Normative Recommendations	Practices
Debt Management Policy/Disclosure (e.g., debt ceiling, debt approval by National Assembly, debt issuance, any debt/tax choice policy or guidance, i.e., when to sue pay-go and pay-as-you-use finance)	The German *Schuldenbremse* ("debt brake") as debt ceiling, Binding borrowing constraints
Centralized Execution and Project Management	
Budget/Project Status Reporting	Annually reports
Internal Audit (using budget variance report)	The Centre of Excellence for Sustainable Procurement within the Procurement Office of the Federal Ministry of the Interior
Project Acquisition, Contract Management, and Performance Monitoring	The key role of Federal Ministry of Finance
Budget Status Report/ Internal Auditing	Internal audit by the Federal Audit Office
Infrastructure Maintenance	
Maintenance Planning	Planning through National Reform Program and Federal Transport Infrastructure Plans
Maintenance Funding	Funding through National Reform Program and Federal Transport Infrastructure Plans
Asset Management (e.g., repair over replacement policy)	Replacement policy
Program/performance evaluation	The public-private partnership advisory company, ÖPP Deutschland AG Program evaluation of the ÖPP partnerships by the Federal Audit Office

Section 2

Capital Management and Budgeting in Transitioning Economies

Chapter 4
Capital Budgeting, Infrastructure, and Capital Investment in the Republic of Uzbekistan

Tatyana Guzman
Cleveland State University, USA

ABSTRACT

This chapter offers a macro-level review of the capital budgeting process and practices, capital investment projects, and capital funding in the post-Soviet Republic of Uzbekistan. The chapter discusses some of the major challenges related to capital investment and capital budgeting that Uzbekistan faced after the collapse of the Soviet Union, how the country has overcome some of these challenges in 27 years of independence, and what issues remain unresolved. The chapter additionally describes the most sizeable and impactful recent capital investment projects and the role government played in their financing. Finally, the chapter provides a comparison between capital budgeting practices in Uzbekistan, some post-Soviet republics, and the United States.

INTRODUCTION

Budgeting is a vital part of government financial management. To handle money responsibly, public entities need to have a financial plan that documents how revenues will be generated and how they will be spent. The budget is this financial plan. Proper budgeting practices and financial control are equally important for both operating expenses, such as wages and salaries, utilities, and other current expenditures, and for capital expenditures, such as investment in infrastructure, buildings, and other major structures. Some argue that capital projects have to go through even more scrutiny and control, and, therefore, an even stricter budget process, as capital projects are long lasting, non-recurring, and expensive (Mikesell, 2013).

DOI: 10.4018/978-1-5225-7329-6.ch004

The following book chapter presents a macro-level descriptive analysis of the capital budgeting process and capital investment in one of the former Soviet countries, the Republic of Uzbekistan. The chapter discusses major challenges in the capital investment and capital budgeting that the country faced after the collapse of the Soviet system, how it has overcome these challenges, and the changes that have been made. The chapter addresses the trends in capital investments and explains what drives these trends, reviews the sources of capital funding, discusses which regions benefit from capital investments more and why, and what capital projects are more likely to receive funding from the government sources. It reviews budgeting practices and procedures and discusses the role of main budget players among other important issues. The discussion begins with a general background information on administrative, demographic, and economic structure of the Republic and a little history that can help explain a current state of affairs in Uzbekistan.

BACKGROUND

Uzbekistan is a double land-locked country in Central Asia bordering Kazakhstan, Tajikistan, Kirgizstan, Turkmenistan, and Afghanistan. The Republic, geographically slightly larger than California, is home to about thirty million residents, most of whom are ethnical Uzbeks (83.8 percent of total population in 2017, compared to 72.8 percent in 1991, according to the The State Committee of the Republic of Uzbekistan on Statistics. This is the most highly populated country in Central Asia. The major religion is Islam (Sunnis). Administratively, Uzbekistan includes twelve regions and the autonomous Republic of Karakalpakistan. The capital city is Tashkent. The same president, Islam Karimov, led the country from 1989 until his death in 2016. Current president, Shavkat Mirziyoev was previously a prime minister of Uzbekistan (from 2003-2016) and succeeded president Karimov after his death.

The borders of today's Uzbekistan have historically been situated in a highly developed region lying in the midst of a Silk road, which ascertained trade benefits. The region has been generously endowed with natural resources, such as copper, gold, natural gas, and others. The hot and dry climate has favored growth of cotton, fruits, and vegetables. Prosperity of the region for millennia attracted powerful conquerors from Alexander the Great, to Genghis Khan, and Tamerlane. During the nineteenth century, Central Asia was invaded by Russian empire and after the Revolution of 1917, it became one of fifteen Soviet republics. Abundance of natural resources and seventy years of Soviet presence have undoubtedly affected the path of economic growth in the Republic, impacted the nature of capital budgeting practices, and created a stock of capital assets that Uzbekistan owes to this day.

After the collapse of the Soviet Union, Uzbekistan, like other post-Soviet countries, was left owning a number of sizeable production enterprises, all controlled by the government, and many of them too big for a small republic. All Soviet republics housed large specialized companies, agricultural enterprises, plants, and factories that, by design, were highly dependent on the branches located elsewhere in the USSR. Cotton is one of the leading productions in Uzbekistan economy. The International Cotton Advisory Committee reports that despite taking the 82nd place in the world by its GDP, Uzbekistan is the 6th largest producer and the 3rd largest exporter of cotton in the world, despite the fact that cotton production decreased from about 1.6 million tons in 1990 to only about 1 million ton in 2010 (International Cotton Advisory Committee, 2011). In Soviet times, cotton was processed into threads, fabrics, oil, gunpowder, and other end products in Ukraine, Russia, and other Soviet republics. The aircraft building factory evacuated to Tashkent -the capital of Uzbekistan, during World War II was one of the largest in the former Soviet Union, and at its peak, employed about 20,000 people (Биржевой Лидер, 2013). The factory produced passenger and cargo aircrafts that were similar and mainly sold to the other Soviet republics. Engines and some other major parts of the airplanes were produced in the other republics, while fuselage was built and assembled in Uzbekistan.

When the Soviet system collapsed in 1991, the ties with other Soviet republics were broken. The demand from other links in the production-consumption process housed in other republics no longer existed. These enterprises became too expensive for any individual country, especially quite small ones, like Uzbekistan, to manage and auxiliary infrastructure too costly to support. The move to a market economy also required a major overhaul of the uniform government monopoly and monopsony present at any level and in any industry. All these changes dramatically impacted the industrial composition of Uzbekistan and inventory of its capital assets. For example, Uzbekistan remains a large producer and exporter of cotton fiber. The collapse of the Soviet Union contributed to development of textile and other related cotton processing industries. The aircraft building factory, on the other hand, dramatically cut its production of airplanes (Uzbek airlines became almost the solo buyer of the Uzbek-produced airplanes) and requalified into production of household items, such as kitchen pots and pans. In 2010, the factory applied for bankruptcy and produced its very last airplane in 2012 (Биржевой Лидер, 2013).

CAPITAL INVESTMENT IN UZBEKISTAN

Economy

The composition of the economy and its size have undoubtedly impacted the inventory of public infrastructure and the dynamics and scale of capital investment practices in Uzbekistan. In Soviet times, the Uzbek economy was relatively small and less developed compared to other Soviet republics. In 1990, the last year before the collapse of the Soviet Union, the overall GDP in Uzbekistan was just under 20.5 billion constant 2010 US$. This was higher than the economy of even smaller Kyrgyzstan, Armenia, Tajikistan, and Turkmenistan, but lower than GDP of the remaining eleven Soviet republics (World Bank Group, 2016). And, in per capita terms, Uzbek GDP at only 997 US$ per capita was the lowest among 15 Soviet countries in 1990 (Figure 1 a). For comparison, the per capita GDP in Russia was ten times, and in neighboring Kazakhstan – six times the size of that in Uzbekistan in 1990.

Economies of all post-Soviet republics were hit hard by the collapse of the Soviet Union (Ceka, 2018; Ermasova & Ermasova; 2018, Krupa, 2018). Per capita GDP and GDP growth plummeted in the first years of transition. However, since Uzbekistan has been heavily reliant on mining rather than processing industries, economic recession in the country has been relatively mild compared to other republics (Figure 1 b). But, even with that, Uzbek per capita GDP returned to its pre-recession value only in 2005 (some post-Soviet republics, like Ukraine or Kyrgyzstan, still have not reached their per capita GDP of the 1990). From 2004 GDP growth in Uzbekistan has been between 7 and 10 percent. By 2016, per capita GDP more than doubled from its 1990 value. Nevertheless, because of the low starting point, there is still a long way for the Uzbek economy to recovery. It remains the third smallest of the post-Soviet countries, ahead of only Tajikistan and Kyrgyzstan. In 2016, the per capita GDP in Uzbekistan was about 2,905 US$. For comparison, it was 25,136 US$ on average in European and Central Asian countries and 52,364 US$ in the USA (World Bank Group, 2016).

Figure 1a. Per capita GDP in 15 post-Soviet Republics between 1990 and 2016, in constant 2010 US$
Source: World Bank Group, 2016.

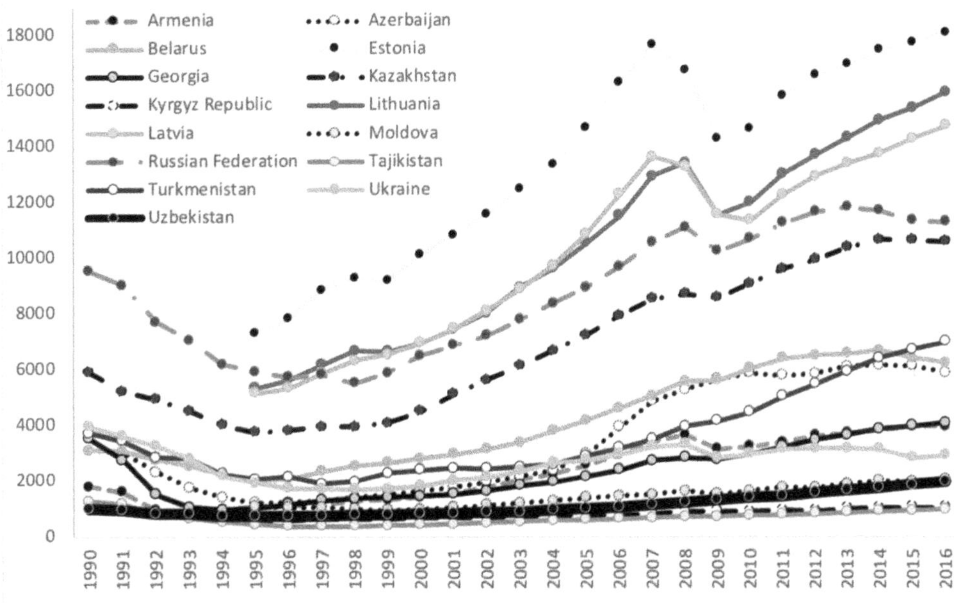

Figure 1b. GDP growth in 15 post-Soviet Republics between 1990 and 2016, in constant 2010 US$
Source: World Bank Group, 2016.

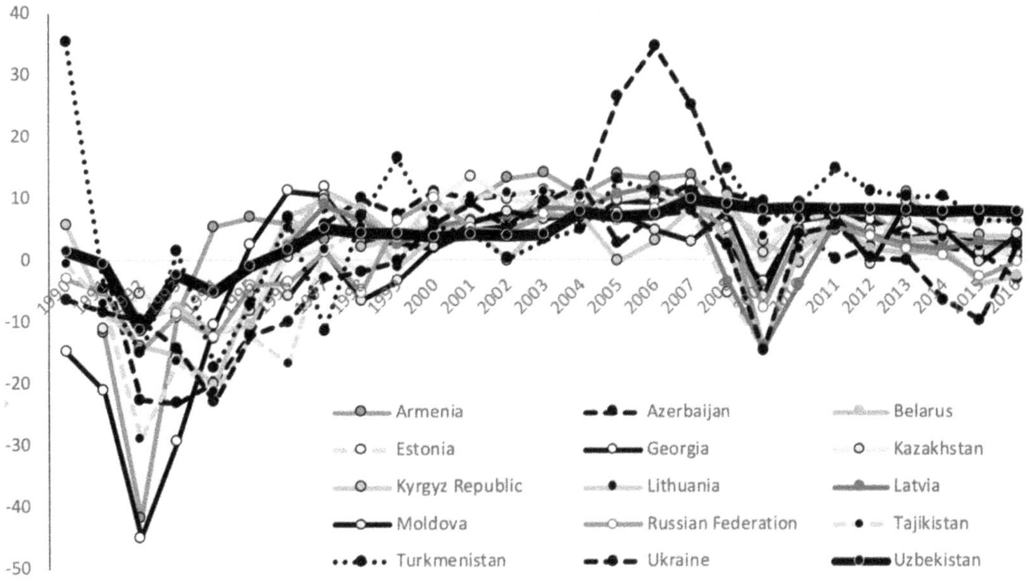

Notes: In both graphs Uzbekistan represents a bold black line; GDP data for Baltic countries -Latvia, Lithuania, Estonia, and Moldova - are available from 1995, GDP growth estimates are from 1996.

The rapid growth of Uzbek economy has been going hand-in-hand with increase in capital investments. From 2006, the amount of capital investments in Uzbekistan almost tripled from 5.35 billion in

Figure 2. Capital investments in Uzbekistan in constant 2010 US$ between 2000 and 2016
Sources: The State Committee of the Republic of Uzbekistan on Statistics; World Bank Group, 2016.

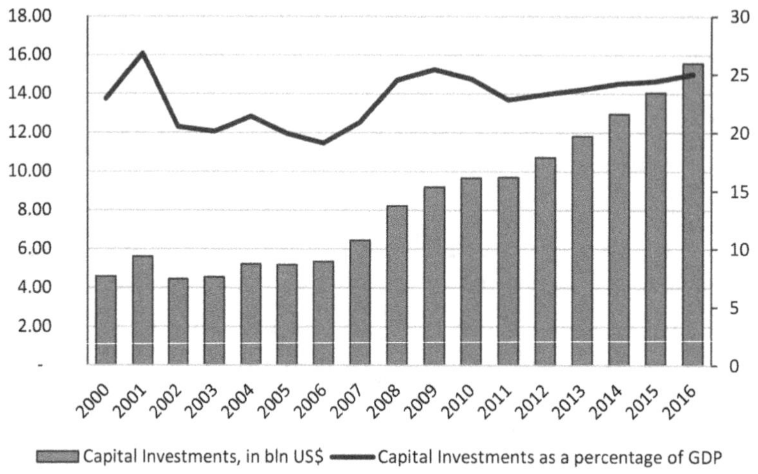

constant 2010 US$ to 15.6 billion US$ (Figure 2). However, as a percentage of GDP, the capital investments have remained almost unchanged at about 25 percent of GDP from 2007.

The per capita total capital investment by region in real 2010 US$ are shown in Figure 3. The capital investments tend to concentrate in and around the capital city Tashkent. Collectively, Tashkent city and Tashkent region score about a quarter of all capital investments in the Republic. Per capita and total capital investment have been consistently increasing over time, especially in Bukhara, Navoiy, and Tashkent regions, the city of Tashkent, and the Republic of Karakalpakistan. In the Navoiy region and the Republic of Karakalpakistan, most of the increase in capital investment is attributed to the development of mining sites and infrastructure that supports them. In Bukhara region, in addition to extraction of natural resources, the capital investments are also largely used to rehabilitate historic sites and build infrastructure around them.

Tashkent, being the largest city in Central Asia, and by far the largest city in Uzbekistan (according to the State Committee of the Republic of Uzbekistan on Statistics over 2.4 million people lived in Tashkent in 2017, and over 5.2 million lived in the capital and Tashkent region together), has been undergoing overall major face lift from ongoing construction of roads, to school buildings, museums, business, and other capital projects that are aimed mainly at attracting tourists and businesses to the Republic.

When capital investments are considered by source (Table 1) only a small percent of them (4.5 percent of total, or 0.7 billion US$ in 2016) come directly from the state budget and additional 11.2 percent (1.75 billion US$) come from budget and off-budget government funds, including the Fund for Reconstruction and Development. However, it is hard to identify the true overall government capital expenditures, as most of the banks and private enterprises (columns 4 and 5 in Table 1) are owned by government or government owns a control share of assets in these entities. Besides, private sector investments include tax expenditures, i.e. revenues forgone due to preferential treatment of certain organizations for the tax purposes[1]. Available statistics also does not allow disintegrating government funds spent on public purposes, like infrastructure, and government funds spent on private purposes, such as oil and gas, energy, telecommunications, and other spheres of the economy controlled by Uzbek government.

Figure 3. Per capita capital investment by regions, in constant 2010 US$
Sources: The State Committee of the Republic of Uzbekistan on Statistics (capital investment data in Uzbek sums); the World Bank (purchasing power parity – measure of inflation, and official exchange rate data).

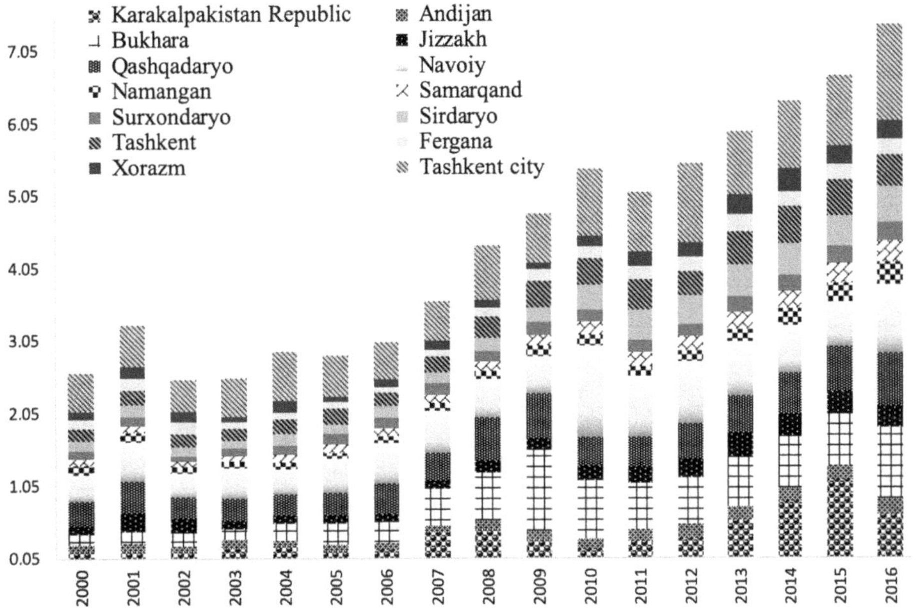

The Sources of Capital Funding

The capital investments in Uzbekistan are provided from multiple sources. Interestingly, the most common way of financing infrastructure projects in many countries around the world - the debt financing – has not been utilized in Uzbekistan in any way. Uzbekistan has never been rated by credit rating agencies and Uzbek government has never issued long or short-term bonds at federal, provincial, or municipal level (Pismennaya, Andrianova, & Doff, 2018).

Public projects generally rely on revenues pledged directly through the state budget, and a number of budget and off-budget funds, including the Ameliorative Fund for Improving Irrigated Lands (Фонд Мелиоративного Улучшения Орошаемых Земель), Fund for Development of Physical Plant of Educational and Medical Enterprises (Фонд Развития Материально-Технической Базы Образовательных и Медицинских Учреждений), Off Budget Fund for Reconstruction, Capital Repairs, and Equipment of Secondary Schools, Professional Colleges, Academic Lyceums, and Medical Enterprises (Внебюджетного Фонда Реконструкции, Капитального Ремонта и Оснащения Общеобразовательных Школ, Профессиональных Колледжей, Академических Лицеев и Медицинских Учреждений), Republican Road Fund (Республиканский Дорожный Фонд при Кабинете Министров Республики Узбекистан), as well as foreign investments, and loans from the Fund for Reconstruction and Development, according to the 2017 Resolution of the President of the Republic of Uzbekistan.

The first three Funds are administered by the Ministry of Finance of the Republic of Uzbekistan, and the last two - the Road Construction Fund and the Fund for Reconstruction and Development (FRD) - are administered directly by the Cabinet of Ministers. All Funds have the managing boards of directors

Table 1. Capital investment by sources of funding and region in 2016

	State Budget	Off-Budget Funds	Bank Loans	Private Sector	Foreign Investment	Total
Uzbekistan total (in bln soum)	2,239.65	5,574.24	26,378.10	10,601.01	4,977.00	49,770
Uzbekistan total (in bln 2010 US$)	0.70	1.75	8.27	3.32	1.56	15.60
Uzbekistan total (in percent of total)	4.50	11.20	53.00	21.30	10.00	100
Karakalpakistan Republic	2.60	12.30	5.60	34.20	45.30	100
Andijan	3.60	13.90	12.80	64.30	5.40	100
Bukhara	1.20	2.90	4.20	37.80	53.90	100
Jizzakh	5.00	10.60	19.10	56.80	8.50	100
Qashqadaryo	1.50	13.70	4.40	51.90	28.50	100
Navoiy	5.10	35.10	6.40	48.00	5.40	100
Namangan	2.80	10.50	15.80	46.00	24.90	100
Samarqand	4.90	7.70	10.80	74.10	2.50	100
Surxondaryo	8.40	10.40	14.90	55.90	10.40	100
Sirdaryo	24.40	12.00	18.10	37.30	8.20	100
Tashkent	5.40	5.50	18.80	55.60	14.70	100
Fergana	11.40	2.80	13.90	58.00	13.90	100
Xorazm	5.30	6.40	13.80	68.20	6.30	100
Tashkent city	4.00	11.50	9.50	60.20	14.80	100

Sources: The State Committee of the Republic of Uzbekistan on Statistics; World Bank Group, 2016.

that include ministers, their deputies, heads of state committees, and other government officials. These Funds receive revenues from earmarked sources, general funds, private grants, and other sources and spend these revenues on specific programs consistent with the missions of the funds. The Ameliorative Fund for Improving Irrigated Lands, for instance, finances the construction of water drainage systems, pumping stations, and hydrotechnical structures, among other things. The Republican Road Fund is devoted to road construction and maintenance projects. The Fund for Reconstruction, Capital Repairs, and Equipment of Secondary Schools, Professional Colleges, Academic Lyceums, and Medical Enterprises is earmarked for capital repairs and new constructions of pre-schools, schools, colleges, and lyceums. And, the Fund for Development of Physical Plant of Educational and Medical Enterprises is earmarked for capital repairs, reconstruction, and new constructions of universities and medical buildings (detailed lists of expenses by each fund are provided annually in the appendices to the Resolution of the President of the Republic of Uzbekistan "On Investment Policy in the Republic of Uzbekistan").

Table 2 shows the share of capital investment by each fund and sources. FRD is the largest single source of capital investment in the Republic (see more about FRD below), directing even more outlays for the capital projects than the state budget and much more than any one of the individual Funds. In 2017, for instance, 881.52 million US$ for capital projects was provided from FRD, while 767.84 million US$ came from the budget, and 485.77 million US$ from the Road Fund, the second largest fund earmarked. Interestingly, all funds, except FRD, offer pay-as-you-go financing to capital projects (expenditures are paid from current revenues), while FRD provides pay-as-you-use (or debt) financing.

Table 2. Capital investments of the Republic of Uzbekistan by the source of funding budgeted for 2017 fiscal year, in million constant (2010) US$

Total Capital Investment	**19,244.01**
Centralized (Government) Investments	*4,922.50*
Budget	767.84
Dedicated Funds, including	1,090.38
- Ameliorative Fund for Improving Irrigated Lands	75.22
- Republican Road Fund	485.77
- Off Budget Fund for Reconstruction, Capital Repairs, and Equipment of Secondary Schools, Professional Colleges, Academic Lyceums, and Medical Enterprises	413.26
- Fund for Development of Physical Plant of Educational and Medical Enterprises	116.13
Fund for Developing Youth Sports	116.96
Fund for Reconstruction and Development	881.52
Foreign Investments and Investments given under Government Guarantees	2,065.80
Non-centralized Investments	*14,321.51*
Investment by Legal Entities (includes tax expenditures)	5,322.17
Credits of commercial banks and other borrowed funds	2,346.57
Direct foreign investments	2,953.62
Investments by individuals	3,699.14

Source: Appendix 1 to the Resolution of the President of the Republic of Uzbekistan on Investment Program of the Republic of Uzbekistan for 2017; World Bank Group, 2016.

The Fund for Reconstruction and Development

The Fund for Reconstruction and Development is the financial institution of the Cabinet of Ministers. It was created in 2006 by the Cabinet of Ministers, the Ministry of Finance, and five major state-controlled banks all of which are represented at the highest level in the board of the FRD directors. The board is led by the prime minister of the Republic of Uzbekistan, and the other members are selected personally by the President of Uzbekistan (Resolution of the President of the Republic of Uzbekistan, 2006).

FRD is tasked with providing government-guaranteed loans for capital projects that are considered strategically important for the Republic (see the description of some of the major recent projects financed by the Fund in the next section). Since its creation, FRD funded 79 major capital investment projects. The Fund was created with 1 billion US$ in assets in 2006, grew to 15 billion US$ in 2015 and is expected to reach 25 billion US$ in assets by 2020 (Sources: FRD web site and US Department of State 2011 and 2016).

It is not immediately obvious how the revenues for FRD are generated. The Resolution of the President of the Republic of Uzbekistan on "Creation of the Fund for Reconstruction and Development of the Republic of Uzbekistan" note that the Fund is financed from the sale of certain government assets, the difference in the world market prices for strategic natural resources and the cut-off prices for these resources set by the President of Uzbekistan, the difference in sale of government assets to foreign investors in foreign currency that exceed the values recorded in the state budget, and other sources. The lack of transparency even in the description of the revenue sources may potentially create incentives for price and budget manipulations whenever the need arises to generate new revenues for the Fund or shift revenues from related sources. The Uzbekistan Investment Climate Statements by the U.S. Department of State consistently argues that FRD was created to "sterilize and accumulate foreign exchange revenues" (see, for instance, US Department of State 2011 and 2016). Yet, the Fund for twelve years now has played one of the key roles in funding many of the major capital construction projects in the Republic.

Foreign Investments

Another large source of capital investment in Uzbekistan are foreign direct investments. These investments constituted 3 billion US$, or over 15 percent of total capital investment in 2017 alone (Table 2). Bukhara region has benefited from foreign investments and credits the most. This region accounted for 29.2 percent of all foreign investments in the Republic in 2016. The second highest share of foreign capital investments, 18.9 percent in 2016, went to Qashqadaryo region. The capital city Tashkent and Tashkent region collectively received 19.8 percent of foreign investments in 2016, according to the State Committee of the Republic of Uzbekistan on Statistics).

The Committee also reported that in at least the last decade, the three major foreign investors in Uzbekistan have by far been Russia (33.7 percent of total foreign investment in 2016), South Korea (20.2 percent in 2016), and China (14.8 percent in 2016). Of individual foreign investors, the 2011 US Department of State Report on Investment Climate in Uzbekistan named Russian Lukoil, the largest single foreign investor in Uzbekistan (200 million US$ in investments and 5 billion US$ in investment commitments), followed by Chinese CNPC (3 billion US$ in total investments and investment commitments), Malaysian PETRONAS (over 500 US$ in investment), UK-owned British American Tobacco (over 300 million US$ in investments), Russian-owned Gazprom (over $400 million in investment), VimpelCom, and MTC - both telecommunication companies with about $200 billion US$ in investment each, and Swiss Nestle (about 20 million US$ in investments) (US Department of State, 2011). The specialization of the largest foreign investors can further speak to the importance of specific industries in Uzbek economy. The four largest of them, Lukoil, CNPC, and PETRONAS are all oil and gas companies, and Gazprom specializes only in gas extraction and production.

Short- and Long-Term Investment Planning

The investment policy of the Republic is revised and updated annually and signed into law in the last two months of the year by the resolution of the President of the Republic of Uzbekistan on "The Investment Program of the Republic of Uzbekistan" for a given year. The resolution is supplemented by a number of documents that provide details of the investment program of the Republic, such as the estimates of the investment by the source of funding; a detailed list of the projects, that includes the cost of the project in a given fiscal year, a total cost of each project, the number of jobs the investment project created, the date of completion, and other relevant information. It also includes a list of funding for investment projects, by agency, and the purpose of the spending coming from the Republican budget, FRD, and every other government off-budget fund.[2] While information contained in the supplements is quite comprehensive, unfortunately, it is backward looking or considers only the next budget year. The forward-looking multi-year comprehensive capital improvement plans are published very infrequently. To the best of the author's knowledge the last time a comprehensive long-term program was published was in 2010. Back then, the plan presented capital investment program for 2011-2015[3]. Every now and then, the long-term improvement plans are published for specific capital purposes, although this also does not happen on a regular basis. In 2013, for example, the President signed into law "Measures on Continuing Improvement of Ameliorated Condition of Irrigated Lands and Rational Usage of Water Resources between 2013 and 2017."

State of Infrastructure

Uzbekistan does not make an inventory of public assets, including infrastructure, openly available for public scrutiny. The condition of existing infrastructure is also not discussed in government reports. It is possible, however, to assess the quality of Uzbek infrastructure from the World Bank score card index, published every two years, that rates the "quality of trade and transport related infrastructure (e.g., ports, railroads, roads, information technology)". Uzbekistan received a score of 2.57 out of 5 on this indicator in 2018 (Ranked 77 out of 160 countries) (source: the World bank). For comparison, this index for the US is 4.05 and for the highest rated country – Germany – is 4.37. For years Uzbekistan has been ranked higher in this indicator than other Central Asian countries and neighboring Kazakhstan. But, it is ranked lower than Baltic counties of the former Soviet Union and Russia. While it is hard to discuss the scope and state of capital assets outside of the information provided by the World Bank, Uzbek government allows for a glimpse into the major capital projects financed by taxpayers' dollars. The description of such projects is offered in the next section.

Recent Major Capital Projects

In the developed countries, including the United States, government owns roads and highways, bridges, schools and other government buildings, water and sewer, and other supporting infrastructure (see chapter 1 in this book for more details), while for-profit enterprises, with a small exemption, remain under the private control. As mentioned earlier, in Soviet Union every industry and enterprise within each industry were owned by government. After the collapse of the USSR Soviet republics, including Uzbekistan, inherited this practice. Uzbekistan continues the legacy to these days with many industries and separate enterprises remaining under the state control, and hence, receiving funding from the general state budget. The bankrupt aircraft building factory mentioned earlier was all, but 10 percent owned by government or government run enterprises («Ferghana» News Agency, 2010). In fact, government controls all industries considered strategic for the Republic – such as mining, energy, telecommunications, and others - monopolizing or maintaining controlling shares in key enterprises in these industries (US Department of State, 2011). In addition, all land in the Republic belongs to government. Private individuals and legal entities may own certain structures, but the land they are on is all state-owned.

One of such major state-owed industries is Uzbekneftegas (Oil and Gas Industry). In 2008, Uzbekneftegas created a joint venture with several South Korean companies to build a massive Ustyurt Gas Chemical Complex in Surgil gas field discovered several years earlier in Karakalpakistan area. The overall construction cost totaled to about 4 billion US$ and continued for four years from 2011 to 2015. The financing was provided by 19 financial institutions with a large portion of funding coming directly from the Uzbekistan state budget and FRD. Information from the Fund for Reconstruction and Development and Uz-Kor Gas Chemical web sites indicates that The Ustyurt Complex currently produces hundreds of millions of cubic meters of gas and tens of thousands of tons of polyethylene, polypropylene, and other related products.

Another recent major capital project is a 1.3 billion US$ expansion of Talimardjan Thermoelectric Power Station located in the southeastern part of Uzbekistan in Qashqadaryo Region. All hydro and thermoelectric stations in Uzbekistan are also government-controlled and receive the majority of their operating and capital funding from the state budget and FRD. The funding and administration of the Talimardjan expansion project was provided by the Decree of the President of Uzbekistan from 2013.

The smaller recent projects highlighted by the Fund for Reconstruction and Development are the $230 million purchase of two Boing-787 airplanes for Uzbekistan Airlines for the long-distance international passenger flights (the purchases are financed and administered by President decrees from 2010, 2014, and 2016), 96.5 million US$ purchase of three electric trains for Uzbekistan Railways (the purchases are financed and administered by President decrees from 2010 and 2015), and the 633.75 million US$ construction of the portion of the railroad in the eastern part of Uzbekistan (the construction is financed and administered by the President decree from 2013) according to the Fund for Reconstruction and Development. Both Uzbekistan Airlines and Uzbekistan Railways are also public entities.

In addition to the projects that are already in place, Uzbek government seriously entertains the ideas of several other major capital endeavors. One of them is the Tashkent City business center. The project meant to improve the attractiveness of Tashkent for tourism and businesses is envisioned to include business offices, private apartments, hotels, and even schools and universities. It is estimated that the construction will last five years since its inception and the total price tag is preliminary estimated at 1 billion US$ (UzbekistanToday, 2017). Uzbek government additionally developed plans for construction of the system of the toll roads in the Republic. The first one will connect the cities of Tashkent, Samarkand, and Bukhara and may be built in as early as 2020. The toll roads are planned to be built in collaboration with a private German company, but before that, the Uzbek government has to pass laws governing public-private partnerships (PPP or P3), which the Republic presently does not have, but plans to adopt in 2018 (The Free Library, 2014).

Budget Process

Another important aspect to consider to better understand the capital budget process and procedures in Uzbekistan, the role Uzbek budget players, and how some important capital budgeting decisions are made is to study the Republican budget process. The process is outlined in the Budget Code of the Republic of Uzbekistan, a most recent version of which was passed in 2013[4]. Theoretically, any budget process should include four stages (Mikesell, 2013). It starts with executive preparations, which is when departments and agencies develop their budgets from the instructions of a central budget office. The central budget office then compiles agencies budgets into a single executive budget that is later considered and voted through by the legislative branch. Once approved, the budget is signed into law by the President, and its execution begins in the first day of a new fiscal year. Following the execution, the budget is audited by internal and external agencies.

The budgeting process in Uzbekistan follows a similar pattern, although the same agencies are involved in budget preparation, execution, and audit stages. Interestingly, the executive budget is audited twice before it is submitted for legislative considerations and by the end of the fiscal year, after it is executed. There are no separate operating and capital budgets, so the budgets are developed and considered legislatively together on the annual basis. There is also no separate capital budgeting process.

The main budgeting players in Uzbekistan are the Cabinet of Ministers, the Ministry of Finance, the Treasurer Department of the Ministry of Finance, and the Audit Chamber in the executive branch, and the Upper Chamber (the Senate) and the Lower Chamber of Oliy Majlis – the legislative branch - each chamber has a Committee on Budget and Economic Reforms. The role of every agency in each stage of the budget process is discussed below – all information on the budget process comes from the Budget Code of the Republic of Uzbekistan (adopted on December 26, 2013).

Budget Preparation

In Uzbekistan, the executive branch consists of ministries and agencies that are managed and administered by the Cabinet of Ministers. The Cabinet of Ministers includes the prime minister, his seven deputies, fourteen ministers, chairmen of state committees, and heads of state management entities. Among multiple other functions, the Cabinet of Ministers coordinates and administers the development of the agencies' capital and operating budgets. The Ministry of Finance is one of the fourteen ministries and the main government agency involved in budget preparation and monitoring budget execution, which plays the role of a central budget office. The Ministry of Finance develops fiscal and budget policies of the Republic and prepares general revenue forecasts. These forecasts and highlights of the fiscal and budget policies are distributed between state agencies.

Agencies financed from the state budget funds, formulate budget requests based on the forecasts and policy guidelines provided by the Ministry of Finance, and revenue and expenditures projections prepared by the local tax collection agencies, municipal budgets, and other documents. The city, provincial budgets, and the budget of the Republic of Karakalpakistan are developed by their finance departments. State agencies are then required to submit budget requests to the Ministry of Finance before July 1st of each fiscal year. The director of the Fund for Reconstruction and Development is also required to submit the budgeted revenues and expenditures to the Audit Chamber and the Ministry of Finance before July 1st of each year.

The Ministry of Finance consolidates agencies' budget requests into the executive budget, prepares budgets for main and off-budget funds, and develops a budget message. The executive budget, fund budgets, including a budget for the Fund for Reconstruction and Development of the Republic of Uzbekistan, the fiscal and budgetary policies, and the budget message are submitted for considerations to the Cabinet of Ministers by September 15 of each year. By September 20th, the Cabinet of Ministers transmits the budget and policy documents for review to the Audit Chamber. The Audit Chamber is given two days to make conclusions and recommendations about proposed budgets and budget policy for the next fiscal year.

Legislative Considerations

The Cabinet of Ministers transmits the budget message, the executive budget, funds' budgets, and executive views on the budget priorities and fiscal policy to Uzbek Parliament, the Oliy Majlis, no later than October 15 of each year. Oliy Majlis is the legislative government branch. It consists of two Chambers; the upper chamber, the Senate, and the lower, the Legislative chamber. The budget considerations fall mainly onto the Committees on Budget and Economic Reforms in each chamber. The Committee on Budget and Economic Reforms is one of the six upper and ten lower chamber committees of Oliy Majlis. The Budget Code of the republic does not specify by which day Oliy Majlis has to approve the budget and the fiscal policy directives and forecasts and by which day the president has to authorize these documents. In practice, though, the budget is signed into law in December of each year by the Resolution of the President of the Republic of Uzbekistan “On Macroeconomic Forecasts and Parameters of the State budget of the Republic of Uzbekistan”.

Budget Execution

The budget execution stage begins from the first days of a new fiscal year, which in Uzbekistan overlaps with the calendar year, and lasts from January 1st to December 31st. Agencies receiving funds from the state budget are required to prepare a “smeta” – a detailed financing plan that includes revenues (coming from the state budget and other sources) and expenditures’ estimates for the year. Only after the approval and registrations of such financial plans, the agencies can receive money from the state budget. The smetas are prepared and approved by the heads of accounting and finance departments and the heads of the state agencies and Funds. Temporary smetas for the first quarter of a fiscal year are approved and registered by December 25th. The smetas for the remainder of the year are compiled based on the approved budget parameters and registered and approved by March 10 of each year. If the smeta is not registered by April 1st, the entity stops receiving funds from the state budget until registration occurs. The smetas of different jurisdictions are audited, registered, and approved by the Ministry of Finance or the finance department of the city administrations

In general, the Cabinet of Ministers is in charge of the execution of the Republican and Funds’ budgets in Uzbekistan. The cities’ and regional administrations as well as the Cabinet of Ministers of the Republic of Karakalpakistan are responsible for budget execution on local levels. These entities regularly monitor in-flow of revenues and out-flow of expenditures. The Ministry of Finance is tasked with balancing budget expenditures and revenues quarterly, including the use of investments. The Budget Code defines the roles of all budget players, the deadlines, the rules of financial reporting, the regulations concerning the transfer of funds between budget categories and between agencies, and provides other regulations related to budget execution.

Audit and Evaluation

The Ministry of Finance plays the most important role in the internal budget audit process. All entities financed from the state budget are required to provide quarterly financial and budget reports on April 1st, July 1st, and October 1st of each year, and the annual financial and budget reports by January 1st to the Ministry of Finance, finance departments of the regional and cities administration and other financing authorities as defined by the Budget Code of the Republic of Uzbekistan. The state tax committee and the state Customer Service Committee prepare reports on revenue generation. The Ministry of Finance provides combined quarterly reports to the Cabinet of Ministers and the comprehensive annual report on budget execution to the Cabinet of Ministers by April 1st of each year. All Budgetary Funds report monthly to the Ministry of Finance on budget execution. The entities financed from the budgetary Funds are required to submit their reports to the Ministry of Finance quarterly.

The external audit of the republican budget is conducted by the Audit Chamber. The Ministry of Finance submits budget reports and Funds’ execution reports to the Audit Chamber not later than April

5th of the year following the report year. The Audit Chamber submits the auditing report to the Cabinet of Ministers by May 10. The Cabinet of Ministers then submits the annual report on budget execution and the Audit chamber report to Oliy Majlis no later than May 15th of the year. The Legislative chambers of Oliy Majlis discuss the submitted reports and approve them with the resolution of the Oliy Majlis, which is then published on the Ministry of Finance web site.

SOLUTIONS AND RECOMMENDATIONS

The understanding of various aspects of capital budgeting and capital investment practices and processes in Uzbekistan helps recognize and highlight certain problem areas and offer potential solutions. The next section summarizes some of these important practices - most of them discussed earlier in the chapter, emphasizing the differences between the Uzbek approach to capital budgeting, capital investment, and similar practices in other post-Soviet countries and the United States and offers suggestions for improvement.

Privatization

While some of the former Soviet republics, like Russia (see Ermasova, chapter 6 of this volume) or Ukraine (see Krupa, chapter 5 of this volume) were quick to privatize a lot of their government resources after the collapse of the Soviet Union, Uzbekistan has been engaging in privatization efforts very slowly. Government ownership in most of the sectors of the Uzbek economy - especially those considered strategic for the Republic - is still extremely extensive. While quick and wide-scaled privatization of assets may also be undesirable, mainly because government loses control and a flow of revenues generated by privatized assets, in many cases, privatization may lead to the favorable outcomes as private sector can often offer a better response to customer needs, a smaller government, and a greater efficiency – i.e. a higher quality of goods and services at lower cost than public sector, among other advantages (Mikesell, 2013).

Today, 27 years after proclaiming independence Uzbekistan is still far from achieving a healthy balance between privatized and government-owned enterprises. A Soviet legacy of prevalent state ownership in telecommunications, transportation (including railroads and airlines), mining, and other spheres is still very relevant in the Republic and continues to occupy a large share of the government capital budgets. Although, privatization efforts are present, their pace is too slow. The US Department of State notes that the 2015 privatization program offered 68 government-owned enterprises for sale to foreign investors and 1,179 enterprises for sale to a private sector (US Department of State, 2016). The 2016 Uzbekistan Investment Climate Statement argues, however, that government will still hold 51percent of assets in some of these enterprises. As to the future efforts, by February 2017 Uzbek government offered 341 state-owned assets for privatization and announced that by 2019 it plans to privatize 675 state-owned assets (US Department of State, 2017).

Uzbekistan Does Not Receive Credit Ratings and Does Not Issue Government Bonds

After the collapse of the Soviet Union in 1991, many former Soviet republics, such as Russia, Ukraine, and neighboring Kazakhstan, have been receiving credit ratings from the mid 1990's (source: Moody's

Investment Services). The United States government has been rated by credit rating agencies for about eighty years now. Uzbekistan has never applied for and received a sovereign credit rating. Uzbekistan also does not issue government bonds, which are used extensively by many governments around the world, including the United States, as a major way of financing capital projects and conducting monetary policy (by buying and selling treasury bonds in the United States). Application for credit ratings would be a major leap for the Republic to access international credit market. It will improve visibility of the country, and it will offer new ways to funding the capital projects. Pismennaya, Andrianova & Doff (2018) note that Uzbekistan may apply for and receive its first credit ratings as early as 2018.

No Regular Long-Term Capital Improvement Plans

While Uzbek government updates and publishes lists of capital projects and details of their financing sources annually, long-term capital improvement plans are rare. To the best of the author's knowledge, the last time such a plan was published in 2010, when a capital investment program for 2011-2015 was presented. In the United States, for example, capital improvement plans are typically prepared for five-to-seven-year periods. Such plans create an avenue for the long-range financial planning, provide a more extensive picture of capital budgeting needs, and can help government prioritize the projects (see, chapter 1 in this volume on the extensive discussion of capital improvement plans).

No Clarity in Criteria for Capital Projects' Selection

While capital improvement programs are published annually for each budget fund, there is no transparency about the process and criteria of capital projects' selection or a selection of contractors for projects' execution. Published documents simply outline what projects will be pursued in the next budget year and how much they will cost.

Lots of Obstacles for Foreign Investments

The Investment Climate Report in Uzbekistan, published annually by the US Department of State, outlines a number of obstacles for foreign companies to conduct business in Uzbekistan. Government corruption, difficulty with currency convertibility, non-uniform interpretation of laws, and multiple other issues have been consistently highlighted in the reports as impedance for foreign investments. Although, the first report after the election of a new president in December of 2016 has sounded a lot more promising and positive (US Department of State, 2017). For instance, the 2017 *Investment Climate Report* noted that Uzbek government introduced a number of measures to improve regulatory system in the Republic. The key government regulations are now published online. Besides, in January 2017 newly elected president Mirziyoev signed into law a new legislation "On Combating Corruption". After the 2017 Investment Climate Report was published, the Uzbek government introduced major changes to currency conversion, basically eliminating black market exchange rates.

No Laws Regulating Public-Private Partnerships

There are no prior practices of public-private partnership (PPP) in capital improvement projects in Uzbekistan, because there are currently no laws regulating such partnerships in the Republic. PPP would open yet another frontier for financing, execution, and later exploitation of capital projects. The Uzbek government plans to draft and pass laws governing PPP later in 2018 (The Free Library, 2014).

Budget Audit Is Conducted Twice

Unlike the United States, where budget is audited by an external agency (Government Accountability Office) only in the end of the budget cycle, the external audit of the executive budget in Uzbekistan is conducted twice: at the executive preparations stage: before the budget is offered to legislative branch for considerations and in the end of the fiscal year during the audit and evaluation stage. Such practice can potentially help identify and fix problems early in the budget cycle, yet it increases the workload of the auditing agency and adds another bureaucratic layer to the budget process.

CONCLUSION

Seventy years of the Soviet ruling has undoubtedly played an important role in shaping economic, cultural, demographic, political, and any other aspects of Uzbek life. Now, 27 years after proclaiming independence, the traces and tracks of Soviet influence are still not only visible but often prevalent. And, while some of the norms brought by the Soviet presence - like broad-spectrum education (World Bank reports a 99.98 percent literacy rate among adult population of Uzbekistan), rapid development of infrastructure, and migration of qualified personnel to the Republic, especially intensified during the World War II - benefited the country a lot, other aspects - like overall government monopoly and excessive specialization of the Republican economies - have contributed to a slow start in the first years of independence and potentially continue to impede growth and development in the Republic. This chapter aimed to review major capital budgeting and capital investment practices in post-Soviet Uzbekistan, compare them to these in the developed countries, like the United States, identify successes and problem areas, and offer some potential ways for improvement.

The discussion in this manuscript shows how far Uzbekistan has progressed since proclaiming independence on September 1st, 1991. The country now has an established, well-identified budget process that includes multiple layers of controls and clearly defined budget players. It has been successfully pursuing a number of important capital improvement projects. The Republic created a designated Fund – the Fund for Reconstruction and Development - to accumulate funds used in financing of some of the major capital projects considered strategic for the country. There is, however, still much inefficiency in the capital budgeting and capital investment areas. There is little transparency around revenue sources for FRD. The US Department of State, for example, warns that the real purpose of the FRD is "sterilization" of foreign revenues. There is a widespread government control of many sectors of the economy, especially those considered strategic for the Republic. There is still a lack of debt financing in the country. The long-term capital improvement plans are rare. A number of these and other issues highlighted in the chapter show there is still a lot of room for improvement.

ACKNOWLEDGMENT

I want to thank Dr. Lyudmila Shibarshova for her guidance and help with data collection. This research received no specific grant from any funding agency in the public, commercial, or not-for-profit sectors.

REFERENCES

Биржевой Лидер. (2013). *Ташкентский Авиазавод Теперь не Будет Производить Самолеты – выводы*. Author.

Стратегия действий по пяти приоритетным направлениям развития Республики Узбекистан в 2017-2021 годах. Указ Президента Республики Узбекистан от 7 февраля 2017 года N°УП-4947. (n.d.). Retrieved from http://strategy.gov.uz/ru/lists/docview/96

Указ Президента Республики Узбекистан. «Об образовании Министерства инновационного развития Республики Узбекистан». (2017). Retrieved from http://uza.uz/ru/documents/ob-obrazovanii-ministerstva-innovatsionnogo-razvitiya-respub-29-11-2017

Budget Code of The Republic of Uzbekistan. (2013). *Budget Code* No. ZRU-360 of December 26, 2013. Retrieved July 23, 2018 from http://lex.uz/pages/getpage.aspx?lact_id=2304140#2311779

Ceka, E. (2018). *Public capital budgeting and management process in Moldova. In Capital management and budgeting in the public sector*. Hershey, PA: IGI Global.

Ermasova, N., & Ermasova, P. (2018). *Public capital budgeting and management process in Russia. In Capital management and budgeting in the public sector*. Hershey, PA: IGI Global.

«Ferghana» News Agency. (2010). *Uzbekistan: Tashkent aircraft factory, named after Chkalov, goes bankrupt*. Retrieved July 23, 2018, from http://enews.fergananews.com/news.php?id=1878

Fund for Reconstruction and Development. (2018). *Uzbekistan*. Retrieved July 23, 2018, from http://ufrd.uz/

Government Portal of the Republic of Uzbekistan. (2018). *Uzbekistan*. English. Retrieved July 23, 2018, from https://www.gov.uz/en

Government Portal of the Republic of Uzbekistan. (2018). *Uzbekistan*. Russian language. Retrieved July 23, 2018, from https://www.gov.uz/ru

International Cotton Advisory Committee. (2011). *Cotton fact sheet Uzbekistan*. Retrieved July 23, 2018, from https://www.icac.org/econ_stats/country_fact_sheets/fact_sheet_uzbekistan_2011.pdf

Krupa, O. (2018). *Capital budgeting and public investment projects in Ukraine. In Capital management and budgeting in the public sector*. Hershey, PA: IGI Global.

Legislative Chamber of the Oliy Majlis of the Republic of Uzbekistan. (n.d.). *Committee on budgeting and economic reforms*. Retrieved July 23, 2018, from http://parliament.gov.uz/en/

Mikesell, J. (2013). *Fiscal administration* (7th ed.). London, UK: Cengage Learning.

Ministry of Finance of the Republic of Uzbekistan. (2018). *Uzbekistan*. Retrieved July 23, 2018, from https://www.mf.uz/en/

Ministry of the Economy of the Republic of Uzbekistan. (2018). *Uzbekistan*. Retrieved July 23, 2018, from https://mineconomy.uz/ru/

Moody's Investors Service. (2018). *19ADAD Uzbekistan*. New York: Moody's Investors Service.

Pismennaya, E., Andrianova, A., & Doff, N. (2018). *Central Asia's most populous country plans first uurobond sale*. Retrieved May 3, 2018, from https://www.bloomberg.com/news/articles/2018-02-22/central-asia-s-most-populous-country-plans-first-eurobond-sale

Resolution of the President of the Republic of Uzbekistan. (2016). *On investment policy in the republic of Uzbekistan in 2017 Nº ПП-2697* (Russian). Retrieved May 5, 2018, from https://nrm.uz/contentf?doc=493240_postanovlenie_prezidenta_respubliki_uzbekistan_ot_23_12_2016_g_n_pp-2697_ob_investicionnoy_programme_respubliki_uzbekistan_na_2017_god&products=1_vse_zakonodatelstvo_uzbekistana

Resolution of the Republic of Uzbekistan. (2017). *Resolution of the republic of Uzbekistan Nº УП-3932 from October 31, 2007*. On Creation of the Ameliorative Fund for Improving Irrigated Lands Regulated by the Cabinet of Ministers of the Republic of Uzbekistan. Retrieved from http://lex.uz/pages/getpage.aspx?actForm=1&lact_id=1262506&ONDATE=31.10.2007percent2000#1262543

The Central Bank of the Republic of Uzbekistan. (2018). *Uzbekistan*. Retrieved July 23, 2018 from http://www.cbu.uz/en/

The Free Library. (2014). *Uzbekistan plans to build toll road*. Retrieved from https://www.thefreelibrary.com/Uzbekistan+plans+to+build+toll+road.-a0531800301

The Permanent Mission of the Republic of Uzbekistan to the United Nations. (2018). *Uzbekistan*. Retrieved July 23, 2018 from https://www.un.int/uzbekistan/uzbekistan/country-facts

The Resolution of the president of the Republic of Uzbekistan Nº УП-3751 from November 5, 2006 on creation of the fund for reconstruction and development of the republic of Uzbekistan. (2006). Retrieved from Norma web site on April 23, 2018 from https://nrm.uz/contentf?doc=103640_ukaz_prezidenta_respubliki_uzbekistan_ot_11_05_2006_g_n_up-3751_o_sozdanii_fonda_rekonstrukcii_i_razvitiya_respubliki_uzbekistan&products=1_

The State Committee of the Republic of Uzbekistan on Statistics. (2018). *Uzbekistan*. Retrieved July 23, 2018, from https://stat.uz/en/

US Department of State. (2011). *Investment climate statement – Uzbekistan*. Retrieved July 23, 2018, from https://www.state.gov/e/eb/rls/othr/ics/2011/157382.htm

US Department of State. (2016). *Investment climate statement – Uzbekistan*. Retrieved from July 23, 2018, https://www.state.gov/e/eb/rls/othr/ics/2016/sca/254497.htm

US Department of State. (2017). *Investment climate statement – Uzbekistan.* Retrieved July 23, 2018, from https://www.state.gov/e/eb/rls/othr/ics/2017/sca/270035.htm

Uz-Kor Gas Chemical. (2018). *Uzbekistan.* Retrieved July 23, 2018, from http://www.uz-kor.com/index.php/en/

UzbekistanToday. (2017). *10 facts about the Tashkent City.* Retrieved July 23, 2018, from http://ut.uz/en/business/10-facts-about-the-tashkent-city/

World Bank. (2000). *The law of republic of Uzbekistan on budget system.* Retrieved July 23, 2018, from http://www1.worldbank.org/publicsector/pe/BudgetLaws/UzbekistanBudgetLaw.doc

World Bank. (2018). *Logistics performance index.* Retrieved July 23, 2018, from https://lpi.worldbank.org/international/scorecard/column/32/C/UZB/2018/R/ECA/2007/I/LMC/2007/C/KAZ/2007/C/KGZ/2007/C/RUS/2018/C/UKR/2018/C/TJK/2018/C/TKM/2018?sort=asc&order=Infrastructure#datatable

World Bank Group. (2016). *World bank group countrysSurvey FY16- Uzbekistan.* Retrieved from http://microdata.worldbank.org/index.php/catalog/2720

ENDNOTES

1 Appendix 1 to the Resolution of the President of the Republic of Uzbekistan on Investment Program of the Republic of Uzbekistan for 2017 (and other years) states that “private sector” capital investments include business tax preferences. The Resolution does not specify what exactly these tax preferences are.

2 All mentioned documents are publicly available (in Russian and Uzbek) in Uzbekistan Informational Portal “Norma”: https://nrm.uz/.

3 The plan “On the acceleration of infrastructure, transport, and communication development in 2011-2015” signed into law by the President of the Republic of Uzbekistan N° ПП-1446 from December 21, 2010. Retrieved from Norma website on April 21, 2018: https://nrm.uz/contentf?doc=218083_postanovlenie_prezidenta_respubliki_uzbekistan_ot_21_12_2010_g_n_pp-1446_ob_uskorenii_razvitiya_infrastruktury_transportnogo_i_kommunikacionnogo_stroitelstva_v_2011-2015_godah&products=1_.

4 The budget code is available only in Russian and Uzbek. This is a link to a Russian version of the Code: http://lex.uz/pages/getpage.aspx?lact_id=2304140#2311779.

Chapter 5
Capital Budgeting and Public Investment Projects in Ukraine

Olha Krupa
Seattle University, USA

ABSTRACT

This chapter discusses the budget process for public capital investments in Ukraine, presents controversies in the current process, and offers several avenues for improvement. In doing so, the author provides a description of the country's normative capital public budgeting framework, presents the institutional setup, and tracks Ukraine's public capital expenditure trends for nearly three decades (1991-2016). The study then discusses implementation, audit, and performance issues in Ukraine's public capital expenditure management and provides recommendations. Because of the country's limited fiscal capacity as compared to its massive infrastructure needs, the author posits that Ukraine can no longer afford to delay or ignore its most pressing public capital investment needs. Because the current list of capital investment proposals is underfunded and too long, the author suggests that the government focuses on finishing strategic, high-priority public projects, while other capital spending proposals target private sector financing once it becomes more readily available.

INTRODUCTION

Considering Ukraine's limited fiscal capacity, the country is in particular need of well-developed, strategic capital budgeting practices. Without this strategic focus, Ukraine will continue lagging behind its nearest neighbors in investment climate, global market competitiveness, and public service provision. Essential to future economic growth, public capital expenditures create an economic multiplier, increase income and employment, and update the country's capital infrastructure. Despite the significance of public capital investments, the detailed comparative cross-country examinations of public capital budgeting processes in public finance literature are rare (Srithongrung, 2008; Ermasova & Ermasova, 2019). Contributing to this important research area, this chapter examines Ukraine's normative public capital expenditure framework and offers several avenues for improvement. The chapter describes project proposal-setting, submission, consideration, implementation, audit, and review stages for public capital expenditures in Ukraine.

DOI: 10.4018/978-1-5225-7329-6.ch005

For much of the twentieth century, Ukraine's extensive public project infrastructure received capital financing through the Soviet command-and-control central planning system. Once Ukraine gained its independence from the USSR in 1991, the country began a jarring, poorly thought out transition from a centrally planned economy to a market economy. Between 1991 and 2018, its challenges included a series of macroeconomic shocks accompanied by hyperinflation, the interrupted, discontinued access to markets, the "fire sale" of the public assets, and the resulting manufacturing collapse (Economist, 2003; Economist, 2015). Compounding these abrupt transformations were government bureaucracy, red tape, and government corruption (Economist, 2017). As a result, between 1991 and 2016, Ukraine lost 13.4 percent of its population and a quarter of its per-capita GDP and became the poorest country in Europe (Organization for Economic Cooperation and Development, 2014; Economist, 2015; World Bank, 2017). Similar transformations occurred in other Soviet republics during that period Ermasova & Ermasova, 2019; Guzman, 2019).

Between 2002 and 2007, Ukraine experienced a short period of macroeconomic stabilization, a credit boom, and economic growth (Duenwald et al., 2005; Economist, 2015). However, that trend has had little effect on renewing the country's aging capital infrastructure, as it was too short to absorb any newly available capital financing. Following the Global Financial Crisis, Ukraine lost its economic momentum. In the summer of 2010, a pro-Russian President Victor Yanukovych came to office, representing the oligarch interests in Eastern Ukraine. He has reversed Ukraine's pro-Western position and triggered the Revolution of Dignity in November 2014 – February 2015. That resulted in his own retreat to Russia, Russian annexation of Crimea, and a war with Russia over Ukraine's Donetsk and Luhansk regions (Economist, 2015; Economist, 2017a; Economist, 2017b).

Although between 1991 and 2017 Ukraine substantially reformed its budgetary system, including the budgeting process for public capital spending, in many regulations and procedures, the elements of the former central planning system remained. Because as many of its capital assets are publicly-funded and publicly-provided, Ukraine still lags behind its Central European neighbors in terms of capital infrastructure development (Dodonov et al., 2002). Some attribute Ukraine's weak connection between the public infrastructure spending and economic growth to its institutional setup (Gramlich, 1994; Dodonov et al., 2002; Economist, 2017b). Exploring privatization effects, studies found that in Ukraine, the recently-privatized public enterprises were associated with higher private investments and that privatization of capital assets has led to a 2 percent increase in multifactor productivity of its firms (Brown et al., 2005; Mykhayliv & Zauner, 2013). These modest positive effects, however, do not justify a rapid decline in manufacturing and employment the country experienced since 1991.

Ukraine's massive, aging infrastructure, which was inherited from the Soviet economy, commands extensive financing for capital asset maintenance and renovations, estimated in excess of 10 billion dollars over the next decade - an enormous amount for a relatively small emerging markets economy (World Bank, 2013). These substantial capital needs, however, are overshadowed by other national spending priorities including social support, healthcare, education, and most recently, defense. Ukraine's public capital expenditures remain relatively low at 3.1 and 3.6 percent of the GDP at the state and local level in 2007 and 2.2 and 1.2 percent of the GDP at the state and local level in 2016 respectively (Verner, 2017). Considering Ukraine's limited options for private infrastructure investments, the country's efforts to attract new funding for infrastructure development and support projects remain a formidable task. In September 2017, Ukraine issued a $3 billion Eurobond but has no other new funding proposed or available; the country largely relies on the IMF loan program. As its fiscal capacity remains limited, most of the funds come from aid packages of the Western countries. In these circumstances, the national and local governments must be especially mindful of their strategic spending priorities regarding capital projects, the timely completion of each project, and the performance outcomes these capital projects deliver.

Under the current public budgeting system circumstances, many capital projects remain unfinished and most are under-funded. At the heart of the public capital budgeting process are three problems: 1) a sharp, continuing decline in the share of public capital investment projects as a percentage of total government spending and as a share of the GDP (Verner, 2017; World Bank 2017), 2) a backlog resulting from of a long list of unfinished capital investment projects, and 3) a lack of strategic focus in project selection, implementation, and evaluation so that the bulk of public capital spending occurs to state-owned enterprises in "mostly private" industries like energy, agriculture, and manufacturing.

The goals of this chapter are to present the institutional framework of Ukraine's public capital investment programs within the context of the country's public finance system, to provide an overview of the select long-term budgeting issues the country faces, and to provide recommendations from a normative perspective of public finance and budgeting literature. To accomplish these objectives, the chapter presents public sector capital expenditure data within the broader system of public finances in Ukraine. The report provides statistical data on public capital spending over time, across industries, and geographic areas. The chapter then discusses the share of public capital investment projects by industry or sector and outlines the regional distribution of public capital financing projects. Drawing from the literature, the chapter raises several important concerns regarding the system of public capital projects and the issue of project prioritization and completion. Of particular interest remain project performance review, compliance, and audit. In closing, the author provides recommendations about the budget process.

BACKGROUND

Located in the center of Europe, Ukraine is the largest European country. Its capital, the city of Kyiv, has been a major metropolis for over a thousand years. Established before 482 AD, the Kyiv kings ruled Ukraine's predecessor the Kievan Rus,' the first Slavic metropolitan state (Encyclopedia Britannica, 2018). Many centuries later, in 1991, Ukraine's independence from the Soviet Union came unexpectedly through a general public referendum.

With over 45 million residents, a highly skilled and educated labor force and rich natural resources, Ukraine's economy was the second most important economic component of the USSR after Russia, "producing about four times the output of the next-ranking republic" (Central Intelligence Agency, 2018). Ukraine's vast agricultural sector produced more than one-fourth of the Soviet agricultural output (Central Intelligence Agency, 2018) and remains one of the leading global producers of grain, sunflower seeds, and other agricultural commodities. Most of its agricultural output is exported to the neighboring states, (among which Russia remains the largest market), the Middle East, and Asia. Ukraine's industrial outputs include a well-diversified, machine building industry, specializing in heavy machinery, unique manufacturing equipment, drilling equipment, drilling and transport pipes for oil and gas, railroad wagons and machinery, transport industry equipment, petrochemicals, and nitro fertilizers. In comparison, the USSR, who has a centrally planned economy, most assets and investments were government-owned. Since the beginning of the 1990s, most of the specialized industrial producers were hastily privatized through the "fire sale" of these public assets. As a result, most of Ukraine's manufacturing capacities have been fully depreciated or decommissioned. The new "private owners" sold many of the functioning factories off for scrap metal; Ukraine still exports scrap metal to Western Europe. Despite losing most of its industrial capacity, Ukraine remains one of the leading global steel and pipe producers. Just like in most post-Soviet republics, the oligarchs fully control the state's economy.

In foreign trade, due to oil and gas dependency and its old Soviet trade connections, Russia remains Ukraine's largest trading partner. In 2016, 9.9 percent of Ukraine's exports went to Russia (mostly oil and gas pipes and agricultural products) and 13.1 percent of Ukraine's imports came from Russia (mostly energy: oil and gas). Its other significant export markets are Egypt (6.2 percent), Poland (6.1 percent), Turkey (5.7 percent), Italy (5.3 percent), India (5.2 percent), and China (5.1 percent). Ukraine's imports come from China (12 percent), Germany (11 percent), Belarus (7.1 percent), Poland (6.9 percent), and the United States (4.3 percent) (Central Intelligence Agency, 2018). Ukraine is also a large exporter of skilled and unskilled labor. In 2017, two million Ukrainians worked in Poland, and many more remain gainfully employed in other industrialized countries (Economist, 2017; Milakovsky, 2017; Vlasiuk, 2017).

In 2000-2007, Ukraine experienced a level of relative prosperity and economic growth attracting some private-sector capital investments through foreign and domestic long-term bank loans, bonds, and private equity issues. However, the global financial crisis drained the availability of any private, long-term financing, and since 2010, Ukraine has been relying solely on government funds to fund its capital investment projects. Table 1 demonstrates how following the global financial crisis, Ukraine has never fully recovered. Its per-capita GDP declined from over 4 thousand USD per capita in 2012 to a little over 2 thousand USD per capita in 2016. While the local-currency GDP has nominally increased, in US dollars it has significantly diminished.

In 2014, the Revolution of Dignity resulted in forceful removal of the pro-Russian President (Victor Yanukovych) that has triggered Russian military intervention in Ukraine, the annexation of Crimea, and a partial occupation of the two Eastern provinces (Economist, 2015; Economist, 2017a; Economist 2017b). As a result of active fighting in these two primarily industrial, export-oriented regions, the industrial manufacturing processes in Eastern Ukraine have been disrupted; shipments and trade came to a standstill thereby leading to an economic meltdown. Because industrial producers in these regions were highly leveraged by Western bank loans, this has also triggered a banking system collapse and two-digit inflation (Economist, 2015; World Bank, 2017).

Although Ukraine's natural resources boast formidable arable lands, mild climate, and a highly skilled labor force, the country has fallen behind its nearest neighbors and the EU-member states in PPP-adjusted per-capita GDP formation since the 1990s. Figure 1 illustrates these trends.

Table 1. Ukraine's economic indicators, 2012-2020

	2012	2013	2014	2015	2016	2017p	2018p	2019*	2020*
Nominal GDP, UAH million	1,405	1,465	1,587	1,980	2,383	2,832	3,195	3,572	3,975
GDP per capita, USD	4,080	4,216	3,119	2,122	2,174	2,358	2,552	2,834	3,132
GDP deflator, percent change	8.1	3.1	14.8	38.4	17.1	16.5	9	7.5	7
Budget Expenditures, percent of GDP	48.9	48.4	44.8	43.2	40.6	44	44.6	43.8	43.4
Capital Expenditures, percent of GDP	2.9	2	1.3	2.2	3.1	3.8	3.8	3.8	4
Public and Guaranteed Debt, percent of GDP	36.6	40.6	70.3	79.4	81.2	85.2	85.1	78.9	73.4

Source: World Bank, 2017.

Figure 1. Ukraine and its neighbors: per capita GDP at purchasing-power parity (in constant 2011 USD), 1990-2015
Source: World Bank, 2017.

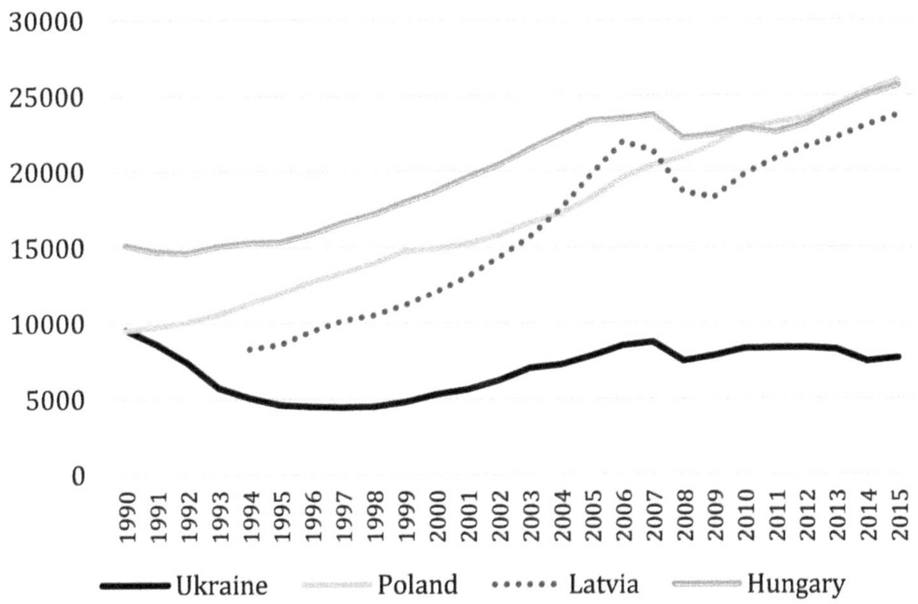

During the last two decades, Ukraine became the poorest country in Europe on GDP per-capita basis (World Bank, 2017). According to the United Nations Development Project representative in Ukraine, in 2017, at least 60 percent of Ukrainians live below the poverty line, and some 1.7 million persons have been internally displaced from its war-torn Eastern regions (Ukrainian News and Information Agency, 2017).

Structure of Government

A unitary state, Ukraine is a semi-presidential republic that consists of 24 provinces (plural – oblasti, singular – oblast'), one Autonomous Republic of Crimea (ARC), and two special municipalities with oblast' status – the city of Kyiv, Ukraine's capital, and the city of Simferopol, the capital of the ARC. Each oblast is governed out of its largest city, a namesake administrative center, (e.g. the city of Lviv is the administrative center of Lvivska oblast; the city of Donetsk is the administrative center of Donetsk oblast, etc.). Within each oblast and each city are smaller districts (plural – rayons, singular – rayon). These are Ukraine's smallest administrative divisions.

Ukraine's chief legislative document is its Constitution. Most recently adopted in 1996 (the first Ukrainian constitution of the Kossack state was adopted by Pylyp Orylk in 1710), it has been amended several times in 2004, 2010, and 2015. The President and the Parliament (Verkhovna Rada or Supreme Council) can both propose Constitutional amendments for Parliamentary consideration; these then must be approved by the Parliament and by a general public referendum. Constitutional articles on individual rights and freedoms, national independence, and territorial integrity cannot be amended (Central Intelligence Agency, 2018).

The country's three branches of government are as follows.

Legislative branch - The highest legislative body is unicameral Verkhovna Rada (the Supreme Council or the Parliament). It consists of 450 seats of which 225 members are directly elected by a simple majority vote and 225 by proportional representation vote. The members of parliament serve 5-year terms (Constitution of Ukraine, 1996). Like most European states, Ukraine uses the civil law system consisting of a judicial review of legislative and sub-legislative acts.

Executive branch - The President is the Chief of State. The Prime Minister, appointed by the President and approved by the Parliament, is the head of the Cabinet of Ministers. The President is elected for a 5-year term by a simple majority vote and is confirmed by the Parliament. Like in most European countries, the President can serve up to 2 terms. Reporting to the Prime Minister are the line Ministers, who govern public agencies in each sector of the economy (e.g. Ministry of Agriculture, Ministry of Foreign Affairs, Ministry of Economic Development and Trade, etc.) (Constitution of Ukraine, 1996).

Judicial branch - The Supreme Court is the highest judicial body consisting of civil, criminal, commercial, and administrative law chambers. Proposed by the Supreme Council of Justice and appointed by the President, its 95 judges serve 5-year terms with up to a 65-year age limit. The Constitutional Court justices are proportionally appointed by the President (6 judges), by the Supreme Council of Justice (6 judges) and by the Parliament (6 judges) and serve non-renewable 9-year terms. Subordinate courts include specialized high courts, Court of Cassation, Courts of Appeal, regional, district, city, town, and rayon courts (Constitution of Ukraine, 1996).

Not prescribed by the Constitution, an artifact of the former Communist party structure network, is the Administration of the President. Actively involved in Ukraine's governance and the system of public finances, the Presidential Administration consists of an impressive central office with its departments duplicating every line Ministry, and its 25 regional offices posted in every oblast of Ukraine.

PUBLIC CAPITAL EXPENDITURES IN UKRAINE

Public sector reforms are essential to Ukraine's transition to a free market system. These critical transformations initiated in the early 1990s to liberalize trade, and since then, much has been accomplished in the budgetary and legislative system. However, in the area of public capital expenditures, there is still much to be done. The structural reforms regarding public capital investment projects have been slow and are still far from the full market transition.

What Are Public Capital Expenditures? Some Definitions

In order to describe and discuss the normative, public capital budgeting process in Ukraine, it is important to delineate which public capital investments and expenditures shall be included in this chapter. In Ukraine, public capital expenditures include all expenditures financed by central and local governments, as well as foreign-funded capital investments channeled through the central government budget. Government-funded capital expenditures shall include direct capital transfers to state-owned (or state-controlled) companies. Investments that these state-owned companies make from their "own" funds, however, are not considered public capital expenditures. These definitions follow expenditure classifications of the Ukrainian Ministry of Statistics and are described in greater detail by the World Bank (1997).

Capital investment projects encompass a plethora of public investment program definitions including capital expenditures, investment projects, national projects, state investment programs, and construction projects. According to the World Bank, these definitions create an environment in which most projects are titled in a way so that they avoid a formal consideration, appraisal, and assessment process ("construction projects") (World Bank, 2013).

Government-funded capital expenditures typically include all construction, capital repairs, and maintenance works. Rehabilitation and renovation costs are aggregated with all other capital expenses. For legislative review and approval, the budget proposals aggregate all of the capital investments. Public capital expenditures are also presented by sector and sometimes even by program and are recorded in budget implementation reports as such (World Bank, 1997; Verner, 2017). Government budgets do not include any international donor funds spent on capital projects outside of centrally budgeted allocations.

Public or Private?

In Ukraine, because of the former command-and-control system of central planning, the distinction between the "public" and "private" sectors has been rather blurred. For example, many traditionally private sectors in the developed countries (e.g. energy, communications, and higher education) are mostly public in Ukraine. Therefore, it is appropriate to assume that the country's public expenditure categories include not only mostly public sector capital expenditures but also many of the mostly private-sector capital investments. For example, these include direct capital spending on agricultural equipment, telecoms, nitro fertilizer production, and airports.

Transitioning away from a centrally planned economy in 1997-2018, Ukraine has privatized many of its key industries. During that time, the list of government-owned and government-run industries has been greatly reduced as Table 2 demonstrates. Table 2 also includes an "aspirational sectoral view" on Ukraine's public capital investment strategy by the World Bank prepared early on in 1997 (World Bank, 1997). With that in mind, this section will present the scope and the trends in Ukraine's public capital investments.

Key Agencies Involved in Project Selection and Approval Process

Before reviewing the process of selection and approval of a public capital expenditure project, listed are the key public agencies involved in the decision-making. The following section then presents project selection and the approval process. Table 3 summarizes the roles of key public institutions engaged in public capital investment process within the central government.

Public Capital Expenditures: Budget Process

In this section, the chapter describes the budgeting process for capital expenditures and raises some questions and concerns about the later stages of the budget cycle. According to international experts, Ukraine's budget reforms in the area of public capital expenditures has been slow, fragmented, and somewhat focused on inputs and technical characteristics of the project (World Bank, 1997; World Bank, 2013). In their view, Ukraine has demonstrated no evidence or political will to reform its public capital expenditure review and approval process. Among the obstacles to a successful reform is the absence of a single strategy or a framework for effectively budgeting for public capital expenditures. A plethora of legal definitions for public capital projects sends project applicants down different budgetary paths. By

Table 2. Ukraine's public and private capital investments: sectoral divisions

	Former Public/Private Sector Mix (1997)	Current Public/Private Sector Mix (2018)	Aspirational Public/Private Sector Mix
All Public	Defense Law and Order Education Health Environmental Protection Power (generation, transmission, distribution) District heating Water and sewage Transport infrastructure (roads, rail, ports, airports, subway) Transport services (roads, rail, ports, airports, subway) Telecommunications (except cellular phones) Coal mining Other mining	Defense Law and Order Environmental Protection	Defense Law and Order Education Health (basic public health; preventive care) Environmental Protection Power (transmission)
Public/Private (Mostly Public)	Housing Banking, Insurance Manufacturing Construction Agriculture Agro-industry Irrigation (networks, on-farm) Trucking Urban bus transport Cellular phone telecommunications	Education Health Transport services (roads, rail, ports, airports, subway) Agriculture (no private land ownership; large farms leased from the state for up to 50 years) Irrigation (networks, on-farm) Coal mining District heating Water and sewage	Power (generation, transmission, distribution) District heating Water and sewage Transport infrastructure (roads, rail, ports, airports, subway) Telecommunications (except cellular phones)
Public/Private (Mostly Public)	Commerce (retail and wholesale)	Power (generation, transmission) Transport infrastructure (roads, rail, ports, airports, subway) Telecommunications (except cellular phones) Housing Urban bus transport Banking, Insurance Manufacturing Construction Other mining	Health (tertiary, curative care) Agricultural infrastructure (market information, restructuring standards, etc.) Transport services (air, airports, rail, subway) Coal mining Housing Banking, insurance
All Private		Agro-industry Trucking Cellular phone telecommunications Commerce (retail and wholesale)	Agriculture Agriculture industry On-farm irrigation Transport services (road, ports) Trucking Cellular telecom Urban bus transport Manufacturing Construction Other mining Commerce (including retail)

Source: adapted from the World Bank, 1997.

Table 3. Central government agencies role regarding public investment projects

Government Agency	Role	Comments
Line Ministries (16) and other Central Government Agencies (53)	• To conceive and prepare projects that directly affect their central functions and implement those that receive funding. • To receive and administer capital requests from agencies and other entities under their control. • Design and implement centrally financed projects including budgeting and contracting.	Excludes state-owned enterprises and sub-national governments
Ministry of Economic Development and Trade (MEDT)	• Policy development degrading PIM • Prepare and review economic appraisals for State Investment Programs • Development and maintenance of a projects database for State Investment Program • Procurement regulatory function	Some (but in limited capacity) capability in project appraisal
Ministry of Finance	• Direct negotiations with many public entities regarding project funding • Project selection • Budget allocations	
Accounting Chamber	The supreme audit institution responsible to Parliament (an equivalent of the CBO in the United States)	Some limited performance audit attempts
Anti-Monopoly Commission	To receive and administer complaints about public procurement procedures	
State Financial Inspection	Compliance audit: controls financial and administrative norms	Under the Ministry of Finance

Source: World Bank, 2013.

prioritizing politically desirable projects, the current capital expenditure process conveniently exploits the country's system of public finances.

As Figure 2 presents, during the project selection and approval stages the applicants can take several paths: engaging several budget agencies and Ministries described above, the budgeting process involves these six steps. First, public agencies (including state-owned enterprises) prepare input driven project requests. In these requests, capital construction cost estimates should conform to the existing input cost norms and standards. Requests can be titled as "public investment projects" (10 percent of the total projects) or "public construction" projects (90 percent of the total projects) (World Bank, 2013). Second, the relevant line Ministries consider feasibility of proposed capital projects: they prepare the projects' technical reviews. At this stage, the projects receive no cost-benefit analysis or economic justification.

Next, proposals entitled "public investment projects" (10 percent of total proposals) are sent to the Ministry of Economic Development and Trade (MEDT), which prepares their economic justification. That process is procedurally focused and relatively quick. The projects are then placed in the MEDT's database. Alternatively, proposals titled "construction projects" are sent directly to the Ministry of Finance via a shortcut (see Figure 2 below). The rationale for using the shortcut is to get ahead of all other projects in the queue by sending the proposal for review and approval by the Ministry of Finance. That both saves time and increases the likelihood that the proposed capital investment project will ever be approved and funded.

Following the review, all public investment projects, whether the MEDT approves them or not, arrive at the Ministry of Finance to compete for the minuscule amount of available funds (World Bank, 2013). At this stage, politically motivated proposals surface to the top of the list. The Ministry of Finance then

Figure 2. Public investment project selection in Ukraine: Use a shortcut!
Source: World Bank, 2013.

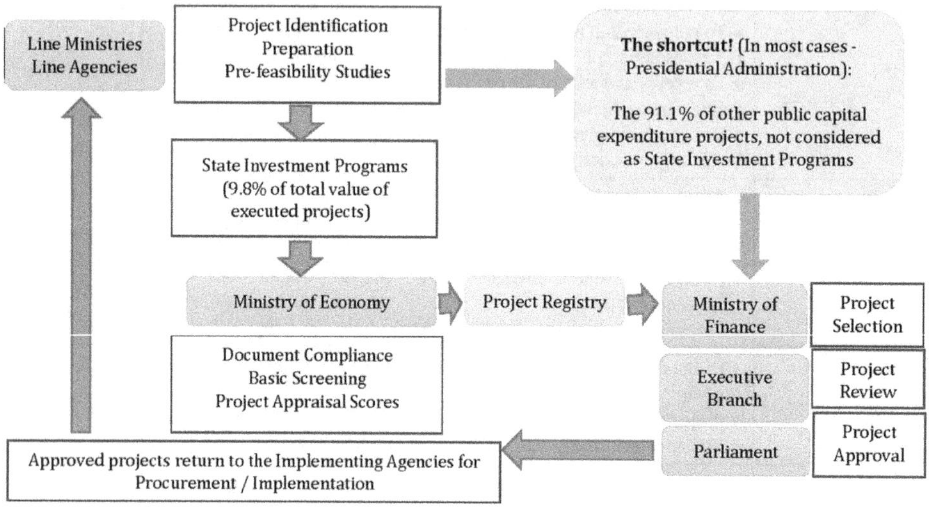

presents capital expenditure projects for legislative approval at the Verkhovna Rada (Supreme Council or the Parliament). Upon approval, public capital investment projects return to the requesting agencies for implementation within the allocated budget authority lines. At this stage, any changes to the allocation lines must be re-approved by the Ministry of Finance and by the Parliament. And finally, while a traditional budget cycle concludes with a public audit and evaluation stage, this is not the case in Ukraine. Whereas the budget laws require the Accounting Chamber to conduct audit and evaluation of each project (Kraan, 2012), de facto this stage of the public budgeting process is being largely ignored (World Bank, 2013). According to that World Bank study (2013), Ukraine's internal audit system does not function effectively. The institutions established to conduct these checks, including the Accounting Chamber, the Anti-Monopoly Committee, and the State Financial Inspection have limited recourse on public capital investment projects. Once executed, these projects are never assessed for performance, economic sensibility, or effectiveness. Those few projects that do receive government funding are implemented at a relatively slow pace: their completion rates varied between 60 and 70 percent completion rate between 2009 and 2011 (World Bank, 2013).

To that end, a holistic review of the scale and scope of public capital spending in Ukraine remains a truly formidable endeavor. Impeding the process are varied, conflicting definitions of what constitutes a public capital investment project, several possible avenues of project consideration and approval, and a lack of accountability and audit after the project completion. The absence of an effective performance management review breaks down the budget cycle and prevents the public from effectively evaluating the efficiency and effectiveness of public capital investments. This interrupts Ukraine's public capital budgeting process.

Key Industries and Trends

Although transition economies are likely to demonstrate temporary declines in capital spending, Ukraine's capital public expenditure cuts have been particularly striking (World Bank, 1997). For example, Figure

1 illustrates that in 1991, Ukraine, Poland, and Latvia embarked upon the free markets' transition at about the same level of per capita GDP. Then, their paths have markedly diverged since. As the country transitioned away from the centrally planned economy, it lost a substantial share of its public capital investments in the 1990s. For example, the share of public capital investment declined from 4.6 percent of the GDP in 1994 to 1.4 percent of the GDP in 1996 and to 0.27 percent in 1997 (World Bank, 1997). This was followed by a moderate increase to 2 percent of the GDP in 2013, and then to 3.1 in 2016 (World Bank, 2017).

Because of these cuts, Ukraine's extensive public infrastructure has fallen into disrepair and now requires substantial maintenance, rehabilitation, and replacement funding. Considering the already constrained fiscal space to cover operating expenses, the need for more funding towards social assistance programs, and the financial challenges of the ongoing war with Russia, public capital investments are not a priority. Ukraine's capital construction projects remain unfinished and under-funded as public moneys are being spent on other high-priority programs. Moreover, political favoritism continues to delay many strategic infrastructure projects.

Regional Distribution of Funding

Among Ukraine's regions, the city of Kyiv, Ukraine's capital, and its namesake province receive the bulk of public capital funding. Forty percent of the total public capital expenditures went to Kyiv and Kyiv oblast in 2016 (Verner, 2017). Among other significant regions are Ukraine's key industrial and defense industry centers - Dnipro, Donetsk, and Kharkiv. Table 4 presents the regional distribution of Ukraine's public capital expenditures between 2010 and 2016. An attentive reader will observe Ukraine's concentration of public capital investment in large industrial centers featuring large populations and strategic industrial bases. The less- industrialized and mostly agricultural regions receive little state capital investments. Table 4 also shows that the relative allocations of public capital investment funds have not markedly changed over time.

Note that upon the Russian occupation of Ukraine's two industrially significant Eastern regions in 2014, public capital investments into the occupied sections of Eastern provinces of Donetsk and Luhansk have stopped[1]. As of the date of the chapter completion, the military conflict in these two industrial centers continues. Ukraine's State Statistical Service reports reflect these data (Verner, 2017)

Sectoral Allocations

Whereas in market economies most of the capital investment funding comes from private investors, in Ukraine, private long-term investments are rare. In Ukraine, the three largest sectors receiving public funds for capital investment projects are the manufacturing sector (or the industrial production sector), the agricultural sector, and the capital construction sector. Combined, these three receive nearly 60 percent of all state capital investment funds as Table 5 lists (Verner, 2017). In what follows, the chapter will describe each of these three largest sectors in more detail.

Agriculture

Ukraine's agricultural sector received 14 percent of all the central government's public capital spending in 2016 (Verner, 2017). Although the share of total capital investments into agriculture has declined from

Table 4. Regional distribution of public capital expenditures, million UAH[2]

	2010	2011	2012	2013	2014	2015	2016
Ukraine Total	181	241	273	250	219	273	359
Cherkaska oblast	3	3	4	3	3	4	6
Chernihivska oblast	2	2	3	3	3	4	5
Chernivetska oblast	2	2	2	2	2	3	3
Dnipropetrovsk oblast	16	22	23	21	20	26	33
Donetsk oblast	15	27	32	28	13	8	12
Ivano-Frankivska oblast	4	4	5	5	7	10	8
Kharkivska oblast	8	13	15	9	8	11	17
Khersonska oblast	2	3	2	2	2	3	5
Khmelnytska oblast	3	4	3	4	4	7	9
Kirovohrad oblast	2	4	5	3	3	4	6
Kyiv City	54	71	80	70	68	88	106
Kyiv oblast	11	18	20	21	20	24	33
Luhansk oblast	6	7	8	11	5	2	4
Lviv oblast	9	12	11	10	10	13	19
Mykolaiv oblast	4	4	5	5	4	6	10
Odesa oblast	10	9	15	12	9	10	17
Poltavska oblast	6	8	10	10	9	8	15

Source: Verner, 2017

Table 5. Sectoral allocations of public capital expenditures in 2010-2016, percent

	2010	2011	2012	2013	2014	2015	2016
Agriculture	6%	7%	7%	7%	8%	11%	14%
Manufacturing	31%	33%	34%	39%	39%	32%	33%
Construction	16%	13%	15%	16%	16%	16%	12%
Automotive industry	10%	10%	9%	9%	9%	8%	8%
Transportation and logistics	11%	11%	12%	7%	7%	7%	7%
Telecoms	5%	4%	4%	4%	4%	8%	4%
Finance and insurance	3%	2%	3%	3%	3%	2%	2%
Real estate	5%	6%	5%	5%	5%	4%	5%
Professional, scientific and technical occupations	3%	4%	3%	1%	1%	1%	2%
General administration	2%	2%	2%	2%	2%	2%	3%
Public administration, defense, and social insurance	4%	5%	4%	3%	3%	5%	6%
Education	1%	1%	1%	0%	0%	1%	1%
Healthcare	1%	1%	1%	1%	1%	1%	1%
Art, sports and recreation	1%	1%	1%	1%	0%	0%	0%
Other	1%	1%	1%	1%	1%	1%	1%

Source: Verner, 2017

22 percent in 1995 (World Bank, 1997) to 6 to 14 percent in 2010-2016 (Verner, 2017), the agricultural sector remains one of the largest recipients of the public funds. In that, food processing receives nearly ¾ of total capital financing, and less than ¼ of total funding goes to water resource management, including rural water supply, drainage, and irrigation. A small percentage of funding goes to land resource management, research, and education, as well as social infrastructure investments such as housing, healthcare, education, and community services in rural areas.

As of 2018, all agricultural lands in Ukraine remain in state ownership. The state land ownership, combined with special political interests, commands a significant portion of public finds that could otherwise be replaced by the private financing. The private financing, however, is limited due to the lack of land ownership rights, and the public debate about the legal status of agricultural land continues as I describe below in detail.

Considering Ukraine's mild climate and vast fertile agricultural farms, the country's agricultural land assets remain very attractive to privatization by foreign and domestic investors. If privatized, Ukraine's public capital investments would no longer be required to support mainstream agribusiness and food processing and could be scaled back to fund land and water resource management, research, and social infrastructure investments. However, privatization of land is not on the agenda. A vast European agricultural country, Ukraine still does not allow private ownership of agricultural land. According to the country's Land Code, agricultural land is considered a national treasure placed under a special protectorate of the state (Land Code of Ukraine, 2002). In the absence of private ownership, the farmers can only lease land from the state through revocable long-term and short-term lease agreements.

Because Ukraine's agricultural lands cannot be privately owned, the country's agricultural sector has failed to attract any private capital infrastructure investments. Lacking protections and assurances with regards to ownership rights to these capital investments, agricultural producers and investors maintain a short term planning horizon (e.g. producers receive short-term credit lines for seeds and fertilizer purchases but no long-term capital investment loans). In these circumstances, direct public subsidies to large local farmers (most frequently, the oligarchs - the lessees of the land on favorable terms) replace private capital investments at the expense of the state budget. Because Ukraine's agricultural products are exported at world market prices, directly benefitting these large agricultural producers, Ukraine's agricultural sector is neither private nor public. Significant farming subsidies flow to private, highly profitable, non-taxable large operators.

Conveniently, Ukraine's land-users[3] (the oligarchs) remain the members of Parliament. They steadfastly lobby for agricultural subsidies because of the importance of farming as a sector of the economy. This populist rhetoric resonates with the voters well; they demonstrate support for national land ownership and support "small, local" farming. The country's issue of land ownership is especially salient because of the aggressive Soviet (1930s) and then German (1940s) highly extractive agricultural policies before and during World War II in Ukraine. Because of these influences, the electorate does not like foreign investors. They are associated with the "invaders", "Nazis", and "exploiters" of rural peoples. Although the land reform, if managed well, could bring a lot of wealth and prosperity, it is not on the public agenda because of these special interests. Because of the special interests and populist rhetoric, Ukraine's land reform remains a formidable task.

Whether Ukraine is able to attract private capital investments into its agribusiness or not, it would be reasonable to continue some public capital investments to support Ukraine's agricultural development. For example, 1) the government should continue to support the agriculture with agro market information systems, grading and health standards for food and agricultural products, 2) the government should continue to provide training and management support programs to farmers, 3) agricultural research and development must be continuously publicly funded through a public system of agricultural colleges and universities, and 4) the government must ensure the public provision for property ownership rights registration, land surveys, financing programs, and the physical and social infrastructure in rural areas.

Manufacturing (Industrial Production)

Manufacturing or industrial production industry, is the largest recipient of Ukraine's public capital investment funds. Between 2010 and 2016, the receipts varied between 31 and 39 percent of the total capital spending (Table 5). Public capital investments flow to the manufacturing sector through these two channels: a) direct receipts from the state budget to state-owned enterprises and b) budgetary credits (government loans), and grants. The central government provides all of these funds.

Nearly two thirds of all public capital is invested into heavy machinery industry and construction. The industry includes metals and mining, natural resource exploration, chemicals and fertilizers, machine building, iron and steel production, construction works, and others. Less than one third of the total capital spending in manufacturing industry supports a limited number of finished consumer goods. Within this sector, Ukraine's largest capital investment projects include:

1. Chornobyl nuclear reactor confinement project. The Government of Ukraine fully funded the concrete nuclear sarcophagus to bury the remnants of the Chernobyl nuclear plant's reactor explosion, A new nuclear reactor confinement is now expected: at a projected cost of EUR 1.5 billion, the project will cover the heavily contaminated site and will be financed by the European Bank of Reconstruction and Development's loan (European Bank of Reconstruction and Development, 2018);
2. Generation and transportation of electric energy including capital upgrades and the new construction;
3. Energy-saving investments;
4. Investments into the oil and gas transportation company Naftogaz, and
5. Other capital investments into various state-owned enterprises including projects on energy savings, competitiveness, and innovation at these state-owned production facilities. Without a doubt, many of these publicly financed enterprises could also use private financing if the appropriate long-term private funding had been available to them on favorable terms.

Housing

Part of the construction industry, public housing and lodging received between 12 and 16 percent of total capital investment expenditures in 2010 and 2016 respectively (Table 5). Most of the public housing projects in Ukraine take a very long time to complete or remain unfinished. The World Bank experts note that despite considerably lower labor costs, the cost of public housing construction is 25-30 percent higher in Ukraine than in Germany (World Bank, 2013) thereby pointing to red tape, inflated cost schedules, and a widespread corruption in government agencies and state and private contractors. A significant share of the public funds dedicated to housing comes from the Chernobyl fund aimed at providing state housing to the Chernobyl nuclear disaster liquidators, victims, and displaced persons.

Of the total capital construction, one quarter of overall spending provides for residential housing, another quarter for non-residential uses (institutional construction such as schools, hospitals, etc.), and about one half for the engineering constructions (e.g. industrial buildings) (Verner, 2017). Within the residential housing, most of the new construction houses public sector workers, socially vulnerable populations, and the employees of state-owned enterprises. Because of high profitability of residential housing construction in the mid-2000s, municipal and private building companies quickly filled in the unmet housing demand in Ukraine. However, because the mortgage industry is in its infancy and inability to finance the mortgages on a large scale, private capital investments into housing remain rather low. After the Great Recession in 2009, private capital financing dried up, and Ukraine's housing sector growth has scaled back considerably.

Several important obstacles prevent private sector construction from a more rapid development. Firstly, building permitting and property collateralization is subject to red tape and corruption. Secondly, the registration process of ownership rights to dwellings and land parcels in cities remains a problem. Third, the legal gridlocks in contract enforcement of rent, mortgage, and utility nonpayers prevent tenant and mortgage evictions. Nonpayers cannot be evicted if a residence includes any minors, residents with disabilities, veterans, and other vulnerable individuals protected by law. That sector is currently under reform.

Because of the above issues in the private housing market, it is likely that the public capital construction programs in housing will remain. It is notable that in Ukraine public housing assignments frequently depend on the occupational, veteran, or family status of the recipient. The public housing programs are not only designed to serve the poor but also to support other residents, community members, and public servants.

CONTROVERSIES AND PROBLEMS

In Western experts' opinions, Ukraine does not appear to have a firm grasp on its public capital growth and development strategy (World Bank, 1997; World Bank, 2013). The analysis of Ukraine's public capital expenditures discovers several controversies and problems in public capital investments. Firstly, considerably less funding is dedicated to public capital investments than during the Soviet rule. Following de-industrialization in the 1990s and shifting from command-and-control economy to a transitional market economy, coupled with significant GDP contraction, Ukraine has significantly limited its fiscal space. Therefore, constrained by low fiscal capacity or the inability to raise and collect additional taxes, the public capital investment funds available have been scarce. Secondly, like many developing economies, Ukraine prioritizes operating government spending over strategic investments. As short-term "band-aid" solutions crowd out strategic investment programs, this results in a fierce competition for already limited funds. Thirdly, the country has also been unable to replace its public capital financing with any significant amount of private investments. Private, long-term bank loans are unavailable because they have dried out after the Global Financial Crisis. Finally, a glut of project submissions and red tape do not effectively address the strategic public capital needs of Ukraine. Many capital projects remain "legacy investments" and do not contribute to the economy and the current priorities of Ukraine. Each fiscal year, public agencies re-submit previously unfunded "frozen" capital proposals to their respective Ministries waiting for funding for their completion. These unfinished projects are in the way of current investment decisions, overcrowd the project investment pipeline, and dilute the scarce public funds available for capital investment.

Central to public capital expenditure reform are several problems. The first problem concerns lingering projects. Ukraine's legacy of unfinished and underfunded projects impedes successful project implementation and assessment. Based on the World Bank's data in 1997, there were 60,000 unfinished capital investment projects, 40,000 in the manufacturing sector and 20,000 in social investment proposals. A quarter of these projects took more than 10 years to complete and 29 of these projects were initiated in the 1970s and 1980s (World Bank, 1997). A more recent World Bank public review notes that while project execution rates have been improving, they remain low (World Bank, 2013).

Lack of strategic planning is the second problem. A team of World Bank experts remarks that there is little in the way of policy based explanation of the need for a project, whether a proposed project might be the best solution for meeting the need of the public or whether there is even a need in the first place (World Bank, 2013). The screenings done by the line Ministries are superficial and compliance focused, strategic investment planning is almost non-existent in public capital investment programs, and public agencies reapply for the limited project funding year after year creating a glut of public sector capital investment proposals. Input based, procedural budgeting is the main focus as opposed to performance-based budgeting (World Bank, 2013).

SOLUTIONS AND RECOMMENDATIONS

To resolve the above concerns, the chapter proposes several short-term to medium-term action steps: (1) it is recommended that the funded agencies finish the existing funded projects and cancel the others. If possible, these cancelled projects could be proposed to private investors once the market conditions are favorable; (2) the new capital financing projects ought to refrain from any new investments into the seemingly-private industries such as agribusiness, industrial manufacturing and construction. Instead, the investments should flow into mostly-public industries; (3) the Ministry of Finance must sharpen its focus on high-priority areas, depending on the country's long-term strategy, and direct other capital proposals to the private sector for financing when that becomes available; (4) from a procedural standpoint of view, new proposals must receive economic justification early on in the project development stage, which can then be reviewed during the project completion and implementation; (5) the project performance review, audit and project evaluation remain the weak links that must be reinforced; (6) Ukraine must make progress towards improving the climate for private-sector investments.

According to World Bank experts (1997; 2013), there has been no lack of interest in private sector investment. But numerous obstacles are in the way to a successful private capital investment campaign. Among the entry barriers are confusing legal framework, non-transparent taxation that is applied in non-equitable ways, bureaucratic hurdles, a nonfunctioning judicial system, corruption, crime, and price distortions. Undoubtedly, it is hard to attract long-term investors in the middle of the war with Russia, but small steps done today to secure the rule of law, investor's rights, and sector transparency may serve Ukrainians well once the war is over.

FUTURE RESEARCH DIRECTIONS

The research this chapter presents could proceed in several interesting directions. One way of exploring Ukraine's public capital budgeting process would be to look at the performance, audit, and evaluation stages of budgeting and compare the normative setting that the legislative documents provide to the *status quo*. A qualitative study could reconnect the existing normative framework with government action plans and the missing link in the budget process. Another study could examine the largest public capital works-in-progress. For example, an examination of the Troyeshchyna bridge project in the city of Kyiv could be interesting, considering the length of time this project has already been underway as well as the fact that there is no completion date in sight, and then explore mitigation strategies to reduce the project backlog. A third direction this research could take is to explore the connections between strategic, long-term goals of the key government agencies and goal implementation strategies in public capital investment projects. All of these research avenues will require using in-depth qualitative survey methods and a more granular data collection.

CONCLUSION

Having gained its independence in 1991, Ukraine experienced a major disruption of trade connections and business activity resulting in a series of significant macroeconomic shocks and hyperinflation. Since then, the country transitioned into a new market-based economy. It elected the President and the Parliament, adopted the Constitution, and assisted by Western advisors, established the basic public budgeting and finance framework. However many of Ukraine's well-intended privatization reforms have resulted in unintended consequences and have resulted in considerable backtracking and economic stagnation. As a result, Ukraine's per capita GDP, industrial output, population growth, life expectancy, and health conditions have markedly declined since the 1990s.

The country's massive aging infrastructure needs command extensive funding for capital asset maintenance and renovations. In the next decade, an estimated 10 billion dollars of public capital spending will be required to maintain the infrastructure needs at their current level (World Bank, 2013). That is a huge sum for a relatively small emerging markets country. However, these needs are overshadowed by other national spending priorities that include social support, healthcare, education, and, most recently, defense. Therefore, the country's public capital expenditures have been relatively low at 3.1 and 3.6 percent of the GDP at the state and local level in 2007 and 2.2 and 1.2 percent of the GDP in 2016 respectively (Verner, 2017) and considering the limited private infrastructure investments opportunities, the country has had limited opportunities to attract private capital infrastructure financing.

In these circumstances, the Ukrainian government must be especially mindful of their capital spending priorities. It ought to mindfully focus on Ukraine's strategic objectives and carefully follow through the timely completion of every government-financed capital project. As a glut of investment proposals overcrowds the Ministry of Economic Development and Trade's project roster, the Ministry of Finance can only fund a small percentage of what is being proposed. As a result, many public capital investment projects remain underfunded and unfinished. Currently, Ukraine's Western advisors remark that there is a lack of strategy and political will to reform the budget process for public capital investments (World Bank, 1997; World Bank, 2013).

This chapter reviews the key elements of Ukraine's public capital budgeting process including agency overview, sectoral development, and geographic distribution of public capital investments. Provided are the definitions, trends, key agencies, and industries receiving public capital investment funds. The chapter describes the capital project selection and approval process with some level of detail and then points to the strategic and procedural issues, which in the opinion of Western experts, prevents Ukraine from successful, focused development and renewal of public capital infrastructure.

Within the public capital budgeting, several areas call for immediate attention. First, streamlining the selection, approval, and implementation process for public investment projects and clarifying which projects are prioritized in receiving government funding will help Ukraine realign its capital spending with the long-term strategic objectives. Currently, a long project waitlist suggests Ukraine's government does not prioritize its capital spending because it lacks a coherent long-term development strategy. A laundry list of unfinished projects remains, and the government agencies soliciting funding continue expanding it. That behavior must be interrupted, and the line ministries must start focusing on a small list of high priority capital spending projects that can be completed. Secondly, the economic justification and cost-benefit analysis of each public capital project must be established. That may help to eliminate conflicting and obsolete proposals in order to strategically prioritize capital spending. Thirdly, some of the government financing continues to flow to mostly private sectors of the economy including agriculture, industrial production, and housing projects whereas the critical needs of the public sector projects remain unfunded. That practice ought to be revisited. Finally, strengthening the closing loop of the budget cycle could help eliminate waste and abuse within the system of public capital investments. The implemented public capital projects must receive budget performance assessment, a reasonably independent audit, and a program evaluation review. This would ensure accountability and compliance in capital investments funded by the public.

ACKNOWLEDGMENT

This research received no specific grant from any funding agency in the public, commercial, or not-for-profit sectors.

REFERENCES

Central Intelligence Agency. (2018). *The world factbook: Ukraine.* Retrieved March 20, 2018, from https://www.cia.gov/library/publications/the-world-factbook/geos/up.html

Dodonov, B., Christian, H., Petra, O., & Sugolov, P. (2002). Efficient infrastructure supply for economic development – the case of Ukraine. *Post-Communist Economies, 14*(2), 149–167. doi:10.1080/14631370220139909

Duenvald, C., Georguiev, N., & Schaechter, A. (2005). *Too much of a good thing? Credit booms in transition economies: The cases of Bulgaria, Romania, and Ukraine.* IMG Working Paper.

Economist. (2003). *Inflation in post-Communist Europe: Whipped.* London, UK: Economist print edition.

Economist. (2015a). *Crisis in Ukraine.* London, UK: Economist print edition.

Economist. (2015b). *War-torn reform. Ukraine's government is making some progress. But much more needs to be done.* London, UK: Economist print edition.

Economist. (2017a). *Plugging the gap. Ukrainian immigrants are powering Poland's economy. Now poles worry that Visa-free travel may lure them to the rest of the EU*. London, UK: Economist print edition.

Economist. (2017b). *Ukraine and Russia are both trapped by the war in Donbas*. London, UK: Economist print edition.

Economist. (2017c). *Ukraine is a mess; The West should press it harder to fight graft*. London, UK: Economist print edition.

Encyclopedia Britannica. (2018). *Ukraine: History*. Assessed April 2, 2018, from https://www.britannica.com/topic/Kievan-Rus

Ermasova, N., & Ermasova, P. (2019). Public capital budgeting and management process in Russia. In Capital management and budgeting in the public sector. Hershey, PA: IGI Global.

European Bank of Reconstruction and Development. (2018). *Chernobyl: A site transformed*. Retrieved April 15, 2018, from http://www.ebrd.com/what-we-do/sectors/nuclear-safety/chernobyl-overview.html

Gramlich, E. M. (1994). Infrastructure investment: A review essay. *Journal of Economic Literature*, *32*, 1176–1196.

Guzman, T. (2019). Capital budgeting, infrastructure, and capital investment in the Republic of Uzbekistan. In Capital management and budgeting in the public sector. Hershey, PA: IGI Global.

Kraan, D. J., von Trapp, L., Kostyleva, V., van Tuinen, J., & Morgner, M. (2013). Budgeting in Ukraine. *OECD Journal on Budgeting*, *12*(2), 69–140. doi:10.1787/budget-12-5k4c1s8n0br0

Land Code of Ukraine. (2002). *Vidomosti Verkhovnoi Rady Ukrainy*, *3-4*, 27.

Milakovsky, B. (2018). *Ukrainians abroad: The economics and politics of labor migration*. Kennan Institute. Retrieved March 2, 2018, from http://www.kennan-focusukraine.org/ukrainians-abroad-the-economics-and-politics-of-labor-migration/

Mykhayliv, D., & Zauner, K. G. (2013). Investment behavior and ownership structures in Ukraine: Soft budget constraints, government ownership and private benefits of control. *Journal of Comparative Economics*, *41*(1), 265–278. doi:10.1016/j.jce.2012.03.001

Organization for Economic Cooperation and Development. (2014). *Territorial reviews: Ukraine 2013*. Retrieved from . doi:10.1787/19900759

Srithongrung, A. (2008). Impacts of state capital management programs on state economic performance. *Public Budgeting & Finance*, *28*(3), 83–107. doi:10.1111/j.1540-5850.2008.00912.x

Ukrainian News and Information Agency. (2017). *Nearly 60% of Ukrainians live below poverty line. Kyiv, Ukraine: Ukrainian news and information agency*. Retrieved April 25, 2018, from https://www.unian.info/society/1850781-nearly-60-of-ukrainians-live-below-poverty-line-un.html

Verner, I. (Ed.). (2017). *Uraina V Tsyfrakh 2016. Statystychnyi Zbirnyk*. Kyiv, Ukraine: State Statistical Service of Ukraine.

Vlasiuk, V. (2017). *Svoboda Vyboru i Trudova Emigratsiya. Ukrainskyi Vybir. EPravda.* Retrieved April 24, 2017, from https://www.epravda.com.ua/columns/2017/02/2/619422

World Bank. (1997). *Public investment managementrReport.* Washington, DC: The World Bank Group.

World Bank. (2013). *Public investment management performance assessment.* Washington, DC: The World Bank Group.

World Bank. (2017). *Ukraine economic update.* Washington, DC: The World Bank Group.

ENDNOTES

1 Not all of the Donetsk and Luhansk oblasts have been occupied: Ukraine retains control over a portion of each of these oblasts.

2 These data exclude the Autonomous Republic of Crimea (ARC), city of Sevastopol, and the Russian-occupied territories in Donetsk and Luhansk regions.

3 Because agricultural operators are neither land owners (agricultural lands are state-owned in Ukraine) nor tenants (the oligarchs do not pay rent for using the vast agricultural resources; any in-kind payments they make to the villagers and farmers cannot be considered market rents), I will call them land-users.

Chapter 6
Public Capital Budgeting and Management Process in Russia

Natalia B. Ermasova
Governors State University, USA

Polina Ermasova
DePaul University, USA

ABSTRACT

This chapter provides a case study from Russia regarding public capital budgeting and management at the federal, state, and local levels. This chapter presents an analysis of four main components of Russian capital budgeting system including (1) long-term public capital planning, (2) annual public budgeting and financing, (3) project execution, and (4) public infrastructure evaluation. This research explains the general challenges of capital budgeting process after the several decades of financial and budget reforms. This chapter presents the structure and classification of the capital budget as well as recent trends in capital expenditure levels in Russia. The authors review the capital resource allocations across sectors based on investment needs and national priorities in Russia. The chapter explains public investment management processes and presents recommendations to improve the efficiency of public capital budgeting in Russia.

INTRODUCTION

This chapter examines the capital budgeting and management processes in Russia. This chapter is written in response to the suggestions of Halachmi and Sekwat (1997), Ammar, Duncombe, and Wright (2001, p.48), Srithongrung (2008, p.83), and Ermasova (2013, p.120) who stated that well-crafted evaluations of capital management practices are limited in number. Given the importance of capital investments, the scope of capital financing, the condition of capital infrastructure, and the shortage of knowledge about capital budgeting practices in Russia, an exploration of this area is important.

Federal government is the most prominent actor in capital budgeting and management in Russia. The political level plays a key role in deciding which projects will be a part of the portfolio appropriation. The political support for a capital project can be more important than cost-benefit estimates, for

DOI: 10.4018/978-1-5225-7329-6.ch006

example, Sochi Olympic Games infrastructure project. During budget execution, the appropriation framework allows some possibility for the government to change and reallocate the funding within the investment portfolio.

This chapter examines the effects of budget reforms on changes in capital budgeting practices with a focus on the federal level. The specific objectives of the chapter include (1) long-term public capital planning, (2) capital budgeting and financing, (3) investment project execution, and (4) public infrastructure maintenance. This chapter begins with a 'Background' section that includes a discussion of the different levels of government. The next section provides an overview of capital budgeting and management at the federal level. This section provides an overview of existing knowledge about capital planning, project management, and asset maintenance. In addition, the section will discuss public-private partnerships, which were rare until recently in Russia. This chapter provides recommendations for policy makers, budget analyst, and debt managers on how to better manage capital infrastructure by providing links to best practices on how to implement these recommendations by exploring innovative solutions in capital budgeting and financing in Russia. This study provides a valuable starting point for future research on comparative studies of capital budgeting in different countries.

BACKGROUND

Previously a part of the Soviet Union, Russia is the largest country in the world by geographic area, but its population is sparse in many parts of the country. In the Soviet Union, all revenue was centralized and then allocated according to the national plan, including capital investments. In the last thirty years, Russia has undergone significant changes since the collapse of the Soviet Union, moving from an isolated, centrally planned economy to a more market based and globally integrated economy.

The governments are structured in three layers: federal, regional, and local. Federal expenditures increased from 16 percent of GDP in 2005 to 18 percent in 2016 (Ermasova, 2008, 2016, World Bank, 2017) (Table 1). Table 1 demonstrates the dynamics of federal expenditures in % of GDP in Russia from 2005 to 2016.

Federal expenditures were 16,181 trillion rubles ($245.66 trillion) in 2017 and were proposed to increase to 15,978 trillion rubles ($242.09 trillion) in 2018 and to 15,964 trillion rubles ($240.2 trillion) in 2019.

Article 5 of the Constitution of Russia, adopted in 1993, creates equal subjects of the Russian Federation (initially 89 but reduced to 85) with equal rights in their relations to federal authorities. Each subject of the Federation has its own foundation laws (constitutions for the republics and charters for all others), political institutions, and legislation. The 85 subjects of the federation include: 22 republics, 46 *oblasts* (provinces), 9 *krays* (territories), 4 autonomous *okrugs* (areas), 1 autonomous raion, and 3 federal cities (Moscow, Sevastopol, and St. Petersburg). City of Moscow has 25 percent of total gross regional product (GRP) and 8 percent of population of the country. There are more than 24,000 local governments with dramatically different levels of economic strength, level of development, and institutional capacities. The major obstacles to economic transition are problems with fiscal federalism (Ermasova & Mikesell, 2016). Russia's fiscal constitution is more centralized than other federal countries.

According to Di Bella, Dynnikova, and Grigoli (2017), the main building blocks are a relatively centralized tax authority and a complex system of federal transfers. The federal government plays a significant role in shaping regional outcomes through the system of federal transfers. Consolidated federal

Table 1. Federal expenditures in % of GDP in Russia from 2005 to 2016

Year	Federal Expenditures in % of GDP
2016	18
2015	17
2014	17
2013	18
2012	17
2011	17
2010	18
2009	20
2008	17
2007	17
2006	17
2005	16

Source: World bank, 2017

transfers from the federal budget or from federal extra budgetary funds (EBFs) to the regions "amounted to 3.5 percent of GDP in 2016, or about 65 percent of federal oil and gas revenues" (Di Bella, Dynnikova, & Grigoli, 2017, p.3). The share of federal transfers in regional revenue varies widely across regions, ranging from 11 percent (Tatarstan) to 90 percent (North Caucasus Federal Region). According to Kraan et al. (2008),"the Budget Code grants large opportunities for reallocation during execution. The strong parliamentary 'powers of the purse' suggested by the detailed classification turned out to be illusionary in view of actual reallocation practices" (p.39). Russian reforms of intergovernmental fiscal relations had been introduced in a trial and error manner as a part of the ongoing political struggles between the federal government and the regions. Vartapetov (2010, p.471) suggests that "the stochastic and often non-transparent system of federal-to-regions grants, coupled with modest revenue and expenditure discretion of sub-national governments, might present a barrier to long-term economic growth in Russia's regions."

The Budget Code of the Russian Federation was adopted in July 1998 and entered into force in 2000. It defines the jurisdictions of the federal and regional governments, regulates their financial relations, prescribes the annual budget preparation and execution, and provides rules for the public debt. The budget process in Russia is comprehensively regulated by the Budget Code of the Russian Federation, which sets the rules and procedures for the preparation, approval, and execution of federal capital budget. This comprehensive legal framework ensures consistent classification and treatment of expenditure and revenue and enables strong central control over government finances, including capital budgeting. The Budget Code and subsequent amendments have established a comprehensive legal framework for investment policy, capital budgeting, and fiscal management at all levels of government. The Budget Code identifies the procedure for investment funding in the Russian Federation.

The Tax Code provides a comprehensive legal framework for taxation in the Russian Federation. Within this federal framework, regional and local governments have a degree of autonomy within the constraints that are set by federal legislation concerning the rate structure, payment dates, and exemptions in regional and local taxation (Bird & Smart, 2001; Ermasova, Mikesell, & Ermasov, 2014; Ermasova

& Mikesell, 2016; Zhuravskaia, 2000). In addition to the Budget Code and Tax Code, there is separate legislation that regulates government accounting, reporting, and financial control.

There were main budget reforms in 1991, 1998, 2006, 2008, and 2013 years that changed capital budgeting in Russia. The federal government was and remains the most prominent actor in capital budgeting and management, but in recent years, more flexibility has been given to lower levels of government and the private sector through public-private partnership (PPP) projects. The important budget reform was in 2006 when the Investment Fund was created, which provides financing for infrastructure investment projects. Investment Fund of the Russian Federation is a part of the federal budget, which is subject to spend on implementation of investment projects based on Public Private Partnership. Another main capital budgeting reform was in 2008 when the Russian government transferred the supervision of capital spending from the Ministry of Economic Development of the Russian Federation to the Ministry of Finance.

The Federal law FZ#392 (2011) established the legal base for the stimulation of territorial development and state support for promotion of investment activities in the regions. In 2013, the federal government approved Resolution#326, which established the list of the 20 regions of the Russian Federation that can establish zones of territorial development. The list includes *Republics of* Adygeya, Altai, Buryatia, Dagestan, Ingushetia, Kabardino-Balkar, Kalmykia, Karachaevo-Cherkessia, Karelia, Northern Osetia – Alania, Tyva, and Chechen; Zabaikalskiy, Kamchatskiy, and Primorskiy *Krais*; Amur, Ivanovo, Kurgan, Magadan *Oblasts* and the Jewish *Autonomous Oblast*. These regions submit a request to the federal government to establish a territorial development zone and propose a long-term socioeconomic development strategy for 12 years. Based on this strategy, the federal center provides the investment support of regional territorial development zone. For example, the federal government supported regional territorial development zones, such as aviation and space cluster in Samara Oblast and biotechnology cluster in Chernogolovka City of Moscow Oblast.

CAPITAL BUDGETING AND MANAGEMENT

Capital Planning

The Ministry of Economic Development of the Russian Federation prepares the macroeconomic forecasts for the federal budget. The macroeconomic assumptions by Ministry of Economic Development and Trade have to be accepted by the Central Bank of the Russian Federation and approved by the Budget Commission. According to IMF (2014), these long-term projections include a section on the development of main fiscal parameters. The Ministry of Economic Development publishes an optimistic and pessimistic macroeconomic scenario based on alternative assumptions for key variables, such as the oil price, the exchange rate, and global economic developments.

The Ministry of Finance developed the Concept of Long-Term Development of the Russian Federation until 2020 (Federal Law#1662, 2008). The Ministry of Economic Development (2013) developed the Forecast of the long-term socio-economic development of the Russian Federation for the period up to 2030. These documents have more detailed assessment of expenditures, including analysis of the sensitivity of public finances to various macroeconomic assumptions. In addition, the Ministry of Finance prepares Public Debt Management Report that includes a qualitative discussion and some illustrative quantification of the impact of global oil prices dynamics on government revenues, balance, and debt.

The Budget Commission plays an important role in capital planning. The Budget Commission's members are the Minister of Finance, the Minister of Economic Development, the Minister of Industry and Energy, the Minister of Defense, the Minister of Education, the Minister of Health Care and Social Development, and the Chair of the Budget Committee of the State Duma. Other ministers can be invited to the meetings of the Budget Commission if their investment projects are discussed. The Prime Minister is the chair of this Commission. The Budget Commission approves the ministerial targets for the new spending initiatives and provides the separations in these targets between current and capital expenditures. If the issues for capital expenditure cannot be resolved between the line ministry and the Ministry of Finance, these issues are submitted for negotiations to the Economic Issues Sub-commission of the Budget Commission that is chaired by the Minister of Economic Development. The outcomes of the reviews are formalized in a memo and submitted to the Budget Commission, which makes the final decisions. The budget documentation includes a consolidated forecast of general government revenue and expenditures (Budget Code, Article 192, Paragraph 44). Budgets at the federal, regional, and municipal levels cover the one- and two-year planning periods. Information on forward plans is provided at the same level of detail for all years in the planning framework. Expenditures are classified by organizational unit, function, economic category, and program. The government updates its expenditure projections for the new budget and planning period each year based on new policy commitments, updated macroeconomic and demographic projections, and any changes in the budget structure that has occurred since the previous year.

The Budget Code introduces the concept of the "federal targeted investment program". According to Article 182 of the Budget Code, the targeted investment program is prepared with the draft of the budget for the following financial year. The federal, targeted investment programs contain data characterizing each investment project for the entire period of its implementation, including the total estimated cost of the project and the breakdown of budgetary allocations by the year of construction. This approach allows for increasing the validity and transparency of planning and implementation of budgetary capital investments. Budget capital investments that are allocated from the federal budget are included in the federal targeted investment program (Article 179.1 of the Russian Federation's Budget Code), which is also an annex to the federal law on the federal budget.

According to the Budget Code, debt is limited to a ceiling equal to the sub-national government's annual budget revenue net of federal grants. Annual borrowing is limited to 15 percent of revenue net of federal grants for regions and 10 percent for municipalities (Article 91 in Budget Code). There are more restrictions on regions and municipalities that rely more heavily on federal transfers. For example, if federal transfers have exceeded 60 percent of a region's own revenue in two of the last three years, then the debt ceiling would be reduced to 50 percent of revenues, and annual borrowing would be limited to 10 percent of revenue net of federal transfers. In addition, the region is required to take action to raise local revenue and rationalize expenditures. The Ministry of Finance monitors compliance with these limits, and any breaches can result in financial sanctions (Budget Code, Article 168).

Capital Budgeting and Financial Management

In the last twenty-five years, capital budgeting changed dramatically in Russia. The Law of the Russian Soviet Federative Socialist Republic (RSFSR) of June 26, 1991 No. 1488-I "On Investment Activities in the RSFSR" was transformed into two laws that define two different approaches to the federal investment: (1) Federal Law No. 39-FZ of February 25, 1999 "On investment activity in the Russian Federation implemented as capital investments" that defines investments in the form of capital investments (investments in fixed assets) and (2) Federal Law No. 160-FZ of July 9, 1999 "On Foreign Investments in the Russian Federation" that regulates the investment activities of foreign investors. The Federal Law No. 39-FZ determines the legal and economic basis of the investing activities performed in the form of capital investments and in the territory of the Russian Federation, and also, it establishes guarantees of equal protection of the rights, interests, and property of subjects of the investing activities performed in the form of capital investments irrespective of patterns of ownership. Federal law No. 160-FZ provides the basic guarantee of rights to foreign investors to investment as well as the earnings and profit gained on them, which are the terms and conditions of entrepreneurship activities of foreign investors in Russia. The goal of this Law is to provide a stable environment for the activities of foreign investors and to compliance of the legal treatment of foreign investments with the provisions of international law and international practices of investment cooperation.

Until 2008, the budget formulation process in Russia was divided between appropriations for current expenditures (coordinated by the Ministry of Finance) and appropriations for capital expenditure (coordinated by the Ministry of Economic Development). The Russian government decided to transfer the supervision of capital spending from the Ministry of Economic Development to the Ministry of Finance in 2008. The concentration of financial supervision in the Ministry of Finance was an important step forward. According to Kraan et al. (2008), the development of various types of "targeted programs" were not well integrated in the regular budget process. The goal of transformation was to improve the capital budget process, provide better linkage between capital and current expenditures, and have a better trade-off between public services.

There are four types of targeted investment programs at the federal level: "Federal Targeted Programs" (FTPs), the "Federal Investment Targeted Programs" (FITP), "Departmental Targeted Programs" (DTP), and "Long-Term Targeted Programs" (LTP). Federal Targeted Programs (FTPs) were created for large-scale investments and scientific programs. The Minister of Economic Development and Trade is responsible for their administration and budget. FTPs often lacked effective management mechanisms and were not well coordinated with the responsible ministries. The Federal Investment Targeted Programs (FITP) compiles information on budget investments in FTPs but also other (related) investments projects. The Minister of Finance is responsible for the budget of the FITP while the Minister of Economic Development and Trade is responsible for the selection of projects. Departmental Targeted Programs (DTPs) are investment programs that are administered and funded by line ministers. Long-Term Targeted Programs (LTPs) were introduced in 2009. LTPs are administered and funded by line ministries, but they are reflected in the budget as separate line items (because of their size and importance).

The Budget Code is the main document for approval and implementation of budgetary investments from the federal budget. The "investments" are defined as a part of the capital expenditures of the budgets (Article 67 Budget Code). The Budget Code establishes that budgetary investments are budget funds allocated for the creation or increased value of federal (municipal) property (Article 6 of the Budget Code). According to the Budget Code of the Russian Federation (Articles 21, 79), the sub-groups "Budget Investments" and "Budgetary Investments to Other Legal Entities" are included in the group, "Capital Investments in State (Municipal) Property Objects," of the unified classification of budget expenditures. The Law on Amendments to the Budget Code proposes that the budget investments in facilities with an estimated cost of investment projects of more than 8 billion rubles must be reflected as a part of the departmental structure, separately for each investment project. The decision about budget investments of 1.5 billion rubles and more are made in the form of normative legal acts. Government of the Russian Federation makes the decisions on the preparation and implementation of an investment project valued at more than 600 million rubles. The chief administrators of federal budget funds make the decisions on the preparation and implementation of projects with a lower cost. The decision about other budget investments are made in the form of legal acts of the chief administrators of budgetary funds (Article 79 Budget Code). In accounting, public capital investments are presented in a separate annex to the budget law, which specifies the addressees, the volume, and purpose of the budget investments (Article 80 Budget Code). The budget investments in objects with the estimated cost of more than 100 million rubles reflect in the consolidated budgetary list separately for each investment project and the corresponding type of expenditure.

The financing of investment projects was selected on a competitive basis in the Russian Federation until January 1, 2005. The Development Budget Fund was a component of the federal budget that was formed as part of capital expenditures of the federal budget, and it was used for lending, investment, and guarantee support of investment projects (Article 1, 3 Federal Law "The Development Budget of the Russian Federation"). The Development Budget Fund was closed in 2005. The Investment Fund of the Russian Federation was established in January 2006 in accordance with the Budget Code of the Russian Federation. The Budget Code (2006) proposes an article introducing the concept of the Investment Fund. Part of the federal budget funds should be used for the implementation of investment projects on the principles of public-private partnership (Article 179-2 of the Budget Code). According to paragraph 16 of the Regulation on the Investment Fund, federal capital investments can be provided in the following forms: a) co-financing on a contractual basis of an investment project with the registration of property rights of the Russian Federation, including financing the costs of managing an investment project, and financing the development of project documentation, b) transferring investment funds to the legal entities, c) granting state guarantees of the Russian Federation for investment projects. State guarantees are provided to commercial organizations participating in an investment project in favor of credit institutions, including credit institutions with foreign investments. The Russian Federation Government Resolution No. 694 of November 23, 2005 "On the Investment Fund of the Russian Federation" established procedures for the formation of the Investment Fund, selection and implementation of investment projects, as well as the conditions for granting state support at the expense of the Investment Fund. The Investment Fund of the Russian Federation represents a part of federal budget funds, which is subject to spending upon implementation of investment projects based on Public Private Partnership. The goals of the Investment Fund of the Russian Federation are following: (1) stimulating socio-economic development by creating needed infrastructure of national significance, (2) contributing to the innovation initiatives, (3) facilitating structural change, (4) financing of regional infrastructure investments programs, and (5) supporting region specific investment projects by creating of transport, engineering, and energy infrastructure of regions. The capital investments from the Investment Fund are carried out within the framework of public-private partnerships (Articles 69, 691, 79, 80 of the Budget Code).

Centralized Execution and Project Management

The central government ministries verify the most important infrastructure needs in the country, prioritize them, and finance public capital projects in Russia. These investment projects are selected on the basis of economic and social impact on more than a single prefecture or region. The following are sources of funding of infrastructure programs: (1) Federal budget, (2) Investment Fund, (3) Regional and local budgets, (4) state companies like Avtodor, (5) natural monopolies (Gazprom, Transneft, Russian Railways); (6) National Wealth Fund (NWF), (7) Pension funds, and (8) private investors.

Table 2 presents the public capital spending for all three levels of government from 1990 to 2016. Table 2 shows that Ratio Investments in fixed capital to GDP decreased from 18.7 percent to 13.9 percent in 1999 and increased to 20.3 percent in 2008. After 2014, this ratio decreased from 16 to 17 percent.

Table 2. Total public capital spending from 1990 to 2016

Years	Investments in Fixed Capital in Current Prices (Million. rub., Before 1998 - Billion Rubles).	Changes to the Previous Year in Comparable Prices (%)	Changes to 1990 Year in Comparable Prices (%)	GDP in Constant Prices 1990 (mln. $)	GDP in Current Prices (Billions rub., Before 1998 - Trillions rubles).	Ratio Investments in Fixed Capital to GDP
1990	249.1	100	100	570400		
1991	210.5	85.1	85.1	541900		
1992	2670.2	60.3	51,3	463300		
1993	27125	88.3	45,3	423000		
1994	108810	75,7	34,3	369300		
1995	266974	89,9	30,8	354100	1428	18.7%
1996	375958	81,9	25,3	341300	2007	18.7%
1997	408797	95,0	24,0	346100	2342	17.5%
1998	407086	88,0	21,1	327600	2629	15.5%
1999	670439	105,3	22,2	348400	4823	13.9%
2000	1165234	117.4	26.1	383400	7305,6	15.9%
2001	1504712	111.7	29.2	402900	8943,6	16.8%
2002	1762407	102.9	30,0	422000	10830,5	16.3%
2003	2186365	112.7	33.8	452800	13208,2	16.6%
2004	2865014	116.8	39.5	485300	17027,2	16.8%
2005	3611109	110.2	43.5	516200	21609,8	16.7%
2006	4730023	117.8	51.3	558300	26917,2	17.6%
2007	6716222	123.8	63.5	606000	33247,5	20.2%
2008	8781616	109.5	69.5	637800	41276,8	21.3%
2009	7976013	86.5	60.1	587900	38807,2	20.6%
2010	9152096	106.3	63.9	614400	46308,5	19.8%
2011	11035652	110.8	70.8	640600	60282,5	18.3%
2012	12586090	106.8	75.6	662600	68163,9	18.5%
2013	13450238	100.8	76.2	671300	73133,9	18.4%
2014	13902645	98.51	75.11	675300	79199,7	17.6%
2015	13897188	89.9	67.5	649640	83387,2	16.7%
2016	14639835	99.1	66.9	656600	86148,6	17.0%

Sources: Federal State Statistics Service (2018), p.37-38 [Статистический сборник России. 2018: Росстат. - М., 2018, С.37-38.] http://www.gks.ru/free_doc/new_site/vvp/vvp-god/tab1.htm; World Bank (2018a). World Bank national accounts data. https://data.worldbank.org/indicator/NY.GDP.MKTP.CD

Federal budget spending goes through the Government Commission. This Commission selects investment projects based on national, regional, and interregional importance. The Federal Treasury publishes monthly information on budget execution, including consolidated receipts and expenditures by sub-national government. Individual regional and municipal governments are required to publish financial information, which follows national standards on at least an annual basis. The official balance sheet does not disclose long-term liabilities associated with government managed pension funds, growing liabilities under PPPs, any of the assets or liabilities of Russia's large public corporations sector, or any sub-soil oil and gas reserves (IMF, 2014, p.52).

The bank, Vnesheconombank, carries out the functions of the financial advisor of the Russian Government. Vnesheconombank prepares its conclusions about the tenability of forecasts in business plans of projects (including the marketing plan) and the compliance of the projects, claiming budgetary allocations from the Fund with the criteria of financial, budgetary and economic effectiveness. The period of project financing from the Fund should not exceed 5 years. The minimum project cost for obtaining money from the Fund is 500 million rubles. The government's Investment Fund of Russia provides funding for major federal PPP projects. By 2012, it had funded projects worth a total of 1.3 trillion rubles (2 percent of GDP).

The investments from the federal, regional, and local budgets bring around 20 percent of total investments in fixed capital (Table 3). The government plays a major role in capital investments in Russia. According to Chakrabarti (2016), the share of the private sector, as a percentage of cumulative infrastructure investments in Russia over 2006–2010, was 16 percent; the US was 29 percent, India — 40 percent, EU new members — 44 percent, EU old members — 64 percent, and Chile — 66 percent. Russia needs to increase private sector participation in infrastructure investments. Table 3 presents the total investments in fixed capital.

The important instruments of financial support from federal level are investment subsidies. Investment subsidies include subsidies for the implementation of federal target programs (FTP) and subsidies for investment in capital construction projects in regions. The total share of these subsidies to the budgets of regions is on average 2 percent, but in the Kaliningrad region, it reaches 24 percent. In Ingushetia and Chechnya the average is 16-18 percent, in the Primorsky Krai and Mordovia it is 13 to 14 percent, and in Dagestan, Kabardino-Balkaria, Tatarstan it is 11 to 12 percent of total revenues. The Krasnodar region received higher shares of federal transfers in budget (from 25 to 31 percent) due to increased investment in Sochi Olympiad project. Sochi Olympiad project was originally budgeted at $12 billion, but the capital expenditures expanded to $51 billion, making Sochi the most expensive Olympics in history (Yaffa, 2014).

There is increasing use of public-private partnerships in infrastructure projects. The private sector provides the latest technologies and valuable expertise, along with the required financing. The President of the European Bank for Reconstruction and Development, Chakrabarti (2016), suggests that PPPs and the private sector cannot substitute public financing and expertise "structuring many potential projects on a PPP basis in the Russian infrastructure market would leverage the role of the public sector in coordinating and leading infrastructure development. This will require the enhanced development of public sector expertise to prepare well-structured PPP projects, something multilateral development bank (MDBs) and international experts can help develop." The Russian government is actively promoting the use of PPPs in a number of sectors, including transport, housing, and utilities. Table 4 presents the public- private partnerships (PPPs) investment from 2005 to 2016 in Russia.

Table 3. The investments in fixed capital (in actual prices, billions rubles)

	2012	2013	2014	2015
Total investments in fixed capital	9595.7	10065.7	10379.6	10485.0
including:				
Equity	4274.6	4549.9	4742.3	5260.3
Credits and subsidies	5321.1	5515.8	5637.3	5224.7
including:				
Banks' credits	806.3	1003.6	1098.7	849.8
Including foreign banks' credits	113.7	107.7	265.2	183.4
Credits from other financial organizations	588.2	626.1	660.1	698.5
Foreign investments		76.4	88.8	122.9
Investments from budget	1712.9	1916.3	1761.3	1921.2
including:				
Federal budget	926.6	1009.9	933.6	1185.5
Regional budget	677.0	753.3	676.6	599.3
Local budget	109.3	153.1	151.1	136.4
Off-budget funds	33.3	27.9	24.0	27.4
funds of organizations and population involved in shared construction	259.5	294.9	367.6	334.8
Including personal funds	197.1	234.7	281.7	252.5
others	1920.9	1570.6	1636.8	1270.1
	In % of total			
Total investments in fixed capital	**100**	**100**	**100**	**100**
including:				
Equity	44.5	45.2	45.7	50.2
Credits and subsidies	55.5	54.8	54.3	49.8
including:				
Banks' credits	8.4	10.0	10.6	8.1
Including foreign banks' credits	1.2	1.1	2.6	1.7
Credits from other financial organizations	6.1	6.2	6.4	6.6
Foreign investments		0.8	0.9	1.2
Investments from budget	17.9	19.0	17.0	18.3
including:				
Federal budget	9.7	10.0	9.0	11.3
Regional budget	7.1	7.5	6.5	5.7
Local budget	1.1	1.5	1.5	1.3
Off-budget funds	0.4	0.3	0.2	0.3
funds of organizations and population involved in shared construction	2.7	2.9	3.5	3.2
Including personal funds	2.1	2.3	2.7	2.4
others	20.0	15.6	15.7	12.1

Source: Finance of Russia, 2016, p. 285 [Финансы России. 2016: Стат.сб./ Росстат. - М., 2016, С.285.]

Table 4. Public private partnerships (PPPs) investment from 2005 to 2016

Years	Public Private Partnerships Investment in Energy (Current US$)	Public Private Partnerships Investment in Transport (Current US$)	Public Private Partnerships Investment in Water and Sanitation (Current US$)
2016	207 010 000	79 400 000	
2015		1 824 300 000	1 200 000 000
2014	262 000 000		
2012	43 000 000	3 900 000 000	100 000 000
2011	4 795 000 000		
2010	5 187 000 000	4 347 900 000	
2007	1 000 000 000		174 000 000
2006			698 700 000
2005	3 000 000		340 300 000

Source: World Bank (2016)

The six state corporations (Deposit Insurance Agency, Vneshekonombank, Fund for Assisting in Housing and Utility Reform, Russian Roads, Olympstroi, and Rosatom) are not included in the annual budget (IMF, 2014). The investment activities of these state corporations involve the implementation of government policies. Some examples include managing road infrastructure (Russian Roads), overseeing the construction of public infrastructure (Olympstroi), and supporting the diversification of the economy (Vneshekonombank). Table 5 provides the programs and financing of the State Company Russian Roads from 2010 to 2019.

The Oil Stabilization Fund was established in 2004. The purpose of the fund was to insure the federal budget against oil price volatility. Revenues were flowing into the Fund from the mineral extraction tax (95 percent) and the export customs duty on oil (100 percent) in excess of the cut-off price of the Oil Stabilization Fund. In 2007, the Oil Stabilization Fund (called the Reserve Fund from 2008) fulfilled two functions, namely insurance against volatility of the oil price and using oil windfalls in a macro

Table 5. The programs and financing of the State Company Russian Roads from 2010 to 2019 (millions of rubles)

Types of Investments	Sum in Millions of Rubles
Total investments, including:	1 392 814
Investments from Investment Fund	1 024 353
Investments from non-budgets funds	368 462
Number of investment projects	23
Reconstruction of roads	964 kilometers
Construction of new roads	959 kilometers
Toll roads	1 295 kilometers

Source: Ministry of Finance of Russia, 2018 [Министерство Финансов России, 2018]

economically responsible way to generate future income streams that help to cover structural budget deficits. The Fund was replaced in 2008 by two funds: (1) the Reserve Fund to fulfill the price volatility insurance function and (2) the National Wealth Fund to fulfill the intergenerational equity function. If the accumulated resources reached 500 billion rubles (about 2 percent of the GDP), the resources of the fund could be used for certain other purposes, such as the repayment of foreign debt. The Reserve Fund and National Wealth Fund are managed by the central bank under guidelines set down by the Finance Ministry. The OECD (2006) recommended defining and reforming the Oil Stabilization Fund by recognizing its two different objectives. One part of the Fund should be considered as a buffer against oil price volatility while the other should be used to generate investment income. The tax base of the Fund should be broadened to include gas revenues. The minimum reserve of the buffer sub-fund should be increased to match the potential impact of a sharp drop in prices. The investment sub-fund should only gradually move to more risky assets to avoid mismanagement and to allow for capacity building.

The National Wealth Fund (NWF) was established in 2008 to help finance Russian pensions but was actually used to fund government backed investment projects. Management of National Wealth Fund aims at capital preservation and a stable level of return on long-term perspective. According to Ministry of Finance Russian Federation (2018), management of NWF assets is executed by the Ministry of Finance of the Russian Federation in accordance with procedure and terms established by the Government of the Russian Federation. Table 6 presents balance of National Wealth Fund from 2015 to 2018 years.

The Reserve Fund was capped at 10 percent of GDP. All revenues exceeding this cap are transferred to the National Wealth Fund. While the National Wealth Fund was designed to cover long-term outlays for social spending, such as supporting the pension system, it was unsealed to finance infrastructure projects and support banks during a crisis. The tax base of the funds has been expanded. In addition to 95 percent of the proceeds of the mineral extraction tax and 100 percent of the export customs duty on oil production and export, 100 percent of the proceeds of the mineral extraction tax and the export customs duty on gas flow into the funds. The Reserve Fund had been almost exhausted and had only $17 billion in it at the end of 2017. What remains of the Reserve Fund has been merged with the National Wealth Fund (NWF) in January 2018. With the closing of the Reserves Fund, all excess oil and gas revenues

Table 6. The National Wealth Fund from 2015 to 2018

Years	Balance of National Wealth Fund (bln.$)	Balance of National Wealth Fund (bln.rub.)	% to GDP
01.01.2018	65.15	3 752.94	3.9%
12.01.2017	66.94	3 904.76	4.2%
06.01.2017	74.18	4 192.30	4.5%
01.01.2017	71.87	4 359.16	4.7%
12.01.2016	71.26	4 628.09	5.4%
06.01.2016	72.99	4 823.19	5.6%
01.01.2016	71.72	5 227.18	6.1%
12.01.2015	72.22	4 784.05	5.7%
08.01.2015	74.56	4 398.15	5.3%

Source: Ministry of Finance of Russia, 2018 [Министерство Финансов России, 2018] https://www.minfin.ru/ru/perfomance/nationalwealthfund/statistics/

earned by the government will now be paid into the NWF as part of the "budget rule" that has recently been reintroduced – a rule that means excess revenues earned from raw material exports is sterilized in the fund, so it cannot force the appreciation of the currency. According to Tanas & Andrianova (2017), Finance Minister Siluanov said that the government would still complete all planned investments in infrastructure from the $74.2 billion National Wealth Fund.

Infrastructure Maintenance

Current levels of investment funding are far below what is needed to properly maintain, improve, and expand public infrastructure in Russia to avoid the economic costs and inefficiencies. World Economic Forum (2015) shows that the lack of capital investments over the last 20 years has dropped Russia to 93rd place globally in quality of overall infrastructure. Only the quality of railway infrastructure in Russia has a relatively high level (31st). All other areas (quality of roads and highways, dams, port infrastructure, air transport infrastructure, and electricity supply) need improvement. Data by Federal State Statistics Service (2018) demonstrates a very high level of depreciations (47-48 percent) and a very low level of replacement of fixed assets (Table 7). According to estimates by McKinsey Global Institute (2015), the minimum need for infrastructure investments maintenance is around $57-67 trillion from 2013 through 2030 (Ganelin & Vasin, 2014). Other former Soviet republics, like Moldova (see Ceka, chapter 7 of this volume), Uzbekistan (see Guzman, chapter 4 of this volume), or Ukraine (see Krupa, chapter 5 of this volume) have the same problems with high level of depreciation of fixed assets after the collapse of the Soviet Union.

The Russian railway system includes a total of 150,000 kilometers (93,210 miles) of rails. It is one of the most extensive railway systems in the world. Due to three decades of insufficient investment in maintenance and capital improvement, the railway infrastructure has badly deteriorated. Around 30 percent of freight cars, 40 percent of passenger cars, and nearly half the locomotives have such poor quality that they should be replaced immediately (Ganelin & Vasilev, 2014). The traffic handling capacity in the most developed areas decreased dramatically in recent years and is essentially no longer capable of coping with growing demand. According to Ganelin and Vasin (2014, p.21), "this situation has given rise to massive traffic jams (average speed on downtown Moscow roads is 20 kph compared to 40 kph in large European cities). It has also created bottlenecks on railroads and reduced the speed of rolling stock (average speed of freight trains decreased by 12 percent to 300 km per day in 2013)." To improve this situation, federal government increased the budget financing of transport infrastructure (Table 8).

Russia has a large number of detailed federal and regional special purpose programs devoted to the development of transportation infrastructure. By 2020, the infrastructure investment plan should reach $650 billion ($90 billion per year on average). The bulk of transport infrastructure investment will be directed to road construction (45 percent), while rail transport will take 20 percent (including the

Table 7. Degree of depreciation of fixed assets

	2010	2011	2012	2013	2014	2015	2016
Degree of depreciation of fixed assets (at the end of the year), %	47.1	47.9	47.7	48.2	49.4	47.7	48.1
Rate of replacement of fixed assets (in constant prices), %	3.7	4.6	4.8	4.6	4.35	3.9	3.7

Source: Federal State Statistics Service (2018), p.11 [Статистический сборник России (2018). Москва:Росстат, 2018, с.11.]

Table 8. The volume of budget financing in the transport sector in 2012 -2014 (mln.rub.)

	2012	2013	2014
Investment fund	27132.6	3657.2	14352.5
Budget investments in capital infrastructure, not included in the federal targeted programs	268.3	924.9	1 520.0

Source: Ministry of Finance (2018). [Министерство Финансов России, 2018]

Moscow-Kazan High-Speed Railway and subway facilities). Pipeline transport should account for 30 percent, while ports and airports will comprise the remaining 5 percent (Ganelin & Vasin, 2014). For example, the government of Moscow is planning to invest over 3 trillion rubles ($45,454 billion) in infrastructure until 2020. The key large-scale project involves expanding the Moscow Subway with a total cost of investments around 1.4 trillion rubles. This project will expand the total length of subway lines by 50 percent (460 km), including the deployment of 72 new stations. Another project is the investment in the expansion of the road network (1.4 trillion rubles). This project will finance construction of new roads (78 km) and reconstruction of existing roads (400 km). These investment projects will be funded on public-private partnership (PPP) terms.

One example of a successful infrastructure public-private partnership PPPs projects is Pulkovo Airport (St. Petersburg's air travel hub and Russia's fourth-largest airport). After completion of infrastructure project from 2010 to 2014, the airport handled and served 13.3 million passengers, approximately 60 percent greater than in 2010 when Northern Capital Gateway (NCG) became the airport operator and developer. NCG successfully completed a 1.2 billion euros airport development and reconstruction program in 2014. This infrastructure project modernized Pulkovo Airport and achieved the current capacity of 17 million passengers per year. The President of the European Bank for Reconstruction and Development, Chakrabarti (2016), suggested that Russian infrastructure projects are generally very complex, not only legally, but also financially and technically "With the notable exception of Pulkovo airport, none of the other transport infrastructure PPPs has yet completed the construction stage. To build a sustainable infrastructure PPP pipeline, PPP units need to be more actively used on both federal and regional levels to concentrate expertise and improve coordination in the origination and preparation of projects " (p.1).

In Russia, the rate of investment in infrastructure was around 3.6 to 4.2 percent of the GDP (OECD, 2016). The government provides around 65 percent of infrastructure investments. The significant parts of infrastructure investments are the construction of city roads, water supply systems, and municipal infrastructure facilities. Due to financial unattractiveness of infrastructure investments and the lack of legal framework to facilitate private sector participation, infrastructure investments are generally provided by state and local government owned entities. The budget-funded infrastructure was around some $1.4 trillion in 2014. In comparison, the volume of private investment in infrastructure was around $700 billion in 2014. Table 9 presents estimated aggregate investments in transport infrastructure from 2010 to 2020.

The Russian government uses many strategies and programs dedicated to infrastructure development in Russia. In total, 325 infrastructure projects are planned to begin in the period from 2015 to 2030. According to Ernst & Young (2018), the majority of the infrastructure projects (51 percent) are planned to begin in the period from 2015 to 2020 with some projects planned to finish in 2030. Most investment projects are located in Western Russia, which has higher population density and features more economic activity than the Eastern part of the country.

Table 10 presents the number of planned investments projects from 2015 to 2030 in Russia.

Table 9. Estimated aggregate investments in transport infrastructure, RUB bln

Types of Transport Infrastructure	2010	2011	2012	2013	2014	2015	2016	2017	2018	2019	2020
Federal roads	238	296	375	428	427	495	640	714	664	732	791
Regional roads	308	360	548	620	448	470	493	518	544	571	600
Railroads	198	234	288	274	233	277	277	277	168	168	168
Airports	22	37	59	67	55	47	52	56	57	57	54
Total investments in transport infrastructure	1508	1984	2022	2229	2110	2445	2774	2924	2743	2527	2430
% of GDP	3.3%	3.5%	3.2%	3.3%	3.0%	3.2%	3.4%	3.3%	2.8%	2.4%	2.2%

Source: Ganelin and Vasin (2014), p.23

The greatest amount of infrastructure projects is planned for railway transport infrastructure maintenance and new development, including the program of high speed railway development through 2030. The second to largest direction of planned infrastructure investments is road and bridge construction. These projects of road and bridge construction are under the jurisdiction of the state corporation Avtodor. Russian government prepared the Russian transport strategy through 2030. Another direction of planned infrastructure investments is the power and utilities construction, including electric power supply, water supply, and gas supply infrastructure projects.

CONCLUSION

The processes for capital investment planning are complicated and not well coordinated within the budget process in Russia. Separate planning of capital expenditure and related current expenditure for maintenance has led to negative consequences, such as uncompleted construction projects, prolongation of construction terms, and high exploitation costs of completed projects. According to Kraan et al. (2008), it is recommended that the present planning procedures for various kinds of "targeted programs" should be simplified. A planning document should be created under the responsible ministry that would cover both capital and operating spending on investment projects. The investment planning is not entirely integrated in the regular budget process of the line ministries that are responsible for the relevant policy sector. Such integration requires that the Minister of Transport have authority over infrastructure, the

Table 10. Infrastructure projects from 2015 to 2030 in Russia

Status of Investments Projects	Number of Projects	Sum of Planned Financing, in Billions of US$
Completed investment projects	59	31.8
In progress	189	329.5
Planned investment projects	77	608.1
Total number of investment projects	325	969.4

Source: Ernst & Young (2018). Russian infrastructure in the global context.. http://www.ey.com/ru/en/issues/business-environment/ey-road-to-2030-russian-infrastructure-in-global-context

Minister of Defense over weapon systems, the Minister of Urban Development over public housing, etc. If Russia wants to go this way, it is recommended to better coordinate the investment planning procedures.

OECD countries usually have only a single sectoral planning document for the medium and long term like for transport, defense, water resources, etc. This document treats both capital and current expenditures and the resulting performance in a fully integrated way. It is entirely under the authority of the sectoral minister. This minister is also responsible for the administration and funding of all investment projects in his/her sector. Possibly, the Long-Term Targeted Programs (LTPs) that are foreseen in the amended Budget Code can evolve into this type of document, but this would require a considerable simplification and cleanup of the remaining procedures and institutional setup. In the future, it may be useful to maintain a "light" form of coordination in the Ministry of Economic Development; for instance, it could be by way of a "knowledge center" that can perform cost-benefit analysis on project proposals and provide line ministries with advice about technical aspects of investment projects.

The Investment Fund plays a key role in the infrastructure, financing process. The Investment Fund of the Russian Federation is a part of federal budget funds, which is subject to spend on implementation of investment projects based on Public Private Partnership. The Investment Fund of the Russian Federation presented in the annual budget alongside other, budget-financed, public investments. According to Kraan et al. (2008), the Investment Fund is not well integrated in the budget process. The tools for using the Investment Fund's resources are not properly developed and do not allow prioritizing of the projects. The under-use of the Investment Fund's resources and accumulation of its reserves are the results of these problems. To improve this situation, federal government should implement strategic plans for prioritization projects in the Investment Fund.

The supervision of capital spending was transferred from the Ministry of Economic Development to the Minister of Finance in 2006. The Government Commission selects investment projects based on national, regional, and interregional importance. The acquisition of government investments are controlled by the Budget Code and approved through the annual budget process. The lack of a capital budget on the federal level systematically penalizes capital investment because the political incentives embedded in the budgeting process. For example, the Ministry of Finance is most likely to fund programs like the infrastructure project for Sochi Olympic Games or the bridge to Crimea. Based on the theory and research reviewed above, the present study made the following assertions: (1) there is rising concern for effective planning and budgeting for life-cycle costs to reduce wasteful expenditures down stream, and (2) despite the concern, there is an absence of success at planning for maintenance funding. It would be important to evaluate which projects for maintenance funding are likely to have the greatest impact on productivity and safety.

Russia uses conditional and unconditional intergovernmental investment grants to finance infrastructure. The transfer systems have been structured in ways that are non-transparent, subject to negotiation between central and regional government, and create significant incentives for inefficiency. In practice, the federal transfer structure represents a "patchwork quilt" of federal grants (unconditional grants, subsidies, and subventions, other transfers), making the importance of these funds vary dramatically across the Russian regions (Ermasova, 2008; Ermasova & Mikesell, 2015). It would be important to improve the transfer system.

There is the gap between infrastructure needs and ability of the governments to finance infrastructure investments. Asset maintenance has been found to be the weakest area in capital management. Investment programs are often revised and underfinanced (Ganelin & Vasin, 2014). Movchan (2016, p.1) highlights another important problem: "around 50 percent of all money allocated for infrastructure projects is lost to corruption and inefficiency." The average implementation rate of federal programs is 85 to 90 percent, while the regional programs have a lower level of this rate. There is general acceptance that infrastructure needs require attention in Russia. First, additional funding sources would be helpful. A second category of solutions involves improving the intergovernmental transfer system. Third, public-private partnerships should be increasingly used for infrastructure projects. Appendix 1 provides summary of capital budgeting and management in Russia.

President of the European Bank for Reconstruction and Development, Chakrabarti (2016), highlights that "Russia has unique long-term potential for infrastructure development due to the healthy state of public finances, current high demand for infrastructure development and good prospects for such demand to continue" (p.1).

ACKNOWLEDGMENT

We want to thank Dr. John Mikesell for his guidance and for his exceptional and outstanding support of our research.

REFERENCES

Ammar, A., Duncombe, R., & Wright, A. (2001). Evaluating capital management: A new approach. *Public Budgeting & Finance*, *2*(1), 47–69. doi:10.1111/0275-1100.00058

Bird, R., & Smart, M. (2001). Intergovernmental fiscal transfers: Some lessons from international experience. In *Symposium on Intergovernmental Transfers in Asian Countries: Issues and Practices, Asian Tax and Public Policy Program*. Hitotsubashi University. Retrieved October 13, 2017, from http:// www1.worldbank.org/publicsector/learningprogram/Decentralization/IFTlessons.pdf

Budget Code of the Russian Federation. (1998). *Budget code N145-F3 from July 31, 1998 (with amendments up until July 23, 2013)*. Retrieved October 13, 2017, from http://www1.worldbank.org/publicsector/pe/BudgetLaws/Budget_Code_Russia_Eng1998.pdf

Ceka, E. (2018). *Public capital budgeting and management process in Moldova. In Capital management and budgeting in the public sector*. Hershey, PA: IGI Global.

Chakrabarti, S. (2016). *Key issues for infrastructure development in Russia*. Retrieved February 1, 2018, from http://www.ey.com/ru/en/issues/business-environment/ey-road-to-2030-infrastracture-development-in-russia-viewpoint-suma-chakrabarti

Constitution of the Russian Federation. (1993). *Constitution of the Russian Federation*. Retrieved February 1, 2018, from http://www.constitution.ru/en/10003000-01.htm

Di Bella, G., Dynnikova, O., & Grigoli, F. (2017). *Fiscal federalism and regional performance*. International Monetary Fund (Working Paper).

Ermasova, N. (2008). *Budget system* (3rd ed.). Moscow: Urait.

Ermasova, N. (2013). Capital budgeting in the states after the great recession. *State & Local Government Review*, *45*(2), 119–130. doi:10.1177/0160323X13487079

Ermasova, N. (2016). *Budget systems in Russia* (2nd ed.). Moscow: UNITY.

Ermasova, N., & Mikesell, J. (2016). Fiscal disparity and equalization in the Russian Federation. *Post-Communist Economies*, *28*(1), 1–15. doi:10.1080/14631377.2015.1084726

Ermasova, N., Mikesell, J., & Ermasov, S. (2014). Impact of recession on total revenue of regional governments in Russia. *Business Systems & Economics*, *4*(2), 139–154. doi:10.13165/VSE-14-4-2-03

Ernst & Young. (2018). *Russian infrastructure in the global context*. Retrieved February 1, 2018, from http://www.ey.com/ru/en/issues/business-environment/ey-road-to-2030-russian-infrastructure-in-global-context

Federal State Statistics Service. (2018*). Investments in Russia in 2017* [Инвестиции России в 2017]. Retrieved May, 24, 2018, from http://www.gks.ru/free_doc/doc_2017/invest.pdf

Ganelin, M., & Vasin, S. (2014). *Russian infrastructure. A big ship sails far* (Industry report). Retrieved May 24, 2018, from http://www.gazprombank.ru/upload/iblock/007/gpb_russian%20infrastructure_eng_150714.pdf

Guzman, T. (2018). *Capital budgeting, infrastructure and capital investment in Republic of Uzbekistan. In Capital management and budgeting in the public sector*. Hershey, PA: IGI Global.

Halachmi, A., & Sekwat, A. (1997). Strategic capital budgeting and planning: Prospects at the county level. *Public Budgeting and Financial Management*, *1*(1), 578–596.

IMF. (2014). *Fiscal transparency evaluation for the Russian Federation*. International Monetary Fund Country Report No. 14/ 134.

Kraan, D., Bergvall, D., Hawkesworth, I., Kostyleva, V., & Witt, M. (2008). Budgeting in Russia. *OECD Journal on Budgeting*, *8*(2), 1–58.

Krupa, O. (2018). *Capital budgeting and public investment projects in Ukraine. In Capital management and budgeting in the public sector*. Hershey, PA: IGI Global.

McKinsey Global Institute Report. (2015). *Bridging infrastructure gaps has the world made progress*? Retrieved May, 24, 2018, from https://www.mckinsey.com/~/media/mckinsey/industries/capital/mgi-bridging-infrastructure-gaps-discussion-paper.ashx

Ministry of Finance Russian Federation. (2018). *Investment management*. Retrieved February 1, 2018, from http://old.minfin.ru/en/nationalwealthfund/management/

Minitry of Economic Development. (2013). *Forecast of the long-term socio-economic development of the Russian Federation for the period up to 2030*. Retrieved July 13, 2018, from http://economy.gov.ru/minec/activity/sections/macro/prognoz/doc20130325_06

Movchan, A. (2016). *Is investment in infrastructure the answer to Russia's economic problems?* Retrieved May 24, 2018, from https://carnegie.ru/commentary/63484

Nations Encyclopedia. (2017). *Russia - Infrastructure, power, and communications*. Retrieved May 24, 2018, from http://www.nationsencyclopedia.com/economies/Europe/Russia-INFRASTRUCTURE-POWER-AND-COMMUNICATIONS.html#ixzz5GUjvot1F

OECD. (2006). *OECD economic surveys: Russian Federation, 17, OECD Publishing, Paris. Resolution No. 326 (2013б April 10). Resolution of federal government on April 10, 2013. On Approval of the List of RF Constituents where Territorial Development Zones May be Established.*

Resolution No. 694. (2005, November 23). On the investment fund of the Russian Federation. Retrieved May 24, 2018, from http://pravo.gov.ru/proxy/ips/?docbody=&nd=102101231&rdk=&backlink=1

Srithongrung, A. (2008). Impacts of state capital management programs on state economic performance. *Public Budgeting & Finance*, *28*(3), 83–107. doi:10.1111/j.1540-5850.2008.00912.x

Tanas, O., & Andrianova, A. (2017, June 19). *Russia eyes a $90 billion sovereign wealth fund. Bloomberg News*. Retrieved March 1, 2018, from https://www.bloomberg.com/news/articles/2017-06-19/russia-to-discuss-merging-wealth-funds-into-90-7-billion-coffer

Tax Code of the Russian Federation. (2018). *Tax code* [Налоговый Кодекс Российской Федерации]. Retrieved March 1, 2018, from http://nalogovyykodeks.ru/

The Federal law FZ#1662-R. (2008) *Concept of long-term social and economic development of the Russian Federation for the period to 2020* [О Концепции долгосрочного социально-экономического развития Российской Федерации на период до 2020 года]. Retrieved February 10, 2018, from http://www.consultant.ru/document/cons_doc_LAW_82134/

The Federal Law FZ#392. (2011). On zones of territorial development in the Russian Federation and on amendments to some legislation of the Russian Federation.

Vartapetov, K. (2010). Russia's federal fiscal grants: Regional equalisation and growth. *Post-Communist Economies*, *22*(4), 471–481. doi:10.1080/14631377.2010.518452

World Bank. (2016). *Private participation in infrastructure project database*. Retrieved March 21, 2018, from https://data.worldbank.org/indicator/IE.PPN.WATR.CD?locations=RU&view=chart

World Bank. (2017). *Russia's recovery: How strong are its shoots? Russia Economic Report*. Retrieved May 18, 2018, from https://openknowledge.worldbank.org/bitstream/handle/10986/28930/30-11-2017-17-58-52-forwebNovFINALRERENGfull.pdf?sequence=7

World Bank. (2018a). *World Bank national accounts data*. Retrieved May 17, 2018, from https://data.worldbank.org/indicator/NY.GDP.MKTP.CD

World Bank. (2018b). *Gross fix capital formation*. Retrieved May 17, 2018, fromhttps://data.worldbank.org/indicator/NE.GDI.FTOT.CD?locations=DE

Yaffa, J. (2014). *The waste and corruption of Vladimir Putin's 2014 winter Olympics. Bloomberg Businessweek.* Retrieved February 18, 2018, from https://www.bloomberg.com/news/articles/2014-01-02/the-2014-winter-olympics-in-sochi-cost-51-billion

Zhuravskaia, E. (2000). *Incentives to provide local public goods: Fiscal federalism, Russian style*. Boston: Mimeo. Harvard University.

APPENDIX

Table 11. Summary of capital budgeting and management in Russia

Normative Recommendations	Practices
Long-Term Capital Planning	
Comprehensive/Master Planning	The Ministry of Economic Development issues long-term projections for the economy discussing the external and domestic long-term developments
Strategic Planning	Strategic Planning prepared by the Ministry of Economic Development
Long-term Fiscal Planning	50-60 page document presenting objectives and main directions of tax policy; 100 page document presenting medium-term macroeconomic assumptions, objectives of fiscal policy, projection of general government finances, breakdown of budget expenditure, and sources of financing
Asset Inventory Analysis/Need Analysis	The government produces an estimate of the general government balance sheet which includes most conventional assets and liabilities.
Capital Improvement Program	5 year CIP
Capital Budgeting and Financial Management	
Systematic Priority Ranking	Investment projects are ranked according to cost-benefit analysis, the expected need for the project, and the assessed urgency in constructing the asset
Multi-year Fiscal Forecasting	Long-term social and economic forecast of RF for the period from 2015 to 2030; medium-term economic forecast presenting three to five scenarios for a selected number of macroeconomic and social indicators over the coming three years prepared by the Ministry of Economic Development
Capital Budgeting Process	Three-year budgeting framework. The government's budget submission to parliament. In addition to the proposed law and annexes (about 4,500 pages) the budget submission includes a large volume of accompanying documents for investments
Debt Affordability Analysis	Yes
Operating Reserve	Yes
Debt Management Policy/Disclosure (e.g., debt ceiling, debt approval by National Assembly, debt issuance, any debt/tax choice policy or guidance, etc.)	Debt is limited to a ceiling equal to the sub-national government's annual budget revenue net of federal grants. Annual borrowing is limited to 15 percent of revenue net of federal grants for regions and 10 percent for municipalities (Article 91 in Budget Code)
Centralized Execution and Project Management	
Budget/Project Status Reporting	The Treasury's budget execution reports and financial statements
Internal Audit (using budget variance report)	Internal Audit by Chamber of Accounts (Счетная Палата)
Project Acquisition, Contract Management, and Performance Monitoring	The key role of Federal Ministry of Finance
Budget Status Report/ Internal Auditing	The information on the general government's fixed and financial assets and liabilities is published on an annual basis in the Treasury's year-end financial report and Federal State Statistics Service data
Infrastructure maintenance	
Maintenance Planning	N/A
Maintenance Funding	No mid-term, no long-term policy of maintenance funding
Asset Management (e.g., repair over replacement policy)	Asset Quality Review
Program/performance evaluation	Program evaluation

Chapter 7
Public Capital Budgeting and Management Process in Moldova

Erica Ceka
Northern Illinois University, USA

ABSTRACT

As Moldova works toward building democracy and sustainable development, it is focusing its attention on increasing the effectiveness of public capital investment management. The chapter summarizes the current legal framework and practices in the field of capital management and budgeting in Moldova and compares the processes with a normative framework for effective capital investment management, focusing on capital planning, capital financial management, capital project execution and management, and public infrastructure maintenance. The analysis demonstrates that the public capital management and budgeting process in Moldova at the level of planning, allocation, and implementation of capital budgets falls short of its potential. The case reveals that despite a promising budgetary reform and comprehensive legal framework, the process of capital budgeting and management in Moldova remains ineffective due to institutional, economic, and political constraints.

INTRODUCTION

The theoretical literature on public capital investment emphasizes the importance of capital projects for state economic progress and the overall well-being of the population. Studies suggest that to achieve sustained growth, low-income countries should increase their investments in infrastructure such as transportation, communication, and energy (Dabla-Norris, Brumby, Kyobe, Mills, & Papageorgiou, 2013; Srithorgung, Yusuf, & Kriz, 2019). However, empirical analysis of the public capital decisions of developing countries sometimes provides inconsistent results (Dabla-Norris et al., 2013). In many low-income countries, public capital investments are not productive, and the quality and efficiency of capital projects are often not achieved because of corruption, weak technical expertise, limited information, and capital investment mismanagement (Dabla-Norris et al., 2013; Pritchett, 2000).

DOI: 10.4018/978-1-5225-7329-6.ch007

Moldova is an example of a low-income country that is currently attempting to increase effectiveness of public investments in the capital infrastructure through the creation of relevant administrative procedures. The reform of capital investment management in Moldova was supported by the World Bank and by the European Union through the Technical Assistance Project for Improving Public Finance Management Reform. The international organizations offered their expertise to assist the Moldovan government in developing favorable, legal and administrative frameworks. Undeniably, as a newly formed independent country, Moldova needs assistance from other states that already have experience in making such normative arrangements and that can offer generalized solutions (Morozov, 2014).

After a few decades of reforms and foreign assistance, the capital management and budgeting processes in Moldova fall short of successful practices. The analysis of public expenditures in Moldova performed by the World Bank evaluates all aspects of public capital management and concludes that rather than contributing to the state's economic progress, the capital management and budgetary reform in Moldova has resulted in significant inefficiencies in the allocation and implementation of capital budgets, a large variation in capital budget execution, dependence of capital investments on externally-funded projects and grants, and the lack of an integrated framework for strategic planning and common appraisal methodology for all capital projects (Coulibaly & Diagne, 2014). Scholars (e.g., Esfahani & Ramirez, 2003; Haque & Kneller, 2008; Srithongrung, Yusuf & Kriz, 2019) suggest that governmental capital management practices can deviate from the normative prescriptions of what a government should do due to institutional, political, and managerial contexts.

The major purpose of this chapter is to analyze capital management and budgeting practices in Moldova, comparing them against the normative framework suggested by the theoretical literature (Srithongrung, Yusuf & Kriz, 2019) to identify whether the adoption of the normative principles affects capital investment efficiency and effectiveness. This comparative analysis will focus on the four critical components of the systematic capital management process as described by Srithorgung, Yusuf, and Kriz (2019): (1) public capital planning, (2) capital budgeting and financial management, (3) centralized execution and project management, and (4) public infrastructure maintenance. In addition to the comparative analysis within the normative framework suggested by the scholars, the chapter will also present the unique features of the capital management approach used in Moldova as well as the country's context that affects capital management and budgeting processes.

The chapter makes a twofold contribution to the field of public finance and management. The first contribution is in its focus on Moldova and more specifically, on the country's capital management and budgeting processes and the way they are practiced in this country. Considering the recent efforts taken by the Moldovan government for addressing gaps in public budgeting, specifically in regard to capital investment management, this analysis attempts to increase our understanding of the factors that influence the capital investment decisions of the Moldovan government. The study will enhance the existing literature on capital management and budgeting practices that mainly consists of reports done by the international organizations and a few empirical studies. The second contribution is derived from the comparative perspective of the analysis. Viewed through the normative framework suggested by the scholars (Srithongrung, Yusuf & Kriz, 2019), the case study on Moldova will serve as an example of how capital management and budgeting processes vary in different national contexts, increasing understanding of countries' differences and possible consequences that result from different practices of capital management and budgeting.

This chapter is structured in four parts. The first part provides a brief overview of the country's political, economic, legal, and institutional backgrounds that frame decisions and practices in relation to public capital management as well as the current state of the Moldovan public infrastructure system in terms of accessibility, quality, and quantity. The second part has two sections. The first section presents the theoretical literature on the capital management and budgeting processes, focusing on the four components of the systematic capital management process of the Srithongrung, Ermasova and Yusuf's (2019) normative framework and the key elements of each component of the framework. The second section provides a descriptive analysis of the legal and institutional frameworks that regulate capital management and budgeting processes in Moldova. The third part of the chapter presents distinct features of the country's context that affect its capital management and budgeting processes. The chapter concludes that regardless of the available legal tools, the process of capital budgeting and management remains ineffective due to institutional, information, economic, and political factors.

COUNTRY'S BACKGROUND

The Republic of Moldova is one of the 15 ex-Soviet Union republics that became independent in 1991 after the revolutionary wave of the late 1980s across the entire communist camp in Europe. It is a parliamentary republic in which the president represents the head of state, the prime minister represents the head of the government, and the parliament has legislative authority (Constitution of the Republic of Moldova, 1994). With Romania in the West and Ukraine in the East, Moldova seems to be sandwiched by two big and very different worlds: the powerful European Union to the west and the immense Slavic world to the east. Being the smallest country in the whole Eastern European space, Moldova found itself to be a country with the biggest political, social, and most evidently, economic problems in the region. Cut off from the energetic supplies, centralized funding, and massive subsidies from the Soviet Union to support its industry and agriculture, Moldova was cast, practically overnight, into a deep financial crisis that immediately paralyzed all domains of Moldovan society. The World Bank and other international organizations estimated that "by the FY 2000 Moldovan GDP was about half of what it was in 1990" (Morozov, 2014, p. 148). With the support of the World Bank and the International Monetary Fund (IFM) in the early 1990s, the new Moldovan government launched ample and ambitious reform programs meant to bring a number of changes to the Moldovan economy and prevent it from falling into a total collapse. The country proclaimed commitment to democratic principles and restructured the institutional and legal framework to create free markets and a representative government (Matei, 2013; Morozov, 2014).

Since its emergence, the Moldovan government has been comprised of central and local governments. According to the law on the administrative territorial organization of the Republic of Moldova, there are two levels of local government. The first level is local government that represents villages or cities. The second level includes the regional government, (i.e. districts), municipalities, and the autonomous territorial unit of Gagauz Yeri. The district level is the intermediary level between the national authority and local authorities. There are 32 districts at the second level in the territorial-administrative system of Moldova and about 900 administrative-territorial units (ATUs) at the first level (The National Bureau of Statistics, 2013, p. 14). In the frame of the new reform, the Law on Local Public Finance No. 397-XV (LLPF) represented an effort to create a self-financing system for local governments (Morozov, 2009). The LLPF attempted to provide a procedure through which the local budgets should be designed by the local executive bodies and approved by the local councils. According to this law, budgets of local governments are independent, and upper levels of government may not intervene in this budget autonomy. Local governments have their own revenues and authority to define the purpose of the fund's usage. The only exceptions are special transfers and loans, which are given to local governments from upper level budgets: level II, and, mainly, the state budget (Morozov, 2014). Likewise, the Law on Local Public Administration No. 436-XVI/2006 and the Law on Administrative Decentralization no. 435-XVI/2006 delegate authority to the local governments. Overall, the main purpose of the new legal framework is to determine the fiscal responsibility of the local governments and to establish an efficient mechanism to regulate inter-budgetary relationships between all levels of governance (Matei, 2013; Morozov, 2009, 2014). Given the European Union's standards for decentralization and self-governance, the process of decentralization has been considered a basic policy issue in Moldova (Morozov, 2009).

Although the law regarding local public administration and the law on decentralization gave the local public authorities (LPAs) rights to initiate and decide all matters of local interest, the LPAs lack financial resources to meet local demands for services (Matei, 2013). Therefore, the state still has a strong influence on local governments because of the massive amount of governmental assistance it provides (Morozov, 2009). For example, in 2009 the share of national transfers in local budgets accounted for 65 percent (Kraan, Kostyleva, Forthun, Albrecht, & Olofsson, 2010). Thus, the process of budget development in Moldova is marked by a high dependency of LPAs on the central government (Matei, 2013). In addition, the law on decentralization considers LPAs financially sustainable if their administrative expenditures do not exceed 30 percent of the total revenue. But in the Public Administration Reform Strategy (PARS) 2016-2018, the national government reported that less than 20 percent of the LPAs meet these requirements. Furthermore, the government reported in the PARS that the true fiscal decentralization is not achieved at the level of local government (p. 43).

Creating and developing economic partnerships with the growing European Union and other international economic bodies such as the IFM and the World Bank as well as other ex-Soviet countries has been an impetus for Moldova's economic survival. The Partnership and Cooperation Agreement (PCA) signed with the European Union (EU) in 1994 opened up multiple opportunities to pursue economic recovery through cooperation with EU. This agreement was very important for Moldova because it represented an official start for the dialog on the Moldovan European integration and future potential EU accession. Following suggested strategies and reforms, introducing a new national currency (in 1993), and launching a massive privatization program, the Moldovan government managed to reduce the budget deficit from 6.3 percent of GDP in FY 1999 to 1.1 percent of GDP in 2001 (Morozov, 2014, p.149).

Through the partnerships with international institutions, Moldova received financial support in the form of grants, loans, and technical assistance (Morozov, 2014). During the first decade of its independence, the amount of foreign aid and international assistance that Moldova received from the major donors increased from $62.9 million in FY 2000 to $272.9 million in FY 2010 (Morozov, 2014, p.155). The World Bank reported an increase in capital expenditures that are funded by external sources; the share of which increased from 15 percent in 2006 to 36 percent in 2011 (Coulibaly & Diagne, 2014, p. 12). In his analysis of the Moldovan public finance system, Morozov (2014) noted that during the 2009-2015 period "the highest growth rate in capital spending was observed in externally financed spending. This suggests that Moldovan dependency on foreign assistance for improvement of its infrastructure is increasing" (p. 161). In fact, the trend in budgetary allocations for capital expenditures from the domestic sources increased as well, which can be explained by the commitment of the Moldovan government to leverage resources for externally financed capital projects implemented through partnership agreements (see Table 1).

To transform the country's economy, it was essential for Moldova to improve the infrastructure system, increasing public capital investments in the agriculture, transportation, and energy sectors. However,

Table 1. Capital expenditure in the general budget of Moldova, 2009-2015 (MDL, millions)

Capital Expenditure	2009	2010	2011	2012	2013	2014		2015
						Budget	Proj.	Proj.
Total	3,004	3,431	4,273	5,553	7,120	7,898	8,557	9,418
Domestically financed	**2,274**	2,228	2,714	3,406	4,665	5,063	5,078	5,548
Externally financed	**730**	1,203	1,559	2,147	2,455	2,835	3,480	3,870
External finance to total CE (%)	**24%**	35%	36%	39%	34%	36%	41%	41%

Source: Author's calculation using data in Morozov B. (2014, p. 160)

since its independence, Moldova has not been able to address the investment needs for infrastructure upgrades due to a permanent political and economic crisis that has significantly influenced the access to and coverage of the public infrastructure. After the collapse of the Soviet Union and loss of centralized financial support, the Moldovan government did not have sufficient resources even to maintain the poor and underdeveloped infrastructure built by the previous regime (Morozov, 2014). Then the rise of the communist government in 2001 that significantly increased public sector wages and pensions to support its constituency resulted in a large fiscal deficit (from 1.1 percent to 11.5 percent of GDP between 2001 and 2009, respectively) and the deterioration of the capital infrastructure (Morozov, 2014, pp.150, 154). The last decade brought oligarchs into power who, in just a few years of governing, embezzled about $1 billion from the state banks, which accounts for 15 percent of the country's GDP (Rumney, 2016), affecting the country's economy and, consequently, governmental capacities to fund public infrastructure. The current funding available for capital improvements is insufficient to address infrastructure needs in all capital categories.

According to the Country Report 2017, generated by the IMF, the quality of the public infrastructure in Moldova for almost all sectors is below the average among the neighboring countries. Compared to other low-income countries, Moldova scores higher only for the telecommunication infrastructure and electricity. In terms of infrastructure quantity, the IMF notes that Moldova demonstrates better scores compared to other low-income countries. For example, Moldova offers better access to and coverage of economic infrastructure (e.g., energy and telecommunication networks, roads, and water) and social infrastructure (e.g., hospitals and schools). However, the IMF reports that the access and coverage are limited to certain locations and are not uniform across the country. The analysis of Public Investment Efficiency (PIE) evaluates the institutional framework that shapes public capital investment management across the four stages of the capital investment process: appraisal, selection, implementation, and evaluation. According to the results of this analysis in 2012, Moldova scored 2.33 out of 4 on the PIE index among 71 low- and middle-income countries (see Dabla-Norris et al., 2013 for the list of countries used in the analysis).

There are two capital categories that require special attention from the Moldovan government. The first category relates to the roads and transportation. The second category includes the water and sewage systems. The World Bank reports that by 2014, "only about 26 percent of national roads are in good to fair condition, 54 percent in poor condition and about 20 percent in bad condition. The situation for local roads is worse, with 22 percent in fair condition and the rest in poor to bad condition" (Coulibaly & Diagne, 2014, p. 48). Likewise, the capital investments in the water and sanitation category are not sufficient to halt the deterioration of water supply and sewage systems. The evaluation of the water and sewage systems in Moldova reveals that "as of 2012, 44 percent of registered water supply systems and 40 percent of waste water management systems still required full rehabilitation. The rate of pipe breakage was about 7.4 breaks per km/year in 2010, which is 30 times higher than the rate in well maintained Western European systems" (Coulibaly & Diagne, 2014, p. 60). The needs in this category require a substantial capital investment that the Moldovan government specified in the long-term (2012-2025) national Water and Sanitation Strategy (WSS). The government reported that the total investment needs range between $1.3 to $3.2 billion. Yet the current spending on water and sanitation between 2008 and 2012 was only about $120 million (WWS, p. 51). The government stated that in terms of access to water and sewage systems:

- 44 percent of the population has no access to safe drinking water;
- The quality of most groundwater used for drinking purposes is inadequate due to naturally occurring or anthropogenic pollutants;
- There is a high degree of non-compliance for microbiological samples taken both in urban (9.4 percent) and rural (16.2) areas;
- Water supplied in schools and children's institutions is inadequate (23.8 percent of the samples exceeding the MACs for chemical and microbiological parameters). (p. 48)

The National Development Strategy Moldova 2020 represents a comprehensive strategic document on how to achieve sustainable development, but it envisions infrastructure development in only two categories: 1) roads and transportation and 2) fuel and energy. The largest capital investment category, roads and transportation, includes the capital expenditures mostly related to the maintenance work and basic repair rather than infrastructure development. Despite the established goals, the government is unlikely to achieve its strategic objective to have at least 80 percent of all of the country's roads in good condition by 2020, as specified in the National Development Strategy (Coulibaly & Diagne, 2014). In the fuel and energy category, the allocations are below one percent of the total infrastructure needs.

In its annual Medium Term Expenditure Framework Report (MTEF) 2018-2020, the Ministry of Finance (MOF) stated that "the share of capital expenditures in total spending remains modest and declined to 10 percent of the total budget spending in 2016. In the medium term, more public investment in the infrastructure and other key areas will be needed" (p. 13). The MOF also reported that Moldova has experienced a significant increase in international support in the form of grants and loans for budgetary support and investment projects. According to the national budget in FY 2018, Moldova is scheduled to receive $596.4 million in foreign assistance. There are eight major donors that the Moldovan government recognizes as the most critical partners for the country's development. The donors and their contributions are included in the budget report for citizens prepared by the MOF. They are:

- European Commission ($208.7)
- The World Bank ($112.4)
- IMF ($26.6)
- Global Fund ($4.6)
- European Investment Bank ($111.0)
- Council of Europe Development Bank ($25.5)

- International Fund for Agricultural Development ($10.1)
- European Bank for Reconstruction and Development ($89.0)

Regardless of the impressive number of the adopted laws and international assistance, Moldova has not achieved sustainable economic growth and remains the poorest country in Europe. According to the International Monetary Fund (IMF), the GDP per capita in Moldova is the smallest among the neighborhood countries and the ex-Soviet republics (see Table 2).

CAPITAL MANAGEMENT AND BUDGETING: THEORY AND PRACTICE

The Normative Framework

Public capital expenditures can be attributed to two broad categories, either purchase of capital assets that will provide benefits for an extended period without repeating the investment or spending on capital improvements of already existing capital assets, prolonging their useful life (Mikesell, 2013). In either case, the capital expenditures focus on spending for a multiyear period (Bland, 2014). Capital expenditures can also be classified based on their impact on production of public and private goods and services (Mikesell, 2013). For example, expenditures related to capital investments and capital procurement all contribute to the economic development of the country while procurement of fixed assets, capital repair works, and capital transfers are aimed at improving the efficiency and effectiveness of the government.

Governments differ in their approaches to budgeting and managing capital expenditures. Some use unified budgets consisting of operating expenditures together with capital expenditures in one document, while other governments use separated budgets for each type of expenditure. Many scholars favor a separate capital budgeting process, arguing that “separate consideration contributes to the efficiency and effectiveness” of long-term investments and can stabilize tax rates (Mikesell, 2013, p. 260). The ratio-

Table 2. GDP per capita at purchasing power parity in 2010 and 2016 (USD)

Country	2010	2016
Albania	7 454	10 067
Armenia	5 110	6 712
Georgia	5 114	7 386
Macedonia	9 728	13 136
Moldova	3 083	4 424
Bulgaria	12 851	18 010
Romania	11 860	16 335
Ukraine	6 712	9 739
Estonia	18 519	25 145
Latvia	14 460	20 213
Lithuania	17 185	24 262

Source: The National Development Strategy Moldova 2020 (p. 12)

nale for separate capital budgeting is summarized by six critical reasons: 1) stakes are high, 2) decisions extend for years, 3) spending varies from year to year, 4) implementation takes time, 5) debt financing is often used, and 6) capital projects differ from year to year (Marlowe, Rivenbark, & Vogt, 2009). Another advantage of having a separate capital budget is the possibility for tracking expenditures that result in the purchase of an asset, helping to properly interpret the state of government finances and avoid giving a misleading impression that the government has high operating costs (Goode & Birnbaum, 1956).

Regardless of the budget type, separate or unified, capital expenditures should receive special treatment (Goode & Birnbaum, 1956). Scholars suggest attributing a label, i.e. capital, to expenditures to distinguish between capital and operating costs. The distinction between capital and operating expenditures can be understood in the following terms: capital expenditures "represent collective investment, whereas operating expenditures represent collective consumption" (Goode & Birnbaum, 1956, p. 26). Bland (2014) states that the distinction between two classes of expenditures is based on five differences: type of expenditures, funding sources, levels of risk, timing requirements, and monitoring.

Capital expenditures have a long-term impact on operating costs, either causing an increase in operating expenditures by adding more lines (e.g., interest payments on borrowed capital) or improving governmental service capacity (e.g., building a new service facility, automatization, procurement of new equipment). Since capital expenditures differ from government operating costs and have a long service life, they merit special attention during the planning process (Bland & Nunn, 1992). Comprehensive capital planning helps estimate a country's capital formation and appreciate amortization allowances against capital items recorded as expenditures in the operating budget (Bland, 2014). Such planning will provide a clear picture of the impact of capital investments on the annual budget (Gianakis & McCue, 1999). Capital planning also prevents making mistakes and reduces errors in addressing the public infrastructure needs. In most cases, the decisions regarding fund capital investment projects favor borrowing, which may add financial pressure in times of crisis (Mikesell, 2013). Thus, capital planning can assist governments in evaluating whether the demands for capital improvement match their financial capacity to fund those capital projects (Bland, 2014; Mikesell, 2013).

Srithongrung, Yusuf and Kriz (2019) united the theoretical suggestions in a comprehensive capital management and budgeting normative framework, consisting of four key components: (1) long-term public capital planning, (2) capital budgeting and financial management, (3) project execution, and (4) infrastructure maintenance.

The long-term capital planning component involves the following elements: needs assessment and asset inventory, strategic planning, capital improvement programs, and long-term fiscal planning. The needs assessment is based on economic and demographic data as well as statistics for capital assets and state-funded capital programs. It provides an overview of the predictable long-term capital needs for a five-year period. The strategic planning includes cost estimation of projected capital investments, prioritization of those capital projects within the agency's mission, and availability of resources. The development of a capital improvement program (CIP) with a comprehensive data collection system and reliable estimates of current and projected resources logically derives from the previous two elements. The main purpose of CIP is "to identify and monitor proposed capital projects, and coordinate the financing and timing of their capital improvements in a way that maximizes their return to public" (Gianakis & McCue, 1999, p. 124). CIP also serves as a mechanism that unites financial forecasts with needs and program analyses, helping to identify "how much money will be needed to keep up with infrastructure needs" (Gianakis & McCue, 1999, p. 124). Even if the CIP is not considered a legal document approved by the voters, it is highly important for a government as it assists in making decisions on selection of and funding for capital investment projects.

The fiscal component of the long-term planning focuses on the description and assessment of alternative methods to finance capital investment projects. It presents financing opportunities, including current government revenues, debt financing, international grants, and any participation by the private sector. Long-term public capital planning is a critical component of a systematic capital management process because it reflects a strategic approach to capital management and assists governments in achieving investment efficiency.

The second component of the Srithongrung, Yusuf and Kriz's (SYK) normative framework reflects the process of capital budgeting and financial management with a main purpose to match existing financial resources with capital needs and to ensure fiscal stability. This component includes the following elements: prioritization of capital projects, development of comprehensive financial strategies, and annual budgeting. Capital investment projects can be ranked based on the following criteria: fiscal impact; health and safety effects; economic effects; environmental, aesthetic and social effects; disruption and inconvenience; distributional effects; political feasibility; implication for deferral; amount of uncertainty; effects on surrounding cities; and impact on other capital projects (Bland, 2014). Among other factors that may influence the ranking of capital investment proposals are governmental priorities, community preferences, and the possibility of leveraging external grants or private funding (Bland, 2014). The multi-year revenue and expenditure forecasting helps identify governmental capacities to fund capital investment needs. During a period of budgetary scarcity, it is critical to conduct debt affordability analysis to estimate whether a national debt is too high in comparison with other countries. The importance of annual budgeting is in the potential for performing a continuous reappraisal of capital investment projects every budget cycle as the interest rate, the project costs, project demands, and even project priority may change (Bland, 2014; Gianakis & McCue, 1999).

The third component of the SYK normative framework emphasizes the importance of centralized execution and project management, and it consists of the following elements: project acquisition and contract management, budget status report, and internal auditing of the capital investment projects. When capital investment projects are coordinated by a central budget office, it has a positive impact on capital investment efficiency and effectiveness. Therefore, it is recommended that capital projects should be submitted to a central budget office that will ultimately determine and report the effects of the capital requests on the national budget and the state debt capacity. The creation of a database that captures the information of the state-wide capital project should also be practiced by a central budget office.

The fourth component of the SYK normative framework reflects recommendations related to infrastructure maintenance such as maintenance planning, maintenance funding, asset management, and program evaluation. To establish that the capital needs included in the CIP are based on actual needs, the SYK normative framework recommends adopting an asset management system that performs a regular assessment of the conditions of the capital assets to reserve resources for repairs and upgrades needed to extend the useful life of capital assets and to prevent costly replacements. According to SYK normative framework recommendations, there should be a reserve fund for emergencies in case the capital item may require immediate repair. The infrastructure maintenance can be included either in the capital or operating budget or in the special maintenance and repair budget (Ermasova, 2013).

Capital Management and Budgeting in Moldova

Capital Planning

The Moldovan Law on the Budgetary System and the Budgetary Process (LBSBP) No. 847 specifies that the capital formation is determined by the central government based on the national revenue accounts and associated fiscal forecasts. To estimate a country's capital formation, the Moldovan government made a clear distinction between capital and operating expenditures in a budget by providing a classification of what type of expenditures are considered capital (Annex 7 to the LBSBP). As reported on the Ministry of Finance website, the capital expenditures are recorded in the Moldovan budget in accordance with the classification of the Government Finance Statistics 2001.

The system does not require a separation of government capital and operating budgets, and thus, the capital expenditures and operating costs are included in one budget document. The public capital expenditures are planned, executed, and reported together with the current operating expenditures as an integral part of the state budget in compliance with the budgetary procedures as established by the Law on Public Finances and Fiscal Responsibilities (LPFFR) No. 181. The rationale for having a unified budget is connected to the principle of performance when performance-based programs are used to prepare and report budgets, allowing the government to more easily measure program costs and allocate resources among competing programs. In this unified public budget, capital expenditures and transfers of a capital nature are presented among other expenditures with a distinction between the physical and financial characteristics of capital assets. Consequently, the Parliament approves the operational and capital expenditures together as a package for each budget category.

The Moldovan government has adopted an improved economic classification system, employing the Government Finance Statistics recommended by the IMF. The current state budget includes the following six categories as capital expenditures: 1) *Capital investments:* purchase of assets used in the production of services or goods and expected to produce long-term benefits (e.g., construction of buildings, bridges); 2) *Capital procurement:* purchases of strategic stock, land, and intangible assets; 3) *Fixed assets:* procurement of assets with a usage period extending beyond one fiscal year and a value higher than 6,000 Moldovan lei (≈ $350); 4) *Capital repair works:* refurbishments of assets accumulated through capital investment; 5) *Capital transfers within the country:* any intra-budgetary transfers, transfers to state-owned enterprises or state funds (e.g., road fund); and 6) *Capital transfers to implement externally-funded projects:* the share of government funds and external grants and/or loans in capital projects (Coulibaly & Diagne, 2014, p. 10).

To guarantee the efficient and effective management of capital investments as well as the implementation of capital investment projects (CIP) in 2013, the Moldovan government adopted the Law on Public Capital Investments (LPCI) No. 1029. The LPCI provides two guiding principles of resource allocation for capital investment: (1) the priority in resource allocation is given to the completion of ongoing projects and (2) the development of the new CIPs must be based on the government's priorities at the national and local levels as specified in the strategic planning documents.

Capital investment projects financed from the pubic budget are planned, approved and managed in accordance with legal provisions. First, CIPs are prioritized based on their alignment with policy priorities and objectives set in medium-term strategic planning documents. Second, the allocation of resources for capital investment projects and their implementation reports are based on performance. Third, CIPs must demonstrate the efficient and effective use of public resources, ensuring a high degree of cost-effectiveness. Fourth, CIPs must demonstrate sustainability by taking into account the operating and maintenance costs after project completion. Fifth, CIPs must demonstrate the availability of budgetary resources and the capacity to implement the project (see Chapter II, article 7 of the LPCI for a more detailed description).

Long-term capital planning includes the following four phases:

- Establishment of a general limit for capital investment expenditures;
- Analysis and evaluation of the existing portfolio of capital investment projects;
- Identification of priorities for capital investment;
- Determination of capital expenditure limits (MOF, web resource).

The government requires that expenditures related to capital investment projects be included in the budget only if the procedures for preparing capital projects have been followed. The planning cycle for new capital investment projects consists of five stages: 1) project identification and preliminary assessment, 2) development of project documentation, 3) analysis and approval of funding, 4) implementation and monitoring, and 5) final evaluation.

According to the LPCI, in each of the stages, some public institutions play more active roles than others. In the first stage, the leading role is taken by the public agency that initiates the CIP. The agency should identify the purpose, objective, and preliminary results of the new CIP, and then evaluate the proposal against the following twelve selection criteria established by the government:

1. The proposed CIP must address capital problems identified through the needs assessment.
2. The proposed CIP must correspond to the national government's policy priorities.
3. CIP objectives are clear, measurable, achievable, and realistic with reasonable deadlines.
4. The CIP stipulates how to measure project results and achievements after implementation.
5. Different alternatives to achieve goals and measure results are considered.
6. Selected alternatives are justified.
7. Capital costs are realistic and justified through various scenarios and calculations.
8. Current costs are realistic and justified through various scenarios and calculations.
9. Sources to fund the proposed CIP have been identified.
10. Participants are identified and ready to become involved.
11. A clear and realistic implementation plan has been developed.
12. The proposed CIP has a high probability of achieving its objectives and results.

To move the CIP to the next stage, the LPCI specifies that the proposals should meet expectations for all selection criteria at each stage of the evaluation. In this process, the proposal is initiated by the lowest level of government, where relevant ministries and institutions should offer consultancy to the CIP initiating agency in needs assessment and preliminary selection. At the second stage, the CIP initiating agency should develop project documents and submit them to the relevant ministries of the upper level of government for analysis and approval. During the third stage, the main lead is taken by the relevant ministry or the upper-level public institution that evaluates project proposals and writes an informative note about the preliminary evaluation to the initiating agency, requesting more information and details. In cases of a positive decision, the package of documents for the approved proposal is submitted to the MOF. At this stage, the MOF prepares an informative note regarding the evaluation results for each proposal and combines the proposals from the central and local public administration authorities into one register. This register is submitted to the governmental Capital Investment Division for further evaluation and approval of the projects considered for funding.

Capital Budgeting and Financial Management

Based on standards set by the World Bank, the Moldovan government has attempted to improve its financial management by introducing a Medium-Term Expenditure Framework (MTEF) with three-year macroeconomic forecasting. The MTEF has a strategic meaning for long-term planning purposes and includes all components of the national public budget, containing elements of sectoral analysis and strategic planning with expenditure plans. Three main principles guide implementation of the MTEF: "(i) a top-down allocation of the budget envelope; (ii) a bottom-up estimation of the current and medium-term costs of existing and new policies; and (iii) a process of matching costs with available resources in the context of the annual budget cycle" (Kraan, Kostyleva, Forthun, Albrecht, & Oloffson, 2010, p. 18). The MTEF is seen as an instrument of public finance management as it focuses on ensuring better links between resource allocation and policy priorities and on improving decision making in budget management. Achieving efficiency of public resources is critical to sustainable improvement of public service delivery. The MOF recommends using the MTEF as a tool for increasing the effectiveness and efficiency of existing programs and redirecting resources to the highest priorities.

The MTEF cycle is based on a rolling framework that overlaps with the previous and following cycles by two years. The MOF sets the preliminary spending limits for a three-year period as a guideline for the expenditure development. After the budget proposals are submitted by governmental departments and ministries, the MOF incorporates proposals into one budget document and presents it to the Parliament for approval. For example, the MTEF 2016-2018 presents a picture of the revenues and expenditures for all three years separately, but Parliament approves the budget only for the 2016 fiscal year, while 2017 and 2018 become budget forecasts. The next year the forecast for 2017 becomes a budget for approval, while 2018 remains as a forecast and a new year three (2019) is added to the MTEF.

To improve capital investment decisions for multi-year CIPs, the MTEF separately provides progress information on financial implementation by central and local public authorities beyond the planning year. For each capital improvement proposal, the Moldovan government provides the Parliament with separate information tables collected from the MTEF budgets developed by public agencies for analysis. Those information tables list all future financial implications of capital investment projects (usually for the next two years after the fiscal year under review). Information on the ongoing projects is structured in conformity with the requirements of international organizations and consists of the following:

(a) Total estimated project cost, (b) Actual expenditure prior to the current budget year, (c) Balance to complete at the beginning of the current budget year, (d) Current budget plan, (e) Balance to complete at the end of the current budget year, (f) Planned expenditure in the budget planning year by source of funds, and (g) Estimated expenditures in the two years after the budget planning year. (Coulibaly & Diagne, 2014, p. 27)

As prescribed by the LPCI, the government can justify its decisions based on the results of the technical-economic evaluations and sufficient analysis of the cost-effectiveness of CIPs due to expectation for their long-term usage. Also the proposals should demonstrate a connection with government priorities and the socio-economic context, reflecting the needs of target users or groups. Fiscal, environmental, and social impacts play a significant role in project selection. In addition, the capacity of the implementation agency to run the project and analysis of risks and spatial planning problems are taken into consideration.

The MOF sets up four critical points to assist the allocation decisions. First, the expenditures should be in close correlation with the country's strategic priorities: The National Development Strategy "Moldova 2020," the Association Agreement between the Republic of Moldova and/or the EU and the Government Action Program 2016-2018. Second, a priority in resource allocation should be given to the programs that will have a greater impact on the achievement of government policy objectives. Third, project proposals should be correlated with the available external funding provided through development partners and other sources. Fourth, resources should be targeted toward high-level priorities based on getting a high-value-for-money ratio.

Spending for capital items is expected to be covered by other sources not normally used to fund operating costs, and the money is usually borrowed because it is anticipated that capital items will yield a return on investment in future years (Bland, 2014). However, the World Bank (2008) reported that "Moldova's capital markets are narrow with only a handful of corporate stocks being publicly traded, and thus are not yet perceived as a source of financing" (Coulibaly & Diagne, 2014, p. 6). As the capital needs are high and cannot be covered by the domestic financing, the capital expenditures are funded through loans and grants offered by the international organizations (see Table 3). The amount of loans for investment projects offered to Moldova in FY 2018 is about twice as big as those in the previous year, which significantly increases the country's debt. In accordance with the Law on Public Sector Debt and State Guarantees No. 419-XVI (adopted on December 22, 2006), the national debt and debt ceiling are approved by the Parliament. The central government debt is managed by the MOF that acts as a governmental representative in debt administration, while the National Bank of Moldova (NBM) manages debt contracted on the NBM name. Local public authorities manage debt and issue guarantees on local debt contracts.

The Moldovan government practices a three-year Medium Term Debt Management (MTDM) strategy, covering about 90 percent of the total national debt. The fifth chapter of the MTDM strategy includes the evaluation of risks associated with the central government debt portfolio. The Public Debt Department (PDD) manages the governmental debt portfolio, including all external and domestic loans, and issues the governmental guarantees. Debt service, debt statistics, and development of the borrowing plans are also responsibilities of the PDD. There are 15 units in the PDD that oversee external and domestic debt, perform analysis of risks, and control lending. The Treasury Department is responsible for cash planning and forecasting for budget execution and reporting.

Table 3. The structure of the international assistance (USD, millions)

		2016	2017	2018 Projected
Grants	Investment Projects	16.2	39.4	36.2
	Budgetary Support	47.2	25.7	123.8
Loans	Investment Projects	76.6	134.5	266.1
	Budgetary Support	153.7	135.2	170.2

Source: The Ministry of Finance of Moldova (2018)

In their report on the debt management performance of Moldova, the World Bank (2008) stated that

overall Moldova scores high on the managerial structure, coordination with monetary policy, policies and procedures for domestic borrowing, and debt records. Aspects of legal framework as well as debt reporting were also highly rated. In the area of coordination with fiscal policy, policies and procedures for external borrowing, loan guarantees, on-lending and debt-related transactions, as well as cash flow forecasting and cash balance management Moldova meets the minimum requirements for effective debt management. (p. 6)

Centralized Execution and Project Management

According to the Law on Public Procurement No.131 of July 3, 2015, the CIP implementation starts with preparing all necessary documentation for public acquisition procedures, selecting contracting organizations, and establishing guidelines for supervision of work. All acquisitions related to the implementation of the CIP are carried out in accordance with the public procurement legislation. The Public Procurement Agency (PPA) is responsible for examining, monitoring, and verifying compliance of all public procurement contracts with the existing public procurement procedures. The PPA has a responsibility to register all procurement contracts in a country-wide procurement register and to maintain the public procurement registry. However, the PPA registers each procurement contract as an individual entry, but it does not reflect procurement contracts in connection to the CIP (Coulibaly & Diagne, 2014).

As established by the LPCI, the CIP initiating agency becomes responsible for implementation and reporting, while the upper level agencies monitor the implementation and report the project status and results based on information provided by the implementation agency. Execution of the CIP must be done in accordance with the approved financial limits, activity plans, and time frames. The CIP implementation plan must clearly specify the project's activities, estimated completion dates for each activity, and cost-benefit description for each activity. The implementation plan must also present all relevant documentation, including approval from the appropriate institutions and experts up to the final stage of the CIP implementation.

The proper management and monitoring of CIPs is the responsibility of both the central public authority (i.e., MOF) and the local public authority that initiates the CIP. The LPCI specifies the basic responsibilities of the MOF in the process of managing capital investment projects, which include a) updating the baseline and determining the overall capital expenditure limits, b) examining the sectoral spending strategies and analyzing the proposals of the central public authorities to adjust the expenditure limits on capital investments, c) coordinating the process of allocating the sectoral limits of capital investment expenditures to the components of the national public budget and to central public authorities, and d) submitting the list of capital investment projects for approval to the Moldovan government.

The LPCI establishes the role of the local public agencies in the CIP implementation and reporting. According to the LPCI, the head of the agency that initiates the CIP should ensure that the CIP has a project manager to coordinate implementation and monitoring as well as to submit implementation reports in accordance with the MOF requests and other relevant laws. The implementation report should reflect the following a) a description of the CIP, including the purpose and objectives; b) the performance indicators for the CIP related to the purpose and objectives; c) the actual CIP expenses up to the reporting date; d) proposed changes that would require an increase in the allocation limits with appropriate justification; e) recommendations and solutions to overcome changes in the implementation; and f) other critical (e.g., technical, financial, environmental) factors that may affect the CIP implementation. The ongoing CIP monitoring report is submitted by the implementation agency to the MOF annually.

After CIP implementation is completed, the implementing agency submits the final report to the MOF, focusing on compliance of the CIP implementation with the initial project deadline, resource allocation, and technical aspects. The report also must include a description of any discrepancies between the initial implementation plan in terms of activities and the de-facto implementation with a comprehensive explanation of what caused the deviation. The report is analyzed by the MOF and is then presented to the Capital Investment Division for examination and final approval. There is a very strict financial control in Moldova with rigid procedures to ensure that projects achieve their objectives. However, the reporting requirements are weak because they are based only on annual financial indicators related to the disbursement of funds within the reported period. Internal auditing is not performed, and therefore, the problems are not identified at the early stages (Coulibaly & Diagne, 2014).

Infrastructure Maintenance

With the support of the European Union Technical Assistance for Improving the Public Finance Management Reform, the Moldovan government is currently in the process of developing an information system that includes all CIPs in one national registry. The first purpose of this system is to maintain records of existing capital projects at any stage of their implementation, offering public authorities at all levels access to the inventory. The second purpose is to provide a way for the national government to evaluate ongoing projects that do not match their priorities. The third purpose of the development of a national information system is the possibility for a systematic capital needs assessment and further identification of strategic directions for capital investments (Coulibaly & Diagne, 2014).

Capital assets are recorded as capital expenditures in the current state budget, reflecting the total cost of the annual commitment for the capital purchase, but capital revenues and capital depreciation allowances are not included in the annual public budget. Although the Moldovan government has managed to integrate capital expenditures in multi-year budget planning, in most cases, those expenditures represent costs associated with new capital projects rather than planned improvements of already existing capital assets. When the public agency initiates a new capital investment project, it must include in the proposal availability of funds or sources for maintenance that are sufficient to cover operation for the first two years of the capital object once the object gets in use. Capital expenditures related to the maintenance of the object and depreciation allowances become the responsibility of the receiving agency where asset formation takes place. The Ministry of Transportation, for example, will have to reflect costs related to the maintenance and depreciation allowances of new buses that were purchased in the frame of a capital investment project as operating expenditures in its annual budget.

According to the law on public finances, the maintenance of capital assets and asset appraisal has been moved from the national budget into the budgets of the public agencies that initiate capital investment projects. The capital assets are reflected in financial reports based on their initial value. The initial value is the sum of the purchase cost (including all relevant taxes), the cost for constructing or manufacturing the capital asset, the cost to prepare all documents, and any installation costs as well as other expenses related to the preparation of a capital asset for usage. Modification of the initial value of capital assets is only allowed in cases of procurement of additional equipment, upgrading, reconstruction, and/or partial liquidation of the respective objects. The capital repair of capital assets and special constructions are not considered maintenance expenditures but instead increase the initial value. In cases when the capital repair of buildings and special construction is carried out over a period of more than one budgetary year, the initial value of the respective fixed assets shall be increased by the amount of the expenses incurred for capital repairs in the year of execution. By allowing implementing agencies to allocate funds for infrastructure repair and maintenance for current and future years of asset usage as part of their budgets, the government improved the proposal development and prioritization processes (Coulibaly & Diagne, 2014).

Consequences

The analysis of capital management and budgeting in Moldova demonstrates that the capital management practices are constrained by the institutional, informational, fiscal, and political factors. Despite the improved legal framework for public investment management, the capital infrastructure projects in all areas remain underfinanced. According to the MOF report (2018), "the share of capital expenditures in total spending remains modest and declined to 10 percent of the total budget spending in 2016. In the medium term, more public investment in infrastructure and other key areas will be needed" (p. 13).

The underinvestment in infrastructure and other capital projects can be explained by the fact that the function of public administration in Moldova is framed in the hierarchical dimension (Matei, 2013, p. 193). Because of the reforms and changes in political power, local governments experience limitation of fiscal autonomy, blurred line of authority between national and local public administration, as well as intervention of national government in issues that are local in nature (Morozov, 2009). The limitation in some taxing powers and a weak self-financing capacity of local governments affect the overall quality of capital planning and long-term fiscal planning. Public agencies are discouraged from engaging in any meaningful planning because limits on capital expenditures are established by the MOF in advance without taking into consideration the actual financial needs to cover capital investments (Coulibaly & Diagne, 2014). The local public administrations and public agencies lack discretion to make decisions on selecting perspective projects, being bounded by the centralized priorities. Since the prioritization process is aligned to the national priorities but local governments do not have sufficient financial resources to independently fund local projects, the infrastructure needs at the community level remain underfinanced. For example, the World Bank notes that with the decentralization, the local governments did not manage to halt the deterioration of the water and sewage systems (Coulibaly & Diagne, 2014, p. 59). At the local level, governments lack the institutional capacity to mobilize and manage additional funds to invest in repairs and maintenance of the existing infrastructure, resulting in high inequalities in access to sewage (only 5 percent of the rural population is connected to sewage systems) and improved sanitation (Coulibaly & Diagne, 2014, p. 61). The extent to which public agencies are constrained by the established revenue limits leads to their incapability to attract additional resources for solving local problems, to assure their own revenues, and to bring innovation for capital improvement projects. Hence, capital projects with a high local priority are postponed due to incapability of public agencies to generate revenues in favor of those capital projects that have available international or national funding.

Moldova practices multiyear planning, such as MTEF, based on a programmatic approach that covers a three-year period. The MTEF serves as a mechanism that unites fiscal forecasts with programmatic and capital needs in one strategic document. The central and local public authorities can separately evaluate implementation of each capital investment project beyond the planning year at each level in the system. Such an activity allows performance of fiscal analysis to ensure continuity of funding for high-priority projects or to identify projects that have already lost their priority. However, the development of the national registry of capital assets is still in process. Therefore, at the central level, there is a lack of information on the assets' condition. To update existing assets according to their current values is challenging and is done mainly on the accounting principles rather than the actual physical condition of the capital assets. As a result, the capital planning and fiscal forecast is affected by the lack of reliable data and a systematic information collection process.

While the expenditure amounts for capital investment projects are presented for each spending category, the source of funding is included in the report in an aggregated form, making it difficult to determine how many CIPs are funded in each category and/or the source of the funding. It can be added that the indicators of performance are not related to the qualitative achievements of the program targets but mostly reflect financial information serving little purpose for resource allocation decisions. The MTEF mostly includes expenditures on new capital investment projects, while the operating and maintenance costs of already completed CIPs are included in the budgets of the agencies that receive the assets. Without reliable data, capital investment planning remains basically ad hoc (Coulibaly & Diagne, 2014).

The capital management and budgeting process in Moldova lacks a separate capital budget, which significantly affects governmental decisions on capital investment spending. Despite so many categories of capital expenditures, the budgetary positions are not transparent, offering little information on the two biggest categories of the capital expenditures. While most of the categories are self-explanatory and point directly to the type of capital expenditures, the capital transfers within the country and the capital transfer to implement externally-funded projects do not provide sufficient information to understand the purpose and destination of those expenditures. Often outlays covered by the capital transfer label do not represent capital expenditures, rather the costs are related to the maintenance and operation of services and, as a result, are arbitrary (Coulibaly & Diagne, 2014). The inclusion of the operating costs into the capital transfer category allows the government to neglect limitations on government operation expenditures. Also such practices may lead to partial avoidance of the political checks, as the size of the capital transfers would remain unchanged. The issue of misclassification of capital expenditures also affects the country's statistics. For example, by correcting a mistake in classification of the expenditures for the Road Fund covered by the capital transfer within a country in 2011, the share of the capital spending in the country's GDP would decrease from six to five percent (Coulibaly & Diagne, 2014).

The annual nature of public budgets often creates challenges for public officials and their financial boards regarding how to manage multi-year capital planning and commitments in the annual budget process. In many countries with annual budgets, governments usually renew funding for multi-year contracts that were signed under a forward commitment without any interruptions in payment. In the case of Moldova, multi-year contractual commitments are allowed; however, appropriations and payments must be required annually. Thus, the annual renewal of the contracts results in delays of payments and execution of project implementation.

The prioritization of capital proposals is affected by a lack of funds and dependence of Moldova on foreign assistance for capital infrastructure improvement (Morozov, 2014). The domestically-financed capital investments are replaced by the externally-funded capital expenditures in almost all budgetary categories. However, in some of the categories, the share of external finance reached more than a half of the total amount allocated for capital expenditure in a given category. The analysis of the national budgets for FY 2009-2015 and the budgetary allocations for capital projects in such categories as agriculture, energy, environmental protection, and transportation and road construction in 2009-2015 reveals a significant increase in transfers for the implementation of capital projects financed from external sources. For example, in the agriculture category, the share of external finance for capital project implementation increased from 40 percent in 2009 to 86 percent in 2015, while the foreign contribution for capital project in the environmental protection category almost tripled, moving from 25 percent in 2009 to 74 percent in 2015 (see Table 4).

A lack of sufficient funds to cover capital expenditures also affects the ranking of capital proposals. Although the priority system could help determine the selection of capital projects, it is challenging to choose when most of the capital investment needs are critical for a country's development. In such cases, cost-benefit analysis is one of the best tools in establishing the ranking of capital proposals. Yet, cost-benefit analysis is not always a determinant in project selection, as sometimes other priorities may outweigh economic benefits. Thus, the encouragement to correlate capital proposals with the available external funding provided through development partners and other sources increases the priority of those proposals that are in the interest range of the international donors (Coulibaly & Diagne, 2014). The funding gap for all capital infrastructure needs is so high that at the level of the central public authority, the Moldovan government mostly relies on external financial support to implement capital investment projects. For example, the national budget for FY 2018 indicates that 85 percent of total costs for capital investments are covered by foreign assistance (see Table 5).

Given the unstable politico-economic context of Moldova with the constant shift in governmental priorities from one year to the next, ongoing capital projects have to compete for financing with new investment proposals, risking being "frozen" until a better time. For example, in 2010 Parliament significantly cut budget allocation for three out of fourteen ongoing capital projects submitted by the government. In 2011, the government's budget proposal did not include four capital projects funded in

Table 4. Trend in CIPs funding in major sectors 2009-2015 (MDL, million, unless otherwise noted)

Capital Expenditures (CE)	2009	2010	2011	2012	2013	2014	2015
Agriculture (total CE)	429.6	408.6	498.3	888.3	997.5	1,516.9	1,851.9
From foreign sources	171.2	194.9	183.9	519.3	599.1	939.8	1,592.6
% External Finance to Total Capital Expenditure	40%	48%	37%	58%	60%	62%	86%
Environment protection (total CE)	56.3	58.7	69.7	92.1	109.7	115.4	54.7
From foreign sources	14.1	13.7	7.7	31.7	48.3	51.6	40.5
% External Finance to Total Capital Expenditure	25%	23%	11%	34%	44%	45%	74%
Transportation and road constructions (total CE)	450.6	835.9	1,051	1,673.1	2,224.7	2,500.3	1,580.8
From foreign sources	101.5	107.5	202	539.6	902	1,421.8	868.3
% External Finance to Total Capital Expenditure	23%	13%	19%	32%	41%	57%	55%
Energy and fuel (total CE)	75.3	153.2	61.6	169.9	242.03	162.05	85.7
From foreign sources	75.3	153.2	58.2	67.3	42.9	129.4	85.5
% External Finance to Total Capital Expenditure	100%	100%	95%	40%	18%	80%	99%

Source: Author's calculations using the BOOST database, the Ministry of Finance

Table 5. Capital investments per central public authority for FY 2018 (MDL, thousands)

Central Public Authority	Total	Funding Sources:		% Foreign Assistance in Total Capital Budget
		Domestic Funds	Foreign Assistance	
Ministry of Finance	68403.20	45595.40	22807.80	33%
Ministry of Justice	222713.70	89313.30	133400.40	60%
Ministry of Internal Affairs	123456.40	84545.80	38910.60	32%
Ministry of Economy and Infrastrucutre	2577708.20	80277.30	2497430.90	97%
Ministry of Agriculture, Regional Development, and Ecology	157820.10	14632.90	143187.20	91%
Ministry of Education and Culture	145414.60	145414.60		-
Ministry of Health and Social Protection	39997.10	39223.00	774.10	2%
Social Investment Fund	1180		1180.0	100%
TOTAL	336693.3	499002.3	2837691.0	85%

Source: Author's calculations using the 2018 National Budget Document (Annex 4)

previous years with some projects being in operation since 2001 and 2007. As a result, the efficiency and effectiveness of public capital expenditures decreased due to an inconsistency in funding and an increased implementation period for many capital projects (Coulibaly & Diagne, 2014).

The main reason for development of capital investment proposals and approval for funding still has short-term political considerations, often disregarding government strategic priorities. At the level of the allocation of funds, the decisions are made by members of the Parliament who do not debate the allocation priorities in terms of macro-economic or performance indicators but based on political factors (Coulibaly & Diagne, 2014). There is a visible inconsistency between the government and Parliament capital investment priorities. For example, governmental priorities for capital investment for 2011 targeted completion of ongoing projects in water-supply and sanitation, but the Parliament allocated resources for building cultural centers and pre-school facilities. The Parliament also favors small ongoing capital projects at the national level, disregarding capital investment proposals submitted by local public authorities. For example, in 2010 and 2011 more than 75 percent of the government proposals for capital investment suffered a significant budgetary cut (Coulibaly & Diagne, 2014).

The problem of political biases in project funding happens because of economic constraints on satisfying all capital infrastructure needs. Politicians can be under the pressure of the government to fund those capital projects that are included in the budget proposals and reflect governmental priorities or to focus their attention on those capital proposals that perhaps are not included in the budget but will more likely satisfy voters. The MOF is guided by the fiscal possibilities and opportunities to leverage external funding pushing the government's and international donors' agendas, while politicians choose to fund those capital projects that are consistent with their political agenda. Although the priority system could help determine selection of capital projects, it is challenging to choose when most of the capital investment needs are critical for the country's development. This reality suggests that Parliament generally approves those capital investment projects that reflect voter preferences using the state funds and those that reflect the country's strategic priorities funded by international donors.

CONCLUSION

The capital management process in the Republic of Moldova has been significantly improved through a series of fiscal reforms, mirroring the best practices of other countries, and it is characterized by a variety of legal and institutional arrangements. An example of this is the governmental decision on Public Capital Investments No. 1029 that sets up the guiding principles and responsibilities in the field of capital investments. Through this decision, the government also regulates the process of capital investment, project development, and resource allocation for such projects. The MOF supports the implementation of this decision by developing the Capital Management and Budgeting Instructions No. 185 that are used in planning, approval, implementation, and monitoring of capital investment projects. The Law on Public Finances and Fiscal Responsibility No. 181 adds more budgetary techniques and requirements to improve capital investment management.

By introducing comprehensive capital investment planning, the government has enhanced the quality of governmental decisions in the resource allocation and implementation of capital investment projects. The development of a legal framework ensured a better connection between allocation decisions and governmental priorities. Through a restructuring of the institutional framework and creation of the centralized capital management unit to supervise and monitor implementation of capital investment projects, the Moldovan government has attempted to improve execution of such projects. A significant step has been made toward improvement of the legal mechanism regarding maintenance of capital assets. Overall, the legal framework of capital management and budgeting recently adopted by the Moldovan government mirrors the SY normative prescriptions and, thus, has become more oriented toward efficiency and effectiveness.

Regardless of the legal and institutional developments as well as the governmental commitment to achieve the reform's objectives, the capital management process in Moldova falls short of successful practices due to the country's context. First, the extent of institutional constraints and centralized control became one of the most frustrating problems in the process of capital planning and budgeting. The Moldovan local public administration has limited financial autonomy and is highly dependent on the national government during the budget development process. Local public agencies and sectoral ministries do not have a sufficient degree of discretion in determining capital investment priorities as well as flexibility in resource allocation. The public agencies also lack discretion in selecting capital projects since they are bound by centralized priorities, spending limits, and requirements to include only projects that have guaranteed funding.

Second, the analysis reveals that capital investment planning and fiscal forecast in Moldova are not based on reliable data provided in a regular manner. The procedures that regulate budgeting, accounting, and reporting are not sufficiently adjusted to make the information meaningful and useful for decisions on the state's public finances. The medium-term planning is affected by the information deficit because local public agencies provide information with a delay or because the information included in the planning documents are used for project prioritization and not taken from the asset management registry. In addition, there is little information available to provide a clear distinction between estimations of the current programs expenditures (i.e., sectoral policies) and future spending limits.

Third, the analysis demonstrates that the capital management and budgeting process in Moldova is affected by the country's political conditions. In many cases capital investment proposals are approved for funding based on the legislators' short-term political considerations that disregard governmental priorities. The country's unstable political situation and a high fractionalization among politicians lead to a delay in capital project implementation or even to a total stoppage of funding. In addition, since the entire budgetary process is based on the negotiation results between the government and politicians, there is a perception among local public authorities that the capital planning does not have any relevance to the real budget process.

Fourth, the findings suggest that the decisions of the Moldovan government on capital investments for infrastructure improvements are affected by a high dependency on international assistance because the country lacks financial resources to cover its capital investment needs. Therefore, the country significantly reduced domestically-financed capital investments, replacing them by the externally-funded capital improvement projects. The project ranking is affected the most by the country's dependency on foreign aid because the prioritization is based on the availability of the external funding provided through development partners rather than on cost-benefit analysis.

As noted by the scholars, the way a government practices capital management might deviate from the normative framework suggested by the literature. This chapter illustrates that even when the recommendations are incorporated in the legal framework, a country's specific context can prevent successful implementation of capital management and budgeting processes. The analysis results suggest that capital management and budgeting practices in Moldova are shaped by the country's socio-economic background, institutional and informational constraints, political uncertainties, and dependence on foreign assistance. While some of the factors, such as poverty, cannot be addressed in a short-term period, others could be improved to create better opportunities for capital investment.

REFERENCES

Bland, R. L. (2014). *Budgeting: A guide for local governments.* Intl City County Management Assn.

Bland, R. L., & Nunn, S. (1992). The impact of capital spending on municipal operating budgets. *Public Budgeting & Finance*, *12*(2), 32–47. doi:10.1111/1540-5850.00936

Constitution of the Republic of Moldova. (1994). Retrieved January 4, 2018, from http://lex.justice.md/document_rom.php?id=44B9F30E:7AC17731

Coulibaly, K. S., & Diagne, M. F. (2014). *Capital expenditures: Making public investment work for competitiveness and inclusive growth in Moldova.* The World Bank Report No. 76310-MD.

Dabla-Norris, E., Brumby, J., Kyobe, A., Mills, Z., & Papageorgiou, C. (2012). Investing in public investment: An index of public investment efficiency. *Journal of Economic Growth*, *17*(3), 235–266. doi:10.100710887-012-9078-5

Ermasova, N. (2013). Capital budgeting in the states after the great recession. *State & Local Government Review*, *45*(2), 119–130. doi:10.1177/0160323X13487079

Esfahani, H. S., & Ramírez, M. T. (2003). Institutions, infrastructure, and economic growth. *Journal of Development Economics*, *70*(2), 443–477. doi:10.1016/S0304-3878(02)00105-0

Gianakis, G. A., & McCue, C. P. (1999). *Local government budgeting: A managerial approach.* Greenwood Publishing Group.

Goode, R., & Birnbaum, E. A. (1956). Government Capital Budgets. *Staff Papers*, *5*(1), 23–46. doi:10.2307/3866136

Haque, M. E., & Kneller, R. (2008). *Public investment and growth: The role of corruption.* Centre for Growth and Business Cycle Research discussion paper series, 98.

International Monetary Fund. (2001). *Government finance statistics manual* (*GFSM 2001*). Retrieved September 10, 2017, from http://www.imf.org/external/pubs/ft/gfs/manual/index.htm

International Monetary Fund. (2017). *Public investment, efficiency and growth: The case Of Moldova.* IMF Country Report No. 17/399. Retrieved June 15, 2018, from https://www.imf.md/press/cr17399-MoldovaSIP.pdf

Kraan, D. J., Kostyleva, V., Forthun, C., Albrecht, J., & Olofsson, R. (2010). Budgeting in Moldova. *OECD Journal on Budgeting*, *10*(3), 115. doi:10.1787/budget-10-5km36kl2k3hf

Marlowe, J., William, C., Rivenbark, W., & Vogt, A. J. (2009). *Capital budgeting and finance: A guide for local governments*. ICMA Press.

Matei, L. (2013). Republic of Moldova: Toward a European administration. In *Public Administration in Post-Communist Countries* (pp. 205–230). Routledge. doi:10.1201/b14237-10

Mikesell, J. (2013). *Fiscal administration*. Cengage Learning.

Ministry of Finance of the Republic of Moldova. (2017). *Report on medium term expenditure framework*. Retrieved March 25, 2018, from http://mf.gov.md/sites/default/files/documente%20relevante/evaluarea_cbtm_2017-2019_1.pdf

Ministry of Finance of the Republic of Moldova. (2018). *The budget for the citizens*. Retrieved July 12, 2018, from http://mf.gov.md/sites/default/files/Buget%20Cetateni%202018.pdf

Morozov, B. (2009). Degree of fiscal decentralization in republic of Moldova. *The NISPAcee Journal of Public Administration and Policy*, *2*(1), 89–109.

Morozov, B. (2014). Republic of Moldova: 20 years of independence and experiments with public finance system. *International Public Management Review*, *15*(2), 133–165.

National Bureau of Statistics the Republic of Moldova. (2013). *Territorial statistics*. Retrieved July 25, 2018, from http://www.statistica.md/public/files/publicatii_electronice/Statistica_teritoriala/Statistica_teritoriala_2013.pdf

National Government of the Republic of Moldova. (1996). *Law on the budgetary system and the budgetary process No. 847.* Retrieved January 8, 2018, from http://lex.justice.md/md/311518/

National Government of the Republic of Moldova. (2003). *Law on local public finance No. 397-XV.* Retrieved October 25, 2017, from http://cis-legislation.com/document.fwx?rgn=7085

National Government of the Republic of Moldova. (2006). *Law on administrative decentralization, no. 435-XVI.* Retrieved October 25, 2017, from http://cis-legislation.com/document.fwx?rgn=18455

National Government of the Republic of Moldova. (2006). *Law on local public administration no. 436-XVI.* Retrieved October 25, 2017, from http://lex.justice.md/document_rom.php?id=C8E304A4:037190E8

National Government of the Republic of Moldova. (2006). *Law on public sector debt and state guarantees No. 419-XVI.* Retrieved July 25, 2018, from https://cis-legislation.com/document.fwx?rgn=18036

National Government of the Republic of Moldova. (2010). *National development strategy Moldova 2020.* Retrieved March 3, 2018, from http://particip.gov.md/public/files/Moldova_2020_ENG1.pdf

National Government of the Republic of Moldova. (2012). *Republic of Moldova's water supply & sanitation strategy.* Retrieved April 18, 2018, from http://www.serviciilocale.md/public/files/2nd_Draft_WSS_Strategy_October_final_Eng.pdf

National Government of the Republic of Moldova. (2013). *Public law on capital investment management No.1029.* Retrieved December 10, 2017, from http://lex.justice.md/index.php?action=view&view=doc&lang=1&id=350859

National Government of the Republic of Moldova. (2014). *Law on public finances and fiscal responsibilities no. 181.* Retrieved August 15, 2017, from http://lex.justice.md/md/354213/

Pritchett, L. (2000). The tyranny of concepts: CUDIE (cumulated, depreciated, investment effort) is not capital. *Journal of Economic Growth, 5*(4), 361–384. doi:10.1023/A:1026551519329

Rumney, E. (in press). EU aid to Moldova made little difference, say auditors. *Public Finance International.* Retrieved March 2, 2018, from http://www.publicfinanceinternational.org/news/2016/09/eu-aid-moldova-made-little-difference-say-auditors

Srithongrung, A., Ermasova, N., & Yusuf, J.-E. (2019). Capital budgeting and management in Russia. In Capital management and budgeting in the public sector. Hershey, PA: IGI Global.

Srithongrung, A., Yusuf, J.-E., & Kriz, K. A. (2019). A systematic public capital management and budgeting process. In *Capital management and budgeting in the public sector*. Hershey, PA: IGI Global.

World Bank. (2008). *Debt management performance assessment. Republic of Moldova.* Retrieved July 25, 2018, from http://siteresources.worldbank.org/INTDEBTDEPT/Resources/468980-1226602826665/DeMPAMoldovaFinal_EN.pdf

Chapter 8
Capital Management and Budgeting Processes in Albania

Jane Beckett-Camarata
Pennsylvania State University – Harrisburg, USA

ABSTRACT

This chapter investigates, analyzes, and compares capital management and budgeting processes in Albania and the implications for road and highway infrastructure investment. It is a case study of Albania's capital management and budgeting processes seen through the framework of the Srithongrung, Yusuf, and Kriz normative model. The analysis and insights derived suggest a mixed picture of the contribution that the current capital management and budgeting processes make on the country's capital investment and its economic growth and development. Albania's capital management and budgeting processes are not consistent with the normative framework as follows: (1) the fragmentation and political involvement in capital improvement planning (CIP), (2) forecasting bias and fragmentation in the forecasting process resulting in misalignment and lack of prioritizing new capital investments, (3) shortcomings in the capital financing strategies stemming from court decisions and weak budgetary controls, (4) centralized execution and project management in monitoring highways maintenance.

INTRODUCTION

Although the normative model framework for public capital asset management and capital budgeting processes (long-term capital planning, annual capital budgeting, capital budget execution and public spending evaluation) are largely and fully adopted and used by US state and local governments (Ermasova, 2013), there is limited knowledge of the framework's applicability to central governments internationally. However, there are EU country comparisons of public infrastructure quantity and quality in aggregated, WDI, IMF, FAD databases. Using the EU average as equal to 1.0, the quality of Albania's overall infrastructure is 0.75/1.0 in comparison to other EU countries, placing it substantially below the norm, below Russia, Poland and Italy, but above Ukraine, Moldova, Serbia, Montenegro and Bosnia and Herzegovina (WDI, IMF, IMF FAD database, 2018). Additionally, using the EU average as equal to 1.0, Albania, at .35/1.0, is even further below the norm relative to the quantity of public infrastructure expenditures, with only four other EU members below (WDI, IMF, IMF FAD database, 2018).

DOI: 10.4018/978-1-5225-7329-6.ch008

The capital management and budgeting components and activities identified in the normative framework, taken together, enhance a government's capacity to be responsive to public infrastructure needs while concurrently maintaining strong financial condition. The objective of this chapter is to fill a portion of this void by providing an understanding of Albanian capital management and budget processes viz-a-viz the normative framework and the implications of its use for enhancing effective public infrastructure investment. Following the identified components and activities in the normative framework can enhance efficiency and effectiveness in the acquisition of public infrastructure systems (Srithongrung and Kriz, (2012). Using the normative model framework of Srithongrung, Ermasova, Yusuf (2019), this chapter investigates and analyzes past and current capital management and budgeting processes in Albania.

Albania is in southeastern Europe, bordering the Adriatic Sea and the Ionian Sea, between Greece to the south, Macedonia to the east, and Montenegro and Kosovo to the north. Albania is about 70 kilometers from the coast of Italy, across the Strait of Otranto. The country is primarily mountainous with small plains along its coast. The population of Albania is about 2.9 million (INSTAT, 2017) in which about half live in urban areas. Tirana, the capital, has a population of 764,000 (INSTAT, 2017) or almost 20% of Albania's total citizenry. About 20% of the population is below 15 years old, about 70% is between 15-64 years old, and 10% is 65 or older (INSTAT, 2017).

Although Albania's economy continues to grow, the country is still one of the poorest in Europe. The informal economy is large, as one would expect in economies that were Planned Economies not that long ago. The transport sector, especially roads and highways, is well below standard, which is another expected condition under the country's previous planned economic system and has been a long-standing barrier to sustained economic growth. Major sectors of Albanian Capital Investment include Energy, Telecommunications, and Transport. Within the Transport Sector there are several sub-sectors which include airports, ports, and roads and highways.

Because Albania is still transitioning to a market economy and all sectors are undergoing major change, this study of Albanian Capital Management and Budgeting Processes has focused initially on one, roads and highways, since this sub-sector is such a critical component of the country's economy. Subsequent research will address capital management and budgeting in the other sub-sectors.

The study is organized as follows: The next section discusses the background of the Albanian road and highway infrastructure system. The third section provides analysis of the Albanian Capital Management and Budget Processes viz a viz the normative model. The final section presents the Conclusion.

BACKGROUND

This section introduces the unique features of the Albanian road and highway infrastructure system. The country went through a period of infrastructure modernization in the 1980s. Part of this modernization was the building and/or upgrading of their national transportation system. During this time, new roads and highways were constructed. The relatively limited use of roads and highways following construction combined with their regular routine maintenance, kept the infrastructure in good condition for a decade. Starting in the 1990s, however, there has been a period of increased social and economic mobility and autonomy and, consequently, greater use of roads and highways. (Dalakoglou, 2012). The natural result is an increased need for more effective capital management and budgeting procedures to support the planning, budgeting, acquisition, maintenance, and improvement of Albania's capital assets especially road and highway infrastructure.

A country's public infrastructure system is an output of its capital management and budgeting processes (Srithongrung, Erasamova, & Yusuf, 2019). Srithongrung and Kriz empirically confirmed that public capital management and budgeting practices enhance citizen quality of life through the quantity and quality of public infrastructure (2012). Therefore, it is important to understand the Albanian road and highway infrastructure system in the context of its capital budgeting and management processes. In Albania, transportation alternatives are very limited; therefore, roads and highways are the predominant means of land transportation and are the critical link for both freight-commerce and personal mobility. Thus, roads and highways in Albania are an especially important component of the country's public infrastructure system. Ongoing road and highway maintenance can bring significant benefit to Albanian communities by providing better access to education, markets, and centers of commerce.

Albania inherited poor road and highway infrastructure in part because of the existence of the country's planned economic system under Communist rule. Following democratic elections in 1992 and the subsequent move to a market economy, Albania has experienced rapid growth in automobile ownership, and the resulting need was to develop road and highway transport infrastructure (World Bank, 2013). Increased traffic and inadequate capital budgeting for road and highway asset maintenance expenditures and road and highway capacity limitations have increased the rate of deterioration of the country's road and highway transportation network and costs to road-users (World Bank, 2013). When Albania began transitioning to a market economy, the demand for private automobiles dramatically increased from 25 per 1,000 population in 1989, to 118 per 1,000 population in 2013 (World Bank, 2013). In addition, one of the major capital budget and management issues is that there has been little formal identification of, or regular monitoring of, the country's capital asset conditions. Rather, the priority has been to initiate infrastructure capital assets with little emphasis on budgeting for maintenance.

The Albanian Road Authority (ARA) is responsible for the construction, operation, and maintenance of the national road and highway network. The overall length of the road and highway network in Albania is approximately 15,000 km (World Bank, 2013). The road and highway network is made up of about 3,400 km of national roads and highways administered by the Ministry of Transport and maintained by the Albanian Road Authority. The local road network consists of: 4,441 km of district roads, which are maintained by district road departments within the Regional Road Authorities under the Ministry of the Interior; 4,980 km of communal roads including private access roads, which provide rural communal links, and are maintained by 309 communes; and 2,500 km of urban or municipal roads, which are maintained by the road departments of 65 Municipalities (World Bank, 2013).

The next section will provide relevant background information on the Albania's evolving political and economic systems, government institutions, and public administration practices that impact the Capital Budgeting and Management processes in Albania. The Socialist Party came out of the last elections with a clear mandate for continued reform, especially in the areas of property rights and strengthening the public sector (IMF, 2015).

The Albanian public sector is made up of national central administrative functions at the national level, state territorial functions, local governments, state enterprises and utilities, and numerous miscellaneous institutions. The focus of this study's discussion is on the national level. This section describes the Executive, Legislative and Judicial branches and the Public Sector.

Albania is a parliamentary republic. The current Constitution was adopted by referendum on November 22, 1998. Since 1912, Albania has used different models of governance including: (1) an international protectorate, (2) a monarchy, (3) a state-party regime, and (4) a parliamentary republic. Awareness of these models is important to understanding the evolution of Capital Planning discussed later in the Capital Planning Section. As a parliamentary republic, the Office of President, as the head of state, has also taken different forms during each of these models of governance. The President of Albania is the head of state and is indirectly elected to a five-year term by Parliament through secret vote that requires a three-fifths majority of the votes of all members. The President may be elected for a second five-year term. The Prime Minister is the head of the Albanian government. According to the Constitution, the Prime Minister is the most senior minister of the cabinet in the Executive Branch. In the Albanian Parliamentary System, the Prime Minister is appointed by the President, and ministers are nominated by the President.

Albania's evolving political system is important in this context because government integrity issues, especially in the Executive Branch, impact capital budgeting and management processes. For example, political pressure to justify and maintain growth in spending has resulted in overly optimistic revenue forecasts to support spending increases, which as could be expected, have negatively impacted capital funding (MoF, 2014).

The Albanian parliament is unicameral. It has 140 deputies elected for a 4-year term under a closed-list, regional proportional representation system. The Parliament is made up of no less than 140 members elected based on direct, universal, periodic and equal suffrage by secret ballot. Article 45 of the Constitution guarantees the right to vote. Albanian citizens exercise their power through their elected representatives in the Parliament. There are 15 permanent committees. Parliament has the authority to increase or decrease aggregate spending. Legislative control of the Capital Budget is exercised through an Economic Committee which oversees the economic, fiscal, and budget areas including legislative budget analyses. Under the market economy, effective Capital Management and Budgeting is a consequence of financial discipline that requires the adherence to long-term capital planning, annual capital budgeting, capital budget execution, and public spending evaluation. While the political climate is improving, the Albanian Parliament has been seriously hampered in the past because of political standoffs between the ruling majority and the opposition, a lack of constructive dialogue, and the mutual suspicion characteristic of Albanian politics (EUR, 2016). It is expected that under such political disharmony the needed efficient, financial structures and budgetary discipline would lack priority.

The Judicial branch is based on the French legal system. It is a three-tiered, independent judicial system governed by the constitution and national legislation enacted by Parliament. The judicial branch of Albania is divided into three main institutions; the 'Highest Courts', which includes the Supreme Court and the Constitutional Court, the 'Intermediate Courts' such as the Courts of Appeals, Court of Appeals for Serious Crimes, and the Administrative Court of Appeals. Also included are the 'First Instance Courts' such as the District Courts and the Court of First Instance for Serious Crimes. Hearings are often held in the judge's private office, which raises the possibility of undue influence (EUR2016). The functioning of the Judicial System continues to be highly politicized and there is not a high degree of independence and impartiality (EUR, 2016). The court system is further undermined by lack of sufficient financial and human resources. These issues are important because government integrity issues, especially in the judiciary, impact capital budgeting and management due to the lack of independence and impartiality in enforcement of contracts in capital projects.

Although there is an ongoing decentralization process, the Albanian public sector is centralized. The Albanian public sector is also small. Total public spending is approximately 30.3% of Albanian GDP (Heritage.org, 2018). The economy is dominated by agriculture, which employs about half of the workforce, and services including tourism (Heritage.org, 2018).

Historically, Albania has not invested sufficiently in upgrading its' public sector institutions, and many central administrative agencies continue to be underequipped, especially in up-to-date, digital technology, to manage its transition to a market economy, to provide the regulatory/administrative framework for the market, to establish relations with the international community, and to negotiate and manage aid flows (Durata, undated). The public sector, which includes central and local government as well as publicly-owned companies, employs about 164,000 people out of 600,000 non-agricultural jobs in the country (Balkan Insight, 3/18/18). Central government employment is approximately 81,000, of which about 9,000 are core civil service (Balkan Insight, 3/18/18). This core civil service category is the backbone of a professional public administration with hiring and firing procedures regulated by a specific law (Balkan Insight, 3/18/18). The Albanian core civil service, however, is not fully defined and not protected under the law, and as a result, it is underpaid and, expectedly of poor quality (Durata, undated).

Allocation of Albanian public sector, human resources is inefficient, with some areas experiencing over-staffing and low productivity, while others, especially in central administration, are both under-staffed and under-qualified (Durata, undated). The lack of hiring transparency impedes development of Albania civil service reform. Base salaries for civil servants are at or below poverty rates, and for top officials, they are only slightly above poverty rates. This situation leads to several negative effects such as corruption, position grade inflation, salary compression, low quality, and low motivation (Durata, undated). A high number (30%) of core civil service jobs are still being filled illegally by direct appointment (Balkan Insight, 3/18/18).

The Albanian Government's public administration reform strategy includes two key elements that impact its capital budgets: (i) strengthen public expenditure management and (ii) strengthen human resource management. The public expenditure management reform strategy component addresses five elements of the public expenditure management system (relative to strengthening human resource capability in the areas of:

1. Budget formulation
2. Budget execution (treasury),
3. Macroeconomic and fiscal forecasting,
4. Accounting,
5. Procurement, and
6. Management of the Ministry of Finance (MoF, 2014).

A stronger capital project management capability component (e.g., accounting, audit, procurement, disbursement management, monitoring and evaluation) is not in place but is especially needed.

CAPITAL BUDGETING AND MANAGEMENT IN ALBANIA

Capital Planning at the National Level

This section contrasts the Albanian capital management and budget processes with the normative framework. The central study question is: How do the Albanian Capital Management and Budget processes compare with the normative model?

The Ministry of Transport and Infrastructure (MOTI) has overall responsibility for initiating policy and coordination of transport, including roads and highways. The MOTI also has overall oversight of transport, in addition to setting sector policies, such as developing sub-sectoral budgets and performing regulatory functions. The Albanian Road Authority (ARA) is responsible for national road network asset management. It is also responsible for the construction, upgrading, rehabilitation, and maintenance of the national road network, including capital planning, capital budget formulation, and implementation. The ARA is accountable to MOTI and has responsibility for national road network infrastructure management. The ARA Management Board has oversight of the ARA. Formal coordination is through a capital project board or team. The ARA Board is made up of the Ministries of transport, finance, economy, local government, and three representatives of private sector organizations.

Long-term planning should be established for future capital project acquisition. This phase of the capital budgeting framework is especially important since it "includes comprehensive and strategic physical planning, capital needs analysis, project cost estimation, project priority ranking, and capital projects programming based on the acquisition phase and sequential order of projects (Bunch, 2013; Marlowe, Rivenbark, and Vogt, 2009, Millar, 1988; Steiss, 2005, Vogt, 2004)" (Srithongrung, 2018, p. 52). The evolution of long-term capital planning is linked to Albania's evolving models of governance. While capital planning is now beginning to be emphasized, the long-term capital asset planning and forecasting component of the Capital Budget process is still evolving, and thus impacts the other phase of the capital budget framework. Ideally, long-term economic forecasting and planning are the prerequisites of good capital planning (Ammar, Duncombe & Wright, 2001). The Albanian road and highway maintenance system especially depends on effective capital planning and budgeting systems. For overall capital planning and maintenance, the Department of Planning and Budget within the Ministry of Finance is responsible for preparing medium-term budgets and forecasts (World Bank, 2013). Medium-term budget frameworks cover three to four years and attempt to improve the inherent quality and uncertainty issues of medium-term fiscal planning with descriptive estimates (OECD, 2016). The Albanian Capital Planning function should be more closely aligned with capital project procurement, implementation and contract management functions to ensure that forecasts and budgets are aligned and updated regularly. The capital budgets include forecasts of investment spending.

The capital planning process should include formal coordination across departments, including estimated benefits of the project and projected life-cycle costs (Ammar, Duncombe and Wright, 2001). Unfortunately, capital budget formulation in Albania has been negatively impacted by inaccuracy in macro-economic assumptions in revenue forecasts (IMF, 2015). These forecasts are politically motivated, based on the need to justify and maintain growth in spending in general and in capital investments in particular (IMF, 2015). The Albanian Council of Ministers has had to cut expenditures, primarily capital expenditures (which dropped from 8.8% of GDP in 2009 to 5.8% of GDP in 2010) in the middle of the fiscal year, as well as cut administration and low priority sector expenditures. Because of this situation, in mid-year 2010 and 2011, there were substantial budget revisions for example (OECD, 2014). As a result, since current capital budget project expenditures take precedence, the limited new capital revenue negatively impacted the initiation of even new capital projects.

The Capital Improvement Plan (CIP) provides an opportunity to revise planned projects and acquisitions considering recent developments and add new projects if needed (Vogt, 2004) usually updated annually. The Capital budget is the first year of the CIP. Capital investments and capital projects are normally identified and prioritized through the Capital Improvement Plan. However, the Albanian process for initiating, appraising, prioritizing, approving and contracting for capital improvements planning does not follow the steps in an organized manner (MoF, 2014) because the process is politicized, fragmented, and lacks adequate staffing. Activities such as initiating capital assets, appraising, etc. are necessary to drive a capital improvement program, which is "...a list of the major capital projects and acquisition needed over a five-six-year period, appropriation of expenditures to be incurred for the identified projects, financial sources for the project funding, and the impacts of the projected outcomes on the future operating budget" (Vogt, 2004, p. 19). Cost-benefit analysis is conducted for major Albanian capital projects over a certain threshold, but the results are not published (MoF, 2014), are not reviewed, and as a result, are of limited use in developing the CIP. This is a hindrance to adequately developing the Capital Budget, since it helps to consolidate, prioritize, and organize uneven capital needs which vary from year to year (Srithongrung, 2018; Giannakis and McCue, 1999).

Information must be produced for each Albanian capital project in the CIP (MoF, 2014) as follows:

- Project Justification
- Full Description of the Project
- Alternative Approaches
- Total Project Cost
- Cost for the Budget Year
- Cost for Two Out Years and Remaining Cost
- Recurrent Cost Impact because of the Investment Project
- *Forecasted Project Revenues, if any (Author's note: see discussion below for long term forecasting and is relationship to forecasted project revenues)
- Donor Funding, if any
- Net Budget Cost

The Prime Minister's Office is responsible for long-term fiscal projections. Albania produces six-to-seven-year fiscal projections and revises the projections every seven years. The Albanian Ministry of Finance prepares medium-term fiscal forecasts, which are the basis for the Capital Improvement Plan. Three-year forecasts are created, and summary tables are published in the *Macroeconomic and Fiscal Framework* at the beginning of the medium-term budget process. These forecasts, which set out in the Medium-term Budget, are updated and published after the final budget is approved (IMF, 2015). Specifically, the medium-term forecast report is prepared by the Macroeconomic and Fiscal Policy Department (MFPD) of the MoF with input from the Budget Analysis, Policy and Programming Directorate (BAPPD), and the Budget Management and Monitoring Directorate (BMMD).

The Tax Office also provides input on revenue forecasts. Tax and revenue targets are used for revenue estimates for the budget. Inflation estimates are tied to the Albanian Central Bank's assumptions. The Central Bank, however, does not project economic growth. The Statistics Offices provides data used in the forecasts but does not develop the forecasts. Economic assumptions published by IMF are used as a point of comparison. Comparisons also include data on Albania's principle trading partners: Greece, Italy and Kosovo. The forecast developed in January is updated in July (mid-year). The revised forecast is the basis for revisions to the MTBF (OCED, 2014). *However, while the Albanian long-term fiscal forecasts are updated regularly, the new/updated forecasts do not explain how or why the new/updated reports differ from the previous forecast, nor do they compare how the forecasts differ from the actual

(IMF, 2015). As a result, this makes capital budget revenue, especially at the project level, difficult to plan for and rely on, particularly by contractors. This is especially true during priority planning (discussed below) as well as project management.

Capital Budgeting and Financial Management at the National Level

This component involves consolidating the proposed capital projects by fiscal year, selecting projects based on agreed upon criteria, estimating project cost, and recommending annual appropriation through a separate capital budget document.

Capital projects in Albania are identified in the Capital Budget Proposal, but only projects listed in the first year of the capital improvement plan (capital budget proposal) are budgeted for. The Ministry of Finance (MoF) is responsible for compiling the government-funded Capital Budget in Albania. The capital budgeting priority planning process typically involves preparing capital requests by individual agencies and submission of their requests to the central agency (Bozeman, 2004). The Albanian Capital Budget includes both Government-funded projects and foreign-funded projects. Albania includes a list of multi-year capital projects in rank order. The projects are ranked based on political priorities, funding availability, and national sector strategies. As noted previously, political priorities are a major factor in priority ranking. In practice, the process for initiating, appraising, and approving Albania's capital projects has been "much less orderly than intended and would be desirable" (MoF, 2014) because of political involvement.

Prioritizing road and highway infrastructure investments in the Capital Budget is critical to ensure its sustainable maintenance and management (IMF, 2014). Prioritization of investments in roads and highways, based on criteria used in generally accepted capital asset industry standards is needed to ensure the sector's continued contribution to economic growth and road and highway's sustainable maintenance and management. The Capital Project Plan, feasibility study, and other economic/financial analyses must be completed and submitted with the Capital Budget Proposal. Project proposals are submitted to the MoF's Project Management Investment Directorate (PIMD) in the Budget Office for review. Project plans are also integrated into the MTBP for the individual line ministry.

The Annual Albanian budget process can be described as "top-down" (OECD, 2016). In top-down budgeting, the Chief Executive determines the aggregate fiscal revenue and expenditure targets (expenditure and revenue levels) based on medium-term fiscal objectives and current economic conditions (OECD, 2016). Within this aggregate, "...ceilings are set and (approved by the cabinet) reflecting existing commitments, political priorities in general, and key new policy initiatives (OCED, 2016, p. 6.) To be effective, top-down budgeting processes require "...rigorous and prudent economic forecasts..." and fiscal management practices (OECD, 2016, p. 6). Budget conflicts are resolved by the Albanian Finance Minister.

Albania has no budget balance rules (OCED, 2016). In the past, revenue from privatization has been used to finance the Albanian operating budget, and no distinction was made between revenue from privatization in the operating and capital budget (IMF, 2015). This resulted in the undermining of the government's capital asset position and increased pressure on the capital budget. The operating budget increased because of the one-time asset sales at the expense of the capital budget (IMF, 2015).

The budget process for capital investment projects in Albania has been impacted by budget cuts necessary to adjust for unrealized revenue, which has in turn restricted capital project investment. According to the *Public Expenditure and Financial Accountability Report,* "...insufficient attention is being paid to implementation capacity, capital expenditure targets for investment programs are being set at overly optimistic levels despite poor past performance" (PEFA, 2012, p. 9). Although, the report did note that Ministries such as Transport achieve planned levels (PEFA, 2012). Project arrears have a direct impact on budget formulation for investment projects in Albania (OCED, 2016). Funding for prior commitments has preempted funding of some new projects. While capital expenditures are separated in the budget, it is clear capital spending is inadequate for both building and maintaining the country's infrastructure. Capital budget planning has been negatively impacted by budget forecasts, which have been overestimated by about 2% of GDP. The overestimation resulted in unrealistic budgets (IMF, 2015). Because of the unrealistic spending plans, the government was forced to cut the budget, as described above, including the capital budget, during the fiscal year.

Capital financing strategies, until 2008, involved sustained high rates of economic growth averaging about 6.2 percent (World Bank, 2015), but the global financial crisis beginning in 2008, and the subsequent Eurozone crisis, resulted in a significant economic slowdown. After 2008, as revenues declined and budgets for public investments were reduced, many capital projects including the transport sector continued as initially planned using commercial loans (World Bank, 2015). However, in 2013, new construction commitments, weak budgetary controls (IMF, 2014), and serious loan payment arrears discussed in a later section, drove up the cost of non-performing loans and negatively impacted the Albanian Capital Budget (World Bank, 2015).

Previous studies have demonstrated that "Spending based on the availability of revenue may result in fluctuating capital outlay which, in turn, creates a relatively high cost for project acquisitions" (Srithongrung, 2018, p. 48). Capital projects tend to be sequential and normally take between two to three years to be completed (Srithongrung, 2018; Gatti, 2012). When capital projects are interrupted for any reason, the cost of the project is not the same as planned (Srithongrung, 2018; Gattti, 2012; Steiss, 2005). Table 1 presents the Albanian basic indicators and macroeconomic framework.

Table 1. Albanian basic indicators and macroeconomic framework, 2013-2017

Albanian Basic Indicators	2013	2014	2015	2016	2017 (est.)
Real sector		(Growth rate in percent)			
Real GDP	1.0	1.8	2.2	3.4	3.9
Consumer Price Index (avg.)	1.9	1.6	1.9	1.3	2.1
Consumer Price Index (eop)	1.8	0.7	1.9	2.2	2.3
GDP deflator	0.3	1.5	0.1	-0.2	2.1
Saving-investment balance		(Percent of GDP)			
Foreign savings	9.3	10.8	8.6	7.6	8.0
National savings	17.9	15.9	16.3	15.9	16.2
Public	-0.8	0.6	0.7	1.2	1.2
Private	18.7	15.4	15.6	14.7	15.0
Investment	27.2	26.7	25.0	23.5	24.2
Public	5.1	5.0	4.7	4.6	4.6
Private	22.1	21.7	20.2	18.9	19.6

continued on following page

Table 1. Continued

Albanian Basic Indicators	2013	2014	2015	2016	2017 (est.)
Fiscal sector		(Percent of GDP)			
Revenues and grants	24.0	26.3	26.4	27.4	28.2
Tax revenue	22.0	24.1	23.9	24.9	25.9
Expenditures	29.2	32.2	31.0	29.6	30.2
Primary	26.0	29.3	28.3	27.2	28.1
Interest	3.2	2.9	2.7	2.5	2.1
Overall balance (excluding arrears payment)	-5.2	-5.9	-4.6	-2.3	-2.0
Primary balance (excluding arrears payment)	-2.0	-3.0	-1.9	0.2	0.1
Net domestic financing	4.4	3.4	-1.3	0.9	-1.7
of which: Privatization receipts	1.2	0.0	0.1	0.2	0.0
Foreign financing	0.8	2.5	5.0	1.3	3.7
Public Debt	70.4	72.0	74.1	73.3	71.5
Domestic	43.4	42.4	39.7	39.0	35.3
of which: Unpaid bills and arrears	4.8	1.9	1.0	0.9	…
External (including publicly guaranteed)	27.0	29.6	34.4	34.3	36.2
Monetary Indicators		(Growth rate in percent)			
Broad money growth	2.3	4.0	1.8	3.9	4.3
Private credit growth	-1.4	2.0	-2.8	0.4	0.9
Velocity	1.2	1.2	1.2	1.2	1.2
Interest rate (3-mth T-bills, end-period)	3.4	3.1	1.5	1.2	…
BoA repo rate (in percent)	3.0	2.3	1.8	1.3	…
External sector		(Percent of GDP, unless otherwise indicated)			
Trade balance (goods and services)	-18.0	-19.0	-17.3	-16.9	-16.5
Current account balance	-9.3	-10.8	-8.6	-7.6	-8.0
Gross international reserves (in billions of Euros)	2.0	2.2	2.9	2.9	2.9
(In months of imports of goods and services)	5.4	5.6	7.6	7.2	6.4
(Relative to external debt service)	4.9	2.9	2.6	3.6	3.1
(In percent of broad money)	24.6	25.7	32.5	31.5	29.5
Change in real exchange rate (eop, in percent)	1.0	2.3	1.5	3.9	…
Memorandum items Nominal GDP (in billions of lek)	1350	1395	1428	1473	1562
Output gap (percent, - = gap)	-0.7	-1.2	-1.6	-1.2	-0.6

Sources: Albanian authorities; and IMF staff estimates and projections.

IMF credit outstanding for Albania is estimated to be 3.1 percent of GDP or 12.5 percent of gross reserves in 2017 (IMF, 2017). Debt service to the IMF alone is expected to peak in 2022 at around 0.4 percent of GDP and 1.9 percent of international reserves. External public debt is projected to peak at 35.30 percent of GDP and peak at about 40 percent of GDP in 2018 before falling to 34 percent of GDP in 2022 (IMF, 2017). Risks to repayment capacity are mitigated by Albania's robust reserve coverage, strong record of repaying the Fund, and the authorities' stated commitment to continue implementation of reforms (IMF, 2017).

The overall fiscal balance has improved by 2.1 percentage points of GDP between 2013 and 2017 mostly through higher revenues (IMF, 2017). However, Albania's public debt and gross financing needs still remain high, and room for policy maneuver is limited. Albanian authorities reiterated their commitment to lower the debt ratio below 60 percent of GDP by 2021, consistent with the 45 percent of GDP debt objective under the Organic Budget Law (IMF, 2017). These objectives strike an appropriate balance between reducing debt sustainability risks and maintaining the quality of adjustment, on the one hand, with the need for a growth-friendly adjustment that accommodates the cost of structural reforms on the other (IMF, 2017).

Albania's public debt has increased to 71.5 percent of GDP in 2017 (IMF, 2017). Stress tests suggest that the risks largely come from a combined macro-fiscal shock, pushing up public debt to 80 percent of GDP by 2020 IMF, 2017). The key limitations to reducing public debt are: (1) high rollover needs (20 percent of GDP in 2018 since about two-fifths of domestic debt was short term at the end of 2017), (2) efforts to replace short-term domestic debt with longer-term external borrowing raised exposure to exchange rate fluctuation risks; and lack of non-bank institutional investors, leaving high exposure to government bonds (25 percent of total assets) (IMF, 2017, p. 7). High debt may hinder economic recovery, which means greater vulnerability to rollover requirements and higher vulnerability to shifts in market perception. Public and private external debt service is expected to rise gradually through the medium-term, increasing to 11 percent of GDP in 2020 as the 2015 Eurobond issuance is amortized. MoF expects to roll over this debt and accrue new debt through increased commercial borrowing in the medium-term (IMF, 2017).

High reliance on domestic banks poses a systemic risk of a sovereign-banking feedback loop. While significant progress has been made, efforts to extend the average debt maturity need to continue. The illiquid secondary market has led investors to seek short-term instruments that are held to maturity. The Albanian government has indicated that increased reliance on external commercial borrowing was needed to overcome domestic financing constraints and meet public investment goals. Nevertheless, the Government states that the size and timing of the issuance would consider the risks to external debt sustainability.

Albania's credit rating is B+/B, with a stable outlook (S&P Report, 2018). The average maturity of government debt has lengthened considerably over the past three years. With the exception of the domestic portion of debt, average maturity remains relatively short at slightly above two years. Domestic debt accounts for just over 50% of total public sector debt, and approximately 49% of total government debt is denominated in foreign currency. Albania's banking system holds the largest share of domestic debt, and about 24% of the banking system's assets are government securities. Foreign Direct Investment (FDI) is the country's primary external financing source, and capital projects will continue to be a major source of FDI. Albania's external debt is relatively low, which reflects external funding relying on foreign equity. Net external debt declined to 8% of current account receipts but is anticipated to increase to 15% by 2020 (S&P, 2018). In addition, the long-term Capital Project debt has increased nearly 17% between 2016 and 2017 (IMF Country Report 18/123, 2018).

Albania uses a revenue-availability approach to capital investment spending. This approach results in routine interruption of the prioritization of capital projects because of unexpected revenue shortages

(Moak and Hillhouse, 1975). Governments who use the revenue-availability approach, "…tend to make abrupt decisions to finance capital projects on an emergency basis" (Srithongrung, 2018, p. 48).

In an attempt to avoid the abrupt decision making and avoid capital funding on an emergency basis, the MoF conducts Debt Affordability Analysis. According to the MoF, in the framework of existing debt service and borrowing, the Medium-Term Debt Management Strategy (MTDMS) analyzes and assesses the domestic market and international capital markets conditions, defining the financial instruments most likely available. The domestic market is continuously analyzed primarily with the banking system in order to identify the demand for government financial instruments and long-term securities. External investments are analyzed in order to identify the country risk perceived and all possible costs added by the risk. The analysis conducted estimates that in the medium term 2016-2018 the Albanian government will be able to use the following financing alternative (IMF, European Department, 2018, p. 35-38).

1.3.1. In the domestic market *- Treasury bills; - Bonds; In the domestic market, the banking system is characterized by satisfactory levels of liquidity and the credit risk perceived by investors is not high. This will enable the Albanian government to refinance the current debt and domestic deficit through the instruments listed above.*

1.3.2. In international markets *- Eurobond - PBG. Consists in a partial guarantee issued by World Bank in favor of Albanian government in order to borrow in international markets at a more favorable cost compared to the market. - Loans for financing projects. This group includes all loans in the form of loans used to finance development projects which are defined as a priority by the government, with the aim to further develop strategic economic sectors of the country. Loans with commercial interest rates are available, but with a relatively high maturity. - Budget support within the framework of the agreements with international financial institutions (World Bank, IMF, etc). (Medium-Term Debt Management Strategy, MoF, 2016-2018, p. 24-25)*

Working with the IMF, Albania's Capital Debt Affordability Analysis is further enhanced by the IMF's findings and recommendations (IMF, European Department, 2018, p. 35-38).

Annex III. Debt Sustainability Analysis (DSA):

After the substantial fiscal adjustment during 2014-2016, fiscal consolidation has continued at a slower pace. However, Albania's debt remains high and poses significant risks. Rollover needs are gradually declining but remain sizable. Over the medium term, continued fiscal consolidation and steadfast implementation of structural reforms will be crucial. for reducing the risks to debt sustainability. The authorities broadly agreed with this assessment.

Capital Budget Execution and Project Management

This component involves monitoring capital project acquisitions and establishing central project status reporting to prevent waste, fraud, and cost overruns. The Directorate of Public Investment Management within the Ministry of Finance tracks the execution of capital projects and programs by sector to monitor the capital program process and project cycle. The Albanian budget law provides for specific appropriations for state revenues (grants, taxes, and non-tax revenues) and state expenditures (current, capital and special revenue fund expenditures). Current and capital expenditures are identified for line ministries. Albania's Executive Budget has 128 line-item classifications and provides no flexibility to transfer funds within the Budget. Albania MoF allows line agencies to reallocate funds, with ex-ante approval of the legislature. For capital investment expenditures, Albania allows revenue carry-forwards, and line ministries can carry-forward revenue for multi-year capital contracts but for no more than three years (OECD, 2016). Albania has implemented a new Capital Management and Budget system, which is based on government priorities, sectoral policies, and improved domestic and external budget resource allocation. This new system was designed to link capital investment needs to the MTBP and to priorities within an assessment of available financing. It is also designed to ensure that public investments are coordinated over the MTBP timeframe. However, the new process has been slow to be implemented because of the ongoing problems with politicization of the budgeting process, lack of adequate training of staff, inadequate staff levels and weak budgetary controls in capital investment.

Albania's project acquisition and contract management are based on a public procurement, planning, preparation and implementation systems, which are transparent and efficient (EUR Report, 2016). Project/contract management is a critical element of effective capital asset acquisition and management. This is especially important because the consequences of a mistake can include significant project delays and cost overruns. The contract management segment of project management ensures that projects are completed on time and within budget. The basis of good capital project management is careful tracking of progress against the schedule and budget and frequent reporting to top management (Posner, 1998).

Budget status monitoring is carried out in four government units involved in different aspects of capital budget monitoring. One of those, the Directorate of Public Investment Management within the Ministry of Finance (MoF), tracks the implementation of capital projects and programs by sector to monitor the capital program progress and project cycle management. Only two staff in the Capital Investment Department focus on capital budget monitoring. Consequently, there is a problem in that MoF does very little review of capital investment project plans or cost-benefit analysis. With such limited staffing and fragmentation, it has little capacity to verify the accuracy of capital budget assumptions and only monitors output. As noted previously, Capital Budget formulation in Albania has been significantly impacted by inaccuracy in revenue forecasts (World Bank, 2015). MoF has little capacity to verify the accuracy of the assumptions and only monitors output and only monitors (actual versus projected) costs for projects over a certain threshold. Audits consist of a review of the planning, design, construction, and management of the roads and highways maintenance (World Bank, 2013).

The Albanian legislature also monitors the capital budget during the fiscal year through quarterly and yearly reports presented by the Ministry of Finance. Budget execution and monitoring reports are prepared by the authorizing officer of the government unit at least four times a year (Article 65, Organic Budget Law). Within one month after the end of the quarterly report period, the Minister of Finance presents the budget monitoring and implementation reports to the Council of Ministers and the Legislature.

Capital Infrastructure Maintenance

The final component involves assessing current and future use of public infrastructure to project future capital projects needs and to set aside maintenance cost based on depreciation rates. Road maintenance is a basic requirement for economic growth because it contributes to the value of almost all the country's goods and services (World Bank, 2015). Both regular and periodic maintenance and improvement to roads and highways also reduces the cost of transportation and improves the quality of life. As a result, the economy grows because goods and services become more competitive. Inadequate road and highway maintenance leads to rapid road deterioration and slows down the realization of expected benefits from road improvements. Although there is general recognition in Albania of the importance of both routine and periodic maintenance, it is still not adequately financed or implemented (World Bank, 2015). Now, only 25% of the local road network is in a "maintainable" condition (Berger, 2010). This means that, for example, approximately 8,000 km of local roads need to be rehabilitated (Berger,2010).

Albania has very little in the way of a systematic asset inventory/need analysis. There is currently inadequate regular monitoring of asset conditions, and records of the road inventory needs to be updated (World Bank, 2015; Berger,2010). Experience from road and highway capital asset needs analysis in other countries indicated that low road maintenance expenditures adversely impact sustainability of road investments (World Bank, 2015). Records of road and highway structures inventory need to be updated and little information is collected on traffic volumes or axle loads. Such deficiencies impede the development of a professional approach to road asset management, financing [and evaluation] (IMF, 2014).

The capital maintenance function is divided into maintenance planning and maintenance funding (Ammar, Duncombe and Wright, 2001). Capital maintenance planning involves systematically estimating the condition of capital stock and determining required funding to bring existing infrastructure up to an acceptable condition (Ammar, Duncombe and Wright, 2001). Capital maintenance planning should be tied directly to assessment of the condition of the capital asset with the asset management system as the link (Ammar, Duncombe, and Wright, 2001). The system should combine capital asset condition information with depreciation and replacement cost (Ammar, Duncombe, and Wright, 2001). Committing adequate funds to maintenance requires political leadership engaging in fiscal discipline (Ammar, Duncombe and Wright, 2001).

Because historically Albania has not systematically planned for and adequately budgeted for periodic road maintenance in its capital budget, road maintenance has been underfunded. The World Bank is working with Albania to monitor, plan, budget for, and maintain both its routine and periodic road maintenance. Road maintenance, especially periodic maintenance, is the "Achilles heel" of most capital management systems (Ammar, Duncombe and Wright, 2001). The cost to eliminate the periodic maintenance backlog on Primary and Secondary Roads to prevent further deterioration is estimated to be $400 million (USD) over a five-year period (Jovanovic, 2017). What Albania needs is to develop and implement an adequately funded, cost-effective road and highway maintenance system, which will support the safe operation of the road and delivers both routine and periodic maintenance to the required levels of service (Jokanovic, 2017).

Albania budgets a lump-sum for maintenance of existing capital assets such as roads and highways. They also include a lump-sum for operating costs for new capital investments such as new roads and highways. Average expenditure of local roads in Albania, for example, is between 32,000-40,000 leg per km per year (Jokanovic, 2017), which is considered low compared to other countries. Maintenance funding covers routine road maintenance only and does not include periodic maintenance. At the local level, authorities let the roads deteriorate until a contract must be let because the road must be repaired immediately due to the amount of damage. No effort has been made to fund the required road work as maintenance and "a substantial amount of [routine] maintenance has been offloaded to the capital budget thereby saving immediate maintenance expenditure at the expense of future increased costs" to capital (Jokanovic, 2017). Recurrent expenditures averaged only 10 percent of total expenditures at the national level over the period 2007-2011 (IMF, 2014). In 2010, for example, the level of recurrent expenditure on the national road network amounted to some US $3 million, about 30 percent of what is estimated for routine and winter (periodic) maintenance (Berger, 2010).

There is also acknowledged budgetary "arrears" problem specifically in construction of roads and highways. The Ministry of Finance has stated that the problem stems from contractors continuing to build on multi-year projects from their own expense above the limit of the annual budget for capital expenditures, which creates claims on the following years' budgets, although this practice does not carry any contractual rights and there are no formal "arrears" (OCED, 2014). Multi-year capital commitments are not regulated in the Albanian Budget Law. The practice of making informal commitments arises from the technical issue related to the costs of discontinuing the projects, a political issue from pressure to expand development and a procedural issue since contractors cannot apply for new projects unless they have finished 70% of old project contracts (OCED, 2014). Because of these unauthorized commitments, which constitute "arrears", the Ministry of Transport's budget for 2012 and 2013 only included ongoing capital investment projects and not new projects (OCED, 2014).

As seen from road and highway asset funding with Albanian roads and highways, the primary emphasis has been on developing the national road network, however, these investments have not been adequately maintained (World Bank, 2011). Road maintenance planning and management is an on-going capital activity, which requires current and accurate information on road and highway asset inventory and condition. Where structural road failure has occurred, the affected section was included in future reconstruction projects, and no effort was made to fund the routine work as maintenance in the current budget (Jokanovic, 2017). The central Albanian road asset management issue is the need to adequately plan and budget for both routine and periodic maintenance.

The Albanian Ministry of Finance monitors (actual versus projected) costs for projects over a certain threshold. The audits consist of a review of the planning, design, construction and management of the roads and highways maintenance (World Bank, 2013).

ANALYSIS

Capital Planning

The capital planning function should be more closely aligned with capital project, implementation, and contract management processes to ensure that timely and accurate expenditures are recorded for capital projects. Prioritization in the Capital Improvement Plan for both new capital investments in roads and highways as well as for capital investment in both routine and periodic maintenance is critical to ensuring continued Albania's economic growth and sustainable road and highway maintenance and management. Routine maintenance is small-scale repair conducted frequently, such as pot-hole patching and grass cutting. It is usually conducted on a regular basis, weekly, or monthly. Periodic road maintenance, on the other hand, is normally conducted on a section of a road at a longer interval, tend to be large scale, require specialized equipment and specially trained personnel. While the Albanian budget process does include a process for prioritizing new capital investments in the Medium-Term Budget Plan that attempts to prioritize new capital investments, what is needed is a better aligned and more cohesive process for balancing the need for new capital investment, especially projects that have greater economic impact, with the need to adequately budget for both routine maintenance in the operating budget and budget for higher level periodic road and highway maintenance funding in the capital budget. The capital planning function should include more formal coordination and less fragmentation across departments. The CIP should also include estimated costs-benefits of the project and projected life-cycle costs.

Capital Budgeting and Financial Management

As noted previously, capital improvement planning within the Albanian Budget Process is still evolving. The issue with macroeconomic forecasts prepared by the Macroeconomic and Fiscal Policy Department of the MoF is the need to include a comparative explanation of how and why the updated forecasts differ from previous forecasts as well as to compare who they differ from so that the forecasts are understood in context with past forecasts. Further, the excessive political involvement in capital contracts, while difficult to change because of long-standing cultural precedence, should be better managed within the overall framework of capital improvement planning and capital budgeting, especially using a forecasting advisory panel. For example, the Durres-Kukes highway linking Albania with Kosovo is highly political and justified by Albanian political officials as important to the cultural linkages of the two countries. The contract to build the first stage of the highway connecting Tirana with the Kosovo border was awarded in 2006 on a fast-track procurement process. Costs on that highway escalated to 950 m EUR because the contract was signed without an agreed cost limit or detailed construction plan. The fast-track Albanian tender process (four short-listed firms were evaluated based on their ability to do the job without including a price) was contrary to Albanian Law. Albania was not able to borrow from international financial institutions because both the World Bank and IMF did not support the project (Balkan Insight, 4/10/18). Consequently, Albania was forced to borrow from commercial banks at above market rates.

The recognized weaknesses and inefficiencies in the Albanian capital management and budgeting system and the high degree of political involvement in the capital planning process have made private financing of infrastructure investment attractive. Public-Private Partnership (PPP) initiatives, if they are managed effectively by capable, up-to-date public financial administrators, can be a viable option to mobilize private investment, increase efficiency, and provide Value for the Money. PPP investments, however, involve fiscal risks in all stages of the project cycle, including budget preparation, procurement, financing and managing contracts. While Albania has used PPP previously, albeit somewhat ineffectively, it is planning to use them more extensively in the future. To ensure that any new PPP ventures benefit Albania appropriately, the government will need to significantly improve the capabilities and capacity of its budgetary and financial management. Further, it needs to support and encourage Albanian financial managers to take a much stronger lead in planning and managing partnerships and any ensuing fiscal risks and costs.

The *Albanian National Strategy for Development and Integration* sets forth the policy for capital investment and the MTBP financial constraints (MoF, 2014). *The National Strategy for Development and Integration 2014-2020*, together with sector strategies, cross-sector strategies, Master Plans, and Action Plans are the basis for master planning and strategy development (MoF, 2014). These documents, taken together, define priorities and long-term and medium-term objectives. The Albanian government plans to spend an estimated USD 200 million on infrastructure in 2017 primarily for roads (Export.Gov, 9/26/16). It has been suggested that the rehabilitation and upgrading of secondary roads that are not part of the Master Plan be established, which sets up priorities and annual investment requirements on rehabilitation and improvement of local and rural roads (Berger, 2010).

Albania should focus on improving the functioning of the primary market for domestic government debt and developing a liquid secondary market. Eurobond markets to amortize FX swap debt while being vigilant of risks posed by excessive reliance on FX swap and non-concessional borrowing. These efforts will help attract new investors, extend maturity, and lower liquidity. Strengthening communication and coordination among the stakeholders on liquidity and debt management is also important to avoid excess volatility of T-bill rates.

Capital Budget Execution and Project Management

Authorization for large capital projects tends to be more complex and is often a multistep process (Marlowe, Rivenbark and Vogt, 2009). As noted previously, Albania is developing a strategy for completing or closing projects during MTBP period 2015-2017 to address the issues with capital budget execution. Revision of capital budget project plans need to be conducted at least quarterly to mitigate the budgetary arrears problem in construction of roads and highway. This will identify situations where projects are exceeding their budgeted amount and reduce claims on the following fiscal year budget, as well as help to identify costs of discontinuing the projects.

Because of the large amount of arrears in capital investment road and highway projects and inadequate road asset management, there is inadequate funding for required road maintenance especially periodic maintenance. Budgeting for routine capital maintenance has been should be charged to the annual budget, while periodic maintenance should be charged to the capital budget.

Capital Infrastructure Maintenance Component

Routine and periodic maintenance are not adequately funded or supported because of insufficient monitoring of road and highway asset conditions, and as a result, a large percentage of Albanian roads need major rehabilitation. There is a need for a more effective capital budget process, which identifies and includes adequate funding for sustainable road asset management and maintenance, especially periodic road maintenance is critical.

Where unidentified structural road problems have occurred, the affected section of the road should be included in the operating budget for current reconstruction projects and routine work funded as maintenance in the operating budget. The central Albanian road asset management issue is the need to adequately plan and budget for both routine and *periodic* maintenance.

This study investigated the Albanian capital management and budgeting processes using the Normative Model. When compared to the normative model, there are patterns to the weaknesses in the country's capital management and budget system which have important practical effects for road and highway infrastructure investment. The shortcomings stem from the lack of sound financial and judicial structures and lack of budgetary discipline because of political disharmony and the evolving transition to a market economy. Political pressure to maintain spending levels has created the climate for overly optimistic forecasting to support spending increases, which in turn have negatively impacted the capital budget. The study revealed patterns of under-staffing and underqualified civil service hiring, which has led to opportunities for corruption and low employee quality.

This is especially challenging in adequately staffing the ministries that are responsible for: budget formulation, budget execution, forecasting, accounting, procurement, disbursement management, monitoring, and evaluation. The study also shows pattern of fragmentation in the capital planning process, with overlapping responsibilities among the various line ministries. While the CIP process is in place, the process is not followed, is politicized, fragmented, and lacks adequate and capable staffing.

This shortcoming is especially acute because the Albanian CIP is based on the forecasts in the Medium-Term Budget. Regarding shortcomings in budget execution, the new Capital Management and

Budget system has been slow to be implemented because of ongoing problems such as pattern of political interference, lack of adequate staff training and inadequate staff levels. The shortcomings in capital road maintenance funding reveal a pattern of ineffective, systematic capital road maintenance monitoring and record keeping. The pattern of shortcomings in capital project expenditure monitoring have also resulted in budgetary arrears. The arrears are the result of a lack of contract monitoring as contractors continue to build well after the annual capital project appropriation limit is reached on an individual project.

The Albanian processes and practices exhibit identifiable patterns (when compared to the Normative Model) that suggest the critical need for strengthening the long-term capital planning and management process. Additionally, the patterns highlight the need for the acquisition and training of competent, capable public financial managers to effectively and efficiently identify, monitor and manage Albania's economy and fiscal future. This conclusion is further supported, given the planned increases in capital investment, by the need for these managers to counterbalance both the negative effects of political decisions and any unanticipated revenue shortfalls on capital investment.

CONCLUSION

This study of the Capital Management and Budgeting in Albania investigated and examined the public-sector processes as they compare with, relate to, and impact Albanian public infrastructure investment using the current processes compared to those specified in the Normative Model framework of Srithongrung, Yusuf, and Kriz (2019). This section of the study summarizes the processes' deficiencies and provides insights and implications that can be drawn from and derived from the study investigation.

Briefly, the study analysis indicated that Albania's shortcomings in the current capital management and budgeting processes applied to road and highway infrastructure investment has contributed to and created several economic limitations that, in turn, have negatively impacted the country's growth and development. Specifically, Albania's capital management and budgeting processes are not consistent with the normative framework as follows: (1) *Capital Planning Component*, especially the fragmentation and political involvement in capital improvement planning (CIP) process, (2) *Capital Budgeting and Financial Management Component,* particularly the significant bias and fragmentation in the forecasting process has resulted in misalignment and lack of prioritizing new capital investments in line with the actual strategic macro and fiscal situation; (3) *Capital Budget Execution and Project Management Component, specifically (a) shortcomings in the capital financing strategies* processes stemming from court decisions and (b) weak budgetary control which resulted in arrears on many capital contracts, and (4) *Capital Infrastructure Maintenance Component*, principally inadequate financing of capital asset management and maintenance funding.

REFERENCES

Albania Institute of Statistics (INSTAT). (2017). *Government of Albania.* Retrieved October 13, 2018, from http://www.instat.gov.al/en/themes/economy-and-finance/national-accounts-gdp/

Albania Organic Budget Law. (2010). *Republic of Albania.* National Assembly, No. 10-355 (2/12/10). Retrieved October 13, 2018, from http://www1.worldbank.org/publicsector/pe/BudgetLaws/Albania-OrganicBudget1998.pdf

Ammar, S., Duncombe, W., & Wright, R. (2001). Evaluating capital management: A new approach. *Public Budgeting & Finance*, *21*(4), 47–69. doi:10.1111/0275-1100.00058

Balkan Insight. (2018). *Albania Civil Service Watch*. Retrieved May 4, 2018, from http://www.balkaninsight.com/en/page/albania-home

Balkan Insight. (2018). *Albania-Kosovo Highway Costs Soar to 2 Billion Euros*. Retrieved May 4, 2018, from http://www.balkaninsight.com/en/page/albania-home

Berger, L. (2010). *Five Year Review of Albanian National Transport Plan*. ANTPS.

Bozeman, B. (2004). *All Organization are Public: Comparing Public and Private Organizations*. New York: Beard Books.

Bunch, B. (2013). Capital planning and budgeting. In J. Bartle, B. Hildreth, & J. Marlowe (Eds.), Management policies in local government finance (6th ed.; pp. 253-277). Washington, DC: ICMA Press.

Dalakoglou, D. (2012). The road from capitalism to capitalism: Infrastructures of (post) socialism in Albania. *Mobility: Roads and Authorities*, *7*(4), 571–586. doi:10.1080/17450101.2012.718939

Durata, T. (n.d.). *An overview of public administration in Albania*. Retrieved May 4, 2018, from https://scholar.google.com/scholar?rlz=1C1CHBF_enUS786US786&um=1&ie=UTF-8&lr&cites=388660522110937877

Ermasova, N. (2012). *Capital budgeting at the state level: an empirical analysis from the economic downturn through the present* (PhD Dissertation). SPEA, IU.

Ermasova, N. (2013). Capital budgeting in the states after the Great Recession. *State & Local Government Review*, *45*(2), 119–130. doi:10.1177/0160323X13487079

EU Report. (2016). *European Commission Staff Working Document*. Retrieved May 4, 2018, from https://ec.europa.eu/neighbourhood-enlargement/sites/near/files/20180417-albania-report.pdf

Export. Gov. (2017). *Albania market overview*. Retrieved May 4, 2018, from https://www.export.gov/article?series=a0pt0000000PAt7AAG&type=Country_Commercial__kav

Gatti, S. (2012). *Project finance in theory and practice: Designing, structuring and financing private and public projects*. Waltham, MA: Elsevier.

Giannakis, G. & McCue, C. (1999). *Local government budgeting: A managerial approach*. Westport, CT: Quorum Books.

Heritage Foundation. (2018). *Index of economic freedom*. Retrieved July 23, 2018 from https://www.heritage.org/index/country/albania

International Monetary Fund. (2014). *Albanian financial system stability assessment*. Retrieved July 23, 2018, from https://www.imf.org/en/Publications/CR/Issues/2016/12/31/Albania-Financial-System-Stability-Assessment-41424

International Monetary Fund. (2016). *Staff country report-Albania and IMF no. 16/142*. Retrieved July 23, 2018, from https://www.imf.org/en/Publications/CR/Issues/2016/12/31/Albania-Selected-Issues-16142

International Monetary Fund. (2017). *Albania selected issues report no. 17/364*. Retrieved July 23, 2018, from https://www.imf.org/en/Publications/CR/Issues/2016/12/31/Albania-Selected-Issues-43939

International Monetary Fund. (2018). *Public infrastructure in the western Balkans*. Retrieved July 23, 2018, from https://www.imf.org/en/Publications/Departmental-Papers-Policy-Papers/Issues/2018/02/07/Public-Infrastructure-in-the-Western-Balkans-Opportunities-and-Challenges-45547

International Monetary Fund. (2018). *Country report no. 18/123*. p. 35-38. Retrieved July 23, 2018, from https://www.imf.org/en/Publications/CR/Issues/2016/12/30/Albania-Selected-Issues-and-Statistical-Appendix-16403

Jokanovic, I., Crujic, B., Zeijic, D., & Crujic, D. (2017). Article. *Journal of Civil Engineering*, *12*(2), 71–78.

Krepsik, K. (2014). Budgeting in Albania. *OCED Journal on Budgeting*, *3*(32), 1–23.

Marlowe, J., Rivenbark, W. C., & Vogt, A. J. (2009). *Capital budgeting and finance: A guide for local government*. Washington, DC: ICMA Press.

Ministry of Finance. (2014). *Public financial management strategy 2000-2015*. Government of Albania.

Moak, L. I., & Hillhouse, A. M. (1975). *Concepts and practices in local government finance*. Chicago: Municipal Finance Officers Association.

OECD. (2017). Albania budgeting. *OECD Journal on Budgeting, 1*(2). doi:10.1787/budget-v16-2-en

Posner, P. (1998). *Budgeting for capital. Government Accountability Office*. GAO.

Srithongrung, A. (2018). Capital budgeting and management practices: Smoothing out rough spots in capital outlay. *Public Budgeting & Finance*, *38*(1), 47–69. doi:10.1111/pbaf.12167

Srithongrung, A., & Kriz, K. (2012). From public infrastructure to national economic growth: Do systemic Investment practices matter? *International Public Management Review*, *13*(2), 1–32.

Srithongrung, S., Ermasova, N., & Yusuf, W. (2019). *Capital management and budgeting in the public sector*. Hershey, PA: IGI.

Standard & Poor. (2018). *Rating: Albania credit rating*. Retrieved July 23, 2018, from https://tradingeconomics.com/albania/rating

Steiss, A. W. (2005). *Strategic Facilities Planning: Capital Budgeting and Debt Administration*. Lanham, MD: Lexington Books.

Vogt, J. A. (2004). *Capital budget and finance: A guide for local governments*. International City/County Management Association.

World Bank. (2012). *Policy briefs: Albania*. Retrieved July 23, 2018 from http://www.worldbank.org/content/dam/Worldbank/document/eca/Albania-Policy-Briefs-2013.pdf

World Bank. (2013). *Albanian country profile*. Retrieved July 23, 2018 from https://openknowledge.worldbank.org/handle/10986/20829

World Bank. (2015). *Albanian public expenditure and financial accountability assessment* (PEFA 2015). Retrieved July 23, 2018 from, http://documents.worldbank.org/curated/en/904191521826887529/Albania-Public-expenditure-and-financial-accountability-PEFA-performance-assessment-report

World Bank. (2018). *Medium-term debt management strategy*. MoF. Retrieved July 23, 2018, from https://openknowledge.worldbank.org/handle/10986/17637

APPENDIX

Table 2. Summary of Comparisons of the Normative Model with Albanian Processes and Practices

Normative Model Recommendations	Albanian Processes and Practices
1. Long-term Capital Planning	
Comprehensive/Master Planning	Yes. (noted in strategic planning section)
Strategic Planning	The *Albanian National Strategy for Development and Integration* sets forth the policy for capital investment and the MTBP financial constraints (MoF, 2014). *The National Strategy for Development and Integration 2014-2020,* together with sector strategies, cross-sector strategies, Master Plans, and Action Plans are the basis for master planning and strategy development (MoF, 2014)
Long-term Fiscal Planning	For overall capital planning and maintenance, the Department of Planning and Budget within the Ministry of Finance is responsible for preparing medium-term budgets and forecasts (World Bank, 2013). Medium-term budget frameworks cover three to four years and attempt to improve the inherent quality and uncertainty issues of medium-term fiscal planning with descriptive estimates (OECD, 2016)
Asset Inventory Analysis/Need Analysis	No. Albania has very little in the way of a systematic asset inventory/need analysis. There is currently little regular monitoring of asset conditions, and records of the road inventory needs to be updated.
Capital Improvement Program	Yes. However, the Albanian process for initiating, appraising, prioritizing, approving and contracting for capital improvements planning does not follow the steps in an organized manner (MoF, 2014) because the process is politicized, fragmented, and lacks adequate staffing
2. Capital Budgeting and Financial Management	
Systematic Priority Ranking	Yes, but not too general. Priority given only to projects listed in the first year of the capital improvement plan (capital budget proposal) and investments in roads and highways.
Multi-year Fiscal Forecasting	The Prime Minister's Office is responsible for long-term fiscal projections. Albania produces six to seven years fiscal projections and revises the projections every seven years. The Albanian Ministry of Finance prepares medium-term fiscal forecasts, which are the basis for the Capital Improvement Plan
Capital Budgeting Process (e.g., resource allocation decisions—incremental or programmatic, separate capital budget document, definition of capital expenditure, specific level for each year for investment VS consumption ratio)	Yes. The annual Albanian budget process can be described as "top-down" with a set ceiling. Albania has no budget balance rules. The capital expenditures are separated in the budget, it is clear capital spending is inadequate for both building and maintaining the country's infrastructure. Albania uses a revenue-availability approach to capital investment spending. This approach results in routine interruption of the prioritization of capital projects because of unexpected revenue shortages
Debt Affordability Analysis	High debt may hinder economic recovery. High debt also means increased vulnerability to increased rollover requirements and higher vulnerability to shifts in market.
Operating Reserve	Bank of Albania committed to holding sufficient level of foreign reserves. At the end of the third quarter 2017, international reserves estimated to cover about 6.5 months of imports of goods and services and about 170% of the short-term debt.
Debt Management Policy/ Disclosure (e.g., debt ceiling, debt approval by National Assembly, debt issuance, any debt/tax choice policy or guidance, i.e., when to sue pay-go and pay-as-you-use finance)	Debt Management Policy objective is downward trajectory of public debt as a ratio to GDP beginning in 2016. Public debt is expected to fall to about 68.7% of GDP in 2018; 66.4% of GDP in 2019 and 63.5% in 2020. Medium-term indicative target for public debt is its reduction below 60% in 2021.

continued on following page

Table 2. Continued

Normative Model Recommendations	Albanian Processes and Practices
3. Capital Budget Execution and Project Management	
Budget/Project Status Reporting	Yes. There are four government units involved in capital budget monitoring: Ministry of Finance, Capital Investment Department, Public Investment Management, The Albanian legislature. The Albanian legislature also monitors the capital budget during the fiscal year through quarterly and yearly reports presented by the Ministry of Finance. Budget execution and monitoring reports are prepared by the authorizing officer of the government unit at least four times a year (Article 65, Organic Budget Law). Within one month after the end of the quarterly report period, the Minister of Finance presents the budget monitoring and implementation reports to the Council of Ministers and the Legislature.
Internal Audit (using budget variance report)	Yes. The Albania Ministry of Finance monitors (actual versus projected) costs for projects over a certain threshold. The audits consist of a review of the planning, design, construction and management of the roads and highways maintenance
Project Acquisition, Contract Management, and Performance Monitoring	Yes, there is a public procurement system and planning, preparation and implementation systems are in place.
4. Infrastructure maintenance	
Maintenance Planning	Yes. Although there is general recognition in Albania of the importance of both routine and periodic maintenance, it is still not adequately financed or implemented (World Bank, 2015). Now, only 25% of the local road network is in a "maintainable" condition (Berger, 2010).
Maintenance Funding	Yes. Albania budgets a lump-sum for maintenance of existing capital assets such as roads and highways. They also include a lump-sum for operating costs for new capital investments such as new roads and highways
Asset Management (e.g., repair over replacement policy)	Yes, but only for roads
Program/performance evaluation	Yes, but only for roads There is, however, insufficient ongoing routine monitoring of road and highway asset conditions.

Section 3

Capital Management and Budgeting in Other Economies

Chapter 9
Infrastructure Development in Burkina Faso:
The Story of Public Capital Budgeting

Kouliga Koala
Old Dominion University, USA

Joshua Steinfeld
Old Dominion University, USA

ABSTRACT

In Burkina Faso, the public capital management and budgeting framework is the MTEF. The budgeting method is the PBB. While Burkina has a budgeting framework and method, it is not clear how effectively they work when it comes to capital budgeting for infrastructure development, unlike developed countries where the framework and method are completely developed and clearly laid out. It is important to understand how Burkina integrates components of a normative framework such as long-term public capital planning, capital budgeting and financial management, centralized execution and project management, and infrastructure maintenance. The chapter focuses on providing a comparison of capital budgeting in Burkina and the normative framework. Exploring the literature and government documents, the authors show that Burkina theoretically addresses some of the elements of the normative components while practically, the country's use of most elements is weak and non-existent. The unique factors that inhibit the normative framework are highlighted and ten recommendations are provided.

INTRODUCTION

Burkina Faso became independent from France on August 5, 1960 under the name of Upper Volta. Burkina Faso has a total area of 274,000 square kilometers and a population of more than 18 million people (World Bank Group, 2017; Jeune Afrique, 2017). As of 2016, approximately 30.3 percent of the population lived in urban areas. While the official language of Burkina is French, more than 60 national languages are spoken, representing different ethnic groups including the mossi, the fulanis, the gurunsi, the bisansi, the dagari, the lobi, the samo, the dioula, and others.

DOI: 10.4018/978-1-5225-7329-6.ch009

Geographically, Burkina Faso is landlocked and surrounded by six countries. Regionally located in the heart of West Africa, it is a member of the Economic Community of West African States (ECOWAS). Burkina is also a member of the West Africa Economic and Monetary Union (WAEMU) composed of eight countries that use the Communauté financiére d'Afrique (Financial Community of Africa) currency (FCFA) and speak the same language, French, except Guinea-Bissau which speaks Portuguese. These regional organizations influence in one way or the other the development policies of Burkina including financial and public procurement policies. There is a strong regional effort to achieve integrated economic and infrastructure development for the benefits of free movement of people and a larger regional market. These efforts concerned mostly major infrastructure development projects with individual neighboring countries.

While Burkina Faso inscribes itself in line with the regional dynamism of infrastructure development in Africa, it also focuses on national infrastructure projects and programs as part of its national development strategies. In its state of development, schools, roads, transportation, health facilities, water, and sewerage are among the most pressing infrastructure areas where Burkina Faso has significant infrastructure gaps. In 2011, the World Bank estimated that the country would need to invest 11 percent of Gross Domestic Product (GDP) toward infrastructure over 10 years to close the gap with the continent's leading performers (O'Sullivan and Lima, 2016). In addition to capital requirements, there are a host of governance challenges to improving infrastructure. At a national assembly meeting in 2016, the Ministry of Territorial Administration and Decentralization pointed out that the slow work of public administration, the procedures of technical and financial partners, difficulties in the public procurement procedures, and deficiencies in companies and service providers are some of the main causes of ineffective execution of projects.

Governance issues and ineffective management are coupled with resources constraints. To remedy, Burkina Faso adopted the Medium-Term Expenditure Framework (MTEF) and the Program-Based Budget (PBB) as the budgeting framework and method. While there are benefits to these systems, the Ministry of Finance (MINEFID) identified the deficiencies of the current budgeting system including the lack of coherence between the MTEF framework and sectorial policies, the lack of sectorial policies, the difficulties in harmonizing MTEF with PBB, and the non-respect of MTEF portfolios (CAFRAD, 2018). The system is mined with cost overruns as well. Thus, there is a need to explore different avenues for better solutions. Key's (1940) simple question of "how do we decide to allocate X amount to program A instead of B" is not only a practical one but also calls to thinking about normative and theoretical approaches to orient public spending (*also see* Mukherjee & Henderson,1987). A normative framework lays out steps in the budgeting process and articulates the practices needed to be successful. This chapter presents the current use of MTEF in Burkina while analyzing its fit with the elements of normative capital budgeting framework.

The comparison is necessary because of previous success of the implementation of normative frameworks in other countries. Srithongrung, Ermasova, and Yusuf (2019) believed that the normative public capital management and budgeting process was largely adopted and fully practiced by state and local governments in the U.S. However, there is limited knowledge as to how the framework is practiced by central governments globally. There is also the belief that the framework may serve as a capital management and budgeting tool that is useful for the development of public infrastructure (Ermasova 2012, 2013a, 2013b). As such, its application may as well contribute to enhance the quality of life, attract business relocation, and improve equity in access to public infrastructure in developing countries such as Burkina Faso.

The methodology for conducting the comparative analysis consists of the content review of the literature on capital budgeting on developing countries and in Burkina Faso. The major budgeting framework, policies, budget laws and relevant reports of the government of Burkina Faso are reviewed. The common issues, shortcomings, problems, and themes that appear frequently will be the focus for further discussion in the chapter. The recommendations are based on scholars' views of the capital budgeting and the knowledge from budgeting documents.

The review comprises the following agenda: The first part in this chapter introduces the background of the country such as the government structure and institutional arrangements. The second part presents Burkina's public infrastructure system in terms of accessibility, quality, and quantity. The third part presents the country's current budgeting framework and method. The fourth part analyzes and discusses the country's public capital management and budgeting in terms of the four aspects of the normative framework. The fifth part summarizes the main factors that influence the capital management and budgeting practices. The sixth part presents the national perspectives and challenges.

This research is relevant as it brings Burkina in the literature of capital budgeting as an example of a developing nation with minimal resources and a younger public administrative system that is yet to mature. It presents the use of MTEF and PBB and a comparison against a normative framework. As the information is presented in English, a larger audience is reached. Burkina Faso, in general, is absent from the literature in the Anglophone literature. The research process allows discovering scholars on capital budgeting in developing countries such as Burkina Faso.

BACKGROUND: GOVERNMENT AND STRUCTURE

Government and Administration

Burkina has had a complex and turbulent history of governance systems. From 1960 until today, the country has had two republics and seven exceptional regimes through military coups or non-democratic takeover. Burkina Faso is currently at its fifth republic. As a republic, it is a semi-presidential and democratic system with the president as the head of state and the prime minister as the head of government. The government is composed of 33 ministries that carry out the operations of the strategic action of government across the different sectors. The government has three branches: the executive, the judiciary, and the legislative. The country is divided into thirteen regions administered by governors. The regions are subdivided into a total of 45 provinces, each administered by a high commissioner. The provinces are in turn subdivided into 351 departments composed of 49 urban and 302 rural departments, each administered by a prefect. There is a total of 8,438 villages each led by a village development committee (CVD) (Labopresse.net, 2018; Agence EcoFin, 2018). The government has two main levels: the central government and the local government. The local government is composed of two levels: the region, which serves as an intermediate between the central government and the municipalities; and the municipalities. Local government has been an important part of the Burkinabe public administration through revived laws aimed at decentralization in recent years.

Decentralization

The first constitution was adopted on June 2, 1991. Since then, the country has undertaken steps towards decentralization. In 2004, the country adopted the General Code of Territorial Collectivities, extending decentralization to all parts of the country. This was a major milestone where the central government decided to extend, delegate, and share responsibilities with local governments. On the one hand, decentralization was undertaken as part of a stronger and more effective democratic governance. On the other hand, it was the push from donors to decentralize that made it possible. Thus, Article 2 reads: "Decentralization guarantees the right of territorial collectivities to freely administer themselves and manage their own affairs in order to promote local and area-based development and reinforce local governance" (Loi des Finances, 2017). Decentralization was followed by de-concentration of public services. Today, there are a total of 364 local collectivities in Burkina (Region.bf, 2014). Communes or municipalities are legally responsible for public policy and administration including land management, territorial management and urbanism, environment and management of natural resources, construction and maintenance of healthcare facilities, education, water, energy, slaughterhouses, managing markets, and other policy domains (Englebert and Sangare, 2014).

The goal of decentralization is also to give autonomy to the local governments to self-govern and self-finance. However, Englebert and Sangare (2014) highlighted the lack of administrative autonomy because of the oversight of de-concentrated institutions. Added to that is the lack of financial autonomy as municipalities are not able to raise enough revenues to cover their expenses. The communes adopt their own budgets, which must be approved by the Ministry of Territorial Administration and Decentralization (MTAD) and the Ministry of Economy, Finance, and Development (MINEFID). Therefore, these municipalities remain heavily dependent on national budget and donors for functioning.

Structure of Local Governments

MTAD is currently in charge of territorial administration through coordination of territorial affairs. It provides support to area-based development through the capacity building of local authorities as well as to the implementation of government's decentralization policy. The MINEFID, through the Directorate General of Territorial Development, Local and Regional Development formulates area-based development policies and ensures that such policy frameworks are translated into programs and projects. The mission of the MINEFID is to support the implementation and monitoring of the government's fiscal, financial, and economic policies and strategic planning. In terms of decentralization, the MINEFID oversees the financial management of territorial collectivities and has the responsibility for territorial planning and regional and local development (MINEFID, 2010). Other ministries involved include the Ministry of Agriculture, Hydraulics and Fishery Resources (MAHRH), Directorate General of Rural Land Tenure and Farmer Organizations (DGFROP), Ministry of Animal Resources (MRA), Department of Studies and Planning (DEP), Department of Pastoral and Land Development (DGAEP), and the Ministry of Environment and Livelihoods (MECV).

STATE OF PUBLIC INFRASTRUCTURE OF BURKINA FASO

Infrastructure development sectors that are important in Burkina include, among others, roads, water and sanitation, power, and air transport. This section presents a background for the state of infrastructure across the country's major sectors as a means of providing a context for the country's capital budgeting.

Transportation

Roads

According to the Ministry of Infrastructure and Transport, as of 2013, Burkina had a classified road network of 15,304 km, of which 3642 km or 24 percent are paved. Roads are important for general connectivity. In an economy based on agriculture, road density is one of the main determinants of the cash income from agricultural sales in Burkina, along with agriculture yield, high-value crops, and direct selling to markets (World Bank, 2009). The road network provides regional, national, and international connectivity, linking the major capital city of Ouagadougou to international border crossings and provincial capitals in the interior. However, there remains some obstacles to the appropriate road maintenance as pointed out by Briceño-Garmendia and Domínguez-Torres (2011). The first factor is the disruption of the historic corridor providing Burkina access to the port of Abidjan in Côte d'Ivoire during the decade-long political crisis. This shifted traffic from the Abidjan-Ouagadougou Corridor to new corridors connecting Ouagadougou to Tema in Ghana, Lome in Togo, and Cotonou in Benin. These corridors were not designed for the subsequent increase in traffic, leading to an accelerated deterioration of roads and further maintenance and rehabilitation (Briceño-Garmendia and Domínguez-Torres, 2011). Another issue is overloading, which exerts considerable weight on the road infrastructure itself, leading to degradation and deterioration. Burkina faces the challenge of enforcing potential controls. For example, the control to ensure that there is no overloading should be first exercised at freight-origination points or ports rather than en route where it is more difficult to penalize. This requires regional agreements between Burkina and neighboring countries (Briceño-Garmendia and Domínguez-Torres, 2011).

The second factor deals with funding, where the current practice of collecting a fuel levy is unsustainable because it amounts to 20 to 30 cents per liter of gasoline consumed. This levy is unaffordable for many Burkinabe users. An alternative source of funding is needed in which neighboring countries could agree to not only endorse and enforce overloading regulations and facilitate the modernization of transport and logistics services in general, but also to agree to share the rehabilitation and maintenance costs as well as benefits of the regional corridors across countries (Briceño-Garmendia and Domínguez-Torres, 2011).

Railways

Burkina Faso has a transnational railway line jointly owned with Côte d'Ivoire. The railroad company, the Societe Internationale de Transport Africain par Rail (SITARAIL), was established in 1995 as a result of the merger of the national railways of the two countries. The rail line links the port of Abidjan to Ouagadougou and is a key conduit for bulk freight from and into the landlocked hinterland of Burkina. According to Briceño-Garmendia and Domínguez-Torres (2011), benchmarking with other African rail lines indicates that SITARAIL is one of the strongest performers on a wide range of operational indicators, including labor productivity, traffic volumes, and average tariffs. Strong traffic growth took place during the first five years of the concession or incentives, from 1995 to 2000, when the volume of freight almost doubled from 450 million to 700 million tons/km (Briceño-Garmendia and Domínguez-Torres, 2011). The Ministry of Infrastructure puts the total length of railroad at 622 km of which 518 km are in use. The length has not changed since 2002 due to high costs of building the railroad.

In spite of its strong operational performance, SITARAIL is in financial distress due to war-related losses of $38.6 million, including physical damage ($5.7 million), loss of income to employees ($9.7 million), nonpayment of state-owned asset-holding companies' debt ($8.6 million), concession fee payments or incentives ($1.1 million), and loss of revenues ($13.5 million). Consequently, SITARAIL's future depends on the ability of its public and private partners to revise the current concession contract to restore the company's long-term financial viability.

SITARAIL is a lease type of public-private partnership (PPP). But since the beginning of the concession or incentives, this arrangement has not generated enough revenues to allow both the payment of the state-owned asset-holding companies and the financing of rehabilitation of the railway infrastructure and rolling stock. Investment needs for the railway network over the next 10 years have been estimated at $240 million, of which $100 million for freight rolling stock would be covered by SITARAIL, $60 million for infrastructure rehabilitation and passenger rolling stock by Burkina, and $80 million for infrastructure rehabilitation and passenger rolling stock by Côte d'Ivoire.

Air Transport

Burkina is a minor player in air transportation in West Africa; it has less than half a million seats per year across all traffic categories. The country has two international airports, located in Ouagadougou and Bobo Dioulasso. In 2013, approximately 230,000 passengers arrived and departed at Ouagadougou airport as compared to approximately 6500 passengers at Bobo-Dioulasso airport. These figures represent a 19.8 percent increase in passengers at Ouagadougou airport and a 60 percent increase in the number of passengers at Bobo-Dioulasso airport compared to 2012 (Ministry of Transport, 2015).

Across the region, there has been a tendency for aircraft fleets to be scaled down in size to facilitate the consolidation of routes toward a hub-and-spoke system. The aircraft fleet serving Burkina has been renewed rapidly in recent years with the share of modern aircraft rising from 73 percent in 2004 to 93 percent in 2007 (Briceño-Garmendia and Domínguez-Torres, 2011). Burkina has a nationalized airline. Air Burkina was founded in the 1960s and later became part of Air Afrique. When Air Afrique collapsed in 2001, the government of Burkina privatized Air Burkina. The airline is now partially owned by the Aga Khan fund and serves Europe, including flights to Paris, Orly, and Marseille. Regular African destinations include Benin, Côte d'Ivoire, Gabon, Ghana, Mali, Niger, Senegal, and Togo; and works in code share with Air Mali (Ministry of Transport, 2015, p.20). The domestic market is barely developed and therefore very thin—Burkina has the third-smallest domestic market in Sub-Saharan Africa, next to Mali and Côte d'Ivoire.

Burkina continues to face safety and security issues in air transport. Burkina has not undertaken the U.S. Federal Aviation Administration/International Aviation Safety Assessment (FAA/IASA) audit and none of its carriers have passed the International Air Transport Association/IATA International Safety Audit (IATA/IOSA) (Briceño-Garmendia and Domínguez-Torres, 2011). Burkina's existing airport is unsuitable, and the country needs to address capacity constraints and security issues. The immediate challenge for the government is to keep the existing airport in an operational condition by upgrading installations to follow international standards.

Water and Sanitation

As a landlocked country, one of the obstacles is the lack of hydraulic resources. With an urban growth rate of 5.2 percent per annum, it is projected that 40 percent of the population will be living in urban centers by 2030, in particular in informal settlements (World Bank, 2017). This puts pressure on the need for water and sewage infrastructure. Burkina Faso has made progress with the help of international organizations. The World Bank supported the Urban Water Sector Project (UWSP) 2009-2018 funded by 12 donors, including the International Development Agency (IDA) and Trust Funds of about US$266 million. Under UWSP, the implementation of the Ouagadougou Water Supply Project from the Ziga Dam 2001–2017 cost US$70 million. The results were access to improved sources of drinking water. First, access went up from 54 percent in 2001 to 90 percent in 2016, of which 63 percent is served by household connections and 27 percent served by standpipes. Second, there has been a significant drop in water connections fees, from US$250 to US$50 per household connection. Third, the implementation of 160,200 new household connections, including peri-urban settlements and the installation of 711 standpipes were realized (World Bank, 2017).

Another project in the area of water and sanitation is the Community-Based Rural Development project (CBRD) 2001–2013 financed at US$35 million. As a result, about 1.4 million people in rural areas gained access to clean water that improves the health of rural populations and reduces time spent, especially by women, in collecting water. The World Bank (2017) stated that the public agency in charge of water distribution, the Office National de l'Eau et de l'Assainissement (ONEA) and Burkina's state-owned water and sanitation utility, is today ranked among the top performing water utilities in Sub-Saharan Africa. The agency has a staff productivity of 2.9 staff per 1000 connections and a bill collection ratio of 97.7 percent (World Bank, 2017). Despite improvement and overall access in the country both in rural and urban areas for 72.4 percent of people in the country, as of 2016, disparities exist in terms of access to improved water supplies between urban and rural areas. Particularly access to adequate sanitation facilities remain low in both urban and rural areas, at 36.1 percent and 13.7 percent (World Bank, 2017).

Power

Threatened by lack of rainfall and inaccessibility to waterways, Burkina relies on man-made sources and its neighbors for power and energy. Burkina has taken steps to encourage the private sector by improving the legal and regulatory framework of the energy sector. In recent years, there has been a systematic effort by the Burkinabe authorities to increase power trade with neighbors in the regional West African Power Pool (WAPP). Investment has been carried out to integrate the national power system into a unified regional electricity market by building interconnections with Côte d'Ivoire. The connections to major cities of Bobo-Dioulasso-Ouagadougou became functional by 2014. Another supply with Ghana started in 2011.

According to the World Bank (2017), today, Burkina imports 15 percent of the electricity consumed. The power capacity from neighbors comes at much lower prices. An emphasis on increasing power trade brings benefits on many fronts. From the cost perspective, it is well documented that costs per kilowatt-hour (kWh) of power produced by the Société Nationale d'électricité du Burkina Faso (SONABEL), the state-owned energy agency, are just short of US35 cents, among the highest in Africa, mostly driven by fuel prices. Even with high tariffs, the current level of power costs calls for subsidies and represent fiscal costs on the order of US$50 million per year. Imported electricity has been negotiated for at US7 cents/kWh, roughly 20 percent of the cost of domestic production (Briceño-Garmendia and Domínguez-Torres, 2011).

Burkina's power supply is insufficient to meet increasing demand. Only about 18 percent of the population has access to electricity equating to 40% in urban areas and 3 percent in rural areas. Per capita consumption is 44 kWh in Burkina, compared with 100 kWh in Cameroon, 200 kWh in Senegal, and 270 kWh in Côte d'Ivoire. Approximately 90 percent of the population relies on wood energy such as firewood and charcoal. Further, SONABEL has faced system transmission and distribution losses of over 60 percent, much higher than the internationally accepted norm of 10 percent (Briceño-Garmendia and Domínguez-Torres, 2011).

BUDGETING FRAMEWORK AND METHOD OF BURKINA FASO

Medium-Term Expenditure Framework (MTEF)

The Burkinabe government officials need to understand the capital budgeting process. Srithongrung (2008) defined capital budgeting as "a process or system of administrative procedures that relates a long-term capital improvement program (CIP) to the methods that will be used to pay for those improvements and provide for the implementation of these long-term financial and physical plans" (p.85). The CIP itself is a list of the major capital projects and acquisitions needed over a five- to six-year period. With the CIP, the appropriation of expenditures to be incurred by the identified projects as well as the financial sources for the project funding, and the impacts of projected outcomes on the future operating budget need to be highlighted (Srithongrung, 2008). Maintenance planning to assess the condition of capital stock and tying that information to the actual use and wear and tear of infrastructure, the depreciation schedule, and replacement and repair costs are key (Srithongrung, 2008).

Since 2000, Burkina Faso used the MTEF. MTEF was recommended to Burkina by partners such as the World Bank. It consists of a top-down resource envelope, a bottom-up estimation of the current and medium-term costs of existing policy, and ultimately, the matching of these costs with available resources in the context of the annual budget process (See Figure 2). Key elements of the institutional change of the MTEF are the harmonization of donor assistance procedures with the budget procedures of the government and the alignment of donor assistance to the MTEF and the budget process (Chukwuma, 2005). The Burkinabe authorities also highlighted the importance of aid integration in the budget for better planning of resources in order to achieve realistic development objectives.

Chukwuma (2005) argued that MTEF was the result of decline in budgetary performance. This was due to the diminishing of governance caused by a combination of the floundering of public sector capacity, severe political conflict and instability, and in some cases civil war. It was also due to the stagnation of domestic resource mobilization and the increasing dependence on external loans and grants in budget funding.

In Burkina Faso, MTEF would be adopted conjointly with the experimentation of PBB. The use of PBB within six ministries had some limitations for multi-year estimates. MTEF was therefore adopted in 2000 as a better alternative to PBB. It was believed to provide all the measures affecting the revenues and expenditures inscribed in the budget with the goal of impacting the conjuncture (Circulaire Budgetaire, 2017). The Public Expenditure Management Handbook (1998) similarly supported that the objectives of an MTEF consist of improving the macroeconomic balance, the allocation of resources to strategic priorities between and within sectors, the commitment to predictability of both policy and funding, and assisting line agencies with a hard budget constraint (Jacobs, 2008).

The process however cannot yield results unless certain conditions are met. The successful implementation of MTEF requires a reliable budget system, the capacity to collect and produce economic data and forecasts, the production of timely and accurate financial reports, the ability to measure the future budgetary impacts of policy decisions, and the mastery over volatile and uncertain fiscal conditions (Downes, 2013). Are those conditions met in the case of MTEF in Burkina Faso? It is important to look at the development strategies and how the government is planning to achieve them. Below is a chart of the MTEF approach.

Figure 1 shows the process of the MTEF with macro-economic and fiscal considerations as preliminary steps. At the government level, the actual process starts with the budget call circular, the portfolios are prepared, the budget is then negotiated and reconciled, and finally the portfolios are compiled. The final adoption is voted at the national assembly in the case of Burkina Faso.

Figure 1. MTEF Approach
Adapted from: What is MTEF and Why is it Important? (www1.worldbank.org/publicsector/pe/MTEFprocess.doc)

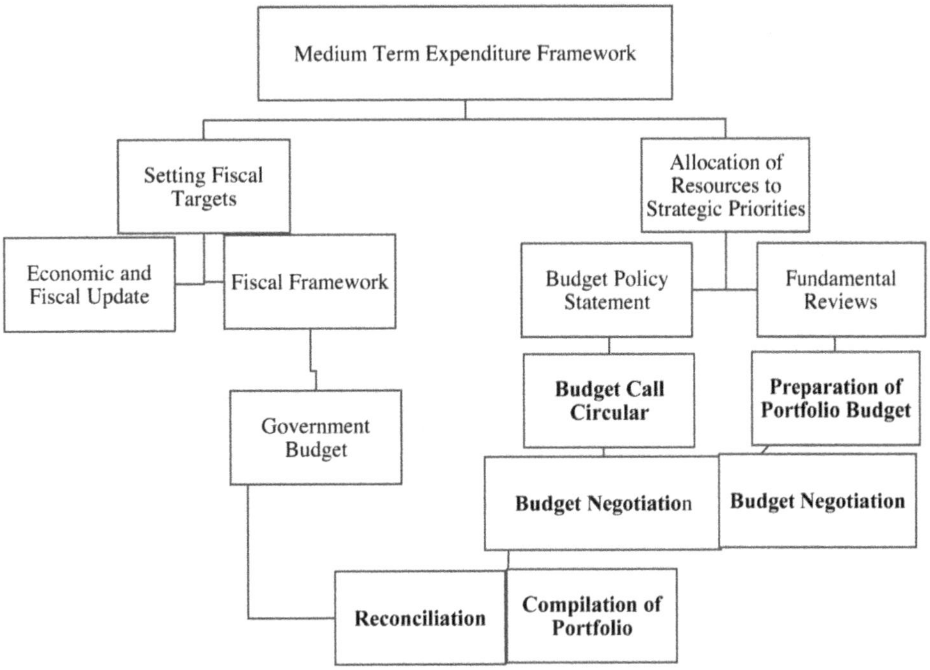

Program-Based Budgeting (PBB)

According to the World Bank (2017), the National Economic and Social Development Plan (PNDES) 2016-2020 based on PBB amounts to FCFA 15,478 billion, approximately US$26.3 billion. PBB is a departure from line item budgeting based on means to a results-based budget. The administrative organization is substituted with the organization by program. A program consists of actions with same purposes and contributing to reach the global objectives defined by government as part of its strategic planning (Circulaire Budgetaire, 2017). The process of PBB is also a strategy for focusing on programs and performance.

According to the Loi Organique N°073-2015/CNT of November 2015, which called for the use of PBB, every ministry and president of institution is the main authorizing officer of expenditures for program funding and of supplementary budgets for their institution. The ministries and institutions design the programs and endowments. The program is meant to correspond to a general office or a group of general offices, or group of public agencies. The total number of programs per ministry is limited to seven. Each program is to be composed of actions and activities. A person responsible to coordinate and monitor the activities is designated at the Council of Ministers. Every ministry designates a program manager for each program in their department. That principal manager is responsible for the allocation of credits between programs and endowments and the allocation between different actions with respect to their mission. The manager is in control of the results of offices implementing the program and is in charge of the mechanisms of internal control and management control. The objectives, expected results, performance indicators, and cost of necessary resources must be determined.

In terms of decentralization, the ministries are responsible for providing the local collectivities with financial resources within reasonable deadlines. Six ministries are mainly concerned with this transfer. The transfer includes the financial resources for the operation, maintenance, and implementation of work in the areas concerned by the transfer. The ministries add a note indicating the expected results. The results are then agreed upon by the territorial collectivities, which would have agreed to accountability principles.

Investment projects are subject to feasibility studies before they are included in the budget. This practice is meant to prevent operations where costs exceed the capacity of the national budget. The Ministry of Finance has the responsibility to ensure that the priorities are included in the proposals considering the available budget. The elaboration, adoption, and execution of the 2017 Public Procurement Plans (PPM) uses the integrated Information System of Public Procurement (SIMP).

ANALYSIS AND DISCUSSION OF BURKINA'S BUDGETING PRACTICES AND THE NORMATIVE FRAMEWORK

Development Strategy and Plan of Burkina Faso

The current development plan since 2015 is the PNDES for a medium term 2016-2020. The budget for meeting the PNDES priorities, as understood by Burkina under the MTEF, is the financial translation of alternative national policies, where elaboration is subject to constraints while taking into account the international and sub-regional environment as well as the internal conjuncture. The resource constraints oblige the government to implement budget policies that recommend defining priorities and strategic choices to effectively orient the resource allocation process (Circulaire Budgetaire, 2017).

The medium-term budget policy is articulated around three main priorities divided into three strategic axes (see Figure 2). The first is reforming the institutions and modernizing the administration such as security, the judicial system, fight against corruption, and budget management. The second is developing the human capital such as public health, education, employment and training, access to clean drinking water, and sanitation. The third is reinforcing the sectors conducive to economic growth and job creation such as agriculture, animal breeding, mining, transportation infrastructure, power and energy, small businesses, manufacturing, and information, communication and technology (Circulaire Budgetaire, 2017).

The major axes encompass all development projects in all domains of developments of which capital projects are part of. While the strategic plan covers a five-year period, there is no separate capital budgeting document that is an aggregate of national capital projects for infrastructure development. In other words, each ministry or department proposed the capital projects as line-items during the PBB process. The projects are thus only specific to the ministry's plan and programs.

Long-Term Public Capital Planning

Burkina Faso has a medium-term framework of 3 years, which is the recommendation for using MTEF. The strategic plan for national development is however based on a 5-year period (IMF, 2017). While the normative model uses the CIP, Burkina Faso uses the Le Programme Triennal D'investissement Public Glissant (PTIP-G) or PIP which describes public investments, the priorities, and orientations. Fundamentally, the PIP is more of a process of integrating aid assistance in the budget planning. In short, Burkina Faso has no CIP process. Put otherwise, there is no unified comprehensive master plan of major infrastructure projects. The strategic plan is part of the priority of line ministers but not linked to an existing master plan. Funds for new infrastructure and repairs are expected to be included in line ministries' appropriations. No separate funding exists for maintenance and repairs. Similarly, there is no aggregate asset inventory analysis.

Burkina Faso believes that a multi-year planning strategy is ineffective with regards to regional, national and international factors impacting the financial sources (Figure 3). Donations for projects and programs are significant and changes in donors' countries politics or economic situations are not elements under the control of the country for effective forecasting. Another factor therefore is the political instability that creates uncertainty for investors who fear losses if they made long-term commitments.

Figure 2. Major Axes of the Strategic Plan of Burkina Faso

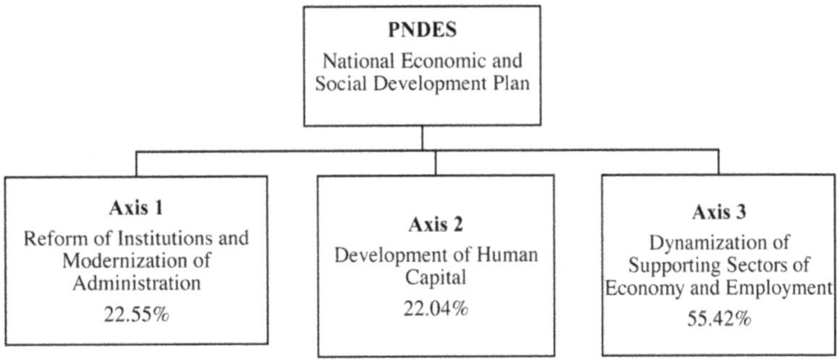

Thus, MTEF seems to provide more assurance as it resembles a "check-and-report as you go" system. In that sense, risk is minimal, and changes could be brought to projects that are not performing efficiently. The fiscal planning follows the three-year MTEF planning with the budget being revisited each time it is adopted on a rolling basis.

The planning process is influenced by donors and the need to integrate aid into the budget. Donor impact is significant because the country was dependent on aid for financing 80 percent of the value of investment programs and projects (Zongo, 2011). Burkina Fasohas, since then, worked towards integrating aid into the budget through the development of guidelines for programs such as the PTIP-G or the three-year public investment program and Le Programme d'investissement Public (PIP) or the Public Investment Program. The PTIP-G establishes the coherent framework of public investment with the main orientations of government policies such as the strategic development goals, sectorial policies, and medium-term plans. The purpose is to ensure budget transparency and visibility of investments. As such, it is composed of programs and projects in which conventions were signed, projects being executed or ongoing projects, and projects that are about to begin; projects and programs that studies are completed and funding was acquired; projects and programs being considered and studied.

The elaboration of PTIP-G and PIP begins with the preparation of the national budget. In terms of institutional arrangement and integration, a technical committee is put in place and is composed of general and specialized offices and the inter-ministerial committee. In terms of inclusion and inscription of projects into PTIP-G, Article 3 Decree n°2007-775/PRES/PM/MEF of September 9, 2007 on general regulation of projects and programs stipulates that any development project and program approved by the State must be listed in the integrated bank of projects and PIP in title 5 "Investissements exécutés par l'Etat." PIP consists of ongoing projects being executed and projects where funding was acquired and ready to start in the year budgeted for. It is composed of core projects and national projects. In its contents, the PIP presents the annual investment program in terms of project type, ministries or execution institutions, planning sources, and modes of financing.

One of the challenges is that projects that were signed during the year would not be included in the PIP. Also, the lack of knowledge of donors' procedures by project managers may lead to poor programming and frequent amendment to the budget. This is especially true for projects where borrowing procedures delay the execution, or when there is lack of knowledge of projects by the department and aid management entities. There are also difficulties in accounting for non-profit aid.

Revenues and Expenditures Strategies

In terms of capital budgeting and financial management, there is an extensive description of the revenue mobilization and expenditures. The expenditure estimates are matched with tendential, pessimistic, and optimistic hypotheses. However, these are not based on multi-fiscal year forecasting. As mentioned earlier, Burkina Faso discarded that option as it was thought to be ineffective.

The strategies and priorities following the MTEF, as stated in the 2017 budget, include reforming the institutions and modernizing the administration, developing the human capital, and reinforcing the sectors conducive to economic growth and job creation. These priorities are at the center of planning national budget, capital transfer, strategic budgetary choices, and the priority investment program (PIP). The revenues and expenditures are clearly laid out even though they are part of the overall budget process and the strategic plan of government. In other words, the capital funds are generally budgeted as part of the line ministers' appropriations. Thus, it can be said that Burkina has a systematic priority ranking except to restate the fact that this ranking is not tied to a separate capital budgeting.

Burkina Faso deals with public investment programs, the equivalent of CIP as part of major investment determination. In the description of revenues and expenditures, as shown in Figures 3 and 4, investments are separated from consumption. In terms of debt, Burkina Faso, per the finance law, puts a ceiling of CFA 50 billion on loans and discourages borrowing by the line ministries which is in line with policies in the n°2009-150/PRES/PM/MEF decree on regulation of public debt and public debt management (Loi de Finance, 2018). This is to ensure that the government does not spend beyond its financial capacities. The figures show how revenues are mobilized and projects funded. The next step is understanding the centralized execution and project management.

Where Do the Country's Revenues Come From?

Figure 3 provides a view of the revenues of the national budget and the amount that each source contributes to the overall budget. The tax revenues, in the amount of 1607.98 billion, is the amount from levy and taxes such as value added taxes. The non-fiscal revenues of 148.67 billion come from pecuniary penalties. The financial product revenues of 0.76 billion are the interests from deposits and exchange rate gains. Program donations of 3.37 billion are partners' contribution to the national budget. The amount for "donations, projects and legacies" of 174.22 billion are resources contributed by partners for the financing of targeted investment projects.

Figure 3. Revenue Sources (Currency is in FCFA)
Adapted from: 2018 Budget Citoyen

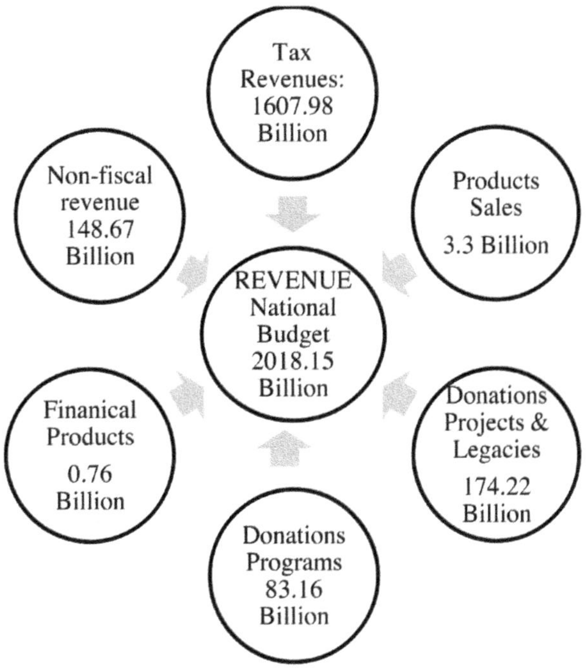

Figure 4. Expenditure Types (Currency is in FCFA)
Adapted from: 2018 Budget Citoyen

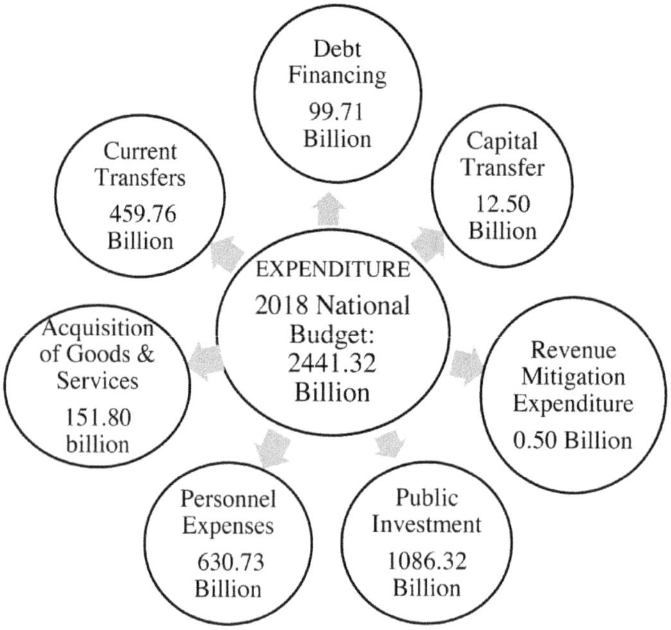

What Are Revenues Used for?

Figure 4 provide a view of the expenditures and the amount from the budget that is spent on each type of expenditures. The debt financing of 99.71 Billion is the financial amount spent as interest on debt. The expenditures of current transfers of 459.76 billion do not include the capital transfers of 12.50 billion. The amount of 1086.32 billion is spent on public investment projects. A total of 630.73 billion is spent on personnel expenses. The amount of 0.50 billion is spent on revenue mitigation. A total of 151.80 billion is used for the acquisition of goods and services.

Centralized Execution and Project Management

The centralized execution in Burkina Faso can be considered as a process of integration of capital budgeting practices into the project management to make it more effective. For example, Burkina's budget balance had a deficit of FCFA 308.42 billion as of March 31, 2018. The deficit is due to the low level of mobilization of ordinary revenues. If the level of revenue mobilization were to remain the same, the main approach will be to observe some prudence in the execution of expenditures. Thus, Burkina Faso emphasized effective execution to reduce the deficit.

There are integration and monitoring or accountability mechanisms in place to ensure effectiveness. On the one hand, MINEFID, per the finance law, issued a trimestral report on the budget execution and management of the treasury. Public procurement is another mechanism. The public procurement plan shows 3,164 applications as of March 31, 2018 on SIMP 2 for a total of FCFA 463.48 billion against 2302 applications for a total amount of FCFA 549.07 over the same period in 2017. That is an increase of 862 applications and a reduction by FCFA 85.59 billion in value. Public procurement has been one area through which the government integrates performance management into the budgeting systems. For example, procurement regulation agency (ARCOP) issued their 2015, 2016, and 2017 reports on the performance of ministries using 6 to 14 and 17 indicators in key ministries and regional and local governments.

On the other hand, the hierarchical structure plays a role in the execution, monitoring, and reporting for accountability purposes as discussed in PBB. According to Article 7 of the Loi Organique, the president or ministry of each institution exercises a permanent control over the entities under their authority to ensure that revenues collected are deposited in the public treasury. The ministries make decisions using monthly reports that are submitted to MINEFID. In terms of appropriations, the President of Burkina has the responsibility for the expenses related to the Presidency and subordinated services. Presidents of institutions have responsibility over their institutions. The Prime Minister and parliamentary ministers have responsibility over their respective fiscal domains. MINEFID has responsibility for the transfers made to territorial collectivities and inter-ministerial local governments or communes (See Article 19 of Loi Organique). For non-constitutional institutions, the main authorizing officer of credits in the name of their institutions is the head. The authorizing officer may delegate all or part of their power to public agents.

All ministries and presidents of institutions, the President, and the six ministries who work with the territorial collectivities, have responsibilities over the portfolios and the agencies to which any fund is transferred. Trimestral or monthly reports are used as control mechanisms and budget status reports. The system of reports flow through the accountability chain following the hierarchy in the administration. Furthermore, the adoption of program-based budgeting systems with its focus on results-oriented funding has been a strategy for integrating performance management into the system. For example, for the expenses and expenditures, the "circulaire budgetaire 2017" requires all actors to specify the objectives, the expected outcomes, the performance indicators, and the cost to meet the objectives.

O'Sullivan and Lima (2010) advised that good investment budget management is one of the keys to prospects of success in the implementation of the PNDES. They praised the recent initiatives undertaken by the Burkinabe authorities including the revised procurement code, which will contribute to significantly improving investment budget execution (O'Sullivan and Lima, 2010). Koala (2016) investigated public procurement management and found that the regulation and monitoring authority was transferred to a newly created agency, the Autorite de Regulation de la Commande Publique (ARCOP), to ensure transparency, accountability, and effective execution. Previously, the government played both roles. ARCOP has developed some performance measures, by which projects are evaluated to show whether or not expected results are achieved.

Another accountability approach is placing a ceiling on certain types of finances. Article 29 stipulates that the ceiling for advance payment that the public treasury may allow territorial collectivities for the fiscal year 2018 is FCFA 1.75 billion. Article 30 stipulates that the ceiling of loans allowed by the public treasury is FCFA 50 billion. The interest rate of the loan and the modalities of reimbursement are specified by the public treasury.

Infrastructure Maintenance

Maintenance should have been a priority in Burkina Faso. Because there are few resources to replace and build newer infrastructure, focusing on maintaining has the advantage of long-lasting infrastructure. The country would alleviate the financial burden of spending money to rebuild from scratch. Unfortunately, less emphasis is put on maintenance, and therefore, less funding is set aside. This is also due to budget constraints and donors' mishandling of the national priorities. MTEF has been criticized for neglecting the maintenance aspect in its approach to budgeting. This is a critical weakness of MTEF.

In short, Burkina Faso does not have maintenance planning and maintenance funding processes. It is even less clear whether repairing has priority over replacement with new infrastructure. The lack of maintenance funding and planning means that basic regulations are not put in place to prevent damaging practices such as overloading of trucks and non-payment of fees. Thus, part of the problem is the inability to collect and levy enough resources that will contribute to maintenance. In cases where levy is significant, there is less control to prevent financial mismanagement and opportunistic behavior (Delavallade, 2007). The inability to function properly is due to several variables and unfavorable factors.

FACTORS AFFECTING CAPITAL MANAGEMENT AND BUDGETING

Political Leadership and Budgetary Implications

Leadership, especially political leadership, plays a significant role in large and long-term development projects. De Renzio (2011), for example, investigated the domestic and external factors affecting the outcomes of reforms aimed at improving the quality of government budget institutions across a sample of 16 aid-dependent countries including Burkina Faso from 1997-2007. The results were that economic and political stability, government leadership and commitment to reforms, and the centralization of budget institutions are preconditions for successful budget reform outcomes. Government leadership is needed to assure donors of better budget governance, better coordination of technical assistance and general budget support. De Renzio (2011) argued that effective leadership would reduce the perverse incentives induced by aid fragmentation. While effective leadership is necessary, Burkina Faso has gone at least six decades without true leadership.

Early Regime Changes 1960-1983

Burkina Faso became independent from France in 1960, with Maurice Yameogo, elected first president on December 11, 1959. The regime appeared conservative and to have western aligned foreign policy (Englebert, 1996). Yameogo was re-elected president for a second term on October 3,1965 but was forced to resign following popular unrest in 1966. General Sangoule Lamizana took power on January 3, 1966 and established a military regime. Ndiaye and Siri (2016) described this period as a period of contractionary fiscal policies and strong control over expenditures and an increase in government revenue with an introduction of discretionary tax known as "contribution patriotique." In other words, there was reduction in government expenditures characterized by layoff of civil servants, wage cuts of 10 percent in the civil service, removal of housing allowances, and reduction of subsidies. There was no budget deficit and no fiscal policy in 1966-1970. Even though there was no deficit, the contractionary fiscal policies did not emphasize the development of a significant infrastructure master plan, which would call for capital budgeting planning.

The situation remained the same as a result of coups and union strikes. In October 1980, teacher union strikes spread over the country and led to a paralysis in government. A Coup d' Etat brought Colonel Saye Zerbo to power on November 25, 1980. Two years later, another coup led by Commandant Jean-

Baptiste Ouedraogo overthrew Colonel Zerbo. A section of the army, in turn, overthrew Ouedraogo leading to a major revolution on October 15, 1983 led by Captain Thomas Sankara. Sankara re-baptized Upper Volta to Burkina Faso. The period was characterized by a gradual expansionary fiscal policy regime. The policies were geared towards investment in industry and creation of public enterprises and infrastructure; investment in social sectors such as health, wage increases, housing and frequent subsidies to state enterprises (Ndiaye and Siri, 2016). The expansionary policies under Sankara were successful in the development of infrastructures such as manufacturing infrastructures, schools, and roads, but the revolutionary regime lasted only four years and faced external aid reduction.

The Period of Transformational Leadership

Sankara was a revolutionary and transformational leader who wanted to change the culture and had new vision for the country (Ott, Parkes, & Simpson, 2003). More intensely than their predecessors, the Burkinabe revolutionaries had vast programs of infrastructure development, education, environmental protection, and promotion of human and women rights. Sankara specifically called on African countries at an African Union Summit to come together and oppose the repayment of debt on the basis that the financial system was based on imbalanced partnerships and asymmetric decision-making power. The result was less assistance. Ndiaye and Siri (2016) argued that military coups experienced in the 1970s and 1980s contributed to the observed peaks in capital flight in 1974, 1980, and 1987. The capital flight is the flow of financial assets out of Burkina Faso to donor countries due to factors such inflation, change in currency rates, economic crises or political instability. At times, foreign experts designed by donors to implement the programs are being paid with a high percentage of donated funds. In a country with limited resources, external investment, expertise and technical assistance that might be helpful were driven away. For countries such as France, the revolution created some ideological conflicts between capitalism and socialism as the revolution was seen as upholding a socialist agenda.

The Mixed Period: Democracy or Authoritarianism – October 1987-October 2014

The new President, Blaise Compaore, declared the dissolution of Sankara's government in October 1987 and proceeded to what he called "the Rectification." The Rectification meant governing for the best interest of the Burkinabe by correcting the mistakes made by his predecessor. From 1987 to 1991, Compaore's regime was still military and adopted a moderate fiscal expansion with market-oriented policies (Ndiaye and Siri, 2016). It was soon followed by the Fourth Republic from 1991 to 2014. This civilian regime adopted fiscal contraction and a moderate fiscal expansion characterized by removal of state subsidies, investment in social sectors, and infrastructure. However, the real purpose of democratization and reform efforts was to maintain power control (Hilgers, 2010). The system was mined with semi-authoritarian tendencies such as patronage, corruption, and partisan factionalism (Harsch, 1998; Harsch, 2009). This fiscal contraction policy remained passive concerning major infrastructure development policies. The initiatives such as the large dams and irrigation have increased agricultural and electricity provision capacities in some regions. However, the achievements were judged minimal for the 27 years of rule (Hilgers & Loada, 2013; Koussoube et al, 2014). Furthermore, the ruling period could have been an opportunity for enormous master plans to build the country's infrastructure. This missed opportunity left the market and economy chaotic and incapable of supporting sophisticated projects.

Economic and Market Capabilities of Burkina Faso

Burkina's economy is driven by agriculture such as cotton, millet, corn, animal breeding, including cattle and poultry, and other natural resources. The production is mostly used for food and local consumption. Only a small quantity is commercialized or exported to other countries. The major mining resources include gold, zinc, and manganese. According to the World Bank Group (2017), the gold mining industry, cotton, and grain production paved the way for an acceleration of economic growth in 2016, growing the real GDP at a year-over-year rate of 5.9 percent.

Public finances deteriorated in 2016. The fiscal deficit increased to 3.1 percent from 2 percent of GDP in 2015 as a result of rising investment expenditures and civil service wages and tax revenues that failed to increase at the same pace. Despite the deficit, Burkina has improved its external position in 2016, with a current account deficit of 6.8 percent of GDP, compared to 8 percent in 2015. External support and the resumption of foreign direct investments (FDI), particularly in the mining sector, helped narrow the external deficit. According to *Jeune Afrique*, FDI accounts for US$309 million.

The Burkinabe economy also suffers from the small size of the private sector market and the non-existence of quasi-governmental sectors. This does not allow the country to tackle problems of public provision related to project selection, infrastructure maintenance, inefficient pricing, capture and corruption, institutional design, and renegotiation (Engel et al., 2014). The lack of a large market and expertise from the private sector for capital investment still affects the ability to provide public services. Since 2005, the country is engaged in aggressive public procurement reforms through decrees and separation of control and regulation functions to ensure transparency and efficiency. Koala (2016) found the system has improved. However, the limited funds and the incapacity of certain local governments to absorb credits remain a challenge, an issue that is in part due to the limited market capability and expertise. This weakness also implies that the country is greatly in need of public-private partnerships (PPPs).

Debt and Foreign Aid

Even though Burkina did not experience the extreme balance-of-payments crises and debt problems and budget deficits that shook much of Africa throughout the 1970s and 1980s due to extremely prudent policies (Savadogo & Wetta. 1992), the small size of the market forced the country to rely on external sources. If economic growth is not sustained over a long period of time, the lack of deficit might not be effective to prevent future deficit. Thus, as the budget deficit occurs, foreign aid and borrowing become part of the budget planning. Donors helped in exchange for democratic and economic reforms and infrastructure developments. There was also fear of aid perversity, the belief that aid may produce the opposite effect while it was proven that deep cutbacks in external assistance are more likely to hurt rather than help the cause of democracy and market reform in many African countries including Burkina Faso (Goldsmith, 2001). Wright, Dietrich & Ariotti (2015) found that donor's exchanging aid for judicial independence in 121 countries including Burkina has been successful at times but failed during times when judicial reform is costly politically. This shows the eventual impact of political events on capital projects. The reality is that foreign aid continues to be a part of the investment efforts of Burkina Faso. The challenge is not only how to ensure its reliability, continuation, and feasibility necessary for long-term planning, but also, how Burkina Faso can maintain a steady progress based on its priorities while managing aid and donor's expectations.

For example, one of the issues with debt is capital flight. Boyce and Ndikumana (2001) found that external borrowing is the single most important determinant of capital flight. From 1970-1996, roughly 80 cents on every dollar that flowed into the region from foreign loans flowed back out as capital flight in the same year. Ndiaye & Siri (2016) argued that ineffective regulation of foreign exchange operations, tax administration weaknesses, and collusion between politico-administrative elites and the business world lead to capital flight. Thus, better tax revenues, the growth rate of GDP, and changes in economic policy regimes reduced the level of capital flight whereas total natural resource rents, external debt, and political violence increased the magnitude of capital flight. Capital flight reduces the chances of obtaining and sustaining loans for investments in infrastructure projects. Donors tend to respond to events by withdrawing their commitments and allocated funds.

The solution is a focus on national natural resources and debt relief strategies to prevent a new cycle of external borrowing and capital flight. To succeed, substantial reforms on the part of both creditors and debtors to promote responsible lending and accountability of debt management are necessary (Duncombe & Schroeder,1988; Ndiaye & Siri, 2016). Sankara had argued against aid stating that "aid should work to assassinate aid" and any aid that would result in debt was considered exploitation (Englebert, 1996). Overall, potentialities and challenges lay ahead of the Burkinabe government and people in envisioning effective and viable infrastructure development policies.

Summary of Factor Variables

From the review of the state of infrastructure in Burkina Faso, the budgeting practices and the political context, the chapter identified four (4) factor variables that inhibit the successful application of the capital budgeting as envisioned by the normative framework. They include the lack of a separate capital budgeting and skills therein, the lack of resources for financing capital projects, the lack of funding for maintenance and lack of assessment, and the lack of accountability in the implementation of capital projects. For example, the lack of careful and long-term capital planning leads to unrealistic project funding estimates, fiscal planning, inexistent master plan and asset inventories, deadlines, cost overruns, and non-completed projects.

The review highlighted six (6) practices that are inconsistent with the normative recommendations. The practices presented by order of importance as follows:

1. The insufficient mobilization of national or internal revenues: This issue leads to project failures as the country fails to follow through with adequate financial resources over the long-term.
2. The general lack of resources for financing capital projects: This issue, both with regards to the national capacity and external assistance, limits the ambitions of the country and the ministries to propose expensive development projects that are likely to be struck down during the budgeting process.
3. The instability in donor assistance, debt, and capital flight: This challenge reduces not only the financial resources, but also drives away technical expertise necessary for infrastructural planning.
4. The small size of market and weak private sector investment: This reality discourages the investors from engaging in big infrastructure projects that are key, but may not evolve beyond their embryonic stage if started.

5. The lack of expertise and technology to build large and durable infrastructure: This shortcoming refers to the lack of skills in capital budgeting planning and sophisticated technological tools for undertaking major infrastructure projects with durable and quality outcomes.
6. The lack of continuously effective political leadership and political will: This phenomenon disrupted the government and development plans, diverted investors' attentions, and made the country vulnerable to financial deficits due to slow or interrupted production, productivity, trade, and resource mobilization.

NATIONAL PERSPECTIVES AND CHALLENGES

Economically, the African Bank Group (2018) and the World Bank (2017) confirm that the real GDP growth increased 5.9 percent from 2015 to 2016, and 6.7 percent from 2016 to 2017 due to gains in mining, higher investment in construction, a healthy commercial sector, and improvements in agriculture. This economic growth is expected to sustain at 6.6 percent in 2018. This is attributed to the NESDP/PNDES 2016-2020 public investment program. In terms of mining and cotton, the higher prices will continue to boost economic performance, thus reducing the budget deficit to 4.8 percent of GDP in 2018 and 2.9 percent in 2019. Public debt associated with the NESDP/PNDES was estimated at 36.9 percent of GDP in 2017, far below the convergence criteria of 70 percent set by WAEMU. Inflation was an estimated 1.5 percent in 2017, after falling 0.2 percent in 2016, and is likely to remain below 2 percent in 2018-2019.

However, this outlook for growth depends on several sources of instability, including terrorism, adverse weather for farming, persistent social unrest, and price volatility for gold and cotton. Since 2015, Burkina has suffered a series of terrorist attacks that killed more than 70 people and slowed the economic recovery (African Bank Group, 2018). It may divert resources or discourage investment in key projects across the country as well as discourage local and foreign investments in major projects. Today, minimizing security threats has become an essential element of predicting investment decisions.

In terms of the 2018 national budget, the total revenues of 2,018,157,960,000 FCFA against the total expenditures of 2,441,317,986,000 yields a deficit of 423,163,026,000 FCFA (*faso.net,* See Figure 3 and 4). The World Bank Group as shown in the water projects earlier assist with additional funding. Thus, partnership packages with larger partners can be a part of the strategy, but this should be done with a leadership that is convincing and credible with a vision for building the infrastructure of the country.

Politically, Burkina is moving towards more democratic governance that will bring credibility and stability in the legal and regulatory system to help with growing the economy and attracting partners. The concerns that the fall of the Compaore regime in 2014 will rush the military to take over and retain a central political role were short-lived (Frere & Englebert, 2015).

CONCLUSION

The review and analysis of the state of infrastructure of Burkina Faso show features of the infrastructure of a developing country. The need for infrastructure is enormous and the baseline initiatives have been taken. Looking at sectors such as roads, airports, water and sanitation, power, railways, and information and technology, the progress sometimes made is undermined by challenges related to funding and maintenance.

The chapter shows that less emphasis is put on maintenance and therefore less funding is set-aside in this area. The reason is that there are budget constraints forcing policymakers to budget for the main or overall projects. Another reason is that donors who support certain projects often fail to account for maintenance funding. As shown at the beginning of the chapter, the lack of maintenance funding itself reduces the level of control needed; thus, exacerbating the deterioration of the infrastructure.

The chapter further argues that Burkina Faso only marginally follows the normative framework of capital budgeting. It is important to note that the assessment was based on the overall budget process, as Burkina does not have a separate capital budget as such. Thus, while MTEF is used as the framework, it is applied to the overall national budget system. MTEF is not a framework specifically designed for capital budgeting. It appears, therefore, that the MTEF in its design differs from the normative capital budgeting framework. The CIP in the normative framework corresponds to the PIP in Burkina Faso. The PIP however has been designed as a process for integrating aid into the budget as a tool for satisfying donor's transparency measures.

Moreover, in comparing the MTEF and the normative framework, it appears in terms of capital planning that the normative framework is based on a long-term planning strategy of five years or more while the MTEF is limited to three-years in Burkina Faso. The planning in Burkina is embedded in the overall budget process. In terms of capital budgeting and management, Burkina emphasizes the priorities of national budget, capital transfer, strategic budgetary choices, and the Priority Investment Program (PIP). Revenues sources, expenditure targets, and the strategies for execution are laid out. In terms of centralized execution and project management, Burkina relies on the hierarchical structure of the administration for control and auditing. The ministries, the presidents of institution, and the President of Burkina are expected to ensure control and are accountable for any outcomes of the agencies under their control. For local governments, the ministries that transfer funds to local governments have the responsibility to ensure control.

The chapter contends that the lack of a separate capital budgeting and skills therein, the lack of resources for financing capital projects, the lack of funding for maintenance and lack of assessment, and the lack of accountability in the implementation of capital projects inhibit systematic capital budgeting practice. The factors inconsistent with the normative recommendations include the lack of careful and long term capital planning, the insufficient mobilization of national or internal revenues, the instability in donor assistance, debt and capital flight, the size of market and private sector investment, the lack of expertise and technology, the lack of political leadership and political will, and the recent terrorist threat; all reducing the chances of an effective capital project planning. Srithongrung (2008) and Mikesell (2003) found that systematic capital management programs indirectly enhance a state economy through efficient and effective capital spending policies. Politically, Srithongrung & Kriz (2012) found that government management and political institutions indirectly affected national productivity through the physical condition and accessibility of core public infrastructure in 25 developing countries.

In light of the findings, it can be concluded that Burkina Faso adopted the MTEF to allow flexibility in making changes between years and in the short-term and to be in line with the country's financial capabilities and donors' expectations. The closest explanation that the normative framework might not be a viable option is that the economic and financial markets and political institutions are not large and strong enough to allow and support the kind of planning that such framework stipulates. Nonetheless, certain sectors have shown successes with long-term planning including the case of water and sanitation. Thus, while the framework may not be applied to the overall system, some of its aspects may be useful for specific projects in Burkina Faso (Boex et al., 2000). Moving forward however, long-term planning of capital projects and master plans will be a more viable solution (Ammar et al., 2001).

REFERENCES

African Development Bank (ADF). (2018). *Burkina Faso economic outlook*. Retrieved July 23, 2018, https://www.afdb.org/en/countries/west-africa/burkina-faso/burkina-faso-economic-outlook/

Agence EcoFin. (2018). *Burkina Faso: Composition du nouveau gouvernement*. Retrieved July 23, 2018, https://www.agenceecofin.com/politique/0102-53952-burkina-faso-composition-du-nouveau-gouvernement

Ammar, S., Duncombe, W., & Wright, R. (2001). Evaluating capital management: A new approach. *Public Budgeting & Finance*, *21*(4), 47–69. doi:10.1111/0275-1100.00058

Association des Régions du Burkina Faso (ARBF). (n.d.). *Presentations des regions*. Retrieved July 23, 2018, http://www.regions.bf/spip.php?page=regions&id_rubrique=19

Boex, L. F., Martinez-Vazquez, J., & McNab, R. M. (2000). Multi-year budgeting: A review of international practices and lessons for developing and transitional economies. *Public Budgeting & Finance*, *20*(2), 91–112. doi:10.1111/0275-1100.00013

Briceño-Garmendia, C., & Domínguez-Torres, C. (2011). *Burkina Faso's infrastructure: A continental perspective. Africa infrastructure country diagnostic*. Washington, DC: The World Bank.

Budget citoyen. (2017). *Budget 2018*. Retrieved from http://www.dgb.gov.bf/index.php?option=com_edocman&view=document&id=148.

Burkina Faso. (2018). *Evaluation des projets et programmes de développement*. Retrieved July 23, 2018, from http://www.finances.gov.bf/index.php?option=com_content&view=article&id=286:burkina-faso-evaluation-des-projets-et-programmes-de =371.

Cadre Budgetaire a Moyen-Term. (2015). *Cadre budgetaire a moyen-term 2016-2018*. Retrieved July 23, 2018, http://www.dgb.gov.bf/index.php?option=com_edocman&view=document&id=372

CAFRAD. (2018). *What is MTEF and why it is important? A Brief Overview*. Retrieved July 23, 2018, from http://old.cafrad.int/Workshops/Tanger21-23_04_09/Session4_2.pdf

Chukwuma, O. (2005). *The medium-term expenditure framework: The challenges of budget integration in Sub-Saharan African countries*. World Bank Working Paper Series, 82.

Circulaire Budgetaire. (2016). *Cadre budgetaire 2017*. Retrieved July 23, 2018, http://www.dgb.gov.bf/index.php?option=com_edocman&view=document&id=149

Circulaire Budgetaire. (2017). *Cadre budgetaire 2017.* Retrieved July 23, 2018, http://www.dgb.gov.bf/index.php?option=com_edocman&view=document&id=146

De Renzio, P. (2011). *Buying better governance: The political economy of budget reforms in aid-dependent countries, 1997-2007.* PQDT - UK & Ireland.

De Renzio, P., & Angemi, D. (2012). Comrades or culprits? Donor engagement and budget transparency in aid-dependent countries. *Public Administration and Development, 32*(2), 167–180. doi:10.1002/pad.1603

De Renzio, P., & Masud, H. (2011). Measuring and promoting budget transparency: The open budget index as a research and advocacy tool. *Governance: An International Journal of Policy, Administration and Institutions, 24*(3), 607–616. doi:10.1111/j.1468-0491.2011.01539.x

Delavallade, C. (2007). Lutte contre la corruption au Burkina Faso et réformes de la gestion budgétaire. *Afrique Contemporaine, 3*(3), 271–288. doi:10.3917/afco.223.0271

Downes. (2013). *Medium-term expenditure frameworks (MTEF): Logic, benefits, limitations.* Retrieved July 23, 2018, from https://wpqr4.adb.org/lotusquickr/cop.../0/.../4%20MTEF%20-%20R%20Downes.pdf

Duncombe, W., & Schroeder, L. (1988). The effects of tax instability on budgeting and financial management in developing countries. *International Journal of Public Administration, 11*(3), 271–309. doi:10.1080/01900698808524590

Engel, E., Fischer, R. D., & Galetovic, A. (2014). *The Economics of public-private partnerships: A basic guide.* New York: Cambridge University Press. doi:10.1017/CBO9781139565615

Englebert, P. (1996). *Unsteady statehood in West Africa.* Burkina Faso: Westview Press.

Englebert, P., & Sangaré, N. (2014). Burkina Faso: Limited decentralization under tight oversight. In J. T. Dickovick & J. S. Wunsch (Eds.), *Decentralization in Africa: The paradox of stata strength* (pp. 45–68). Boulder, CO: Lynne Rienner.

Enquête sur le Budget Ouvert 2017. (2017). *International budget partnership.* Retrieved July 23, 2018 from https://www.internationalbudget.org/wp-content/uploads/burkina-faso-open-budget-survey-2017-summary-french.pdf

Ermasova, N. (2012). *Capital budgeting at the state level: an empirical analysis from the economic downturn through the present* (PhD Dissertation). SPEA, IU.

Ermasova, N. (2013a). Capital budgeting in the states after the great recession. *State & Local Government Review, 45*(2), 119–130. doi:10.1177/0160323X13487079

Ermasova, N. (2013b). The improvement of capital budgeting at the state level in the USA. *Public Administration Review, 2*(2), 92.

Frère, M. S., & Englebert, P. (2015). Briefing: Burkina Faso—the fall of Blaise Compaoré. *African Affairs, 114*(455), 295–307. doi:10.1093/afraf/adv010

Goldsmith, A. A. (2001). Foreign aid and statehood in Africa. *International Organization, 55*(1), 123–148. doi:10.1162/002081801551432

Harsch, E. (1998). Burkina Faso in the winds of liberalization. *Review of African Political Economy, 78*(78), 625–641. doi:10.1080/03056249808704348

Harsch, E. (2009). Urban protest in Burkina Faso. *African Affairs, 108*(431), 263–288. doi:10.1093/afraf/adp018

Hilgers, M. (2010). Evolution of political regime and evolution of popular political representations in Burkina Faso. *African Journal of Political Science and International Relations, 4*(9), 324–350.

Hilgers, M., & Loada, A. (2013). Tensions et protestations dans un régime semi-autoritaire: Croissance des révoltes populaires et maintien du pouvoir au Burkina Faso. *Politique Africaine (Paris, France), 3*(3), 187–208. doi:10.3917/polaf.131.0187

IMF. (2017). *Medium term expenditure frameworks: From concept to practice. Preliminary Lessons from Africa*. Retrieved July 23, 2018, from www.dif.mp.gov.in/spmg/MTEFManual_PWD.pdf

Jacobs, M. D. F. (2008). A review of capital budgeting practices (No. 8-160). International Monetary Fund.

Jeune Afrique. (2018). *Chronologie Burkina Faso*. Retrieved July 23, 2018, from http://www.jeuneafrique.com/pays/burkina-faso/chronologie/

Koala, K. (2016). *The enforcement of the 2008 decree on general public procurement procedures and service delegation in Burkina Faso: Its influence on the management system*. Mankato: Minnesota State University.

Koussoube, E., Loada, A., Nebie, G., & Raffinot, M. (2014). *Political economy of growth and poverty in Burkina Faso: Power, institutions and rents* (Working Paper No. DT/ 2014-01). Dauphine Université Paris.

LOI n°055-2004/AN du 21 décembre 2004 portant code général des collectivités territoriales au Burkina Faso (JO spécial n°2 du 20/4/2005).

Marlowe, J., Rivenbark, W. C., & Vogt, A. J. (2009). *Capital budgeting and finance a guide for local governments* (2nd ed.). Washington, DC: ICMA PRESS.

Mikesell, J. (2003). *Fiscal administration analysis and applications for the public sector* (6th ed.). Belmont, CA: Wadsworth.

Ministere des Infrastructures du Desenclavement et des Transports. (2015). *Tableau de Bord 2013 du Ministère des infrastructures, du désenclavement et des transports*. Retrieved July 23, 2018, from http://cns.bf/IMG/pdf/tableau_de_bord_midt_2013-vf.pdf

Ministre de l'Economie et des Finances. (2009). *L'expérience du Burkina Faso en matière d'élaboration du Cadre de Dépenses à Moyen Terme (CDMT)*. Retrieved July 23, 2018, from https://www.slideshare.net/AfricanCoP/lexprience-du-burkina-faso-en-matire-dlaboration-du-cadre-de-dpenses-moyen-terme-cdmt

Mukherjee, T. K., & Henderson, G. V. (1987). The capital budgeting process: Theory and practice. *Interfaces, 17*(2), 78–90. doi:10.1287/inte.17.2.78

Ndiaye, A. S., & Siri, A. (2016). Capital flight from Burkina Faso: Drivers and impact on tax revenue. *African Development Review, 28*(S1), 100–112. doi:10.1111/1467-8268.12184

Ndikumana, L., & Boyce, J. K. (2003). Public debts and private assets: Explaining capital flight from Sub-Saharan African countries. *World Development, 31*(1), 107–130. doi:10.1016/S0305-750X(02)00181-X

O'Sullivan, L., & Lima, F. (2016). *Scaling Up Public Investment, Growth And Debt Sustainability IMF Country Report No. 16/391*. Retrieved July 23, 2018, from https://www.imf.org/external/pubs/ft/scr/2016/cr16391.pdf

Press Release No. 2018/105/AFR. (2018). *Burkina Faso: World bank approves $50 Million to boost private investment and job creation*. Retrieved July 23, 2018, from https://www.worldbank.org/en/news/press-release/2018/03/29/burkina-faso-world-bank-approves-50-million-to-boost-private-investment-and-job-creation

Public Expenditure Management Handbook. (1998). *Burkina Faso*. Retrieved July 23, 2018, from http://www1.worldbank.org/publicsector/pe/handbook/pem98.pdf

Sankara, T. (2007). *We Are thehHeirs of the world's revolutions: Speeches from the Burkina Faso revolution 1983-87* (2nd ed.). Atlanta, GA: Pathfinder Press.

Savadogo, K., & Wetta, C. (1992). *The impact of self-imposed adjustment: The case of Burkina Faso*, 1983–9. In G. A. Cornia, R. van der Hoeven, & T. Mkandawire (Eds.), *Africa's Recovery in the 1990s* (pp. 53–71). London: Palgrave Macmillan. doi:10.1007/978-1-349-22344-2_3

Srithongrung, A. (2008). The impacts of state capital management programs on state economic performance. *Public Budgeting & Finance, 28*(3), 83–107. doi:10.1111/j.1540-5850.2008.00912.x

Srithongrung, A. (2018). Capital budgeting and management practices: Smoothing out rough spots in government outlays. *Public Budgeting & Finance, 38*(1), 47–71. doi:10.1111/pbaf.12167

Srithongrung, A., Ermasova, N., & Yusuf, J.-E. (2019). *Capital management and budgeting in the public sector*. Hershey, PA: IGI.

Srithongrung, A., & Kriz, K. A. (2012). From public infrastructure to national economic growth: Do systematic investment practices matter? *International Public Management Review, 13*(2), 19–50.

World Bank. (2010). *Local development, institutions and climate change in Burkina Faso: Situation analysis and operational recommendations. Social Development Department. Area-based Development and Climate Change*. Retrieved July 23, 2018, from http://siteresources.worldbank.org/EXTSOCIALDEVELOPMENT/Resources/244362-1232059926563/5747581-1239131985528/5999762-1242914244952/BurkinaReportFinal_EN.pdf

World Bank. (2017). *Burkina Faso: Developing infrastructure and an enabling environment for sustained access to water and sanitation services for the urban poor*. Retrieved July 23, 2018 from http://www.worldbank.org/en/results/2017/07/28/burkina-faso-developing-infrastructure-and-an-enabling-environment-for-sustained-access-to-water-and-sanitation-services-for-the-urban-poor

Wright, J., Dietrich, S., & Ariotti, M. (2015). *Foreign aid and judicial independence*. Retrieved July 23, 2018, from https://pdfs.semanticscholar.org/e2e8/31f2c1edc2c25fa0f1ae20fbb789475937fb.Pdf

Zongo. (2011). Rencontre IATI-Pays Partenaires. *Integration De L'aide Dans Le Budget*. Et Le Programme D'investissement Public (Pip).

Chapter 10
Thai Public Capital Budget and Management Process

Arwiphawee Srithongrung
University of Illinois at Springfield, USA

Kenneth A. Kriz
https://orcid.org/0000-0001-8050-8506
University of Illinois at Springfield, USA

ABSTRACT

This chapter describes the public capital budgeting process in Thailand. Public infrastructure is very centralized; local governments do not play a large role in public infrastructure investment. The country's long-term physical planning is fragmented and lacks an effective long-term fiscal planning. The budget process is dominated by senior civil servants in the Bureau of the Budget, the Ministry of Finance, Bank of Thailand, and the National Economic and Social Development Board. Expensive projects financed by long-term debt bypass the budget process, and as a result, a comprehensive list of annually approved projects is unavailable to the public. This leads to public investment being driven almost entirely by debt capacity. Because of these factors, Thai governments have invested too little in public infrastructure, and the infrastructure investment is uneven across sectors.

INTRODUCTION

This chapter describes the public capital management and budgeting process in Thailand along with the country's social, legal, economic, and public administration institutions. Thailand is an emerging economy in Southeast Asia. At one time, it was a relatively poor country by international standards. But from the 1960s to the late 2000s, it grew rapidly. Along with the strong economic growth, the country's public infrastructure system demands also grew, especially for urban transit systems. Public infrastructure quality and quantity are significant factors contributing to growth (Srithongrung & Kriz, 2012). Therefore, it is imperative to develop an understanding of Thai public capital management and budgeting processes. The goal of these processes is to acquire public infrastructure in the most efficient and effective manner (Srithongrung, 2008).

DOI: 10.4018/978-1-5225-7329-6.ch010

This chapter is comprised of five sections. The first section describes the country's socio-economic and demographic characteristics along with the structure of its public administration. The local government's institutional arrangement is also discussed given that Thailand has been attempting to make basic public infrastructure (e.g., local road and water services) available at the local level since the 1999 Decentralization Act was enacted (Chardchawan, 2006, 2010; Krueathep, 2010). The second section provides an overview of the country's public infrastructure systems along with an objective evaluation drawn from the international public capital literature and analysis of secondary data. The third section describes the four main components of the Thai public capital management and budgeting process: planning, budgeting and financing, execution, and evaluation. The fourth section evaluates whether the Thai processes adhere to the normative framework set forth in the introduction to this volume and identifies the strengths and weaknesses of the process. This section also provides critical analysis of the linkages between the capital management and budgeting processes and the quality and quantity of public infrastructure delivered to the public. The last section concludes with observations regarding the processes and future propositions for the relationship among institutions, management processes, and outcomes.

BACKGROUND

Socio-Economic Characteristics

Thailand, an ASEAN nation, has a population of 68.86 million (World Bank, 2018). From 1960 to 2016, the population grew at an annual average rate of 1.7 percent. However, in more recent years, the growth rate has been slower; from 2010 to 2016 the Thai population increased only about 0.8 percent for the entire period (Thailand Bureau of Census, 2018). As with many countries, its population is aging. Its median age in 1960 was 19 years old. As of 2015, that figure was 38 years (Thailand Bureau of Census, 2018). The country is experiencing urbanization as in many other countries in the region. In 1960, only 18 percent of the population lived in urban areas. Recently, the urban population had increased to 49 percent of the country total (UN Statistics Division, 2018). The country has an average population density of 131 people per square kilometer (Statistics Times, 2018). Thailand's density ranks 5th out of the 10 ASEAN countries with Singapore as the most density (8,226 population per square kilometer) and Lao People's Democratic Republic as the least dense country (20 population per square kilometer) (Statistics Times, 2018). This suggests that Thailand, as a relatively less dense country, will have greater infrastructure demands compared to the size of the population. Bangkok, the capital city of Thailand, is the densest city with 5,294 people per square kilometer (Thailand Bureau of Census, 2018). Much of the density growth of Bangkok has been attributed to migration from Northeast region of the country (Thailand Bureau of Census, 2018). Despite the slow overall population growth, the urbanization has led to urban sprawl and rapidly increasing population density. This has, in turn, increased the demand for public infrastructure systems important to urban development (such as transit and expressway construction). Meanwhile, public infrastructure projects supporting rural development (such as water, sewerage, energy, and information infrastructure systems) must be increased to help create jobs and slow migration from rural to urban areas.

In 2017, Gross Domestic Product (GDP) was $455 billion or $6,729 per capita. The unemployment rate was 1.2 percent (National Economic and Social Development Board, 2018). Once very high, Thai economic growth has slowed in recent years. In 2016, real GDP increased by 3 percent, somewhat slower than the 6 percent average growth rate from 1960 to 2016. The real annual growth rate in four of the last five years has been 3 percent or less (the World Bank, 2018).

Thailand is classified as an Upper-Middle income country with an average annual household income of $10,272 (National Economic and Social Development Board - NESDB, 2018). Income inequality has been improving over the past twenty years. The Gini Index for Thailand decreased from 0.453 in 1981 to 0.378 in 2013 (World Bank, 2018). In 2017, Thailand experienced a trade surplus with exports of $235 billion and imports of $203 billion. The country has maintained a low inflation rate; in 2017, it was 0.7 percent (NESDB, 2018). Basic economic sectors include electronics manufacturing, automotive manufacturing, machinery and equipment manufacturing, and agriculture. Major exports include machinery and equipment, computer parts and accessories, vehicle parts and accessories, integrated circuits, and petrochemical products (NESDB, 2018). Thailand's private investment growth has been sluggish recently with rates of 0.5 percent in 2016 and 1.7 percent in 2017. Public investment has grown more rapidly, but the growth has been volatile, as we will discuss below.

Combined, the economic data suggests that the Thai economy has expanded in the long run, contributing to better living standards both in terms of average income and equality compared to a half century ago. However, its economy has slowed recently with falling economic growth rates and decreasing private investment. A portion of this slowing growth may be due to economic interruptions because of political regime changes and accompanying unrest. Furthermore, the statistics reveal a divergence between public and private investment; public investment is increasing while private investment growth has been slow. The growth in public investment may be explained by the current military administration announcing a new investment plan to boost the country's economic performance. This plan features increased investment in public infrastructure, information technology, and agricultural technology (NESDB, 2017).

Legal Institutions

Thailand is a constitutional monarchy. The Thai government is comprised of executive, legislative, and judicial branches. Thailand adopted a new constitution in April 2017. According to the new document, Parliament is comprised of 700 elected and appointed officers. The House of Representatives (lower chamber) is comprised of 350 directly elected officials and 150 officers from political party lists determined by the percentage of votes each of the major parties received in the elections (The Office of Senate Secretary, Thailand National Assembly, 2017). The Senate is comprised of 200 officers appointed by the King. The Prime Minister (PM) is selected by the House of Representatives and governs an administration consisting of 19 ministries. The PM selects the Ministers and Deputy Ministers from the House of Representatives to advise, set, direct, administer, implement, and supervise policies and activities in each of the individual ministries. The PM, Ministers, and Deputy Ministers from the Council of Ministers are equivalent to the Cabinet in the U.S. government.

The Cabinet prepares a budget for consideration by the Parliament and submits to the Parliament bills affecting governmental policy and procedures (Thailand Law Forum, 1997). In addition to the budget bill, the Cabinet has the power to submit urgent legislation to the King for immediate implementation by Royal Decree (Thailand Law Forum, 1997). This legal institution grants most power to the executive branch. The legislative branch initiates legislation. For the Annual Budget Act, the legislative branch reviews the Annual Budget Proposal submitted by the Cabinet, makes changes within limitations specified in the Constitution, and approves it to become the Annual Budget Act. The judicial branch consists of trial courts, appeal courts, and the Supreme Court. The Constitutional Court governs public policy and administration by ruling on the validity of laws, regulations, and government decisions and implementation of the public policies and programs (Thailand Law Forum, 1997).

The executive branch has traditionally dominated the public policy process, including the public capital budgeting process; policy has typically been decided and selected in a top-down manner. Furthermore, as characterized by Riggs (1965), Thailand is a strong bureaucratic state where national policy setting is conducted by a group of high-ranking bureaucrats, military leaders, and career civil servants who tend to come from a limited number of families with high socio-economic status. With this institutional arrangement, citizen participation and input from grassroots are limited.

Public Administration Arrangement

The Administrative Law of 1933 (B.E. 2476) established three layers of Thai administration: central or national, provincial, and local. The central administration (PM and Cabinet) has the most power in formulating and implementing national policies and priorities (Sopchokchai, 2001). Provincial administration consists of 76 provinces and 2 special districts: Bangkok and Pattaya. The North, Northeast, Central, East, West, and South Regions have 9, 20, 21, 7, 5, and 14 provinces, respectively. Five provinces along with Bangkok are in metropolitan areas. The central government administers provincial regional offices of the 19 Ministries, appointing 76 Governors from the pool of qualified civil servants in Ministry of Interior (MOI) to supervise policy implementation in the provinces and report back to the central administration.

Figure 1 presents the local government structure. According to Thailand Department of Local Administration (2018), local administration is comprised of 2,441 municipalities (divided into 30 city municipalities, 178 town municipalities and 2,233 subdistricts), 76 provincial administrative organizations (PAO), and 5,333 Tambon Administration Organizations (TAO).

According to the 1999 Act, local authorities have the freedom to manage and provide local public services (Sopchokchai, 2001). Each of these local government units has its own executive and legislative branches, and all officials are directly elected by residents (Sopchokchai, 2001). However, local government officials overseeing public project initiatives must coordinate with provincial and central government officials, as they are advised and approved by the Ministry of Interior (MOI) (Sopchokchai, 2001; Kittipanyasiri, 2015). This arrangement weakens local government autonomy and results in strong national and provincial government structures.

According to the 2017 Constitution, local governments are responsible for providing basic public services and public projects. This arrangement is purported to lead to better quality of life and self-sustainability in the long-term (The Office of Senate Secretary, Thailand National Assembly, 2017). Local government services include small-scale public service projects (e.g., village roads, water wells, dikes, village playgrounds, and small sport stadiums) and supplementary vocational and economic development programs. These locally initiated programs and projects must be financed by a local government's own-source revenue, shared Value Added Tax (VAT) and income tax revenue, and central government grants and subsidies allocated by the MOI. The central government is responsible for helping local governments establish their public finance systems. These activities range from identifying and developing existing own-revenue sources to providing basic public infrastructure to attract new jobs and expand tax bases. The Constitution also designates that the central government shall allocate enough public budgetary resources to support local governments until they become financially self-sustainable (The Office of Senate Secretary, Thailand National Assembly, 2017).

Figure 1. Thai Public Administration Structure
Source: Adapted from National Economic and Social Development Board (NESDB) (2017)

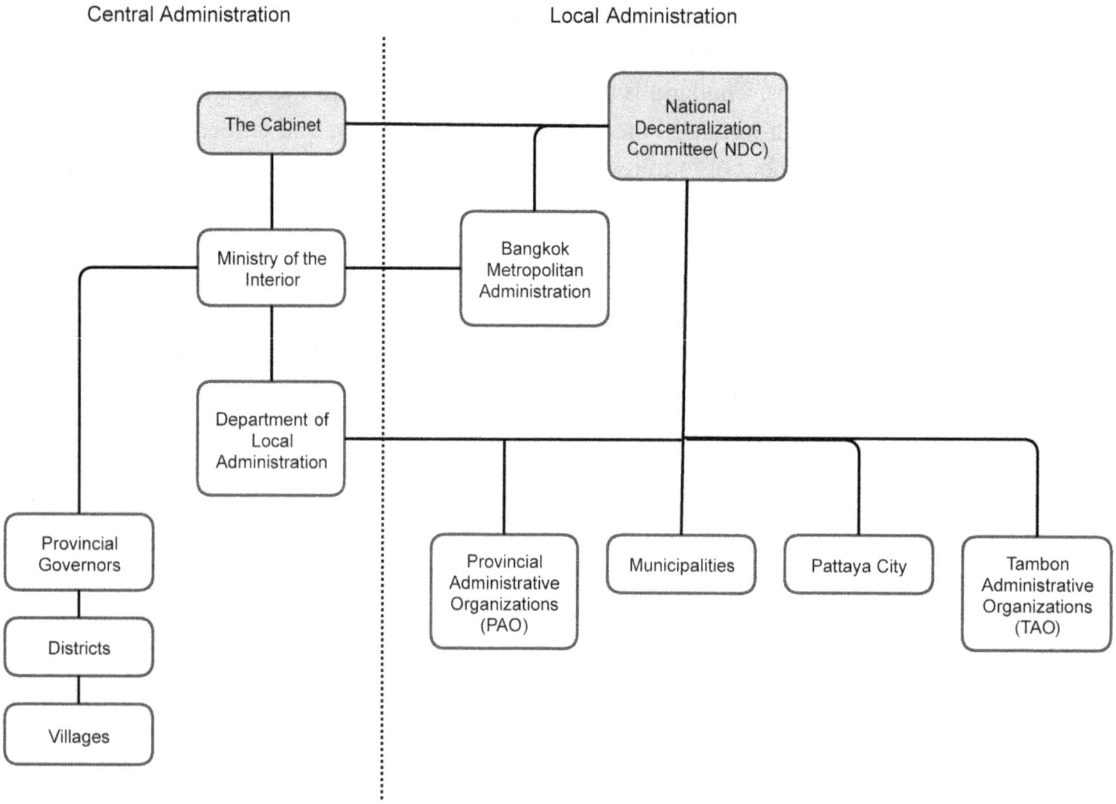

In practice, Thai public administration is highly centralized mainly due to the lack of own-source revenue at the subnational level, insufficient central budgetary support, and excessive control exercised by the central government (justified by a view that local governments lack administrative capacity). Local governments rely on the central government to finance public infrastructure projects, as they do not have enough own-source revenue and the required approval by the Ministry of Interior (Kittipanyasiri, 2015; Sudhipongpracha & Wongpredee, 2015). Also, the central government's shared revenue and grants are not distributed based on specific purposes and clear formulas (Kittipanyasiri, 2015; Sopchokchai, 2001). Central grants and subsidies are unstable across administrations, depending on political and administrative ideologies (Pungprawat, 2009). Urgently needed public projects must be developed through lobbying the regional offices of the central government through the budget allocation process (Sudhipongpracha & Wongpredee, 2015). The allocation is based on national policy priorities and central government discretion (Sudhipongpracha & Wongpredee, 2015). The public projects initiated and implemented by local governments tend to be excessively scrutinized by the Office of the Auditor General to protect the Ministry of Interior (MOI) from being encumbered since MOI's public projects tend to be overlapped and delayed (Kittipanyasiri, 2015). Finally, provincial and municipal governments can borrow from commercial banks that may or may not resell the debts to public investors; the sources of this commercial bank debt service are local government own-source revenue, which is limited.

Public Infrastructure System and Investment Patterns

Thai public infrastructure systems include electric networks and facilities, water and sewer management systems, secondary and higher education facilities, Internet and telephone service infrastructure, public health and hospital facilities, and multimodal transportation systems. These transportation systems include national and regional airports, air traffic control towers, seaports, railroad facilities, expressways, highways, mass-transit systems, roads, and bridges. Since the 1992 Privatization Act, several public infrastructure systems in urban areas, especially in Bangkok and the Metropolitan region, have been acquired through state enterprise public-private partnerships (PPP). A substantial portion of public infrastructure systems servicing local areas including water services, local roads, and irrigation systems are provided by the central government through departments and agencies in relevant Ministries.

Figure 2 presents central government capital expenditure, Gross Domestic Product (GDP) and percent of central government capital expenditure to GDP in the period ranging from 1990 to 2006. The central government (including state enterprises) is the main public infrastructure provider in the country with its capital spending accounting for 1 to 7 percent of the GDP in the years 1990-2016. As the figure demonstrates, with solid economic growth during the early-mid 1990s (the "Asian Tiger" period), central government capital spending rose from 50 billion Thai baht (THB) to THB 333 billion. After the advent of the Asian Fiscal Crisis in 1997-1998, spending declined precipitously. Since 2004, central government capital spending has averaged 1 to 2 percent of the GDP, despite sustained (nominal) economic growth. This does not compare favorably to rates in other Asian countries (Bangladesh, Bhutan, People's Republic of China, Fiji, Georgia, Hong Kong, China, Indonesia, India, Republic of Korea, Sri Lanka, Maldives, Myanmar, Mongolia, Pakistan, Philippines, Papua New Guinea, Singapore, and Viet Nam), which invest an average of about 5 percent of GDP per year in public capital (The World Bank, 2018). Even with this higher rate of investment, the estimated gap between public infrastructure needs and existing investment for these countries are estimated at nearly $429 billion per year or about 2.4 percent of GDP (The World Bank, 2018). These figures suggest that to keep up with future public infrastructure demands, countries in the region need to invest at an annual rate of 7.4 percent of GDP, suggesting a large gap in Thai public infrastructure investment.

Despite underinvestment in the recent period, Thai public infrastructure seems to be improving in both quantity and quality. Figure 3 presents Thai public capital stock in both nominal and constant values. In nominal terms, Thailand's net total public infrastructure increased from THB 76 billion in 1970 to THB 12.258 trillion in 2014 (Figure 3). Again, we see that Thai public stock accumulated rapidly during the 1990s, but after 2000, constant THB public capital stock grew at an average annual rate of only 3 percent. Over the last fifty years, capital investment has seemed to follow the nation's business cycles with high growth rates during the periods from the mid-1970s to mid-1980s and during the run-up to the Asian fiscal crisis in 1997-1998. During the most recent decade public capital stock grew very slowly. This pattern is consistent with the pattern for central government capital expenditure.

One of the factors that has led to lower capital accumulation in recent years has been a relatively high depreciation rate for public capital. In current dollars, Thailand's public infrastructure depreciation increased from THB 3.3 billion in 1970 to THB 532 billion in 2014. This depreciation rate has caused a problem during recent years. From 2004 to 2014, constant dollar annual Thai public infrastructure stock accumulation averaged approximately 2.7 percent per year. Meanwhile public infrastructure during that same period depreciated at average rate of 3.6 percent per year. In other words, the increase in

Figure 2. Central Government Capital Expenditure: 1990-2016
Data Source: Asian Development Bank (2017), https://sdbs.adb.org/sdbs/

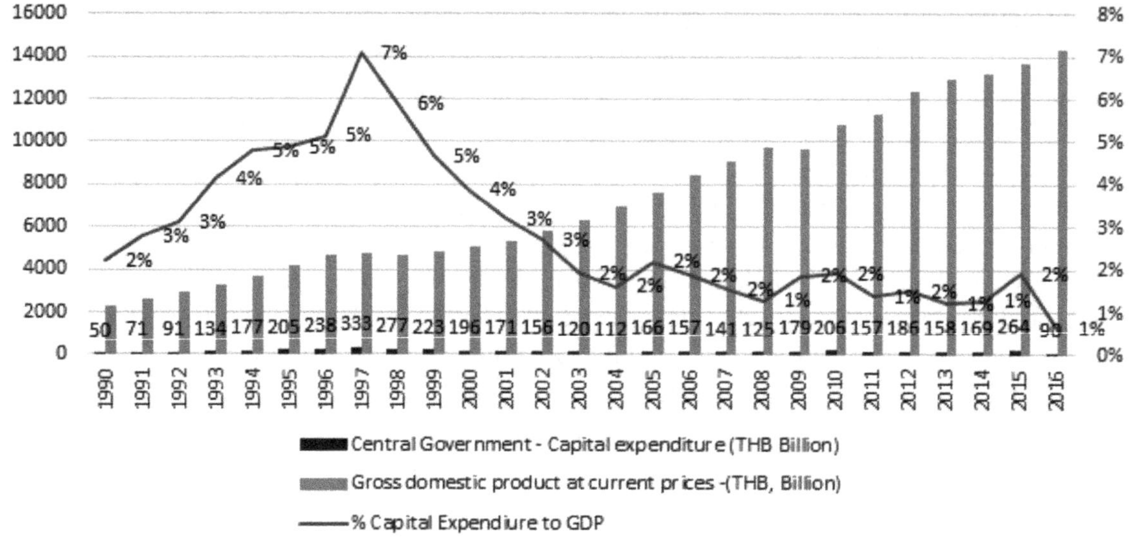

Figure 3. Thai Public Capital Stock, Net of Depreciation (in Millions of Current and Constant 2017 THB) and Annual Growth Rate in Constant 1988 THB (in percent, right axis)
Data Source: Thailand Office of National Economic and Social Development Board (NESDB), http://www.nesdb.go.th/nesdb_en/main.php?filename=national_account

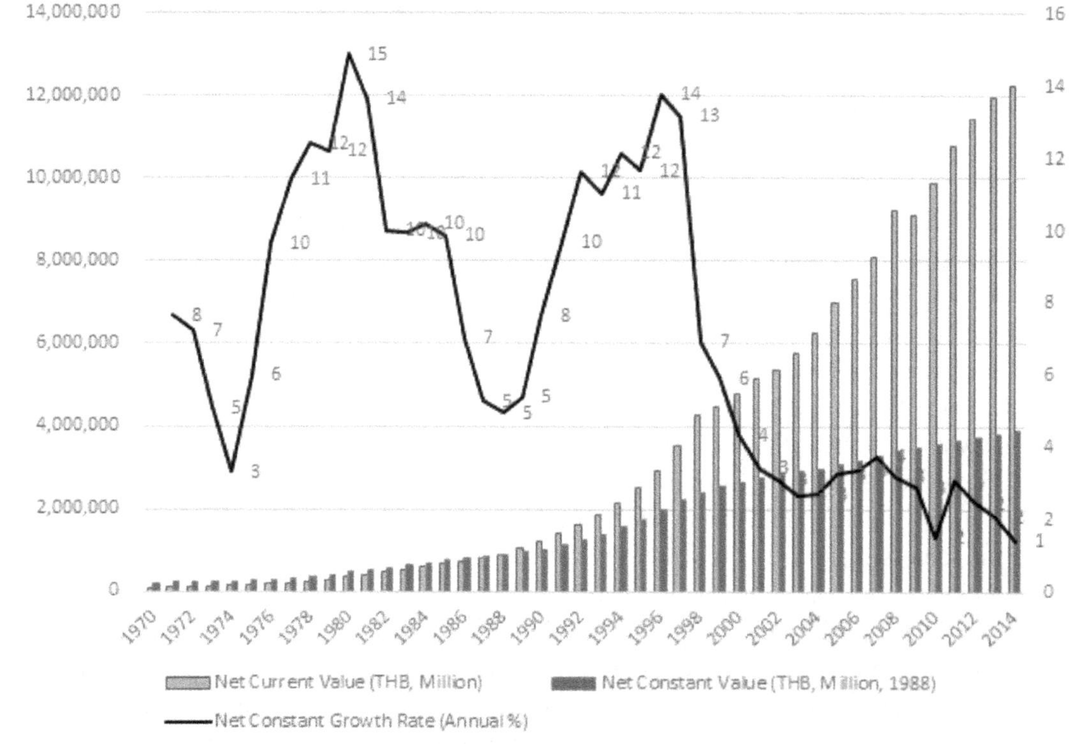

capital stock was not sufficient to replace worn out systems and may not be able to expand to attract and accommodate new business establishments, which is necessary to propel the economy forward.

This view is supported by quality data compiled in the 2016-2017 Global Competitiveness Report (Schwab, 2018), which assesses the capacity, accessibility, and quality of a country's public infrastructure systems in attracting and accommodating new businesses. According to this report, the Thai public infrastructure system ranks 49th in terms of its capacity to attract business investment and productions among 138 countries with a total composite score of 4.39 (on a scale of 1 to 7 ordinary scale, with 7 being excellent). However, in terms of overall quality of public infrastructure, Thailand is below the median, ranking 72nd. Several individual indicators in the Global Competitiveness Report suggest that Thai public infrastructure is unevenly developed, resulting in the overall quality of public infrastructure that is below those of the world's average. For example, for the indicators "availability of airline seat kilometer" and "quality of air transport infrastructure", Thailand is above the median ranking at 15th and 42nd respectively. For the indicators "quality of roads", "quality of port infrastructure," "quality of electricity supply," and "mobile cellular telephone subscriptions per 100 population", Thai public infrastructure ranks near the median at 60th, 65th, 61st and 55th respectively. But for the indicators, "quality of railroad infrastructure" and "fixed telephone line availability per 100 population," Thai public infrastructure is below average, ranking at 77th and 91st respectively. These data indicate that for Thailand, air transportation facilities are relatively good, road, port, electricity and mobile cellular phone service are at the world's average, and railroad and fixed telephone systems are relatively poor. Moreover, the report shows that within the East Asia and Pacific region, Thai's public infrastructure quality falls behind those of South Korea, Hong Kong, Singapore, Malaysia, Japan, and Taiwan, all major competitors for the country in business investment. The same report also suggests that among 14 problematic factors for the public management and economic situation, inadequate supply of infrastructure ranks as high as 7th in terms of priorities for improvement. Thus, increasing overall quality and quantity of public infrastructure as well as balancing the quality of the infrastructure should be the country's policy priority if Thailand were to attract new business investment.

Other studies have pointed to relatively inferior quality of Thai infrastructure. The Economist (2015) assessed that the quality of the railroad systems in the country as relatively poor, limiting the country's overall performance in logistics and freight services. A study by the Thai logistics service asserts that the most important problem for Thailand economic competitiveness is that the country neglects the development and maintenance of freight rail services, while focusing on advancing the national highway and expressway system (Peters, 1998). This results in an imbalance between modes of ground transportation that can raise logistic costs (Peters, 1998). For the countries that have well established supporting infrastructure and services, the logistic cost component is on average about 20 percent to 25 percent of the retail price; however, for Thailand, such cost is about 40 percent of the price (Peters, 1998). The International Monetary Fund (2016) suggests that the country needs to upgrade its infrastructure systems for regional competition and lifting the country's economic growth.

PUBLIC CAPITAL MANAGEMENT AND BUDGETING PROCESS

This section describes the four main components of public capital management and budgeting in Thailand: long-term planning, budgeting and financing, execution, and evaluation.

Long-Term Planning

Thai governments have many systematic practices in long-term planning. There are several plans developed by Office of Prime Ministers and Cabinet; however, none of those plans are aggregated into a capital improvement program (CIP). The main strategic plan that the country uses for national budget planning is the National Economic and Social Development Plan (NESDP). This plan spells out goals, outcomes, objectives, policy, and program priorities as well as broad guidelines for a course of action and indicators to gauge expected outcomes at the end of the plan period. In addition to the NESDP, the country has other strategic plans issued by the central government. For example, in the current military-led administration, there are 8 multi-year plans involving public infrastructure development, including the Transportation Infrastructure Strategic Plan, the Metropolitan Waterworks Authority Water Supply Infrastructure Development Plan, and the Third Provincial Waterworks Authority Strategic Plan. Some of these plans can be considered a comprehensive plan since they are identified based on the current infrastructure needs and future demands projected through socio-economic data. However, each of these plans focuses on a single sector, such as water or transportation. According to the current NESDP, these multi-year plans are considered as supplementary plans; hence, they may appear to be redundant both in terms of timelines and substance. The difference between these single sector, multi-year strategic plans and the NESDP is that the former identify fiscal sources and includes long-term fiscal planning for the public projects while the latter does not.

As discussed earlier, the NESDP is the main 5-year strategic plan for the country, composed by the National Economic and Social Development Board (NESDB) and approved by Parliament. In the formulation of the plan, The World Bank advised the country to use it as a platform for developing national policies (NESDB, 2018). This recommendation seems dubious. Since 1966, Thailand has adopted 12 plans. In each plan, the country's socioeconomic characteristics were analyzed and discussed, and the major goals, targeted outcomes, previous development accomplishments (e.g., economic growth rates

Table 1. The Transportation Infrastructure Strategic Plan, 2015-2022 (Excerpted from Sitthiyot, 2017)

As an example of the multi-year plans, the Transportation Infrastructure Strategic Plan of 2015-2022, formulated in 2015, targets total investment in public transportation of approximately THB 1.913 billion. The main goal of this plan is stated as acquiring a public transportation system that supports the country's vision in becoming a regional hub of business, transportation, and other economic competitiveness (Royal Thai Government, 2016). This plan contains a list of mega transportation projects, a timeline to accomplish the projects, and financing sources for the projects (Sitthiyot, 2017). Examples of projects in this plan include Bangkok and inter-city rail network projects, double-track railway networks (standard gauge), mass transit railways, public bus service system upgrades and improvements, new motorways and expressway projects, and a four-lane road network expansion and upgrading projects, and multi-modal transportation and cross-border logistic center development projects including maritime and air transportation service facilities. Fifty-two percent (THB 1,072 billion) of the plan investments are targeted for the public transportation network in Bangkok and Metropolitan area. Thirty-three percent (THB 624 billion) of the total plan is slated to go for highway networks. The remaining 25 percent (THB 217 billion) is for maritime transportation, Intercity Rail networks, and air transportation (Office of Transport and Traffic Policy and Planning, 2014). In terms of financing sources, the multi-year plan designates that THB 978 billion (52 percent) will be financed through national government and state enterprise borrowing, THB 542 billion (28 percent) will be financed by current revenue appropriated through the annual budget process, THB 298 billion (16 percent) will be financed by public-private partnerships, and the remaining THB 86 billion (4 percent) will be financed through state-enterprise revenues (Office of Transport and Traffic Policy and Planning, 2014).
The multi-year plans listed above have annual action plans stating in detail which projects are to be completed in what time periods, how to acquire the projects, and how to finance the projects. However, these plans were not fully executed. For example, the Transportation Infrastructure Strategic Plan planned to disburse about THB 56 billion, but only THB 1.6 billion was spent, 97 percent less than the planned amount (Sitthiyot, 2017). Part of the reason for the lack of full execution may have been poor fiscal planning. Another interpretation is simply that long-term planning activities are too ambitious compared to available resources.

and literacy rates), and broad strategic plans for the next five-year period are outlined. All plans have the same major goals in fostering economic growth, creating better living standards, and reducing the income gap. These goals are stated clearly as the ultimate socially desirable outcome for the country in all twelve plans (Srithongrung, 2009).

In theory, the plans are meant to address social, economic, and development problems in a sequential manner. The recommended courses of actions and policy priorities for NESDPs are changed with each new plan, depending on available resources, the NESDB's expertise, and previous policy accomplishments. For example, the first plan suggests that the country needs to focus spending on education and social development programs serving the central region, while the second plan designates the same activities, adding income equity programs in rural areas. However, in practice, the abrupt changes in policy priorities and courses of action interrupt policy direction, including long-run public infrastructure spending. Often, the previous plan has not been completed within the first five years and needs to continue, but by the time the following plan comes out, the directions are changed (TDRI, 1998).

At present, the Twelfth Plan (2017 -2021) is in effect. This plan was developed based on the 20-year National Strategic Framework, which did not exist prior to the current administration (which assumed power in 2014). The framework focuses on six dimensions including national security, economic competitiveness, human capital development, social justice and equity, quality of life, and sustainable environment and public management improvement. The Twelfth Plan's analytical section suggests that Thai society will be aging and that there will be a depletion of natural resources and a deterioration in the environment. The plan recognizes the importance of global competitiveness and international trade as well as corporations on the Thai macroeconomics. As a result, the plan recommends that governments accelerate improvement in fundamental strategic development factors such as strategic investments in research and development, the development of science, technology and innovation programs, and the enhancement of labor skills. The plan spells out 10 strategies along with targeted objectives to be achieved in the next five years. These strategies include (1) a strategy for strengthening and realizing the potential of human capital, (2) a strategy for creating a just society and reducing inequality, (3) a strategy for strengthening the economy and underpinning sustainable competitiveness, (4) a strategy for environmentally friendly growth, (5) a strategy for reinforcing national security for the country's progress towards prosperity and sustainability, (6) a strategy for public administration, corruption prevention, and good governance in Thai society, (7) a strategy for advancing infrastructure and logistics, (8) a strategy for development of science, technology, research and innovation, (9) a strategy for regional, urban, and economic zone development, and (10) a strategy for international cooperation for development. Not surprisingly, advancing the country's infrastructure systems is the seventh strategy in the plan.

According to the seventh strategy, by 2021, several development outcomes must be accomplished, including improved transportation and trade facilities, expanded and improved nationwide water supply infrastructure services, and increased infrastructure driven industries. To accomplish the outcomes, the seventh strategy sets forth broad activities, including developing overall infrastructure and logistical systems, increasing the proportion of waterways and railways in freight transportation, raising the usage of public transportation in Bangkok, and expanding Bangkok and other regional airports to meet increasing demands, enhancing tap water production capacity, and expanding coverage of nationwide water supply service facilities. To facilitate the recommended actions, the seventh strategy provides detailed guidelines for annual policy priorities and public expenditures. The plan lists 62 Flagship Projects that the governments should accomplish in the next five years. However, there is no fiscal planning presented along with the projects and the plan in general. In fact, no NESDPs provide long-term fiscal planning.

The NESDBs do not conduct cost-benefit analysis and priority ranking for the included projects (TDRI, 1998). The stated policy priorities tend to be too broad, and as a result, Ministries insert as many projects as possible in hope that they will get acquire some portion of national budget resources. This results in duplicative projects among ministries (TDRI, 1998).

National long-term fiscal planning for public infrastructure financing does not exist. Recently, the country issued the 2018 Fiscal Policy Act, designating the central government to establish the National Fiscal Policy Committee. The committee is to be comprised of the PM, the head of the Ministry of Finance (MOF), the Deputy Directors of MOF and the NESDB, the Bureau of the Budget (BOB) Director, and the President of the Bank of Thailand (BOT) to establish medium-term fiscal policies and plans. The Act designates that the committee determines the amount of borrowing that could be used to finance the country's deficits and public infrastructure. Furthermore, for current revenue, the Act states that in each year, the country needs to allocate at least 20 percent of budgetary resources for capital projects and capital spending must not be below the amount of the deficit in that year. While the Act seems to be prudent in forcing governments to maintain an optimal level of investment, it tends to allow government officials to replace all current revenue used to finance capital projects with borrowing. The Act gives general guidelines for fiscal planning that to borrow, governments must consider fiscal conditions and debt service capacity. The Act allows any department, agency, state enterprise, or local government unit receiving foreign aid, assistance, or grants to not report and transfer the monetary resources to the MOF. While this Act allows flexibility in fiscal planning and may expedite public project implementation, especially those that are big-ticket items, it may make the country's long-term fiscal planning become less focused like the situation with strategic physical planning.

Budgeting and Financing

Finally, despite the plethora of plans and strategies, Thailand lacks a CIP as the final output of the long-term physical and fiscal planning process. None of the three levels of government requires the formulation of a CIP. The Budget Procedure Act B.E. 2502 (1959 Budget Act), which is the main budget law, does not specify how the public capital budget should be planned and prepared. The Thai fiscal year (FY) ranges from October 1 to September 30. Given that the 1959 Budget Act does not require that the national government needs to have a separate capital budget, public capital projects are included with public programs proposed for the operational budget. Capital expenditure is defined as "expenses on equipment, land, buildings, and related expense" (Thailand Bureau of Budget Document, FY 2018, p. 37).

Annual Budget Planning

Since 2004, Thailand has adopted performance based budgeting in which budgetary resources, including capital resources, are allocated based on national goals and expected outcomes. In 2005, Thailand issued the Regulation of the Office of Prime Minister on Budget Management B.E. 2548 (2005 Budget Regulation), which has been used as a blueprint in preparing strategic spending until today. The 2005 Budget Regulation has been modified many times. Its main substance remains that programs and budget requests both at the disaggregated and aggregated levels must be strategically planned to achieve national strategic goals and performance outcomes for Ministries. The Regulation also specifies that Ministries, Departments, Agencies, and State Enterprises should follow BOB instructions tying strategic budget planning to the NESDPs. BOB issues annual budget instructions suggesting that Ministries, Departments, Agencies, and State Enterprises propose their programs and projects in a way that is responsive to the NESDP.

The rules passed in the last several years have changed the structure of government finance. According to the 2005 Budget Regulation, the Ministries are responsible for preparing their annual operation plans based on their strategic service goals, expected short and medium-term outcomes and annual objectives. The Ministries' operational plans are used as the basis for budget request preparation. These requests cut across departments and agencies in each Ministry. The Ministries' annual strategic service goals are set to address long-term national strategic goals. These changes are important to public capital spending because the new operational structure has made public officials identify, select, and propose capital projects that are responsive to national goals. The public projects are approved by the BOB if they are consistent with the NESDP (Personal Interview with BOB Planning Director, June 16, 2008; Thailand Bureau of the Budget, 2018). This process should result in the government having a better direction in proposing and prioritizing public projects.

The national budget planning process starts with BOB, MOF, NESDB, and BOT establishing in a collaborative manner the Long-term Expenditure Forecast (LTEF), which includes projections for the next 20 years for revenue, expenditures, surpluses, and debt service (Figure 4). Next, the MOF, working with BOB, NESDB, and BOT, creates the Medium-term Expenditure Forecast (MTEF), which includes projections for the next 5 years for revenue, expenditures surpluses, and debt service. In establishing the MTEF, the MOF considers key macroeconomic factors, including GDP and its growth rates, export and import volume, inflation, public debt levels, and government financial condition (Pallop, 2004). The BOB then prepares the Annual Strategic Budget Allocation Guidelines (ASBAG) based on the LTEF and MTEF. The BOB's ASBAG integrates the MTEF with policy priorities identified by the current administration, National Plan, and other plans. The ASBAG is the major instrument in converting the NESDP into annual action plans through the budgetary process (Thailand Bureau of the Budget, 2018).

Figure 4. Thai Budget Planning
Source: Thailand Bureau of Budget (2018)

The guidelines form the implementation plan for the 10 strategies of the 12th NESDP (including the Seventh Strategy: Infrastructure Development) within the six dimensions, as identified by the 20-year National Strategic Framework (Thailand Bureau of the Budget, 2018). For public infrastructure, the Seventh Strategy, Strategy for Advancing Infrastructure and Logistics, is divided into two dimensions: Dimension 2, which is economic competitiveness and enhancement, and Dimension 5, which is water, quality of life, and a self-sustainable environment.

Capital Budget Decision-Making Process

After the ASBAG is approved by the Cabinet in July, the central government's Regional Offices and Local Government Units (i.e., PAOs, TAOs, and Municipalities) prepare their annual budget plans. In this activity, the 19 Ministries work with the Regional Offices and Local Government Units to identify local needs. In September, the budget plans are approved by the heads of local governments (such as Governors and other officers appointed by Ministry of Interior and elected officers in PAOs and TAOs) and the Ministries' Operational Committees. By the end of October, budget limits are passed by the PM. These include limits by Ministry, limits by province, and limits by operational plans (as identified in the NESDP and 20-year National Framework), along with targets for personnel, central fund expenditures, and debt. By the end of December, the Cabinet approves and formalizes the budget policy.

In February, Ministries, Departments, Regional Offices, Provinces, and Local Governments submit their budget requests to the BOB. To consolidate the budget requests, the BOB segregates the requests into two groups: operational and capital expenditure (Pungprawat, 2009). In general, both capital and operational budget requests will be included in the national budget proposal if they adhere to the Strategy in the 12th NESDP and are well integrated in one or more dimensions of the 20-year National Strategic Framework (Thailand Bureau of the Budget, 2018 and FY 2018 Annual Budget Proposal). For capital expenditures, ad hoc committees are formed to make decisions. The ad hoc committees include budget analysts and BOB Deputy Director General, who is the chair and has full authority in considering budget requests by the related government agencies (Pungprawat, 2009). In addition to the general program and project selection criteria, proposed capital projects must include clear project acquisition plans and projections for total acquisition expenditures and must be ready to implement after appropriated. Furthermore, for large public projects (the definition of which is unspecified), life cycle costs must be estimated to assure that there will be no negative impacts on the future budgets (FY 2018 Annual Budget Proposal). Since public capital requests, included in the Annual Budget Proposal, will be financed by current revenue, projects tend to be relatively small. For larger, multi-year projects proposed by the Ministries and their agencies, they may be allocated through acquisition phases. In practice, capital expenditures for continuous phases of public projects are priorities in the first round of the BOB budget review (Pungprawat, 2009). In April, the Cabinet reviews the BOB budget proposals and recommends changes. The BOB then makes changes as appropriate. In May, the Cabinet approves the Annual Budget Proposal, with BOB inputs, and converts the Proposal to become the Annual Budget Bill. The PM then presents the Annual Budget Bill to Parliament for consideration.

The Annual Budget Bill approval process starts in the beginning of June with consideration by the House of Representatives. There are three stages for budget consideration including principles, amendment, and final consideration stages. In the principles stage, general administration and government policies are debated and almost all representatives for the opposition parties of the PM (i.e., those that are not in the Cabinet) participate. After the debate, voting occurs, and if the Annual Budget Bill is not passed (by a required majority), the PM must resign, and the Cabinet is dissolved. The second and third stages occur in July and August, respectively. In the amendment stage, committees are set to scrutinize the Budget Bill that is now divided into different articles. The "Scrutiny Committees" include the head of MOF as the committee chair, BOB Director General as the Committee Secretary, and high-ranking officers from MOF, BOB, and NESDB. Testimony by the heads of the Agencies and State Enterprises about the importance and level of the budget occur in this stage. This stage is important since the representatives can negotiate for public projects that will be beneficial to their constituencies (Pungprawat, 2009). The Scrutiny Committees and representatives can propose cuts in department budgets. In the absence of the consensus, majority voting rules are observed. In the third stage, the House of Representatives decides whether they approve the Annual Budget Bill as an entire bill. The process takes 105 days to complete. After the Annual Budget Bill is approved by the House of Representatives, it is transmitted to the Senate who has 20 days to approve the bill. If the bill is not approved by the Senate, it will be transferred back to the House of Representatives. They then can vote (by a simple majority) to favor the bills and if this occurs, the Budget Bill is considered passed by the Parliament and sent to the King for his approval. Upon signing, the Annual Budget Bill becomes the Annual Budget Act.

In Thailand, public projects are approved in one of three different ways depending on the type of government and the size of the projects. Projects that have price tag less than THB 1 billion are included in the Annual Budget Proposal and are financed and executed as a part of the Annual Budget Act (Webster and Theeratham, 2004). For projects that are larger than THB 1 billion, line agencies will submit budget requests for these projects to their Ministry, and then, if approved, it will be sent directly to the Cabinet without passing them through BOB. The Cabinet will ask for comments from the MOF, BOB, and NESDB prior to making a final decision approving the projects. If the projects are approved and will be financed through current revenue, the Cabinet will send them to the BOB to be included in the Annual Budget Proposal. If the project is approved by Cabinet with the intent to use long-term debt as the financing source, it will be sent to the Public Debt Management Office (PDMO) in the MOF to include its cost in the annual debt plan.

If the projects are initiated by a State Enterprise instead of the line agencies, they must be reviewed and approved by the NESDB prior to Cabinet submission. After Cabinet approval, these projects undergo the same route as those proposed by line agencies. PPP projects go through a separate approval process. The 1992 Privatization Act requires that Ministries responsible for PPP projects submit the new project requests to NESDB. However, existing projects with new concessions can be sent directly to MOF. After the NSDEB and MOF approve for new and existing projects, respectively, project requests are transmitted to the Cabinet for approval. After approval, line agencies set Project Execution Committees to execute the bidding process specified in Article 13 of the Joint Venture Act. Article 22 of the Privatization Act requires that line agencies establish Monitoring Committees to monitor construction and operation of the projects (Webster and Theeratham, 2004). Despite the monitoring committee, the PPP projects tend to face fraud problems, which will be discussed in the following section.

Because of the key role played by the Cabinet and Parliament in project approval, they exert disproportionate power in approving capital projects. There are many opportunities for them to exert pressure to support or reject projects according to their preferences. This obviously removes the capital project approval process from neutral, competent bureaucrats. This in turn likely reduces efficiency and effectiveness of public capital projects in Thailand.

Capital Financing

The central government finances public projects through three main financing sources: current revenue appropriated through the Annual Budget Act, domestic and international borrowing, and PPPs. In 2017, total central government capital expenditures were approximately THB 633 billion and outlays were about THB 381 billion. Capital spending as a percentage of overall spending fell from a range of 16 percent to 21 percent in the 2000s to 13 to 14 percent in the 2010s. The capital spending reduction can be attributed to political instability. During the latter period, Parliament was dissolved three times (2006, 2011 and 2013) and two elected PMs were impeached. During the same period, there were two military coups, with a military-led government in effect since 2014. Such political interruptions result in administrative changes and inconsistent public capital spending.

Central government revenue sources used to finance capital projects with current revenue include taxes, sales of assets and services, net revenue from state enterprises, and others. Most of this revenue comes from taxes (THB 2.6 trillion or 92 percent in FY2017) with smaller amounts from State Enterprise revenue (4.6 percent), sales of assets and services (1 percent), and other sources (1.5 percent) (Thailand Budget in Brief, FY 2018, Table II-1 Receipts Estimates). In FY 2017, the central government borrowed THB 553 billion from domestic capital markets to finance budget deficits. This is about 23.3 percent of total net revenue available to the central government.

State enterprises play a major role in Thai public capital investment. Table 2 presents the percentage of public capital outlay spent by State Enterprises as a share of total capital outlays spent by central government. Over the period 2010-2017, State Enterprises spent nearly as much as the central government in acquiring capital projects, except in 2016 and 2017.

One question that surrounds the use of state enterprises is how well they do in executing their budgeted spending. In 2017, the State Enterprise Policy Office (SEPO) reported planned spending THB 344 billion for capital outlay while real capital outlays at about THB 231 billion are about 67 percent of planned spending. This percentage is one of the lower percentages of budgeted spending since 2010.

Table 2. Public capital outlay by central government and state enterprises

Year	State Enterprises (THB Billion)	Central Government (THB Billion)	Total (THB Billion)	State Enterprises as % of total
2010	175	178	353	50%
2011	210	253	463	45%
2012	297	264	561	53%
2013	228	261	489	47%
2014	223	271	494	45%
2015	219	253	472	46%
2016	145	341	486	30%
2017	231	341	572	40%

Source: Author's Calculation Using Data from Budget Appropriation and Expenditure Classified by Economic and Ministry, Ministry of Finance, http://dataservices.mof.go.th/Dataservices/GovernmentExpenditureEconomyMinistry

State enterprise capital spending is highly concentrated in a few industries (Table 3). Petroleum and electricity production infrastructure are the largest investments, accounting for over 90 percent of State Enterprise investment. The large amount of investment in the Petroleum Authority is somewhat curious, given that Thailand is a large net importer of oil (CIA World Factbook, 2018). It may be that the Thai government is attempting to reduce dependence on foreign oil imports.

There is some evidence that local government autonomy may be increasing. Prior to 2009, capital resources were not transferred to the provinces. From 2009 to 2011, provincial governments received capital resources accounting for 0.3 percent to 7 percent of total capital resources. Despite the relatively small dollar amount, this spending may suggest a promising future for local governments to be self-sufficient since they have started receiving support from the central government to acquire basic public infrastructure that can help enhance local economic growth.

Long-Term Debt Finance

There is no fiscal management policy suggesting when projects should be financed through long-term debt. According to the current BOB Director, public spending on capital projects appropriated by the Annual Budget Act is relatively small (Thai Publica, 2014). As mentioned above, based on the authors' calculation, public capital outlays financed by the central government is about 11 percent to 14 percent of total outlay during the period of 2011 - 2017. Thus, the majority of public infrastructure in Thailand is financed by some forms of long-term debt issued by either the central government or by state enterprises.

Table 4 presents the structure of Thai public debt. In 2017, total outstanding public debt was THB 74 trillion, or 41.7 percent of the country's GDP. As shown in the Table, 78 percent of the public debt is

Table 3. Top ten state enterprises, public infrastructure investment, 2017

Top Ten SOE	2017 Planned Spending (THB Million)	% of Total
Petroleum Authority of Thailand (PTT)	195,374	57%
Electricity Generating Authority of Thailand (EGAT)	64,790	19%
Provincial Electricity Authority (PEA)	32,324	9%
Metropolitan Electricity Authority (MEA)	20,442	6%
Thai Airways	15,369	4%
Communication Authority of Thailand (CAT)	6,300	2%
Telephone Organization of Thailand (TOT)	5,264	2%
Thailand Post	2,983	1%
Mass Communication Organization of Thailand (MCOT)	695	0.2%
Dhanarak Asset Development (DAD)	558	0.2%
Forest Industry Organization (FDO)	408	0.1%
Total Planned	344,511	100%

Source: State Enterprise Policy Office: http://www.sepo.go.th/#chart6

Table 4. Public debt structure: 2017

Public Debt Outstanding (THB Millions)	2017	% Total
Direct Government	**57,952,733.92**	**77.9% (of Total Public Debt THB 74.4 Trillion)**
External Debt	1,161,807.73	2.0% (of total Direct Government Debt, THB 57.9 Trillion)
Domestic Debt	56,790,926.19	98.0% (of total Direct Government Debt, THB 57.9 Trillion)
Deficit Financing and Debt Management	39,784,563.59	70.1% (of total Direct Government Domestic Debt, THB 56.7 Trillion)
Bond to Compensate FIDF's Loss	17,460,641.14	30.1% (of total Direct Government Domestic Debt, THB 56.7 Trillion)
Non-Financial State Enterprise Debt	**10,675,778.53**	**14.3% (of Total Public Debt THB 74.4 Trillion)**
Special Financial Institutions Guaranteed Debt	**5,204,757.76**	**7.0% (of Total Public Debt THB 74.4 Trillion)**
FIDF Debt (Liabilities)	**431,908.38**	**0.6% (of Total Public Debt THB 74.4 Trillion)**
Autonomous Agency Debt (VF & EFPO)	**139,040.07**	**0.2%(of Total Public Debt THB 74.4 Trillion)**
Total (1+2+3+4+5)	**74,404,218.66**	**100.0%(of Total Public Debt THB 74.4 Trillion)**
Exchange Rate: Baht/USD	31.7	
Estimated GDP (Million Baht)	178,520,688.89	
% Total Debt to GDP	**41.7%**	
% External Debt to GDP	**0.065%**	

Source: Ministry of Finance, http://dataservices.mof.go.th/Dataservices/PublicDebtOutstanding?language=EN

directly issued by the government, 14 percent is from State Enterprises, and the remaining 8 percent is from special and independent agencies. Of the THB 57.9 trillion in direct government debt, 98 percent is domestic debt and 2 percent is from foreign sources. Most of the direct government domestic debt is used to finance budget deficits. Data for public debt specifically used to finance public projects are not available.[1] However, if we assume that all external debts, non-financial state enterprise debt, and that portion of domestic debt not issued to finance budget deficits were issued for capital projects, we can estimate that capital project-related debt is only about THB 11.8 trillion (6.6 percent of GDP). Therefore, although the overall debt burden for the country is relatively modest, the fact that most of the debt is for non-capital investment is worrisome. Table 4 also shows that public capital project debt is mostly issued by State Enterprises.

Table 5 breaks out outstanding debts by state enterprises. As described above, state enterprise projects can be financed through either current revenue appropriated by BOB or long-term debt with or without MOF guarantees. State enterprises can borrow in both domestic and international markets. In 2016, total domestic outstanding debts by the non-financially-related State Enterprises stand at THB 2.9 trillion and THB 3.9 trillion for guaranteed and non-guaranteed debt respectively. Total international outstanding debts by the non-financially related State Enterprises are about THB 869 billion and THB 1.42 trillion for guaranteed and non-guaranteed respectively. Domestic borrowing is mainly for rail, electricity, petroleum, and expressways projects, while international debt is mainly issued for rail, petroleum, and the national airline.

Table 5. Long-term debt for state enterprise public infrastructure financing, 2016 (THB million)

State Enterprise	MOF Guaranteed Domestic Debts	Non-Guaranteed Domestic Debts	MOF Guaranteed International Debts	Non-Guaranteed International Debts
Total for Non-financial Related SOEs	2,914,337	3,986,401	869,587	1,423,748
Electricity Generating Authority of Thailand (EGAT)	15,000	478,700	6,798	0
Petroleum Authority of Thailand (PTT)	16,000	1,510,673	0	737,624
Expressway Authority of Thailand (EXAT)	256,750	28,100	0	0
Mass Rapid Transit Authority of Thailand (MRT)	0	0	553,907	0
Thai Airway Co. Ltd.	0	733,093	0	686,123
Provincial Electricity Authority (PEA)	0	729,585	6,437	0
State Railway of Thailand (SRT)	1,172,147	0	16,092	0
Telephone Organization of Thailand (TOT)	0	87,378	6,898	0
Metropolitan Waterworks Authority (MWA)	0	0	16,496	0
Metropolitan Electricity Authority (MEA)	0	306,900	0	0

Source: Outstanding Public Debt by State Enterprises, Ministry of Finance, http://dataservices.mof.go.th/Dataservices/GovernmentExpenditureEconomyMinistry

The 2018 Fiscal Discipline Act

The current Thai government has been actively searching for public infrastructure financing sources to finance its ambitious strategic plans. The 2018 Fiscal Discipline Act, enacted around the time of drafting this chapter, provides for potentially greater local autonomy in some aspects of public finance. The 2018 Fiscal Discipline Act appears to be tailored to support government borrowing for developmental projects. In this Act, the new definition of public debts includes all debts issued by the MOF and debts issued by agencies and state enterprises guaranteed by the MOF. Debt issued by agencies and state enterprises not guaranteed by MOF are *not* counted as public debt (Prachachart, 2017). Agencies can issue debts for public infrastructure on their own with or without MOF guarantees. In doing so, the Act only requires that agencies must conduct debt affordability analysis and assess the efficiency and effectiveness of using such long-term debt to finance public projects. The Act allows the MOF to issue debts without approval from BOB and the Cabinet. Such debts can be acquired in two circumstances. The first is when there are emergency needs for projects. The second is when there is a need for projects that can fulfill social and economic development purposes of the country, but the budgetary resources appropriated by Annual Budget Bill are insufficient.

According to the Act, the proceeds from borrowing in both conditions are not required to be recorded in the Annual Budget Bill and be included in the fiscal reserve accounts. Instead, the MOF will save it for disbursement by the responsible agencies. After the debt proceeds are used to acquire the projects, the Cabinet is required to evaluate projects and report the disbursement. If the debt proceeds are not used due to project cancellation or completion with lower than estimated costs, the MOF must deposit the money into the fiscal reserve accounts. If the MOF has not received proceeds from the borrower yet, the MOF must cancel the debt contract.

For local governments, the Act allows the local jurisdictions to borrow to establish strong public infrastructure foundations that can later increase own-source revenue through expansion of the tax base, similar to the logic of tax increment financing in the United States. The Act allows local governments to access capital funding through domestic markets but does not specify the details of the process. If local governments borrow from international capital markets, receiving the loan proceeds in foreign currency, the PM and the Cabinet must approve the loan prior to the borrowing process. This rule is new given that prior to 2018, local governments could not create foreign debts. Although significantly expediting public project acquisition, the Act, at best, may create fragmented fiscal planning and at worse, result in an obscure public debt level due to large amounts of undocumented public project financing.

To evaluate, the Act allows local governments to issue domestic public debt for financing public projects and to receive foreign aid without having to coordinate through the central government. It further reduces monitoring by the central government for borrowing and foreign government assistance. Finally, it expedites the acquisition process by reducing bureaucratic steps in capital project proposal approval. The Act could provide advantages to certain local governments who have access to own source or foreign revenue sources and who have strong fiscal discipline and financial management capacity. However, if a jurisdiction does not have access to revenue sources or lacks financial discipline or financial management capacity, unsustainable public debts could be accumulated. This situation may affect the country's macroeconomic condition if multiple jurisdictions encounter fiscal viability issues at the same time. It is much too early to say which of these outcomes will be realized more in practice.

EXECUTION

Capital project acquisition, monitoring, and internal audit for the projects financed by current revenue as appropriated by Annual Budget Act is governed by the B.E. 2548 Budget Regulation. The law designates that BOB prepares the budget for all projects and programs approved in the Annual Budget Act. After the Annual Budget Bill is passed, agencies and state enterprises are eligible to create obligations and withdraw budget resources from the Treasury according to execution plans proposed to BOB. The MOF, agencies, and state enterprises are authorized to issue public debts after the projects are approved by the Cabinet. For public projects, agency heads must assure that the acquisition plans and the cost estimates for land, equipment, and construction were estimated accurately, and the total project cost must not be above the appropriated level; however, the agency heads can change the input mix to enhance project efficiency. The Regulation allows flexibility in project acquisitions by authoring agency heads to reprogram appropriated budget resources if the reprograming value is less than THB 1 million for equipment or THB 10 million for construction.

The central government monitors public projects by tracking disbursements by agencies and Ministries. The BOB is responsible for creating budget status reports on a quarterly basis to track capital project spending compared to proposed plans. Budget status reports are available for the public on the BOB website. By law, capital project execution is centralized, well monitored, and is consistent with normative recommendations. However, in practice, waste, fraud, and abuse occur frequently, especially for the large capital projects. This is not surprising given that the country's corruption level[2] remains relatively high. Examples of fraud, waste, and abuse are recapped in Table 6 and Table 7.

The two cases given in the tables suggest that the fragmented Thai capital management and budgeting process not only interrupts public infrastructure planning in the first component and creates non-

Table 6. Klong Dan Project (Excerpted from Prombut, 2016)

In 1995 the Cabinet approved a large wastewater treatment and sewer system project located in Samutprakarn province, where heavy industry has operated on land near the ocean for several decades. As a part of an environmental revitalization program to preserve the regional ecological system and sustain the fishing industry, the Pollution Control Department (PCD) within the Ministry of Natural Resources and Environment signed a contract with a private sector consortium in 1997. The private sector consortium was comprised of five construction companies. The contract included at least one company that was a technical expert in wastewater treatment system construction, which oversaw the work of the other companies as contractors. This PPP project was worth THB 23.7 billion and covered 751 acres (1900 Rai in Thai measures) in Klong Dan district. It was envisioned as a turnkey project where private partners would be responsible for executing the entire project including land acquisition, site development, and feasibility studies. The project was financed by a long-term loan from the Asian Development Bank and was scheduled to be completed in 2003.
In 2001, after 80 percent of the project was completed, the project was called off by the PCD after finding corruption in the project. The PCD found that the consortium's wastewater expert, Northwest Wastewater Development (NWD – an English company), withdrew its participation prior to the contract award. The consortium replaced NWD with Opco Co. Ltd, which lacked expertise in wastewater management systems. Meanwhile, the Department of Special Investigation (DSI) detected fraud in land purchases during the period 1998-2000. The Lan Thong Meang Rae Co. Ltd. purchased 751 acres of land from villagers at a below market rate (about THB 38 million) and resold the land to Palm Beach Development, Co. Ltd., which later sold the land to Gateway Development, which in turn, sold the land to the government for THB 1.956 billion. Of the 751 acres, some parcels were public lands, some were acquired by forcing villagers to sell their lands at below market rates, and some were requisitioned by having the Department of Lands issue certificates to purchasers even though the landowners did not wish to sell. DSI found that the executive officers and committees of The Lan Thong Meang Rae Co. Ltd, Palm Beach Development Co. Ltd., Gateway Development, the PPP consortium, and the PPP consulting organization were the same. The Minister of Interior was the President and/or a board member of all the land purchasing companies, construction consortium, and PPP consultation organizations during the period 1998-2000. One member of the PPP consultation committee, an expert in wastewater management from the ADB, was convicted for fraud. This project created a sunk cost of about THB 18.96 billion since the project was never completed. The government may lose another THB 9 billion to a lawsuit brought by the private partners for improper project termination.

Table 7. Hopewell Expressway Project (Excerpted from Peakthaisong, 2017)

The Hopewell expressway project was approved by Cabinet in 1991; it has been the most controversial transportation project in Thailand. The Ministry of Transportation (MOT) signed a PPP contract with Hopewell Holding Co. Ltd., a Hong Kong based company well known in Asia for building mega transportation projects in countries including China and the Philippines. The turnkey contract was for Hopewell to build a three-layer expressway – a four-lane road on the ground level with a "sky train" and "express sky train" on the second and third levels, respectively. These roads and trains were seen as a way to expedite commuting from suburban to downtown areas and held hope for Bangkok residents for solving infamous traffic jams and improving quality of life in Thailand's capital city.[3] The three-layer expressway system was supposed to stretch 60.1 kilometers at its 1999 completion with a THB 80 billion price tag. Under the contract, Hopewell would be the builder and then sole operator for a 30-year period, transferring the asset to the central government after that period. Hopewell was contracted to pay THB 353 billion for the 30-year contract to the government in exchange for building the project, the right to collect user charges for all three transportation facilities and the right to develop 249 acres of the land next to the transportation facility, which belong to the State Railway of Thailand. However, after a military coup in 1992, the project was delayed, and the contract was revised by the new government.
As late as 1997, the project was only 20 percent complete. Hopewell then encountered financial problems during the Asian Fiscal Crisis; it asked the Thai government to provide a guaranteed loan of THB 20 billion to complete the project. The Thai government at that time declined because of the effects of the fiscal crisis on its finances. Hopewell delayed project completion, reasoning that even if the project was completed, it could not make a profit since the project would not generate revenue, and the developed land around the expressway would be devalued due to a stagnant economy. In 1998, a different administration (the fourth one during the project) called off the contract, resulting in Hopewell suing the Thai government for THB 11.188 billion. The private partner also sued the State Railway of Thailand, stating that it failed to adequately clear the site and the land to facilitate project construction, thereby causing a delay in project completion. In 2000, after paying for the land development failure and attempting to cancel the project, the State Railway of Thailand tried to convert the development site including 400 unfinished piers (supports) to be an extension of the existing sky train rail system, minimizing the sunk cost. Hopewell again sued the Thai government for THB 59 billion, accusing the Thai government of improper taking of property awarded to it in the original contract, which it pointed out was not yet expired. In 2012, after severe flooding in Bangkok, some of the piers collapsed due to unfinished portions being submerged for several months.

transparent capital financing in the second component but also encourages or at least allows corruption and waste. That mega-projects (over THB 1 billion) must be financed by either PPP or long-term debts issued by MOF without incorporating them into the Annual Budget Act results in large projects not being monitored by the BOB. Additionally, the institutional arrangements introduce significant uncertainty, as these projects tend to take a long time to complete, covering several administrations. Some administrations may not agree with contracts made by prior governments and simply cancel them. These cases suggest that the Thai government should consider reporting all projects, regardless of size, along with the source of financing in an online database so that the public can scrutinize and monitor them and try to develop a culture where administrations respect contracts left by prior governments.

MAINTENANCE

There are two main activities in the maintenance phase: maintenance planning and maintenance funding. In Thailand, maintenance planning starts with the central government, through the NESDB, compiling and reporting public capital stocks based on the perpetual inventory accounting method. In this accounting method, capital stock depreciation is calculated and reported. Physical condition analysis based on engineering methods are conducted by responsible agencies and departments as well as state enterprises; however, the national government does not compile and report such information in an aggregated manner. Hence, the country does not have data in terms of the demand for future capital projects based on current physical condition and projected future usage. The comparison between current condition and future usage is conducted at the agency and department levels and capital project requests are developed in each fiscal year.

Maintenance funding involves setting aside budgetary resources for depreciation. According to the MOF and BOB, the Thai public capital budgeting and financing process appears to focus on acquiring new public projects rather than focusing on maintenance given that there is no requirement for governments to set aside maintenance funding. This legal requirement results in deterioration of infrastructure.

A fundamental maintenance planning analysis is tracking the rate of use of in-place capital and projecting future demands. This analysis may be difficult in Thailand given that usual methods for detecting demand such as user charge collections are subject to some corruption. For example, in 1998, tolls for Bangkok-Chonburi and Bangpain-Bangplee motorways were stolen by a team of high-ranking officials from the Ministry of Transportation, working with bureaucrats and toll collectors along those routes. An investigation team, led by the Minster of Transportation found that the loop detector systems installed to count the numbers of vehicles per day, recording the weight of the vehicles and categorizing the types of the vehicles (e.g., four-wheeled vehicle) were unusable (Kitsaowapak, 2016). The loop detector installation was contracted out to Tangsirikosol Co. Ltd, who in turn, contracted with a contractor at the price of only 64 percent of the price it charged the government (Kitsaowapak, 2016). It is unclear whether the contractors were involved in installing the unusable loop detector system. Toll collectors, supported by supervisors and high-ranking officials, recycled receipts for the tolls, as most road users do not demand receipts. The investigation team used military officers to count the vehicles on the routes and estimated that the two routes could create approximately THB 143 million a year or THB 400,000 a day in user charges, while the reported toll collection was only THB 4.8 million a year or THB 20,000 a day (Kitsaowapak, 2016). This episode calls into question whether usage analysis would be viable or of value until fundamental issues of fraud, waste and abuse are addressed.

EVALUATION

This section evaluates the Thai capital management and budgeting process based on the normative principles found in the literature.

Long-Term Planning Process

The Thai public capital management process appears to be inconsistent with the normative framework proposed in this book. The country's long-term planning process contains numerous strategic plans, hindering centralized planning and execution. The country lacks a national master plan that spells out a vision of what the nation would want to be in the future. Currently, numerous visions have been developed by different governments but have never been formally elucidated and used as a master plan. For example, during the period 2001- 2006, the PM frequently expressed that the goal was to make Thailand the economic hub in the ASEAN region. As a result, the administration proposed and acquired several relevant infrastructure projects, such as the rapid completion of Suvarnabhumi Airport, which upgraded the quality and capacity of the national airport. That administration also prepared to upgrade and improve road networks throughout the country to support passenger and freight traffic, especially those crossing national borders. This project was not executed by the time the administration was replaced. The current administration does issue the 20-year Strategic Framework with the intent that it be used as a master plan; however, all it does is essentially repeat the goals in the NESDPs.

The 12th NESDP, which is considered as the national comprehensive strategic plan, needs much improvement. Although the NESDP contains socio-economic analysis and integrates analytical results in identifying policy priorities and courses of action, the plan has three flaws that can affect national infrastructure strategy planning. The first is that the plan lacks long-term fiscal planning, detailing how the resources for the development projects will be acquired and to what extent proposed "mega-development" projects would have impacts on the country's fiscal condition. This characteristic makes it difficult for the projects to be actualized in the five-year time frame. For example, in the 12th Plan, the 62 Flagship Projects were described only in terms of location. There was no detail regarding total project cost and proposed financing sources. If the Plan were to integrate long-term fiscal planning, it could be regarded as the national CIP. However, without financial planning, the National Plan is little more than a "wish list".

The second problem is that the NESDP has failed to integrate land use planning and coordinate public infrastructure planning across sectors (ADB, 2014). This results in imbalanced infrastructure development across sectors and regions, leading to an inefficient and inequitable public infrastructure network (ADB, 2014; Peters, 2014). As mentioned above, while Thailand has adequate road systems, including Expressways and Motorways as well as light-rail trains in the Bangkok and Metropolitan areas, its railroad networks for freight and passenger services and water service in rural areas are lagging those of the region (ADB, 2014, Global Competitiveness Report). The last problem is that the plan lacks continuity in their focus on infrastructure development both in terms of sectors and geography. This results in abrupt changes in direction, delayed project execution and an inefficient public infrastructure system as evidenced by projects that were aborted due to changing directions (TDRI, 1998; ADB 2014).

One recommendation to improve the planning component would be to establish a working master plan declaring the country's vision and long-term goals as well as creating a land use plan and development plan. In addition, all single sector strategic multi-year comprehensive plans (e.g., Transportation and Water Development Plans) should be consolidated into NESDPs to coordinate public infrastructure systems so that systems can be developed more consistently. For example, railroad network development will increase public infrastructure demands in other sectors, such as water and waste management and information technology since it will develop businesses and cause migration to rural and regional areas. In addition, instead of adopting a new plan every five years, the county should make the National Plan become a five-year *rolling plan* that can track the progress of project and program accomplishment and most importantly match the capital needs with fiscal capacity.

Budgeting and Financing Process

The decision-making process around budgeting and financial management is fragmented, uncoordinated, and opaque. The process of allocating capital resources and obtaining approval for financing is monopolized by high-ranking officials in four bureaucracies: NESDB, BOB, MOF, BOT, and relevant ministries in the mega-projects. Although the Cabinet, whose members are nationally elected, can provide input through the reviewing and approving process, they rarely call for major changes (Pungprawat, 2009; Ruamporn, no date). Furthermore, when projects with costs more than THB 1 billion need approval, the Cabinet relies on the MOF for the decision and is not reported or recorded in a clearinghouse for large project financing. This appears to be somewhat driven by the fact that the Cabinet does not have the same level of technical expertise as the Ministries they govern. Ministry heads are career civil servants who develop knowledge of needs for projects and competencies in executing them over several years. Further, the Cabinet tends to have little time for reviewing and approving the Budget Proposals submitted by the BOB. This institutional design places the Cabinet in a weak position to develop thorough analyses of proposals. The Cabinet does not appear to be involved in planning for borrowing except for final approval once a deficit occurs, which tends to be in relatively urgent situations precluding much analysis. The National Assembly is the weakest of the budgetary actors since they see the Annual Budget Proposal in its final phase. Although the budget law states that the House of Representatives can scrutinize and cut budgets, they do not have power to insert new projects or reallocate capital resources. The serious legislative debates, which occurred in the first and the second phases, are much more about the legal aspects of the Annual Budget Proposal rather than whether the proposed budget plan will yield efficient and effective infrastructure (Pungprawat, 2009).

The country's definition of capital expenditure is also incomplete, lacking the cutoff values for cost and useful life to be used in classifying a project as a capital investment. The plans could therefore include both major and minor repair and maintenance projects, which tend to compete for project funding. A separate capital budget document is not required, and the budget document is unified containing both operational and capital proposals. The BOB prepares a list of capital projects approved by the Act and segregates the projects into distinct functions, such as water and economic development. In preparing the Annual Budget Proposal, the BOB explicitly states project selection criteria and are listed in the Annual Budget Act. The project selection criteria seems to be consistent with those of the normative concepts. The main three criteria are that projects should be responsive to goals and policy priorities stated in the National Plans, projects must have a feasibility study and be ready to execute once appropriated, and for relatively large public projects (without specifying a value), life cycle cost must be estimated to assure that there will be no negative impacts on the future budgets. However, in practice, several projects that have low benefits are included, given that the Ministries try to insert as many proposals as possible, asserting that all projects are important and pertinent to the NESDPs (TDRI, 1998). Further, when projects are larger than THB 1 billion, the projects tend to bypass BOB and be financed by long-term debt. But since there is no aggregated national CIP and the approval process for large projects bypasses the BOB, annual capital financial planning appears to be weak. This is because once the large projects pass the Cabinet approval, the MOF issues the long-term debt. By law, such debt is not recorded as "capital project debt" but is combined with debt to finance budget deficits and other types of debt. Large projects that are approved and financed are not required to be listed in the Annual Budget Act and thus bypass BOB monitoring in the budget execution phase.

The 2018 Fiscal Discipline Act allows departments, agencies, state enterprises, and local governments units receiving foreign aid, assistance, and grants to not report and transfer monetary resources to the MOF. While this allows flexibility in fiscal planning and may expedite public projects completion, especially for expensive items, it causes a lack of transparency. Coupled with the revision in the B.E 2548 Budget Regulation that public capital budget must be about 20 percent of the total budget or equal to the deficits of each fiscal year, this Act can encourage government officials to hide deficits through an off-budget and may make the country's long-term fiscal planning less focused, affecting the country's financial condition in the long-run. Furthermore, the new definition of the public debts given by this Act does not include state enterprises' foreign and domestic debts not guaranteed by MOF. As shown in the previous section, unfortunately, most state enterprises debts are not guaranteed by MOF and the majority of state enterprise debts are for public capital projects that can create self-revenue once acquired. This implies that public infrastructure projects in Thailand may be less expensive if the debt would otherwise be guaranteed by MOF. Furthermore, this Act could encourage government officials to hide the level of public debts in total since this portion is not included in counting total public outstanding debt.

Given that almost half of public capital expenditures are from State Enterprises, this creates another level of fragmentation in terms of fiscal planning. State Enterprises finance their large projects by issuing long-term debt, and most of these debts are not guaranteed by the MOF. Non-guaranteed debts result in relatively higher cost for public projects, especially for those that can create a stream of revenue once acquired. Like other large projects proposed by the line agencies, large projects of the State Enterprises bypass BOB, and therefore, there is no record of project completion acquired and what projects are to be acquired in the following years by the national government. Combine this with the fact that PPP contributes about twenty percent of total infrastructure, and the possibility of coordination not only among infrastructure sectors but also among administrative levels of government (central, provincial, and local levels) is greatly reduced. Furthermore, infrastructure charges appear not to reflect true costs and benefits of the public service as mentioned in Table 7. For another example, rural wastewater management facilities are often inadequate and outdated because there is not enough revenue collected to cover the full cost of service provision, including depreciation of fixed assets (ADB, 2014). This is due at least in part to weak regulation and lack of enforcement for factories discharging large volumes of wastewater (ADB, 2014).

Execution Process

Project execution in Thailand is legally mandated to be flexible but centrally monitored by BOB and the Comptroller's Office. BOB's budget status report for capital project spending is available on its website. However, once again there are issues with the implementation of projects, as described in the *Klong Dan* and *Hope Well* cases. As shown by the longitudinal statistics mentioned above and as stated by the former BOB Budget Director (Thai Publica, 2014), projects financed through the Annual Budget

Act are relatively insignificant compared to projects financed by debts, which are not required to be reported to BOB. Financial and performance audits are typically one of the main mechanisms for project monitoring in such situations. However, financial audits and reporting seem to be relatively ineffective in Thailand (Andrew, 2006; Kongrungchok & Stanton, 2014). This hinders performance monitoring and transparency, which are important for allocating capital resources in subsequent years and in long-term planning. One study conducted at the end of FY 2007 found that the Thai Bureau of the Budget had not accomplished a systematic performance measurement yet for that fiscal year (Personal Interview with BOB Officer, June 2007). This lack of effective auditing and monitoring may allow for inefficiencies and even outright corruption to become pervasive, especially when Thailand's corruption index score is reportedly relatively high among the East Asian Countries (Kaufmann, Kraay, & Mastruzzi, 2008).

Maintenance Process

As described in the previous section, the maintenance process in Thailand is inconsistent with best practice. It is difficult to identify maintenance funding since the unified budget document treats capital projects as a line item in programs proposed by Ministries. Further, major repair (in lieu of replacement) is not one of the three prioritizing criteria in the Annual Budget Act, therefore, maintenance is overlooked while new projects are highlighted. It has been found that Thai railroad systems are exceptionally outdated, if not completely abandoned (Peters, 1998; ADB, 2014; Global Competitiveness Reports, 2018; Webster & Theeratham, 2004). Furthermore, corruption in toll collection, such as that discussed in the case of Bangkok-Chonburi and Bangpain-Bangplee motorways, and uncollected sewer charges due to the fear that manufacturing and industrial plants will leave areas supposed to be charging them, (ADB, 2014) obstructs the Thai government from obtaining real performance data that can be useful for maintenance planning and funding.

Linkages Between the Processes and the Investment Patterns

To summarize, the major problems in the Thai public capital management and budgeting process are (1) fragmented and unfocused long-term physical and fiscal planning processes, (2) lack of transparency and coordination in annual capital resource allocation and financing, especially when debts are involved, and (3) unexpected changes in administration due to political instability resulting in discontinuity of project acquisition. Long-term planning is unfocused and interrupted by frequent changes in political leadership.

The country's lack of transparency and coordination of public capital resources, especially for high-cost projects, further produces a situation where public capital financing is haphazard and mostly is driven by debt capacity concerns. High cost projects are approved at various times during each fiscal year, and there is no way to know whether the projects are redundant since there is no CIP. During good times, public investment appears to soar, but during bad times, public investment is stagnant. Haphazard planning and investment driven by debt capacity has resulted in volatile public capital outlays with the overall mediocre growth rates of public infrastructure accumulation, which in turn, may stifle the country's economic performance. Unexpected administrative changes due to political instability cause failure in public project execution. In addition, the institutional rule that large projects (over THB 1 billion) are not included in the BOB's central budget project status report tends to encourage corruption and yield relatively large sunk costs as many projects were left incomplete. These problems have led to a situation where public infrastructure is unevenly developed across sectors. Unfortunately, the sectors in which the country does not perform well (e.g., railroad freight services and wastewater services) (ADB, 2014) tend to be important for the goal of increasing economic competitiveness (Peters, 1998). Further, capital replacement rates less than the rate of capital depreciation lead to lagging productivity and economic growth.

CONCLUSION

This chapter describes public capital management and budgeting processes in Thailand. Thailand is a strong bureaucratic state. The policy implementation process is highly centralized and top-down with limited local government autonomy and citizen input. The long-term physical and fiscal planning process is fragmented with several strategic plans in different areas of government. A consolidated master plan does not exist. Instead, a strategic framework issued by the current military-led administration essentially repeats the same information as promulgated in five-year comprehensive plans (the NESDPs). The NESDPs contain lists of desired capital projects, but since they are not accompanied by long-term plans for construction, acquisition, and financing, they are little more than "wish lists". The budgeting process is dominated by the four bureaucratic organization: the BOB, MOF, NSEDB, and BOT, with limited roles for Parliament. The Annual Budget Act is a unified budget but does not contain a complete definition of capital projects. While project prioritization criteria appears to be consistent with the framework we discuss in the book, all projects relevant to the NESDPs are included (BOB, 2018), and Ministries tend to insert as many projects as possible, documenting that they are relevant to NESDPs.

The financial process is fragmented, uncoordinated, and opaque. Large projects, funded by long-term debt, bypass the BOB in the approval process; hence, they are not documented in an aggregated list of the approved and financed projects. Since there is no CIP, there is no plan to set or monitor annual debt levels in funding large projects over THB 1 billion. The 2018 Fiscal Discipline Act, while meaning to encourage public capital investment, expedites high cost project acquisition by authorizing agencies to borrow after Cabinet approval without having to include the projects into the budget document. This reduces transparency in financing. The execution process is flexible and centralized as mandated by law, but in practice, several cases suggest that the country's auditing and evaluation system is ineffective. Maintenance planning and funding are not present in the legal frameworks and documented management practices. These conditions in Thailand, especially for planning and financing, result in two serious problems: (1) public capital financing is haphazard and mostly is driven by debt capacity concerns and (2) public capital outlays are volatile, with resulting uneven growth rates of public infrastructure provision.

REFERENCES

Andrew, M. (2006). Beyond Best Practice and "Basics First" in Adopting Performance Budgeting Reform. *Public Administration and Development*, *26*(1), 147–161. doi:10.1002/pad.401

Asian Development Bank. (2014). *A comparative infrastructure development assessment of the Republic of Korea and the Kingdom of Thailand*. Manila, Philippines: Asian development bank Press.

Asian Development Bank. (2017). *Thailand*. Retrieved July, 1 2018, from https://sdbs.adb.org/sdbs/

Asian Development Bank—ADB. (2018). *Key indicators for Asia and the pacific 2017*. Retrieved July 1, 2018, from www.adb.org/statistics

Budget—BOB. (2018). *FY 2019 budget development process and practices*. Retrieved March 19, 2018, from http://www.bb.go.th/bbweb/?page_id=6013

Central Intelligence Agency (CIA). (2018). *The world factbook: East & Southeast Asia: Thailand*. Retrieved June 4, 2018, from https://www.cia.gov/library/publications/the-world-factbook/geos/th.html

Chardchawan, S. (2006). Chapter 2: Decentralization under threat? In Impacts of the CEO Governor Policy upon Thai Local Government. Academic Press.

International Monetary Fund. (2016). Thailand: Staff report for the 2016 article IV consultation. *IMF Country Report*, *16*(139).

Kaufman, G. G., Krueger, T. H., & Hunter, W. C. (1999). *The Asian financial crisis: Origins, implications and solutions*. New York: Springer.

Kaufmann, D., Kraay, A., & Mastruzzi, M. (2008). *Governance matters VII: Governance indicators for 1996-2007*. Retrieved October 6, 2018, from http://info.worldbank.org/governance/wgi/mc_chart.asp

Kitsaowapak, J. (2016). *Expressway is a cheating way (In Thai), TV program by mass communication organization of Thailand (M.C.O.T.)*. Retrieved May 1, 2018, from https://www.youtube.com/watch?v=Tj5tP-2ypus

Kittipanyasiri, A. (2015). *Planning and budgeting for the capital improvement in Thai Municipalities: Problems in the development of Thai municipal self-governing capacity*. Retrieved October 6, 2018, from http://documents.worldbank.org/curated/en/993671468118138134/pdf/674860ESW0P11800190 06020120RB0EDITS.pdf

Kongrungchok, A. (2014). *Limitations of Thai local government internal auditing in detecting risks*. Retrieved September 10, 2018, from http://globalbizresearch.org/Singapore_Conference/pdf/pdf/S454.pdf

Krueathep, W. (2010). *Bad luck or bad budgeting: A comparative analysis of municipal fiscal conditions in Thailand* (Unpublished Ph.D. Dissertation). Rutgers, State University of New Jersey.

National Economic and Social Development Board—NESDB. (2018). *NESDB economic development report*. Retrieved April 28, 2018, from http://www.nesdb.go.th/ewt_dl_link.php?nid=7384

National Economic and Social Development Board—NESDB. (2018). *NESDB economic report*. Retrieved May 1, 2018, from http://www.nesdb.go.th/ewt_dl_link.php?nid=7384

National Economic and Social Development Board—NESDB. (2018). *NESDB economic development report*. Retrieved April 28, 2018, from http://www.nesdb.go.th/ewt_dl_link.php?nid=7384

National Economic and Social Development Board—NESDB. (2018). *Decentralization and the budget for social services at Tambon administrativelLevel*. Retrieved September 10, 2018, from http://social.nesdb.go.th/social/

Newspaper, P. (2017). *2018 Public debt law with new definition of public debt excluding nonguaranteed loans by state enterprise*. Retrieved April, 1 2018, from https://www.prachachat.net/politics/news-72566

Peakthaisong, O. (2017). *Hopewell or hopeless? (In Thai), TV program by mass communication organization of Thailand (M.C.O.T.)*. Retrieved May 1, 2018, from https://www.youtube.com/watch?v=CoDg1pg_sUs

Peters, H. J. (1998). *Thailand trade and infrastructure. Conference on Thailand's Dynamic Economic Recovery and Competitiveness*. Session 5- Removing Bottlenecks to Productivity (I) Infrastructure.

Prombut, S. (2016). *Klong dan: Cheating project (In Thai), TV program by* mass *communication organization of Thailand (M.C.O.T.)*. Retrieved May 1, 2018, from https://www.youtube.com/watch?v=66xw0Jv9Qxw

Pungprawat, K. (2009). Budgeting system and bureau of the budget in Thailand. Chulalongkorn. *Journal of Economics*, *21*(1), 49–71.

Riggs, F. W. (1966). Thailand; the modernization of a bureaucratic polity. Honolulu, HI: East West Center Press.

Royal Thai Government. (2016). *Transportation infrastructure development*. Author.

Saksophonkul, P. (2004). *Wiwattanakarn kotmai withikarn ngobpramarn lae karn patiroop rabob ngobpramarn khong pratet Thai*.Thailand Bureau of Budget Library.

Schwab, K. (2018). *World economic forum: The global competitiveness report 2016-2017*. Retrieved May 1, 2018, from http://www3.weforum.org/docs/GCR2016-2017/05FullReport/TheGlobalCompetitivenessReport2016-2017_FINAL.pdf

Sitthiyot, T. (2017). The truth about Thailand's transport infrastructure development and financing. *Nomura Journal of Asian Capital Markets*, *2*(1), 38–43.

Sopchokchai, O. (2001). Good local governance and anti-corruption through people's participation: A case of Thailand. *Public Sector Reform Project*, *1*(1), 1–14.

Srithongrung, A. (2009). The effects of results-oriented budgeting on government spending patterns in Thailand. *International Public Management Review, 10*(1), 59-89.

Srithongrung, A., & Kriz, K. (2012). From Public Infrastructure to National Economic Growth: Do Strategic Investment Practices Matter? *International Public Management Review*, *13*(2), 19–50.

State Enterprise Policy Office. (2018). *State enterprise disbursement statistics*. Retrieved March 15, 2018, from http://www.sepo.go.th/#chart6

Statistics Times. (2015). *List of countries by population density*. Retrieved April 20, 2018, from http://statisticstimes.com/population/countries-by-population-density.php

Sudhipongpracha, T., & Wongpreedee, A. (2016). Decentralizing decentralized governance: Community empowerment and coproduction of municipal public work in Northeast Thailand. *Community Development Journal: An International Forum*, *51*(2), 302–319. doi:10.1093/cdj/bsv026

Thai Publica. (2014). *Constitutional court diagnosis for THB 2,000,000 million borrowing for transportation mega projects*. Retrieved March 16, 2018, from https://thaipublica.org/2014/04/mega-projects-constitutional-court/

Thailand Bureau of Census. (2018). *2010 Thailand population and housing census*. Retrieved April 28, 2018, from http://popcensus.nso.go.th/file/popcensus-10-01-56-T.pdf

Thailand Bureau of Census. (2018). 2010 *Thailand population and housing census*, Retrieved April 28, 2018, from http://popcensus.nso.go.th/file/popcensus-10-01-56-T.pdf

Thailand Bureau of the Budget—BOB. (2018). *FY 2018 budget in brief.* Retrieved February 3, 2018, from http://www.bb.go.th/bbweb/?page_id=6039

Thailand Bureau of the Budget—BOB. (2018). *FY 2019 budget preparation directions and principles*. Retrieved April 15, 2018, from http://www.bb.go.th/bbweb/

Thailand Department of Local Administration—DLA. (2018). *Local organization data (in Thai)*. Retrieved September 10, 2018, from http://www.dla.go.th/work/abt/

Thailand Development Research Institution—TDRI. (2004). *A study report of new budgeting system*. Retrieved June 11, 2007, from http://www.bb.go.th/bbhome/index.asp

Thailand Law Forum. (1997). *Thai government structure under Thailand's 1997 (B.E. 2540) constitution*. Retrieved April 12, 2018, from http://www.thailawforum.com/articles/briggsgov.html

Thailand Ministry of Finance—MOT. (2018). *Fiscal statistics: Budget appropriation and expenditure classified by rconomic and ministry*. Retrieved March 15, 2018, from http://dataservices.mof.go.th/Dataservices/GovernmentExpenditureEconomyMinistry

Thailand Ministry of Finance—MOT. (2018). *Fiscal statistics: Outstanding public debt by state enterprises*. Retrieved March 15, 2018, from http://dataservices.mof.go.th/Dataservices/GovernmentExpenditureEconomyMinistry

Thailand National Statistical Office. (2018). *Summary of labor force survey 2017*. Retrieved April 22, 2018, from http://web.nso.go.th/index.htm

Thailand Office of National Economic and Social Development Board (NESDB). (n.d.). Retrieved from http://www.nesdb.go.th/nesdb_en/main.php?filename=national_account

The Economist. (2015). *China, Japan and the case for Thailand*. Retrieved April 2, 2018, from http://country.eiu.com/article.aspx?articleid=1843787968&Country=Thailand&topic=Economy

The Office of Senate Secretary, Thailand National Assembly. (2017). *B.E. 2560 (2017) Thai constitution*. Bangkok, Thailand: National Assembly Press.

The World Bank. (2018). *Infrastructure needs, Asia and the Pacific*, Retrieved April 22, 2018, from https://data.adb.org/dataset/infrastructure-needs-asia-and-pacific

U.S. Federal Reserve Bank of St. Louis. (2018). *International statistics: Crude birth rate for Thailand*, Retrieved March 26, 2018, from https://fred.stlouisfed.org/series/SPDYNCBRTINTHA

Webster, D., & Theeratham, P. (2004). *Policy coordination, planning and infrastructure provision: A case study of Thailand.* Retrieved April 28, 2018, from http://siteresources.worldbank.org/INTEAPINFRASTRUCT/Resources/855084-1137106254308/Thailand.pdf

World Bank. (2007). *Thailand country profile*. Retrieved April 28, 2009, from https://data.worldbank.org/country/thailand?locale=th

World Bank. (2017). *The world by income: FY 2017*. Retrieved April 28, 2018, from http://databank.worldbank.org/data/download/site-content/wdi/maps/2017/world-by-income-wdi-2017.pdf

World Bank. (2018). *Thailand country profile*. Retrieved April 28, 2018, from https://data.worldbank.org/country/thailand?locale=th

World Bank. (2018). *World bank open data*. Retrieved April 28, 2018, from https://data.worldbank.org/country/thailand?locale=th

ENDNOTES

1 As of May 5, 2018, the Public Debt Management Office (PDMO) Website is not accessible by the public. See http://www.pdmo.go.th/en/news.php?page=5&ipp=10.

2 In 2017, Thailand ranked 96th among 180 countries in a widely-cited measure of corruption with total score of 37 (with an index value of 1 indicating the most theoretically corrupt and 100 indicating no corruption). This rank and number have not changed from those reported in 2012 (Transparency International, 2018, http://www.transparency.org/cpi2016).

3 In Bangkok, Thailand, those who live in suburban areas are middle to low-income, while those with high incomes live in high- rise condominiums the central city during the work week and have weekend homes in the suburbs or ex-urban areas. Thus, those who bear the burden of congestion costs are middle- and low-income households who experience delays in their commutes from suburban areas.

Chapter 11
Capital Management and Budgeting Practices in Republic of Korea

Jiseul Kim
University of Nebraska at Omaha, USA

ABSTRACT

The author aims to provide a comprehensive understanding about the current capital management and budgeting practices (CMBP) in the Republic of Korea (hereafter Korea). The book chapter starts with description of the importance of public capital assets and several issues of the current infrastructure system. It then provides the background of Korea's public infrastructure, political regime, and government institutions. Based on the suggested normative framework, the author specifically describes the four major components of CMBP: capital planning, capital budgeting and financial management, centralized execution and project management, infrastructure maintenance. Following the analysis of the current CMBP practices, some of reform ideas are discussed in the conclusion.

INTRODUCTION

Public capital assets including public infrastructure, buildings, equipment, and land acquisitions are the backbone of economic development. Investment in public infrastructure enhances the economy by increasing job creation (Munnell, 1990b), income growth (Aschauer, 1989), and manufacturing industrial outputs (Deno, 1988). During the last 60 years, Korea experienced rapid economic development by investing in public capital infrastructure such as roads, railroads, ports, airports, oil pipelines, communication systems, water and sewer systems, and dams. According to the World Bank (2018), Gross Domestic Product [GDP] per capita in 2016 was $25,458.90 (in constant 2010 USD), which experienced a 2590 percent increase from 1960 when GDP per capita was $944.30 (in constant 2010 USD). The Organization for Economic Co-operation and Development [OECD] (2016) noted that "by 2012, Korea had become the world's leading shipbuilder and fifth-largest car producer" (p. 15). This remarkable economic growth was accompanied by the government's heavy investments in public infrastructure (see Kim et al., 1999).

DOI: 10.4018/978-1-5225-7329-6.ch011

Even if Korea has experienced dramatic growth, issues remain. For instance, some of the current infrastructure systems are inefficient and ineffective (e.g. construction of new roadways in rural areas where there is not much usage). In addition, infrastructure deterioration rates have rapidly increased. In 2014, 31 percent of water, 38 percent of sewage pipes, and 59 percent of water filtration plants ranked in poor condition. In order to address the current infrastructure issues, understanding the current capital management and budgeting practices is significant. However, there is extremely limited understanding about current practices, and it may be difficult for the Korean government to know where to start.

Based on the suggested normative framework, this book chapter aims to describe the detailed process and related institutions. The chapter first provides a brief historical background of Korea's public infrastructure system, the political regime, government system, inter-governmental relationship, and fiscal structure. Second, Korea's major master plans and strategic plans for public infrastructure at the national and local levels will be identified. Third, the prioritization process, general budgeting process, and major financing strategies will be described. Fourth, the current practice for project management will be reviewed. Fifth, the maintenance planning and asset management system will be discussed, as well as how the maintenance budget is allocated. Then, current practices will be analyzed based on the normatively preferred practices. Several suggestions will be introduced in order to address the current issues.

BACKGROUND

Korea is a small peninsula in East Asia with a population of 51.75 million. According to the National Assembly Budget Office [NABO], capital expenditures were 30 trillion KRW in 2017, which is about 7.49 percent of total expenditures. Capital expenditures include construction costs ranging from designing and planning costs, equipment costs, supervision costs, purchase inventories, land purchase, and capital transfer (e.g. to local government). By 2013, Korea's total paved road length exceeded 87,000 km, which included more than 4,100 km of inter-city expressways. The quality of water and sewer systems has improved by 4.5 percent annually in recent years. By 2015, 5,742 electric vehicle charging infrastructures have been established. Korea has experienced rapid economic growth and industrial development during the last few decades, which has taken it from *developing* to a *high-income* country. The rapid economic expansion has been accompanied by the government's major infrastructure investments.

Korean history started in BC 2333 when Gojoseon was established, yet initial development of Korea's current public infrastructure system dates back to the 1960s. At the end of the Korean War, Korea only had 580 km of paved roads. Since then, the government began to heavily invest in public infrastructure. Under the dictatorship of the former president, Park Chung-hee, the central government constructed railroads, roads, ports, and industrial complexes. In the 1960s, the first major inter-city expressway project was initiated by connecting Seoul, the capital city located in the northwest, to Busan, the second largest city located in the southeast. By 1970, the government had constructed 3,194 km of railways and 40,244 km of roadways. By 1971, the government had constructed 407 km of long-distance oil pipeline from Pohang to Seoul and 100 km from Ulsan to Daegu.

In the 1970s, the main goal of the nation was to maximize economic growth. Accordingly, substantial public infrastructure development was required. For instance, in 1970, the transport volume of maritime trade was 43,305,000 tons (31.6 percent of the total trade), which was estimated to increase to 176,000,000 tons by 1981. During this period, the government constructed and expanded docks in several ports for container ships, three major international and 14 domestic airports, oil pipelines, communication systems, parks, water and sewer systems, dams, public libraries, and public hospitals.

In the 1980s, the main national goal was regionally balanced economic growth. The government promoted the population decentralization policy by constructing and expanding infrastructure in undeveloped regions, while blocking new construction of large-scale projects in Seoul and some of its satellite cities. During this period, the government selected 15 cities around the country as the growth pole cities and allocated resources for improving the regions' roadways. In addition, the government further developed the nations' water and sewer systems in order to improve citizens' quality of life. For example, eight multipurpose dams, and the Geumgang and Nakdonggang estuary dams were constructed.

Along with the tremendously increased size of the economy and rapid urbanization in the 1990s the nation was faced with several major problems, including (1) shortages of transportation systems, (2) insufficient water supply, and (3) low levels of wastewater treatment due to the rapidly increased industrial pollution. In 1990, 1,321 km of inter-city roadways experienced traffic congestion, which resulted in higher logistic costs. In addition, more railroads, ports, and airports were required to satisfy increased transportation needs. Accordingly, the government invested heavily in the national transportation systems by constructing 1,500 km of inter-city expressways, 5,000 km of national and local roadways, express and inter-city railway networks, new airports and several seaports. Also, the government substantially developed local water and sewer systems.

Following the establishment of the Republic in 1948 after 35 years of Japanese colonization (1910-1945), the Korean War began in 1950, which divided the country into two territories: South and North. Korea has been in armistice status since 1953. Since the First Republic in 1948, Korea has experienced dynamic political changes and has moved toward a democratic society with several citizen protests and uprisings. In 1948, the Constitution of the Republic of Korea was adopted. In the 1950s, the first president, Rhee Syn-man, governed the country with a dictatorship. He started to build public infrastructure including schools, roads, and communication networks. In reaction to his dictatorship, in 1960, Korean students protested for democracy and forced the dictator Rhee to resign, which is often called the *April 19 Revolution*.

However, the short democratic regime of the Second Republic was defeated by a military coup led by General Park Chung-hee in 1961, and the Third Republic was established in 1963. During his presidency, he oppressed the media. He initiated the first Comprehensive National Territorial Plan in the 1970s and laid the foundation for the new public infrastructure of Korea. The repressive authoritarian regime led by the dictator Park lasted until 1979 when he was assassinated. In 1980, General Chun Doo-whan took power with his military coup, and student, professor, and labor groups took up arms against the government and sought democratization and human rights; this is called the *May 18 Gwangju Democratic Uprising*. Hundreds of citizens were killed by Chun's military coup during the uprising.

In 1987, Korea initiated constitutional reform in reaction to the massive citizens' protest called *the 6.10 Democracy Movement*, which led to the on-going process of democratization. After Rho Tae-woo's presidency, Korea entered the era of civilian democracy in President Kim Young-sam's regime in 1993. In 1997, Kim Dae-jung won the presidential election, which was the first turnover from a popularly elected government of one party to a different party. In 2003, Roh Moo-hyun, a former human rights lawyer, was elected president. He communicated well with ordinary people and pursued *Participatory Government* by breaking away from the old authoritarian regimes. The former president, Rho focused on sustainable development in many areas including social integration, citizens' health improvement, economic development, and environmental protection.

In 2007, the conservative candidate Lee Myung-bak, an ex-Hyundai construction CEO and former mayor of Seoul (nicknamed *the Bulldozer*), won the presidential election. He proposed pragmatic policies by aiming to improve economic growth. However, with the global economic crisis in 2008, his plans became an illusion, and participatory government dissolved back into tensions. Scholars found that some of his plans such as dredging the nation's rivers to push forward his canal plan against scientific and economic judgment veered quite dangerously towards future crisis (see Doucette, 2010).

The current president Moon Jae-in, of the Democratic Party, was elected in 2017 following the impeachment of the former President Park Geun-hye, the nation's first female president and the daughter of the Cold War military dictator Park Chung-hee. Citizens were outraged by a corruption scandal, and a South Korea court removed her from office. Currently, President Moon pursues reform of Chaebol (family-owned conglomerates) by reducing corporate corruption and improving government transparency. As a part of his policies in 2018, the government introduced the National Participatory Budgeting Institution, which ensures that citizens not only propose budgets, but also participate in the project evaluation and prioritization process.

Korea adopted a presidential system of government in 1948, with the separation of power among the executive, legislature, and judiciary branches. According to the Constitution as of 2018, the president serves a single five-year term and is elected by a nationwide, direct, equal, and secret ballot. The presidential system of Korea incorporates some characteristics of a parliamentary system in that the government has a prime minister and not a vice president, and has a state council, that deliberates on important policies that fall within the power of the executive. According to the Constitution, the president appoints a prime minister and the chair of the Board of Audit and Inspection with the approval of the National Assembly, and appoints cabinet members and ministers with the recommendation of the prime minister.

Korea has a unicameral legislature, and the legislative power is vested in the National Assembly. Members of the National Assembly serve four years. Since there is no appropriation act, the legislature cannot initiate budget increases or introduce new budget items, it only has authority to reduce the budget (Ok, 2015). Also, Korea's president does not have veto authority over the legislature's budget approval. An incumbent member in the National Assembly is able to be appointed as a minister of the executive department and serve concurrent positions. Also, both members of the National Assembly and the executive branch can introduce legislative bills. The legislative bills introduced by the executive branch are often called government bills.

During the authoritarian era (1973-1988), 1,633 bills were introduced, and 65 percent of the bills were driven by the executive branch. Since the democratization of the Korean political system, legislative bills have increased dramatically. From 1988 to 2016, the total number of introduced bills was 17,822. During this period, government bills were only 6 percent of the total with the rest of the bills introduced by the members of the National Assembly. Even though the portion of introduced government bills has decreased dramatically, Namkoong and Kim (2018) stated that "it is common that legislative members of the ruling party introduce bills prepared by the executive branch" (11). In other words, the president of Korea is able to exercise power through the ruling party. The power of presidents has been firmly institutionalized since the beginning of the Republic and through the authoritarian government period from the 1960s to the 1980s. Namkoong and Kim (2018) stated that "strong presidential leadership has been considered inevitable because of the ongoing confrontational circumstances between North and South Korea" (9).

Korea's judiciary branch consists of the Supreme Court, High Courts, District and Branch Courts, and Specialized Courts. Based on the Constitution, all Courts evaluate all legal conflicts. The Chief Justice of the Supreme Court and justices of other Courts are appointed by the president with the consent of the National Assembly, and judges of the Courts are appointed by the Chief justices with the consent of the Council of Supreme Court Justices. The Chief Justice serves a single six-year term, justices can serve multiple six-year term, and judges can serve multiple 10-year terms.

The Constitutional Court of Korea was established in 1988, which addressed legal conflicts including the impeachment of politicians, the dissolution of a political party, the constitutionality of legislation, and safeguarding human rights. Currently, the president appoints nine justices. Three come from nominees of the president, three are elected by the National Assembly, and three come from nominees of the Justice Chief of the Korean Supreme Court. Nine justices serve six-year terms, which can be renewable. The equal composition of the court increases their independency for law interpretation power.

Korea is mainly divided by the central government and the local-self-governments (hereafter local governments). The central government's budget consists of 1 general account, 18 special accounts, and 64 funds as of 2013. The general account is used for maintaining public order and safety, education, housing, social infrastructure, and general government functions. The special accounts are used only for specific projects or other designated areas, and funds are used for specific purposes and operated independently from the budget (The Ministry of Economy and Finance [MOEF], 2014). The main revenue sources of the general account include various taxes (e.g. income taxes and value-added tax) and non-tax revenues (e.g. proceeds from the sale of shares of state-owned enterprises). The special account revenues are collected from special tax revenues (e.g. liquor tax) and non-tax revenues (e.g. charges and loan repayment). Fund revenues come from contributions and charges.

Local governments are made up of 244 general offices including 17 metropolitan units and 227 basic units and 17 educational offices (MOEF, 2014, p. 6). Similar to the central government, the finances of the general offices consist of general accounts, special accounts, and funds. In 1999, the local governments went through the first local elections. Even though the central government initiates many infrastructure projects and provides funds, local governments provide various capital assets including parks, roads, railroads, ports, school, water and sewer systems, and electricity. Despite the central government trying to transfer capital management authority to localities, there is limited budget and finance authority in local governments.

The local government tax system is governed by the central government, and there is no variation in the budget system among the same level of local government. In terms of revenue, local governments depend greatly on the central government, as 41.8 percent of the total local budget in 2013 came from the dependent sources (e.g. subsidy from national treasury), while 34.3 percent came from local taxes, 21.3 percent from non-tax revenues, and 2.6 percent came from local government debt. Some of the local governments (e.g. Seoul Metropolitan City) with higher financial independency may initiate projects and rely on their own sources. However, they are still influenced by the central governments' policy and decisions. The main reason is that local governments are bound by the Local Finance Act in most of their practices. For example, the Local Finance Act states that the Ministry of the Interior and Safety regulates local government bond limits and the issuance process. Thus, if Seoul needs to issue debt over the limit, it needs to discuss it with the MSF.

During the last decade, both central and local governments in Korea adopted a series of innovations in budgeting practices (Son, Kang, Jang, and Choi, 2014). For example, the central government adopted program budgeting in 2007, and local governments implemented it in 2008. Program budgeting contains identification of goals and strategy, analysis of programs and financial plans, the coordination of strategic planning and program accounting, and detailed description of activities. Even though the program budget includes a capital spending category, there is currently no specific guidance to define capital spending. Therefore, governments often include operating spending in the capital spending category and vice versa. This practice may generate a bias in allocating resources. Since the costs for capital projects are relatively larger than other expenditures, officials may cut spending for capital projects during times of fiscal stress, ending up increasing life cycle costs of capital assets.

PUBLIC CAPITAL MANAGEMENT AND BUDGETING PRACTICES

Capital Planning

Master Plans

Since the 1970s, investments in infrastructure assets have been based on national and urban planning. As seen in Figure 1, at the national level, there are two major master plans: the Comprehensive National Territorial Plan [CNTP] and the Seoul Metropolitan Area Readjustment Plan [SMRP]. At the local level, there are three main master plans: the Metropolitan Area Plan [MAP], the City Management Plan [CMP] and the Basic City Plan [BCP]. Detailed descriptions will be made.

The most influential master plan that contributed to the current economic growth, citizens' quality of life, and global competitiveness is the Comprehensive National Territorial Plan [CNTP]. In the 1970s, the government initiated the CNTP to address the nation's urgent infrastructure needs and started to prioritize projects in the longer-term perspective by introducing the 10-Year master plan (1971). CNTPs mainly develop national goals, policies, and territorial development strategies based on economic and other environmental factors. There have been four CNTPs and three modifications since 1971, yet, none of them includes a financial plan for capital projects. The first and second CNTPs contributed to the na-

Figure 1. National and urban planning
Source: Drawn by the author

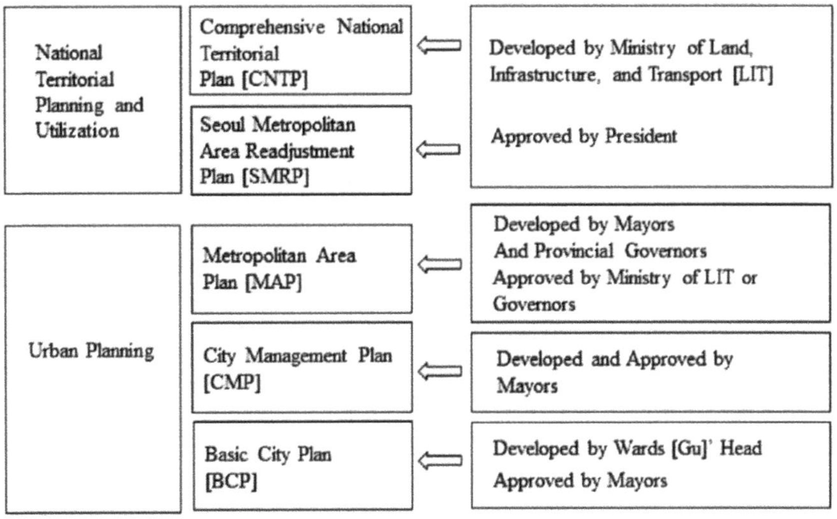

tion's economic growth by constructing infrastructure such as roads, railroads, industrial complexes, and dams, as well as reorganizing urban spatial structure. The third CNTP started to recognize the importance of local development. In the fourth CNTP (2000-2020), government extended the planning period to 20 years and emphasized balanced regional development. During this period, government constructed a new administrative capital in Korea. In the current system, the Ministry of Land, Infrastructure, and Transport [LIT] develops the CNTP by organizing the requests from the central government, local governments, research institutions, and experts, which is then approved by the president.

The Seoul Metropolitan Area Readjustment Plan [SMRP] is a 15-year master plan developed by LIT. The first SMRP (1982-1996) was developed when the nation experienced a rapid population concentration phenomenon in the Seoul Metropolitan area. The 15-year SMRP had to address the nation's goals for regionally balanced economic growth and population decentralization policy. Accordingly, the SMRP developed such strategies as constructing an inter-regional transportation system, constructing subway and railways in the area, improving water and sewer systems in the area, and constructing industrial building and facilities outside of the area. Since then, two more SMRPs have been developed. The current SMRP (2006-2020) has four main goals for the Seoul Metropolitan area: enhancing high quality of life, global competitiveness, infrastructure for sustainable development, and balanced development with local governments. The SMRP aims to address the current problems and suggests strategies to develop infrastructure to meet the goals.

The Metropolitan Area Plan [MAP] is a 20-year master plan, which provides goals and strategies for development in two or more jurisdictions. MAPs can be developed by mayors and provincial governors when two or more cities or counties have shared plans for long-term development. If the scope of the plan lies within a state, the governor should approve the plan. If it is beyond one state, the plan should be approved by the minister of LIT or governors. Local governments develop the City Management Plan and the Basic City Plan for their own master plans, which are generally coordinated with the upper government goals. Since 2005, CMP and BCP have been approved by governors, which facilitated decentralization in urban planning of Korean local governments.

Preliminary Feasibility Study

The Preliminary Feasibility Study [PFS] was introduced in 1999 in order to improve efficient allocation of resources for publicly financed projects. According to the National Finance Act, Article 38, total project costs should be as at least 50 billion KRW, and government contribution toward the investment should be at least 30 billion KRW. Projects include construction projects initiated by the central and local governments and private entities as well as other projects such as information, R&D, social welfare, and education. There is no specific PFS institution at the local level; local governments submit project requests to agencies and departments of the central government if the projects need subsidies from the central government and meet the criteria suggested by the National Finance Act, Article 38.

Based on the general guideline, Korea Development Institute [KDI] is in charge of conducting the entire process of PFS and examines efficiency and appropriateness of a project. Accordingly, KDI conducts various analyses including economic analysis (e.g. benefit-costs analysis, sensitivity analysis, financial analysis, demand analysis, technical review), policy analysis (e.g. risk analysis, financial feasibility analysis, coordinating with policy goals, environmental effect evaluation), and regional balanced devolvement analysis (e.g. regional economic effects, under-development index). In 2001, the government introduced the Analytic Hierarchy Process [AHP] analysis technique, which is a comprehensive evaluation technique. If AHP is more than 0.5, projects are considered to be valid. As seen in Table 1, 631 projects were examined from years 1999 to 2015. The Preliminary Feasibility Study primarily focuses on economic and policy adequateness as well as technical viability.

National Budget Operational Plan

The National Budget Operational Plan [NBOP] was introduced in 2004 to provide budget goals and strategies in the mid-term perspective. This plan provides financial management evaluation for the previous years, and mid-term investment plans based on policy, financial, and performance goals. It also suggests the expected performance or outcome after the five-year investment. The plan is developed based on each ministry and agency's Mid-term Program Plan. In addition, various actors including citizens, experts and interest groups can participate in the public debate for developing the NBOP, then the Ministry of Economy and Finance develops and updates a plan each year.

Mid-Term Local Financial Plans

In 1988, the Mid-term Local Financial Plan [MLFP] was introduced due to the realization that local budget allocation does not fully address the national goals and plans. These plans are required to be coordinated with national and local plans and have been updated annually since 1993, and they have been recommended to be coordinated with local governments' program budgets since 1997. According to the current guideline (2018-2022) developed by the Ministry of the Interior and Safety [MIS], MLFP is a 5- year plan, which should reflect a local government's vision and policy priorities as well as develop resource allocation strategies by forecasting their revenues and expenditure flows. It also identifies projects that require the Investment Appraisal and local debt and provides an understanding about consolidated budget balance. All local governments should submit these plans to MIS along with their budgets, which enables the Minister of MIS to develop a comprehensive plan.

Investment Appraisal

According to the Local Finance Act, Article 37, a head of a local government shall conduct the Investment Appraisal for budget bills on finance investment projects, which require creating debts or other burdens in addition to budgets. Projects that undergo the Preliminary Feasibility Study can be exempt from the Investment Appraisal. There are several purposes of institutionalization of the Investment Appraisal (Son et al., 2008). It aims to improve efficient and effective investment for public projects given limited resources. Moreover, it aims to prioritize projects based on several analyses and coordination with other plans. In order to achieve rational and feasible analyses, an evaluation department is required

Table 1. Number of projects in preliminary feasibility study

Year	99'	00'	01'	02'	03'	04'	05'	06'	07'	08'	09'	10'	11'	12'	13'	14'	15'	Total
Projects	20	30	41	30	32	55	30	32	46	38	63	48	43	35	13	36	19	631
Source: KDI																		

to use several analytic techniques including operation research, systems analysis, cost-benefit analysis, simple cost analysis, cost-goal analysis, cost-constraint analysis, cost-effectiveness analysis, and financial analysis. Based on the analyses and the recommendations from the investment appraisal committees, the head of the local government decides which projects to fund, and local debt can be issued.

The Ministry of the Interior and Safety determines debt Affordability. In 2006, a local debt issuance limitation was adopted. According to the Local Finance Act, MIS shall determine the local debt limit every year based on debt service obligations, debt service schedules, and financial capacity. Also, MIS uses a benchmark by setting a different percentage of debt issuance eligibility depending on the level of local governments and their population size. As long as the total debt issuance amount of a local government does not go over the limit set by MIS, the local government can issue debt with local council approval. If the total debt amount would be go over the debt limit, the local government shall request their debt issuance and get approval from MIS.

Capital Budgeting and Financial Management

Project Prioritization and Selection Process

The Preliminary Feasibility Study [PFS] is a critical nationwide institution for prioritization of financing large new public infrastructure construction. As seen in Figure 2, the head of each agency selects projects and prioritizes them based on the Ministry of Economy and Finance [MOEF]'s project guidelines, the National Budget Operation Plans [NBOP], and master plans. Once they receive project requests, MOEF has authority to prioritize and select projects. In order to make rational decisions, Korea Development Institute [KDI] conducts comprehensive analyses for each requested project. Depending on the type

Figure 2. Project selection process
Source: Drawn by the author based on KDI website

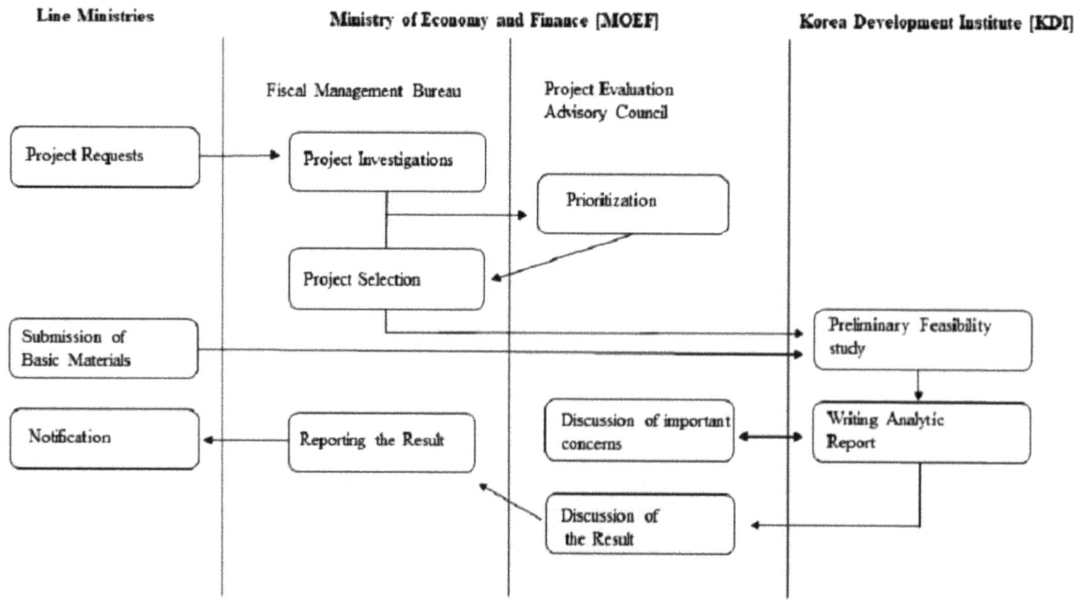

of project, the analyses can be analyzed in the mid-term or the long-term perspective. After analyzing each project, KDI scores projects. In this process, KDI receives various opinions from academia, citizen experts, and other research institutions, and considers them in the analytic report. Based on the report, MOEF selects projects and notifies heads of agencies.

Budgeting Process

Figure 3 illustrates the budgeting process of the central government. Projects are typically selected two years prior to the budget implementation year (*t*-2). One year prior to the budget implementation year (*t*-1), the budget is prepared by MOEF and adopted by the General Assembly. By January 31, ministries and agencies submit a Mid-term Program Plan [MPP] to MOEF. MPP is a five-year investment plan for new projects and major existing projects with clarifying performance goals and annual spending strategies. The plan is developed based on each department or agency's program but does not separate capital spending from maintenance spending in the life-cycle approach. Based on MPPs, MOEF develops 5-year National Budget Operational Plans [NBOP] from June to August and submits them to the General Assembly by September 3. The NBOP is very descriptive and only provides an aggregated expected investment level and outcomes in each sector. Thus, it is technically unclear how the budget is actually allocated and how it improves outcomes.

After the cabinet meeting and the President's approval for the Mid-term Program Plans, MOEF provides ministries and agencies a guideline for the next year's budget and expenditure limit by March 31. Ministries and agencies then submit budget requests to MOEF by May 31. By September 3, MOEF develops the next year's budget and submits it to the National Assembly for budget deliberation. Government funds are comprised of a general account, special account, and fund account, and the budget is mainly classified by organization, function and economic category. Korea does not have a separate

Figure 3. Budgeting process
Source: Drawn by the author

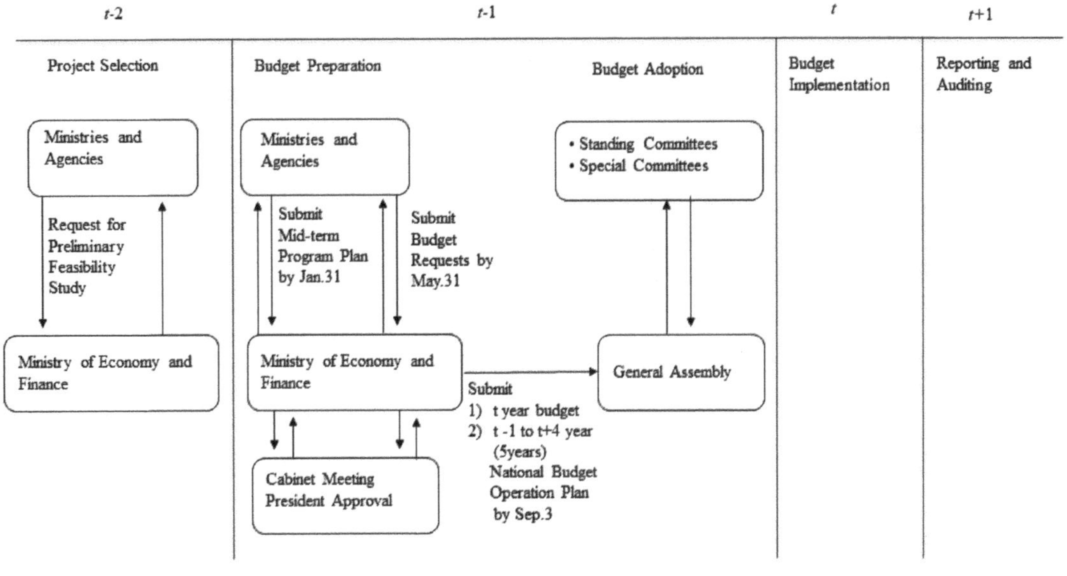

capital budget at the central or local levels. The expenditure budget specifies 7 economic categories including capital spending and several line-items lie under the capital spending category including land purchases, construction costs, tangible and intangible assets' acquisition, borrowing costs, investment payments, and security purchases.

In the budget adoption process, there are sequential activities: (1) government delivers administrative policy speech, (2) standing committees conduct preliminary evaluation, (3) special committees finalize budget evaluation, and (4) the finalized budget goes through the deliberation and approval process in a plenary session of the General Assembly. After the budget adoption and the President's approval, MOEF allocates the budget to each ministry and agency, which is then implemented in t period. In the $t+1$ period, national financial statements are developed by MOEF, audited by the Board of Audit and Inspection, and submitted to the General Assembly for deliberation and approval.

Similar to the central government, local governments develop the Mid-term Local Financial Plan. Departments in a local government then develop project plans, and request technological evaluation and the Investment Appraisal from the responsible departments. Based on the analyses and the recommendations from the Investment Appraisal committees, the head of the local government decides which projects get funded. The results of the investment decision are submitted to the budget department, and local debt is issued. In this process, MIS provides guidelines about MLFP to local governments and receives the comprehensive local plans from them. MIS not only participates in the IA process by evaluating and approving plans for issuing local government bonds, but also sets the local government bond limits.

The Local Finance Act guides local governments' budgets. Based on MIS's guideline and standards, local governments develop their budget and get budget approval from local councils. The budget is mainly structured by functions and by categories. Functions include general administration, public safety, education, culture and tourism, social welfare, industry, transportation, territorial and regional development, environment protection, healthcare, science, agriculture, forestry, and maritime, etc. Budget classification includes 8 categories, one of which is capital expenditure.

Financing Strategy for Public Infrastructure

There are four major funding mechanisms for public infrastructure: government budget, earmarked revenue, debt, and private investments. The government budget is allocated to construct, improve, and maintain public infrastructure, which is based on budget pools from the general account, special account, and fund account. For example, one of the 2018 national budget goals is improving economic productivity by constructing roads and railroads, and the industrial complex (NABO, 2018). In order to address the national goal, various infrastructure projects that underwent PFS are funded by the government budget. Also, the government budget for maintaining infrastructure can be allocated, which is not included in PFS. In 2018, 57 billion KRW is included in the national budget for deteriorating urban railroads in Seoul and Busan.

Some of the earmarked revenues go to specific public infrastructure. At the national level, a person who produces and/or imports gasoline oil and similar alternative oil should pay 475 won/ ℓ in *Transportation, Energy, Environment Tax*, and a person who produces and/or imports diesel oil and similar alternative oil should pay 340 won/ ℓ (MOEF, 2015). These taxes are mostly used for road construction and improvement. At the local level, some taxes for specific buildings like theaters and department stores are collected through *Community Resource and Facility Tax* and used specifically for public assets such as fire protection facilities and sanitation facilities.

Issuing debt is one important financing strategy for public assets of local governments. Generally, the purpose of the central government's debt is to stabilize the economy. The central government mainly relies on government bonds (e.g. Korea Treasury Bonds, National Housing Bond, and Foreign Exchange Equalization Fund Bonds) and special bonds (e.g. Monetary Stabilization Bond issued by Bank of Korea and bank bonds). On the other hand, local debt is mainly issued for financing public infrastructure such as subway, roads, and water and sewer systems.

According to the MIS (2017)'s report, local government debt was 26.42 trillion won as of 2016: 68.25 percent came from municipal bonds (46.5 percent from industrial development bonds and 21.7 percent from subway construction bonds), 13.4 percent came from bank bonds, and 22 percent came from borrowing from the central and private banks. Local government debt is generally paid back through local government taxes and non-tax revenues from the general and special accounts.

Finally, public-private partnership (P3) has become an important financing strategy for public infrastructure such as roads, ports, railroads, school facilities, and environmental facilities. Both the central and local governments have signed P3 agreements for public infrastructure projects. In August 1994, the government enacted the Promotion of Private Capital into Social Overhead Capital Investment Act. There are four principles for selecting projects with private capital. First, projects should provide quality of services to citizens who are willing to pay user fees. Second, projects should have positive return on investment given the limited government subsidies. Third, projects are expected to be constructed in a targeted period and generate revenues in the early years of the life cycle. Fourth, projects are expected to have higher efficiency and effectiveness compared to government construction. P3 projects do not need to undergo the Preliminary Feasibility Study because P3 and PFS are developed based on separate laws. While PFS should disclose all evaluation results, the capital investment act does not allow disclosure of some private investors' information. Thus, P3 project plans are separately evaluated by government.

Major types of P3 in Korea are Build-Transfer-Own [BTO] and Build-Transfer-Lease [BTL]. Until 2016, 702 projects had been constructed and operated through P3; 231 projects were through BTO, and 471 projects were through BTL. Generally, projects that can charge service fees to users are financed through BTO, while projects that cannot charge fees are financed through BTL. BTO projects include roads, railroads, and ports, and BTL projects include school facilities, military housing, sewer system, and cultural and welfare facilities. As of 2017, 16 inter-city expressways are operated by private parties, 5 speed roadways are under construction, and 2 inter-city expressways are in planning for construction through private parties.

Centralized Execution and Project Management

Total Project Cost Management

Korea has adopted Total Project Cost Management [TPCM]. The aim of TPCM is to improve financial efficiency by managing total project cost in every stage. The National Finance Act defines public projects that undergo TPCM as ones that take two or more years to complete, and the total project costs should be more than 50 billion KRW. Also, government contribution to the investment should be at least 30 billion KRW. The Minister of MOEF develops a guideline for TPCM and provides it to heads of ministries and agencies. Based on the MOEF's guideline, each ministry and agency should evaluate infrastructure projects (e.g. a project scale, the total project cost, and a construction period) in every phase of infrastructure development. However, TPCM does not include the cost items related to operation, maintenance, or simple improvement of the projects. In addition, some projects do not undergo TPCM, including P3 projects and projects supported by the national treasury's debt or a pre-determined fixed budget. In 2017, 856 projects were evaluated under TPCM, which was almost double the size in the year 2000 when 483 projects were evaluated.

KDI is in charge of managing the total project cost of public infrastructure assets. There are four ways to conduct TPCM. First, based on the MOEF's guideline, some projects are selected for Feasibility Re-evaluation [FR]. FR is generally conducted when the total project cost of the project is perceived to be increased. FR aims to prevent project cost overruns and to find efficient alternatives to manage the projects. If projects are not feasible, projects may be stopped or delayed. Second, other projects that do not undergo FR are also evaluated based on MOEF's guideline. The evaluation is similar to but simpler than FR. Third, demand estimation is re-evaluated in every phase of infrastructure development, ensuring feasible construction and operation. Fourth, a project's feasibility is re-examined when a department or agency requests a project design change and/or to increase the level of total project cost after asset construction has started.

Infrastructure Maintenance

Maintenance Planning

Since 2003, the Ministry of Land, Infrastructure, and Transport [MLIT] has developed a five-year long Basic Plan of the Safety and Maintenance for Infrastructure [BPSM], which is a national plan of public infrastructure facilities maintenance for the central and local governments and private parties that construct and manage the infrastructure facilities. In order to obtain accurate information for infrastructure facilities, the Minister of MLIT coordinates with heads of each agency and ministry and reflects their evaluation in developing the BPSM. The document has been updated every five years, and there have been four reports for BPSM so far. The BPSM identifies five-year long government visions and policy goals for facilities' safety and maintenance, performance measures and strategies to attain the identified visions and goals, and annual operating schedules. It also shows several other analyses including mega trends of the society, current issues of infrastructure deterioration and safety, environmental characteristics, and evaluation of the previous plan.

For instance, the fourth BPSM (2018-2022) evaluates the third BPSM (2013-2017) by suggesting that two of the three goals were attained: no accidents in the first and the second types of infrastructure facilities and maintaining 95 percent safety level for the first and the second types of infrastructure. However, the report suggested that one goal, lowering citizens' dissatisfaction level about facilities safety by 5 percent, was not attained because citizens experienced several crises from the third type facilities, such as the Sewol Ferry Disaster in 2014, and the fracture of a part of the Jeongneungcheon high-level road in 2016. The Sewol Ferry sank on April 16, 2014 and 304 passengers and crewmembers died in the disaster. Yet, there is still no clue as to why it happened. The Jeongneungcheon high-level road connects Majangdong to the Dongbu arterial highway, which was completed in 1998: one of the tendons was fractured due to internal deterioration, and the road was blocked from use for about a month.

As a result, the fourth BPSM (2018-2022) contains a vision, establishing sustainable facilities management for responding to future needs, and generates four major goals: 1) improving facilities with longer life and safety, 2) *smart facilities* with advanced technologies such as Internet of things [IoT], big data, artificial intelligence [AI] and drones, 3) facilities that can improve economic growth, and 4) facilities that provide trust to citizens. Performance measures include 1) safety grades for the first and the second types of facilities should be at least 95 percent and regular checkups for the third type should be more than 90 percent, 2) budgets for advanced technologies for maintaining facilities should be increased by more than 20 percent, 3) new employees with advanced knowledge in technologies should be increased by 10 percent, and 4) increasing citizens' satisfaction about facilities safety by 10 percent.

Maintenance Funding

When departments submit budget requests, they may request a maintenance budget to MOEF. According to the National Finance Act, maintenance expenditures should not be included in the Preliminary Feasibility Study. Maintenance expenditures are allocated through the general budgeting process, meaning the maintenance funding sources come from government revenues (e.g. income taxes) and compete with other operating budget items. The 2018 national budget report does not provide a detailed maintenance budget allocation process, yet it reveals that some departments receive estimated lump-sum budgets for asset operation and maintenance.

There are two departments—MLIT and the Ministry of Oceans and Fisheries [MOF]— that receive lump-sum operation and maintenance budgets for public infrastructure. Two other departments—the Ministry of Agriculture, Food, and Rural Affairs and Cultural Heritage Administration — receive estimated lump-sum budgets for water facilities' improvement and cultural properties' maintenance. As seen in Table 2, for example, MLIT was budgeted 561.5 billion KRW in 2018, which is about a 66.6 percent increase from 2014. Interestingly, MOF's maintenance budget in 2018 experienced about a 50 percent decrease since 2014. MLIT and MOF have discretion to allocate this fund as long as it meets the broad budget descriptions.

Asset Management

In 1994, the Sungsoo Bridge, built in 1979, collapsed as a result of shoddy construction. In reaction to the catastrophe, Korea enacted the Facility Safety Special Law in 1995, which requires infrastructure managing entities (including the central and local governments and private entities) to periodically examine the safety of infrastructure assets. It also emphasizes constant maintenance and improvement based on the established infrastructure performance levels. Performance evaluation can be done through the Korea Institute of Facilities Safety or other safety evaluation organizations based on the decision of the managing entity, which is reported to the Minister of MLIT. Managing entities generally cover all expenses of performance evaluation of the infrastructure facilities, and they can request the budget to the MOEF (Table 2).

The Korean government has a centralized information system for infrastructure facilities. As an affiliated organization of MLIT, in 1995, the Korea Infrastructure Safety Corporation [KISC] was established and takes charge of managing the asset management system. KISC operates the information system, which includes management plans, facility designs, regular checkups, safety reports, performance reports, etc. They also develop performance measures and ensure that national major infrastructure facilities meet the pre-determined performance goals as well as disclosing the information to the public. Managing entities evaluate infrastructure asset performance based on the guidelines. Based on the performance information, MLIT develops upcoming maintenance plans.

Table 2. Capital spending

Unit: One Billion KRW	2014		2015		2016		2017	2018
	Budget	Actual	Budget	Actual	Budget	Actual	Budget	Budget
MLIT								
Road operation and maintenance	337.0	324.5	477.6	453.2	502.1	501.4	517.5	561.5
MOF								
Port operation and maintenance	64.5	61.6	64.0	55.1	60.8	50.8	50.0	32.5
Data from Analysis on 2018 Budget								

ANALYSIS

The normative framework suggests four main components: long-term capital planning, capital budgeting, financial management execution and project management, and infrastructure maintenance.

Capital Planning

Specifically, strategic and comprehensive long-term planning is recommended to promote efficient investment as it 1) strategizes capital management practices, 2) provides a multi-year investment time-frame, and 3) prevents unexpected budget cuts for the projects. The central and local governments have several long-term master plans including CNTP, SMRP, MAP, CMP, and/or BCP. These comprehensive plans identify policy goals and strategies as well as analyze socioeconomic and environmental characteristics in the multi-year perspectives. Also, there are two strategic planning institutions: the Preliminary Feasibility Study and the Investment Appraisal. At the national level, the current PFS is helpful to evaluate investment needs and cost effectiveness, as well as to prioritize projects by linking the nation's master plans. At the local level, IA is useful to examine efficiency and effectiveness of investment for public projects, as well as to prioritize projects by coordinating with MLFP and NBOP. Many analytic techniques such as forecasting and cost-benefit analysis have been utilized for rational decision-making.

However, there are still limitations in the current system, in that it is less clear how the existing projects are coordinated with the new project selection process. Feasibility Re-evaluation enables examination of the current projects, yet its purpose is to meet the Total Project Cost Management requirement and improve fiscal efficiency. Also, none of the plans identifies specific capital expenditure needs and strategizes financing methods for this purpose. It would be useful for governments to adopt a Capital Improvement Program [CIP] by incorporating long-term strategic financial plans with physical plans. In order to establish the effective system of a CIP, the government needs to change the current budgeting process by differentiating the capital budget from the current program budget. That way, the government can clarify financing strategies for specific capital uses. In addition, in the planning process, it may be useful to have a mechanism to discern whether investing in new projects is more beneficial than investing in the existing stock given that significant amounts of the current public infrastructure of Korea are outdated.

Capital Budgeting and Financial Management

According to the normative recommendation, governments are advised to have a solid prioritization process in the budgeting process and have prudent fiscal and debt management. Korea has a well-constructed project prioritization process through PFS at the national level and IA at the local level. PFS uses various rational analytic techniques to understand economic and policy adequacy and technical viability. PFS utilizes several analytic tools including but not limited to forecasting revenues and expenditures, b/c analysis, sensitivity analysis, demand analysis, risk analysis, financial feasibility analysis, environmental effect evaluation, and regional economic effects analysis. Overall feasibility is then examined using the Analytic Hierarchy Process [AHP] analysis technique.

However, there is a possibility that politics may affect the project selection process. For example, in order to initiate the four-river projects, in 2009, the former president Lee Myung-bak changed the enforcement ordinance for PFS in the National Finance Act by adding the word, *prevention.* By doing so, the core four-river projects, such as constructing 16 beams, didn't need to undergo PFS and were able to be immediately funded by the central government. The project selection process is problematic as it did not go through the typical PFS and other potential urgent projects were not able to be considered for the use of limited government resources. Ultimately, this raises a question of democratic and accountable decision- making for public capital assets (see the U.S. local case suggested by Ebdon and Landow, 2012).

At the local level, a government develops the Mid-term Local Financial Plan, which provides revenue and expenditure forecasting. Using the information, various proposed projects are evaluated and prioritized through IA. IA also utilizes various techniques including but not limited to systems analysis, cost-benefit analysis, and financial analysis. Based on the analyses and the recommendations from the investment appraisal committees, projects are selected and local debt is issued. In this process, however, local governments are significantly affected by the central government's decision.

The current system does not separate capital budgets from the operating budgets, rather the budget is allocated for programs. Thus, it is very difficult to identify the exact capital and maintenance needs and their funding sources. Korea needs to consider adopting a capital budget institution to allocate and manage resources for capital projects that last more than one year (Marlowe, Rivenbark, and Vogt, 2009). In this process, government can strategize efficient and effective funding strategies by determining the optimal mixture of resources including pay-as-you-go and debt financing. Many argue that strategic capital management and budgeting practices are crucial for effective and efficient resource allocation given limited government resources (e.g. Ebdon 2001, 2003, 2004, 2007, Ermasova, 2013; Kim and Ebdon, 2017, Marlowe, 2013; Pagano, 1984; Srithongrung, 2008, 2010a, 2010b, 2012, Yusuf and Jordan, 2018).

Large capital projects usually have a longer service life, meaning future taxpayers can also enjoy the infrastructure. In this sense, debt financing ensures cost distribution between generations and stabilizes the current tax rates. Thus, a separate consideration for capital budgets can enhance intergenerational equity by using debt financing and imposing debt costs for future taxpayers (Mikesell, 2003). However, it would be very difficult to have a capital budget for the central government as national debt is generally used for fiscal stabilization reasons. It may be more appropriate that local governments of Korea adopt the institution as debt is only used for financing public infrastructure.

Project Management

As suggested by normative recommendation, Korea has a centralized system for evaluating the feasibility of projects to prevent cost overruns and improve efficient budget allocation. Centralized project management is known to increase government accountability, capital program effectiveness, and funding efficiency. However, there is little information about 1) mechanisms of monitoring process and internal reports, 2) frequency of monitoring and reports, 3) how to track the use of funds, and 4) how the capital assets that are less than 50 billion won are managed. In order to understand the detailed practices, case studies through interviews and surveys would be recommended.

Infrastructure Maintenance

Normative recommendations suggest having both maintenance planning and maintenance funding. At the national level, Korea has developed a Basic Plan of the Safety and Maintenance for Infrastructure, which is a multi-year plan of public infrastructure facilities maintenance for entities that construct and manage the infrastructure facilities. The plan has identified performance measures and promoted an asset management system by addressing national policy goals. Yet, performance measures for infrastructure condition should be enhanced as the current measures merely reflect the years that public infrastructure has been used.

For example, 4.02 percent of major public infrastructure (e.g. bridges, tunnels, dams, buildings, and water and sewer systems) exceeded 30 years of life as of 2015. Depending on who uses the facilities, how the facilities are used, and other environmental factors, the level of deterioration can differ (see Ostrom Schroeder, and Wynne, 1993). Thus, more accurate investigation of the current infrastructure condition may be necessary in order to make an appropriate plan for asset maintenance. In addition, it is critical to improve current planning by incorporating a life cycle cost perspective, which enables an understanding of when to allocate maintenance budgets to maximize assets' useful life and minimize the total life-cycle costs.

Also, there need to be funding mechanisms for asset maintenance. Maintenance activities are invisible and easy to delay, as they do not bring an immediate outcome (Jimenez and Pagano, 2012). For example, the deteriorated water system of Korea covered more than 30,000 km and the cost from water leakage of 60 million tons every year was estimated at $420 million. Yet, the Ministry of Environment delayed maintenance activities due to the invisible characteristics of leakage (Chung et al., 2006). The problem is that delayed maintenance can result in significant infrastructure catastrophes. In order to prevent such infrastructure catastrophe, adequate maintenance practices are desirable.

Currently, both the central and local governments have reserve funds or rainy-day funds, from setting aside 1 percent of the budget. However, these funds are not specifically used for maintenance but for all government activities. Also, the central government allocates lump-sum budgets for operation and maintenance spending, yet they are only for two major ministries: MLIT and MOF. There is lack of evidence about how the limited maintenance funds are prioritized. Having specific funding mechanisms for asset maintenance may improve asset condition by improving maintenance resource allocation, hence preventing potential infrastructure crises. Kim, Chen, and Ebdon (2018) found that state highway maintenance spending had a mediating effect on improving state highway condition in the U.S. context. Also, a more thorough process for asset maintenance prioritization could be helpful for adequate resource allocation. It may be helpful to have an institution to determine the efficiency and effectiveness of investing in either existing assets or new assets. Further research should be conducted in this area.

CONCLUSION

This chapter describes the comprehensive capital management and budgeting practices in Korea for the first time. This chapter aims to provide the overall picture of capital management and budgeting practices in Korea. Data was mostly from various government reports, which are accessible on government websites. Based on the accessible information, the author was able to analyze the current practices in Korea.

This chapter suggests that Korea has implemented various good institutions for CMBP including 1) master, strategic, and fiscal plans, 2) rational evaluation tools for project selection, 3) various realistic financing strategies, 4) centralized cost management, and 5) centralized maintenance planning and asset management systems. However, there are still several limitations in the current CMBP. First, there is no CIP and a separate capital budget in the current budgeting process. Second, politics may affect the rational decision-making process. Third, there is limited information about detailed practices of project management. Fourth, there is lack of understanding about asset maintenance in the life cycle cost perspective, so that preventive maintenance may not be prioritized. Fifth, there is lack of evidence about how the maintenance budget is allocated.

In order to prevent current issues of inefficient and ineffective resource allocation, deteriorating infrastructure, and their negative impact on society, several institutional reforms should be thoroughly considered and implemented. First, local governments are encouraged to introduce a CIP along with a separate capital budget in the budget allocation process, which could strategize financing and physical plans and potentially improve inter-generational equity. Second, government can improve integrated information about monitoring, fund tracking, and internal reporting for all capital assets. Third, more thorough and well-measured information for asset condition and life cycle costs should be developed. Fourth, maintenance funding mechanisms for asset maintenance should be introduced in order to improve preventive maintenance and reduce life-cycle cost, as well as improve asset conditions. These institutions may help to determine whether government should invest in new projects or existing projects given limited budgets. Also, they will help to optimize financing strategy by minimizing life-cycle costs.

Fundamentally, the absence of an Appropriation Act may cause inefficiency and ineffectiveness in budget allocation, as it may not link budgeting with outcomes. However, policy implementation is a complex process and there may be other numerous factors affecting the chain of causality (Pressman and Wildavsky, 1973). In the current system, detailed descriptions for budgeting have not been legalized, and the budget only shows revenue and expenditure items with aggregated amounts (Ok, 2015). It is also unclear how budgets are implemented. Along with several capital management and budgeting institutions suggested in this chapter, fundamental institutional aspects such as the adoption of an Appropriation Act may need to be thoroughly examined in further research.

REFERENCES

Aschauer, D. A. (1989). Is public expenditure productive? *Journal of Monetary Economics, 23*(2), 177–200. doi:10.1016/0304-3932(89)90047-0

Chung, S., Hong, T., Han, S., Son, J., & Lee, S. (2006). Life cycle cost analysis based optimal maintenance and rehabilitation for underground infrastructure management. *KSCE Journal of Civil Engineering, 10*(4), 243–253. doi:10.1007/BF02830778

Deno, K. T. (1988). The effect of public capital on U.S. manufacturing activity: 1970 to 1978. *Southern Economic Journal, 55*(1), 400–411. doi:10.2307/1059112

Doucette, J. (2010). The terminal crisis of the "Participatory Government" and the election of Lee Myung-Bak. *Journal of Contemporary Asia, 40*(1), 22–43. doi:10.1080/00472330903270338

Ebdon, C. (2001). *Capital planning in the states: Internal decision-making. Learning Paper Series.* Retrieved July 23, 2018, from www.maxwell.syr.edu/gpp/pdfs/CM_State_Learning_Paper.pdf

Ebdon, C. (2003). Capital management. In K. Alan (Ed.), *Paths to performance in state and local government: Final report from the Maxwell School* (pp. 71–100). Syracuse, NY: Syracuse University, Campbell Public Affairs Institute.

Ebdon, C. (2004). Capital management practices in U.S. counties. *Public Works Management & Policy, 8*(3), 192–202. doi:10.1177/1087724X03259604

Ebdon, C. (2007). Underpinning government: Capital and infrastructure management in state and local government. In P. Ingraham (Ed.), *In pursuit of performance; Management systems in local government* (pp. 57–81). Baltimore, MD: The Johns Hopkins University Press.

Ebdon, C., & Landow, P. (2012). The Balancing Act: Using private money for public projects. *Public Budgeting & Finance, 32*(1), 58–79. doi:10.1111/j.1540-5850.2011.01002.x

Ermasova, N. (2013). The improvement of capital budgeting at the State level in the USA. *Public Administration Review, 2*(2), 92–104.

Ha, Y. (2010). *Public budgeting & financial management.* Seoul, South Korea: Dasan Publisher. (in Korean)

Jimenez, B. S., & Pagano, M. A. (2012). What factors affect management quality? State infrastructure management and the government performance project. *Public Works Management & Policy, 17*(2), 124–151. doi:10.1177/1087724X11419308

Kim, J., Chen, C., & Ebdon, C. (2018). Effects of the GASB no. 34 infrastructure reporting standards on state highway infrastructure quality: A panel data analysis. *Journal of Public Budgeting, Accounting & Financial Management, 30*(2), 1–24.

Kim, J., & Ebdon, C. (2017). Have the GASB no.34 infrastructure reporting requirements affected state highway spending? *Journal of Public Budgeting, Accounting & Financial Management, 29*(3), 347–374.

Kim, S., Koo, J., & Lee, Y. (1999). Infrastructure and production efficiency: An analysis on the Korean manufacturing industry. *Contemporary Economic Policy*, *17*(3), 390–400. doi:10.1111/j.1465-7287.1999.tb00691.x

Marlowe, J. (2013). Strategy, priority-setting, and municipal capital budget reform: Three cases from the great recession. *Journal of Public Budgeting, Accounting and Financial Management*, *25*(4), 693–718.

Marlowe, J., Rivenbark, W. C., & Vogt, A. J. (2009). *Capital budgeting and finance: A guide for local governments* (2nd ed.). Washington, DC: ICMA Press.

Mikesell, J. (2003). *Fiscal administration: Analysis and applications for the public sector*. Boston, MA: Cengage Learning.

Ministry of Economy and Finance [MOEF]. (2014). *The budget system of Korea*. Retrieved July 23, 2018, from http://english.mosf.go.kr/images/TheBudgetSystemofKorea.pdf

Ministry of Economy and Finance [MOEF]. (2015). *A guide to Korea taxation*. Author.

Ministry of the Interior and Safety. (2017). *Local government debts*. Retrieved July 23, 2018 from http://lofin.mois.go.kr/portal/bbs/bbsDetail.do?listSubCd=FSL432&bbsCd=FSL1004&subCd=FSL432&code=fsl&leftCd=1&currPage=1&ansTag=N&seq=54101&searchWd=

Munnell, A. H. (1990b). How does public infrastructure affect regional economic performance? In A. Munnell (Ed.), *Is there a shortfall in public capital investment? Proceedings of a conference* (pp. 69-103). Boston, MA: Federal Reserve Bank of Boston.

Namkoong, K., & Kim, I. (2018). Foundation of public administration and policy in South Korea. In K. Namkoong, K. Cho, & S. Kim (Eds.), *Public administration and policy in Korea: Its evolution and challenges*. Paris: OECD publishing.

National Assembly Budget Office. (2018). *Analysis on 2018 Budget*. Retrieved July 23, 2018, from http://korea.nabo.go.kr/eng/publications.do?psStep=view&psPage=3&shSearch=&shKeyword=&shDivisionCD=&shPubYear=&shPubCD=pubRecent&pubSID=910

Ok, D. (2015). Toward fiscal democracy: Power structure and budgeting system. Seoul, South Korea: 21Century Books Publication. (in Korean)

Ostrom, E., Schroeder, L., & Wynne, S. (1993). *Institutional incentives and sustainable development: Infrastructure policies in perspective (Theoretical lenses on public policy)*. Boulder, CO: Westview Press.

Pagano, M. A. (1984). Notes on capital budgeting. *Public Budgeting & Finance*, *4*(3), 31–40. doi:10.1111/1540-5850.00648

Pressman, J. L., & Wildavsky, A. (1984). *Implementation*. Berkeley, CA: University of California Press.

Son, H., Kang, I., Jang, N., & Choi, G. (2014). Local budgeting system (4th ed.). Seoul, South Korea: Daeyoung Cultural Publication. (in Korean)

Srithongrung, A. (2008). The impacts of state capital management programs on state economic performance: An empirical analysis. *Public Budgeting & Finance*, *28*(3), 83–107. doi:10.1111/j.1540-5850.2008.00912.x

Srithongrung, A. (2010a). State capital improvement programs and institutional arrangements for capital budgeting: The case of Illinois. *Journal of Public Budgeting, Accounting & Financial Management, 22*(3), 407–430.

Srithongrung, A. (2010b). The impacts of state economic capital management programs on State economic performance. *Public Budgeting & Finance, 23*(3), 83–107. doi:10.1111/j.1540-5850.2008.00912.x

Srithongrung, A., & Kriz, K. A. (2012). From public infrastructure to national economic growth: Do systematic investment practices matter? *International Public Management Review, 13*(2), 19–50.

World Bank. (2018). *GDP per capita.* Retrieved July 23, 2018, from https://data.worldbank.org/indicator/NY.GDP.PCAP.KD?end=1960&locations=KR-GH-JP&name_desc=false&start=1960&view=bar

Yusuf, J.-E., & Jordan, M. (2018). State transportation planning: Linking quantifiable performance measures and infrastructure condition outcomes. *Public Works Management & Policy, 23*(1), 58–77. doi:10.1177/1087724X17715266

ENDNOTES

1. 1,000 KRW is about 1 USD.
2. BTO is a structure in which ownership of the facility is transferred to the government upon completion of construction while the private partner receives operational rights. The private partner provides services to users and enjoys return on its investment by charging user fees.
3. BTL is a structure where the private partner recovers its investment on facilities by receiving funds from the central or local government. The government payments include lease payment and operational costs, which are determined based on its operational performance in a given period of time. Ownership of the facility is transferred to the government upon completion of construction, and the private partner receives operational rights.
4. The Facilities Safety and Management Act refers infrastructure facilities as roadways, bridges, tunnel, ports, dams, building, and other types of facilities defined by the central and local governments.
5. Interpretation of the acronyms are shown in Table 3 in the Appendix.

APPENDIX

Table 3.

Acronyms	Interpretation
AHP	The Analytic Hierarchy Process
BCP	The Basic City Plan
BPSM	Basic Plan of the Safety and Maintenance for Infrastructure
BTL	Build-Transfer-Lease
BTO	Build-Transfer-Own
CMP	The City Management Plan
CNTP	The Comprehensive National Territorial Plan
FR	Feasibility Re-evaluation
KDI	Korea Development Institute
KISC	The Korea Infrastructure Safety Corporation
LIT	The Ministry of Land, Infrastructure, and Transport
MAP	The Metropolitan Area Plan
NBOP	The National Budget Operational Plan
MIS	The Ministry of the Interior and Safety
MLFP	The Mid-term Local Financial Plan
MLIT	The Ministry of Land, Infrastructure, and Transport
MOF	The Ministry of Oceans and Fisheries
MPP	The Mid-term Program Plan
MOEF	The Ministry of Economy and Finance
NABO	The National Assembly Budget Office
PFS	The Preliminary Feasibility Study
SMRP	The Seoul Metropolitan Area Readjustment Plan
TPCM	Total Project Cost Management

Chapter 12
Capital Management and Budgeting in Taiwan

Wei-Jie Liao
University of Nebraska at Omaha, USA

Nai-Ling Kuo
National Taiwan University, Taiwan

ABSTRACT

In this chapter, the authors provide an overview of Taiwan's public infrastructure system using the recommended normative framework presented in Chapter 1. In general, most of Taiwan's practices fit the requirements suggested in Chapter 1. However, there are still rooms for improvements in prioritization, debt affordability analysis, and infrastructure maintenance. In addition, the build-operate-transfer (BOT) model and the so-called "Mosquito Buildings" also feature Taiwan's capital management and budgeting process and are discussed in this chapter. Nowadays, Taiwanese governments place much emphasis on disaster prevention, environmental protection, and renewable energy. These new trends may also affect Taiwan's capital management and budgeting process.

INTRODUCTION

Taiwan's public infrastructure is generally of good quality. In this chapter, we discuss Taiwan's capital management and budgeting processes. In the first section, we provide background on Taiwan's history, politics, public infrastructure system, and governmental structure. Next, the capital management and budgeting processes in Taiwan are presented in terms of long-term capital planning, capital budgeting and financial management, centralized execution and project management, and infrastructure maintenance. We analyze similarities and differences between Taiwan's practices and the required elements suggested in Chapter 1. Furthermore, we discuss the Build-Operate-Transfer (BOT) model and disused public buildings (so-called "mosquito buildings")[1], as they also feature in Taiwan's capital management and budgeting processes. We identify several issues related to the BOT model and "mosquito buildings" and discuss how Taiwanese governments respond to them. We expect that the case of Taiwan can contribute to comparative analysis of capital management and budgeting in the public sector.

DOI: 10.4018/978-1-5225-7329-6.ch012

BACKGROUND

Taiwan is located in East Asia with a population of 23.56 million recorded at the end of 2017. It is one of the most densely populated places in the world — its population density is 651 people per square kilometer (1,686 people per square mile). Before the 19th century, Taiwan was ruled by the Dutch, the Spanish, and the Qing Dynasty of China. After the 1894 War of Jiawu, Taiwan was ceded to Japan by the Qing Dynasty. The Japanese Empire completed numerous important public infrastructure projects in Taiwan, such as the West Coast Railway Line and several hydroelectric power stations. After Japan's surrender to the Allies ended World War II in 1945, the Republic of China (ROC) took control of Taiwan. In 1949, ROC's ruling party, the Kuomintang (KMT), lost the Chinese Civil War to the Chinese Communist Party and retreated to Taiwan. Meanwhile, President Chiang Kai-shek declared martial law and started a one-party dictatorship in Taiwan. It was not until the 1980s that martial law was lifted and democratic reforms in Taiwan began. Currently, the two major political parties in Taiwan are the KMT (the major party of the Pan-Blue Coalition, which favors the Chinese nationalist identity) and the Democratic Progressive Party (DPP; the major party of the Pan-Green Coalition, which favors the Taiwanese identity). Taiwan has already experienced three governing party changes since the first direct presidential election in 1996.

During the second half of the 20th century, Taiwan experienced rapid economic growth and was known as one of the "Four Asian Tigers," along with Hong Kong, Singapore, and South Korea. According to the International Monetary Fund (2017), Taiwan is currently one of the 25 largest economies in the world, measured by nominal gross domestic product (GDP) or purchasing power parity.

Taiwan lies in the Northwestern Pacific area, the western edge of the Pacific Ring of Fire. Due to its location, Taiwan usually experiences a few earthquakes and typhoons every year. In the past two decades, several catastrophic natural disasters (e.g., the 921 Earthquake in 1999 and Typhoon Morakot in 2009) have caused serious damage in Taiwan. Thus, Taiwanese governments have set high standards for public infrastructure systems (e.g., strict building codes for earthquake resistance and high flood protection standards) and have tried hard to improve the capacity for disaster management.

Transportation, energy, and water are three major types of public infrastructure in Taiwan. Transportation infrastructure in Taiwan is highly accessible and of high quality. There are 4 major international airports, 8 major domestic airports, and 4 major international ports. Among them, Taiwan Taoyuan International Airport is one of the 50 busiest airports in the world with 44.9 million passengers in 2017 (Port Authority of NY & NJ, 2018). Due to the high population density, rail transport in Taiwan is well-developed, including a conventional railway system circling the island, a high-speed rail along the west coast of Taiwan, and 4 rapid transit systems in the special municipalities. The highway system in Taiwan, including 8 national highways and 12 expressways, is also in good shape.

Energy infrastructure in Taiwan is mostly managed by the Taiwan Power Company, a government-owned electric power industry. There are 4 nuclear power plants, 21 fossil fuel power stations, and 16 hydroelectric power stations in Taiwan. They together have more than 44,000 megawatts (MW) of power generating capacity per year (Taiwan Power Company, 2018). After Japan's 2011 Fukushima Daiichi Nuclear Disaster, the Taiwanese government decided to phase out nuclear power and promote renewable energy (e.g., wind power and solar energy).

Dams and levees are important water infrastructure in Taiwan. Since most rivers in Taiwan are short and steep, Taiwan has built more than 30 dams to collect and store water. The levees of major rivers in Taiwan are designed to contain a flood with a 100-year return period, while the levees of Tamsui River, the major river in Taipei, are designed to contain a flood with a 200-year return period. In 2017, more than 93.9 percent of Taiwanese people enjoyed clean tap water (Water Resource Agency, 2018). However, deteriorating pipeline causes high tap water leakage rates, recorded 19.55 percent in 2012 and 15.49 percent in 2017 (Taiwan Water Corporation, 2018). Sewers are usually ignored by Taiwanese governments since they tend not to be visible. The average sewage treatment connection rate in Taiwan is about 56 percent (Construction and Planning Agency, 2018). Compared to OECD countries, recorded 77 percent in average in 2013 (OECD, 2015), sewers seem to be ignored nationwide in Taiwan with the exception of Taipei City and New Taipei City that both reached the average level of OECD countries in 2017.

Taiwan's system of government is a semi-presidential republic under which citizens directly elect the president and legislators, and the elected president appoints the prime minister (the head of the Executive Yuan). Figure 1 shows the government structure of Taiwan. The central government includes five branches (Yuans): the executive, the legislative, the judiciary, the examination, and the control Yuans. The Executive Yuan consists of 12 ministries and 8 commissions, which submit departmental budgets and execute the legal budgets. The Legislative Yuan is a unicameral legislature with 113 legislators, who are responsible for budget review and approval. The central government's budgets are audited by the supreme audit institution, the National Audit Office of the Control Yuan.

There are 22 municipal governments in Taiwan, including 6 special municipalities, 3 county-level cities, and 13 counties[2]. Citizens directly elect mayors of special municipalities or county-level cities, magistrates of counties, and councilors. Municipal governments compose and execute their own budgets annually. The budgets are reviewed and approved by city/county councils. Nevertheless, Taiwan still performs some degree of fiscal centralization (Lee & Clark, 2011, p.92). That is because most municipal governments rely heavily on intergovernmental transfers from the central government.

Figure 1. The Structure of Governments in Taiwan
Source: The Authors

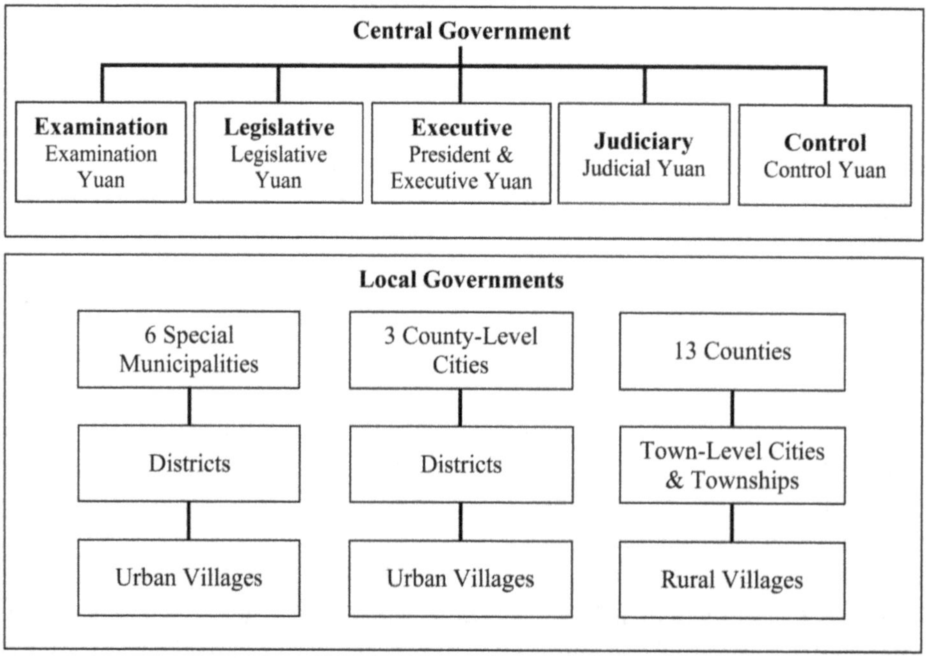

The central government is in charge of most large-scale public infrastructure, such as airports, ports, railways, highways, bridges, dams, levees, and power plants. On the other hand, local governments engage in smaller-scale public infrastructure, including roads, sidewalks, parks, street lights, schools, natatoriums, parking garages, and incinerators. Program grants (conditional grants) or matching grants from the central government are important sources for the construction of local public infrastructure, especially when it is aligned with the central government's policy directions. Most public infrastructure projects in Taiwan are funded through annual budgets. While some multi-year projects for special purposes (e.g., national defense and disaster recovery) are funded through special budgets. Other projects, especially transportation or utility infrastructure, adopts the user-pays principle to cover the operating expenses or to repay the debt incurred for construction.

In the past ten years, the central government's revenues and expenditures remained quite stable. In 2017, the central government's actual general fund expenditures were NT$ 1.93 trillion (US$ 64.33 billion)[3]. Among them, 84.3 percent (NT$ 1.63 trillion; about US$ 54.33 billion) were operating expenses and 15.7percent (NT$ 303 billion; about US$ 10.1 billion) were capital expenditures.

CAPITAL MANAGEMENT AND BUDGETING PROCESSES IN TAIWAN

Long-Term Capital Planning

The normative framework in Chapter 1 recommends that a capital budgeting system should include multi-year comprehensive strategic plans. In Taiwan, there are two major types of long-term capital planning. One is established by public administrators (the National Development Plan, hereinafter, NDP), and the other is established by presidents and prime ministers. The former is the multi-year comprehensive strategic planning for public infrastructure investment, while the latter is usually based on the president's campaign promises and the suggestions of his or her core staff.

NDP developed by the National Development Council (NDC) is the most important comprehensive strategic plan in Taiwan[4]. In recent years, each NDP covers a four-year period, which is aligned with the presidential term. It is usually developed on the basis of the president's policy directions and is announced one year after the presidential inauguration. Each NDP includes a situation analysis (both internal and external), a set of development strategies, several macroeconomic targets, and several detailed policy directions. In recent years, the NDC has also developed annual NDPs, which are more detailed and are updated annually (National Development Council, 2018a). Generally speaking, the NDPs are important guidelines for both the central and local governments in Taiwan.

Since the 1970s, presidents and prime ministers in Taiwan have usually announced a series of long-term, large-scale capital projects right after their inauguration. Table 1 lists the long-term capital projects proposed by presidents and prime ministers. In 1974, Prime Minister Chiang Ching-kuo proposed the Ten Major Construction Projects in response to the 1973 Oil Crisis and the lack of public infrastructure in Taiwan. These projects were the first large-scale capital projects to be implemented in Taiwan since 1949. Many important capital projects were built during this period, such as Taiwan Taoyuan International Airport, Taichung Port, North-Link Line Railway, Sun Yat-sen National Highway, and the first nuclear power plant. In the 1980s, the Chiang administration followed up with the Twelve Construction

Table 1. Large-scale capital projects proposed by presidents and prime ministers

Capital Programs	Years	Presidents (Party)	Major Projects
Ten Major Construction Projects	1974 - 1979	Chiang Kai-shek, Chiang Ching-kuo (KMT)	Transportation (highway, railway, airport, port, shipyard), energy (1st nuclear power plant, oil refinery), steel mill
Twelve Construction Projects	1980 - 1985	Chiang Ching-kuo (KMT)	Transportation (South-Link Line Railway, cross-island highways, port expansion), energy (2nd and 3rd nuclear power plant), irrigation systems, levees, public housing
Fourteen Construction Projects	1984 - 1990	Chiang Ching-kuo Lee Teng-hui (KMT)	Transportation (railway and highway expansion, Taipei Metropolitan Area Railway Underground Project, Taipei Metro), energy (4th nuclear power plant), flood control
New Ten Major Construction Projects	2004 - 2008	Chen Shui-bian (DPP)	Transportation (highway, railway MRT-ization, new rapid transit systems, port expansion), sewage systems, Internet infrastructure, performing arts centers and museums
i-Taiwan 12 Projects	2009 - 2011	Ma Ying-jeou (KMT)	Transportation (rapid transit systems expansion, airport and port expansion, Taoyuan Aerotropolis), flood control, sewage systems, industrial innovation and upgrading (industrial and research park upgrade), free wireless broadband
Forward-Looking Infrastructure Development Plan	2017 - 2021	Tsai Ing-wen (DPP)	Transportation (new railway and rapid transit systems), renewable energy, water supply and flood control, the DIGI+ plan

Source: The Authors

Projects and the Fourteen Construction Projects. These projects also focused on transportation and energy infrastructure, such as expanding railway and highway systems, building Taipei Metro, and constructing new nuclear power plants.

In the past two decades, presidents have viewed building large-scale capital projects as a way to expand domestic demand and to foster economic growth. Each president has proposed a series of capital projects amounting to at least NT$ 400 billion (US$ 13.33 billion). In 2003, President Chen Shui-bian proposed the New Ten Major Construction Projects. Following the success of Taipei Metro, rapid transit systems became a focal point in these projects. New rapid transit systems and railway MRT-ization were proposed by the Chen administration. Besides transportation infrastructure, Internet infrastructure and art centers were first mentioned in these projects. In 2008, President Ma Ying-jeou developed the i-Taiwan 12 Projects based on his campaign promises. The expansion of Taiwan Taoyuan International Airport and the Taoyuan Aerotropolis were important parts of these projects. Industrial innovation and upgrading were also highly emphasized. Thus, projects related to industrial and research parks were proposed. In 2017, President Tsai Ing-wen issued the Forward-Looking Infrastructure Development Plan. This plan placed much emphasis on track construction, renewable energy, water infrastructure, and digital infrastructure.

Overall, there are four main themes in the projects proposed by presidents and prime ministers: transportation, energy, water, and digital infrastructure. First, since transportation infrastructure is highly related to citizens' daily life, such projects are proposed by every president and prime minister. Some transportation projects may be self-liquidating, such as Taiwan Taoyuan International Airport, national highways, and Taipei Metro. However, some may become burdens for governments. For example, Kaohsiung Metro, the rapid transit system in Taiwan's third largest metropolitan area, faces debt problems since its ridership is not as high as expected (Lee, 2017)[5]. Thus, as President Tsai Ing-wen's Forward-Looking Infrastructure Development Plan intends to build several new rapid transit systems, it may be questioned whether metropolitan areas other than the Greater Taipei Area can afford rapid transit systems (Chu, 2017).

Second, energy infrastructure has experienced a huge change in focus. In the 1970s and 1980s, the central government placed much emphasis on developing nuclear power in response to the increasing demand for electricity caused by rapid economic growth. However, after Japan's 2011 Fukushima Daiichi Nuclear Disaster, Taiwan's nuclear power policy became highly debated. There have been several anti-nuclear protests since 2011. In 2016, President Tsai Ing-wen decided to phase out nuclear power generation by 2025 and to promote the use of renewable energy.

Third, since Taiwan experiences several typhoons and floods every year, water infrastructure, especially infrastructure for flood control, is also a focal point for presidents and prime ministers. The central government often makes special budgets for flood control. For instance, in the 2000s, the Chen administration spent NT$ 31.6 billion (US$ 1.05 billion) on the Keelung River Integrated Flood Control Plan, and the Chen and Ma administrations spent NT$ 75.5 billion (US$ 2.52 billion) on the Flood-Prone Areas Management Plan. Last but not least, in the so-called Digital Age, developing digital infrastructure is imperative. Thus, digital infrastructure has always been included in long-term capital projects since 2000.

In addition to long-term capital planning, different types of pre-evaluations of capital projects are required in Taiwan. According to Article 34 of the *Budget Act*, a new major public construction project should be accompanied by a cost-benefit analysis. The *Environmental Impact Assessment Act* requires environmental impact assessments to be conducted before constructing major projects. The *Soil and Water Conservation Act* also requires a soil and water conservation plan before constructing on sloping fields or in a forest zone. However, most governments in Taiwan do not pay much attention to pre-evaluations. Sometimes, pre-evaluations may even be unreliable. For instance, as mentioned above, in the case of Kaohsiung Metro, the daily ridership was highly overestimated in the cost-benefit analysis. In some cases, if a project's benefits do not outweigh its costs, politicians may exaggerate its social benefits, which may be hard to quantify. Because of this, politics usually needs to be taken into consideration in decision-making processes.

Capital Budgeting and Financial Management

The normative framework suggests that governments should have multi-year fiscal forecasting as well as systematic priority ranking. In Taiwan, multi-year revenue and expenditure forecasting is conducted by the central government. Each year, the Directorate General of Budget, Accounting, and Statistics (DGBAS) announces the Four-Year Medium-Term Budget Estimates. Then, each ministry or commission makes its medium-term plan and annual budget based on the DGBAS's budget estimates. Marlowe, Rivenbark, and Vogt (2009, p.70) provided several approaches for prioritizing capital projects, such as urgency-of-need criteria, a weighted rating system, and organizational goals. In practice, to meet the requirement of the *Rules of Preliminary Process and Screening for Major Public Construction Programs*, central agencies in Taiwan will prioritize their own capital projects first, and then the NDC will prioritize the large-scale capital projects of that fiscal year and present the prioritization to the Executive Yuan. However, there are no well-constructed prioritization criteria.

The annual public budget is consisted of operating and capital budgets. Most small-scale capital projects and infrastructure maintenance are funded through the annual capital budget, while large-scale capital projects can be funded through the annual capital budget, capital project funds, or special budgets.

The *Budget Act* allows government agencies to establish capital project funds for major public construction projects[6]. Money in the capital project funds is separated from the general fund and can only be used on specific capital projects. Establishing capital project funds may be a good way to fund capital projects since those funds can accumulate resources for specific capital projects and may not be diverted to cover general fund shortfalls. However, this has not been a popular way for Taiwanese governments to fund capital projects. At the time of writing, there is only one capital project fund established by the Ministry of National Defense (MND), the Fund for Reconstruction of the Military Barracks.

In recent years, proposing a special budget has become a popular way for the central government to fund large-scale capital projects. According to Article 83 of the *Budget Act*, the Executive Yuan can propose a multi-year special budget outside of the annual budget when facing the following four situations: national defense emergencies or wars, major national economic events, major calamities, or major political events that take place irregularly or once every few years. Since special budgets are proposed outside of the annual budget, the central government usually does not have excess revenues and needs to issue public debt to fund them. Table 2 lists the special budgets related to public infrastructure after 2000. Notably, the large-scale capital projects proposed by the presidents, including President Chen Shui-bian's New Ten Major Construction Projects, President Ma Ying-jeou's i-Taiwan 12 Projects, and President Tsai Ing-wen's Forward-Looking Infrastructure Development Plan, have all been funded through special budgets. These three special budgets proposed by presidents have created an outstanding level of public debt amounting to NT$ 1.04 trillion (US$ 34.67 billion)[7].

Debt financing has become a popular financial instrument for Taiwanese governments at all levels since it can meet increasing public demand without raising taxes or cutting other expenses and can immediately raise enough funds for large-scale investments[8]. Taiwanese governments seldom conduct debt

Table 2. Special budgets related to public infrastructure, 2001 - 2019

Special Budgets	Years	Presidents (Party)	Budget (Billion NT$)
Post-921 Earthquake Reconstruction Plan	2001 - 2002	Chen Shui-bian (DPP)	100.0
Keelung River Integrated Flood Control Plan	2002 - 2005	Chen Shui-bian (DPP)	31.6
New Ten Major Construction Projects	2004 - 2008	Chen Shui-bian (DPP)	430.0
Flood-Prone Areas Management Plan	2006 - 2010	Chen Shui-bian (DPP) Ma Ying-jeou (KMT)	75.5
Shimen Reservoir and its Catchments Management Plan	2006 - 2011	Chen Shui-bian (DPP) Ma Ying-jeou (KMT)	25.0
i-Taiwan 12 Projects	2009 - 2011	Ma Ying-jeou (KMT)	499.2
Post-Typhoon Morakot Reconstruction Plan	2009 - 2012	Ma Ying-jeou (KMT)	116.5
Integrated River Basin Management Plan	2014 - 2019	Ma Ying-jeou (KMT) Tsai Ing-wen (DPP)	66.0
Forward-Looking Infrastructure Development Plan (Stage 1)	2017 - 2018	Tsai Ing-wen (DPP)	107.1

Source: DGBAS. (2018). Special Budget. Retrieved April 25, 2018 from https://eng.dgbas.gov.tw/np.asp?ctNode=5255

affordability analysis before issuing debt; however, Taiwan does have strict debt limits and debt disclosure requirements which are covered by the *Public Debt Act*. According to Article 5 of the *Public Debt Act*, "public debt with a maturity of one year or more incurred by the central government ... may not exceed 40.6 percent of the average of nominal GDP for the previous three fiscal years." At the municipal level, special municipalities are subject to debt limits similar to the central government[9], while counties and county-level cities cannot incur debt of more than 50 percent of their annual expenditure budget. Once a government reaches 90 percent of its debt limit, it will be required to draw up a debt improvement plan. Once a government exceeds its debt limit, it will not be able to incur any new debt. In 2018, only Miaoli County and Yilan County exceeded the debt limits. The central and other municipal governments all abided by the *Public Debt Act*. Kuo and Liao (2018) found that mayors or magistrates in Taiwan tend to borrow more money to construct new capital projects in their second term when they cannot run for another reelection and do not need to worry about the government's future fiscal condition.

As for debt disclosure, Article 10 of the *Public Debt Act* requires that both the central and municipal governments report their debt information to the Ministry of Finance (MOF) as well as make their debt information public on their websites monthly. However, only the total debt amount is required to be disclosed. It may be hard for citizens to know the detailed items and amounts borrowed for each project.

The normative framework also suggests that governments should set up rainy day funds for unanticipated revenue shortfalls or unexpected expenditures. Governments in Taiwan do not have rainy day funds to retain their year-end surpluses. Instead, they are required by Article 22 of the *Budget Act* to set aside a part of their annual budget and name the budget item as "reserves[10]." These "reserves" cannot be retained if they are not used up by the end of the year. In addition, the *Disaster Prevention and Protection Act* also requires municipal governments to prepare "reserves" in their annual budget for disaster response and recovery.

Centralized Execution and Project Management

In Taiwan, different authorities, either government agencies or government-owned corporations, may be in charge of different types of public infrastructure. Table 3 lists the authorities of public infrastructure. Utility infrastructure, such as water and energy infrastructure, is managed by government-owned corporations, like the Taiwan Water Corporation and the Taiwan Power Company. Transportation infrastructure is usually maintained by agencies of the Ministry of Transportation and Communications (MOTC). However, some transportation infrastructure is managed by government-owned corporations, such as Taiwan Taoyuan International Airport, Taiwan High Speed Rail (THSR), and the rapid transit systems. In general, government-owned corporations are expected to take responsibility for their profits and losses and have more flexibility in procurement and hiring than government agencies.

Despite the fact that different authorities manage different types of public infrastructure, Taiwan does have a central committee called the Public Construction Committee (PCC), which supervises and monitors capital project construction as the normative framework suggests. The PCC was established in 1995. In 2001, the PCC created the Public Construction Management Information System (the PCMI System) in order to improve its internal control. In 2005, the *Freedom of Government Information Law* (the *FGI Law*) was announced. Article 7 of the *FGI Law* requires governments at all levels to make contracts and documents related to capital projects and procurements available to the public actively and in a timely manner. Thus, information related to public construction, such as the contractor, the contract amount, the funding sources, the expected construction time, and the progress of the construction can

Table 3. Infrastructure-Related Government Agencies or Government-Owned Corporations

Types of Authorities	Types of Public Infrastructure	Names of Government Agencies or Government-Owned Corporations
Government Agencies	Airports	Civil Aeronautics Administration, MOTC
	National Highways	Freeway Bureau, MOTC
	Provincial Highways and Bridges	Directorate General of Highways, MOTC
	Railway	Taiwan Railways Administration, MOTC
	Dams and Levees	Water Resources Agency, Ministry of Economic Affairs
Government-Owned Corporations	Airport (Taiwan Taoyuan International Airport)	Taoyuan International Airport Corporation
	Ports	Taiwan International Ports Corporation
	THSR	Taiwan High Speed Rail Corporation (THSRC)
	Rapid Transit Systems	(Five different rapid transit corporations)
	Tap Water (except for Taipei City) *	Taiwan Water Corporation
	Energy and Electricity	Taiwan Power Company

Source: The Authors.
*Note: * Tap water in Taipei City is managed by Taipei Water Department, Taipei City Government.*

now be found on the online PCMI System (Public Construction Committee, 2018c). With the help of the *FGI Law* and the PCMI System, capital management and budgeting processes in Taiwan have become increasingly transparent. Citizens and the media can now easily access information related to public construction projects. In recent years, the PCC has also created a list of large-scale public construction projects, which monitors ongoing projects with a budget over NT$ 100 million (US$ 3.33 million) (Public Construction Committee, 2018b).

Like operating budgets, capital budgets are internally audited by government agencies themselves. The central and local governments release their monthly accounting reports on their official websites. Monthly and year-to-date actual revenues and expenses are revealed in the reports. However, monthly budgeted revenues and expenses are usually not included in the reports. Most government agencies only present their budgets on a yearly basis. Thus, it may be difficult to conduct budget variance analysis, which compares the budgeted amount of revenues or expenses with the actual amount monthly.

Generally speaking, public construction projects can be implemented by governments themselves, or through contracting-out or BOT. Since the public sector in Taiwan usually has limited resources, and the private sector is usually affluent and skillful, contracting-out and BOT are feasible ways to build public infrastructure. BOT is a type of public-private partnership (PPP), which has been frequently used in Taiwan, especially in the past two decades. Nowadays, many transportation facilities, lodgings, and hospitals are built through BOT. For instance, THSR is one of the largest BOT projects in the world. In 2000, the *Act for Promotion of Private Participation in Infrastructure Projects* (hereinafter, the *PPIP Act*) was announced "to upgrade the level of public services, to expedite social economic development, and to encourage private participation in infrastructure projects." This act has fostered the use of BOT in Taiwanese governments at all levels. Since BOT is a notable feature of Taiwan's capital management, we further discuss it in the section on the special features of Taiwan's capital management and budgeting processes.

Procurement is an important process in the project execution stage. Since the Taiwanese government announced the *Government Procurement Act* (*GPA*) in 1998, the procurement process has become more systematic and more transparent. Article 18 of the *GPA* lists three different bidding procedures for procurement: open, selective, and limited bidding procedures. Most of the time, if the procurement is greater than NT$ 1 million (US$ 33.3 thousand), governments are required to apply open bidding procedures. Only under certain circumstances listed in Article 20 and 22 of the *GPA* can governments apply selective or limited bidding procedures[11].

According to Article 52 of the *GPA*, contracts can be awarded on the basis of either the lowest bidding principle or the most advantageous bidding principle[12], which should be specified in the bidding documentation. Hsieh (2012) found that there is a debate between adopting the lowest bidding principle and adopting the most advantageous bidding principle. The lowest bidding principle may help governments lower the cost of public infrastructure but sometimes may reduce its quality. The most advantageous bidding principle may help governments find the best contractor for public construction projects, but sometimes corruption may occur during the evaluation process since the evaluation may be subjective. Nowadays, public administrators in Taiwan prefer the lowest bidding principle to the most advantageous bidding principle, since they believe that the lowest bidding principle may be more objective and less expensive. Most important of all, adopting the lowest bidding principle may prevent them from being accused of corruption.

Since the lowest bidding principle is prevalent, contractors may lower the bidding price in order to win the bid. After winning the bid, they usually request large amounts of supplemental budgets when building public construction projects. According to Article 79 of the *Budget Act*, if expenses increase due to major incidents, government agencies may apply for supplemental budgets. Yao (2016) found that supplemental budgets are frequently used in public construction projects. More than half of public construction projects applied for supplemental budgets. The major justifications given by contractors when requesting supplemental budgets include raw material price increases, construction delays, and natural disasters. For example, the construction of the National Kaohsiung Center for the Arts was one of the New Ten Major Construction Projects proposed by the Chen administration in the 2000s. In 2005, its original budget was NT$ 8.36 billion (US$ 278.67 million). However, this project was delayed for several years, and the contractor requested a large supplemental budget. Its budget has now been raised by 28.6 percent to NT$ 10.75 billion (US$ 358.33 million) (Public Construction Committee, 2018b). Although applying for a supplemental budget may sometimes be reasonable, this budget tool should not be used habitually. The executive branch should apply for a supplemental budget only when necessary (e.g., when natural disasters cause damage to ongoing projects), and the legislative branch should review the proposed supplemental budget carefully.

Infrastructure Maintenance

Much of the public infrastructure in Taiwan was constructed in the 1970s and 1980s, when Taiwan experienced rapid economic growth. Thus, aging public infrastructure has now become a serious problem for governments at all levels and has made infrastructure maintenance and replacement important. There are several emerging issues related to aging public infrastructure and its maintenance. For instance, many government buildings, school buildings, and bridges are old and may not meet modern construction standards. Thus, these buildings need to be renovated or reconstructed. Moreover, as mentioned above, old pipes in Taiwan may cause high tap water leakage rates and may contain lead, a heavy metal that can harm health. These pipes need to be replaced as soon as possible. In addition, reservoir sedimentation poses a serious threat to major dams in Taiwan by reducing their storage capacity. Although the central government keeps dredging reservoirs, heavy sediment deposits continue to outpace dredging efforts.

Even though infrastructure maintenance is clearly important for Taiwan, it has long been neglected by most Taiwanese governments, since it is less visible compared to new capital projects. In general, governments place emphasis on infrastructure maintenance only when major disasters cause severe damage or when infrastructure failures are highly visible to citizens. For example, the Reconstruction Project of Old and Damaged Bridges was proposed by the Directorate General of Highways, MOTC after the Hou-Fong Bridge in Taichung was destroyed by Typhoon Sinlaku in 2008.

Some infrastructure failures, such as potholes and sidewalk damage, are highly visible since they are related to citizens' daily life. Thus, governments may pay more attention to the maintenance or repair of these projects. For instance, road maintenance and improvement have become major concerns in recent years. In 2009, the Taipei City Government first implemented the "Road Smoothing Project" to resurface roads and reduce the number of manhole covers on roads[13]. The "Road Smoothing Project" has since been adopted and regularly implemented by many other municipal governments. In addition, since the late 2000s, many municipalities in Taiwan have established "1999 Citizen Hotlines." Citizens can now report infrastructure damage easily and request governments to respond in a timely manner.

Generally speaking, Taiwan does not have systematic maintenance planning as the normative framework suggests. Although different types of infrastructure may have different maintenance regulations[14], there is no general law for infrastructure maintenance (Yeh, 2017). According to the National Development Council (2016), there is also a lack of regular condition assessment of public infrastructure. Some public infrastructure may suffer from low usage, lack of maintenance, or even insolvency and become disused public buildings (called "mosquito buildings" in Taiwan). Nowadays, "mosquito buildings" have attracted much attention among Taiwanese people as public information becomes increasingly transparent. As a Taiwanese saying goes, "policy mistakes may be worse than corruption." How to deal with existing "mosquito buildings" and prevent new ones from being constructed are important issues to both the central and local governments in Taiwan. Since the problem of "mosquito buildings" is a hot topic in Taiwan, we discuss it in the section on the special features of Taiwan's capital management and budgeting processes.

Most Taiwanese governments do not have a maintenance fund. Maintenance funding is usually included in government agencies' annual operating budget. As mentioned above, only the MND has established a capital project fund for maintenance and replacement. When an emergency occurs, government agencies can use the "reserves" set aside in their annual budget to respond to it immediately. Later, the central government can make a multi-year special budget for a post-disaster reconstruction plan.

As for asset management, governments in Taiwan monitor and maintain the value of their own assets, but there is no general law for asset management. Instead, there is guidance on the durable years of fixed assets and depletion rates of depletable assets released by the MOF that shows when assets should be replaced. Taiwanese governments are also required to evaluate the execution progress and performance of capital projects every year. Moreover, when a large-scale capital project is selected as a "Yuan-Monitored Project," both the agency and the NDC will conduct performance evaluation and report to the Executive Yuan.

Overview Discussion and Analysis

In general, Taiwan's capital management and budgeting processes correspond to the steps suggested by the normative framework. In the capital planning stage, the NDC announces the medium-term NDP every four years and updates the annual NDP. In the financial management stage, the DGBAS provides multi-year revenue and expenditure forecasting every year. The *Budget Act* has strict debt limits and debt disclosure requirements. Overall, the central government and most municipal governments follow the debt rules. In the project execution stage, the PCC monitors major capital projects and provides project information publicly for online search. The *GPA* regulates project acquisition. The mechanisms aligned with the normative framework work well and make Taiwan's capital management efficient and effective.

However, we do find some practices that do not follow the normative framework. In the financial management stage, even though project prioritization is required, there is no clear prioritization criteria. Moreover, Taiwanese governments place less emphasis on debt affordability analysis than on debt limits. In addition, governments in Taiwan do not have rainy day funds, but they do set aside part of their annual budget as "reserves" to cover unanticipated emergencies. In the infrastructure maintenance stage, comprehensive maintenance planning and condition assessment are in general neglected in Taiwan. However, regular condition assessment may help governments assess future needs as well as reduce the number of "mosquito buildings." Taiwanese governments should develop mechanisms suggested by the normative framework as soon as possible. In recent years, the NDC has developed the Framework for Life-Cycle Performance Management of Public Infrastructure as well as the Public Infrastructure Project Reviewing, Early Warning, and Exit Mechanism (National Development Council, 2018b). The newly developed framework covers all four stages of the systematic capital management processes suggested by the normative framework. Both the framework and the mechanism are expected to better monitor public infrastructure projects and to reduce waste.

In addition, there are several other issues we would like to address here. First, environmental protection has become a prominent issue in Taiwan. Some capital projects have been terminated or changed because of their possible environmental impact. For example, the New Central Cross-Island Highway (from Xinyi, Nantou to Yuli, Hualien) was terminated in 1986 since the proposed route might cut through Yushan National Park, which is a protected area for wildlife. Another example is the Suhua Highway (from Suao, Yilan to Hualien). The existing Suhua Provincial Highway is often closed due to heavy rain and landslides, so the MOTC proposed to build the new Suhua National Highway in the 1990s. However, the project failed in 2008, as environmental impact assessment showed some environmental issues. Thus, in 2010, the MOTC proposed an alternative project, the Suhua Provincial Highway Improvement Project, to improve the existing route.

Second, as mentioned in the background section, Taiwan usually experiences several natural disasters every year. Therefore, disaster prevention, preparedness, response, and recovery are all important in Taiwan's capital management. Higher standards have been set for public infrastructure systems. In the past two decades, the central government has made two special budgets for disaster recovery: the Post-921 Earthquake Reconstruction Plan and the Post-Typhoon Morakot Reconstruction Plan. It is highly possible that Taiwan will encounter other natural disasters in the future. Thus, Taiwanese governments should work hard to prevent disasters and mitigate possible damage.

Last but not least, there may exist disparities between municipalities in terms of public infrastructure provision and financing. Generally speaking, the public infrastructure in the metropolitan areas is well-developed, while public infrastructure in rural areas, especially in the eastern part of Taiwan and the offshore islands, is still wanting. In order to narrow the urban-rural gap, the central government established two special funds for rural areas in the early 2010s: the Hualien-Taitung Area Sustainable Development Fund (NT$ 40 billion, about US$ 1.33 billion) and the Offshore Islands Development Fund (NT$ 30 billion, about US$ 1 billion).

In capital management and budgeting processes, BOT is frequently used by Taiwanese governments to construct public infrastructure projects. We view it as the first special feature of Taiwan's capital management. In addition, there are plenty of "mosquito buildings" all over Taiwan that have emerged from either lack of planning and pre-evaluation or lack of maintenance. We consider managing "mosquito buildings" to be the second special feature of Taiwan's capital management. In the following section, we discuss these two special features in detail.

SPECIAL FEATURES OF TAIWAN'S CAPITAL MANAGEMENT AND BUDGETING PROCESSES

The Build-Operate-Transfer (BOT) Model

The level and quality of public infrastructure are considered important indicators of the extent to which a country is developed (Nurre, Cavdaroglu, Mitchell, Sharkey, & Wallace, 2012). Nevertheless, in the past two decades, many countries have not had sufficient funds to carry out public infrastructure projects. This may be primarily due to both the growth of entitlements and to worldwide economic recessions. To cure under financing of public infrastructure, private entities are invited to participate in public infrastructure projects through PPP (Grimsey & Lewis, 2002). PPP may improve efficiency, foster innovation, and save public money (Chou & Pramudawardhani, 2015). However, accountability and transparency may be major challenges to PPP (Kuo & Cheng, 2018; Marlowe et al., 2009, p.111).

According to the World Bank (2016), there are numerous forms of PPP, including private participating infrastructure projects that are established through: (1) management and operating agreements, (2) leases or affermage, (3) concessions, BOT, or Design-Build-Operate, and (4) joint ventures. Among them, BOT is a typical structure for long-term capital project financing. As mentioned above, when a government decides to build a public facility, it may choose to build it by itself, to contract-out, or to use BOT. If the government chooses BOT, it will first sign a contract with a private contractor, allowing the contractor to build a new public facility and granting the contractor a concession period (usually more than ten years) to operate and maintain the facility. By the end of the concession period, the contractor has to transfer the facility to the government.

The concept of BOT was developed as early as the 18th century, while its first application was in Turkey in 1984 (McCarthy & Tiong, 1991). Since then, BOT has been widely adopted to build new public infrastructure all over the world. BOT has some variants that are usually used for existing projects, such as Renovate-Operate-Transfer (ROT) and Operate-Transfer (OT). Generally speaking, large-scale capital projects usually involve high risks due to their long time frames, large costs, and irreversible nature (Lewis & Hildreth, 2013, p.231). BOT-type models are proposed because the public and private sectors can share financial burdens and other socioeconomic risks of public infrastructure construction and operation. Most importantly, a successful BOT needs careful risk management to prevent it from failing (Ebrahimnejad, Mousavi, & Seyrafianpour, 2010).

It was not until the mid-1990s that BOT-type models gained the attention of Taiwanese governments. The *Statute for Encouragement of Private Participation in Transportation Infrastructure Projects* was promulgated in December 1994. The Executive Yuan approved the project named "Promoting Public Construction through BOT" in August 1995. In the following two years, the Executive Yuan decided to promote and expand the application of BOT-type models to public infrastructure projects other than transportation facilities. In 2000, the *PPIP Act* was promulgated, and its latest amendment was in 2015. The *PPIP Act* is the main act governing the implementation of BOT-type models, and the Department for the Promotion of Private Participation of the MOF is now in charge of it[15]. To attract more private entities to build public infrastructure projects through BOT-type models, both the central and local governments provide several incentives for private contractors, such as regulatory relaxation, preferential land rentals, expropriation of private-owned land, promise of affiliated commercial facilities, tax incentives, and loan credits (Kuo & Cheng, 2018, pp. 226-228; Wang & Chen, 2016).

The establishment of a legal framework and incentive mechanisms make the use of BOT-type models in public infrastructure projects a trend in Taiwan. BOT is the most commonly used form of PPP in Taiwan. Table 4 shows the major BOT projects in Taiwan. The BOT model is adopted to provide various types of public infrastructure, such as commercial, sanitation and medical, sports, and transportation infrastructure. Both the central and local governments use BOT for public infrastructure projects. Most of the major BOT projects render fifty years of concession or more to private contractors. In some cases, like Kaohsiung Arena, THSR, and Kaohsiung Metro, governments also provide some funding for public infrastructure projects[16].

BOT is a frequently used method for public infrastructure projects, but how important is it to Taiwan? According to the 2017 Taiwan PPP Investor's Manual released by the MOF, there were 1,464 BOT-related contracts signed between 2002 and 2016, creating more than 230,000 job opportunities. The contracts amounted to NT$ 1.2 trillion (US$ 40 billion) and were estimated to save NT$ 1.5 trillion (US$ 50 billion) in government expenditures and to add NT$ 760.5 billion (US$ 25.35 billion) in government revenues. The estimated worth of BOT investment opportunities from mid-2017 to mid-2018 was NT$ 200 billion (US$ 6.67 billion). Compared to the central and local governments' aggregate expenditure, which is about NT$ 2.7 trillion (US$ 90 billion), BOT saves a significant amount of public money.

Nevertheless, not all BOT projects in Taiwan are successful. The failure cases may also provide valuable lessons to other projects. Wang and Chen (2016) reviewed five controversial BOT cases in Taiwan: THSR, the Taipei Dome complex, Taiwan Highway Electronic Toll Collection (ETC) System, Taipei Bus Station, and Songshan Cultural and Creative Park and found several controversies surrounding BOT in Taiwan. First, asymmetric information and low levels of transparency during bidding processes may cause agency problems, either related to adverse selection or moral hazards. In the case of ETC, the Far Eastern Group did not have the best technology, but it eventually won the bid by pretending it could do the best job. In the case of THSR, the THSRC won the bid by promising to build the railway with zero net cost from the central government. However, after winning the bid, the THSRC faced difficulties in raising funds and asked the central government for funding of NT$ 105.7 billion (US$ 3.52 billion).

Second, the promise of affiliated commercial facilities in or around BOT sites as an incentive mechanism could be problematic. Private contractors may run public infrastructure less carefully and pay most attention to the monopoly business in or around BOT sites, which may violate the spirit of PPP. For example, in the case of the Taipei Dome complex, the Taipei City Government signed a BOT contract with the Farglory Group in 2006, allowing the contractor to build a multi-use stadium and a shopping mall, which it would operate for fifty years. However, the contractor changed the design of the building

Table 4. Examples of major BOT projects in Taiwan

Projects	Facility Types	Government Authorities in Charge	Contractors	Concession Periods	Private Investment in NT$ (% of the Total Costs)	Government Funding in NT$ (% of the Total Costs)
Taipei 101 (Taipei World Financial Center)	Commercial	Taipei City Government	Taipei Financial Center Corporation	70 Years (1997 - 2067)	58 Billion (100.00%)	-
Shuang-Ho Hospital	Sanitation and Medical	Ministry of Health and Welfare	Taipei Medical University	50 Years (2004 - 2054)	7 Billion (100.00%)	-
Tainan Municipal An-Nan Hospital	Sanitation and Medical	Tainan City Government	China Medical University	50 Years (2010 - 2060)	4 Billion (100.00%)	-
New Taipei Municipal Tu-Cheng Hospital	Sanitation and Medical	New Taipei City Government	Chang Gung Medical Foundation	50 Years (2014 - 2064)	6.7 Billion (100.00%)	-
Kaohsiung Arena	Sports	Kaohsiung City Government	Kegel Sports International Co., Ltd.	50 Years (2004 - 2054)	6.3 Billion (80.77%)	1.5 Billion (19.23%)
Taipei Dome complex *	Sports	Taipei City Government	Farglory Group	50 Years (2006 - 2056)	37 Billion (100.00%)	-
THSR **	Transportation	MOTC	THSRC	70 Years (1997 - 2067)	336.6 Billion (76.10%)	105.7 Billion (23.90%)
Kaohsiung Metro	Transportation	Kaohsiung City Government	Kaohsiung Rapid Transit Corporation	36 Years (2001 - 2037)	30.5 Billion (16.81%)	150.9 Billion (83.19%)
Taiwan Highway ETC System	Transportation	Freeway Bureau, MOTC	Far Eastern Electronic Toll Collection Co, Ltd	20 Years (2004 - 2024)	10 Billion (100.00%)	-
Taipei Bus Station	Transportation	Taipei City Government	Radium Life Tech Co., Ltd.	50 Years (2004 - 2054)	10.9 Billion (100.00%)	-
Taipei Port Container Terminal Project	Transportation	MOTC	Taipei Port Container Terminal Corp.	50 Years (2004 - 2054)	20.3 Billion (100.00%)	-
Nangang and Songshan Train Station Complex	Transportation	Taiwan Railways Administration, MOTC	Ruentex Group	50 Years (2006 - 2056)	12 Billion (100.00%)	-
Taipei City Hall Bus Station	Transportation	Taipei City Government	Uni-President Development Corp.	50 Years (2006 - 2056)	10.8 Billion (100.00%)	-

Source: The Authors and the 2017 Taiwan PPP Investor's Manual, MOF.
*Note: * The Taipei Dome complex has been suspended since 2015.*
*** THSR is so far the largest BOT case in Taiwan.*

to expand the affiliated commercial facilities without the Taipei City Government's permission. Thus, the construction of the Taipei Dome complex has now been suspended for more than three years.

Taiwanese governments now try hard to fix these problems by amending regulations or bidding processes. For example, the Taipei City Government revised its bidding processes in 2015 and increased the number of outside experts on the selection committee to two-thirds. The percentage of affiliated commercial facilities of a BOT project has also been regulated in Taipei since 2015. These reforms are expected to improve the quality of public infrastructure funded through the BOT model.

Managing "Mosquito Buildings"

Like many governments all over the world, Taiwanese governments now face the problem of limited resources and need to cut unnecessary expenses. In addition, citizens can now access government information more easily since it becomes more transparent in recent years. Under these circumstances, the problem of disused public buildings or so-called "mosquito buildings" has become a focal point for governments as well as citizens. For example, artist Jui-Chung Yao has been discovering and photographing "mosquito buildings" since 2010. Until now, he has discovered more than 400 "mosquito buildings" all over Taiwan and has published a book series "Mirage: Disused Public Property in Taiwan" in which he documents them.

Generally speaking, there are three possible causes of "mosquito buildings." First, politicians in Taiwan often make campaign promises related to public construction projects without conducting thorough pre-evaluations. Thus, when these projects are put into practice, they may not be cost-effective and may suffer from low usage or insolvency. Second, Taiwanese governments were affluent in the 1990s as Taiwan had just experienced a period of rapid economic growth. The central government kept encouraging local governments to build public retail markets, natatoriums, parking garages, and incinerators without considering actual demand[17]. Many of these buildings have now become "mosquito buildings" (Yao, 2016). Third, governments in Taiwan usually neglect the importance of infrastructure maintenance or are unable to afford maintenance expenses. Therefore, even though some public infrastructure projects are not badly designed, they may still become "mosquito buildings" due to mismanagement.

"Mosquito buildings" may become burdens for governments because they sometimes still need to budget for them. Furthermore, some abandoned "mosquito buildings" may even become hot spots of crime. Thus, it may be necessary to activate or terminate "mosquito buildings" to make better use of the buildings or land involved. However, it is not easy to terminate "mosquito buildings," as was seen in the case of Hengchun Airport, a former military airfield built during World War II. In 2003, the central government decided to spend NT$ 539 million (US$ 17.97 million) converting it into a civil airport, since it is near Kenting National Park, a popular tourist spot in Pingtung County. However, the airport is often forced to close due to strong winds so has not processed any passengers since 2014. The Civil Aeronautics Administration (CAA), MOTC has to spend NT$ 60 million (US$ 2 million) per year on the airport's personnel expenses and maintenance. It may be intuitive that the airport should be closed or be converted back to a military airfield, but the Pingtung County Government keeps forcing the CAA not to do so, arguing that Hengchun Airport should be expanded to attract more airlines and tourists (Pan, 2018).

Nowadays, activating "mosquito buildings" has become a major concern for Taiwanese governments at all levels. Therefore, the Public Construction Committee (2018a) has created a list of disused public properties, which includes more than 100 "mosquito buildings." Most "mosquito buildings" are public retail markets, natatoriums, parking garages, and incinerators. The total construction costs of these "mosquito buildings" exceeded NT$ 20 billion (US$ 666.67 million). The PCC's list provides detailed information about those "mosquito buildings," such as their associated authorities, construction costs, current conditions, and future plans. Citizens are also invited to report "mosquito buildings" in their neighborhoods and provide suggestions for activating "mosquito buildings." Sometimes, citizens may come up with innovative ideas that government officials have never considered. Some BOT-type models, such as ROT or OT, may also be helpful for activating "mosquito buildings."

In order to prevent new "mosquito buildings" from being built, governments should first conduct reliable pre-evaluations to see whether projects are cost-effective or self-liquidating. The pre-evaluations should be based on trustworthy and professional forecasting or assessment. Second, decision-makers should be responsible for the projects they propose and should be held accountable. Last but not least, governments should conduct regular condition assessments to decide whether public infrastructure should be modified or terminated. With these efforts, we hope the number of "mosquito buildings" can be reduced and governments can make better use of limited resources.

CONCLUSION

Overall, Taiwan's public infrastructure system is well-developed. Citizens can easily gain access to public infrastructure of high quality. Most of Taiwan's capital management and budgeting processes follow the recommended normative framework presented in Chapter 1. For example, Taiwan has a four-year NDP, multi-year revenue and expenditure forecasting, and strict debt limits and debt disclosure requirements. Also, the PCC plays an important role in monitoring public infrastructure projects. However, Taiwanese governments should place more emphasis on pre-evaluations, needs analysis, prioritization, debt affordability analysis, and infrastructure maintenance as the normative framework suggests. Although a Taiwanese saying goes that "politics should not override professional judgment," politics is usually involved in Taiwan's capital management and budgeting processes. Taiwanese governments should make the processes less political and more professional by conducting more reliable pre-evaluations and making decisions based on professional analyses.

Some noteworthy trends have been evident in Taiwan's capital management and budgeting processes in recent years. First, environmental protection has been highly valued by governments as well as citizens. Environmental impact assessment is required before carrying out large-scale capital projects. Some projects may be terminated or modified due to environmental factors. Second, Taiwan usually experiences several natural disasters every year. As a result, higher standards for the public infrastructure system have been set up to enhance its ability to prevent and withstand natural disasters. Third, Taiwanese governments now place more emphasis on renewable energy, such as wind power and solar energy, in the hope of ensuring a clean, safe, and sustainable power generating system.

From the case of Taiwan, we first conclude that the BOT model may be an ideal way to build public infrastructure, especially when governments have limited resources and the private sector is affluent. Using BOT, governments may not need to afford huge construction costs and can share risk with the contractors. However, BOT processes may be less transparent than ordinary procurement processes. Sometimes, the contractors care more about the affiliated commercial facilities than the projects themselves. These problems should be dealt with properly when adopting the BOT model. Second, there exist many "mosquito buildings" in Taiwan, either due to a lack of thorough pre-evaluations or due to mismanagement. These existing "mosquito buildings" may become burdens for governments or hot spots of crime. Thus, Taiwanese governments try hard to activate or demolish these buildings. The PCC has created a list of "mosquito buildings" to monitor the process of activating these buildings. The private sector may play an important role in managing "mosquito buildings." For example, citizens are already invited to report "mosquito buildings" and to come up with ways to deal with these buildings. ROT or OT could be adopted to activate existing "mosquito buildings." Moreover, reliable pre-evaluations of capital projects should be conducted to prevent new "mosquito buildings" from being built and to make good use of limited resources.

ACKNOWLEDGMENT

The authors would like to thank the editors of the book, the two anonymous reviewers, and Dr. Carol Ebdon for their constructive comments and suggestions.

REFERENCES

Chou, J. S., & Pramudawardhani, D. (2015). Cross-country comparisons of key drivers, critical success factors and risk allocation for public-private partnership projects. *International Journal of Project Management, 33*(5), 1136–1150. doi:10.1016/j.ijproman.2014.12.003

Chu, S. C. (2017). President Tsai Ing-wen will spend NT $400 Billion on railway construction. *Business Weekly*. Retrieved May 6, 2018, from https://wealth.businessweekly.com.tw/GArticle.aspx?id=ARTL000088021

Construction and Planning Agency, Ministry of Interior. (2018). Sewage treatment connection tates [Data file]. Retrieved April 25, 2018, from https://www.cpami.gov.tw/filesys/file/chinese/dept/sew/sew1071.ods

Directorate General of Budget, Accounting, and Statistics. (2018). *Special budget*. Retrieved April 25, 2018, from https://eng.dgbas.gov.tw/np.asp?ctNode=5255

Ebrahimnejad, S., Mousavi, S., & Seyrafianpour, H. (2010). Risk identification and assessment for build-operate-transfer projects: A fuzzy multi attribute decision making model. *Expert Systems with Applications, 37*(1), 575–586. doi:10.1016/j.eswa.2009.05.037

Grimsey, D., & Lewis, M. (2002). Evaluating the risks of public private partnerships for infrastructure projects. *International Journal of Project Management, 20*(2), 107–118. doi:10.1016/S0263-7863(00)00040-5

Hsieh, T. Y. (2012). *Wandering between the lowest bid and the most advantageous bid*. National Policy Foundation Research Report. Retrieved April 25, 2018, from https://www.npf.org.tw/2/10493

International Monetary Fund. (2017). World economic outlook database [Data file]. Retrieved April 18, 2018, from https://www.imf.org/external/pubs/ft/weo/2017/02/weodata/index.aspx

Kuo, N. L., & Liao, W. J. (2018). Determinants of public debt in Taiwanese municipalities. *Public Finance Review (Taiwan), 47*(1), 1–18.

Kuo, Y. Y., & Cheng, M. H. (2018). Budgeting and financial management of public infrastructure: The experience of Taiwan. In *Value for money: Budget and financial management reform in the people's Republic of China, Taiwan and Australia* (pp. 221–250). Canberra, Australia: ANU Press. doi:10.22459/VM.01.2018.11

Lee, C. H. (2017, April 26). Can Kaohsiung metro become successful? *Global Views Monthly*. Retrieved April 25, 2018, from https://www.gvm.com.tw/article.html?id=22919

Lee, T. P., & Clark, C. (2011). The limits of budget reform in Taiwan. In C. Menifield (Ed.), *Comparative public budgeting: A global perspective* (pp. 91–105). Sudbury, MA: Jones & Bartlett Learning.

Lewis, C., & Hildreth, W. (2013). *Politics and capital budgeting. In Budgeting: Politics & power* (pp. 224–249). New York, NY: Oxford University Press.

Marlowe, J., Rivenbark, W., & Vogt, A. J. (2009). *Capital budgeting and finance: A guide for local governments* (2nd ed.). Washington, DC: ICMA Press.

McCarthy, S., & Tiong, R. (1991). Financial and contractual aspects of build-operate-transfer projects. *International Journal of Project Management*, *9*(4), 222–227. doi:10.1016/0263-7863(91)90030-Y

Ministry of Finance. (2017). *2017 Taiwan PPP investor's manual*. Retrieved May 6, 2018, from https://ppp.mof.gov.tw/ppp.website/DownFile.aspx?fromto=website&ReferId=pKRKH4r%2bKq4%3d

National Development Council. (2016). *Framework for life-cycle performance management of public infrastructure*. Retrieved April 25, 2018, from https://goo.gl/h3t3FL

National Development Council. (2018a). *Plans for national development*. Retrieved April 25, 2018, from https://www.ndc.gov.tw/en/Content_List.aspx?n=16081B8F505ABB7B

National Development Council. (2018b). *Projects control*. Retrieved May 6, 2018, from https://www.ndc.gov.tw/Content_List.aspx?n=22C3B697A101DF19

Nurre, S., Cavdaroglu, B., Mitchell, J., Sharkey, T., & Wallace, W. (2012). Restoring infrastructure systems: An integrated network design and scheduling (INDS) problem. *European Journal of Operational Research*, *223*(3), 794–806. doi:10.1016/j.ejor.2012.07.010

OECD. (2015). *Environment at a glance 2015*. Retrieved April 25, 2018, from https://www.oecd-ilibrary.org/environment/environment-at-a-glance-2015/sewage-treatment-connection-rates-of-population_9789264235199-table30-en

Pan, C. C. (2018, January 8). The NT$ 600 million Hengchun airport has become a Qigong center. *China Times*. Retrieved May 6, 2018, from http://www.chinatimes.com/newspapers/20180108000491-260114

Port Authority of NY & NJ. (2018). *2017 annual airport traffic report*. Retrieved April 18, 2018, from https://www.panynj.gov/airports/pdf-traffic/ATR2017.pdf

Public Construction Committee. (2018a). *List of disused public properties*. Retrieved April 28, 2018, from http://cmdweb.pcc.gov.tw/pccms/morac/idle_owasys.detail_list?ikind=D&ictrm=N

Public Construction Committee. (2018b). *List of large-scale public construction projects*. Retrieved April 25, 2018, from http://cmdweb.pcc.gov.tw/pccms/pwreport/showpeople_hm106.show_detail

Public Construction Committee. (2018c). *Public construction management information system*. Retrieved April 25, 2018, from http://cmdweb.pcc.gov.tw/pccms/owa/guesmap.userinn

Taiwan Power Company. (2018). Generating capacity of power stations [Data file]. Retrieved April 18, 2018, from http://stpc00601.taipower.com.tw/loadGraph/loadGraph/genshx.html

Taiwan Water Corporation. (2018). Leakage rate of Taiwan water company [Data file]. Retrieved April 25, 2018 from, https://www.water.gov.tw/opendata/prot2.csv

Wang, W. Y., & Chen, C. T. (2016). *Opportunities and challenges of BOT: The Taiwan experience.* NTU Center for Public Policy and Law Research Report. Retrieved April 25, 2018, from http://www.cppl.ntu.edu.tw/research/2015research/10407final.pdf

Water Resource Agency. (2018). Saturation of water supply [Data file]. Retrieved April 18, 2018, from https://www.wra.gov.tw/6950/7169/7316/7324/24043/

World Bank. (2016). *Types of public-private partnership agreements.* Retrieved May 6, 2018, from https://ppp.worldbank.org/public-private-partnership/agreements

Yao, J. C. (2016). *Mirage: Disused public property in Taiwan.* Taipei, Taiwan: Garden City Publishers.

Yeh, R. S. (2017, March 28). The Government should institutionalize public infrastructure maintenance. *Engineers Times*. Retrieved May 6, 2018, from https://goo.gl/km1ZLU

ENDNOTES

1 In Taiwan, people usually call disused public buildings "mosquito buildings" as they tend to be hotbeds for mosquito breeding. In this chapter, the term "mosquito buildings" is used for "disused public buildings."

2 Special municipality is the highest rank of local government in Taiwan. According to Article 4 of the *Local Government Act*, municipalities with a population of more than 1.25 million can be reformed into special municipalities. Generally speaking, special municipalities can receive more intergovernmental transfers from the central government and may have higher debt limits than other municipalities. There are currently six special municipalities in Taiwan: Taipei City, Kaohsiung City, New Taipei City, Taichung City, Taoyuan City, and Tainan City.

3 1 U.S. Dollar (US$) equals approximately 30 New Taiwan Dollars (NT$).

4 The National Development Plan (NDP) was first announced in 1953 and was known as the Taiwan Economic Development Plan (TEDP) before the early 1990s. In the past, the TEDP and the NDP were developed by the Council for Economic Planning and Development (CEPD). In 2014, the CEPD was merged with the Research, Development and Evaluation Commission (RDEC) to form the National Development Council (NDC). Thus, the NDC is now in charge of developing the NDP.

5 According to Global Views Monthly, in the cost-benefit analysis of Kaohsiung Metro, the daily ridership was expected to be 237,000 in 2008. However, the actual number turned out to be 110,000. The overestimation of the ridership has resulted in a heavy financial burden for Kaohsiung Metro.

6 According to Article 4 of the *Budget Act*, there are six types of special funds outside of the general fund: the enterprise fund, debt service fund, trust fund, operations fund, special revenue fund, and capital project fund.

7 President Chen Shui-bien's New Ten Major Construction Projects borrowed NT$ 430 billion (US$ 14.33 billion). President Ma Ying-jeou's i-Taiwan 12 Projects borrowed NT$ 499.2 billion (US$ 16.64 billion). President Tsai Ing-wen's Forward-Looking Infrastructure Development Plan has so far borrowed NT$ 107 billion (US$ 3.57 billion) and will borrow another NT$ 313 billion (US$ 10.43 billion) in the next three fiscal years.

8 In 2017, the central government's revenue was NT$ 1.92 trillion (US$ 64 billion), while its debt with a maturity of one year or more (long-term debt) was NT$ 5.36 trillion (US$ 178.67 billion), which was 32.14 percent of the average of nominal GDP for the previous three fiscal years. In the same year, local governments' aggregate revenue was NT$ 830 billion (US$ 27.67 billion), while their aggregate long-term debt was NT$ 854 billion (US$ 28.47 billion).

9 In 2018, the long-term debt incurred by special municipalities may not exceed the following percentages of the average of nominal GDP for the previous three fiscal years: Taipei City: 2.49%; Kaohsiung City: 1.82%; New Taipei City: 1.00%; Taichung City: 0.87%; Taoyuan City: 0.76%; and Tainan City: 0.71%.

10 In Taiwan, governments have "first reserve" and "secondary reserve" in the annual budget. Each government agency has the "first reserve" in its departmental budget, which amounts to 1 percent of its operating budget. The "secondary reserve" is set under the general budget (e.g., the Executive Yuan's budget or municipalities' general budget). The amount is determined by governments' financial conditions.

11 For example, when the qualification requirements for suppliers are complicated, governments may apply selective bidding procedures. When there is no bid in response to open bidding procedures or selective bidding procedures, governments may apply limited bidding procedures.

12 According to the *GPA*, if a government applies the lowest bidding principle, a bidder whose bid meets the government's requirements and is the lowest bid should be the winning bidder. If a government applies the most advantageous bidding principle, the government should comprehensively evaluate the bidders' technology, quality, and price, and decide who is the winning bidder based on this evaluation.

13 According to Article 23 of the *Urban Road Act*, local road maintenance is funded through local governments' annual budgets, grants from upper-level governments, donations from the private sector, benefit-fees for road construction, road user charges, and vehicle fuel fees. In the case of Taipei City, the Taipei City Government set up a 6-year's "Road Smoothing Project" (2009 - 2014) to improve the road quality. The main funding source was the government's annual capital budgets.

14 For instance, Technical Directions for Hydraulic Structures Inspection and Safety Evaluation provides instructions for dam maintenance. Regulations for Construction and Maintenance of Railway provides details of railway maintenance.

15 Other acts related to BOT include the Mass Rapid Transit Act, the National Property Act, the Local Government Public Property Administration Act, the Commercial Port Law, the Electricity Act, etc.

16 In Taiwan, governments can co-finance or subsidize BOT projects if needed. According to Article 4 of the *PPIP Act*, a government or government-owned enterprise can provide funding for a BOT project no more than 20 percent of its total costs. According to Article 25 of the *Statute for Encouragement of Private Participation in Transportation Infrastructure Projects*, a government can subsidize part of interest on the loan for a BOT project related to transportation infrastructure if it evaluates that "the private entity does not have adequate self-financing ability."

17 For example, in the 1990s, the MOTC promoted "a parking garage for every town" policy; the Environment Protection Agency also proposed "an incinerator for every municipality" policy.

Chapter 13
The Vietnam Capital Management and Budgeting Case Study

Lien Nguyen
Old Dominion University, USA

Meagan M. Jordan
Old Dominion University, USA

Thuy Thi Nguyen
Ministry of Finance of Vietnam, Vietnam

ABSTRACT

Divided into four parts, this chapter examines infrastructure investment in Vietnam through the lens of a normative framework for capital management and budgeting. Part 1 provides an overview of the country's socio-economic, political, and financial background that would affect the capital management processes. Part 2 introduces the status of Vietnam's infrastructure and its challenges. Part 3 is a comprehensive review of current procedures and processes of capital planning, budgeting, implementation, and maintenance being practiced in Vietnam. The authors then compare and contrast Vietnam's practices with the recommended provisions of the normative framework. Part 4 reviews the probable consequences associated with infrastructure inefficiency, which are implied by Vietnam's inconsistent practices with the framework. This chapter culminates with conclusions and recommendations for capital management and budgeting that are more specific to a developing country like Vietnam.

INTRODUCTION

The normative framework for capital public management and capital budgeting processes is recommended to have four components: (1) long-term public capital planning, (2) capital budgeting and financial management, (3) project execution, and (4) infrastructure maintenance. In the United States, this framework is widely adopted and used by state and local governments (Ermasova, 2013a, 2013b).

DOI: 10.4018/978-1-5225-7329-6.ch013

The application of the four components results in efficiency and effectiveness in public investment (Srithongrung, 2008). However, there is limited knowledge as to how the normative framework is globally practiced. Government practices are also influenced by country-specific factors including economic, political, legal and managerial situations (Srithongrung, 2010). The purpose of this chapter is to fill in this gap by illustrating Vietnam's capital management and budgeting processes in comparison with the normative framework. The chapter also reviews Vietnam's contextual factors that potentially influence their capital management and budgeting practices. The first section describes Vietnam's socio-economic and political background. The second introduces Vietnam's infrastructure system and its challenges. The third section compares Vietnam's capital and management practices to the normative framework, and the final section analyzes and discusses any implications or associated consequences.

THE COUNTRY'S SOCIO-ECONOMIC, POLITICAL AND FINANCIAL BACKGROUND

Socio-Economic Background

Vietnam is a socialist-communist country in South-East Asia. It is geographically located at the heart of the Asia-Pacific region, bordering China in the north, Cambodia and Laos in the west, and the South China Sea and the Pacific Ocean in the east and south (Dang & Pheng, 2015). By 2015, the World Bank (WB) reported Vietnam's population as more than 91 million, which makes Vietnam the 14th-largest nation in the world. About 70 percent of the population is from the age of 15–64 years old (Trading Economics, 2016). In addition, an educated workforce and low labor costs are advantageous to Vietnam for attracting more investors (Magennis, Dang, Le, Fish, & Bui, 2017). Vietnam is divided into 63 cities and provinces. The two largest socioeconomic centers are Hanoi, the capital city in the north with a population of about 7.2 million people, and Ho Chi Minh City in the south with a population of about 8.1 million (General Statistics Office of Vietnam, 2015).

After the northern-based, Democratic Republic of Vietnam merged with the southern-based, Republic of Vietnam to form the autonomous Socialist Republic of Vietnam in 1975, Vietnam started its reconstruction to restore the country's economy that was damaged by the war. During this period, its economy remained in serious crisis with inflation soaring from 125 percent in 1980 to 774 percent in 1986 (Harvie & Tran, 1997). The centrally planned, subsidy-based and relatively autarkic framework followed by Vietnam was considered to contribute to its economic failure (Institute of World Economy Vietnam, 1995). In 1986, the Sixth National Party Congress approved a radical reform, the "economic renovation" or "*Doi Moi,*" that was intended to facilitate the transition from a centralized economy to a "socialist-oriented market economy". Major policy changes initiated by *Doi Moi* combined government planning with free-market incentives (Dang & Pheng, 2015).

Vietnam's economic structure consists of three major sectors: agriculture sector, service sector, and manufacturing and construction sector. As the result of industrialization during *Doi Moi*, Vietnam's economy became less dependent on agriculture and moved toward the rise of the manufacturing and construction sector (Dang & Pheng, 2015). The expanding growth of this sector appears to correspond to the rising level of infrastructure investment in Vietnam. As one of the most open economies in the world, Vietnam has been seeking regional and global opportunities for further international integration.

It joined the World Trade Organization in 2007 and has signed sixteen bilateral and multilateral trade agreements. It recently participated in new free trade agreements such as Vietnam-European Union Free Trade Agreement and the Trans-Pacific Partnership (World Bank, 2017a). Consequently, Vietnam recorded a massive inflow of foreign direct investment, which brought an explosion of infrastructure development in the forms of office buildings, hotels, industrial zones, resident parks (Tran, 2009).

Thirty years after the launch of the *Doi Moi*, Vietnam is considered a development success story—marked by remarkable poverty reduction and economic growth. Vietnam reached the middle-income status in 2009. The poverty rate went down to 13.5 percent in 2014 (World Bank, 2017a). Since then, Vietnam's GDP has expanded more than fivefold. According to the Asian Development Bank (ADB), Vietnam's GDP was 6.2 percent in 2016, which makes the country one of the fastest-growing economies globally (Magennis et al., 2017). Vietnam has been able to transform itself from "a centrally-planned economy with heavy bureaucracy and subsidies to a socialist-oriented market economy characterized by strong dynamism and growing entrepreneurship" (Earnst & Young, 2013, p. 14). Accompanied by a massive expansion in international trade and significant inflows of foreign direct investment, Vietnam's economy has integrated deeply into the regional and global economies bringing about improvements in the economics and welfare of the Vietnamese people, especially significant increases in access and quality of services (World Bank, 2017a).

Despite notable achievements, the *Doi Moi* also has its downsides, and the development challenges of Vietnam persist. For instance, foreign capital flowed primarily to urban areas, and many areas lacked access to capital and productive land. Productivity across the three economic sectors was uneven, and environmental degradation worsened. Inequalities between the rich and the poor developed, and disparities between urban and rural centers grew (Tromme, 2016). Fragmented decentralization incurred since "the scope has mostly limited to fiscal and administrative reform rather political or personnel decentralization" (Vu, 2016, p. 188). Furthermore, and prominently, public sector corruption flourished (Tromme, 2016). Steinfeld and Thai (2013) expressed concern about corruption being the major challenge of Vietnam along with the South China maritime dispute[1] and the growing unhappiness of Vietnamese citizens (Steinfeld & Thai, 2013).

The Governmental System

Vietnam's political system is based on the principle of *democratic centralism* where pluralist opinions and conflicting views should be widely discussed at all levels of the hierarchy. However, while taking these opinions into account, the Communist Party of Vietnam is the one who makes political and economic decisions (McCargo, 2004, p. 55). The political system of Vietnam is composed of the Communist Party of Vietnam, the State system, and other social and political organizations as in Figure 1 (Government Portal of Vietnam, 2018).

The Communist Party of Vietnam

Since Vietnam's reunification, the Communist Party of Vietnam is the only ruling party in the country and has a leading role in setting the broad parameters of the national policy of Vietnam. The most important economic strategies are outlined in the resolutions of the Party Congress. "The actual role of the Party in state management is opaque" (Van Arkadie & Mallon, 2004, p. 59). However, the Party

Figure 1. The political system in Vietnam (Government Portal of Vietnam, 2018)
Source: Adapted from Government Portal of Vietnam, 2018

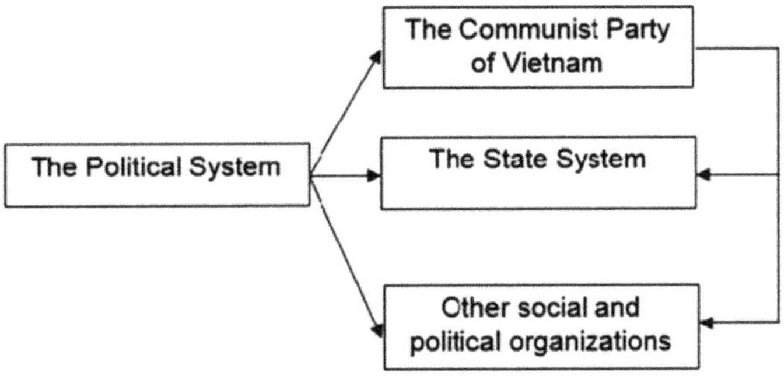

maintains control by filling all key positions in all government agencies. For instance, the Prime Minister, President, and Chairman of the National Assembly are members of the Political Bureau (Politburo), the Party leaders. Party cells function parallel to state agencies at all levels (Van Arkadie & Mallon, 2004).

The State System

All State powers are centralized in one supreme body, the National Assembly (NA), which is a unicameral legislature where almost 90 percent of its legislators are Communist Party members (Magennis et al., 2017). In Figure 2, the NA is superior to both the executive and judicial branches and is vested with constitutional and legislative power. Generally, the NA has three main functions: scrutinizing legislation, reviewing government plans and budgets, and supervising the performance of implementation (Vietnam

Figure 2. The state system (Dan Luat, 2016)
Source: Excerpted and adapted from Dan Luat, 2016

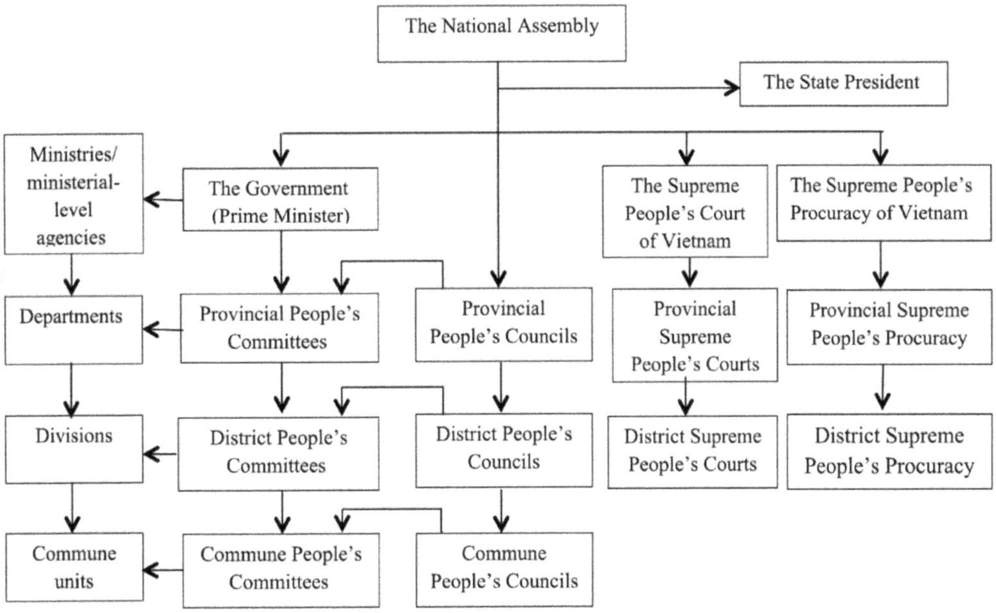

Net, 2010). Subject to the Communist Party's direction, the NA's role has become increasingly important in overseeing all government functions in recent years, and it acts with authority over government performance (Van Arkadie & Mallon, 2004).

The government is the executive arm of the NA and the highest administrative body responsible for executing and managing all national policies (Magennis et al., 2017). The Prime Minister of Vietnam, nominated by the President and approved by the NA, leads a cabinet currently composed of deputy prime ministers, the heads of government ministries, and various state organizations (Government Portal of Vietnam, 2018). Vietnam is a hierarchical, top-down administrative system. Currently, Vietnam has four tiers of government. In addition to the central government, there are three local levels: (1) 63 provinces (includes 5 major cities), (2) 713 district-level cities and towns, and (3) 11,162 wards and commune (see Figure 2). "Each tier of government has both legislative and executive authorities" (Morgan & Trinh, 2017, p. 334).

In the central government, capital planning and budgeting are administered by the ministry of planning and investment (MPI). However, the MPI must coordinate with the ministry of finance (MOF) to formulate the detailed allocation plan for the medium-term and annual public investment plan (Prime Minister's Office of Vietnam, 2017a). Their respective subordinates, the Department of Planning and Investment and Department of Finance, similarly act as facilitators for capital planning and budgeting and fund allocation at the local government level.

Other Social and Political Organizations

There are a number of social and political organizations in Vietnam that have a role in the political and governing system, such as the Vietnam Fatherland Front, Vietnam Labour Confederation, Women's Association, Ho Chi Minh Communist Youth's Union, the Vietnam Veterans' Association, and professional associations. For instance, the Vietnam Fatherland Front is one of the authorities in charge of developing and implementing public investment plans. It is also responsible for public supervision of capital investment projects as regulated in Article 95 of the Public Investment Law (National Assembly of Vietnam, 2014).

Public Finance System

The State Budget Law, first enacted in 1996 and revised several times since then, is the key legislation underpinning budget management in Vietnam. Vietnam is one of a few countries that utilize a single, unified State budget which must ultimately be ratified by the NA. The State budget encompasses the central government budget and the consolidated provincial–district–commune budgets (see Figure 3). Each provincial budget encompasses the provincial budget plus all of the district budgets within the boundaries of the province, and so forth. This nested budgetary arrangement or "Matruska-doll" model means lower level budgets are components of higher level budgets (Asian Development Bank, 2016a).

Each budgetary level is approved by the relevant People's Councils and by the upper-tier provincial People's Committees. The executive organs prepare and finalize their detailed budgets to be approved by the elected organs (Figure 3). The NA approves the State Budget, which includes the Central Budget with details by ministry and the aggregated revenue and expenditure for each provincial budget (Asian Development Bank, 2016a). Vietnam has a rules-based system of intergovernmental fiscal transfers, including balancing transfer and targeted transfer, to narrow horizontal and vertical imbalance. Horizontal

Figure 3. Administrative and budget system (Asian Development Bank, 2016a)
Source: Adapted from Asian Development Bank, 2016a

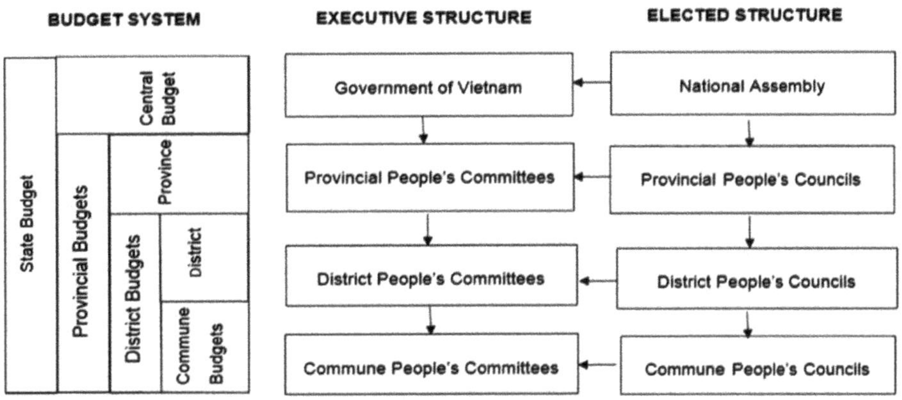

imbalance (across regions) exists because of differences in the fiscal capacities of local governments. It is quite common in Vietnam because some big provinces/cities like Ho Chi Minh city contribute significantly to the State budget, 31.8 percent in 2016 (Le, 2016). Vertical imbalance occurs when there are differences within a region's own expenditure and fiscal revenue (Di Liddo, Longobardi, & Porcelli, 2016). State Budget Law allows local budgets to possess a deficit (National Assembly of Vietnam, 2015). The balancing transfer is given to the provinces without any conditions on allocation, while it is conditional for targeted transfer (Nguyen, 2016). Currently, in Vietnam, there are 50 provinces (out of the 63 provinces) that have received balancing transfers from the central governments (Nguyen, 2016).

Although this nested budget system ensures the uniformity of the budget, it reduces the fiscal autonomy of local governments and complicates budget preparation and monitoring with its bottom-up budgeting and top-down decision-making (Nguyen, 2016). The outcomes of the entire process must be finally integrated into the single State budget (Nguyen-Hoang & Schroeder, 2010). In addition, the nested budget system does not facilitate fiscal accountability of the lower levels of government because the higher levels of government have certain "veto rights" over budgets adopted by provincial and sub-provincial authorities (Rab et al., 2015).

PUBLIC SECTOR INFRASTRUCTURE AND ITS CHALLENGES

Introduction to Vietnam Infrastructure

The government of Vietnam was able to sustain a high level of infrastructure investment at 10 percent of GDP on average during 1995-2007 putting Vietnam ahead of most East Asian economies (Nguyen & Dapice, 2009, p. 2). More recently, Vietnam continued to lead the region in infrastructure investment averaging 8 percent of GDP between 2008 and 2015 (Verougstraete & Tran, 2017), which was much higher than the world average at 3.8 percent of GDP (Inderst, 2016). The commitment to infrastructure is set to continue in the medium term according to the MPI. Vietnam needs some $480 billion to fund urgent infrastructure investments by 2020 (Vietnam Net, 2017).

Significant investment in public infrastructure brings about documented achievements. Generally, infrastructure development is imperative for delivering essential public services, increasing productivity levels, and promoting job opportunities (Verougstraete & Tran, 2017). However, challenges, such as poor quality and disadvantaged infrastructure competitiveness are restraining the country's development. Despite the recent improvement in overall ranking, the competitiveness of Vietnam's infrastructure system is still modest in comparison with more advanced South-East Asian economies (Nguyen & Dapice, 2009). In 2016, Vietnam's overall infrastructure competitiveness ranked 79th out of 138 compared to Thailand and Malaysia at 43rd and 22nd, respectively (Schwab, 2016). Also, Vietnam's logistics costs (costs of managing import and export of goods) have seen an upward trend and has been estimated around 20-25 percent of Vietnam's GDP in recent years, which is far higher than that of a developed country's range of 10-13 percent (Vietnam News, 2015). Low quality infrastructure is one of the contributing factors to the increase in logistical costs (Dang & Pheng, 2015).

There are four major infrastructure sectors: transportation, power, information communication technology, and water and wastewater. To provide context for the country's capital management and budgeting, the following presents a background of the condition and future demand for infrastructure investment.

Transportation Sector

The transportation sector consists of roadways, railways, airways, and marine and inland waterways and has a total projected need of $45 million between 2016-2020. The roadways sub-sector is progressing more rapidly than others and is reported to have the largest share of total investment needs in the transportation sector at 67 percent or $29 billion (Verougstraete & Tran, 2017). Roadways are the dominant means of transport and accounts for 67 percent cargo moved (Dang & Pheng, 2015). ADB assesses that "the road network consists predominantly of unpaved, narrow, local road sections; therefore, traffic is greatly affected by environmental and weather conditions" (Asian Development Bank, 2012, p.5).

Among other subsectors, there are several notable concerns. The main line of the railway, a 1,726 km track linking Ho Chi Minh to Hanoi, is aging and poses various dangers as it passes through the residential urban area (Lovells, Boots, & Harris, 2016). In regards to ports, along with the increasing port congestion (Dang & Pheng, 2015), Vietnam has no "world class" deep-water port that could accommodate "mother ships" (Nguyen & Dapice, 2009, p. 7), and exports are transshipped to Hong Kong or Singapore before being dispatched to foreign markets, increasing transaction costs on export activities (Duong, 2014, p. 404). As stated in the Socio-Economic Development Plan 2016-2020, future demands for continued improvement include development in a number of projects on North-South roads, the upgrade of existing railroad-gauge widening, a North-South high-speed train, and Long Thanh International Airport (Verougstraete & Tran, 2017).

Power Sector

Vietnam's power sector consists of four main fuel sources: hydropower, coal, gas and oil. These contribute to total power generation at 43 percent, 34 percent, 19 percent and 4 percent, respectively. Hydropower dependence exposes Vietnam to risks of seasonal fluctuation and dam safety in the rainy season. During the dry season, the power supply usually falls short due to reduction in production of hydroelectricity as the result of lower flows of water, while the electrical demand typically rises (Nguyen & Dapice, 2009). The government of Vietnam is also concerned about the safety of hundreds of dams for hydropower plants because during the heavy rainy season, they could turn into "water bombs," threatening the lives of millions of people residing in the low-land areas (Muoi, 2013). Nguyen and Dapice (2009) recommend installing more thermal power to solve the seasonal problem of electricity generation. The power supply is pushed to capacity. Electricity of Vietnam reported that by the end of 2014 100% percent of the country's districts and 98 percent of the households had connected to the power grid. Vietnam expects electricity consumption to grow by 10-12 percent annually through 2020. Therefore, an additional power supply is needed to avoid shortages to meet the growing demand (Verougstraete & Tran, 2017).

Information Communication Technology (ICT) Sector

Vietnam's government has prioritized upgrading the ICT infrastructure because it is vital for the development of the country's "economic transition and global integration" (Verougstraete & Tran, 2017, p. 17). Investments in ICT infrastructure are expected to produce wide-reaching innovation throughout the country, including remote areas. These efforts include increasing penetration rates of telephone and internet as well as 100 percent connectivity of all areas to broadband networks via fiber optic cable and satellite. Ultimately, this investment would support the use of ICT in e-commerce and services. Vietnam expects "the number of the internet users will account for over 70 percent by 2020" (Verougstraete & Tran, 2017, p. 17)

Water/Wastewater Sector

Vietnam's investment in the water/wastewater sector is lagging behind other areas of infrastructure. Most of the population, in both urban and rural areas, has access to improved water, 99.1 percent and 96.7 percent, respectively. Provincial water companies, which can be wholly or partially a state-owned enterprise (SOE), are the dominant suppliers of urban water. However, the provision of wastewater treatment is at a much lower level for both urban and rural areas. Fewer than 10 percent of households in urban areas have treated wastewater, which is normally financed by individual households. The revenue generated from historically low tariffs is not sufficient to cover the investment costs needed to modernize wastewater treatment. The 10 percent surcharge for water provision introduced in some cities is a start, but it does not demonstrate a country-wide commitment to the water/wastewater infrastructure sector (Verougstraete & Tran, 2017). The economic growth and urbanization have led to huge pressures on infrastructure systems, such as sewerage and drainage systems, which are outdated and cannot keep up with the pace of growth (Pham & Kuyama, 2013). Wastewater and storm water problems become particularly serious in the big and business concentrated cities.

Infrastructure Investment Challenges

Literature on infrastructure investment in developing countries identify challenges as financial and management issues. The former includes under-investment in infrastructure, allocations of public capital, public resource constraints, and private financing. Management concerns are cost overruns, benefit shortfalls, project planning, or corruption (Dang & Pheng, 2015). Vietnam is also experiencing both financial and managerial issues in its infrastructure development (Nguyen & Dapice, 2009).

Infrastructure Financing Challenges

Despite current high levels of infrastructure investment, financial resources are not sufficient to accommodate infrastructure investment needs (Verougstraete & Tran, 2017; Warlters, 2006). Estimations of annual demand for capital investment in Vietnam range from $16.7 billion to $25 billion by the ADB and WB. United Nations Economic and Social Commission for Asia and the Pacific estimates that Vietnam will need about $20.2 billion annually (Verougstraete & Tran, 2017, p. 47). However, the current State budget, which includes official development assistance (ODA) and government bonds, covers less than half of this amount, creating an estimated financing gap annually of around $12 billion (Verougstraete & Tran, 2017).

In addition, the share of spending on infrastructure projects in Vietnam mainly comes from the public sector. The State budget has accounted for about two-thirds of the infrastructure investment in Vietnam during 2009-2015 (Verougstraete & Tran, 2017). According to ADB estimates, private investment in Vietnam's infrastructure could be less than 10 percent of the national total compared to as much as 30 percent in India (Yap & Nguyen, 2017). Public funding is estimated to be able to meet only one-third of planned spending. Therefore, Vietnam needs to consider innovative solutions to attract more private financing of infrastructure in the coming years.

Infrastructure Management Challenges

The level of infrastructure development in Vietnam has not improved at the same pace as its high level of investment over the past decades (Dang & Pheng, 2015). As indicated by ADB, "expenditure has not translated into improving infrastructure and service delivery (Asian Development Bank, 2016b, p.1). Overall, "Vietnam is the least efficient users of capital based on the incremental capital-output ratio" (ICOR) among selected Asian economies (Nguyen & Dapice, 2009, p. 4). In 2014, the ICOR for Vietnam was 5.2, meaning that it takes Vietnam $5.2 on investment to produce an additional $1.00 of income. Comparatively, the ICOR was $4.9 for India, $4.6 for Malaysia, $4.5 for Thailand, and $3.7 for the Philippines (Asian Development Bank, 2016b).

In the planning stage, poor project selection or prioritization is the most frequently cited problem. Scholars and practitioners consistently find issues of inappropriate planning in Vietnam. According to Warlters (2006), during the planning, it is becoming increasingly difficult to select investment projects with high economic returns. Similarly, it is challenging to direct investment in infrastructure because there is a mismatch between projects identified politically as preferred investment targets and those that would otherwise be chosen by investors on the basis of economic viability (Lovells et al., 2016).

In the implementation stage, many other efficiency problems have been identified, especially in the large construction projects, such as poor performance of existing civil engineering. Many roads in Vietnam are still in bad condition due to inadequate structural design, construction, and poor maintenance (Vo, 2007). Even some newly built major municipal roads and bridges suffer severe quality problems (Vo, 2007). Le-Hoai, Dai Lee, and Lee (2008) indicate that delay and cost overruns are two additional major problems in large construction projects. Vietnam's unit cost for infrastructure projects increases rapidly over time and are relatively higher than that of other countries. The unit cost of an expressway raised to $18.2 million/km during 2009-2013 from $9.8 million/km during 2006-2012 (Nguyen & Dapice, 2009; Vu, 2012).

Vietnam is exposed to a number of other management challenges that are relevant to the country's context. Governance issues, including corruption, also influence the efficiency of infrastructure investment. World Bank (2017a) reports "systemic fraud and corruption issues that have been observed including kickbacks, conflicts of interest, fraudulent document submissions, and use of unauthorized subcontractors" (p. 24). The involvement of State-owned Enterprises (SOEs) in infrastructure development also poses challenges because they are not independent of the corresponding ministry who is formally responsible for implementation, which leads to problems with infrastructure quality and fiscal capacity (Verougstraete & Tran, 2017). The coordination among tiers of government is not smooth (Warlters, 2006). Ambiguous expenditure assignments among central and local governments may cause a spending overlap, resulting in inefficiency (Morgan & Trinh, 2017). Vietnam has become a more decentralized country, administratively and fiscally, which challenges the capacity of a sub-national subordinate to manage its capital investment effectively (Asian Development Bank, 2016b). Further discussion of these challenges and their impacts are found in the Analysis part.

Dang and Pheng (2014) identified the top 27 ranking inefficiency problems and classified them into five factors which are found in Vietnam: (1) insufficient institutional capacity of the government, (2) lack of transparency and accountability in infrastructure development, (3) lack of an effective land acquisition framework, (4) inadequate forecasting capacity, and (5) insufficient building capacity of local firms (p. 8).

The case of Vietnam is a contradiction of high infrastructure investment and inefficient performance, which raises significant questions about how the capital management and budgeting process works. Are there any specific features of Vietnam's capital management and budgeting process associated with the current challenges? What are the possible consequences for capital management? The next section examines the country's current capital management practices.

CAPITAL MANAGEMENT AND BUDGETING PROCESS IN VIETNAM

To promote public investment reform, Vietnam recently enacted laws and relevant decrees to regulate and guide the formulating, assessment, prioritization, approval, implementation, and inspection of public investment projects. Public Investment Law, which went into effect in 2015 and State Budget Law, amended in 2015, are the most important legislation and will guide the presentation of Part III. One of the most notable elements of these two legal documents is the introduction of the Medium-Term Investment Plan and the Medium-Term Financial Plan, which introduce multiple year investment and budgeting plans and are expected to address longstanding issues of alignment between plans and budgets (World Bank, 2017b).

Capital Planning

Strategic Planning

A series of legal documentation outlines the Vietnamese government's guidance of the development of social-economic planning (see Table 1) (Vu, 2012). Despite Vietnam's move to the decentralizing planning in the 2000s, Vietnam's central government is still involved in setting the nation-wide social and economic plan (Vu, 2012). The Prime Minister still directly approves most of the national level planning strategies and programs. A formal consultative decision-making process at all government levels

Table 1. Legal documents guiding socio-economic development planning

Legal Documents	Preparation	Approval	Duration
Central Level			
Ten-year Socio-Economic Development Strategies	Chaired by the Government	Central Executive Committee of the Communist Party	10 years and above
Five-year Socio-Economic Development Plan	Chaired by the Government	The National Assembly	Five-year
Public Investment Programs	Chaired by MPI	The Prime Minister	Five-year
Annual Social-Economic Development Plans	Chaired by MPI	The Government	One year
Region, Locality, and Sector			
Social-Economic Development Plans for Special region/Territory	Chaired by MPI	The Prime Minister	10 years and above
Social-Economic Development Plans for Provincial level	Provincial People's Committees coordinate with Line Ministries	The Prime Minister	10 years and above
Master plan for developing the major national industries, sectors and products	Line Ministries coordinate with Localities	The Prime Minister	10 years and above
Social-Economic Development Plans for District level	District People's Committees	Provincial People's Committees.	10 years and above
Sectoral Development Plans at provincial level	Line Departments	Provincial People's Committees	

Source: Adapted from (Vu, 2012)

involves a wide range of actors including the Party, legislature (NA and People's Council), the state management body (government and People's Committee) and the executive (Bartholomew, Leurs, & McCarty, 2005). While the process conforms to the consensual-seeking principle, the level of influence of that the consultation has on decision making is not clear (Dang & Pheng, 2015).

As in Table 1, the government, led by the Prime Minister and assisted by the MPI, prepares the ten-year Socio-Economic Development Strategies and the five-year Socio-Economic Development Plans and submits to the Party and the NA for approval. The most recent Socio-Economic Development Strategies for 2011–2020 lays out the foundation for the country's medium-term development strategy and highlights the need for structural reform, equity, and emerging issues of macroeconomic stability (Verougstraete & Tran, 2017). The Socio-Economic Development Plan for 2016-2020 lays out the actions needed to translate the strategies into reality, provides a framework and direction for preparation, and ultimately gets approval of the annual plan. The two documents also serve as the basis for the formulation of sectoral and local development plans, including economic infrastructure development. Accompanying the five-year Socio-Economic Development Plan is a Public Investment Program that forms the basis for developing a framework of capital allocation among investments (Dang & Pheng, 2015 cited from MPI).

Master Planning

The Vietnamese government periodically develops master plans for each key infrastructure sector and publishes lists of projects to be developed within the scope of those master plans (Lovells et al., 2016).

In recent years, Vietnam's Prime Minister has issued many decisions to approve master plans to develop the infrastructure system with a vision towards 2020 and beyond. Such master plans include:

- *Decision 1734 of December 2008 for development of high-speed road transportation systems (Decision 1734)*
- *Decision 1436 of September 2009 for development of railway systems (Decision 1436)*
- *Decision 21 of January 2009 for development of air transportation (Decision 21)*
- *Decision 2190 of December 2009 for development of seaports systems (Decision 2190)*
- *Decision 05, Decision 06 and Decision 07 of January 2011 addressing the transportation systems in the North, the South and the Central areas of Vietnam, respectively (Lovells et al., 2016, p.321).*

According to (Lovells et al., 2016), it is more realistic to view the various master plans as setting general but non-binding targets. The master plans identify key developmental needs with terms of 5 or 10 years for attracting investments toward such targets. A master plan acts as the guidelines for relevant ministries, industrial agencies, and/or provincial local authorities to develop their specific development plan, but it does not impose any strict legal obligations on any of these governmental organizations (Lovells et al., 2016). Despite the urgent need for infrastructure development and targets set by various master plans, there is no clear prioritization of one single infrastructure sector over others (Lovells et al., 2016). As a consequence, the constrained budget is spread widely and equally among the infrastructure sectors, which may negatively affect the investment efficiency and effectiveness.

Capital Investment Planning Process

For individual investment projects, the Public Investment Law classifies capital investment into four groups depending on the significance and size. They are: important national projects, Group-A, Group-B, and Group-C (National Assembly of Vietnam, 2014). Each type of project, depending on sources of financing, is subjected to a different approval authority. The important national projects along with special projects, such as ODA funded or concessional loans[2] on national defense, have to be approved by the Prime Minister following the resolution issued by the NA. Head of line ministries and central regulatory bodies are granted authority to decide on Group-A, Group-B and Group-C investment projects financed by the domestic state budget, government bond, ODA and overseas concessional loans. The Chairman/Chairwoman of the provincial People's Committee has the authority to decide on Group-A, Group-B and Group-C investment projects under the provincial administration. The Chairman/Chairwoman of the People's Committee of a district or commune has the authority to decide on Group-B and Group-C projects financed by local balanced fund allocated from the State budget at district or communal administrative levels (National Assembly of Vietnam, 2014).

Figure 4 illustrates the general process of formation and adoption of a medium-term plan for public investment. Following the guidance from the government and MPI, Ministries, regulatory authorities, and local authorities are responsible for formulating plans for public investment based on the approved sectoral development planning and other relevant plans. The MPI leads the coordination and consolidates these submitted public investment plans into Public Investment Programs (Arrow A in Figure 4) including the list of investments and investment budgets. The MOF is in charge of estimating the total funds for the Public Investment Program. The MPI then assesses such plans and the capital allocation and sends back the assessment results to relevant Ministries, Regulatory authorities, and local authorities

Figure 4. Vietnam's national planning system (Dang & Pheng, 2014)
Source: Adapted from Dang & Pheng, 2014

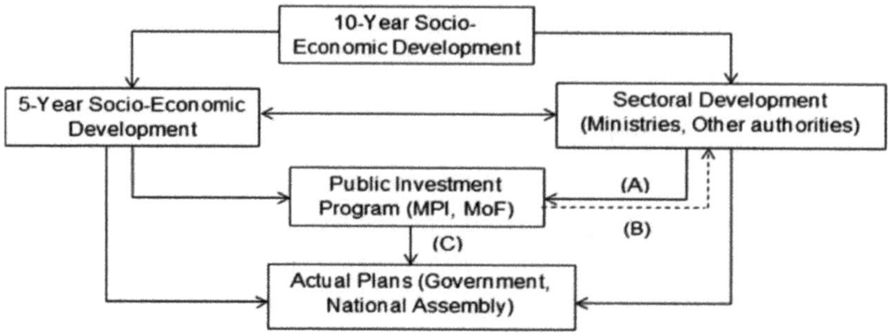

for revision and completion (Arrow B in Figure 4). The final investment plans are submitted again to the MPI who finalizes and presents them to the Government (Arrow C in Figure 4). The Government will submit the national public investment plan to NA for approval (National Assembly of Vietnam, 2014).

The NA, on November 10, 2016, passed a resolution on the first medium-term public investment plan for the 2016-2020 period with a total maximum budget of $89.56 billion; $50.2 billion is from the central budget and $39.4 billion is from the local budgets (Anh, 2016). Public investment plans are classified using three criteria: time limit, level of decentralization and capital sources. As a result, there are annual and medium-term plans; national, central and local plans; and investment plans funded by central budget, by local revenue, by ODA, by concessional loans, and so on (National Assembly of Vietnam, 2014).

Capital Budgeting and Financial Management

Vietnam has a system of "dual budgeting" in which the MOF prepares the fiscal framework and the recurrent budget estimates, while the MPI prepares the Public Investment Program and the investment budget (Bartholomew et al., 2005). This budget system separates the cost of a project's development from its subsequent operating costs (Spackman, 2002). According to the WB, this process has resulted in serious imbalances between recurrent and capital expenditure. Separate planning of capital brings the danger of over-investment because capital is often seen as inherently more virtuous or at least more politically rewarding when not considered with the annual spending for operations (Spackman, 2002, p. 11).

Allocation Priority

There are three main sources of funding for 2016-2020 medium term investment plan: domestic capital, government bond, and foreign capital. The domestic capital first allocation priority is allocated to repay the outstanding debts in infrastructure construction (the value of approved workloads without being allotted to pay yet) prior to December 31, 2014. The next priorities are reciprocal capital for projects using ODA, concessional loans, or investments of the State in public private partnerships (PPPs) and investments into transferred projects completed in this time period. The remaining will be allocated for new projects. For government bonds, the capital allocation will be given to national important projects in transportation and irrigation as listed in the index of Resolution 726/NQ-UBTVQH13. The remaining of this funding source will be used for new urgent capital projects and in mountainous, ethnic minority, and remote areas. The external capital shall be disbursed and allocated according to the central government's budget specified in the agreement signed for specific project of the 2016-2020 period (National Assembly of Vietnam, 2016)

Medium-Term Expenditure Frameworks (MTEF) and Annual Budgeting

Most recently the financing scheme for capital projects is pay-as-you-go basis. Local governments send their need to the central government where the MPI and MOF make a recommendation for financing projects. However, the available budget is insufficient to pay for all capitals requirement by local governments (Verougstraete & Tran, 2017). Currently, the new State Budget Law lays out a plan for the introduction of medium-term expenditure framework (MTEF) to strengthen budget planning with the introduction of the 5-Year Financial Plan (5YFP) and the 3-Year Financial Budgetary Plan (3YFBP) (National Assembly of Vietnam, 2015). This MTEF implementation expects to match with the medium-term capital planning to avoid funding mismatch and fiscal instability when dealing with multi-year capital projects.

The MTEF is known as a multi-year public expenditure planning exercise (Pearson, 2002). It is also known as a rolling budget and as a whole-of-government strategic policy and expenditure framework (Mundial, 1998). In Vietnam's application, the 5YFP is drawn up for a five-year period in accordance with the five-year Socio-Economic Development Plan, and the 3YFBP is formulated annually for three consecutive years, including the year of budget estimation and two additional years based on a rolling approach. Both plans are formulated and submitted by central agencies (national level) and provinces (sub-national level) (Chu, 2017).

For 5YFP, both national and provincial 5YFPs focus on determining overall objectives, specifying financial and budgetary targets, and setting the ceiling for the period. It specifies State budget indicators including revenues, expenditures, and budget balance. It also specifies debt indicators and anticipates risks that may be associated with budget balance and debt indicators (Prime Minister's Office of Vietnam, 2017b). The MOF completes, and the NA approves the national 5YFP. The MPI provides a 5-year economic forecast of the economy as a basis for revenue forecasting covering key macroeconomic variables. The 5YFP at the provincial level is formulated by the provincial People's Committees and decided by the People's Councils after getting opinions of the MOF and MPI.

For 3YFBP, it is formulated annually for three years, whereas the first year represents the budget year and provides detailed estimates of revenues and expenditures, the structure of revenues and expenditures, and the budget deficit. The two subsequent years provide the forecasts of state revenue, expenditure, budget balance, and other relevant information to guide resource allocation for each tier of government for budget estimates of the respective years (Prime Minister's Office of Vietnam, 2017b).

At the national level, the MOF in cooperation with the MPI is in charge of consolidating the national 3YFBP and submits it to the Government and the NA for consideration and discussion. At the provincial level, the Department of Finance coordinates with Department of Planning and Investment to have 3YFBP reported to the provincial People's Committees and approved the People's Councils (Prime Minister's Office of Vietnam, 2017b).

Financial Strategies

The majority of funding for Vietnam's investment on infrastructure over the past 20 years is supported by State budget and the ODA. However, these sources of funding are not sustainable in the mid-to-long-term because of the persistently high budget deficits in recent years and declining ODA[3] since Vietnam achieved its middle-income status (Campbell, Huynh, & Nguyen, 2015). In addition, Vietnam intends to mobilize funds other than State funds and restrict borrowing from foreign creditors under MOF guarantees (Campbell et al., 2015). Private investment through several market-based approaches for funding such as PPP will potentially supplement the identified funding gap for infrastructure, which is around $12 billion a year (Campbell et al., 2015; Verougstraete & Tran, 2017).

State Financing

State financing for infrastructure in Vietnam takes different forms, including direct fiscal support, which typically falls under capital or development expenditures allocated to local governments, regional sectors, and specific projects. In addition, Vietnam Development Bank, wholly owned by the government, plays a significant role in providing financing to infrastructure projects under the execution and management of SOEs and local provinces. This bank's sources of funding include State capital allocation and ODA on-lending. The Vietnam Development Bank also issues bonds and take loans from domestic and foreign lenders (The Vietnam Development Bank, 2018). The government of Vietnam also provides guarantees for SOEs and major infrastructure projects, which enter fiscal accounts as contingent liabilities. However, the proportion of public capital expenditure in the State budget has been significantly reduced recently due to the structural allocation of the State budget (Verougstraete & Tran, 2017).

Official Development Assistance (ODA)

Vietnam is known as one of the largest ODA recipient countries in the last decade. In Figure 5, Japan is the largest bilateral donor to Vietnam, followed by Korea and Germany (Organization for Economic Cooperation and Development-Development Assistance Committee, 2016). International development associations are the second largest donors, which include WB and ADB, who maintain relatively large funding and typically focus on infrastructure development. Donors had committed to loan Vietnam about $85 billion during 1993-2014. However, due to Vietnam's rising income status, the ODA commitment is on the decline with $4.2, $3.2, and $2.9 billion committed for 2014, 2015, and 2016 (Verougstraete & Tran, 2017).

Figure 5. Top ten donors of gross ODA for Vietnam (OECD-DAC, 2016)
Source: Organization for Economic Cooperation and Development-Development Assistance Committee, 2016)

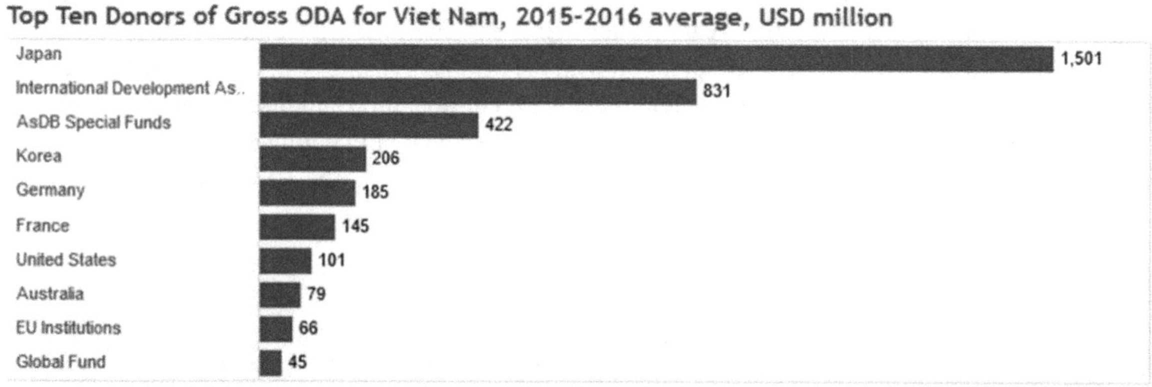

Public Private Partnerships (PPPs)

In the context of declining State budget and limited availability of ODA, private financing through PPPs has become a significant channel for infrastructure development in Vietnam. Private investments have increased steadily between 2000-2016. During that period, infrastructure projects have attracted a total of $12.85 billion from private investments with 61 percent and 16 percent of that going to electricity and ICT (Verougstraete & Tran, 2017, p. 34). Roads and water infrastructures have received the least investment at three percent and two percent, respectively (Verougstraete & Tran, 2017).

In order to create a robust regulatory environment for PPPs, Vietnam has issued a number of laws, decrees, and circulars governing the implementation of investment in PPP for infrastructure projects. In 2015, the new PPP decree provides basic principles and general regulations to ensure flexibility for PPP projects of different scales and in different infrastructure sectors (Campbell et al., 2015). In line with the issuance of the new PPP decree, the Prime Minister approved a list of 127 foreign investment projects through 2020 with an estimated value of $60 billion, and the majority are to be conducted as PPPs (Campbell et al., 2015, p. 2). One of the successful factors of the PPP program is the development of "bankable" infrastructure projects. Bankable projects are structured so that investors are repaid if the funded projects perform adequately; therefore, investors are likely to finance local infrastructure projects that they anticipate will generate sufficient revenue (Verougstraete & Tran, 2017).

Centralized Execution and Project Management

Public investment management in Vietnam is governed by various laws including the State Budget Law, Construction Law, and Investment Law, which have been described as fragmented (Kim & Nguyen, 2013, p. 9), loose, and overlapping (Thai, 2008). The enactment of the Law on Public Investment in 2015 regulates the management and use of capital budget, state management of public investment, and rights and obligation of involved parties and is expected to address the problems identified with previous legislation (Kim & Nguyen, 2013). This next section discusses two key processes of the project execution stage.

Project Procurement

According to Article 1 of Law on Public Procurement, infrastructure investments financed by the State budget, capital investment projects of SOE, and other capital investment that have at least 30 percent or at least VND 500 billion of total capital in the project are subject to competitive bidding except for some circumstances provided by Article 21-27 (National Assembly of Vietnam, 2013). Alternatively, ODA projects are not subject to Vietnam's procurement rules. Investment projects funded by ODA loans and grants are normally governed by regulations in accordance with loan agreements between the Vietnamese government and the donors (National Assembly of Vietnam, 2013).

Implementation and Monitoring

The Ministries, regulatory authorities, local authorities, the People's Committees of districts, and units using the capital budget for public investment are assigned by law to manage their own projects. The main tasks include carrying out the projects by following the approved budget and schedule, conducting bidding and appointing a contractor, making payment to and supervising the contractor, and inspecting the implementation of the public investment plan (National Assembly of Vietnam, 2014). In practice, each of the above entities who uses the capital budget for public investment will establish a Project Management Unit to be responsible for daily implementation. For instance, the Ministry of Industry and Trade is the project owner of an electricity factory project and will assign a department within the Ministry to implement the project.

Regarding project monitoring and supervision, the MPI is tasked with supervision and inspection of the implementation of the annual and medium-term plans for public investment of the Ministries, central authorities and the People's Committees of provinces. In addition, the State Audit of Vietnam conducts the annual independent audit of public investment projects at the request of the National Assembly, Government, and Prime Minister (National Assembly of Vietnam, 2014). The general purpose is to ensure legal compliance and effective management of public expenditure and report any misappropriation of state funds, corruption, or incurred loss. Recently, the State Audit Office of Vietnam has announced a plan to focus on major public investment projects in the transportation sector (Tuoi Tre News, 2017).

Infrastructure Maintenance and Evaluation

In Vietnam, the Law on the Management and Use of State Assets of 2008, which was replaced by the Law on the Management and Use of Public Property in 2017, covers state management of public property, policies on management and use of public property, and the rights and obligations of involved parties. Maintenance planning is under the scope of this Law. The 2008 version creates fundamental changes for the asset management in Vietnam. They include:

(i) For the first time the State was able to assess and compile data on three types of assets: land, property and motor vehicles and other assets at or above the value of VND 500 million; (ii) The right to manage and use assets was transferred to agencies and units in association with the expansion of financial autonomy; and (iii) New asset management mechanisms were adopted which are more transparent and market based. (World Bank, 2017b, p.40)

It is the role of the MOF to ensure the consistent enforcement of this law as well as manage the current public asset management databases. The WB has funded the Vietnam Road Asset Management Project to support efforts to improve the efficiency and sustainability of road asset management and maintenance practices performed on national roads in Vietnam (World Bank, 2017a).

For maintenance funding, the relevant Minister is responsible for issuing legal documents for different infrastructure sectors. For instance, the Minister of Transport is responsible for issuing regulations on road administration and maintenance (National Assembly of Vietnam, 2008). As a result, the Ministry of Transport has issued relevant circulars on guiding management, operation, and maintenance of roadways, national railway. Legislation has also passed that requires all provinces to include the cost of road maintenance in their Medium-Term Expenditure Plans (World Bank, 2017a).

AN ANALYSIS ON VIETNAM'S PRACTICES AND DISCUSSIONS OF POSSIBLE CONSEQUENCES

This section reviews the four components of the normative framework, compares Vietnam's capital management practices with the framework's recommendations, highlights inconsistences, and discusses possible consequences. In general, the capital management and budgeting processes in Vietnam also undergo the four main stages as outlined in the normative framework: long-term capital planning, budgeting and financial management, project management, and infrastructure maintenance. However, at each stage, there are distinctive variations from the framework. For instance, capital budgeting processes are closely similar to the normative framework while the capital planning has a great deal of variation. Additionally, there are country-specific features which significantly affect capital management and budgeting practices, such as SOEs' involvement in capital management, corruption challenges, and the mixture of financing sources, political factors, and other economic and fiscal conditions.

Long Term Capital Planning

The normative framework offers comprehensive guidance on steps and tools involved in the planning process, which involves multi-year project and finance planning. In form, under the requirement of the Public Investment Law, Vietnam also builds multi-year capital planning in line with priorities of the national five-year Socio-Economic Development Plans and longer-term strategies, the ten-year Socio-Economic Development Strategies. The capital plans consist of projects inventory and total estimation of cost as well as the source of financing. However, the current Vietnam's infrastructure planning still appears to deviate from the normative capital planning in numerous ways.

Three deviations from the normative framework reflect a weakness in project assessment. First, the normative framework suggests that need assessment relies on the assessment of facility condition and the agency's mission, strategic planning, and programmatic-based activities, which Vietnam is following. However, there are so many strategic and master plans that it is difficult to ensure consistency. They are also too broadly defined, which allows any project to fit within them (World Bank, 2017b). In addition, Vietnam's public asset management and assessment are inadequate, resulting in inaccurate documentation of facility condition (World Bank, 2017b). Thus, facility conditions would mislead the need assessments.

Second, there is a lack of clarity in assessment criteria. The normative framework suggests that government should establish clear and objective criteria for project selection to reflect community priorities and investment targets. Such criteria are established in Vietnam, but they are either not detailed enough or not consistent or sufficient for project assessment. In fact, there is the absence of methodologies and guidelines on the preliminary assessment of the socio-economic effectiveness of a public investment program (Jenkins, Miklyaev, Afra, & Hashemi, 2017). As a consequence, it leads to poor project selection. In an assessment of piloting prioritization infrastructure project, Marcelo, Mandri-Perrott, House, and Schwartz (2016) find that data among project feasibility studies are not comparable, which may be a consequence of inconsistent rules, guidelines, and standards. In addition, Marcelo et al. (2016) also find an inherent bias towards infrastructure projects in wealthier or urban regions, which also indicates a weakness of selection and definition of evaluation metrics. Without the clear objective and comparable criteria, the assessors may find it difficult to compare or prioritize among projects. Assessors may bias their assessment.

Third, the lack of independence and capacity of the assessor are constraints on the formal assessment as a basis for project selection. Formal appraisal mechanisms are often not independent because the responsible agencies are subordinate to authorities who are ultimately project owners (Asian Development Bank, 2016b). Assessors are not capable of evaluating large scale and complex projects due to lack of professional or technical knowledge related to project appraisal. There are cases of pro forma appraisals to create the appearance of satisfying the appraisal requirement when the projects have been approved by a political decision (Vu, 2012). The pressure of time also impacts the quality of appraisal. For instance, for project Group A, Group B, and Group C, the time limits are 40, 30, and 20 days. These time frames are likely insufficient for complicated assessment workloads (Vu, 2012).

Altogether, problems associated with need assessments, evaluation criteria, and project assessment make the investment project prioritization and project selection in Vietnam problematic. In this context, Vietnam's ineffective assessment process is extremely susceptible to political pressure on project selection and corruption. As a result, until 2015, "many projects were included in the investment plan without being subject to adequately detailed costing or appraisal" (World Bank, 2017b, p.48).

Fourth, the normative framework requires a long-term financial projection that indicates the aggregate amount of resources available for public capital projects in each year based on the individual sources of revenue. Vietnam also has a financial plan included in the capital plan; however, there is always a mismatch between investment needs and available capital resources. This problem may originate from Vietnam's dual budgeting system, which creates the separation between investment decision-making and budget allocation. Most infrastructure sectors and corresponding line-ministries can decide their own investment inventory and scope of investment project. However, the MOF is the one who arranges capital sources. This planning leads to individual provinces or infrastructure sectors competing for scarce resources distributed by MOF. As a consequence, the investment projects proposed by provinces and line ministry keep growing long with an unaffordable budget (Vu, 2012).

Such a mismatch of funding is the most challenging issue in the planning process. The current outstanding construction debts are the obvious and material consequences for the government. Funding allocated to clear these debts in the coming years will reduce financial availability for other priorities. At the same time, incomplete projects waiting for funding may anticipate the delay and incur an extra cost due to such delay. The contractors who are implementing the project also suffer from late payment, and the citizens are forced to wait for long periods for such public services to be delivered.

Capital Budgeting and Financial Management

The weaknesses in Vietnam's budgeting processes regarding prioritizing capital projects have been previously discussed; however, contextual influences strain efforts to maintain prudent fiscal and debt management practices. Vietnam's first priority is to clear outstanding debts in construction infrastructure, which is a consequence of the previous mismatch between capital plan and finance plan. Although the amount of outstanding debt is not officially available, it is estimated at $1.7 billion[4] (Phuc, 2017). Although Vietnam conducts multi-year fiscal planning as required under Medium-term expenditure frameworks, the adoption of this practice only began in 2017. This adoption is expected to eliminate the outstanding construction debts and improve financial stability in the future.

As a proportion of GDP, Vietnam's public debt has increased rapidly over the past few years. Approaching the statutory thresholds of 65 percent, it has reached 61 percent as of 2015, resulting in a high interest payment. The normative framework suggests that a high debt service is more than 15 percent of operating expenditures (Simonsen, Robbins & Brown, 2003). Using the framework's formula, interest payment as a percent of operating expenditure instead of GDP in the 2017 budget was approximately computed at 11 percent[5] of recurrent spending, which places Vietnam at a moderate level. As mandated by State Budget Law, Vietnam is also maintaining an operating reserve of 2 percent-4 percent of total budget at both central and local levels to cover natural disasters and other emergencies. Spending decisions of these reserves at central and local governments rest with the Government and the People's Committee, respectively (National Assembly of Vietnam, 2015).

Centralized Execution and Project Management

Vietnam does not follow the recommended practice from the framework of having a central body to supervise project construction, monitor project performance, track the use of funds, and report funded project progress to the public and central government. Instead, the implementation and supervision of project construction are administered directly by the line ministry, who is the owner/proposal of that project. However, MPI and its subordinate do play the coordination role at central and local government level. They provide guidelines, instructions, and a formal application process for submitting capital project requests based on legislative mandates. Despite its coordination role for capital management and budgeting, the MPI has no such public nationwide, web-based secure application that captures capital project information.

Despite such inconsistence with the framework, it is hard to assess whether such differences cause any problems for Vietnam because the context is so different. Decentralization has been intensive in Vietnam in recent years. An example is fiscal decentralization; the local governments manage more than 50 percent of capital funding (World Bank, 2017b). Capital planning is also delegated to the local government. The recommendation of centralized execution may not be appropriate for Vietnam.

Infrastructure Maintenance

As recommended by the framework, Vietnam implements both maintenance planning and maintenance funding. As mentioned earlier, the recently enacted Law on the Management and Use of Public Property of 2017 governs maintenance planning. However, the implementation is still in a low pace; the current changes are not sufficiently robust and comprehensive. For instance, the waste of assets and leakage of resources are not determined in a timely fashion. "As such the value of an asset has not been maximized" (World Bank, 2017b, p. 40). The government needs to strengthen the utilization and public asset management.

In Vietnam, the maintenance funding regulation is promulgated by respective line ministry for relevant sectors. For instance, the Roadway Maintenance Fund established in 2013 is the largest maintenance fund responsible for roadway maintenance. Whereas, the Central Fund is responsible for national roadways and the Local Fund is responsible for local roadways. At the national level this fund earns revenues from two sources: user fees and a transfer from the State budget. This fund reports that 50 percent of the maintenance demand is satisfied. The Central government also develops the database to manage the road infrastructure as well as roadway asset system for future operation and maintenance (Phan, 2017). This maintenance funding application is similar to the framework's recommended practice of having a separate appropriation bill or a special maintenance and repair budget (Ermasova, 2013a).

One of the long-standing issues related to maintenance funding in Vietnam is the relationship between the spending on capital projects and the spending on recurrent operation and maintenance (O&M). This is apparent in almost all infrastructure sectors but is particularly serious in the transport sector. "In the transport sector, over-spending on capital projects and under-spending on maintenance at both national and provincial levels have long been a concern", because preserving a road in good condition is less costly than its rehabilitation or reconstruction (World Bank, 2017b, p.49).

Potential Consequences Resulting From Vietnam's Context

Corruption Culture

Corruption is perceived to be widespread in Vietnam, which ranks 107th out of 180 countries in Transparency International's 2017 rankings. Vietnam's score of 35 is below average on a scale identifies 0 as highly corrupt and 100 as very clean (International Transparency, 2017). Corruption in Vietnam is thought to have increased since *Doi Moi* (Tromme, 2016). Despite many achievements, *Doi Moi* policies offered more spoils for abuse and bribery (Vu, 2010).

A number of recent studies and surveys illustrate the pervasiveness, scale, and cost of corruption. According to the Provincial Competitiveness Index, the majority of firms (51–70 percent) paid a bribe to access government services between 1996 and 2014. In a 2015 World Bank Enterprise Survey, 91 percent of firms reported they were expected to make informal payments to public officials to "get things done," which was a far higher number than the regional average. Firms also report that connections to the state are important to succeed in business, affecting access to land and other resources. This commercialization of relationships between state and markets also impedes investment and development of the private sector. (World Bank, 2017a, p.15)

With around 10 percent of GDP being channeled into capital investment, this is a prominent area for potential corruption. There have been several documented corruption scandals in connection with infrastructure projects (Warlters, 2006). The two recent scandals are related to Japanese ODA-funded projects. First, in April 2006, the Ministry of Transport was alleged to have embezzled millions of dollars of public funds by rewarding contractors that were closely affiliated to politicians in the Ministry (Tromme, 2016). Second, Japan Transportation Consultants Inc. admitted having bribed the officials from Vietnam Railways' project management unit to win bids for ODA projects (Tromme, 2016). These corruption cases adversely influence the ODA funding from Japan. ODA is one of the main financing sources for infrastructure investment, and Japan is the largest bilateral donor to Vietnam. The negative impact on Vietnam's reputation can extend to other ODA donors.

Corruption is believed to arise at most stages of the infrastructure project cycle, both planning and implementation stages (Warlters, 2006, p. xvi). Gueorguiev and Malesky (2012) found clear evidence of corruption during the business registration process (planning) and procurement procedures (implementation) in Vietnam. A majority of cases involve corruption during procurement. In fact, the two above examples of corruption scandals happened during the procurement process – contractors bribed for favorable award decisions. The involvement of corruption in the bidding process may diminish competition and result in awards to an unqualified contractor that may lead to poor project performance as well as poor quality of infrastructures. Collusion among bidders and the use of inadequate and inferior materials are also common corrupt practices (Warlters, 2006).

Corruption and transparency issues of public procurement are concerns in Vietnam. While competitive bidding is the required for most infrastructure projects, directly awarding contracts to SOEs and subsidized companies is a common practice (Verougstraete & Tran, 2017; World Bank, 2017b). A current investigation by the MPI indicates that 69 out of 71 Build-Operation-Transfer projects in the transportation sector during 2011-2015 were awarded directly to the contractors without competitive bidding (Verougstraete & Tran, 2017). Additionally, reform is needed to ensure independent dispute settlement and to resolve the conflicting instructions in contract implementation. WB contends that "Vietnam has made a great effort in public procurement reform; however, most of the achievements have been in establishing the legislative framework. Implementation remains a challenge" (World Bank, 2017b, p. 39).

Political and Administrative Factors

The literature on infrastructure planning and delivery in developing countries indicates that "political leaders and government bureaucrats can use investments in infrastructure construction as a tool for securing political positions or competing for scarce funds" (Dang & Pheng, 2014, p. 2). As a consequence, infrastructure planning and decision making become political rather than rational. Nguyen and Dapice (2009) offer the construction the Ho Chi Minh highway, which is parallel to the existing Highway 1, as an example of a project that was economically non-viable but approved under political pressure (p. 6). The new highway cuts through mountains of central Vietnam, tracing the path of the famous wartime Ho Chi Minh Trail. Such a geographical location makes the road's construction costly ($2 billion for 1,230 km), and the road is easily exposed to flood damage. More importantly, it does not create a lot of new traffic because it connects poor provinces. It is more cost effective to build a limited-access highway and railway to connect to coastal plans, which fits better with Vietnam's geography. Given the financial constraints, the allocation of this large project would curtail funding for other needed industrial clusters that influence Vietnam's long-term growth. The newly built Ho Chi Minh highway was underutilized, and therefore, an inefficient investment (Nguyen & Dapice, 2009). Today, despite the evolving body of investment legislation, the tension between politically driven projects and investors' need for project viability remains (Lovells et al., 2016).

Since Vietnam is a highly-decentralized administrative structure, both central government and local government have respective distinctive roles in infrastructure development. Such progressive devolution to its subnational governments is a reason for its wide spreading of capital investment (Asian Development Bank, 2016b). Individual provinces select and undertake their own infrastructure projects, and investment decisions are driven mainly by administrative consideration with lack of reference to strategic national priorities and market-based mechanisms for resource allocation (World Bank, 2013). With more than a half of the State budget now administered by the subnational government, many provinces are too small to enable efficient planning of infrastructure, leading to a proliferation of under-utilized airports, deep-sea ports, and industrial parks (Asian Development Bank, 2016b). As reported by the Vietnam Development Report of 2012, there are nearly 260 industrial parks, 18 economic zones, 24 deep sea ports and 20 operating airports. These numbers are excessively high in relation to the size of Vietnam's economy (World Bank, 2013). Accordingly, the average industrial park's occupancy rate is only 46 percent, and the utilization rate of Cai Mep-Thi Vai's seaport is less than 30 percent. Clearly, regionally focused and political decision making without national or inter-regional consideration has resulted in inefficiencies and over developed and underutilized infrastructure projects (World Bank, 2013).

State Owned Enterprises (SOEs)

World Bank (2011) raise concerns about the conflict of interest when discussing SOEs. An SOE, centrally or local owned by an investment owner, is involved in design and implementation of infrastructure projects. A typical example is the case of the Ministry of Construction. An SOE affiliated with the Ministry of Construction may participate in design and implementation of large construction contracts where the Ministry of Construction is also the project owner (World Bank, 2011). Without independent assessment of project design and budget estimation, for instance, this conflict of interest may imply higher costs for the construction project. Vietnam's effort to equitize these SOEs has been recognized; however, the State still owns the majority of shares of these enterprises. Thus, ownership-right of these SOEs remains with the ministries in most cases (World Bank, 2011). In addition, Warlters (2006) expresses concern regarding the capacity of SOEs. For example, "The Ministry of Transport has over 200 SOEs, of which over 100 are engaged in construction. Many of these enterprises are excessively indebted" (p. xiv). Ultimately, the strained capacity of these SOEs affect the quality of work and cause delayed implementation (Warlters, 2006).

Dependence on Foreign Donors and Other Issues

The mixed sources of finance for infrastructure also influence capital budgeting and management. There are some common issues associated with ODA in Vietnam, such as differences in procedures and inconsistency between the Vietnamese legal system for construction projects and international practices and regulations of foreign donors. These problems impact implementation of ODA projects and disbursement of ODA funds that lead to delays in projects, irrelevant designs, and increased costs. Furthermore, the ODA loans are often attached with donor's binding conditions, including policy reform and limited contractor selection. These conditions result in higher borrowing costs as well as less opportunity for local contractors (Verougstraete & Tran, 2017).

Other conditions include fiscal conditions, inefficient domestic resource mobilization, and an inadequate system for monitoring risks also affect the capital budgeting and management. The government of Vietnam's rising debt levels and short average time-to-maturity of domestic government bonds (4.44 years by the end of 2015) impose refinancing pressures upon the government with about 50 percent of Vietnam's domestic public debt maturing in the next three years (World Bank, 2017b, p. 21). In addition, high debt service payment, volatile fiscal revenues, and vulnerabilities in the domestic banking sector also pose threats to future fiscal stability (World Bank, 2017a).

CONCLUSION

The case of Vietnam illustrates an example of a developing country with remarkable economic growth and a strong commitment to public infrastructure development, as evidenced by its high percentage of investment. The review of infrastructure indicates that the transportation sector and power sector are the two largest shares of capital investment, while the water and wastewater sector is the least developed infrastructure sector. Despite the commitment, Vietnam's infrastructure competitiveness and quality are still weak compared to other countries in the region, and the need for vast improvement remains. Financial and managerial problems are identified as the two main challenges that undermine public investment efficiency in Vietnam. While financial challenges receive significant consideration through government efforts in maintaining foreign investment inflows and seeking private financing through PPP, more managerial efforts are needed to improve the quality of infrastructure and the efficiency of planning and allocating resources.

The analysis of Vietnam's capital management and budgeting processes using the normative framework reveals that Vietnam also experiences the four components of the framework. While the budgeting and maintenance practices appear to be similar to the recommendations, the analysis indicates some differences in capital planning and the management compared to the normative. Lack of a sufficient financial plan supporting the capital investment plan is the most problematic issue creating a haphazard capital investment agenda when many infrastructure projects have commenced without the financial allocation available to complete them. The recent introduction of medium-term investment and financial planning is expected to address this problem. Vietnam should also pay further attention to address the inappropriate planning that deviate from the framework, including inadequate needs assessment, lack of independent evaluation, and problematic project prioritization. Vietnam's vast corruption, involvement of SOEs in infrastructure investment, dependence on foreign donors, and current fiscal condition also negatively affect investment effectiveness. Finally, while comparing Vietnam's practices and the normative framework, the legal regulations are not far from the normative framework, but the actual implementation or enforcement creates a more significant deviation.

Lastly, the framework is recommended for developed countries like the United States, and there are differences in practice that exist for developing countries like Vietnam. As a developing country, demand for infrastructure is quite high, and it keeps growing. The country may require a higher percentage of debt service as a proportion of operating expenditure to accommodate such infrastructure needs. In addition, most of the external debt is from ODA (94 percent) (Minh, 2016), which is more favorable (lower interest) than other commercial debts. The recommended debt level should be reconsidered accordingly. Another example is the recommendation in favor of centralized execution and centralized budgeting which appears not to be adopted in Vietnam since the project management units are widespread among ministries and localities. Notably, in the context of substantial devolution and the nested budget system, local governments share responsibilities with the central government and administer about 50 percent of Vietnam's capital budget. The recommended practices of an adapted normative framework that accommodates various political and structural organizations as well as the status of economic development could still benefit developing countries' efforts regarding effective capital budgeting and management.

REFERENCES

Anh, D. (2016). $90 billion for public investment in 2016-2020. *Vietnam Economic Times*. Retrieved May 15, 2018, from http://vneconomictimes.com/article/vietnam-today/90-billion-for-public-investment-in-2016-2020

Asian Development Bank. (2012). *Transport sector assessment, strategy, and road map*. Retrieved May 15, 2018, from https://www.adb.org/sites/default/files/institutional-document/33360/files/vie-transport-assessment.pdf

Asian Development Bank. (2016a). *Public financial management systems—Viet Nam: Key elements from a financial management perspective*. Retrieved from https://www.adb.org/sites/default/files/institutional-document/225661/public-finmgt-systems-vie.pdf

Asian Development Bank. (2016b). *Sector assessment (summary): Public sector management (public expenditure and fiscal management)*. Retrieved May 15, 2018, from https://www.adb.org/sites/default/files/linked-documents/50051-001-ssa.pdf

Bartholomew, A., Leurs, R., & McCarty, A. (2005). *Joint evaluation of general budget support 1994-2004*. Vietnam Country Report: August.

Campbell, S., Huynh, L., & Nguyen, N. (2015). *The new PPP decree – Vietnam's solution for infrastructure development*. Retrieved from http://www.hlaseanhorizon.com/_uploads/pdfs/New_PPP_Decree_in_Vietnam.pdf

Chu, N. A. (2017). *Medium-term expenditure framework on subnational level in Vietnam*. Retrieved from http://gizmacro.ciem.org.vn/Content/files/Final%20Outline%201_Medium%20Term%20Expenditure%20Framework%20on%20Subnational%20Level.pdf

Dan Luat. (2016). *Sơ đồ tổ chức bộ máy nhà nước theo Hiến pháp 2013*. Retrieved from https://danluat.thuvienphapluat.vn/so-do-to-chuc-bo-may-nha-nuoc-theo-hien-phap-2013-144432.aspx

Dang, G., & Pheng, L. S. (2014). Critical factors affecting the efficient use of public investments in infrastructure in Vietnam. *Journal of Infrastructure Systems*, *21*(3), 05014007.

Dang, G., & Pheng, L. S. (2015). *Infrastructure investments in developing economies*. Springer. doi:10.1007/978-981-287-248-7

Di Liddo, G., Longobardi, E., & Porcelli, F. (2016). Measuring horizontal fiscal imbalance: The case of Italian municipalities. *Local Government Studies*, *42*(3), 385–419. doi:10.1080/03003930.2016.1150836

Duong, T. N. (2014). Vietnam country report. *Financing ASEAN Connectivity*, 401-429.

Earnst & Young. (2013). *Doing business in Vietnam*. Retrieved May 15, 2018, from http://www.ey.com/Publication/vwLUAssets/Doing_Business_in_Vietnam/$FILE/Doing_Business_in_Vietnam_16000319.pdf

Ermasova, N. (2013a). Capital budgeting in the states after the Great Recession. *State & Local Government Review*, *45*(2), 119–130. doi:10.1177/0160323X13487079

Ermasova, N. (2013b). The improvement of capital budgeting at the state level in the USA. *Public Administration Review*, *2*(2), 92–104.

General Statistics Office of Vietnam. (2015). *Vietnam*. Retrieved May 15, 2018, from http://www.gso.gov.vn/default_en.aspx?tabid=774

Government Portal of Vietnam. (2018). *Political system.* Retrieved May 25, 2018 from http://www.chinhphu.vn/portal/page/portal/English/TheSocialistRepublicOfVietnam/AboutVietnam/AboutVietnamDetail?categoryId=10000103&articleId=10001578

Gueorguiev, D., & Malesky, E. (2012). Foreign investment and bribery: A firm-level analysis of corruption in Vietnam. *Journal of Asian Economics, 23*(2), 111–129. doi:10.1016/j.asieco.2011.11.006

Harvie, C., & Tran, V. H. (1997). *Vietnam's reforms and economic growth.* Springer. doi:10.1057/9780230389472

Inderst, G. (2016). ADBI working paper series, infrastructure investment, private finance, and institutional investors: Asia from a global perspective. A. D. B. Institute.

Institute of World Economy (Vietnam). (1995). *Vietnam's economic renovation and foreign economic policies*. Social Sciences Publishing House.

International Transparency. (2017). *Corruption perceptions index 2017.* Retrieved May 15, 2018, from https://www.transparency.org/news/feature/corruption_perceptions_index_2017

Jenkins, G. P., Miklyaev, M., Afra, S., & Hashemi, M. (2017). *Prioritization of public investment projects in Vietnam (No. 2017-08).* JDI Executive Programs.

Kim, H., & Nguyen, V. V. (2013). *Improving the Efficiency of the Public Investment in Vietnam through the Korean Experiences.* Seoul: Korea Development Institute. Retrieved May 15, 2018, from https://www.kdevelopedia.org/mnt/idas/asset/2014/04/17/DOC/PDF/04201404170131443070648.pdf

Le, P. (2016). Ho Chi Minh City contributed 31.8% to the state budget. *Phap Luat*. Retrieved May 5, 2018, from http://plo.vn/kinh-te/tphcm-dong-gop-toi-318-cho-ngan-sach-ca-nuoc-643798.html

Le-Hoai, L., Dai Lee, Y., & Lee, J. Y. (2008). Delay and cost overruns in Vietnam large construction projects: A comparison with other selected countries. *KSCE Journal of Civil Engineering, 12*(6), 367–377. doi:10.100712205-008-0367-7

Lovells, H., Boots, S., & Harris, J. (2016). Vietnam infrastructure: Needs and challenges. In *The Principles of Project Finance* (pp. 319–336). London, UK: Routledge.

Magennis, B., Dang, H., Le, C., Fish, R., & Bui, L. (2017). *Legal guide to investment in Vietnam.* Retrieved May 5, 2018, from http://www.vietnamlaws.com/pdf/LegalGuidetoInvestmentinVietNam.pdf

Marcelo, D., Mandri-Perrott, C., House, S., & Schwartz, J. (2016). An alternative approach to project selection: The infrastructure prioritization framework. *World Bank Working Paper.*

McCargo, D. (2004). *Rethinking Vietnam.* London, UK: Psychology Press. doi:10.4324/9780203569467

Minh, D. (2016). *ODA accounts for 94% of government external debt. Vietnam Financial Review.* Retrieved June 1, 2018, from http://thoibaotaichinhvietnam.vn/pages/thoi-su/2016-01-19/oda-chiem-94-danh-muc-no-nuoc-ngoai-cua-chinh-phu-28031.aspx

Morgan, P. J., & Trinh, L. Q. (2017). 10. Fiscal decentralization and local budget deficits in Viet Nam: An empirical analysis. *Central and Local Government Relations in Asia, 1*(1), 323–333.

Mundial, B. (1998). *Public expenditure management handbook*. Washington, DC: World Bank. Retrieved from http://www1.worldbank.org/publicsector/pe/handbook/pem98.pdf

Muoi, N. P. (2013). *Vietnam worried about dam safety in rainy season*. Retrieved June 1, 2018 from https://blogs.wsj.com/indonesiarealtime/2013/08/31/vietnam-worried-about-dam-safety-in-rainy-season/

National Assembly of Vietnam. (2008). *Law on road traffic*. Retrieved June 1, 2018, from http://www.moj.gov.vn/vbpq/en/lists/vn%20bn%20php%20lut/view_detail.aspx?itemid=10506

National Assembly of Vietnam. (2013). *Public procurement law*. Retrieved June 1, 2018, from https://www.hcmiu.edu.vn/Portals/1/Docs/vanbanphapluat/english/43-2013-QH13%20Luat%20Dau%20thau.pdf

National Assembly of Vietnam. (2014). *Public investment law*. Retrieved June 1, 2018, from http://www.fetp.edu.vn/cache/MPP7-541-R9.3E-Law%20on%20Public%20Investment%202014--The%20National%20Assembly-2015-01-07-11214028.pdf

National Assembly of Vietnam. (2015). *State budget law*. Retrieved June 1, 2018, from http://www.economica.vn/Content/files/LAW%20%26%20REG/83_2015_QH13%20Law%20on%20State%20budget.pdf

National Assembly of Vietnam. (2016). *Resolution on medium-term public investment plan of 2016 - 2020 Period*. Retrieved June 14, 2018, from https://vanbanphapluat.co/resolution-26-2016-qh14-on-medium-term-public-investment-plan-of-2016-2020-period

Nguyen, T. T. (2016). *Fiscal decentralization trends in Vietnam: Developments and reforms*. Paper presented at the Public Administration and Policy, Hong Kong.

Nguyen, X. T., & Dapice, D. (2009). *Vietnam's infrastructure constraints*. Ash institute for democratic governance and innovation.

Nguyen-Hoang, P., & Schroeder, L. (2010). An analysis of quasi-decentralized budgeting in Vietnam. *International Journal of Public Administration*, *33*(12-13), 698–709. doi:10.1080/01900692.2010.514449

Organization for Economic Cooperation and Development-Development Assistance Committee. (2016). *Top Ten Donors of Gross ODA for Viet Nam*. Retrieved June 14, 2018 from https://public.tableau.com/views/OECDDACAidataglancebyrecipient_new/Recipients?:embed=y&:display_count=yes&:showTabs=y&:toolbar=no?&:showVizHome=no

Pearson, M. (2002). Medium term expenditure frameworks (MTEFs). DFID's Health Systems Resource Centre for the UK Department for International Development.

Pham, N. B., & Kuyama, T. (2013). *Urban domestic wastewater management In Vietnam - Challenges And opportunities*. Water Environment Partnership in Asia (Policy Brief).

Phan, T. (2017). Road maintenance fund: revenue-expenditure transparency and ict application. *Vietnam Governmental Portal News*. Retrieved June, 4 2018, from http://baochinhphu.vn/Kinh-te/Quy-Bao-tri-duong-bo-Tiep-tuc-minh-bach-thuchi-va-ung-dung-KHCN/317684.vgp

Phuc, N. (2017). *The problem of outstanding construction Debt. Financial Review- Ministry of Finance.* Retrieved June, 4 2018, from http://thoibaotaichinhvietnam.vn/pages/kinh-doanh/2017-06-28/nhuc-nhoi-no-dong-xay-dung-co-ban-44919.aspx

Prime Minister's Office of Vietnam. (2017). *Decree 86/2017/ND-CP defining the functions, tasks, powers and organizational structure of the Ministry of Planning And Investment.* Retrieved June, 4, 2018, from http://www.mpi.gov.vn/en/Pages/cnnv.aspx

Prime Minister's Office of Vietnam. (2017). *Decree 45/2017/ND-CP detailing the formulation of five-year finance plans and three-year finance-state budget plans.* Retrieved June, 4 2018, from https://vanbanphapluat.co/decree-45-2017-nd-cp-formulation-of-five-year-finance-plans-three-year-finance-state-budget-plans

Rab, H. N., Hong, D. Q., Martinez-Vasquez, J., Iyer, I., Shah, A. M., Monkam, K. F. N., . . . Minh, N. V. (2015). *Fiscal decentralization review in Vietnam: making the whole greater than the sum the parts.*

Schwab, K. (2016). *The global competitiveness report 2016-2017, ed.* Paper presented at the WE Forum.

Simonsen, B., Robbins, M. D., & Brown, R. (2003). Debt affordability. Encyclopedia of public administration and public policy. AJ, 1, 308.

Spackman, M. (2002). Multi-year perspective in budgeting and public investment planning. *Draft background paper for discussion at session III, 1*, 46.

Srithongrung, A. (2008). The impacts of state capital management programs on state economic performance. *Public Budgeting & Finance*, *28*(3), 83–107. doi:10.1111/j.1540-5850.2008.00912.x

Srithongrung, A. (2010). State capital improvement programs and institutional arrangements for capital budgeting: The case of Illinois. *Journal of Public Budgeting, Accounting & Financial Management*, *22*(3), 407–430.

Steinfeld, J. M., & Thai, K. V. (2013). Political economy of Vietnam: Market reform, growth, and the state. *Maryland Series in Contemporary Asian Studies, 2013*(3).

Thai, N. Q. (2008). *Public investment efficiency in Vietnam.* Retrieved June 1, 2018, from https://www.kdi.re.kr/data/download/attach/8580_2-4_6.pdf

The Vietnam Development Bank. (2018). Retrieved June 1, 2018, from http://en.vdb.gov.vn/

Trading Economics. (2016). *Vietnam - Population ages 15-64.* Retrieved June 1, 2018, from https://tradingeconomics.com/vietnam/population-ages-15-64-percent-of-total-wb-data.html

Tran, T. Q. (2009). Sudden surge in FDI and infrastructure bottlenecks: The case in Vietnam. *ASEAN Economic Bulletin*, *26*(1), 58–76. doi:10.1355/AE26-1E

Tromme, M. (2016). Corruption and corruption research in Vietnam-an overview. *Crime, Law, and Social Change*, *65*(4-5), 287–306. doi:10.100710611-016-9605-y

Tuoi Tre News. (2017). *Vietnam to audit public investment, BOT projects.* Retrieved June 1, 2018, from https://tuoitrenews.vn/news/society/20171206/vietnam-to-audit-public-investment-bot-projects/43009.html

Van Arkadie, B., & Mallon, R. (2004). *Viet Nam: A transition tiger?* ANU E Press. Retrieved June 1, 2018, from https://press.anu.edu.au/publications/viet-nam-%E2%80%94-transition-tiger

Verougstraete, M., & Tran, H. D. (2017). *Infrastructure financing strategies for sustainable development in Viet Nam.* Retrieved June 1, 2018, from http://www.unescap.org/sites/default/files/20170915%20National%20Study%20-%20Infrastructure%20Financing%20-%20Viet%20%20Nam.pdf

Vietnam Net. (2010). *Political system.* Retrieved from http://english.vietnamnet.vn/fms/vietnam-reference/general-information/439/political-system--part-2-.html

Vietnam Net. (2017). *Vietnam looks to private sector to fund infrastructure.* Retrieved June 1, 2018, from http://english.vietnamnet.vn/fms/business/179988/vietnam-looks-to-private-sector-to-fund-infrastructure.html

Vietnam News. (2015). *Vietnam logistics costs hurting competitiveness.* Retrieved June 1, 2018, from https://vietnamnews.vn/economy/277203/vn-logistics-costs-hurting-competitiveness.html#PRv2fKESKzSuvcFB.97

Vo, T. (2007). Challenges, prospects and strategies for CLMV development: The case of Vietnam. *Development strategy for CLMV in the age of economic integration*, 497-515.

Vu, A. T. T. (2016). Vietnam decentralization amidst fragmentation. *Journal of Southeast Asian Economies, 33*(2), 188–208.

Vu, Q. V. (2010). *Abuse of power in a one-party controlled state with market driven economy: A case study of Vietnam.* Paper presented at the Conference on Authoritarianism in East Asia at the City University of Hong Kong.

Vu, T. T. A. (2012). Quản Lý và Phân cấp Quản Lý Đầu Tư Công Thực Trạng ở Việt Nam và Kinh nghiệm Quốc Tế. *Chương trình giảng dạy kinh tế Fulbright.*

Warlters, M. (2006). *Vietnam's infrastructure challenge—Infrastructure strategy: Cross-sectoral issues.* Washington, DC: World Bank.

World Bank. (2011). *Vietnam - Second public investment reform operation program (English).* Washington, DC: World Bank. Retrieved June 1, 2018, from http://documents.worldbank.org/curated/en/354081468142787169/Vietnam-Second-Public-Investment-Reform-Operation-Program

World Bank. (2013). *Assessment of the financing framework for municipal infrastructure in Vietnam.* Washington, DC: World Bank. Retrieved June 1, 2018, from https://openknowledge.worldbank.org/handle/10986/17568

World Bank. (2017a). *Vietnam - Country partnership framework for the period FY18-FY22 (English).* Washington, DC: World Bank Group. Retrieved June 1, 2018, from http://documents.worldbank.org/curated/en/173771496368868576/Vietnam-Country-partnership-framework-for-the-period-FY18-FY22

World Bank. (2017b). *Vietnam public expenditure review (Vol. 2): Fiscal policies towards sustainability, efficiency, and equity - Overview report (English).* Washington, DC: World Bank Group. Retrieved June 1, 2018, from http://documents.worldbank.org/curated/en/279261508765803168/Fiscal-Policies-towards-Sustainability-Efficiency-and-Equity-Overview-Report

Yap, K. L. M., & Nguyen, U. (2017). *In Asia's infrastructure race, Vietnam is among the leaders.* Retrieved July, 2 2018, from https://www.bloomberg.com/news/articles/2017-03-22/in-asia-s-infrastructure-race-vietnam-is-among-the-leaders

ENDNOTES

1 The maritime dispute over the South China Sea is an ongoing conflict among Asian countries, including Vietnam and China, in the Southeast region. In addition to the navigational rights of the Sea, the maritime dispute extends to the occupation of island archipelagos and mineral rights (Steinfeld & Thai, 2013, p. 51).

2 A concessional loan is the loan that is extended on terms substantially more generous than market loan but its grant element does not reach the ODA grant element threshold (https://stats.oecd.org/glossary/detail.asp?ID=5901).

3 The level of official development assistance from other countries is inversely based on the income status of the recipient country.

4 Converted to equivalent USD by authors.

5 Computed by authors.

Section 4
Conclusion

Chapter 14
Summary, Initial Observations, and Getting to a Tentative Theory of Public Investment Behavior

Arwiphawee Srithongrung
University of Illinois at Springfield, USA

Juita-Elena (Wie) Yusuf
https://orcid.org/0000-0003-3599-1417
Old Dominion University, USA

ABSTRACT

This chapter evaluates the 12 countries' capital management practices according to the systematic public capital management and budgeting process described in Chapter 1. The chapter characterizes and classifies the management practices of the twelve countries based on the authors' evaluation using the case study descriptions. The authors offer some initial observations based on comparisons across the case study countries and analysis of relationships between capital management and budgeting practices and political, economic, and public sector variables. The chapter proposes a tentative theory of public investment behavior and offers five propositions regarding the factors driving different practices across the case study countries and the consequences of a systematic capital management and budgeting process.

INTRODUCTION

In addition to describing how public capital management and budgeting is practiced in different countries, another purpose of this book is to propose a tentative theory of public investment to add to the public finance literature. The previous chapters describe public capital management and budgeting practices in twelve case study countries. An understanding of the differences in public capital budgeting and management practices across the twelve countries should provide a foundation toward theory building in public capital management to explain factors that contribute to variations in public capital management. The

DOI: 10.4018/978-1-5225-7329-6.ch014

individual country case studies presented in this book suggest that capital management and budgeting practices vary regardless of geographical location and government regimes.

This chapter evaluates the twelve countries' capital management practices according to the systematic public capital management and budgeting process described in Chapter 1. The chapter then characterizes and classifies the management practices of the twelve countries based on the editors' evaluation using the case study descriptions. Finally, based on existing frameworks and theories from public finance and entrepreneurial finance (such as information asymmetry, expected utility, transaction cost, prospect theory and investment bias) the chapter proposes a tentative theory of the factors driving different practices across the case study countries.

Note that the tentative theory proposed in this chapter is just a starting point in developing public capital management theory at the international level. This proposed theory needs a larger sample of countries to improve its descriptive and predictive capacity. Despite the important roles of public infrastructure on a country's economic growth, less is known regarding the causes of different capital management practices in providing and arranging public infrastructure systems. Thus, we hope that this book will inspire comparative public administration and international development theorists to build a stronger knowledge base.

The Systematic Process as a Yardstick: Recapitulation

As described in Chapter 1, the normative public finance literature recommends systematic public capital management and budgeting practices for a public infrastructure system that is useful and responsive to the public's capital needs and has reasonable cost compared to its useful life. The systematic process includes long-term capital planning, budgeting and financial management, centralized execution and project management, and infrastructure maintenance. Long-term capital planning includes establishing strategic and fiscal plans based on a government jurisdiction's comprehensive planning and public infrastructure need analyses. The comprehensive plan is a master plan that spells out broad policies for the community's long-term land use, expansion, and containment. The strategic plan describes policies and management practices that will make the best use of available resources to implement the community's vision as stated in the master plan. Long-term fiscal planning is about projecting revenue and expenditure in order to understand future capital financing capacity and capital needs. Long-term fiscal planning may not and cannot be completely accurate given that projections will be subject to error, especially for those in the far out-years. However, the projected results give a rough idea in terms of resources available and the future of a community. Capital inventory and needs analysis identify gaps between existing public infrastructure and future needs based on community growth and socio-economic profiles. If these planning practices are implemented, the community should have a Capital Improvement Program (CIP) which is a comprehensive list of capital projects a community will need within the next 5-7 years along with plans to finance the projects and the impacts of the projects on future budgets. This component will enhance *allocative efficiency* of public capital investment since the systematic review suggests what projects to invest in based on the community's needs and vision, and how to finance the projects based on available resources and the community's projected growth.

The second component is budgeting and financial management, which includes having a separate capital budget, debt management policies, and capital financing policies. The separate capital budget contains appropriation and recommendations for capital projects along with available resources. The recommended capital projects in the capital budget are usually the projects listed in the first-year of the CIP. Given that capital needs tend to exceed available resources, the first-year CIP projects will need to be systematically prioritized using such techniques as cost-benefit analyses or project ranking systems. The separate capital budget is useful in that it provides a special review of the recommended capital projects relative to available capital financing sources in the next fiscal year. If capital projects are included in the operational budget, the two types of public spending (i.e., investment and consumption) will compete for limited resources. With a separate capital budget (i.e., a dual budgeting system) decisionmakers and appointed officials can balance between consumption and investment. In this second component of the systematic capital management and budgeting process, sound financial management practices including debt capacity analysis, long-term budget forecasts, and maintaining some operational reserve funds should be adopted and practiced in order to help enhance the community's credit rating, thus yielding low capital costs. Overall, this component will enhance *scale economy* for public investment since the recommended practices ensure that the community invests in its public infrastructure at the optimal level commensurate with current and future financing capacity as well as future needs.

The third component is centralized execution and project management, which emphasizes establishing a central unit or agency responsible for project management, monitoring contractor performance, and executing the capital budget. The centralized capital project management agency maintains, updates, and discloses the capital budget status indicating how much appropriated funds have been expended and how much are left. The managers in the centralized capital project management agency should perform simple internal audits such as budget variance analysis to identify whether capital spending is implemented as planned. The focus is on preventing waste, fraud, and cost overruns that can severely affect financial status of a jurisdiction. The goal of this component is to ensure that public infrastructure is acquired at the lowest cost possible (*economic efficiency*).

The last component of the systematic capital management and budgeting process focuses on maintenance planning and maintenance funding. Maintenance planning involves asset management and determining what public facilities should be repaired or replaced based on physical condition and current and future use. Major repairs may be considered when it will extend the facility's useful life for a significant number of years. Replacement may be considered when repair will not yield cost savings and demands are projected to increase. Maintenance funding involves setting aside funds to pay for repair and replacement. These two activities help government avoid infrastructure backlogs and reduce the need to finance repair and replacement projects on an emergency basis.

EVALUATION OF THE CASE STUDY COUNTRIES' MANAGEMENT PRACTICES

As described in the previous chapters, public capital management and budgeting practices vary from country to country regardless of their geographical locations and government regimes. In this section, the systematic capital management and budgeting process described in Chapter 1 is used as a yardstick to evaluate the twelve case study countries' practices.

Table 1 presents performance evaluation results in which the case study countries' capital management and budgeting practices are compared with the normative practices in the four components of the systematic capital management and budgeting process. The evaluations were performed according to the rubric described below.

Table 1. Evaluation of case study countries' capital management and budgeting practices

Country	Component				
	Long-term Capital Planning	Capital Budgeting and Financial Management	Centralized Execution and Project Management	Infrastructure Maintenance	Total Score
Albania	Fair	Fair	Excellent	Poor	9
Burkina Faso	Fair	Poor	Poor	Poor	5
Germany	Good	Good	Good	Fair	11
Korea	Fair	Good	Excellent	Good	12
Moldova	Fair	Fair	Fair	Good	9
Russia	Fair	Poor	Poor	Poor	5
Taiwan	Fair	Good	Excellent	Poor	10
Thailand	Fair	Good	Fair	Good	10
Ukraine	Poor	Fair	Poor	Fair	6
United States (Subnational)	Good	Good	Good	Poor	10
Uzbekistan	Poor	Fair	Good	Fair	8
Vietnam	Good	Excellent	Fair	Good	12

Source: Evaluation by the authors

- An '*excellent*' rating suggests that *all* of the recommended activities in a component are adopted and fully implemented. While there may be small deviations from the normative practices, such deviations do not severely affect the quality of management. The important practices across the four components of the systematic process include having a CIP (component 1), having a separate capital budget (component 2), practicing centralized project management and monitoring (component 3), and practicing maintenance planning and funding (component 4). For any component, if the important practices are designated by written policies or laws and are reported by the case study authors as being implemented, an 'excellent' rating is assigned. These written rules, policies, and laws ensure that the recommended practices are adopted and implemented regardless of fiscal or political conditions. The authors of the case studies may mention political involvement and even some corruptions, but as long as the practices are designated by laws, such negative aspects may have only a marginal effect.
- A rating of '*good*' suggests that the *majority* of the systematic practices recommended in a component are adopted and fully implemented. The adopted practices are well adhered to the systematic capital management and budgeting process and are clearly stated in a country's management policies or laws. Only a minority of practices deviate from those of the systematic process and are not designated by written policies or laws, and as a result, such practices may or may not be executed depending on the current administration and available expertise. The case study authors may mention political intervention in the resource allocation process or some corruption in implementation, which may affect the quality of capital management and budgeting.
- A '*fair*' rating suggests that a *minority* of the systematic practices recommended for a component are adopted. The adopted practices may not completely adhere to the systematic capital man-

agement and budgeting process and are not clearly stated in a country's management policies or required by laws. However, the adopted practices as described by the case study authors are considered evidence of implementation. Most of the practices in the component deviate from those of the systematic process and are not designated by written policies or laws. As a result, the important practices may or may not be executed depending on current administration and available expertise. Sometimes the authors explicitly mention lack of administrative and management expertise as an obstacle to completely implementing the recommended practices. The authors may mention political intervention in the resource allocation process or high levels of corruptions in implementation. Such practices, as documented in the country case studies, appear to significantly affect the efficiency of public capital spending.

- A rating of '*poor*' suggests that *none* of the systematic practices recommended in a component are adopted and implemented. Laws and management policies governing important practices in the component do not exist and there is no description by the case study authors of the implementation of such practices. The authors primarily mention the lack of administrative and management practices, high levels of corruptions, and high degrees of political involvement in the budgeting process. Such negative aspects likely affect both the quality of the public capital management process and efficiency of public capital spending, especially since countries with poor capital management practices tend to obtain capital projects with relatively high costs due to corruption or mismanagement.

Each element of the rating scale was given a corresponding score; excellent, good, fair and poor were given scores of 4, 3, 2, and 1, respectively. For each country a total score was calculated across all components (shown in the last column of Table 1). The maximum points possible is 16, indicating that the country's process fully adheres to the systematic capital management and budgeting process discussed in Chapter 1. The minimum total point possible of 4 indicates that the country's process deviates extensively from normative practices. For these countries, political issues, lack of administrative expertise, and corruption can easily penetrate the process.

As presented in Table 1, Vietnam and Korea received the highest scores with 12 total points, followed by Germany (11 points). This indicates close adherence to the systematic capital management and budgeting process recommended by the literature. Taiwan, Thailand and USA had 10 total points. At the other end, Burkina Faso and Russia had the lowest scores (5 points). Based on these scores, we can organize the countries into quartiles:

- **Fourth quartile:** Vietnam, Korea, and Germany.
- **Third quartile:** USA, Taiwan, and Thailand.
- **Second quartile:** Albania, Moldova, and Uzbekistan.
- **First quartile:** Ukraine, Russia and Burkina Faso.

Note that even within the quartiles, the countries may not have the same government regime or may not be geographically located in close proximity. For example, in the fourth quartile Vietnam and Korea are both in Asia, but the former is a communist state while the latter is a presidential republic. In the third quartile, the United States is a federal republic located on the American continent while Thailand and Taiwan are in Asia. Thailand, while under a Monarchy System where the national government has the most power, is presently under military regime. Taiwan is a semi-presidential republic. Similar differences exist across the remaining groups. These simple comparisons suggest that the level of sophistication in public capital management and budgeting practices may not be simply explained by a country's geographical location or government regime. But, if the geographical location and government regimes do not explain capital management and budgeting practices, then what is driving the differences shown in Table 1? This chapter is focused on tentatively answering this question.

Long-Term Capital Planning

For the long-term capital planning component of the systematic process, Vietnam, USA, and Germany were rated as *good*; Albania, Burkina Faso, Korea, Moldova, Russia, Taiwan, and Thailand were rated as *fair*; and Ukraine and Uzbekistan were rated as *poor*. The countries rated *good* have a CIP in which physical planning is well integrated with fiscal planning. The CIP in Vietnam and Germany are designated by public investment laws. Vietnam's CIP, referred to as the Public Investment Program, lists and classifies capital projects following Articles 7-10 of the Public Investment Act of 2014. The USA and Germany have federal systems in which the national governments distribute capital planning and budgeting powers to subnational levels. While the United States does not have a CIP at the national level, Germany has a national CIP that is designated by law (The Act to Promote Economic Stability and Growth) that requires the government to establish a 5-year rolling capital plan based on budget forecasts. Furthermore, as required by law, the German government must present the annually rolling CIP to the Ministry of Finance so that the capital project plan can be actualized instead of being just a wish list.

The majority of the state and local governments in the USA have a CIP (Ebdon, 2004; Ermasova, 2013). Although these CIPs are not designated by laws like those of Vietnam and Germany, they tend to be based on long-term fiscal planning (Ebdon, 2004). Like the USA and Germany, the Vietnamese government uses budget forecasts in long-term planning by integrating forecasts into comprehensive plans. However, unlike those of subnational governments in the USA, the long-term capital plans in Germany and Vietnam are not integrated. Instead, they have multiple sectoral plans based on the numbers of infrastructure sectors or service functions (i.e., transportation, water and sewerage, energy). Such unintegrated plans may result in duplicative and uncoordinated projects. Having sectoral instead of integrated capital plans is the only flaw keeping Vietnam and Germany from receiving an *excellent* rating for this component. However, despite not having integrated plans, Germany has a National Development Policy for executing and coordinating investment projects across the Länders and municipality levels. Furthermore, in practice, the impacts of capital projects (e.g., future operational savings or increasing future operational costs) are incorporated into the CIP and approved by the federal Ministry of Finance. Capital resources are equally allocated among the Länders and the national and subnational levels. Furthermore, Germany is the only case study country study that conducts capital needs analysis based on future demands.

Among the countries rated as *fair* (Albania, Burkina Faso, Korea, Moldova, Russia, Taiwan, and Thailand), only Korea and Burkina Faso have an informal CIP that is not required by law. Korea's CIP (the Comprehensive National Territorial Plan or CNTP), has been used since 1971, but does not integrate capital planning with fiscal planning. The Korean government practices medium-term expenditure forecast and integrates its results into an operational budget plan. From the case study, however, it is unclear whether forecasting results are integrated into the CNTP. Burkina Faso's CIP, also known as the Public Investment Program, is required by international donors, prepared based on simple fiscal capacity projections (i.e., donors' plans), and is used as a tool to consolidate international aid.

All countries in the *fair* category, with the exception of Russia and Burkina Faso, have comprehensive plans, but the governments seem to have difficulty integrating plans across sectors and sorting through the responsibility for public infrastructure provision between national and subnational levels. The latter may be a consequence of having a strong national government or lacking expertise at the subnational governments. For example, the author of the Korea case study notes that Korean subnational governments do not have much autonomy in public administration functions.

To illustrate this point, Korea has five types of comprehensive plans: the CNTP, the Seoul Metropolitan Area Readjustment Plan, Metropolitan Area Plan, City Management Plan and Basic City Plan. Thailand has at least eight comprehensive infrastructure plans including the Transportation Infrastructure Plan (2015-2022), Second Industrial Logistics Master Plans (2017-2021), Thailand Power Efficiency Plan (2015-2016), Alternative Energy Development Plan (2015-2036), Digital Economy and Society Development Plan (2015-2036), Metropolitan Waterworks Authority Water Supply Infrastructure Development Plan (2018-2047), and Third Provincial Waterworks Authority Strategic Plan (2017-2021).

Moldova, Taiwan and Albania have more integrated comprehensive plans. Moldova's current long-term comprehensive plan, it's National Development Strategy "Moldova 2020," covers two sectors – transportation and energy – and spells out the objectives of infrastructure development. The Albanian comprehensive plan integrates all sectors into the plan. However, the comprehensive plan is part of the strategic plan which has a shorter time-frame and, as a result, the comprehensive plan automatically adopts this short-term framework and is not useful in spelling out long-term vision and goals.

Taiwan has a unique comprehensive planning practice in that it sorts public infrastructure provision between national and subnational levels. As implied by the case study author, this practice may be a consequence of the nationally-elected officials' need to be involved in the country's long-term infrastructure planning based on their campaign promises and re-election expectation. The President or Prime Minister prepares the Capital Improvement Program (e.g., Prime Minister Chiang Ching-kuo's Ten Major Construction Projects 1974-1979; President Ma Ying-jeou's i-Taiwan 12 Projects 2009-2011) that cover only large-scale capital projects and are associated with political campaign promises. These plans seem to have relatively short time frames. In addition, the Taiwanese national government is responsible for multi-year comprehensive planning (covering relatively large-scale capital projects) such as the Economic Development and National Development Plans. Meanwhile, local governments have autonomy to prepare their own comprehensive plans and have the capacity to finance their own smaller-scale capital projects. Like Albania, Taiwan's comprehensive planning is contained within strategic planning, resulting in a comprehensive plan that does not address long-term vision and public infrastructure needs.

Burkina Faso and Thailand each have a separate strategic plan that applies economic analyses to make decisions about social and economic development policies (which tend to involve public infrastructure). The Moldovan Ministry of Finance develops a strategic plan that identifies how budgetary resources should be used (e.g., budget allocation should be related to the country's strategic priorities). However, none of the case study countries categorized as *fair* in terms of long-term capital planning conduct capital needs analysis.

Uzbekistan and Ukraine were rated as *poor*. Based on the case study, Ukraine appears to not adopt any long-term capital planning activities recommended by the systematic process. The case study author notes that the country has a long wish list of capital projects but since comprehensive planning, long-term fiscal planning, and strategic planning do not exist, it is difficult to realize the wish list. Uzbekistan is a strong authoritarian state, and its plans tend to be developed based on the President's views. The Investment Program of the Republic of Uzbekistan has a one-year time frame; the plan is revised annually, signed by the President and becomes law. Uzbekistan has an informal CIP that is produced infrequently since it is not required by law. The most recent CIP was issued in 2010 and covered project needs for the period 2011-2015. Periodically, the President issues a large-scale capital improvement program as a special CIP that is signed into law. The most recent special CIP (Measures on Continuing Improvement of Ameliorated Condition of Irrigated Lands and Rational Usage of Water Resource: 2013-2017) focused only on the water sector and was not comprehensive.

Budgeting and Financial Management

For the budgeting and financial management component, Vietnam received an *excellent* rating, exhibiting the best practices among all case study countries. Vietnam has a dual budget system including separate capital and operational budgets. The country has established financial policies related to debt affordability analysis, designating that public infrastructure be financed by domestic bonds (rather than international capital markets), and setting aside budgetary resources for debt services incurred for public infrastructure acquisition. Although the country presently uses only a small amount of long-term debt, the policy clearly sets a foundation for future capital spending that corresponds with the country's growth and debt capacity. The State Budget Law of 2015 mandates that Vietnamese central and local governments maintain an operating reserve of 2% to 4% of the total budget to cover natural disasters and emergencies. This policy implies that the Vietnamese government is putting some effort into maintaining financial discipline. Project prioritization criteria for projects financed by domestic bonds are designed to improve the standard of living. The criteria, listed according to their priority order, include capital projects serving those in mountainous areas, those who are ethnic minority, and those in remote areas; capital projects supporting health and hospital services; transportation projects; irrigation projects; and education projects. The authors of the Vietnam case study note that although the prioritization criteria are set, project selection and prioritization is still affected by politics. However, we note that the establishment of management institutions and laws may alleviate some concerns regarding politics and corruptions. The Vietnamese government is innovative in its approach to capital financing. Through the Vietnam Development Bank, the government borrows money supplies from the domestic capital market and then allocates directly to local governments and state-owned enterprises for capital projects. The case study authors note that this motivates private partners to work with local governments and, as a result, local governments can invest in more capital projects. PPPs are used often in Vietnam, especially for information technology and electricity-related projects. As mentioned in the case study, Vietnam does have corruption and an administrative expertise problem; however, in our view, the country is putting a good amount of effort into establishing systematic capital budgeting and financial management practices.

Germany, Korea, Taiwan, Thailand and the United States were rated *good* in terms of budgeting and financial management. Taiwan and Thailand are similar in that although they do not have separate capital budgets, their capital resource allocation is conducted through a built-in capital budgeting process. The built-in capital budgeting process is supported by a combination of traditional practices and some laws (e.g., a law requiring debt capacity analysis). The laws are helpful in shielding capital spending from competing with operational programs. Both countries include small-scale capital projects (e.g., less than THB 1 million for Thailand) in the annual budgeting process so these projects must compete for resources with operational programs. Large-scale capital projects have their own approval and financing paths. In Taiwan large capital projects are proposed and approved separately from the annual capital budgeting process and financed through long-term debt and a multi-year process. In Thailand, large capital projects are financed through long-term debt issued by the Ministry of Finance and debt proceeds are sent directly to the responsible ministries and state-owned enterprises. Budgeting and financial management practices are better in Taiwan compared to Thailand because the Taiwanese national government has special capital project funds to finance large-scale capital projects allowing the government to pay some project costs with current revenue. Such practices can significantly reduce the amount of debt.

Given that these built-in practices tend to allow flexibility in capital financing, both Taiwan and Thailand have relatively strong financial management laws compared to other case study countries. In Taiwan, Article 5 of the Public Debt Management Act designates that national debt must not exceed 40.6% of the country GDP and local governments cannot incur debt in excess of 50% of total annul expenditure proposed in their budgets. Article 10 of the same act mandates that governments must periodically publicly disclose their debt. In Thailand, the Fiscal Discipline Act of 2018 designates that the national government must appoint fiscal committees that mainly comprise of Ministry of Finance Directors, Bureau of Budget Director, Bank of Thailand's President and board members, and National Social and Economic Development board members to determine annual debt amounts based on long- and medium-term budget forecasts. The act does not require public disclosure of debt. Furthermore, this act allows local governments, public agencies, and state-owned enterprises to borrow directly from international and domestic capital markets without reporting to or sending debt proceeds to the Ministry of Finance. While this practice expedites capital project acquisition, it is not transparent and the lack of consolidation of public debt makes it difficult to monitor. The Fiscal Discipline Act of 2018 creates some opaqueness in the country's financial system.

Germany and Korea do not have a separate capital budget, but more than half of state and local governments in the USA have separate capital budgets. In Germany and the USA subnational governments, the executive branches or those responsible for preparing budget documents propose capital projects based on policy priorities. According to the authors of the USA country case study, a majority of state governments have debt limits and practice debt affordability analysis. Germany has public investment funds (from debt proceeds of bond issuances) which attract private partners for PPP projects. The European Stability and Growth Pact requires that Germany's Council of Economic Experts conducts financial forecasts to identify future resources especially those needed for capital projects. In Korea, debt affordability analysis for the central government and local governments is determined by the Ministry of Finance and Ministry of Interior, respectively. According to Korea's Local Finance Act, local governments' debts limit must be annually determined and legislated based on the annual fiscal situations of the jurisdiction.

Among the countries rated as *good,* only Korea has a systematic project prioritization process. At the national level, Korea uses criteria stated in the Preliminary Feasibility Study to systematically prioritize large capital projects. At the local level, the country uses criteria stated in the Local Finance Act. In Taiwan and Germany, the ministries proposing capital projects are responsible for prioritizing their capital projects based on policy priorities of top management and political leaders.

Taiwan and Germany have operational reserves that are designated by law. Taiwan's Article 22 of the Budget Act requires that the national government set aside resources in general revenue funds as budget reserves. The Disaster Prevention and Protection Act of Taiwan requires that local governments prepare reserve funds. In Germany, the Stability and Growth Act requires that the federal government establish reserve funds. According to the author of the Korean case study, operational reserves are designated by law but are not set aside for capital projects.

Albania, Moldova, Ukraine and Uzbekistan are in the same group receiving a rating of *fair* for this component. Albania is the only country in this group with a dual budgeting system and separate capital budget. However, the case study author notes that public capital spending is severely inadequate compared to the country's needs. Furthermore, the capital resource allocation process is severely affected by national politics. The Albanian Prime Minister's Office develops the long-term expenditure forecast (6-7 years) and the Ministry of Finance forecasts medium-term expenditures that are the basis for the CIP. However, Albania severely lacks financial expertise in forecasting and has no laws enforcing good financial practices such as maintaining operational reserves, conducting debt capacity analysis, and enforcing debt limits. As a result, operational reserves, debt affordability analysis, and debt management policies and practices do not exist.

In Moldova, the Public Finance and Fiscal Responsibility Act does not require a separate capital budget; operational spending competes directly with capital spending. The Moldovan and Ukrainian governments similarly lack technical expertise in budget forecasting and have no financial management laws or policies requiring operational reserves, debt affordability analysis, debt limit, and debt disclosure. According to the Moldova case study, the capital project prioritization process appears to be relatively systematic compared to those of Albania and Ukraine. Moldova's government adheres to the country's strategic plan and allocates capital resource based on the predicted usefulness of the projects. However, the national government tends to not distribute powers to its local governments.

Uzbekistan also does not have financial management laws or policies to enforce fiscal discipline, and the country case study does not document the presence of strong financial management practices. The government has a capital financing policy designating that resources in all funds including the General Fund are used as current revenue to finance capital projects while resources in the Fund for Reconstruction and Development (FRD) are used for capital project debt financing, which generally is in the form of commercial bank loans and private sector lending. The Uzbek government combines capital projects serving citizens and those supporting national oil and gas production, which can result in lopsided resource allocation toward national gas and oil production facilities and inadequate capital projects servicing citizens and enhancing quality of life.

Russia and Burkina Faso were assigned ratings of *poor* for their budgeting and financial management practices. Both countries do not have a separate capital budget. They do not have laws or written policies enforcing fiscal discipline or guiding capital financing and debt management. Burkina Faso's public debt is monitored by the West African Economic and Monetary Union, and the country's debt level (37% of GDP) is well below the Union's debt limit (70% of GDP). According to the authors of the Russia case study, the government used to have a formal definition of capital expenditure (as real-estate and other long-term investments that will increase the value of federal properties) and a separate capital budget, but such practices no longer exist. There is no specific information on whether the Russian government systematically prioritizes public capital projects and no information on the overall financial management as it applies to capital expenditures.

Centralized Execution and Project Management

Albania, Korea and Taiwan received *excellent* ratings in this component given that the national governments in these countries centralize the monitoring process for project acquisition. The Korean government manages and monitors capital project acquisition and capital resource disbursement across all acquisition phases to ensure efficiency and prevent waste and fraud. In Albania, Article 65 of the Organic Budget Law designates that the Ministry of Finance prepares and presents budget monitoring results to the Council of Ministers and Legislature on a quarterly basis. The Capital Investment Department and Public

Investment Management Committees track all capital projects and report budget disbursements to the Ministry of Finance. In addition to the internal fiscal audit, performance auditing is practiced with the Capital Investment Department frequently reviewing the progress of project acquisition and comparing progression against plans. However, these auditing practices apply only to road and highway projects.

Taiwan is the best performer in this group, primarily because it integrates information technology into project management and monitoring. Different ministries, agencies and state-owned enterprises are responsible for project execution, but there is a central Public Construction Committee (PCC) that supervises and monitors project acquisition and capital budget disbursement. In 2001, the PCC established the Public Construction Management Information system which integrates information technology with project execution and monitoring to improve capacity for internal control. Information related to public construction including contractors, contracting amount, budgetary resources and disbursement, expected time to complete, and progress toward completion are periodically updated and available in an online clearinghouse for all approved capital projects. Such progressive practice is important for public scrutiny and centralized monitoring to detect waste and fraud prior to project completion. In terms of contract management Article 18 of the Government Procurement Act requires that the government use open tendering procedures for capital projects valued at or more than NT$1 million. According to Article 52 of the same act, the contract must be awarded based on the principles of lowest cost or most advantageous tender. These examples show that Taiwanese project execution activities closely conform to those recommended by the systematic process. While the case study authors mention corruption as a possible concern, we note that the laws regarding public procurement and the relatively high degrees of public disclosure for project implementation should alleviate some of the consequences of corruption in procurement processes.

Germany, USA, and Uzbekistan received ratings of *good* for this component. The Budget Code of the Republic of Uzbekistan requires that the Ministry of Finance monitor and track all projects financed by the national budget on a quarterly basis. The Ministry compiles capital disbursement and project acquisition information by requiring all agencies receiving resources from national budgetary funds to report, on a monthly basis, project acquisition progress and disbursement information and activities. In the USA, most subnational governments do not have a central committee or agency monitoring public capital project acquisition; however, in practice, local governments are subject to state laws requiring financial audits and financial statements at the conclusion of the fiscal year. For example, the Government Accounting Standards Board recommends financial audit practices for states and localities according to Generally Accepted Accounting Principles. Note, however, that these financial audits are ex-post controls that take place after the fiscal year is over, and therefore may not be able to help these subnational governments detect waste and fraud in the early stages of capital project acquisition. Germany's system is similar to those of the subnational governments in the USA except that Germany's federal government also prepares an annual financial report in addition to those of its local jurisdictions.

Moldova, Thailand and Vietnam received ratings of *fair*. The three countries have line agencies and ministries responsible for monitoring capital projects, supervising project acquisition, and reporting progress to the central government. This ex-post auditing, however, is inferior to ex-ante auditing that can detect waste and fraud early. Thailand is the only country in this group that requires line agencies and ministries to report capital disbursements to the Bureau of Budget which then displays project status reports online. However, public capital projects financed through the annual budgeting process (monitored by the Bureau of Budget) is only a small percentage of total capital spending. Large capital projects are subject to a special built-in capital budgeting and approval process, but Thailand does not have a central unit that tracks capital project acquisition and disbursement for these projects. In practice, the Ministry of Finance monitors large-scale projects financed by long-term debt, but the monitoring and tracking of progress is dispersed. There is no clearinghouse that provides information about approved capital projects, contributing to opaqueness and lack of transparency to the public.

The Moldovan and Thai governments have specific acts governing the public procurement process. In Thailand, Article 22 of the Privatization Act requires that line agencies responsible for public projects establish Monitoring Committees to monitor project execution. In Moldova, the Public Procurement Act created a public procurement agency to monitor contracted projects, verify that all public procurement processes comply with the procedures designated by the act, and provide reports on procurement contracts. The Moldovan government can improve its performance in this component by establishing a central agency to compile, track, and report all approved capital projects, not just those that are contracted out. Vietnam does not have a centralized committee or agency to monitor public projects and does not have any public procurement laws such as those in Thailand and Moldova. Like the USA, Vietnam's fiscal audit is an ex-post audit and is implemented for only large-scale capital projects.

Burkina Faso, Russia and Ukraine rank last among the case study countries in terms of centralized execution and project management practices, receiving ratings of *poor*. Burkina Faso and Russia simply do not any have any centralized project monitoring processes, internal auditing practices, or public procurement rules or laws. The Ukrainian government has put in place internal auditing and project acquisition monitoring; the Accounting Chamber, Anti-Monopoly Committee and State Financial Inspection are responsible for tracking and supervising public project acquisition and capital disbursement nationwide. However, in practice, the Ukraine case study author notes that these three units do not perform these assigned functions. The Ministry of Economic Development and Trade is responsible for developing and maintaining project status reports for all investment programs. However, the case study author notes that once projects are started, they are rarely monitored or assessed. As a result, Ukraine is notorious for having projects that are rarely completed causing significant amounts of sunk costs in acquiring public infrastructure. As noted by the case study author, the World Bank (1997) estimated that since 1970, 60,000 projects were not finished and about 15,000 projects took at least 10 years to accomplish.

Infrastructure Maintenance

Vietnam, Korea, Thailand and Moldova received *good* ratings for the infrastructure maintenance component. These four countries have maintenance planning established; however, asset management practices in Vietnam and Korea are not very sophisticated. With the assistance of the European Union, the Moldovan government is currently developing an information system and inventory of all capital projects. For maintenance planning, the Thai government is the most sophisticated. Its National Social and Economic Development Board (NSEDB) compiles, estimates and reports public infrastructure stock based on a perpetual inventory method. The NSEDB uses this information and projections of future demand as a starting point for recommending the types of public investment for the country. However, as mentioned by the authors of the Thailand case study, in practice ministries and agencies tend to make projects appear to be consistent with the NSEDB's plans so that the projects can be funded, making the NSEDB project selection criteria ineffective. Thailand's maintenance funding process is also incomplete. While there are public resources available each year for repair, these resources are incorporated into the annual operating budget instead of being set aside for maintenance.

The Moldovan government integrates maintenance funding into the annual budgeting process with maintenance funding annually determined based on depreciation rates of existing infrastructure. The Moldovan government emphasizes accounting for public capital assets based on historical records of investment, major repairs and upgrades, and depreciation rates, recognizing that such accounting information will help guide capital resource allocation and project selection. The Vietnamese government sets aside resources for public facilities in various sectors and separates maintenance allocation from annual budgeting.

Germany, Ukraine, and Uzbekistan were rated *fair* for this component. Since inheriting its public facilities from the former Soviet economy, the Ukrainian government has put some effort into asset management although it does not have in place maintenance planning and funding. The case study author notes that most of the public capital spending is to repair (rather than replace) aging facilities. Uzbekistan has a maintenance funding system. For example, the country maintains the Republican Road Fund in which earmarked revenue and surplus from natural resource exports are used to finance road maintenance. Germany's Basic Law requires the government to create and sustain a maintenance fund containing earmarked revenue and surplus general revenue. However, the case study author notes that in the last decade, Germany has faced problems in maintenance funding as public investment slowed and the country experienced infrastructure aging and backlog.

Albania, Taiwan, Burkina Faso, Russia and U.S.A received *poor* ratings for infrastructure maintenance. The Albanian government periodically assesses its capital stock, but the maintenance planning system is not well established. The country sets aside some maintenance funding, but only for roads and highways, and as noted in the country case study, even with maintenance funds being set aside, Albanian roads remain inadequate. Furthermore, because of the focus on transportation, infrastructure in other sectors are not maintained. The remaining governments rated as *poor* do not have any maintenance planning and funding systems. The authors of the case studies specifically mention inadequate maintenance performance in general, resulting in aging public infrastructure (subnational governments in the USA), useless public buildings and so called "mosquito buildings" (Taiwan), and inadequate public infrastructure (Burkina Faso and Russia).

INITIAL OBSERVATIONS

We are interested in the question of what drives differences in public capital management and budgeting practices across different countries. As a first step in answering this question we observe the case study countries' economic profile to identify patterns of relationships between economic performance and public capital management and budgeting practices. Table 2 presents the total scores for the countries' public capital management and budgeting processes, based on the evaluation rubric described in the previous section, along with categorization according to the International Monetary Fund (IMF) income group, total population in 2015, total GDP in 2015, per capita GDP in 2015 and per capita GDP in 1990. Simple visual inspection does not suggest any patterns to the relationships between a country's capital management and budgeting total score and economic performance measured as income group, GDP, and population size. We confirm our visual observation by performing correlation analysis. The statistical results (shown in Table 3) indicate no relationship between economic performance and the capital management and budgeting process.

Table 2. Summary of capital management and budgeting total scores and economic performance data for case study countries

Rank	Country	Capital Management & Budgeting Total Score	IMF Income Group*	2015 Population (million)**	2015 GDP (billion)***	2015 Per Capita GDP***	1990 Per Capita GDP****
1st	Korea	12	AE	50.7	1,740	34,314	8,276
1st	Vietnam	12	LIDC	91.7	536	5,849	939
3rd	Germany	11	AE	81.1	3,618	44,615	19,433
4th	Taiwan	10	AE	23.5	977	41,569	8,178
4th	Thailand	10	EM	65.1	1,020	15,662	4,298
4th	United States	10	AE	321.2	16,940	52,740	23,955
5th	Albania	9	EM	2.9	30	10,190	2,722
5th	Moldova	9	LIDC	4.1	22	5,454	4,162
6th	Uzbekistan	8	LIDC	31.3	284	9,078	1,985
7th	Ukraine	6	EM	42.8	395	9,238	6,763
8th	Burkina Faso	5	LIDC	18.5	27	1,444	546
8th	Russia	5	EM	144.3	3,363	23,303	8,013

Source: Authors' evaluation of capital management and budgeting practices; International Monetary Fund's Economic Outlook Database (2018); Population Reference Bureau (2015); and The World Bank (2018)

Notes:

* Income groups: Low income developing countries (LIDC), Emerging markets (EM), Advanced economies (AE); Retrieved from International Monetary Fund (2018)

** For mid-year 2015; from Population Reference Bureau (2015)

*** Financial data are in real USD based year 2011; from IMF (2018)

**** 1990 Per Capita GDP is in current USD; from The World Bank (2018)

In the economic development literature, the convergence hypothesis asserts that a country starting off its economy at a low-income level will grow faster than those starting off with higher income, and eventually, the former's economy will catch up with those of high-income economies (Barro & Lee, 1994; Baumol, 1986; Ben-David, 1996; Galor, 1996; Knack, 1996). This hypothesis is used to explain why some countries develop faster than others. However, as shown in the last row of Table 3, the cor-

Table 3. Correlation coefficients for the relationship between capital management and budgeting practices and economic performance

	Correlation Coefficient
Capital Management and Budgeting Total Score	1.000
IMF Income Group	0.389
2015 Population (million)	0.109
2015 GDP (billion)	0.159
2015 Per Capita GDP	0.427
1990 Per Capita GDP	0.273

relation between the 1990 GDP per capita and the total score for the capital management and budgeting process (r = 0.273) is not in the negative direction and is weak. We note that this simple correlation analysis is utilized to detect patterns and is not intended for statistical confirmation purposes due to the small number of case study countries.[1]

Next, we observe a country's public administration institutions in order to find some clues about the relationship between public administration functions and structures, and the public capital management and budgeting process. To do this we obtained data from the Quality of Government (QoG) 2015 Expert Survey II (Dahlström, Teorell, Dahlberg, Hartman, Lindberg & Nistotskaya, 2015), which provides an assessment of the organizational design of public bureaucracies and bureaucratic behavior across countries.[2] Using our country case studies we examine the correlations between a country's public administration functions and structures (from the QoG 2015 Expert Survey II) and the capital management and budgeting total scores we assigned to that country. The goal of this exercise is to obtain some preliminary insights into factors that may explain why the quality of capital management and budgeting varies across countries. By looking at the sign, magnitude, and statistical significance of the correlation coefficients, we hope to develop some ideas about (1) the direction of the relationship between institutional factors and capital management and budgeting, (2) the strength of these relationships, and (3) unobservable factors that may affect capital management and budgeting practices.

Among the 59 variables included in the 2015 Quality of Government Expert Survey II, five public administration institutional variables were statistically significant ($p<.05$) and in the expected direction, exhibiting strong relationships between capital management and budgeting total scores and public administration institutions (see Figure 1). The five public administration institutions are: merit-based

Figure 1. Spearman's Rho exhibiting direction and magnitude of the relationship between capital management and budgeting total score and public administration institutional factors

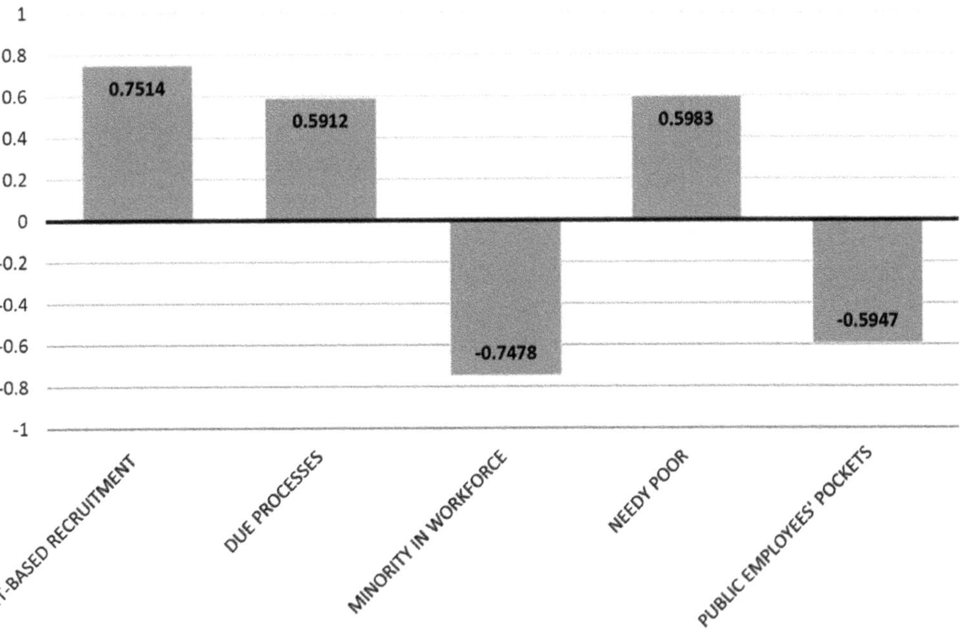

recruitment, due process in public human resource management, the extent to which minorities are represented in the public employee workforce, the percent to which public spending for needy poor recipients are received by needy poor groups, and the percent to which public spending for needy poor recipients go into public employees' own pockets.[3]

Case study countries that have a merit-based system for hiring and retaining public sector employees tend to have higher quality capital management and budgeting practices. Likewise, countries with due process in hiring, firing, promoting, and paying public sector employees tend to have higher quality practices. This is as expected given that capital management and budgeting require technical expertise and skills to perform activities such as revenue forecasts, debt affordability analysis, cost-benefit analysis, and ranking public projects based on a systematic scoring process. Merit-based recruitment and due process in human resource management tend to ensure the public workforce has skilled labor with technical expertise and, as a result, the management tools, procedures, and implementation processes these employees undertake will result in systematic capital management and budgeting practices.

The relationships between capital management and budgeting and whether public spending for the needy poor goes to the needy poor or into public employees' own pockets are also not surprising. In any objective resource allocation process, the allocation decision is focused on enhancing quality of life and targeting the needy poor reflects such a priority. If, for some reason, there is corruption in diverting public resource towards public employees themselves to be used for their own purposes, that tends to reflect capital management and budgeting practices that are relatively poor quality. Combined, these relationships suggest that capital management and budgeting practices may be better in countries where public-sector corruption is relatively low.

The relationship between minority representation in the public sector workforce and capital management and budgeting is negative with a relatively large magnitude, suggesting that diversity and pressure from a pluralistic society may contribute to weakening of the capital management and budgeting process. This is not surprising particularly in the context of capital management and budgeting practices that select projects and allocate reasons based on economic analysis and reasoning, where the winners and losers of such objective practices may not correspond to the diverse wants of society and public employees seeking to meet these diverse interests.

We also examine the correlations between capital management and budgeting total scores and political, economic, and public sector factors included in the QoG Standard Dataset Project (Teorell, Dahlberg, Holmberg, Rothstein, Alvarado & Svensson, 2018). The QoG Standard Dataset consists of 2,100 variables compiled from 100 publicly-available data sources (e.g., from the World Bank, International Monetary Fund). We found several interesting relationships between the capital management and budgeting total scores and QoG Standard Dataset variables (statistically significant at .05 level, exhibiting relatively large magnitude and in the expected direction).[4]

Four variables are worth mentioning. First, the variable representing the share of government consumption to GDP has a large and significant correlation coefficient (-0.7929), suggesting that about 79% of the capital management and budgeting total score is negatively related to the share of government consumption to GDP. This negative relationship implies that countries whose governments consume relatively less on non-durable goods and services tend to have stronger capital management and budgeting practices. Conversely, the QoG Standard Dataset does not contain public investment data; however, since government spending includes public consumption and investment, we posit that it is therefore quite likely that the size of public investment (i.e., public capital spending) is related to the capital management and budgeting process.

Second, the share of merchandise imports to GDP has a large and significant correlation coefficient (-0.7005). This hints at issues related to a country's openness to trade, but since the share of merchandise exports to GDP is not statistically significant, we cannot conclude that the level of economic openness is related to capital management and budgeting. However, this variable suggests general patterns where a government that is saving-oriented (i.e., consumes less and imports less world merchandise) tends to have a better capital management and budgeting process. Government savings orientation may be an important clue for understanding factors underlying variations in the quality of capital management and budgeting in different countries.

Third, the correlation coefficient for the variable representing the number of years since the last amendment to the Constitution was adopted is positive (0.8023) and statistically significant suggesting that countries with stable laws tend to have higher quality capital management and budgeting practices. Finally, an additional public administration institutions variable, the Bayesian Corruption Index (a composite index of the perceived overall level of corruption and defined as the "abuse of public power for private gain" published by Transparency International and the World Bank), is negatively related to the capital management and budgeting total score (correlation coefficient of -0.7825). This suggests that public capital management and budgeting practices become weak in an environment where corruption is widespread.

An Emerging Theme

We further examine the relationship between capital management and budgeting practices to the share of government consumption. Specifically, Figure 2 shows the relationship between capital management and budgeting total scores (on the Y-Axis) and the share of government consumption to GDP (on the X-Axis), highlighting an emerging theme that comes out of this comparison of government consumption and public capital management and budgeting practices. As shown in Figure 2, the Albanian government is average in terms of its capital management and budgeting practices (total score of 9) and its share of government consumption (21%) is at about the average across all case study countries. Countries with shares of government consumption that are below the average tend to have above average capital management and budgeting total scores. For example, Vietnam and Korea have high capital management and budgeting total scores (total scores of 12) and below average government consumption to GDP (11% for Vietnam and 15% for Korea). Shares of government consumption were similarly below average for the USA, Thailand, and Taiwan, and correspondingly their capital management and budgeting practices were above average.

The same pattern manifests when looking at countries with shares of government consumption to GDP that are above the average. As Burkina Faso's profile illustrates, the share of government consumption is above average (23%) and the country's capital management and budgeting total score is below average (total score of 5). The former Soviet Union countries (with the exception of Moldova) and Burkina Faso are consistent with the emerging theme; their capital management and budgeting performance scores are all below average and their shares of government consumption are above average.

Given that transitioning economies are quite unique compared to the rest of the world in terms of government regimes, management culture, and other factors, we look at the profiles of the countries in this sub-group: Moldova, Russia, Ukraine, and Uzbekistan. As a whole these countries seem to conform to the emerging theme, but when individual countries are compared, the patterns are not consistent with the emerging theme. One likely explanation for this is the different levels and types of technical assistance

Figure 2. Correlation between capital management and budgeting practices and share of government consumption to GDP
Source: Analysis by the authors

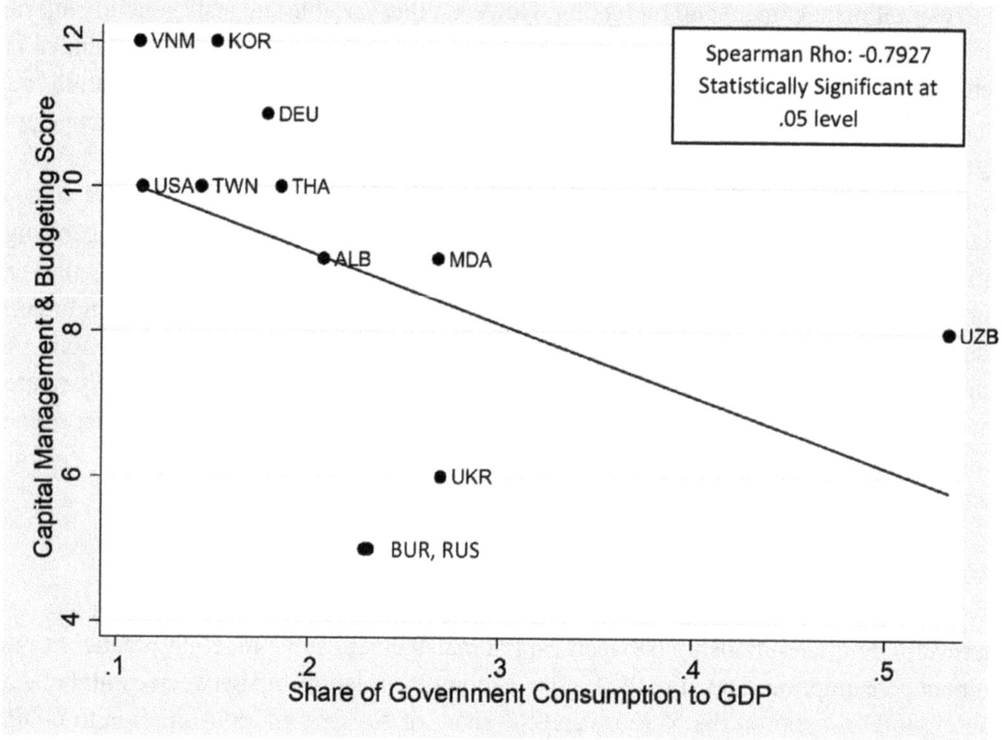

that these countries receive given their status as transitioning economies. For example, at present the Moldovan government is actively pursuing European Union membership. As presented in the case study, the country is receiving technical assistance from the European Union in setting up its management and budgeting processes. Significant parts of the capital management and budgeting total scores assigned to Moldova are the result of the recently established public budgeting and financial management rules and laws that resulted from this external technical assistance. Had the Moldovan government not received technical assistance, its capital management and budgeting total score would be well below average. Uzbekistan's capital management and budgeting total score was 8, and we would expect its shares of government consumption to be slightly above average. However, the country's capital management and budgeting process is unstable and depends on the levels of capital investment and the President's decisions that tend to be haphazard. Similarly, according to the emerging theme, Russia should have better capital management and budgeting practices than those of Ukraine since its share of consumption is less than those of Ukraine. However, data in Figure 3 shows the opposite. Based on this sub-group analysis, we recognize that we do not clearly understand these former Soviet Union countries, except the explanation that compared to the entire group they perform worse than the average and tend to have larger than average shares of government consumption (except for Moldova). Our limited country case studies are not enough to reveal significant themes in this subgroup. Furthermore, we believe that the countries in this group deserve special analysis and additional research is needed.

A TENTATIVE THEORY OF PUBLIC INVESTMENT BEHAVIOR

Based on the extant literature in international development and public finance, coupled with our initial observations from comparing the case study countries, we develop a tentative theory for explaining variations in public capital management and budgeting processes across countries. With this tentative theory, which we call a tentative theory of public investment behavior, we also posit several propositions regarding antecedents and outcomes of the public capital management and budgeting process.

The practices recommended by the public finance literature suggest that to have a high-quality capital management and budgeting process, a government must have human capital with some degree of technical competency and expertise to conduct such complex tasks as financial planning and forecasting, cost-benefit analysis, systematic project ranking, and capital inventory analyses. According to the initial observations just discussed, we see a strong relationship between capital management and budgeting total scores and merit-based practices and due process in public sector recruitment, hiring, promotion and dismissal. Such processes are key for ensuring high levels of talent and expertise within public sector organizations. Employees bring to their organization important skills and expertise which in turn, set the management styles and work processes of the organization (Wright, 2004; Bloom, Genakos, Sadun, & Reenen, 2012). Collectively, talented and expert labor apply their skills and professional viewpoints to the work of the organization, resulting in more sophisticated working practices that are conducive to systematic decision-making processes (Wright, 2004; Bloom, Genakos, Sadun, & Reenen, 2012; Kontoghiorghes, & Kalomyra, 2009). Thus, our first two propositions within this tentative capital management and budgeting theory are stated as follows:

Proposition 1: The more extensive meritocratic recruitment and retention are practiced in a country's public sector human resource management, the better the country's quality of capital management and budgeting.

Proposition 2: The more due process is present in the country's public sector human resource management, the better the country's quality of capital management and budgeting.

A strong capital management and budgeting process not only requires a merit-based employment structure with an emphasis on due process, but also requires objective and ethical public sector employees. Not surprisingly, then, we observe a strong relationship between the quality of the capital management and budgeting process and levels of corruption. For example, our initial observations suggest that in a country where the capital management and budgeting process is of relatively high quality, the implementation of public programs and delivery of public services tend to successfully distribute resources to the needy poor. In contrast, in a country where the capital management and budgeting process is of relatively low quality, public program implementation and public service delivery tend to divert resources into public employees' pockets. Likewise, as mentioned above, a country with relatively poor capital management and budgeting practices would have a relatively high Bayesian Corruption Index.

The international development literature is mixed regarding the effects of corruption, suggesting that corruption may either 'grease' or 'sand' the wheels in terms of economic activities and economic development (see for example Ahmed & Asmaa, 2016; Aidt, 2009; Blackburn & Forgues-Puccio, 2009; DiRienzo & Das, 2015; Ibrahim, Kumi, & Yeboah, 2015; Méon & Sekkat, 2005; Saastamoinen & Kuosmanen, 2014). The 'greasing the wheels' hypothesis suggests that corruption expedites public program implementation while the 'sanding the wheels' hypothesis instead suggests that corruption impedes the public service process. At the international level, Lambsdorff (2003) finds that corruption, especially with regards to capital spending, reduces efficiency in providing public infrastructure. Given that the systematic capital management and budgeting process requires accountability, public disclosure, and open-bidding processes in centralized execution and project management, it is not surprising that we observe higher quality capital management and budgeting practices in environments where corruption is generally not present. Thus, our third proposition is:

Proposition 3: The less corruption that exists in a country's public sector, the better the country's quality of capital management and budgeting.

In the entrepreneurial finance literature, scholars have studied angel investors' behavior and investment decision making (Maula, Autio, & Arenius, 2005; Maxwell, Jeffrey, & Lévesque, 2011; C. Mitteness, Sudek, & Cardon, 2012; C. R. Mitteness, Baucus, & Sudek, 2012; Smith, Harrison, & Mason, 2010; Wiltbank, Read, Dew, & Sarasvathy, 2009). Angel investors are wealthy individuals who act as informal venture capitalists investing own capital directly into early stage ventures (Wiltbank et al., 2009). Forrester (2014) finds that angel investors' decisions cannot be explained by traditional finance theories such as expectancy theory where cognitive processes are used in deliberation and decision making. Instead, because of information asymmetry, especially in terms of predicting future returns on investment, angel investors are influenced by cognitive biases formed through personal experiences, including risk perception (Forrester, 2014).

To deal with uncertainty, angel investors rely on heuristics to determine the level of cognitive process needed for instances of decision making. More specifically, angel investors must decide on the need for due diligence (i.e., activities, time, effort and resources to gather information on the potential investment) which often involves technical and complicated tasks such as background checks, analysis of the size of the target market, determination of growth potential, cash flow projection, and asset valuation (Forrester, 2014). There is evidence in the entrepreneurial finance literature that angel investors reduce information asymmetry by performing activities related to due diligence (Mason & Harrison, 2003; Stuart & Abetti, 1990) and that time spent on due diligence reduces such asymmetry, thus improving angel investment returns (Wiltbank & Boeker, 2007). More importantly, time spent on due diligence increases with the percentage of wealth invested by the angel investor (DeGennaro & Dwyer, 2014; Mitteness et al., 2012; Smith et al., 2010; Wiltbank & Boeker, 2007). Specifically, Wiltbank et al., (2009) find that due diligence was significantly and positively related to investment size; where more due diligence is performed, more money is being put into the new venture.

This connection between the practice of due diligence and investment behavior may be extended to the situation of public investment at the country level. In the analysis of the twelve country case studies presented in this book we see that countries with a meritocratic public workforce tend to have higher quality capital management and budgeting practices (equivalent to practicing more due diligence), which, in turn, relates to low consumption levels (equivalent to high investment levels). Wiltbank et al. (2009) also find that angel investors who perform due diligence become confident and tend to invest more than others. We would similarly reason that a country with a highly skilled workforce (recruited and retained through a merit-based system) would have the expertise to conduct reasonable due diligence (i.e., having systematic capital management and budgeting practices) that would result in high levels of public investment.

The entrepreneurial finance literature also notes differences in how novice angel investors and experienced angel investors approach investment decision making. Specifically, novice angel investors perform more due diligence (e.g., spend more time asking questions) than do experienced angel investors (Smith et al., 2010). At the country level we can see parallels between novice angel investors and countries with a saving orientation. Novice investors have less experience and therefore emphasize due diligence as a way to overcome challenges arising from information asymmetry. Savings-oriented countries may emphasize due diligence and a systematic decision-making process for public investment to overcome challenges of information asymmetry that arise due to a strong focus on managing general consumption.

Based on applying findings from the entrepreneurial finance literature and our initial observations from the country case studies, our final three propositions are as follows:

Proposition 4: The greater the country's saving orientation, the better the country's quality of capital management and budgeting.

Proposition 5: The more extensive meritocratic recruitment and retention are practiced in a country's public sector human resource management, the higher the country's public investment level.

Proposition 6: The better the country's quality of capital management and budgeting, the higher the country's public investment level.

Figure 3 summarizes our tentative theory of public investment behavior that connects the extent to which a country undertakes due diligence in its public investment decision making (i.e., having a systematic capital management and budgeting process) to possible antecedents and outcomes. The arrows on the left side of Figure 3 show administrative factors that may influence the extent to which a country adopts high quality capital management and budgeting practices. These factors correspond to Propositions 1, 2, 3, and 4. For example, consistent with Propositions 1 and 2, a country with a skilled public workforce supported by a human resource management system that is merit-based and incorporates due process will tend to put in place a systematic capital management and budgeting process. High levels of corruption in a country can also result in strong opposition to putting in place a systematic capital management and budgeting process, as such a process involves practices that remove both subjectivity and opportunities for public sector officials and employees to personally benefit from public investment decisions. As such, countries with public investment decision making that takes place in an environment marked by corruption will have lower quality capital management and budgeting practices (Proposition 3).

Approaches to public investment may also be contingent on risk aversion, levels of emphasis or experience, and resources. Countries with a saving orientation are more likely to commit time and resources to a systematic capital management and budgeting process, with an expectation of reducing risks, addressing uncertainty, and generating higher rates of return on its investment. In contrast, consumption-maximizing countries focus on consumption rather than investment and are reluctant to implement a systematic capital management and budgeting process when they are not expecting high rate of returns on their limited public investments relative to high transaction costs. We expect the opposite to hold as well, in that savings-oriented countries will, due to concerns about information asymmetry, put in place better quality capital management and budgeting practices (Proposition 4).

Figure 3 also shows that skillful public workforce and public investment level (i.e., investment orientation) are interrelated. Specifically, Proposition 5 suggests that public sector human resource management can result in relatively high level of public investment. Finally, Figure 3 suggests that when a country

Figure 3. A tentative theory of public investment behavior
Source: Authors' syntheses

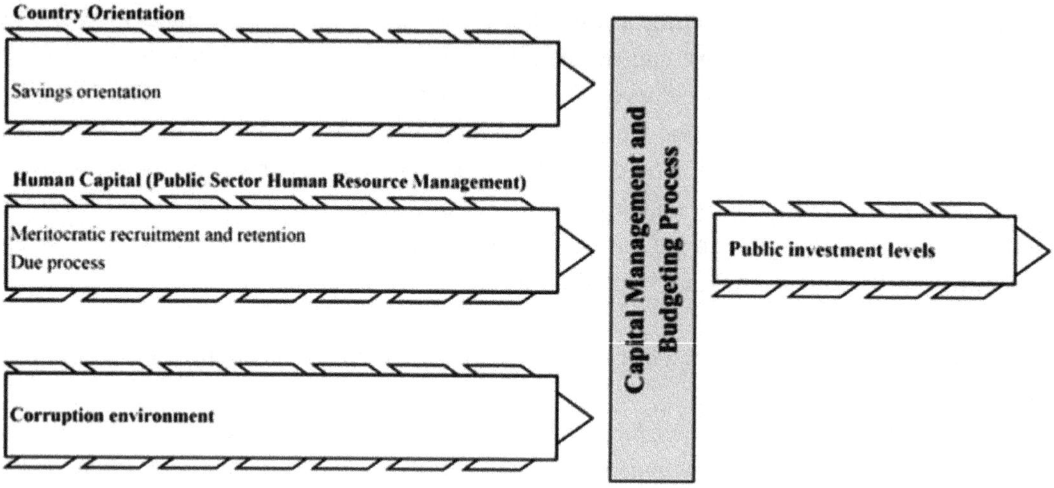

adopts and implements high quality capital management and budgeting process, its investment level tends to be relatively high because the due diligence practices in public investment makes the government become confidence in committing relatively high resources (Proposition 6). To summarize, Figure 3 suggests that the antecedents of the systematic capital management and budgeting process include saving orientation, meritocratic recruitment and retention in public sectors, due process in public sectors, and corruption environment while the outcome of the systematic capital management and budgeting process is a high level of public investment.

CONCLUSION

This book began with the description of a systematic capital management and budgeting process that is intended to be useful and responsive to the public's capital needs and supports a public infrastructure system that has reasonable cost compared to its useful life. This systematic process includes four components: long-term capital planning, budgeting and financial management, centralized execution and project management, and infrastructure maintenance. The book then provides twelve country case studies that describe public capital management and budgeting practices in Albania, Burkina Faso, Germany, Korea, Moldova, Russia, Taiwan, Thailand, Ukraine, Uzbekistan, USA, and Vietnam.

Analysis of these country case studies show that there are variations across the countries in terms of their public capital management and budgeting practices. Beyond these differences we also find that capital management and budgeting practices are related to various public sector factors. We use these initial observations to propose a tentative theory along with several propositions that connect the systematic capital management and budgeting process to possible antecedents. While we note that this theory is tentative, it does suggest some venues for further study of factors affecting how countries approach capital management and budgeting. Furthermore, the tentative theory offers a starting point for thinking about implications of the systematic approach to capital management and budgeting in terms of key public investment outcomes (such as levels of public investment, quality and quantity of public infrastructure, private sector investment, etc.) and governance factors such as openness and transparency, corruption, and accountability.

REFERENCES

Ahmed, F. G., & Asmaa, M. E. (2016). Growth and corruption in Arab countries: What type of relationship connects them? *Journal of Economics and International Finance*, *8*(5), 44–55. doi:10.5897/JEIF2015.0675

Aidt, T. S. (2009). Corruption, institutions, and economic development. *Oxford Review of Economic Policy*, *25*(2), 271–291. doi:10.1093/oxrep/grp012

Barro, R. J., & Lee, J.-W. (1994). Losers and winners in economic growth. *The World Bank Economic Review*, *7*(s1), 267-298.

Baumol, W. J. (1986). Productivity growth, convergence, and welfare: What the long-run data show. *The American Economic Review*, 1072–1085.

Ben-David, D. (1996). Trade and convergence among countries. *Journal of International Economics*, *40*(3-4), 279–298. doi:10.1016/0022-1996(95)01405-5

Blackburn, K., & Forgues-Puccio, G. F. (2009). Why is corruption less harmful in some countries than in others? *Journal of Economic Behavior & Organization*, *72*(3), 797–810. doi:10.1016/j.jebo.2009.08.009

Bloom, N., Genakos, C., Sadun, R., & Reenen, J. V. (2012). Management practices across firms and countries. *The Academy of Management Perspectives*, *26*(1), 23–42. doi:10.5465/amp.2011.0077

Dahlström, C., Teorell, J., Dahlberg, S., Hartmann, F., Lindberg, A., & Nistotskaya, M. (2015). *The QoG Expert Survey II Report*. Retrieved December 10, 2018, from https://gupea.ub.gu.se/bitstream/2077/39869/1/gupea_2077_39869_1.pdf

DeGennaro, R. P., & Dwyer, G. P. (2014). Expected returns to stock investments by angel investors in groups. *European Financial Management*, *20*(4), 739–755. doi:10.1111/eufm.12002

DiRienzo, C., & Das, J. (2015). Innovation and role of corruption and diversity: A cross-country study. *International Journal of Cross Cultural Management*, *15*(1), 51–72. doi:10.1177/1470595814554790

Ebdon, C. (2004). Capital management practices in U.S. counties. *Public Works Management & Policy*, *8*(3), 192–202. doi:10.1177/1087724X03259604

Ermasova, N. (2013). The improvement of capital budgeting at the state level in the USA. *Public Administration Review*, *2*(2), 92–104.

Forrester, R. C. (2014). *Behavioral finance: Factors influencing angel investor decisions.* (Unpublished doctoral dissertation). Kennesaw State University, Kennesaw, GA. Retrieved December 10, 2018, from https://digitalcommons.kennesaw.edu/cgi/viewcontent.cgi?article=1639&context=etd

Galor, O. (1996). Convergence? Inferences from theoretical models. *Economic Journal, 106*(437), 1056–1069. doi:10.2307/2235378

Ibrahim, M., Kumi, E., & Yeboah, T. (2015). Greasing or sanding the wheels? Effect of corruption on economic growth in sub-Saharan Africa. *African Journal of Economic and Sustainable Development, 4*(2), 157–173. doi:10.1504/AJESD.2015.069858

International Monetary Fund. (2018). *Economic outlook database*. Retrieved October 15, 2018, from https://www.imf.org/external/pubs/ft/weo/2018/02/weodata/index.aspx

Knack, S. (1996). Institutions and the convergence hypothesis: The cross-national evidence. *Public Choice, 87*(3-4), 207–228. doi:10.1007/BF00118645

Kontoghiorghes, C., & Kalomyra, F. (2009). The association between talent retention, antecedent factors, and consequent organizational performance. *S.A.M. Advanced Management Journal, 74*(1), 29–36.

Lambsdorff, J. G. (2003). How corruption affects productivity. *Kyklos, 56*(4), 457–474. doi:10.1046/j.0023-5962.2003.00233.x

Mason, C. M., & Harrison, R. T. (2003). "Auditioning for money": What do technology investors look for at the initial screening stage? *Journal of Private Equity, 6*(2), 29–42. doi:10.3905/jpe.2003.320037

Maula, M., Autio, E., & Arenius, P. (2005). What drives micro-angel investments? *Small Business Economics, 25*(5), 459–475. doi:10.100711187-004-2278-4

Maxwell, A. L., Jeffrey, S. A., & Lévesque, M. (2011). Business angel early stage decision making. *Journal of Business Venturing, 26*(2), 212–225. doi:10.1016/j.jbusvent.2009.09.002

Méon, P.-G., & Sekkat, K. (2005). Does corruption grease or sand the wheels of growth? *Public Choice, 122*(1-2), 69–97. doi:10.100711127-005-3988-0

Mitteness, C., Sudek, R., & Cardon, M. S. (2012). Angel investor characteristics that determine whether perceived passion leads to higher evaluations of funding potential. *Journal of Business Venturing, 27*(5), 592–606. doi:10.1016/j.jbusvent.2011.11.003

Mitteness, C. R., Baucus, M. S., & Sudek, R. (2012). Horse vs. jockey? How stage of funding process and industry experience affect the evaluations of angel investors. *Venture Capital, 14*(4), 241–267. doi:10.1080/13691066.2012.689474

Population Reference Bureau. (2015). *2015 world population datasheet*. Retrieved October 15, 2018, from https://www.prb.org/wp-content/uploads/2015/12/2015-world-population-data-sheet_eng.pdf

Saastamoinen, A., & Kuosmanen, T. (2014). Is corruption grease, grit or a gamble? Corruption increases variance of productivity across countries. *Applied Economics, 46*(23), 2833–2849. doi:10.1080/00036846.2014.914149

Smith, D. J., Harrison, R. T., & Mason, C. M. (2010). Experience, heuristics and learning: The angel investment process. *Frontiers of Entrepreneurship Research, 30*(2), Article 3.

Stuart, R. W., & Abetti, P. A. (1990). Impact of entrepreneurial and management experience on early performance. *Journal of Business Venturing, 5*(3), 151–162. doi:10.1016/0883-9026(90)90029-S

Teorell, J., Dahlberg, S., Holmberg, S., Rothstein, B., Alvarado, N., Svensson, P., & Svensson, R. (2018). *The Quality of Government Standard Dataset, version Jan18*. Gothenburg, Sweden: University of Gothenburg, The Quality of Government Institute. Retrieved December 10, 2018, from https://qog.pol.gu.se/data/datadownloads/qogstandarddata

Thomas, M. A. (2010). What do the worldwide governance indicators measure? *European Journal of Development Research*, *22*(1), 31–54. doi:10.1057/ejdr.2009.32

Wiltbank, R., & Boeker, W. (2007). *Returns to angel investors in groups*. Lenexa, KS: Angel Capital Education Foundation. Retrieved December 10, 2018, from https://www.angelcapitalassociation.org/data/Documents/Resources/AngelGroupResarch/1d%20-%20Resources%20-%20Research/6%20RSCH_-_ACEF_-_Returns_to_Angel_Investor_in_Groups.pdf

Wiltbank, R., Read, S., Dew, N., & Sarasvathy, S. D. (2009). Prediction and control under uncertainty: Outcomes in angel investing. *Journal of Business Venturing*, *24*(2), 116–133. doi:10.1016/j.jbusvent.2007.11.004

World Bank. (1997). *Public investment management report*. Washington, DC: The World Bank Group.

World Bank. (2018). *GDP per capita, PPP (current international $), World Bank, International Comparison Program database*. Retrieved October 15, 2018, from https://data.worldbank.org/indicator/NY.GDP.PCAP.PP.CD

Wright, K. (2004). Personal knowledge management: Supporting Individual Knowledge Worker Performance. *Knowledge Management Research and Practice*, *3*(3), 156–165. doi:10.1057/palgrave.kmrp.8500061

ENDNOTES

1 We also want to determine the relationship between the 1960 per capita GDP and the Capital Management and Budgeting score (CMB). Unfortunately, the former Soviet Union member countries, which include almost half of the case study countries, do not have GDP data prior to 1990.Thus, we are unable to inspect the income convergence pattern using 1960 GDP data.

2 The 2015 Expert Survey II is part of the Quality of Government (QoG) project sponsored by the Quality of Government Institute, University of Gothenburg, Sweden. The QoG Expert Survey is a longitudinal project to collect data on the organizational design of public bureaucracies and bureaucratic behavior in different countries. According to Dahlström et al. (2015), the purpose of the QoG Expert Surveys is to provide quantitative assessment of the organizational design of public bureaucracies and bureaucratic behavior across countries. Conceptually, the survey questionnaires were written based on Evans and Rauch's pioneering research on Weberian bureaucracies, New Public Management, and administrative impartiality. The 2015 Expert Survey II's respondents include 1,294 public administrators across 159 countries (Dahlström et al., 2015). The Quality of Government Institute compiled and updated the list of survey respondents, who are public administrators in each country (Dahlström et al., 2015). Each country has at least 3 public administrator respondents.

3 These public administration institutions are operationalized by the QoG Expert Survey as follows:
• Merit-based recruitment: Public sector employees are hired via a formal examination system.
• Due process in public human resource management: The practice of hiring, firing, promoting and paying public sector employees follows the provisions of the laws and other legal documents regulating these processes.
• Minorities are represented in the public employee workplace: Key ethnic and religious groups in society are proportionally represented among public sector employees.
• Public spending reaches the needy poor: The percentage of funds that would reach the needy poor in a hypothetical situation where a typical public sector employee is given the task to distribute an amount equivalent to USD 1000 per capita to the needy poor in the country.
• Public spending goes into public employees' pockets: The percentage of funds that would go into the public employee's own pocket in a hypothetical situation where a typical public sector employee is given the task to distribute an amount equivalent to USD 1000 per capita to the needy poor in the country.

4 The complete list of the correlation coefficients for these 80 variables can be obtained from the editors.

Compilation of References

«Ferghana» News Agency. (2010). *Uzbekistan: Tashkent aircraft factory, named after Chkalov, goes bankrupt.* Retrieved July 23, 2018, from http://enews.fergananews.com/news.php?id=1878

Adams, C. T. (1988). *The Politics of Capital Investment: The Case of Philadelphia.* Albany, NY: State University of New York Press.

Afonso, W. B. (2014). Local Government Capital Spending During and After Recessions: A Cause for Concern? *International Journal of Public Administration, 37*(8), 494–505. doi:10.1080/01900692.2013.865646

African Development Bank (ADF). (2018). *Burkina Faso economic outlook.* Retrieved July 23, 2018, https://www.afdb.org/en/countries/west-africa/burkina-faso/burkina-faso-economic-outlook/

Agence EcoFin. (2018). *Burkina Faso: Composition du nouveau gouvernement.* Retrieved July 23, 2018, https://www.agenceecofin.com/politique/0102-53952-burkina-faso-composition-du-nouveau-gouvernement

Ahmed, F. G., & Asmaa, M. E. (2016). Growth and corruption in Arab countries: What type of relationship connects them? *Journal of Economics and International Finance, 8*(5), 44–55. doi:10.5897/JEIF2015.0675

Aidt, T. S. (2009). Corruption, institutions, and economic development. *Oxford Review of Economic Policy, 25*(2), 271–291. doi:10.1093/oxrep/grp012

Albania Institute of Statistics (INSTAT). (2017). *Government of Albania.* Retrieved October 13, 2018, from http://www.instat.gov.al/en/themes/economy-and-finance/national-accounts-gdp/

Albania Organic Budget Law. (2010). *Republic of Albania.* National Assembly, No. 10-355 (2/12/10). Retrieved October 13, 2018, from http://www1.worldbank.org/publicsector/pe/BudgetLaws/AlbaniaOrganicBudget1998.pdf

American Society of Civil Engineers. (2013). *Failure to act: The impact of current infrastructure investment on America's economic future.* Retrieved May 2, 2018, from https://www.asce.org/uploadedFiles/Issues_and_Advocacy/Our_Initiatives/Infrastructure/Content_Pieces/failure-to-act-economic-impact-summary-report.pdf

American Society of Civil Engineers. (2013). *The 2013 report card.* Retrieved May 2, 2018, from http://www.infrastructurereportcard.org/a/documents/2013-Report-Card.pdf

American Society of Civil Engineers. (2017). *The infrastructure report card.* Retrieved May 2, 2018, from https://www.infrastructurerportcard.org/wp-content-uploads/2016/10/Grades-Chart.png

Ammar, S., Duncombe, W., & Wright, R. (2001). Evaluating capital management: A new approach. *Public Budgeting & Finance, 21*(4), 47–69. doi:10.1111/0275-1100.00058

Andrew, M. (2006). Beyond Best Practice and "Basics First" in Adopting Performance Budgeting Reform. *Public Administration and Development, 26*(1), 147–161. doi:10.1002/pad.401

Anh, D. (2016). $90 billion for public investment in 2016-2020. *Vietnam Economic Times*. Retrieved May 15, 2018, from http://vneconomictimes.com/article/vietnam-today/90-billion-for-public-investment-in-2016-2020

Aronson, J. R., & Schwartz, E. (2004). *Management Policies in Local Government Finance* (5th ed.). Washington, DC: International National City/County Management Association.

Aschauer, D. A. (1989). Is public expenditure productive? *Journal of Monetary Economics, 23*(2), 177–200. doi:10.1016/0304-3932(89)90047-0

Asian Development Bank. (2012). *Transport sector assessment, strategy, and road map*. Retrieved May 15, 2018, from https://www.adb.org/sites/default/files/institutional-document/33360/files/vie-transport-assessment.pdf

Asian Development Bank. (2014). *A comparative infrastructure development assessment of the Republic of Korea and the Kingdom of Thailand*. Manila, Philippines: Asian development bank Press.

Asian Development Bank. (2016a). *Public financial management systems—Viet Nam: Key elements from a financial management perspective*. Retrieved from https://www.adb.org/sites/default/files/institutional-document/225661/public-finmgt-systems-vie.pdf

Asian Development Bank. (2016b). *Sector assessment (summary): Public sector management (public expenditure and fiscal management)*. Retrieved May 15, 2018, from https://www.adb.org/sites/default/files/linked-documents/50051-001-ssa.pdf

Asian Development Bank. (2017). *Thailand*. Retrieved July, 1 2018, from https://sdbs.adb.org/sdbs/

Asian Development Bank—ADB. (2018). *Key indicators for Asia and the pacific 2017*. Retrieved July 1, 2018, from www.adb.org/statistics

Association des Régions du Burkina Faso (ARBF). (n.d.). *Presentations des regions*. Retrieved July 23, 2018, http://www.regions.bf/spip.php?page=regions&id_rubrique=19

Axelrod, D. (1988). *Budgeting for modern government*. St. Martin's Press.

Baldry, D. (1998). The Evaluation of risk management in public sector capital projects. *International Journal of Project Management, 16*(1), 35–41. doi:10.1016/S0263-7863(97)00015-X

Balkan Insight. (2018). *Albania Civil Service Watch*. Retrieved May 4, 2018, from http://www.balkaninsight.com/en/page/albania-home

Balkan Insight. (2018). *Albania-Kosovo Highway Costs Soar to 2 Billion Euros*. Retrieved May 4, 2018, from http://www.balkaninsight.com/en/page/albania-home

Barro, R. J., & Lee, J.-W. (1994). Losers and winners in economic growth. *The World Bank Economic Review, 7*(s1), 267-298.

Bartholomew, A., Leurs, R., & McCarty, A. (2005). *Joint evaluation of general budget support 1994-2004*. Vietnam Country Report: August.

Basic Law. (2017). *Basic law* [Grundgesetz]. Berlin: German Bundestag Public Relations Division. Retrieved May 21, 2018, from https://www.btg-bestellservice.de/pdf/80201000.pdf

Batina, R. G. (1998). On the long run Effects of public capital and disaggregated public capital on aggregate output. *International Tax and Public Finance, 5*(1), 259–263.

Baumol, W. J. (1986). Productivity growth, convergence, and welfare: What the long-run data show. *The American Economic Review*, 1072–1085.

Beckett-Camarata, J. (2003). An examination of the relationship between the municipal strategic plan and the capital budget and its effect on financial performance. *Journal of Public Budgeting, Accounting &. Financial Management, 15*(1), 23–40.

Beckett-Camarata, J. (2008). Capital Budgeting. In J. Rabin (Ed.), *Encyclopedia of Public Administration and Public Policy*. Taylor & Francis.

Ben-David, D. (1996). Trade and convergence among countries. *Journal of International Economics, 40*(3-4), 279–298. doi:10.1016/0022-1996(95)01405-5

Berger, L. (2010). *Five Year Review of Albanian National Transport Plan*. ANTPS.

Bird, R., & Smart, M. (2001). Intergovernmental fiscal transfers: Some lessons from international experience. In *Symposium on Intergovernmental Transfers in Asian Countries: Issues and Practices, Asian Tax and Public Policy Program*. Hitotsubashi University. Retrieved October 13, 2017, from http:// www1.worldbank.org/publicsector/learningprogram/ Decentralization/IFTlessons.pdf

Blackburn, K., & Forgues-Puccio, G. F. (2009). Why is corruption less harmful in some countries than in others? *Journal of Economic Behavior & Organization, 72*(3), 797–810. doi:10.1016/j.jebo.2009.08.009

Bland, R. L. (2014). *Budgeting: A guide for local governments*. Intl City County Management Assn.

Bland, R. L., & Nunn, S. (1992). The impact of capital spending on municipal operating budgets. *Public Budgeting & Finance, 12*(2), 32–47. doi:10.1111/1540-5850.00936

Bloom, N., Genakos, C., Sadun, R., & Reenen, J. V. (2012). Management practices across firms and countries. *The Academy of Management Perspectives, 26*(1), 23–42. doi:10.5465/amp.2011.0077

Boex, L. F., Martinez-Vazquez, J., & McNab, R. M. (2000). Multi-year budgeting: A review of international practices and lessons for developing and transitional economies. *Public Budgeting & Finance, 20*(2), 91–112. doi:10.1111/0275-1100.00013

Bozeman, B. (2004). *All Organization are Public: Comparing Public and Private Organizations*. New York: Beard Books.

Braun, P. J. (2006). Infrastructure Demands Versus Debts. In Managing Local Government Finance. International City and County Management Association (ICMA) Publishers.

Briceño-Garmendia, C., & Domínguez-Torres, C. (2011). *Burkina Faso's infrastructure: A continental perspective. Africa infrastructure country diagnostic*. Washington, DC: The World Bank.

Brown, K. (1999). *Report of the president's commission to study capital budgeting*. Washington, DC: U.S. Government Printing Office.

Budget citoyen. (2017). *Budget 2018*. Retrieved from http://www.dgb.gov.bf/index.php?option=com_edocman&view=document&id=148.

Budget Code of The Republic of Uzbekistan. (2013). *Budget Code* No. ZRU-360 of December 26, 2013. Retrieved July 23, 2018 from http://lex.uz/pages/getpage.aspx?lact_id=2304140#2311779

Budget Code of the Russian Federation. (1998). *Budget code N145-F3 from July 31, 1998 (with amendments up until July 23, 2013)*. Retrieved October 13, 2017, from http://www1.worldbank.org/publicsector/pe/BudgetLaws/Budget_Code_Russia_Eng1998.pdf

Budget—BOB. (2018). *FY 2019 budget development process and practices*. Retrieved March 19, 2018, from http://www.bb.go.th/bbweb/?page_id=6013

Bunch, B. (2013). Capital planning and budgeting. In J. Bartle, B. Hildreth, & J. Marlowe (Eds.), Management policies in local government finance (6th ed.; pp. 253-277). Washington, DC: ICMA Press.

Burger, P., & Hawkesworth, I. (2013). Capital Budgeting and Procurement Practices. *OECD Journal on Budgeting*, *13*(1), 57–104. doi:10.1787/budget-13-5k3w580lh1q7

Burkina Faso. (2018). *Evaluation des projets et programmes de développement.* Retrieved July 23, 2018, from http://www.finances.gov.bf/index.php?option=com_content&view=article&id=286:burkina-faso-evaluation-des-projets-et-programmes-de =371.

Business Roundtable. (2016). *Road to growth: The case for investing in America's transportation infrastructure.* Retrieved January 28, 2018, from http://businessroundtable.org/sites/default/files/2015.09.16%20Infrastructure%20Report%20-%20Final.pdf

Cadre Budgetaire a Moyen-Term. (2015). *Cadre budgetaire a moyen-term 2016-2018.* Retrieved July 23, 2018, http://www.dgb.gov.bf/index.php?option=com_edocman&view=document&id=372

CAFRAD. (2018). *What is MTEF and why it is important? A Brief Overview.* Retrieved July 23, 2018, from http://old.cafrad.int/Workshops/Tanger21-23_04_09/Session4_2.pdf

Calia, R. (2001). Are all public spending programs equal? Priority setting approaches for government budgeting. *Government Finance Review*, *17*(4), 18–18.

Campbell, S., Huynh, L., & Nguyen, N. (2015). *The new PPP decree – Vietnam's solution for infrastructure development.* Retrieved from http://www.hlaseanhorizon.com/_uploads/pdfs/New_PPP_Decree_in_Vietnam.pdf

Ceka, E. (2018). *Public capital budgeting and management process in Moldova. In Capital management and budgeting in the public sector*. Hershey, PA: IGI Global.

Central Intelligence Agency (CIA). (2018). *The world factbook: East & Southeast Asia: Thailand.* Retrieved June 4, 2018, from https://www.cia.gov/library/publications/the-world-factbook/geos/th.html

Central Intelligence Agency. (2018). *The world factbook: Ukraine.* Retrieved March 20, 2018, from https://www.cia.gov/library/publications/the-world-factbook/geos/up.html

Chakrabarti, S. (2016). *Key issues for infrastructure development in Russia.* Retrieved February 1, 2018, from http://www.ey.com/ru/en/issues/business-environment/ey-road-to-2030-infrastracture-development-in-russia-viewpoint-suma-chakrabarti

Chandra, A., & Thompson, E. (2000). Does public infrastructure affect economic activity? Evidence from rural interstate highway system. *Journal of Regional Science*, *27*(3), 419–437.

Chan, Y.-C. L. (2004). Use of Capital Budgeting Techniques and an Analytic Approach to Capital Investment Decisions in Canadian Municipal Governments. *Public Budgeting & Finance*, *24*(2), 40–58. doi:10.1111/j.0275-1100.2004.02402003.x

Chardchawan, S. (2006). Chapter 2: Decentralization under threat? In Impacts of the CEO Governor Policy upon Thai Local Government. Academic Press.

Chen, C., & Bartle, J. (2017). *Infrastructure financing: A guide for local government managers. A policy issue white paper for ICMA and GFOA.* Retrieved May 28, 2018, from https://digitalcommons.unomaha.edu/cgi/viewcontent.cgi?article=1076&context=pubadfacpub

Chou, J. S., & Pramudawardhani, D. (2015). Cross-country comparisons of key drivers, critical success factors and risk allocation for public-private partnership projects. *International Journal of Project Management*, *33*(5), 1136–1150. doi:10.1016/j.ijproman.2014.12.003

Chu, N. A. (2017). *Medium-term expenditure framework on subnational level in Vietnam*. Retrieved from http://giz-macro.ciem.org.vn/Content/files/Final%20Outline%201_Medium%20Term%20Expenditure%20Framework%20on%20Subnational%20Level.pdf

Chu, S. C. (2017). President Tsai Ing-wen will spend NT $400 Billion on railway construction. *Business Weekly*. Retrieved May 6, 2018, from https://wealth.businessweekly.com.tw/GArticle.aspx?id=ARTL000088021

Chukwuma, O. (2005). *The medium-term expenditure framework: The challenges of budget integration in Sub-Saharan African countries*. World Bank Working Paper Series, 82.

Chung, S., Hong, T., Han, S., Son, J., & Lee, S. (2006). Life cycle cost analysis based optimal maintenance and rehabilitation for underground infrastructure management. *KSCE Journal of Civil Engineering*, *10*(4), 243–253. doi:10.1007/BF02830778

CIA. (2018). *Germany*. Retrieved April 14, 2018, from https://www.cia.gov/library/publications/the-world-factbook/geos/gm.html

Circulaire Budgetaire. (2016). *Cadre budgetaire 2017*. Retrieved July 23, 2018, http://www.dgb.gov.bf/index.php?option=com_edocman&view=document&id=149

Circulaire Budgetaire. (2017). *Cadre budgetaire 2017*. Retrieved July 23, 2018, http://www.dgb.gov.bf/index.php?option=com_edocman&view=document&id=146

CNN. (2018, April 8). *Flint water crisis fast cacts. CNN*. Retrieved April 28, 2018, from https://www.cnn.com/2016/03/04/us/flint-water-crisis-fast-facts/index.html

Commission to Study Capital Budgeting. (1999). *Report of the president's commission to study capital budgeting*. Retrieved May 2, 2016, from https://clintonwhitehouse2.archives.gov/pcscb/report.pdf

Congressional Budget Office. (2006). *Comparing budget and accounting measures of the federal government's fiscal condition*. Retrieved May 2, 2017, from https://www.cbo.gov/publication/18262

Congressional Budget Office. (2008). *Capital budgeting*. Retrieved May 2, 2017, from https://www.cbo.gov/publication/41689

Congressional Budget Office. (2014). *Estimated impact of the American recovery and reinvestment act on employment and economic output in 2013*. Retrieved May 2, 2017, from https://www.cbo.gov/publication/45122

Congressional Budget Office. (2015). *Public spending on transportation and water infrastructure: 1956 to 2014*. Retrieved May 2, 2017, from https://www.cbo.gov/publication/49910

Constitution of the Republic of Moldova. (1994). Retrieved January 4, 2018, from http://lex.justice.md/document_rom.php?id=44B9F30E:7AC17731

Constitution of the Russian Federation. (1993). *Constitution of the Russian Federation*. Retrieved February 1, 2018, from http://www.constitution.ru/en/10003000-01.htm

Construction and Planning Agency, Ministry of Interior. (2018). Sewage treatment connection tates [Data file]. Retrieved April 25, 2018, from https://www.cpami.gov.tw/filesys/file/chinese/dept/sew/sew1071.ods

Coulibaly, K. S., & Diagne, M. F. (2014). *Capital expenditures: Making public investment work for competitiveness and inclusive growth in Moldova.* The World Bank Report No. 76310-MD.

Dabla-Norris, E., Brumby, J., Kyobe, A., Mills, Z., & Papageorgiou, C. (2012). Investing in public investment: An index of public investment efficiency. *Journal of Economic Growth, 17*(3), 235–266. doi:10.100710887-012-9078-5

Dahlström, C., Teorell, J., Dahlberg, S., Hartmann, F., Lindberg, A., & Nistotskaya, M. (2015). *The QoG Expert Survey II Report.* Retrieved December 10, 2018, from https://gupea.ub.gu.se/bitstream/2077/39869/1/gupea_2077_39869_1.pdf

Dalakoglou, D. (2012). The road from capitalism to capitalism: Infrastructures of (post) socialism in Albania. *Mobility: Roads and Authorities, 7*(4), 571–586. doi:10.1080/17450101.2012.718939

Dan Luat. (2016). *Sơ đồ tổ chức bộ máy nhà nước theo Hiến pháp 2013.* Retrieved from https://danluat.thuvienphapluat.vn/so-do-to-chuc-bo-may-nha-nuoc-theo-hien-phap-2013-144432.aspx

Dang, G., & Pheng, L. S. (2014). Critical factors affecting the efficient use of public investments in infrastructure in Vietnam. *Journal of Infrastructure Systems, 21*(3), 05014007.

Dang, G., & Pheng, L. S. (2015). *Infrastructure investments in developing economies.* Springer. doi:10.1007/978-981-287-248-7

Darr, D. (1998). The Benefits of Long-Range Capital Planning—The Virginia Experience. *Public Budgeting & Finance, 18*(3), 42–53. doi:10.1046/j.0275-1100.1998.01141.x

Dastidar, K. G., & Mukherjee, D. (2014). Corruption in delegated public procurement auctions. *European Journal of Political Economy, 35*, 122–127. doi:10.1016/j.ejpoleco.2014.05.003

De Renzio, P. (2011). *Buying better governance: The political economy of budget reforms in aid-dependent countries, 1997-2007.* PQDT - UK & Ireland.

De Renzio, P., & Angemi, D. (2012). Comrades or culprits? Donor engagement and budget transparency in aid-dependent countries. *Public Administration and Development, 32*(2), 167–180. doi:10.1002/pad.1603

De Renzio, P., & Masud, H. (2011). Measuring and promoting budget transparency: The open budget index as a research and advocacy tool. *Governance: An International Journal of Policy, Administration and Institutions, 24*(3), 607–616. doi:10.1111/j.1468-0491.2011.01539.x

DeGennaro, R. P., & Dwyer, G. P. (2014). Expected returns to stock investments by angel investors in groups. *European Financial Management, 20*(4), 739–755. doi:10.1111/eufm.12002

Delavallade, C. (2007). Lutte contre la corruption au Burkina Faso et réformes de la gestion budgétaire. *Afrique Contemporaine, 3*(3), 271–288. doi:10.3917/afco.223.0271

Deno, K. T. (1988). The effect of public capital on U.S. manufacturing activity: 1970 to 1978. *Southern Economic Journal, 55*(1), 400–411. doi:10.2307/1059112

Department of the Treasury & Council of Economic Advisers. (2010). *An economic analysis of infrastructure investment, a report.* Retrieved May 22, 2018, from http://www.treasury.gov/resource-center/economic-policy/Documents/infrastructure_investment_report.pdf

Department of the Treasury. (2014). *Deferred maintenance. Financial management service, United States government supplemental information (Unaudited) for the years ended September 30, 2013, and 2012.* Retrieved May 8, 2017, from https://www.fiscal.treasury.gov/fsreports/rpt/finrep/finrep13/supp_info/fr_supplement_info_defer_maint.htm

Di Bella, G., Dynnikova, O., & Grigoli, F. (2017). *Fiscal federalism and regional performance.* International Monetary Fund (Working Paper).

Di Liddo, G., Longobardi, E., & Porcelli, F. (2016). Measuring horizontal fiscal imbalance: The case of Italian municipalities. *Local Government Studies, 42*(3), 385–419. doi:10.1080/03003930.2016.1150836

Directorate General of Budget, Accounting, and Statistics. (2018). *Special budget.* Retrieved April 25, 2018, from https://eng.dgbas.gov.tw/np.asp?ctNode=5255

DiRienzo, C., & Das, J. (2015). Innovation and role of corruption and diversity: A cross-country study. *International Journal of Cross Cultural Management, 15*(1), 51–72. doi:10.1177/1470595814554790

Dodonov, B., Christian, H., Petra, O., & Sugolov, P. (2002). Efficient infrastructure supply for economic development – the case of Ukraine. *Post-Communist Economies, 14*(2), 149–167. doi:10.1080/14631370220139909

Doucette, J. (2010). The terminal crisis of the "Participatory Government" and the election of Lee Myung-Bak. *Journal of Contemporary Asia, 40*(1), 22–43. doi:10.1080/00472330903270338

Dowall, D. E. (2001). Rethinking statewide infrastructure policies: Lessons from California and beyond. *Public Works Management & Policy, 6*(1), 5–17. doi:10.1177/1087724X0161002

Downes. (2013). *Medium-term expenditure frameworks (MTEF): Logic, benefits, limitations.* Retrieved July 23, 2018, from https://wpqr4.adb.org/lotusquickr/cop.../0/.../4%20MTEF%20-%20R%20Downes.pdf

Duenvald, C., Georguiev, N., & Schaechter, A. (2005). *Too much of a good thing? Credit booms in transition economies: The cases of Bulgaria, Romania, and Ukraine.* IMG Working Paper.

Duncombe, W., & Schroeder, L. (1988). The effects of tax instability on budgeting and financial management in developing countries. *International Journal of Public Administration, 11*(3), 271–309. doi:10.1080/01900698808524590

Duong, T. N. (2014). Vietnam country report. *Financing ASEAN Connectivity*, 401-429.

Dupont-Morales, M. A., & Harris, J. E. (1994). Strengthening Accountability: Incorporating Strategic Planning and Performance Measurement into Budgeting. *Public Productivity & Management Review, 17*(3), 231–239. doi:10.2307/3380655

Durata, T. (n.d.). *An overview of public administration in Albania.* Retrieved May 4, 2018, from https://scholar.google.com/scholar?rlz=1C1CHBF_enUS786US786&um=1&ie=UTF-8&lr&cites=3886605221109 37877

Earnst & Young. (2013). *Doing business in Vietnam.* Retrieved May 15, 2018, from http://www.ey.com/Publication/vwLUAssets/Doing_Business_in_Vietnam/$FILE/Doing_Business_in_Vietnam_16000319.pdf

Ebdon, C. (2001). *Capital planning in the states: Internal decision-making. Learning Paper Series.* Retrieved July 23, 2018, from www.maxwell.syr.edu/gpp/pdfs/CM_State_Learning_Paper.pdf

Ebdon, C. (2003). Capital management. In K. Alan (Ed.), *Paths to performance in state and local government: Final report from the Maxwell School* (pp. 71–100). Syracuse, NY: Syracuse University, Campbell Public Affairs Institute.

Ebdon, C. (2004). Capital Management Practices in U.S. Counties. *Public Works Management & Policy, 8*(3), 192–202. doi:10.1177/1087724X03259604

Ebdon, C. (2007). Underpinning government: Capital and infrastructure management in state and local government. In P. Ingraham (Ed.), *In pursuit of performance: Management systems in state and local government* (pp. 57–81). Johns Hopkins University Press.

Ebdon, C. (2007). Underpinning government: Capital and infrastructure management in state and local government. In P. Ingraham (Ed.), *In pursuit of performance; Management systems in local government* (pp. 57–81). Baltimore, MD: The Johns Hopkins University Press.

Ebdon, C., & Landow, P. (2012). The balancing act: Using private money for public projects. *Public Budgeting & Finance, 32*(1), 58–79. doi:10.1111/j.1540-5850.2011.01002.x

Ebrahimnejad, S., Mousavi, S., & Seyrafianpour, H. (2010). Risk identification and assessment for build-operate-transfer projects: A fuzzy multi attribute decision making model. *Expert Systems with Applications, 37*(1), 575–586. doi:10.1016/j.eswa.2009.05.037

Economist. (2003). *Inflation in post-Communist Europe: Whipped.* London, UK: Economist print edition.

Economist. (2015a). *Crisis in Ukraine.* London, UK: Economist print edition.

Economist. (2015b). *War-torn reform. Ukraine's government is making some progress. But much more needs to be done.* London, UK: Economist print edition.

Economist. (2017a). *Plugging the gap. Ukrainian immigrants are powering Poland's economy. Now poles worry that Visa-free travel may lure them to the rest of the EU.* London, UK: Economist print edition.

Economist. (2017b). *Ukraine and Russia are both trapped by the war in Donbas.* London, UK: Economist print edition.

Economist. (2017c). *Ukraine is a mess; The West should press it harder to fight graft.* London, UK: Economist print edition.

Encyclopedia Britannica. (2018). *Ukraine: History.* Assessed April 2, 2018, from https://www.britannica.com/topic/Kievan-Rus

Energy Tax Act. (2006). *Energiesteuergesetz.* Retrieved May 21, 2018, from https://hylaw.eu/database/national-legislation/germany/energy-tax-act-energiesteuergesetz-energiestg

Engel, E., Fischer, R. D., & Galetovic, A. (2014). *The Economics of public-private partnerships: A basic guide.* New York: Cambridge University Press. doi:10.1017/CBO9781139565615

Englebert, P. (1996). *Unsteady statehood in West Africa.* Burkina Faso: Westview Press.

Englebert, P., & Sangaré, N. (2014). Burkina Faso: Limited decentralization under tight oversight. In J. T. Dickovick & J. S. Wunsch (Eds.), *Decentralization in Africa: The paradox of stata strength* (pp. 45–68). Boulder, CO: Lynne Rienner.

Enquête sur le Budget Ouvert 2017. (2017). *International budget partnership.* Retrieved July 23, 2018 from https://www.internationalbudget.org/wp-content/uploads/burkina-faso-open-budget-survey-2017-summary-french.pdf

Ermasova, N. (2012). *Capital budgeting at the state level: an empirical analysis from the economic downturn through the present* (PhD Dissertation). SPEA, IU.

Ermasova, N. (2012). *Capital budgeting at the state level: An empirical analysis from the economic downturn through the present* (PhD Dissertation). SPEA, IU.

Ermasova, N., & Ermasova, P. (2019). Public capital budgeting and management process in Russia. In Capital management and budgeting in the public sector. Hershey, PA: IGI Global.

Ermasova, N. (2008). *Budget system* (3rd ed.). Moscow: Urait.

Ermasova, N. (2013). The capital budgeting at the state level during the Great Recession: The results of survey. *State & Local Government Review, 45*(2), 119–130. doi:10.1177/0160323X13487079

Ermasova, N. (2013). The improvement of capital budgeting at the State level in the USA. *Public Administration Review, 2*(2), 92–104.

Ermasova, N. (2013b). The improvement of capital budgeting at the state level in the USA. *Public Administration Review, 2*(2), 92.

Ermasova, N. (2016). *Budget systems in Russia* (2nd ed.). Moscow: UNITY.

Ermasova, N., & Ermasova, P. (2018). *Public capital budgeting and management process in Russia. In Capital management and budgeting in the public sector*. Hershey, PA: IGI Global.

Ermasova, N., & Mikesell, J. (2016). Fiscal disparity and equalization in the Russian Federation. *Post-Communist Economies, 28*(1), 1–15. doi:10.1080/14631377.2015.1084726

Ermasova, N., Mikesell, J., & Ermasov, S. (2014). Impact of recession on total revenue of regional governments in Russia. *Business Systems & Economics, 4*(2), 139–154. doi:10.13165/VSE-14-4-2-03

Ernst & Young. (2018). *Russian infrastructure in the global context.* Retrieved February 1, 2018, from http://www.ey.com/ru/en/issues/business-environment/ey-road-to-2030-russian-infrastructure-in-global-context

Esfahani, H. S., & Ramírez, M. T. (2003). Institutions, infrastructure, and economic growth. *Journal of Development Economics, 70*(2), 443–477. doi:10.1016/S0304-3878(02)00105-0

EU Report. (2016). *European Commission Staff Working Document.* Retrieved May 4, 2018, from https://ec.europa.eu/neighbourhood-enlargement/sites/near/files/20180417-albania-report.pdf

European Bank of Reconstruction and Development. (2018). *Chernobyl: A site transformed.* Retrieved April 15, 2018, from http://www.ebrd.com/what-we-do/sectors/nuclear-safety/chernobyl-overview.html

Export. Gov. (2017). *Albania market overview.* Retrieved May 4, 2018, from https://www.export.gov/article?series=a0pt0000000PAt7AAG&type=Country_Commercial__kav

Federal Accounting Standards Advisory Board. (2011). *Deferred maintenance and repairs amending statements of federal financial accounting standards 6, 14, 29 and 32: Statement of federal financial accounting standards exposure draft.* Retrieved May 22, 2018, from http://fasab.gov/pdffiles/exposure_dmr_2011jun27.pdf

Federal Aviation Administration. (2017). *Airport and airway trust fund.* Retrieved May 24, 2018, from http://www.faa.gov/about/budget/aatf

Federal Highway Toll Act. (2011). *Gesetz über die Erhebung von streckenbezogenen Gebühren für die Benutzung von Bundesautobahnen und Bundesstrassen*, July 12, 2011, BGBL. I at 1378, § 11.

Federal Minister of Transport and Digital Infrastructure. (2014). *Federal transport infrastructure plan till 2030.* Retrieved May 24, 2018, from https://www.bmvi.de/SharedDocs/EN/Documents/G/ftip-2030.pdf?__blob=publicationFile

Federal Ministry for Economic Affairs and Energy. (2016). *National reform programme 2016.* Retrieved May 22, 2018, from https://www.bmwi.de/Redaktion/EN/Publikationen/national-reform-programme-2016.pdf?__blob=publicationFile&v=7

Federal Real Property Council. (2016). 2016 *guidance for real property inventory reporting.* Retrieved May 24, 2018, from https://www.gsa.gov/cdnstatic/FY_2016_FRPP_Data_Dictionary_May_16__2016.pdf

Federal State Statistics Service. (2018). *Investments in Russia in 2017* [Инвестиции России в 2017]. Retrieved May, 24, 2018, from http://www.gks.ru/free_doc/doc_2017/invest.pdf

Fisher, R. C. (2016). *State and local public finance.* New York: Routledge.

Forrester, R. C. (2014). *Behavioral finance: Factors influencing angel investor decisions.* (Unpublished doctoral dissertation). Kennesaw State University, Kennesaw, GA. Retrieved December 10, 2018, from https://digitalcommons.kennesaw.edu/cgi/viewcontent.cgi?article=1639&context=etd

Forrester, J. P. (1993). Municipal capital budgeting: An examination. *Public Budgeting & Finance*, *3*(1), 85–103. doi:10.1111/1540-5850.00977

Forte, D. (1989). From reactive to proactive fiscal planning: The results of strategic planning in McKinney, Texas. *Government Finance Review*, *54*(4), 7–11.

Frankel, E., & Wachs, M. (2017). More than money: Infrastructure and governance. *Public Works Management & Policy*, *22*(1), 6–11. doi:10.1177/1087724X16667728

Fratzscher, M. (2015*). Why Germany needs to invest. World Economic Forum.* Retrieved April 15, 2018, from https://www.weforum.org/agenda/2015/05/why-germany-needs-to-invest/

Fratzscher, M. (2014). *Die Deutschland-Illusion: Warum wir unsere Wirtschaft überschätzen und Europa brauchen.* Berlin: Carl Hanser Verlag.

Fratzscher, M. (2018). *The Germany illusion: Between economic euphoria and despair.* London: Oxford Press. doi:10.1093/oso/9780190676575.001.0001

Frère, M. S., & Englebert, P. (2015). Briefing: Burkina Faso—the fall of Blaise Compaoré. *African Affairs*, *114*(455), 295–307. doi:10.1093/afraf/adv010

Fund for Reconstruction and Development. (2018). *Uzbekistan.* Retrieved July 23, 2018, from http://ufrd.uz/

Galor, O. (1996). Convergence? Inferences from theoretical models. *Economic Journal*, *106*(437), 1056–1069. doi:10.2307/2235378

Gamper, C. (2012). Public investment across levels of government: The case of Brandenburg, Germany. Report for the 28th OECD Territorial Development Policy Committee, 4-5 Dec 2012.

Ganelin, M., & Vasin, S. (2014). *Russian infrastructure. A big ship sails far* (Industry report). Retrieved May 24, 2018, from http://www.gazprombank.ru/upload/iblock/007/gpb_russian%20infrastructure_eng_150714.pdf

GAO. (1997). *GAO/AIMD-97-88, federal investment outlays*. Fiscal Years 1981-2002 (Letter report, 05/21/1997).

GAO. (2004). *Agency implementation of capital planning principles is mixed.* GAO-04-138.

GAO. (2016). *Process exists for prioritizing asset maintenance decisions, but evaluation could improve efforts.* GAO-17-136.

Gatti, S. (2012). *Project finance in theory and practice: Designing, structuring and financing private and public projects.* Waltham, MA: Elsevier.

Gatti, S. (2012). *Project Finance in Theory and Practice: Designing, Structuring, and Financing Private and Public Projects*. Waltham, MA: Elsevier.

General Services Administration. (2012). *Federal real property council 2012 guidance for real property inventory reporting*. Washington, DC: Author.

General Statistics Office of Vietnam. (2015). *Vietnam.* Retrieved May 15, 2018, from http://www.gso.gov.vn/default_en.aspx?tabid=774

German Council of Economic Experts. (2018). *Annual report 2017/2018*. Retrieved April 18, 2018, from http://www.wiwi.ruhr-uni-bochum.de/news/dekanat/news01324.html.en

German Finance Ministry. (2014). *Weak investment in Germany? German finance ministry's March 2014 monthly report*. Retrieved April 12, 2018, from https://www.bundesfinanzministerium.de/Content/DE/Monatsberichte/2014/03/Inhalte/Kapitel-3-Analysen/3-3-investitionsschwaeche.html

German Finance Ministry. (2015). *Public investment trends in Germany*. Retrieved April 12, 2018, from http://www.bundesfinanzministerium.de/Content/EN/Standardartikel/Topics/Fiscal_policy/Articles/2015-01-12-public-investment-trends-germany.html

German Finance Ministry. (2018). *Gesamtwirtschaftliches produktionspotenzial und konjunkturkomponenten des bundes: Kapitalstock und investitionen*. Retrieved April 12, 2018, from https://www.bundesfinanzministerium.de/Monatsberichte/2017/01/Inhalte/Kapitel-6-Statistiken/6-3-06-kapitalstock-und-investitionen.html

Gershberg, A., & Benning, J. (1999). *Federal capital investment and the balanced budget amendment: The pros and cons of a federal capital budget* (Research paper). The Nelson A. Rockefeller Institute of Government.

Gianakis, G. A., & McCue, C. P. (1999). *Local government budgeting: A managerial approach*. Greenwood Publishing Group.

Gianakis, G. A., & McCue, C. P. (1999). *Local government budgeting: A managerial approach*. Westport, CT: Quorum Books.

Giannakis, G. & McCue, C. (1999). *Local government budgeting: A managerial approach*. Westport, CT: Quorum Books.

Global Economic Forum. (2008). *Global Report*. Retrieved April 15, 2018, from https://www.weforum.org/reports/world-economic-forum-annual-meeting-2008

Goldsmith, A. A. (2001). Foreign aid and statehood in Africa. *International Organization, 55*(1), 123–148. doi:10.1162/002081801551432

Goode, R., & Birnbaum, E. A. (1956). Government Capital Budgets. *Staff Papers, 5*(1), 23–46. doi:10.2307/3866136

Goubau, T. (2018). *Germany infrastructure projects over US $129 billion of investment*. Retrieved May 21, 2018, from https://www.aproplan.com/blog/quality-management-plan-construction/germany-infrastructure-projects-us129-billion-investment

Government Finance Officer Association—GFOA. (2007). *Best Practice in Capital Project Monitoring and Reporting*. Retrieved October 15, 2018, from http://www.gfoa.org/capital-project-monitoring-and-reporting

Government Finance Officers Association. (2001). *GFOA Recommended Practices: Debt Management. Recommended Practices for State and Local Governments: 89-127 (Development of a Debt Policy, revised 2003)*. Retrieved from http://www.gfoa.org/services/rp/debt/debtmanagement-policy.pdf

Government Finance Officers Association. (2016). *GFOA Best Practice: Incorporating the Capital Budget into the Budget Document* Retrieved from http://www.gfoa.org/incorporating-capital-budget-budget-document

Government Finance Officers Association. (2017). *GFOA Best Practice: Capital Project Monitoring and Reporting*. Retrieved from http://www.gfoa.org/capital-project-monitoring-and-reporting

Government Performance Project—GPP. (2005). *Grading the States 2005: A look inside*. Retrieved September 13, 2005, from http://results.gpponline.org/States.aspx

Government Portal of the Republic of Uzbekistan. (2018). *Uzbekistan*. English. Retrieved July 23, 2018, from https://www.gov.uz/en

Government Portal of the Republic of Uzbekistan. (2018). *Uzbekistan*. Russian language. Retrieved July 23, 2018, from https://www.gov.uz/ru

Government Portal of Vietnam. (2018). *Political system*. Retrieved May 25, 2018 from http://www.chinhphu.vn/portal/page/portal/English/TheSocialistRepublicOfVietnam/AboutVietnam/AboutVietnamDetail?categoryId=10000103&articleId=10001578

Gramlich, E. M. (1994). Infrastructure investment: A review essay. *Journal of Economic Literature*, *32*, 1176–1196.

Grimsey, D., & Lewis, M. (2002). Evaluating the risks of public private partnerships for infrastructure projects. *International Journal of Project Management*, *20*(2), 107–118. doi:10.1016/S0263-7863(00)00040-5

Gueorguiev, D., & Malesky, E. (2012). Foreign investment and bribery: A firm-level analysis of corruption in Vietnam. *Journal of Asian Economics*, *23*(2), 111–129. doi:10.1016/j.asieco.2011.11.006

Guzman, T. (2019). Capital budgeting, infrastructure, and capital investment in the Republic of Uzbekistan. In Capital management and budgeting in the public sector. Hershey, PA: IGI Global.

Guzman, T. (2018). *Capital budgeting, infrastructure and capital investment in Republic of Uzbekistan. In Capital management and budgeting in the public sector*. Hershey, PA: IGI Global.

Halachmi, A., & Sekwat, A. (1997). Strategic capital budgeting and planning: Prospects at the county level. *Journal of Public Budgeting, Accounting & Financial Management*, *8*(4), 578.

Halachmi, A., & Sekwat, A. (1997). Strategic capital budgeting and planning: Prospects at the county level. *Public Budgeting and Financial Management*, *1*(1), 578–596.

Hall, J. H., & Mutshutshu, T. (2013). Capital budgeting techniques employed by selected South African state-owned companies. *Corporate Ownership & Control*, *10*(2), 177–187.

Haque, M. E., & Kneller, R. (2008). *Public investment and growth: The role of corruption*. Centre for Growth and Business Cycle Research discussion paper series, 98.

Harsch, E. (1998). Burkina Faso in the winds of liberalization. *Review of African Political Economy*, *78*(78), 625–641. doi:10.1080/03056249808704348

Harsch, E. (2009). Urban protest in Burkina Faso. *African Affairs*, *108*(431), 263–288. doi:10.1093/afraf/adp018

Harvie, C., & Tran, V. H. (1997). *Vietnam's reforms and economic growth*. Springer. doi:10.1057/9780230389472

Ha, Y. (2010). *Public budgeting & financial management*. Seoul, South Korea: Dasan Publisher. (in Korean)

Heritage Foundation. (2018). *Index of economic freedom*. Retrieved July 23, 2018 from https://www.heritage.org/index/country/albania

Highway Construction Financing Act (Strassenbaufinanzierungsgesetz). (2006). Mar. 28, 1960, BGBL. I at 201, *as last amended* by Verordnung, Oct. 31, 2006, BGBL. I at 2407, art. 3.

Hilgers, M. (2010). Evolution of political regime and evolution of popular political representations in Burkina Faso. *African Journal of Political Science and International Relations*, *4*(9), 324–350.

Hilgers, M., & Loada, A. (2013). Tensions et protestations dans un régime semi-autoritaire: Croissance des révoltes populaires et maintien du pouvoir au Burkina Faso. *Politique Africaine (Paris, France)*, *3*(3), 187–208. doi:10.3917/polaf.131.0187

Holtz-Eakin, D., & Schwartz, A. (1995a). Infrastructure in a structural model of economic growth. *Regional Science and Urban Economics*, *25*(2), 131–151. doi:10.1016/0166-0462(94)02080-Z

Howard, K. (1973). *Changing state budgeting*. Lexington, KY: Council of State Government.

Hsieh, T. Y. (2012). *Wandering between the lowest bid and the most advantageous bid.* National Policy Foundation Research Report. Retrieved April 25, 2018, from https://www.npf.org.tw/2/10493

Ibrahim, M., Kumi, E., & Yeboah, T. (2015). Greasing or sanding the wheels? Effect of corruption on economic growth in sub-Saharan Africa. *African Journal of Economic and Sustainable Development*, *4*(2), 157–173. doi:10.1504/AJESD.2015.069858

IMF. (2014). *Fiscal transparency evaluation for the Russian Federation.* International Monetary Fund Country Report No. 14/ 134.

IMF. (2017). *Medium term expenditure frameworks: From concept to practice. Preliminary Lessons from Africa.* Retrieved July 23, 2018, from www.dif.mp.gov.in/spmg/MTEFManual_PWD.pdf

Inderst, G. (2016). ADBI working paper series, infrastructure investment, private finance, and institutional investors: Asia from a global perspective. A. D. B. Institute.

Ingraham, P. (2007). *In pursuit of performance: Management systems in state and local government.* Johns Hopkins Press.

Institute of World Economy (Vietnam). (1995). *Vietnam's economic renovation and foreign economic policies.* Social Sciences Publishing House.

International Cotton Advisory Committee. (2011). *Cotton fact sheet Uzbekistan.* Retrieved July 23, 2018, from https://www.icac.org/econ_stats/country_fact_sheets/fact_sheet_uzbekistan_2011.pdf

International Monetary Fund. (2001). *Government finance statistics manual* (*GFSM 2001*). Retrieved September 10, 2017, from http://www.imf.org/external/pubs/ft/gfs/manual/index.htm

International Monetary Fund. (2014). *Albanian financial system stability assessment.* Retrieved July 23, 2018, from https://www.imf.org/en/Publications/CR/Issues/2016/12/31/Albania-Financial-System-Stability-Assessment-41424

International Monetary Fund. (2016). *Staff country report-Albania and IMF no. 16/142.* Retrieved July 23, 2018, from https://www.imf.org/en/Publications/CR/Issues/2016/12/31/Albania-Selected-Issues-16142

International Monetary Fund. (2016). Thailand: Staff report for the 2016 article IV consultation. *IMF Country Report*, *16*(139).

International Monetary Fund. (2017). *Albania selected issues report no. 17/364.* Retrieved July 23, 2018, from https://www.imf.org/en/Publications/CR/Issues/2016/12/31/Albania-Selected-Issues-43939

International Monetary Fund. (2017). *Estimating the stock of public capital in 170 countries (Jan 2017 update).* Retrieved December 10, 2018, from https://www.imf.org/external/np/fad/publicinvestment/pdf/csupdate_jan17.pdf

International Monetary Fund. (2017). *Public investment, efficiency and growth: The case Of Moldova.* IMF Country Report No. 17/399. Retrieved June 15, 2018, from https://www.imf.md/press/cr17399-MoldovaSIP.pdf

International Monetary Fund. (2017). World economic outlook database [Data file]. Retrieved April 18, 2018, from https://www.imf.org/external/pubs/ft/weo/2017/02/weodata/index.aspx

International Monetary Fund. (2018). *Country report no. 18/123*. p. 35-38. Retrieved July 23, 2018, from https://www.imf.org/en/Publications/CR/Issues/2016/12/30/Albania-Selected-Issues-and-Statistical-Appendix-16403

International Monetary Fund. (2018). *Economic outlook database*. Retrieved October 15, 2018, from https://www.imf.org/external/pubs/ft/weo/2018/02/weodata/index.aspx

International Monetary Fund. (2018). *Public infrastructure in the western Balkans*. Retrieved July 23, 2018, from https://www.imf.org/en/Publications/Departmental-Papers-Policy-Papers/Issues/2018/02/07/Public-Infrastructure-in-the-Western-Balkans-Opportunities-and-Challenges-45547

International Transparency. (2017). *Corruption perceptions index 2017*. Retrieved May 15, 2018, from https://www.transparency.org/news/feature/corruption_perceptions_index_2017

Istrate, E., & Puentes, R. (2009). *Investing for success examining a federal capital budget and a national infrastructure bank*. Retrieved March 2, 2017, from http://www.brookings.edu/~/media/Files/rc/reports/2009/1210_infrastructure_puentes.pdf

Jacobs, D. F. (2008). *A review of capital budgeting practices*. IMF Working Paper, WP/08/160. International Monetary Fund.

Jacobs, M. D. F. (2008). A review of capital budgeting practices (No. 8-160). International Monetary Fund.

Jenkins, G. P., Miklyaev, M., Afra, S., & Hashemi, M. (2017). *Prioritization of public investment projects in Vietnam (No. 2017-08)*. JDI Executive Programs.

Jeune Afrique. (2018). *Chronologie Burkina Faso*. Retrieved July 23, 2018, from http://www.jeuneafrique.com/pays/burkina-faso/chronologie/

Jimenez, B. S., & Pagano, M. A. (2012). What Factors Affect Management Quality? State Infrastructure Management and the Government Performance Project. *Public Works Management & Policy*, *17*(2), 124–151. doi:10.1177/1087724X11419308

Johansen, E., & Cooper, J. H. (2007). Common Funding Options for Capital Projects. In J. P. Casey & M. J. Mucha (Eds.), *Capital Project Planning and Evaluation: Expanding the Role of the Finance Officer* (Vol. 8, pp. 59–80). Chicago, IL: Government Finance Officers Association.

Johnson, C. (1995). Managing financial resources to meet environmental infrastructure needs: The case of state revolving funds. *Public Productivity and Management Review*, *18*(3), 263–275. doi:10.2307/3380847

Jokanovic, I., Crujic, B., Zeijic, D., & Crujic, D. (2017). Article. *Journal of Civil Engineering*, *12*(2), 71–78.

Jung, A., Müller, A. K., Sauga, M., Schmergal, C., Traufetter, G., & Witsch, K. (2014). Germany ailing infrastructure. *Spiegel*. September 18, 2014. Retrieved April 15, 2018, from http://www.spiegel.de/international/germany/low-german-infrastructure-investment-worries-experts-a-990903.html

Kamensky, J. (1993). Program performance measures: Designing a system to manage for results. *Public Productivity & Management Review*, *16*(4), 395–402. doi:10.2307/3381017

Karnowski, S. (2017, July 30). Minnesota bridge collapse still reverberates 10 years later. *The Chicago Tribune*. Retrieved May 8, 2018, from http://www.chicagotribune.com/news/nationworld/midwest/ct-minnesota-bridge-collapse-anniversary-20170730-story.html

Kaufman, G. G., Krueger, T. H., & Hunter, W. C. (1999). *The Asian financial crisis: Origins, implications and solutions*. New York: Springer.

Kaufmann, D., Kraay, A., & Mastruzzi, M. (2008). *Governance matters VII: Governance indicators for 1996-2007.* Retrieved October 6, 2018, from http://info.worldbank.org/governance/wgi/mc_chart.asp

Kennedy, D. (1967). *Report of the president's commission on budget concepts.* Washington, DC: U.S. Government Printing Office.

KFW. (2015). *European fund for strategic investments (EFSI) launched in Germany. News of KFW Group.* Retrieved April 17, 2018, from https://www.kfw.de/KfW-Group/Newsroom/Aktuelles/News/News-Details_300288.html

Kim, H., & Nguyen, V. V. (2013). *Improving the Efficiency of the Public Investment in Vietnam through the Korean Experiences.* Seoul: Korea Development Institute. Retrieved May 15, 2018, from https://www.kdevelopedia.org/mnt/idas/asset/2014/04/17/DOC/PDF/04201404170131443070648.pdf

Kim, J., Chen, C., & Ebdon, C. (2018). Effects of the GASB no. 34 infrastructure reporting standards on state highway infrastructure quality: A panel data analysis. *Journal of Public Budgeting, Accounting & Financial Management*, *30*(2), 1–24.

Kim, J., & Ebdon, C. (2017). Have the GASB no.34 infrastructure reporting requirements affected state highway spending? *Journal of Public Budgeting, Accounting & Financial Management*, *29*(3), 347–374.

Kim, S., Koo, J., & Lee, Y. (1999). Infrastructure and production efficiency: An analysis on the Korean manufacturing industry. *Contemporary Economic Policy*, *17*(3), 390–400. doi:10.1111/j.1465-7287.1999.tb00691.x

King, L. M. (1995). Operating and capital budget reform in Minnesota: Managing public finances like the future matters. *Government Finance Review*, *11*(1), 7–10.

Kirk, R., & Mallett, W. (2018). *Funding and financing highways and public transportation, congressional research service, January 11, 2018.* Retrieved May 28, 2018, from http://fas.org/sgp/crs/misc/R44674.pdf

Kitsaowapak, J. (2016). *Expressway is a cheating way (In Thai), TV program by mass communication organization of Thailand (M.C.O.T.).* Retrieved May 1, 2018, from https://www.youtube.com/watch?v=Tj5tP-2ypus

Kittipanyasiri, A. (2015). *Planning and budgeting for the capital improvement in Thai Municipalities: Problems in the development of Thai municipal self-governing capacity.* Retrieved October 6, 2018, from http://documents.worldbank.org/curated/en/993671468118138134/pdf/674860ESW0P1180019006020120RB0EDITS.pdf

Knack, S. (1996). Institutions and the convergence hypothesis: The cross-national evidence. *Public Choice*, *87*(3-4), 207–228. doi:10.1007/BF00118645

Koala, K. (2016). *The enforcement of the 2008 decree on general public procurement procedures and service delegation in Burkina Faso: Its influence on the management system.* Mankato: Minnesota State University.

Kongrungchok, A. (2014). *Limitations of Thai local government internal auditing in detecting risks.* Retrieved September 10, 2018, from http://globalbizresearch.org/Singapore_Conference/pdf/pdf/S454.pdf

Kontoghiorghes, C., & Kalomyra, F. (2009). The association between talent retention, antecedent factors, and consequent organizational performance. *S.A.M. Advanced Management Journal*, *74*(1), 29–36.

Koteen, J. (1989). *Strategic Management in Public and Non-profit Organizations.* Praeger.

Koussoube, E., Loada, A., Nebie, G., & Raffinot, M. (2014). *Political economy of growth and poverty in Burkina Faso: Power, institutions and rents* (Working Paper No. DT/ 2014-01). Dauphine Université Paris.

Kraan, D. J., Kostyleva, V., Forthun, C., Albrecht, J., & Olofsson, R. (2010). Budgeting in Moldova. *OECD Journal on Budgeting*, *10*(3), 115. doi:10.1787/budget-10-5km36kl2k3hf

Kraan, D. J., von Trapp, L., Kostyleva, V., van Tuinen, J., & Morgner, M. (2013). Budgeting in Ukraine. *OECD Journal on Budgeting, 12*(2), 69–140. doi:10.1787/budget-12-5k4c1s8n0br0

Kraan, D., Bergvall, D., Hawkesworth, I., Kostyleva, V., & Witt, M. (2008). Budgeting in Russia. *OECD Journal on Budgeting, 8*(2), 1–58.

Krepsik, K. (2014). Budgeting in Albania. *OCED Journal on Budgeting, 3*(32), 1–23.

Krueathep, W. (2010). *Bad luck or bad budgeting: A comparative analysis of municipal fiscal conditions in Thailand* (Unpublished Ph.D. Dissertation). Rutgers, State University of New Jersey.

Krupa, O. (2018). *Capital budgeting and public investment projects in Ukraine. In Capital management and budgeting in the public sector*. Hershey, PA: IGI Global.

Kuo, N. L., & Liao, W. J. (2018). Determinants of public debt in Taiwanese municipalities. *Public Finance Review (Taiwan), 47*(1), 1–18.

Kuo, Y. Y., & Cheng, M. H. (2018). Budgeting and financial management of public infrastructure: The experience of Taiwan. In *Value for money: Budget and financial management reform in the people's Republic of China, Taiwan and Australia* (pp. 221–250). Canberra, Australia: ANU Press. doi:10.22459/VM.01.2018.11

Lambsdorff, J. G. (2003). How corruption affects productivity. *Kyklos, 56*(4), 457–474. doi:10.1046/j.0023-5962.2003.00233.x

Land Code of Ukraine. (2002). *Vidomosti Verkhovnoi Rady Ukrainy, 3-4*, 27.

Le, P. (2016). Ho Chi Minh City contributed 31.8% to the state budget. *Phap Luat*. Retrieved May 5, 2018, from http://plo.vn/kinh-te/tphcm-dong-gop-toi-318-cho-ngan-sach-ca-nuoc-643798.html

Leduc, S., & Wilson, D. (2013). Roads to prosperity or bridges to nowhere? Theory and evidence on the impact of public infrastructure investment. *NBER Macroeconomics Annual, 27*(1), 89–142. doi:10.1086/669173

Lee, C. H. (2017, April 26). Can Kaohsiung metro become successful? *Global Views Monthly*. Retrieved April 25, 2018, from https://www.gvm.com.tw/article.html?id=22919

Lee, T. P., & Clark, C. (2011). The limits of budget reform in Taiwan. In C. Menifield (Ed.), *Comparative public budgeting: A global perspective* (pp. 91–105). Sudbury, MA: Jones & Bartlett Learning.

Legislative Chamber of the Oliy Majlis of the Republic of Uzbekistan. (n.d.). *Committee on budgeting and economic reforms*. Retrieved July 23, 2018, from http://parliament.gov.uz/en/

Le-Hoai, L., Dai Lee, Y., & Lee, J. Y. (2008). Delay and cost overruns in Vietnam large construction projects: A comparison with other selected countries. *KSCE Journal of Civil Engineering, 12*(6), 367–377. doi:10.100712205-008-0367-7

Levine, S., & Augustino, J. (1994). State revolving funds: A model for financing drinking water programs. *Government Finance Review, 12*, 26–44.

Lewis, C., & Hildreth, W. (2013). *Politics and capital budgeting. In Budgeting: Politics & power* (pp. 224–249). New York, NY: Oxford University Press.

Liu, J., Meng, F., & Fellows, R. (2015). An exploratory study of understanding project risk management from the perspective of national culture. *International Journal of Project Management, 33*(3), 564–575. doi:10.1016/j.ijproman.2014.08.004

Lobo, J., & Rantisi, N. (1999). Investment in infrastructure as determinant of metropolitan productivity. *Growth and Change, 30*(1), 106–127. doi:10.1111/0017-4815.00106

LOI n°055-2004/AN du 21 décembre 2004 portant code général des collectivités territoriales au Burkina Faso (JO spécial n°2 du 20/4/2005).

Lopez, G. (2015, August 28). Hurricane Katrina in 7 essential facts. *VOX.* Retrieved May 28, 2018, from https://www.vox.com/2015/8/23/9191907/hurricane-katrina

Lovells, H., Boots, S., & Harris, J. (2016). Vietnam infrastructure: Needs and challenges. In *The Principles of Project Finance* (pp. 319–336). London, UK: Routledge.

Lynde, C., & Richmond, J. (1992). The role of public capital in production. *The Review of Economics and Statistics, 74*(1), 37–44. doi:10.2307/2109540

Magennis, B., Dang, H., Le, C., Fish, R., & Bui, L. (2017). *Legal guide to investment in Vietnam.* Retrieved May 5, 2018, from http://www.vietnamlaws.com/pdf/LegalGuidetoInvestmentinVietNam.pdf

Marcelo, D., Mandri-Perrott, C., House, S., & Schwartz, J. (2016). *An Alternative Approach to Project Selection: The Infrastructure Prioritization Framework.* World Bank Working Paper.

Marcelo, D., Mandri-Perrott, C., House, S., & Schwartz, J. (2016). An alternative approach to project selection: The infrastructure prioritization framework. *World Bank Working Paper.*

Marlowe, J. (2013). Strategy, priority-setting, and municipal capital budget reform: Three cases from the great recession. *Journal of Public Budgeting, Accounting & Financial Management, 25*(4), 693–718.

Marlowe, J. (2013). Strategy, priority-setting, and municipal capital budget reform: Three cases from the great recession. *Journal of Public Budgeting, Accounting and Financial Management, 25*(4), 693–718.

Marlowe, J., Rivenbark, W. C., & Vogt, A. J. (2009). *Capital budgeting and finance a guide for local governments* (2nd ed.). Washington, DC: ICMA PRESS.

Marlowe, J., Rivenbark, W. C., & Vogt, A. J. (2009). *Capital budgeting and finance: A guide for local government.* Washington, DC: ICMA Press.

Mason, C. M., & Harrison, R. T. (2003). "Auditioning for money": What do technology investors look for at the initial screening stage? *Journal of Private Equity, 6*(2), 29–42. doi:10.3905/jpe.2003.320037

Matei, L. (2013). Republic of Moldova: Toward a European administration. In *Public Administration in Post-Communist Countries* (pp. 205–230). Routledge. doi:10.1201/b14237-10

Maula, M., Autio, E., & Arenius, P. (2005). What drives micro-angel investments? *Small Business Economics, 25*(5), 459–475. doi:10.100711187-004-2278-4

Maxwell, A. L., Jeffrey, S. A., & Lévesque, M. (2011). Business angel early stage decision making. *Journal of Business Venturing, 26*(2), 212–225. doi:10.1016/j.jbusvent.2009.09.002

McCargo, D. (2004). *Rethinking Vietnam.* London, UK: Psychology Press. doi:10.4324/9780203569467

McCarthy, S., & Tiong, R. (1991). Financial and contractual aspects of build-operate-transfer projects. *International Journal of Project Management, 9*(4), 222–227. doi:10.1016/0263-7863(91)90030-Y

McKinsey Global Institute Report. (2015). *Bridging infrastructure gaps has the world made progress*? Retrieved May, 24, 2018, from https://www.mckinsey.com/~/media/mckinsey/industries/capital/mgi-bridging-infrastructure-gaps-discussion-paper.ashx

McKinsey Global Institute. (2013). *Game changers: Five opportunities for U.S. growth and renewal*. Retrieved April 2, 2018, from https://www.mckinsey.com/featured-insights/americas/us-game-changers

Méon, P.-G., & Sekkat, K. (2005). Does corruption grease or sand the wheels of growth? *Public Choice*, *122*(1-2), 69–97. doi:10.100711127-005-3988-0

Mikesell, J. (2003). *Fiscal administration analysis and applications for the public sector* (6th ed.). Belmont, CA: Wadsworth.

Mikesell, J. L. (1999). *Fiscal administration: Analysis and applications for the public sector* (5th ed.). New York: Harcourt Brace College Publishers.

Mikesell, J. L. (2017). *Fiscal administration* (10th ed.). Boston, MA: Cengage Learning.

Milakovsky, B. (2018). *Ukrainians abroad: The economics and politics of labor migration*. Kennan Institute. Retrieved March 2, 2018, from http://www.kennan-focusukraine.org/ukrainians-abroad-the-economics-and-politics-of-labor-migration/

Minh, D. (2016). *ODA accounts for 94% of government external debt. Vietnam Financial Review*. Retrieved June 1, 2018, from http://thoibaotaichinhvietnam.vn/pages/thoi-su/2016-01-19/oda-chiem-94-danh-muc-no-nuoc-ngoai-cua-chinh-phu-28031.aspx

Ministere des Infrastructures du Desenclavement et des Transports. (2015). *Tableau de Bord 2013 du Ministère des infrastructures, du désenclavement et des transports*. Retrieved July 23, 2018, from http://cns.bf/IMG/pdf/tableau_de_bord_midt_2013-vf.pdf

Ministre de l'Economie et des Finances. (2009). *L'expérience du Burkina Faso en matière d'élaboration du Cadre de Dépenses à Moyen Terme (CDMT)*. Retrieved July 23, 2018, from https://www.slideshare.net/AfricanCoP/lexprience-du-burkina-faso-en-matire-dlaboration-du-cadre-de-dpenses-moyen-terme-cdmt

Ministry of Economy and Finance [MOEF]. (2014). *The budget system of Korea*. Retrieved July 23, 2018, from http://english.mosf.go.kr/images/TheBudgetSystemofKorea.pdf

Ministry of Economy and Finance [MOEF]. (2015). *A guide to Korea taxation*. Author.

Ministry of Finance of the Republic of Moldova. (2017). *Report on medium term expenditure framework*. Retrieved March 25, 2018, from http://mf.gov.md/sites/default/files/documente%20relevante/evaluarea_cbtm_2017-2019_1.pdf

Ministry of Finance of the Republic of Moldova. (2018). *The budget for the citizens*. Retrieved July 12, 2018, from http://mf.gov.md/sites/default/files/Buget%20Cetateni%202018.pdf

Ministry of Finance of the Republic of Uzbekistan. (2018). *Uzbekistan*. Retrieved July 23, 2018, from https://www.mf.uz/en/

Ministry of Finance Russian Federation. (2018). *Investment management*. Retrieved February 1, 2018, from http://old.minfin.ru/en/nationalwealthfund/management/

Ministry of Finance. (2014). *Public financial management strategy 2000-2015*. Government of Albania.

Ministry of Finance. (2017). *2017 Taiwan PPP investor's manual*. Retrieved May 6, 2018, from https://ppp.mof.gov.tw/ppp.website/DownFile.aspx?fromto=website&ReferId=pKRKH4r%2bKq4%3d

Ministry of the Economy of the Republic of Uzbekistan. (2018). *Uzbekistan*. Retrieved July 23, 2018, from https://mineconomy.uz/ru/

Ministry of the Interior and Safety. (2017). *Local government debts.* Retrieved July 23, 2018 from http://lofin.mois.go.kr/portal/bbs/bbsDetail.do?listSubCd=FSL432&bbsCd=FSL1004&subCd=FSL432&code=fsl&leftCd=1&currPage=1&ansTag=N&seq=54101&searchWd=

Minitry of Economic Development. (2013). *Forecast of the long-term socio-economic development of the Russian Federation for the period up to 2030.* Retrieved July 13, 2018, from http://economy.gov.ru/minec/activity/sections/macro/prognoz/doc20130325_06

Mitteness, C. R., Baucus, M. S., & Sudek, R. (2012). Horse vs. jockey? How stage of funding process and industry experience affect the evaluations of angel investors. *Venture Capital, 14*(4), 241–267. doi:10.1080/13691066.2012.689474

Mitteness, C., Sudek, R., & Cardon, M. S. (2012). Angel investor characteristics that determine whether perceived passion leads to higher evaluations of funding potential. *Journal of Business Venturing, 27*(5), 592–606. doi:10.1016/j.jbusvent.2011.11.003

Moak, L. L., & Killian, K. W. (1963). *Capital programming and capital budgeting.* Chicago, IL: Municipal Finance Officer Association.

Moak, L., & Hillhouse, A. (1975). *Concepts and practices in local government finance.* Chicago, IL: Municipal Finance Officer Association.

Moody's Investors Service. (2018). *19ADAD Uzbekistan.* New York: Moody's Investors Service.

Moomaw, R., Mullen, K., & Williams, M. (2002). Human and knowledge capital: A contribution to empirics of state economic growth. *American Economic Journal, 30*(1), 48–59.

Morgan, P. J., & Trinh, L. Q. (2017). 10. Fiscal decentralization and local budget deficits in Viet Nam: An empirical analysis. *Central and Local Government Relations in Asia, 1*(1), 323–333.

Morozov, B. (2009). Degree of fiscal decentralization in republic of Moldova. *The NISPAcee Journal of Public Administration and Policy, 2*(1), 89–109.

Morozov, B. (2014). Republic of Moldova: 20 years of independence and experiments with public finance system. *International Public Management Review, 15*(2), 133–165.

Motor Vehicle Tax Act. (2002). *Kraftfahrzeugsteuergesetz, repromulgated* Sept. 26, 2002, BGBL. I at 3818, *as amended*, Retrieved May 21, 2018, from http://www.gesetze-im-internet.de/kraftstg/BJNR005090927.html

Movchan, A. (2016). *Is investment in infrastructure the answer to Russia's economic problems*? Retrieved May 24, 2018, from https://carnegie.ru/commentary/63484

Mukherjee, T. K., & Henderson, G. V. (1987). The capital budgeting process: Theory and practice. *Interfaces, 17*(2), 78–90. doi:10.1287/inte.17.2.78

Mundial, B. (1998). *Public expenditure management handbook.* Washington, DC: World Bank. Retrieved from http://www1.worldbank.org/publicsector/pe/handbook/pem98.pdf

Munnell, A. H. (1990b). How does public infrastructure affect regional economic performance? In A. Munnell (Ed.), *Is there a shortfall in public capital investment? Proceedings of a conference* (pp. 69-103). Boston, MA: Federal Reserve Bank of Boston.

Munnell, A. H. (1992). Policy Watch: Infrastructure Investment and Economic Growth. *The Journal of Economic Perspectives, 6*(4), 189–198. doi:10.1257/jep.6.4.189

Muoi, N. P. (2013). *Vietnam worried about dam safety in rainy season.* Retrieved June 1, 2018 from https://blogs.wsj.com/indonesiarealtime/2013/08/31/vietnam-worried-about-dam-safety-in-rainy-season/

Murdick, R. G., & Deming, D. D. (1968). *The Management of Capital Expenditures.* New York City, NY: McGraw Hill.

Mykhayliv, D., & Zauner, K. G. (2013). Investment behavior and ownership structures in Ukraine: Soft budget constraints, government ownership and private benefits of control. *Journal of Comparative Economics, 41*(1), 265–278. doi:10.1016/j.jce.2012.03.001

Namkoong, K., & Kim, I. (2018). Foundation of public administration and policy in South Korea. In K. Namkoong, K. Cho, & S. Kim (Eds.), *Public administration and policy in Korea: Its evolution and challenges.* Paris: OECD publishing.

National Assembly Budget Office. (2018). *Analysis on 2018 Budget.* Retrieved July 23, 2018, from http://korea.nabo.go.kr/eng/publications.do?psStep=view&psPage=3&shSearch=&shKeyword=&shDivisionCD=&shPubYear=&shPubCD=pubRecent&pubSID=910

National Assembly of Vietnam. (2008). *Law on road traffic.* Retrieved June 1, 2018, from http://www.moj.gov.vn/vbpq/en/lists/vn%20bn%20php%20lut/view_detail.aspx?itemid=10506

National Assembly of Vietnam. (2013). *Public procurement law.* Retrieved June 1, 2018, from https://www.hcmiu.edu.vn/Portals/1/Docs/vanbanphapluat/english/43-2013-QH13%20Luat%20Dau%20thau.pdf

National Assembly of Vietnam. (2014). *Public investment law.* Retrieved June 1, 2018, from http://www.fetp.edu.vn/cache/MPP7-541-R9.3E-Law%20on%20Public%20Investment%202014--The%20National%20Assembly-2015-01-07-11214028.pdf

National Assembly of Vietnam. (2015). *State budget law.* Retrieved June 1, 2018, from http://www.economica.vn/Content/files/LAW%20%26%20REG/83_2015_QH13%20Law%20on%20State%20budget.pdf

National Assembly of Vietnam. (2016). *Resolution on medium-term public investment plan of 2016 - 2020 Period.* Retrieved June 14, 2018, from https://vanbanphapluat.co/resolution-26-2016-qh14-on-medium-term-public-investment-plan-of-2016-2020-period

National Association of Manufacturers and Building America's Future Educational Fund. (2013). *Infrastructure: Essential to manufacturing competitiveness.* Retrieved April 2, 2018, from http://www.nam.org/Data-and-Reports/NAM-BAF-Infrastructure-Survey/NAM-BAF-Infrastructure-Survey.pdf

National Association of State Budget Officers (NASBO). (1999). *Capital budgeting in the States-paths to success: A comparative analysis of capital budgeting practices in the States.* Retrieved July 14, 2018, from https://www.nasbo.org/mainsite/reports-data/capital-budgeting-in-the-states/capital-budgeting-archive

National Association of State Budget Officers (NASBO). (2014). *Capital budgeting in the States.* Retrieved July 14, 2018, from https://higherlogicdownload.s3.amazonaws.com/NASBO/9d2d2db1-c943-4f1b-b750-0fca152d64c2/UploadedImages/Reports/Capital%20Budgeting%20in%20the%20States.pdf

National Association of State Budget Officers (NASBO). (2015). *Budget processes in the states.* Retrieved April 2, 2018, from http://www.nasbo.org/publications-data/budget-processes-in-the-states

National Bureau of Statistics the Republic of Moldova. (2013). *Territorial statistics.* Retrieved July 25, 2018, from http://www.statistica.md/public/files/publicatii_electronice/Statistica_teritoriala/Statistica_teritoriala_2013.pdf

National Development Council. (2016). *Framework for life-cycle performance management of public infrastructure.* Retrieved April 25, 2018, from https://goo.gl/h3t3FL

National Development Council. (2018a). *Plans for national development.* Retrieved April 25, 2018, from https://www.ndc.gov.tw/en/Content_List.aspx?n=16081B8F505ABB7B

National Development Council. (2018b). *Projects control.* Retrieved May 6, 2018, from https://www.ndc.gov.tw/Content_List.aspx?n=22C3B697A101DF19

National Economic and Social Development Board—NESDB. (2018). *Decentralization and the budget for social services at Tambon administrativelLevel.* Retrieved September 10, 2018, from http://social.nesdb.go.th/social/

National Economic and Social Development Board—NESDB. (2018). *NESDB economic development report.* Retrieved April 28, 2018, from http://www.nesdb.go.th/ewt_dl_link.php?nid=7384

National Economic and Social Development Board—NESDB. (2018). *NESDB economic report.* Retrieved May 1, 2018, from http://www.nesdb.go.th/ewt_dl_link.php?nid=7384

National Government of the Republic of Moldova. (1996). *Law on the budgetary system and the budgetary process No. 847.* Retrieved January 8, 2018, from http://lex.justice.md/md/311518/

National Government of the Republic of Moldova. (2003). *Law on local public finance No. 397-XV.* Retrieved October 25, 2017, from http://cis-legislation.com/document.fwx?rgn=7085

National Government of the Republic of Moldova. (2006). *Law on administrative decentralization, no. 435-XVI.* Retrieved October 25, 2017, from http://cis-legislation.com/document.fwx?rgn=18455

National Government of the Republic of Moldova. (2006). *Law on local public administration no. 436-XVI.* Retrieved October 25, 2017, from http://lex.justice.md/document_rom.php?id=C8E304A4:037190E8

National Government of the Republic of Moldova. (2006). *Law on public sector debt and state guarantees No. 419-XVI.* Retrieved July 25, 2018, from https://cis-legislation.com/document.fwx?rgn=18036

National Government of the Republic of Moldova. (2010). *National development strategy Moldova 2020.* Retrieved March 3, 2018, from http://particip.gov.md/public/files/Moldova_2020_ENG1.pdf

National Government of the Republic of Moldova. (2012). *Republic of Moldova's water supply & sanitation strategy.* Retrieved April 18, 2018, from http://www.serviciilocale.md/public/files/2nd_Draft_WSS_Strategy_October_final_Eng.pdf

National Government of the Republic of Moldova. (2013). *Public law on capital investment management No.1029.* Retrieved December 10, 2017, from http://lex.justice.md/index.php?action=view&view=doc&lang=1&id=350859

National Government of the Republic of Moldova. (2014). *Law on public finances and fiscal responsibilities no. 181.* Retrieved August 15, 2017, from http://lex.justice.md/md/354213/

National Research Council. (2005). *Key performance indicators for federal facilities portfolios: Federal facilities council technical report number 147.* Washington, DC: The National Academies Press; doi:10.17226/11226

Nations Encyclopedia. (2017). *Russia - Infrastructure, power, and communications.* Retrieved May 24, 2018, from http://www.nationsencyclopedia.com/economies/Europe/Russia-INFRASTRUCTURE-POWER-AND-COMMUNICATIONS.html#ixzz5GUjvot1F

Ndiaye, A. S., & Siri, A. (2016). Capital flight from Burkina Faso: Drivers and impact on tax revenue. *African Development Review, 28*(S1), 100–112. doi:10.1111/1467-8268.12184

Ndikumana, L., & Boyce, J. K. (2003). Public debts and private assets: Explaining capital flight from Sub-Saharan African countries. *World Development, 31*(1), 107–130. doi:10.1016/S0305-750X(02)00181-X

Newspaper, P. (2017). *2018 Public debt law with new definition of public debt excluding nonguaranteed loans by state enterprise*. Retrieved April, 1 2018, from https://www.prachachat.net/politics/news-72566

Nguyen, T. T. (2016). *Fiscal decentralization trends in Vietnam: Developments and reforms.* Paper presented at the Public Administration and Policy, Hong Kong.

Nguyen, X. T., & Dapice, D. (2009). *Vietnam's infrastructure constraints.* Ash institute for democratic governance and innovation.

Nguyen-Hoang, P., & Schroeder, L. (2010). An analysis of quasi-decentralized budgeting in Vietnam. *International Journal of Public Administration, 33*(12-13), 698–709. doi:10.1080/01900692.2010.514449

Nurre, S., Cavdaroglu, B., Mitchell, J., Sharkey, T., & Wallace, W. (2012). Restoring infrastructure systems: An integrated network design and scheduling (INDS) problem. *European Journal of Operational Research, 223*(3), 794–806. doi:10.1016/j.ejor.2012.07.010

O'Sullivan, L., & Lima, F. (2016). *Scaling Up Public Investment, Growth And Debt Sustainability IMF Country Report No. 16/391.* Retrieved July 23, 2018, from https://www.imf.org/external/pubs/ft/scr/2016/cr16391.pdf

OECD. (2006). *OECD economic surveys: Russian Federation, 17, OECD Publishing, Paris. Resolution No. 326 (20136 April 10). Resolution of federal government on April 10, 2013. On Approval of the List of RF Constituents where Territorial Development Zones May be Established.*

OECD. (2014). Budget review: Germany. *OECD Journal on Budgeting, 2*(1), 1–83.

OECD. (2015). *Environment at a glance 2015.* Retrieved April 25, 2018, from https://www.oecd-ilibrary.org/environment/environment-at-a-glance-2015/sewage-treatment-connection-rates-of-population_9789264235199-table30-en

OECD. (2015a). *OECD National Accounts Statistics* (database). Retrieved May 21, 2018, from doi:10.1787/na-dataen

OECD. (2015b). *Implementation toolkit, effective public investment across levels of government.* Retrieved May 21, 2018, from http://www.oecd.org/effective-public-investment-toolkit/

OECD. (2016). *Regional outlook survey.* Retrieved May 21, 2018, from https://www.oecd-ilibrary.org/urban-rural-and-regional-development/oecd-regional-outlook-2016/united-states_9789264260245-48-en

OECD. (2016a). *Subnational governments in OECD countries.* Key data, 2016 edition (brochure).

OECD. (2016b). *Regional Outlook Survey.* Retrieved May 21, 2018, from http://www.oecd.org/regional/oecd-regional-outlook-2016-9789264260245-en.htm

OECD. (2016c). *Overview and preliminary proposal on indicators of co-ordination of public investment for regional development.* Room document discussed in the April 2016 RDPC meeting, unpublished material.

OECD. (2017). Albania budgeting. *OECD Journal on Budgeting, 1*(2). doi:10.1787/budget-v16-2-en

OECD. (2017). *Effective public investments across levels of government: Germany.* Retrieved May 17, 2018, from https://www.oecd.org/effective-public-investment-toolkit/Germany.pdf

OECD. (2018). *National accounts statistics.* Retrieved May 17, 2018, from http://www.oecd.org/sdd/na/

OECD. (2018). *Purchasing power parities (PPP) (indicator).* Retrieved December 10, 2018, from https://data.oecd.org/conversion/purchasing-power-parities-ppp.htm

Office of Management and Budget. (1992). *Circular A–94: Guidelines and discount rates for benefit-cost analysis of federal programs.* Author.

Office of Management and Budget. (2015). *Capital programming guide, V 3.0, supplement to office of management budget circular A-11: Planning, budgeting, and acquisition of capital assets.* Retrieved April 2, 2017, from https://obamawhitehouse.archives.gov/sites/default/files/omb/assets/a11_current_year/a11_2016.pdf

Office of Management and Budget. (2016). *Appendix A - Scorekeeping guidelines* (OMB Circular A-11). Author.

Office of Management and Budget. (2016). *Appendix J - Principles in budgeting for capital asset acquisitions (OMB Circular A-11).* Retrieved April 2, 2018, from https://obamawhitehouse.archives.gov/sites/default/files/omb/assets/a11_current_year/app_j.pdf

Office of Management and Budget. (2017). *Budget of the U.S. government, analytical perspectives, fiscal year 2017.* Retrieved September 26, 2018, from https://www.gpo.gov/fdsys/pkg/BUDGET-2017-PER/pdf/BUDGET-2017-PER-6-4.pdf

Office of Management and Budget. (2017). *Circular A-11.* Retrieved April 2, 2018, from https://www.whitehouse.gov/sites/whitehouse.gov/files/omb/assets/a11_current_year/a11_2017.pdf

Office of Management and Budget. (2018). *Budget of the U.S. government, analytical perspectives, fiscal year 2019.* Retrieved May 24, 2018, from https://fraser.stlouisfed.org/files/docs/publications/usbanalytical/BUDGET-2019-PER.pdf

Ok, D. (2015). Toward fiscal democracy: Power structure and budgeting system. Seoul, South Korea: 21Century Books Publication. (in Korean)

Organization for Economic Cooperation and Development. (2014). *Territorial reviews: Ukraine 2013.* Retrieved from . doi:10.1787/19900759

Organization for Economic Cooperation and Development-Development Assistance Committee. (2016). *Top Ten Donors of Gross ODA for Viet Nam.* Retrieved June 14, 2018 from https://public.tableau.com/views/OECDDACAidataglance-byrecipient_new/Recipients?:embed=y&:display_count=yes&:showTabs=y&:toolbar=no?&:showVizHome=no

Ostrom, E., Schroeder, L., & Wynne, S. (1993). *Institutional incentives and sustainable development: Infrastructure policies in perspective (Theoretical lenses on public policy).* Boulder, CO: Westview Press.

Pagano, M. A. (1984). Notes on capital budgeting. *Public Budgeting & Finance*, *4*(3), 31–40. doi:10.1111/1540-5850.00648

Pagano, M. A., & Perry, D. (2008). Financing Infrastructure in the 21st Century City. *Public Works Management & Policy*, *13*(1), 22–38. doi:10.1177/1087724X08321015

Pan, C. C. (2018, January 8). The NT$ 600 million Hengchun airport has become a Qigong center. *China Times*. Retrieved May 6, 2018, from http://www.chinatimes.com/newspapers/20180108000491-260114

Peakthaisong, O. (2017). *Hopewell or hopeless? (In Thai), TV program by mass communication organization of Thailand (M.C.O.T.).* Retrieved May 1, 2018, from https://www.youtube.com/watch?v=CoDg1pg_sUs

Pearson, M. (2002). Medium term expenditure frameworks (MTEFs). DFID's Health Systems Resource Centre for the UK Department for International Development.

Peters, H. J. (1998). *Thailand trade and infrastructure. Conference on Thailand's Dynamic Economic Recovery and Competitiveness.* Session 5- Removing Bottlenecks to Productivity (I) Infrastructure.

Pham, N. B., & Kuyama, T. (2013). *Urban domestic wastewater management In Vietnam - Challenges And opportunities.* Water Environment Partnership in Asia (Policy Brief).

Phan, T. (2017). Road maintenance fund: revenue-expenditure transparency and ict application. *Vietnam Governmental Portal News.* Retrieved June, 4 2018, from http://baochinhphu.vn/Kinh-te/Quy-Bao-tri-duong-bo-Tiep-tuc-minh-bach-thuchi-va-ung-dung-KHCN/317684.vgp

Phuc, N. (2017). *The problem of outstanding construction Debt. Financial Review- Ministry of Finance*. Retrieved June, 4 2018, from http://thoibaotaichinhvietnam.vn/pages/kinh-doanh/2017-06-28/nhuc-nhoi-no-dong-xay-dung-co-ban-44919.aspx

Pismennaya, E., Andrianova, A., & Doff, N. (2018). *Central Asia's most populous country plans first uurobond sale*. Retrieved May 3, 2018, from https://www.bloomberg.com/news/articles/2018-02-22/central-asia-s-most-populous-country-plans-first-eurobond-sale

Population Reference Bureau. (2015). *2015 world population datasheet*. Retrieved October 15, 2018, from https://www.prb.org/wp-content/uploads/2015/12/2015-world-population-data-sheet_eng.pdf

Port Authority of NY & NJ. (2018). *2017 annual airport traffic report*. Retrieved April 18, 2018, from https://www.panynj.gov/airports/pdf-traffic/ATR2017.pdf

Posner, P. (1998). *Budgeting for capital. Government Accountability Office*. GAO.

Potter, B., & Diamond, J. (1999). *Guidelines for public expenditure management*. Retrieved May 24, 2018, from https://www.imf.org/external/pubs/ft/expend/guide5.htm

Press Release No. 2018/105/AFR. (2018). *Burkina Faso: World bank approves $50 Million to boost private investment and job creation*. Retrieved July 23, 2018, from https://www.worldbank.org/en/news/press-release/2018/03/29/burkina-faso-world-bank-approves-50-million-to-boost-private-investment-and-job-creation

Pressman, J. L., & Wildavsky, A. (1984). *Implementation*. Berkeley, CA: University of California Press.

Price, W. (2002). Innovation in Public Finance: Implications for the Nations Infrastructure. *Public Works Management & Policy*, *7*(1), 63–78.

Prime Minister's Office of Vietnam. (2017). *Decree 45/2017/ND-CP detailing the formulation of five-year finance plans and three-year finance-state budget plans*. Retrieved June, 4 2018, from https://vanbanphapluat.co/decree-45-2017-nd-cp-formulation-of-five-year-finance-plans-three-year-finance-state-budget-plans

Prime Minister's Office of Vietnam. (2017). *Decree 86/2017/ND-CP defining the functions, tasks, powers and organizational structure of the Ministry of Planning And Investment*. Retrieved June, 4, 2018, from http://www.mpi.gov.vn/en/Pages/cnnv.aspx

Pritchett, L. (2000). The tyranny of concepts: CUDIE (cumulated, depreciated, investment effort) is not capital. *Journal of Economic Growth*, *5*(4), 361–384. doi:10.1023/A:1026551519329

Prombut, S. (2016). *Klong dan: Cheating project (In Thai), TV program by* mass *communication organization of Thailand (M.C.O.T.)*. Retrieved May 1, 2018, from https://www.youtube.com/watch?v=66xw0Jv9Qxw

Public Construction Committee. (2018a). *List of disused public properties*. Retrieved April 28, 2018, from http://cmdweb.pcc.gov.tw/pccms/morac/idle_owasys.detail_list?ikind=D&ictrm=N

Public Construction Committee. (2018b). *List of large-scale public construction projects*. Retrieved April 25, 2018, from http://cmdweb.pcc.gov.tw/pccms/pwreport/showpeople_hm106.show_detail

Public Construction Committee. (2018c). *Public construction management information system*. Retrieved April 25, 2018, from http://cmdweb.pcc.gov.tw/pccms/owa/guesmap.userinn

Public Expenditure Management Handbook. (1998). *Burkina Faso*. Retrieved July 23, 2018, from http://www1.worldbank.org/publicsector/pe/handbook/pem98.pdf

Pungprawat, K. (2009). Budgeting system and bureau of the budget in Thailand. Chulalongkorn. *Journal of Economics*, *21*(1), 49–71.

Rab, H. N., Hong, D. Q., Martinez-Vasquez, J., Iyer, I., Shah, A. M., Monkam, K. F. N., . . . Minh, N. V. (2015). *Fiscal decentralization review in Vietnam: making the whole greater than the sum the parts.*

Ratings, F. (2002). *The twelve habits of highly successful finance officers.* Retrieved April 15, 2006, from www.fitchratings.com

Resolution No. 694. (2005, November 23). On the investment fund of the Russian Federation. Retrieved May 24, 2018, from http://pravo.gov.ru/proxy/ips/?docbody=&nd=102101231&rdk=&backlink=1

Resolution of the President of the Republic of Uzbekistan. (2016). *On investment policy in the republic of Uzbekistan in 2017 N° ПП-2697* (Russian). Retrieved May 5, 2018, from https://nrm.uz/contentf?doc=493240_postanovlenie_prezidenta_respubliki_uzbekistan_ot_23_12_2016_g_n_pp-2697_ob_investicionnoy_programme_respubliki_uzbekistan_na_2017_god&products=1_vse_zakonodatelstvo_uzbekistana

Resolution of the Republic of Uzbekistan. (2017). *Resolution of the republic of Uzbekistan N° УП-3932 from October 31, 2007.* On Creation of the Ameliorative Fund for Improving Irrigated Lands Regulated by the Cabinet of Ministers of the Republic of Uzbekistan. Retrieved from http://lex.uz/pages/getpage.aspx?actForm=1&lact_id=1262506&ONDATE=31.10.2007percent2000#1262543

Richard, A., & Daniel, T. (2001). *Managing Public Expenditure: A Reference Book for Transition Countries.* Paris: OECD Publishing.

Riggs, F. W. (1966). Thailand; the modernization of a bureaucratic polity. Honolulu, HI: East West Center Press.

Road Construction Plan. (2013). *Bundeshaushaltsplan.* Retrieved May 21, 2018, from http://www.bundeshaushalt-info.de/fileadmin/de.bundeshaushalt/content_de/dokumente/ 2013/soll/Haushaltsplan-2013.pdf

Robinson, S. G. (1993). Capital Planning and Budgeting. In J. E. Petersen & D. R. Strachota (Eds.), *Local Government Finance: Concepts and Practices* (pp. 65–84). Washington, DC: Government Finance Officers Association.

Royal Thai Government. (2016). *Transportation infrastructure development.* Author.

Rumney, E. (in press). EU aid to Moldova made little difference, say auditors. *Public Finance International.* Retrieved March 2, 2018, from http://www.publicfinanceinternational.org/news/2016/09/eu-aid-moldova-made-little-difference-say-auditors

Saastamoinen, A., & Kuosmanen, T. (2014). Is corruption grease, grit or a gamble? Corruption increases variance of productivity across countries. *Applied Economics*, *46*(23), 2833–2849. doi:10.1080/00036846.2014.914149

Sabol, P., & Puentes, R. (2014). Why isn't cheap debt supporting more infrastructure investment? In The Avenue: Rethinking Metropolitan America, Metropolitan Infrastructure Initiative. The Brookings Institution.

Saksophonkul, P. (2004). *Wiwattanakarn kotmai withikarn ngobpramarn lae karn patiroop rabob ngobpramarn khong pratet Thai.*Thailand Bureau of Budget Library.

Sankara, T. (2007). *We Are thehHeirs of the world's revolutions: Speeches from the Burkina Faso revolution 1983-87* (2nd ed.). Atlanta, GA: Pathfinder Press.

Savadogo, K., & Wetta, C. (1992). *The impact of self-imposed adjustment: The case of Burkina Faso*, 1983–9. In G. A. Cornia, R. van der Hoeven, & T. Mkandawire (Eds.), *Africa's Recovery in the 1990s* (pp. 53–71). London: Palgrave Macmillan. doi:10.1007/978-1-349-22344-2_3

Savas, E. S. (2000). *Privatization and Public-Private Partnerships*. New York: Seven Bridges Press.

Schulz, E. (2016). Germany — yes, Germany — has an infrastructure problem. *CBNC*. Retrieved May 17, 2018, from https://www.cnbc.com/2016/09/14/germany-has-a-crumbling-infrastructure-problem.html

Schwab, K. (2016). *The global competitiveness report 2016-2017, ed.* Paper presented at the WE Forum.

Schwab, K. (2018). *World economic forum: The global competitiveness report 2016-2017*. Retrieved May 1, 2018, from http://www3.weforum.org/docs/GCR2016-2017/05FullReport/TheGlobalCompetitivenessReport2016-2017_FINAL.pdf

Sekwat, A. (1999). Capital budgeting practices among Tennessee municipal governments. *Government Finance Review*, *15*(3), 15–19.

Sermier, E., & Marcone, P. (1993). The Challenge of Governing: Getting Things Done. *Public Productivity & Management Review*, *16*(4), 409–414. doi:10.2307/3381019

Simonsen, B., Robbins, M. D., & Brown, R. (2003). Debt affordability. Encyclopedia of public administration and public policy. AJ, 1, 308.

Simonsen, B., Robbins, M. D., & Brown, R. (2003). Debt affordability. In J. Rabin (Ed.), *Encyclopedia of Public Administration and Public Policy* (pp. 308–312). New York: Marcel Dekker.

Singhvi, S. (1996). Using an affordability analysis to budget capital expenditure. *Healthcare Financial Management*, *50*(6), 70–76. PMID:10158243

Sitthiyot, T. (2017). The truth about Thailand's transport infrastructure development and financing. *Nomura Journal of Asian Capital Markets*, *2*(1), 38–43.

Smith, D. J., Harrison, R. T., & Mason, C. M. (2010). Experience, heuristics and learning: The angel investment process. *Frontiers of Entrepreneurship Research, 30*(2), Article 3.

Son, H., Kang, I., Jang, N., & Choi, G. (2014). Local budgeting system (4th ed.). Seoul, South Korea: Daeyoung Cultural Publication. (in Korean)

Sopchokchai, O. (2001). Good local governance and anti-corruption through people's participation: A case of Thailand. *Public Sector Reform Project*, *1*(1), 1–14.

Spackman, M. (2002). Multi-year perspective in budgeting and public investment planning. *Draft background paper for discussion at session III, 1*, 46.

Spackman, M. (2002, April). *Multi-year Perspective in Budgeting and Public Investment Planning*. Draft background paper for discussion at session III.1 of the OECD Global Forum on Sustainable Development: Conference on Financing Environmental Dimension of Sustainable Development. Retrieved from http://www.oecd.org/unitedkingdom/2081306.pdf

Spackman, M. (2001). Public investment and discounting in European Union member states. *OECD Journal on Budgeting*, *1*(2), 213–260. doi:10.1787/budget-v1-art13-en

Srithongrung, A. (2006). *The impact of state capital budget and management programs on state capital budget decisions and economic performance* (Unpublished D.P.A. Dissertation). Available from Dissertations & Theses @ University of Illinois at Springfield.

Srithongrung, A. (2009). The effects of results-oriented budgeting on government spending patterns in Thailand. *International Public Management Review, 10*(1), 59-89.

Srithongrung, A., Ermasova, N., & Yusuf, J.-E. (2019). Capital budgeting and management in Russia. In Capital management and budgeting in the public sector. Hershey, PA: IGI Global.

Srithongrung, A. (2008). The impacts of state capital management programs on state economic performance: An empirical analysis. *Public Budgeting & Finance*, *28*(3), 83–107. doi:10.1111/j.1540-5850.2008.00912.x

Srithongrung, A. (2010). State capital improvement programs and institutional arrangements for capital budgeting: The case Of Illinois. *Journal of Public Budgeting, Accounting & Financial Management*, *22*(3), 407–430.

Srithongrung, A. (2010a). State capital improvement programs and institutional arrangements for capital budgeting: The case of Illinois. *Journal of Public Budgeting, Accounting & Financial Management*, *22*(3), 407–430.

Srithongrung, A. (2018). Capital budgeting and management practices: Smoothing out rough spots in government outlays. *Public Budgeting & Finance*, *38*(1), 47–71. doi:10.1111/pbaf.12167

Srithongrung, A., & Kriz, K. (2012). From Public Infrastructure to National Economic Growth: Do Strategic Investment Practices Matter? *International Public Management Review*, *13*(2), 19–50.

Srithongrung, A., & Kriz, K. (2012). From public infrastructure to national economic growth: Do systemic Investment practices matter? *International Public Management Review*, *13*(2), 1–32.

Srithongrung, A., & Kriz, K. A. (2012). From public infrastructure to national economic growth: Do systematic investment practices matter? *International Public Management Review*, *13*(2), 19–50.

Srithongrung, A., & Kriz, K. A. (2012). From Public Infrastructure to National Economic Growth: Do Systematic Investment Practices Matter? *International Public Management Review*, *13*(2), 19–50.

Srithongrung, A., Yusuf, J.-E., & Kriz, K. A. (2019). A systematic public capital management and budgeting process. In *Capital management and budgeting in the public sector*. Hershey, PA: IGI Global.

Srithongrung, S., Ermasova, N., & Yusuf, W. (2019). *Capital management and budgeting in the public sector*. Hershey, PA: IGI.

Standard & Poor. (2018). *Rating: Albania credit rating*. Retrieved July 23, 2018, from https://tradingeconomics.com/albania/rating

Stanley, M. T., & Block, S. B. (1984). A survey of multinational capital budgeting. *Financial Review*, *19*(1), 36–54. doi:10.1111/j.1540-6288.1984.tb01083.x

State Enterprise Policy Office. (2018). *State enterprise disbursement statistics*. Retrieved March 15, 2018, from http://www.sepo.go.th/#chart6

Statistics Times. (2015). *List of countries by population density*. Retrieved April 20, 2018, from http://statisticstimes.com/population/countries-by-population-density.php

Statistisches Bundesamt. (2018). *Volkswirtschaftliche Gesamtrechnungen: Arbeitsunterlage Investitionen*. Retrieved July 7, 2018, from https://www.destatis.de/DE/Publikationen/Thematisch/VolkswirtschaftlicheGesamtrechnungen/Inlandsprodukt/InvestitionenPDF_5811108.pdf?__blob=publicationFile

Steinfeld, J. M., & Thai, K. V. (2013). Political economy of Vietnam: Market reform, growth, and the state. *Maryland Series in Contemporary Asian Studies, 2013*(3).

Steiss, A. W. (2005). *Strategic Facilities Planning: Capital Budgeting and Debt Administration*. Lanham, MD: Lexington Books.

Steiss, A. W., & Nwagwu, E. O. C. (2001). *Financial planning and management in public organizations*. New York: Marcel-Dekker.

Stich, B., & Eagle, K. (2005). Planning to Include the Public: Transportation Policy Implementation With Effective Citizen Involvement. *Public Works Management & Policy*, *9*(4), 319–340. doi:10.1177/1087724X05275672

Storm, R., & Feiock, R. (1999). Economic development consequences of state support for higher education. *State & Local Government Review*, *31*(2), 97–105. doi:10.1177/0160323X9903100204

Stuart, R. W., & Abetti, P. A. (1990). Impact of entrepreneurial and management experience on early performance. *Journal of Business Venturing*, *5*(3), 151–162. doi:10.1016/0883-9026(90)90029-S

Sudhipongpracha, T., & Wongpreedee, A. (2016). Decentralizing decentralized governance: Community empowerment and coproduction of municipal public work in Northeast Thailand. *Community Development Journal: An International Forum*, *51*(2), 302–319. doi:10.1093/cdj/bsv026

Taiwan Power Company. (2018). Generating capacity of power stations [Data file]. Retrieved April 18, 2018, from http://stpc00601.taipower.com.tw/loadGraph/loadGraph/genshx.html

Taiwan Water Corporation. (2018). Leakage rate of Taiwan water company [Data file]. Retrieved April 25, 2018 from, https://www.water.gov.tw/opendata/prot2.csv

Tanas, O., & Andrianova, A. (2017, June 19). *Russia eyes a $90 billion sovereign wealth fund. Bloomberg News*. Retrieved March 1, 2018, from https://www.bloomberg.com/news/articles/2017-06-19/russia-to-discuss-merging-wealth-funds-into-90-7-billion-coffer

Tax Code of the Russian Federation. (2018). *Tax code* [Налоговый Кодекс Российской Федерации]. Retrieved March 1, 2018, from http://nalogovyykodeks.ru/

Teorell, J., Dahlberg, S., Holmberg, S., Rothstein, B., Alvarado, N., Svensson, P., & Svensson, R. (2018). *The Quality of Government Standard Dataset, version Jan18*. Gothenburg, Sweden: University of Gothenburg, The Quality of Government Institute. Retrieved December 10, 2018, from https://qog.pol.gu.se/data/datadownloads/qogstandarddata

Thai Publica. (2014). *Constitutional court diagnosis for THB 2,000,000 million borrowing for transportation mega projects*. Retrieved March 16, 2018, from https://thaipublica.org/2014/04/mega-projects-constitutional-court/

Thai, N. Q. (2008). *Public investment efficiency in Vietnam*. Retrieved June 1, 2018, from https://www.kdi.re.kr/data/download/attach/8580_2-4_6.pdf

Thailand Bureau of Census. (2018). 2010 *Thailand population and housing census*, Retrieved April 28, 2018, from http://popcensus.nso.go.th/file/popcensus-10-01-56-T.pdf

Thailand Bureau of Census. (2018). *2010 Thailand population and housing census*. Retrieved April 28, 2018, from http://popcensus.nso.go.th/file/popcensus-10-01-56-T.pdf

Thailand Bureau of the Budget—BOB. (2018). *FY 2018 budget in brief*. Retrieved February 3, 2018, from http://www.bb.go.th/bbweb/?page_id=6039

Thailand Bureau of the Budget—BOB. (2018). *FY 2019 budget preparation directions and principles*. Retrieved April 15, 2018, from http://www.bb.go.th/bbweb/

Thailand Department of Local Administration—DLA. (2018). *Local organization data (in Thai)*. Retrieved September 10, 2018, from http://www.dla.go.th/work/abt/

Thailand Development Research Institution—TDRI. (2004). *A study report of new budgeting system*. Retrieved June 11, 2007, from http://www.bb.go.th/bbhome/index.asp

Thailand Law Forum. (1997). *Thai government structure under Thailand's 1997 (B.E. 2540) constitution*. Retrieved April 12, 2018, from http://www.thailawforum.com/articles/briggsgov.html

Thailand Ministry of Finance—MOT. (2018). *Fiscal statistics: Budget appropriation and expenditure classified by rconomic and ministry*. Retrieved March 15, 2018, from http://dataservices.mof.go.th/Dataservices/GovernmentExpenditureEconomyMinistry

Thailand Ministry of Finance—MOT. (2018). *Fiscal statistics: Outstanding public debt by state enterprises*. Retrieved March 15, 2018, from http://dataservices.mof.go.th/Dataservices/GovernmentExpenditureEconomyMinistry

Thailand National Statistical Office. (2018). *Summary of labor force survey 2017*. Retrieved April 22, 2018, from http://web.nso.go.th/index.htm

Thailand Office of National Economic and Social Development Board (NESDB). (n.d.). Retrieved from http://www.nesdb.go.th/nesdb_en/main.php?filename=national_account

The Central Bank of the Republic of Uzbekistan. (2018). *Uzbekistan*. Retrieved July 23, 2018 from http://www.cbu.uz/en/

The Economist. (2015). *China, Japan and the case for Thailand*. Retrieved April 2, 2018, from http://country.eiu.com/article.aspx?articleid=1843787968&Country=Thailand&topic=Economy

The Federal law FZ#1662-R. (2008) *Concept of long-term social and economic development of the Russian Federation for the period to 2020* [О Концепции долгосрочного социально-экономического развития Российской Федерации на период до 2020 года]. Retrieved February 10, 2018, from http://www.consultant.ru/document/cons_doc_LAW_82134/

The Federal Law FZ#392. (2011). On zones of territorial development in the Russian Federation and on amendments to some legislation of the Russian Federation.

The Free Library. (2014). *Uzbekistan plans to build toll road*. Retrieved from https://www.thefreelibrary.com/Uzbekistan+plans+to+build+toll+road.-a0531800301

The Office of Senate Secretary, Thailand National Assembly. (2017). *B.E. 2560 (2017) Thai constitution*. Bangkok, Thailand: National Assembly Press.

The Permanent Mission of the Republic of Uzbekistan to the United Nations. (2018). *Uzbekistan*. Retrieved July 23, 2018 from https://www.un.int/uzbekistan/uzbekistan/country-facts

The Resolution of the president of the Republic of Uzbekistan N° УП-3751 from November 5, 2006 on creation of the fund for reconstruction and development of the republic of Uzbekistan. (2006). Retrieved from Norma web site on April 23, 2018 from https://nrm.uz/contentf?doc=103640_ukaz_prezidenta_respubliki_uzbekistan_ot_11_05_2006_g_n_up-3751_o_sozdanii_fonda_rekonstrukcii_i_razvitiya_respubliki_uzbekistan&products=1_

The State Committee of the Republic of Uzbekistan on Statistics. (2018). *Uzbekistan*. Retrieved July 23, 2018, from https://stat.uz/en/

The Vietnam Development Bank. (2018). Retrieved June 1, 2018, from http://en.vdb.gov.vn/

The World Bank. (1998). *Public Expenditure Management Handbook*. Washington, DC: The International Bank for Reconstruction and Development.

The World Bank. (2018). *Infrastructure needs, Asia and the Pacific*, Retrieved April 22, 2018, from https://data.adb.org/dataset/infrastructure-needs-asia-and-pacific

The World Bank. (2018). *International LPI - Global Rankings 2018*. Retrieved from https://lpi.worldbank.org/international/global?order=Infrastructure&sort=asc

Thomas, M. A. (2010). What do the worldwide governance indicators measure? *European Journal of Development Research*, *22*(1), 31–54. doi:10.1057/ejdr.2009.32

Tigue, P. (1996). *Capital Improvement Programming: A Guide for Smaller Governments*. Chicago, IL: Government Finance Officers Association.

Trading Economics. (2016). *Vietnam - Population ages 15-64*. Retrieved June 1, 2018, from https://tradingeconomics.com/vietnam/population-ages-15-64-percent-of-total-wb-data.html

Trading Economics. (2018). *Germany government budget*. Retrieved April 15, 2018, from https://tradingeconomics.com/germany/government-budget

Tran, T. Q. (2009). Sudden surge in FDI and infrastructure bottlenecks: The case in Vietnam. *ASEAN Economic Bulletin*, *26*(1), 58–76. doi:10.1355/AE26-1E

Tromme, M. (2016). Corruption and corruption research in Vietnam-an overview. *Crime, Law, and Social Change*, *65*(4-5), 287–306. doi:10.100710611-016-9605-y

Tuoi Tre News. (2017). *Vietnam to audit public investment, BOT projects*. Retrieved June 1, 2018, from https://tuoitrenews.vn/news/society/20171206/vietnam-to-audit-public-investment-bot-projects/43009.html

U.S. Census Bureau. (2012). *Government organization summary report 2012*. Retrieved May 22, 2018, from https://www.census.gov/content/dam/Census/library/publications/2013/econ/g12-cg-org.pdf

U.S. Census Bureau. (2015). *Government finances*. Retrieved May 22, 2018 from https://www.census.gov/govs/local/

U.S. Department of the Treasury. (2018). *FY2017 financial report of the United States government*. Retrieved September 26, 2018, from https://www.fiscal.treasury.gov/fsreports/rpt/finrep/fr/17frusg/02142018_FR(Final).pdf

U.S. Federal Reserve Bank of St. Louis. (2018). *International statistics: Crude birth rate for Thailand*, Retrieved March 26, 2018, from https://fred.stlouisfed.org/series/SPDYNCBRTINTHA

U.S. General Accounting Office. (1998). Executive guide: Leading practices in capital decision-making. GAO/AIMD-99-32. Washington, DC: Author.

U.S. General Accounting Office. (1998). *Executive Guide: Leading Practices in Capital Decision-Making*. Washington, DC: U.S. General Accounting Office. Retrieved from https://www.gao.gov/special.pubs/ai99032.pdf

U.S. Government. (2017). *Financial report, FY2017*. Retrieved May 22, 2018, from https://www.gao.gov/assets/700/690123.pdf

Ukrainian News and Information Agency. (2017). *Nearly 60% of Ukrainians live below poverty line. Kyiv, Ukraine: Ukrainian news and information agency*. Retrieved April 25, 2018, from https://www.unian.info/society/1850781-nearly-60-of-ukrainians-live-below-poverty-line-un.html

US Department of State. (2011). *Investment climate statement – Uzbekistan*. Retrieved July 23, 2018, from https://www.state.gov/e/eb/rls/othr/ics/2011/157382.htm

US Department of State. (2016). *Investment climate statement – Uzbekistan*. Retrieved from July 23, 2018, https://www.state.gov/e/eb/rls/othr/ics/2016/sca/254497.htm

US Department of State. (2017). *Investment climate statement – Uzbekistan*. Retrieved July 23, 2018, from https://www.state.gov/e/eb/rls/othr/ics/2017/sca/270035.htm

UzbekistanToday. (2017). *10 facts about the Tashkent City*. Retrieved July 23, 2018, from http://ut.uz/en/business/10-facts-about-the-tashkent-city/

Uz-Kor Gas Chemical. (2018). *Uzbekistan*. Retrieved July 23, 2018, from http://www.uz-kor.com/index.php/en/

Van Arkadie, B., & Mallon, R. (2004). *Viet Nam: A transition tiger?* ANU E Press. Retrieved June 1, 2018, from https://press.anu.edu.au/publications/viet-nam-%E2%80%94-transition-tiger

Van der Putten, R. (2017). Germany: Infrastructure under threat. *Economic Research by PNP Paribas*. Retrieved April 17, 2018, from economic-research.pnpparibas.com

Vartapetov, K. (2010). Russia's federal fiscal grants: Regional equalisation and growth. *Post-Communist Economies*, *22*(4), 471–481. doi:10.1080/14631377.2010.518452

Vermeer, T., Patton, T., & Styles, K. (2011). Reporting of general infrastructure assets under GASB statement no. 34. *Accounting Horizons*, *25*(2), 381–407. doi:10.2308/acch-10029

Verner, I. (Ed.). (2017). *Uraina V Tsyfrakh 2016. Statystychnyi Zbirnyk*. Kyiv, Ukraine: State Statistical Service of Ukraine.

Verougstraete, M., & Tran, H. D. (2017). *Infrastructure financing strategies for sustainable development in Viet Nam*. Retrieved June 1, 2018, from http://www.unescap.org/sites/default/files/20170915%20National%20Study%20-%20Infrastructure%20Financing%20-%20Viet%20%20Nam.pdf

Vietnam Net. (2010). *Political system*. Retrieved from http://english.vietnamnet.vn/fms/vietnam-reference/general-information/439/political-system--part-2-.html

Vietnam Net. (2017). *Vietnam looks to private sector to fund infrastructure*. Retrieved June 1, 2018, from http://english.vietnamnet.vn/fms/business/179988/vietnam-looks-to-private-sector-to-fund-infrastructure.html

Vietnam News. (2015). *Vietnam logistics costs hurting competitiveness*. Retrieved June 1, 2018, from https://vietnamnews.vn/economy/277203/vn-logistics-costs-hurting-competitiveness.html#PRv2fKESKzSuvcFB.97

Vlasiuk, V. (2017). *Svoboda Vyboru i Trudova Emigratsiya. Ukrainskyi Vybir. EPravda*. Retrieved April 24, 2017, from https://www.epravda.com.ua/columns/2017/02/2/619422

Vo, T. (2007). Challenges, prospects and strategies for CLMV development: The case of Vietnam. *Development strategy for CLMV in the age of economic integration*, 497-515.

Vogt, A. J. (2004). *Capital budgeting and finance: A guide for local governments*. Washington, DC: International City/County Management Association.

Vogt, J. A. (2004). *Capital budget and finance: A guide for local governments*. International City/ County Management Association.

Vu, Q. V. (2010). *Abuse of power in a one-party controlled state with market driven economy: A case study of Vietnam*. Paper presented at the Conference on Authoritarianism in East Asia at the City University of Hong Kong.

Vu, T. T. A. (2012). Quản Lý và Phân cấp Quản Lý Đầu Tư Công Thực Trạng ở Việt Nam và Kinh nghiệm Quốc Tế. *Chương trình giảng dạy kinh tế Fulbright*.

Vu, A. T. T. (2016). Vietnam decentralization amidst fragmentation. *Journal of Southeast Asian Economies*, *33*(2), 188–208.

Wang, W. Y., & Chen, C. T. (2016). *Opportunities and challenges of BOT: The Taiwan experience.* NTU Center for Public Policy and Law Research Report. Retrieved April 25, 2018, from http://www.cppl.ntu.edu.tw/research/2015research/10407final.pdf

Warlters, M. (2006). *Vietnam's infrastructure challenge—Infrastructure strategy: Cross-sectoral issues.* Washington, DC: World Bank.

Water Resource Agency. (2018). Saturation of water supply [Data file]. Retrieved April 18, 2018, from https://www.wra.gov.tw/6950/7169/7316/7324/24043/

Webster, D., & Theeratham, P. (2004). *Policy coordination, planning and infrastructure provision: A case study of Thailand.* Retrieved April 28, 2018, from http://siteresources.worldbank.org/INTEAPINFRASTRUCT/Resources/855084-1137106254308/Thailand.pdf

WEF Global Competitiveness Report. (2017). *Germany.* Retrieved March 17, 2018, from http://reports.weforum.org/global-competitiveness-index-2017-2018/countryeconomy-profiles/#economy=DEU

Werling, J., & Horst, R. (2014*). Catching up: Greater focus needed to achieve a more competitive infrastructure.* National Association of Manufacturers. Retrieved May 28, 2018, from http://www.nam.org/Issues/Infrastructure/Surface-Infrastructure/Infrastructure-Full-Report-2014.pdf

Westerman, N. (2004). Managing the Capital Planning Cycle: Best Practice Examples of Effective Capital Program Management. *Government Finance Review, 20*(3), 26–32.

Westerman, N., & Casey, J. P. (2007). Cost Estimation and Budgeting. In J. P. Casey & M. J. Mucha (Eds.), *Capital Project Planning and Evaluation: Expanding the Role of the Finance Officer* (Vol. 8, pp. 27–44). Chicago: Government Finance Officers Association.

Wigfall, P., & Lynch, T. D. (2003). Capital Budgeting Practices in Local Governments. *Case Studies in Public Budgeting and Financial Management*, 241-252.

Wiltbank, R., & Boeker, W. (2007). *Returns to angel investors in groups.* Lenexa, KS: Angel Capital Education Foundation. Retrieved December 10, 2018, from https://www.angelcapitalassociation.org/data/Documents/Resources/AngelGroupResarch/1d%20-%20Resources%20-%20Research/6%20RSCH_-_ACEF_-_Returns_to_Angel_Investor_in_Groups.pdf

Wiltbank, R., Read, S., Dew, N., & Sarasvathy, S. D. (2009). Prediction and control under uncertainty: Outcomes in angel investing. *Journal of Business Venturing, 24*(2), 116–133. doi:10.1016/j.jbusvent.2007.11.004

World Bank Group. (2016). *World bank group countrysSurvey FY16- Uzbekistan.* Retrieved from http://microdata.worldbank.org/index.php/catalog/2720

World Bank. (1997). *Public investment management report.* Washington, DC: The World Bank Group.

World Bank. (1997). *Public investment managementrReport.* Washington, DC: The World Bank Group.

World Bank. (2000). *The law of republic of Uzbekistan on budget system.* Retrieved July 23, 2018, from http://www1.worldbank.org/publicsector/pe/BudgetLaws/UzbekistanBudgetLaw.doc

World Bank. (2007). *Thailand country profile.* Retrieved April 28, 2009, from https://data.worldbank.org/country/thailand?locale=th

World Bank. (2008). *Debt management performance assessment. Republic of Moldova.* Retrieved July 25, 2018, from http://siteresources.worldbank.org/INTDEBTDEPT/Resources/468980-1226602826665/DeMPAMoldovaFinal_EN.pdf

World Bank. (2010). *Local development, institutions and climate change in Burkina Faso: Situation analysis and operational recommendations. Social Development Department. Area-based Development and Climate Change.* Retrieved July 23, 2018, from http://siteresources.worldbank.org/EXTSOCIALDEVELOPMENT/Resources/244362-1232059926563/5747581-1239131985528/5999762-1242914244952/BurkinaReportFinal_EN.pdf

World Bank. (2011). *Vietnam - Second public investment reform operation program (English).* Washington, DC: World Bank. Retrieved June 1, 2018, from http://documents.worldbank.org/curated/en/354081468142787169/Vietnam-Second-Public-Investment-Reform-Operation-Program

World Bank. (2012). *Policy briefs: Albania.* Retrieved July 23, 2018 from http://www.worldbank.org/content/dam/Worldbank/document/eca/Albania-Policy-Briefs-2013.pdf

World Bank. (2013). *Albanian country profile.* Retrieved July 23, 2018 from https://openknowledge.worldbank.org/handle/10986/20829

World Bank. (2013). *Assessment of the financing framework for municipal infrastructure in Vietnam.* Washington, DC: World Bank. Retrieved June 1, 2018, from https://openknowledge.worldbank.org/handle/10986/17568

World Bank. (2013). *Public investment management performance assessment.* Washington, DC: The World Bank Group.

World Bank. (2015). *Albanian public expenditure and financial accountability assessment* (PEFA 2015). Retrieved July 23, 2018 from, http://documents.worldbank.org/curated/en/904191521826887529/Albania-Public-expenditure-and-financial-accountability-PEFA-performance-assessment-report

World Bank. (2016). *Private participation in infrastructure project database.* Retrieved March 21, 2018, from https://data.worldbank.org/indicator/IE.PPN.WATR.CD?locations=RU&view=chart

World Bank. (2016). *Types of public-private partnership agreements.* Retrieved May 6, 2018, from https://ppp.worldbank.org/public-private-partnership/agreements

World Bank. (2017). *Burkina Faso: Developing infrastructure and an enabling environment for sustained access to water and sanitation services for the urban poor.* Retrieved July 23, 2018 from http://www.worldbank.org/en/results/2017/07/28/burkina-faso-developing-infrastructure-and-an-enabling-environment-for-sustained-access-to-water-and-sanitation-services-for-the-urban-poor

World Bank. (2017). *Russia's recovery: How strong are its shoots? Russia Economic Report.* Retrieved May 18, 2018, from https://openknowledge.worldbank.org/bitstream/handle/10986/28930/30-11-2017-17-58-52-forwebNovFINALRERENGfull.pdf?sequence=7

World Bank. (2017). *The world by income: FY 2017.* Retrieved April 28, 2018, from http://databank.worldbank.org/data/download/site-content/wdi/maps/2017/world-by-income-wdi-2017.pdf

World Bank. (2017). *Ukraine economic update.* Washington, DC: The World Bank Group.

World Bank. (2017a). *Vietnam - Country partnership framework for the period FY18-FY22 (English).* Washington, DC: World Bank Group. Retrieved June 1, 2018, from http://documents.worldbank.org/curated/en/173771496368868576/Vietnam-Country-partnership-framework-for-the-period-FY18-FY22

World Bank. (2017b). *Vietnam public expenditure review (Vol. 2): Fiscal policies towards sustainability, efficiency, and equity - Overview report (English).* Washington, DC: World Bank Group. Retrieved June 1, 2018, from http://documents.worldbank.org/curated/en/279261508765803168/Fiscal-Policies-towards-Sustainability-Efficiency-and-Equity-Overview-Report

World Bank. (2018). *GDP per capita, PPP (current international $), World Bank, International Comparison Program database*. Retrieved October 15, 2018, from https://data.worldbank.org/indicator/NY.GDP.PCAP.PP.CD

World Bank. (2018). *GDP per capita*. Retrieved July 23, 2018, from https://data.worldbank.org/indicator/NY.GDP.PCAP.KD?end=1960&locations=KR-GH-JP&name_desc=false&start=1960&view=bar

World Bank. (2018). *Gross fix capital formation in Germany*. Retrieved May 17, 2018, from https://data.worldbank.org/indicator/NE.GDI.FTOT.CD?locations=DE

World Bank. (2018). *International LPI, Global Rankings 2018*. Retrieved December 19, 2018, from https://lpi.worldbank.org/international/global

World Bank. (2018). *Logistics performance index*. Retrieved July 23, 2018, from https://lpi.worldbank.org/international/scorecard/column/32/C/UZB/2018/R/ECA/2007/I/LMC/2007/C/KAZ/2007/C/KGZ/2007/C/RUS/2018/C/UKR/2018/C/TJK/2018/C/TKM/2018?sort=asc&order=Infrastructure#datatable

World Bank. (2018). *Medium-term debt management strategy*. MoF. Retrieved July 23, 2018, from https://openknowledge.worldbank.org/handle/10986/17637

World Bank. (2018). *Thailand country profile*. Retrieved April 28, 2018, from https://data.worldbank.org/country/thailand?locale=th

World Bank. (2018). *World bank open data*. Retrieved April 28, 2018, from https://data.worldbank.org/country/thailand?locale=th

World Bank. (2018a). *World Bank national accounts data*. Retrieved May 17, 2018, from https://data.worldbank.org/indicator/NY.GDP.MKTP.CD

World Bank. (2018b). *Gross fix capital formation*. Retrieved May 17, 2018, fromhttps://data.worldbank.org/indicator/NE.GDI.FTOT.CD?locations=DE

Wright, J., Dietrich, S., & Ariotti, M. (2015). *Foreign aid and judicial independence*. Retrieved July 23, 2018, from https://pdfs.semanticscholar.org/e2e8/31f2c1edc2c25fa0f1ae20fbb789475937fb.Pdf

Wright, K. (2004). Personal knowledge management: Supporting Individual Knowledge Worker Performance. *Knowledge Management Research and Practice*, *3*(3), 156–165. doi:10.1057/palgrave.kmrp.8500061

Yaffa, J. (2014). *The waste and corruption of Vladimir Putin's 2014 winter Olympics. Bloomberg Businessweek*. Retrieved February 18, 2018, from https://www.bloomberg.com/news/articles/2014-01-02/the-2014-winter-olympics-in-sochi-cost-51-billion

Yao, J. C. (2016). *Mirage: Disused public property in Taiwan*. Taipei, Taiwan: Garden City Publishers.

Yap, K. L. M., & Nguyen, U. (2017). *In Asia's infrastructure race, Vietnam is among the leaders*. Retrieved July, 2 2018, from https://www.bloomberg.com/news/articles/2017-03-22/in-asia-s-infrastructure-race-vietnam-is-among-the-leaders

Yeh, R. S. (2017, March 28). The Government should institutionalize public infrastructure maintenance. *Engineers Times*. Retrieved May 6, 2018, from https://goo.gl/km1ZLU

Yinger, J., Bloom, H., Börsch-Supan, A., & Ladd, H. (1988). *Property Taxes and House Values: The Theory and Estimation of Intrajurisdictional Property Tax Capitalization, Studies in Urban Economics*. Boston: Academic Press.

Yusuf, J.-E., & Jordan, M. (2018). State transportation planning: Linking quantifiable performance measures and infrastructure condition outcomes. *Public Works Management & Policy*, *23*(1), 58–77. doi:10.1177/1087724X17715266

Yusuf, J.-E., & O'Connell, L. (2013). The crisis in state highway finances: Its roots, current effects, and some possible remedies. *Journal of Public Budgeting, Accounting & Financial Management*, *25*(3), 502–521.

Zhuravskaia, E. (2000). *Incentives to provide local public goods: Fiscal federalism, Russian style*. Boston: Mimeo. Harvard University.

Zongo. (2011). Rencontre IATI-Pays Partenaires. *Integration De L'aide Dans Le Budget*. Et Le Programme D'investissement Public (Pip).

Биржевой Лидер. (2013). *Ташкентский Авиазавод Теперь не Будет Производить Самолеты – выводы*. Author.

Стратегия действий по пяти приоритетным направлениям развития Республики Узбекистан в 2017-2021 годах. Указ Президента Республики Узбекистан от 7 февраля 2017 года N°УП-4947. (n.d.). Retrieved from http://strategy.gov.uz/ru/lists/docview/96

Указ Президента Республики Узбекистан. «Об образовании Министерства инновационного развития Республики Узбекистан». (2017). Retrieved from http://uza.uz/ru/documents/ob-obrazovanii-ministerstva-innovatsionnogo-razvitiya-respub-29-11-2017

About the Contributors

Arwiphawee Srithongrung, D.P.A., is a Visiting Research Fellow in Illinois Institute of Public Finance, Center for State Policy and Leadership, University of Illinois at Springfield. Dr. Srithongrung received her Doctor of Public Administration (D.P.A.) from University of Illinois at Springfield. Prior to joining Illinois Institute of Public Finance, she was an Associate Professor (with Tenure) at Wichita State University (2013-2018) and University of Nebraska-Omaha (2006-2013). Dr. Srithongrung has expertise in public budgeting and finance, fiscal policies, economic growth, and performance measurement. In addition to teaching and research experiences, Dr. Srithongrung has assisted state and local governments in several consulting projects including City of Omaha's revenue forecast, State of Nebraska's charitable tax credit analysis, State of Kansas's food sale tax analysis, and City of Wichita's arts and income growth analysis.

Natalia Ermasova is an Associate Professor at Governors State University, IL. She has a PhD of Public Affairs (Indiana University, USA), PhD of Economics (Russia). Her primary research interests are public finance, risk-management, innovation management, and the state capital budgeting. Before starting her work in the USA, she worked as a Professor of Finance in the Volga Region Academy for Civil Services in Russia for 12 years and as Professor of Saratov State University for 2 years. She was Visiting Professor in Germany (Ludwigsburg Academy for Civil Services) and Fulbright Visiting Professor (SPEA, Indiana University). More than 45 books and articles were published in Russia and more than 30 articles published in the USA. Her articles were published in State and Local Government Review, International Journal of Public Administration, SAM Advanced Management Journal, Journal of Management Development.

Juita-Elena (Wie) Yusuf, Ph.D., is an Associate Professor in the School of Public Service at Old Dominion University. Her research interests are in public budgeting and financial management, with a particular interest in transportation and infrastructure finance, and transparency, accountability and public participation.

* * *

Jane Beckett-Camarata is an Associate Teaching Professor. She teaches in the Penn State Harrisburg master's program in public administration. Her finance teaching interests include government revenue systems, public financial management, budgeting, capital budgeting, infrastructure finance, cost accounting, and governmental and managerial accounting. Dr. Beckett-Camarata was a recipient of a

Lilly Foundation Scholar Award for the advancement of teaching excellence. She has taught university courses in Russia and was a Fulbright Scholar at Kharhiv National University in Kharkiv, Ukraine where she taught economic development finance. While at the University of North Wales, Bangor, Wales, she researched the impact of the EU on bank regulation. Dr. Beckett-Camarata has authored many articles and book chapters. Her work has been published in the Public Productivity and Management Review, Journal of Budgeting, Accounting and Financial Management, Municipal Finance Journal, International Journal of Public Administration, American Review of Public Administration, Journal of Business Research, Handbook of Public Sector Economics and Handbook of Globalization, and Governance and Public Administration. She was the recipient of the Baruch College, CUNY distinguished Municipal Leadership and Finance Award which funded her 2005 summer research on changes in New York City's pension fund assets during fiscal crisis. As a former chief financial officer in the Commonwealth of Virginia, she managed operating and capital budgets, financial accounting and reporting, and revenue forecasting. She was instrumental in integrating the strategic plan into the budget and accounting system, and establishing and integrating financial performance measures. She serves as an expert reviewer for the Government Finance Officers Association and as an expert witness for the U.S. Federal Court System in government budgeting. She also serves on the editorial board of several academic journals. Dr. Beckett-Camarata is active in professional organizations including the American Society for Public Administration, where she has served as co-chair of the Finance Committee, Executive Council, and Audit Committee; Association for Budgeting and Financial Management, where she has served on the Board of Directors, the Program Committee and the Curro Award Committee; National Association of Schools of Public Affairs and Administration, where she has served on site visit teams and on the Commission on Peer Review and Accreditation (COPRA); the Government Finance Officers Association; and numerous other organizations. Dr. Beckett-Camarata received a Ph.D. in public policy and administration from Virginia Commonwealth University (1998); master of public administration from the American University (1989); and bachelor of science degree in finance from Syracuse University (1983).

Erica Ceka received her Master of Public Administration at Northern Illinois University in 2012 as a fellow of the Muskie Program, funded by the U.S. Department of State. Currently, she is pursuing her Ph.D. in public administration at NIU (expected degree date August 2019). Her main research interest is on intergovernmental collaboration and performance. She is also interested in studying public budgeting, fiscal decentralization, and transparency. Ceka has a vast experience in international development, previously managing antipoverty and employment generating programs on a national scale as well as serving as a country representative for an international nongovernmental organization in Moldova. She also worked as a regional technical advisor for a UK consortium, consisting of Oxford Policy Management, Institute of Public Policies, and the University of Birmingham. Prior to her study at NIU, Ceka was an elected city board member in her home city.

Carol Ebdon is the Regents/Foundation Professor in the School of Public Administration at the University of Nebraska at Omaha. Her research relates to public budgeting and financial management, and is published in a variety of scholarly journals and books. Dr. Ebdon also served as the Finance Director for the City of Omaha from 2004-2009.

Polina Ermasova is Investments Financial Analyst at Allstate Investments, LLC. Polina graduated with B.Sc. degree in Finance from DePaul University. Following this, she entered a Master of Science in Finance Program in Kellstadt Graduate School of Business at DePaul University. Polina holds a Research Assistant appointment in Kellstadt Graduate School of Business at the DePaul University. She presented her research on many prestigious international conferences. Polina Ermasova possesses a solid financial practitioner experience including various positions she held at Morgan Stanley Wealth Management and BMO Bank. Her primary research interests are investment analysis, capital budgeting, leadership, and business ethics in Russia.

Tatyana Guzman is an Assistant Professor in Maxine Goodman Levin College of Urban Affairs at Cleveland State University. Dr Guzman research interests are in municipal bond market, budgeting, tax preferences, and education finance. She has published articles in peer- and editor-reviewed journals, and authored book chapters and reports. Dr. Guzman has taught undergraduate and graduate level courses in general Public Finance, Budgeting, Research Methods, Statistics, and Economics at Indiana University Bloomington (IUB), Indiana University Purdue University in Indianapolis (IUPUI), and, most recently, in Cleveland State University (CSU). Dr Guzman is originally from Uzbekistan.

Meagan Jordan, Ph.D. is an Associate Professor in Old Dominion University. Dr. Jordan's expertise include Public Budget Theory, Public Financial Management, State and Local Fiscal Policy, State and Local Government Budgets, Public and Nonprofit Strategic Planning, Public Management Ethics. Dr. Jordan has published in numerous articles and book chapters. Her research interests include State and Local Budgeting; State and Local Fiscal Policy; Popular Financial Reporting; Government Financial Transparency; and Public Budget Theory.

Jiseul Kim is a Doctoral Candidate and Instructor from University of Nebraska at Omaha. She received her MPP degree from Arizona State University at Phoenix, during which she received a national scholarship sponsored by the Korean Government. She holds a BA degree in business administration from Kyung Hee University at Seoul. Her research and teaching interests are in public budgeting and financial management, with emphasis on budgetary institutions and institutional performances, capital budgeting and spending, government accounting and financial reporting. Jiseul Kim published two journal articles as the first author, which explore the effects of infrastructure reporting practices required by Government Accounting Standards Board Statement No. 34 on state highway investment and infrastructure quality.

Kouliga Koala is a PhD Candidate in Public Administration and Policy, specializing in Public Procurement at Old Dominion University. Mr. Koala is originally from Burkina Faso and a former Fulbright scholar. He holds a bachelor's in International Relations and History, and a minor in European Studies from Canisius College; a Master of Public Administration and a certificate in Urban Planning from Minnesota State University, Mankato. Mr. Koala has had two papers accepted for publication in the Journal of Public Procurement (JoPP) and in the International Journal of Procurement Management (IJPM).

Kenneth A. Kriz, Ph.D., is University Distinguished Professor at the University of Illinois at Springfield. Dr. Kriz conducts research focusing on subnational debt policy and administration, public pension fund management, government financial risk management, economic and revenue forecasting, and behavioral public finance. Dr. Kriz is a frequent presenter at public economics and public budgeting and financial management conferences and has published more than 40 journal articles and book chapters along with a textbook on quantitative research methods in public administration. Dr. Kriz has consulted with several public and nonprofit organizations on financial and economic matters. Dr. Kriz served as Vice-Chairperson of the City of Omaha, Nebraska Civilian Employees Retirement System from 2006 to 2011 and on the Board of Trustees of the Wichita Police & Fire Retirement System and on the Joint Investment Committee for the city's pension funds from 2014 to 2018. Dr. Kriz was a Fulbright Scholar in the Republic of Estonia during academic year 2004-05 and a Fulbright Senior Specialist in the Czech Republic in 2008.

Olha Krupa is a professor of government finance and public financial management at Seattle University's Institute of Public Service. Her research explores the financial performance of local governments, equity issues in property taxation, and the public finances of transition economies. A Ukraine native, Dr. Krupa is also interested in Ukraine's public sector reform and economic development. Her research appears in Public Finance Review, State and Local Government Review, Journal of Property Tax Assessment and Administration, and State Tax Notes. Prior to joining Seattle University, Dr. Krupa worked at Citigroup Ukraine's corporate and investment bank, the World Bank, Hudson Institute, and the New York Water Municipal Finance Authority. She has an M.A. in international business from Lviv Academy of Commerce (Ukraine), and a Master of Public Administration and a Ph.D. (Public Affairs) from Indiana University – Bloomington.

Nai-Ling Kuo received her Ph.D. in Public Administration and Policy and M.A. in Economics from State University of New York at Albany in 2010 and 2009. She is an Associate Professor in the Graduate Institute of Public Affairs and the Department of Political Science at National Taiwan University. She teaches applied statistics, cost-benefit analysis, fiscal administration, public budgeting and public finance. Her research interests include fiscal finance and budgetary theory, budgetary institutions, public accountability, and tax expenditure. Her recent publications relate to the effectiveness of public money (value for money), fiscal behaviors of local governments in Taiwan, and the influences of citizen dissatisfaction on budgets.

Wei-Jie Liao is a doctoral student in the School of Public Administration at the University of Nebraska at Omaha. He is also a research assistant at the Nebraska State & Local Government Finance Lab. He received both his Bachelor of Arts in Political Science and Master in Public Administration from National Taiwan University. Wei-Jie's areas of specialization are public budgeting & finance and public policy. His research interests include debt management, citizen participation in the budgeting processes, fiscal health, capital budgeting, and performance budgeting.

Lien Nguyen is a doctoral student in the School of Public Service at Old Dominion University in Norfolk, Virginia. Prior to her matriculation through the Ph.D. program, Nguyen, a former Fulbright Scholar, obtained the Master's of Public Administration degree from Old Dominion University, as well as a Bachelor's degree in Economics with a focus on Corporate Accounting from the Academy of Finance in Vietnam. Her current research, as well as, research interests center on infrastructure finance, capital planning & budgeting, and nonprofit governance. Finally, she boasts extensive work experience in Vietnam's national capital investment planning and government procurement as the former Official at Ministry of Planning and Investment in Vietnam.

Thuy Nguyen is a senior researcher at the National Institute for Finance, Ministry of Finance of Vietnam. Her expertise is in the areas of public finance, economic development, fiscal and monetary policies. She is responsible for conducting research, analyzing economic issues, providing advice, contributing to develop the Government's policies and strategies. She obtained her master degree in Economics of Money, Banking and Finance from the University of Sheffield (the United Kingdom) in 2012. She has authored numerous articles on macroeconomics, public finance, fiscal management and has spoken at several international conferences.

Joshua Steinfeld is an Assistant Professor and Director of Certificate in Public Procurement and Management program in the School of Public Service at Old Dominion University. Dr. Steinfeld's areas of expertise include among others Public Procurement, Acquisition, Contracting, Privatization, and Public-Private Partnerships.

Index

Q

R

S

T

U

W

9781522573296